Scandina... Baltic Eu...
on a shoestring

Glenda Bendure
Ned Friary
John Noble
Deanna Swaney
Greg Videon

Scandinavian & Baltic Europe on a shoestring

1st edition

Published by
    Lonely Planet Publications
    Head Office: PO Box 617, Hawthorn, Vic 3122, Australia
    Branches: PO Box 2001A, Berkeley, CA 94702, USA
                  12 Barley Mow Passage, Chiswick, W4 4PH, UK

Printed by
    Colorcraft Ltd, Hong Kong

Front cover
    Hamnoy, Norway (© International Photographic Library)

First Published
    January 1993

Although the authors and publisher have tried to make the information as accurate as possible, they accept no responsibility for any loss, injury or inconvenience sustained by any person using this book.

National Library of Australia Cataloguing in Publication Data

Tony Wheeler

Scandinavian & Baltic Europe on a shoestring

   1st ed.
   Includes index.
   ISBN 0 86442 151 6.

   1. Scandinavia - Guidebooks. 2. Baltic States - Guidebooks
   I. Wheeler, Tony, 1946- . (Series: Lonely Planet on a shoestring).

914.80488

text & maps © Lonely Planet 1993

Glenda Bendure

Glenda Bendure grew up in California's Mojave Desert and first travelled overseas as an AFS high school exchange student to India. She has a sociology degree from the University of California, Santa Cruz.

Ned Friary

Ned Friary grew up near Boston, graduating with a degree in Social Thought & Political Economy from the University of Massachusetts, Amherst.

Glenda and Ned, who wrote the Norway and Denmark chapters of this book, met in Santa Cruz, California. In 1978, with Lonely Planet's *Across Asia on the Cheap* in hand, they flew to London and hit the overland trail through Iran and Afghanistan, and from there on to 3rd-class trains in India and treks in Nepal. The next six years were spent exploring Asia and the Pacific, teaching English in Japan in between jaunts. They now live on Cape Cod in Massachusetts. Ned and Glenda are authors of Lonely Planet's *Hawaii – a travel survival kit* and *Micronesia – a travel survival kit*.

John Noble

John Noble wrote the Estonia, Latvia and Lithuania chapters of this book. He was born and grew up in the valley of the River Ribble, England. After a Cambridge University degree in English and Philosophy and a decade of journalism that led him from the Ribble valley's *Clitheroe Advertiser* via London's *Observer*, *Guardian* and *Times* to Latin America and South-East Asia, he updated Lonely Planet's *Sri Lanka – a travel survival kit*. Since then he has co-authored LP's *Mexico* and the *USSR* travel survival kits; and with his wife Susan Forsyth, helped update *Australia* and *Indonesia*. John, Susan, their daughter Isabella and their son Jack (who arrived while this book was still generating steam from their personal computer) have their home base in the Ribble valley.

Deanna Swaney

After completing her university studies Deanna Swaney, who wrote the Iceland and the Faroe Islands chapters of this book, made the standard European tour and has been addicted to travel ever since. Despite an erstwhile career in computer programming, she managed intermittent forays away from encroaching yuppiedom and, at first opportunity, made a break for South America where she wrote Lonely Planet's *Bolivia – a travel survival kit*. Subsequent travels led through an erratic circuit of island paradises – Arctic and tropical – and resulted in three more travel survival kits: *Tonga, Samoa*, and *Iceland, Greenland & the Faroe Islands*. Deanna, who enjoys the company of moose and bears back home in Alaska, found furry diversity in Africa while researching her next book *Zimbabwe, Botswana & Namibia*.

Greg Videon

Greg Videon wrote the Finland and Sweden chapters of this book. His days in Melbourne daily journalism ended after he visited Scandinavia in 1984. He went to read Swedish, German and Viking Culture at university and in 1989 returned to Sweden as a student. Ambitions to write remain if the work can combine northern Europe and cricket.

From the Authors

Glenda Bendure & Ned Friary In Denmark, thanks to Jan Buschardt (Copenhagen), Trine & Birthe Bøtkjær (Lake District), Lillian Hess and Henrik Hansen (Copenhagen).

In Norway, thanks to Rune Holmberg (Skien), Catherine Ferrier (Stavanger), Shaena Gibbons (Oslo), Jean Charles (Australia), Gerd Strand Larsen of the Bergen Line and the helpful people at various Norwegian tourist offices, particularly Harald Hansen (New York), Asbjörn Gabrielsen (Lofotens), Gunn Sissel Jaklin (Tromsø), Liv Hege Tveit (Bergen), Per Brodal (Oslo), Mari Skavhaug, Roy Aaserud (Trondheim).

John Noble John Noble would like to thank, in order of appearance: Colin Richardson (Notting Hill), Lvudmila Rhokhlova (Rochdale), Vaclovas Sakalouskas (Vilinius), Alexandr Vasilev (Vilinius), Zita Makutiene (Vilinius), Emilija Paplaitiene (Vilinius), Gerald Blazevich (Riga), Janis Schnepsts (Riga), Tiina Koik (Tallinn) and Neil Taylor (Bristol).

Greg Videon Special thanks go to Sveriges Turistråd, Jenny Lundström, Maria Winkler and Gunnela Setterwall; Matkailun Edistämiskeskus, Hanni Kivistö and Sirpa Lotsari; Suomen Retkeilymajajärjestö Ry and Maija-Liisa Aho. Warmest personal thanks to Markus and the Lehtipuu family for their kindness. Thanks also go to:

Finnish Consulate (Melbourne), Lappeenrannan Matkailu Oy, Lahden Kaupungin matkailutoimisto, Saimaan Matkailu Ry and Savonlinna Tourist Service, Pohjois-Karjalan matkailutoimisto, Lieksan Matkailu Oy, Ålands Turistinformation, Rovaniemien Kaupungin matkailutoimisto, Kemi matkailutoimisto, Stockholm Information Service, Uppsala Turist och Kongress AB, Gävle Turistbyrå, Västerås Turistbyrå, Sala Gruvturism, Väsby Kungsgård, Siljan Turism AB, Östersunds Turist-och Kongressbyrå, Luleå Turistbyrå, Gällivare Turistbyrån, Destination Norrköping, Information Jönköping, Jönköpings Länsmuseum, Lunds Kommun Turism och Information, Malmö Turistbyrå, Gotlands Turistförening, Göteborgs Turistbyrå.

My love and gratitude go to Karen and my family for their tolerance and support. This work is dedicated to my late sister.

From the Publisher

This the first edition of Scandinavian & Baltic Europe on a shoestring was edited by Frith Pike. Thanks to Rob van Driesum Adrienne Costanzo and Frith Pike for writing the introductory chapters, to Dan Levin for computer assistance and font creation and to Sharon Wertheim for help with the index. Sally Steward coordinated the language sections written by Peter A Crozier (Danish), Markus Lehtipuu (Finnish), Inga Arnadottir (Icelandic), Doekes Lulofs (Norwegian) and Par Sorme (Swedish). Special thanks to Rob van Driesum, the coordinator of the Europe project, and to Susan Mitra for her support. Frith also thanks all the authors for their cooperation and enthusiasm.

This book was designed by Valerie Tellini, the cartography was coordinated by Chris Lee Ack with help from Sandra Smythe, Sally Woodward and Paul Clifton. Thanks go to those other artists and cartographers who worked on this project, to Ann Jeffree who illustrated the title page and Sandra Smythe who designed the cover.

Warning & Request

Things change – prices go up, schedules change, good places go bad and bad places go bankrupt – nothing stays the same. So if you find things better or worse, recently opened or long since closed, please write and tell us and help make the next edition better.

Your letters will be used to help update future editions and, where possible, important changes will also be included in a Stop Press section in reprints.

We greatly appreciate all information that is sent to us by travellers. Back at Lonely Planet we employ a hard-working readers' letters team to sort through the many letters we receive. The best ones will be rewarded with a free copy of the next edition or another Lonely Planet guide if you prefer. We give away lots of books, but, unfortunately, not every letter/postcard receives one.

Contents

BALTIC STATES

Map Legend

BOUNDARIES

— · — · — · — .... International Boundary
—— · · —— · · —— .... Internal Boundary
+·+·+·+·+·+·+·+ .... National Park or Reserve
- - - - - - - - - - - - .... The Equator

SYMBOLS

⊙ NEW DELHI .... National Capital
● BOMBAY .... Provincial or State Capital
● Pune .... Major Town
◆ Barsi .... Minor Town
■ .... Places to Stay
▼ .... Places to Eat
🏛 .... Post Office
✈ .... Airport
i .... Tourist Information
⊖ .... Bus Station or Terminal
66 .... Highway Route Number
☪✝🕋✝ ...... Mosque, Church, Cathedral
∴ .... Temple or Ruin
✚ .... Hospital
❋ .... Lookout
⚏ .... Lighthouse
⚔ .... Camping Area
⛱ .... Picnic Area
⌂ .... Hut or Chalet
▲ .... Mountain or Hill
▥ .... Stairway
⊢⊣ .... Railway Station
≡ .... Road Bridge
+++++ .... Railway Bridge
⇒ ⇐ .... Road Tunnel
↦ ⇤ .... Railway Tunnel
〰 .... Escarpment or Cliff
⌣ .... Pass
⊓⊓⊓ .... Ancient or Historic Wall

ROUTES

——————— .... Major Road or Highway
- - - - - - - - - - - .... Unsealed Major Road
——————— .... Sealed Road
- - - - - - - - - - - ..... Unsealed Road or Track
═══════ .... City Street
+++++++ .... Railway
◆━━━⊙━━━◆ .... Subway
++++++++++++ .... Tram
.... Walking Track
- - - - - - - - .... Ferry Route
++++++++++ .... Cable Car or Funicular

HYDROGRAPHIC FEATURES

.... River or Creek
.... Lake, Intermittent Lake
.... Coast Line
.... River Flow
.... Waterfall
.... Swamp

.... Icecaps

.... Glacier

OTHER FEATURES

Park, Garden or National Park

.... Built Up Area

.... Pedestrian Mall

.... Plaza or Town Square

.... Cemetery

Note: not all symbols displayed above appear in this book

Introduction

Scandinavian and Baltic Europe encompasses a huge area around the Baltic Sea and out into the cold North Atlantic Ocean offering the visitor rugged wilderness, safe travel, spectacular scenery and amazing sights like the *Aurora Borealis* and the midnight sun.

The countries covered in *Scandinavian & Baltic Europe on a shoestring* have everything from strikingly beautiful fjords, glaciers and mountains to the treeless Arctic tundra. There are cities ranging from cosmopolitan Copenhagen to the East-West blend of Helsinki, from modern Stockholm to the resurging capitals of the newly independent Baltic states (Tallinn in Estonia, Riga in Latvia and Vilnius in Lithuania) with their lively arts and entertainment scenes. Outdoor enthusiasts will find their fill of wilderness activities in Scandinavia from ski-touring in Norway to exploring the glaciers, hot springs and geysers and volcanoes of Iceland or bird-watching in the starkly beautiful Faroe Islands.

The range of attractions in the region is great. Norway has unspoiled fishing villages, rich historic sites including Viking ships and medieval stave churches; Denmark has Viking ruins and unspoiled islands; Sweden has impressive museums and national parks with many walking trails. Visitors to Finland can cruise around giant lakes and experience the Russian influence in the south and see reindeer in the north. The Baltic states offer capital cities whose hearts are architectural treasure troves, as well as interesting islands and coastal areas.

Scandinavian and Baltic Europe is a region of vast differences and vivid contrasts: there are popular swimming beaches along the coast of Denmark in the south while Norway, Sweden and Finland all extend beyond the Arctic Circle in the north. Sweden has managed to combine socialist principles with operating some of the most successful capitalist enterprises on earth. The newly independent Baltic states are hotbeds for local entrepreneurship as two generations of Soviet rule are being discarded.

This book takes you through the region (including the intriguing Kaliningrad area, Russian territory reopened to foreign tourists only since 1991) from predeparture preparations to packing your bag for the return home. There's information on how to get there and how to get around once you've arrived whether it's by ferry across the Baltic Sea or by bicycle along the Danish cycling routes.

Scandinavia is famed for its high costs, but this book details the many ways of minimising them from staying in Denmark's *vandrerhjem* (hostels) to eating at Norway's *konditori* (bakeries). There are extensive recommendations about where to stay including the newest backpacker hostels in the Baltic states and farmhouse accommodation in Iceland. Dining possibilities are covered from Denmark's famous *smørrebrød* to traditional Icelandic dishes you'd probably rather not know about – anyone for *hakarl*, putrefied shark meat?

Scandinavian and Baltic Europe offers the traveller a real chance for adventure exploring natural and political frontiers – all you have to do is go there.

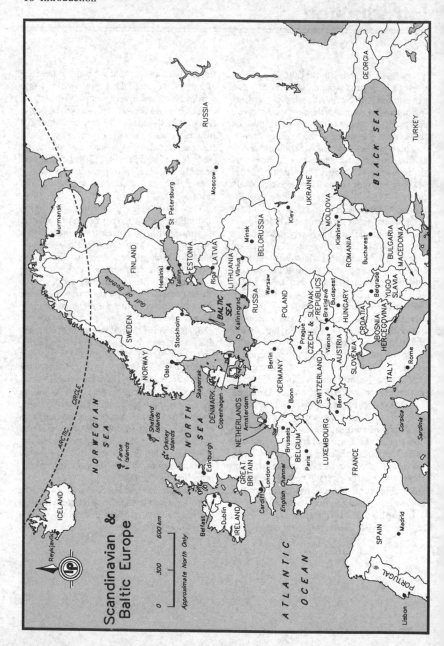

Facts for the Visitor

There are those who say that Europe is so well developed, you don't have to plan a thing when visiting since anything can be arranged on the spot. As any experienced traveller knows, the problems you thought about at home often turn out to be irrelevant, or will sort themselves out once you start moving.

This theory is fine if you've decided to blow the massive inheritance sitting in your bank account but, if your financial status is more modest, some prior knowledge and careful planning can make your hard-earned travel budget stretch further than you thought it would. You'll also want to make sure that the things you plan to see and do will be possible at the particular time of the year you'll be travelling.

PLANNING
Maps
You can't plan without maps. Good maps of various descriptions are easy to get once you're in Europe, but you might want to buy a few beforehand especially if you know your're going to be spending a lot of time in a particular place. The maps in this book will help you get an idea of where you might like to go and will be a useful first reference when you arrive in a city. Falk city maps are very usable and detailed, and their map of Scandinavia is good. Proper road maps are essential if you're driving or cycling.

You can't go wrong with Michelins, and because of their soft covers, they fold up easily so you can fit them in a pocket. Some people prefer the meticulously produced Freytag & Berndt, Kümmerly & Frey or Hallwag maps. The latter have been recommended for Scandinavian countries. The best road maps in Norway are Cappelens, while in Denmark Kort og Matrikelstyrelsen's maps are recommended. In Scandinavia, tourist office country maps can be excellent; they are free and up-to-date. See the Facts for the Visitor section of the Estonia chapter for recommended maps of the Baltic countries.

As a rule, maps published by automobile associations in Europe are excellent, and they're sometimes free to members and associate members.

When to Go
Any time can be the best time to visit Europe, depending on what you want to do. Summer offers the most pleasant climate for outdoor pursuits in northern Europe (see also the climate charts at the back of this book). In general, the short summers in Scandinavia last from mid-June to late August and temperatures can get relatively hot. After August most tourists disappear, school reopens and many summer activities wind down. September is a pleasant time to be there but you most definitely get the impression it's autumn. In the southern part of Sweden, spring is beautiful in early May.

If you want to enjoy concerts and beaches in Denmark, the best time of the year to visit is from late June to August. Otherwise the shoulder seasons from May to June and from September until mid-October are less crowded, most sights are open and the weather is good.

Unless you're into winter sports like skiing or are in search of the Aurora Borealis, from May to September is the best time to visit Norway: it's warmest and the daylight hours are very long even in Oslo and the south. Between late June (after Midsummer) and mid-August is the best time for a visit to Finland: more hostels are open, the weather is at its best and there are fewer public holidays to inconvenience your travel plans unexpectedly.

You won't be the only tourist in Europe during summer, however, as many locals go on summer holidays and celebrate Midsummer with gusto. There are many music festivals and outdoor events. Prices can be high, accommodation fully booked, and the sights packed. You'll find much better deals, and fewer crowds, in the shoulder seasons either side of summer. On the other hand, if you're keen on winter sports such as cross-country skiing, you can get good accommodation deals in some Scandinavian cities during winter. In Iceland things slow down from mid-August and by mid-September the main tourist attractions are inaccessible. Transport services are practically nonexistent during winter but there is skiing in the cities of Reykjavík and Akureyri. In the Faroe Islands tourist facilities only operate from June to September.

If you're visiting the Baltic States, the annual Baltika folklore festival is held in mid-July. The climate is best for travellers in May, June and September; there's snow from mid-December to mid-March or even as late as May in northern and central Scandinavia.

The Climate & When to Go sections in the individual country chapters explain what to expect and when to expect it, and the climate graphs at the end of this book will help you compare different destinations. As a rule, spring and autumn tend to be wetter and windier than summer and winter in Europe. The temperate maritime climate along the Atlantic seaboard means relatively wet conditions all year with moderate extremes in temperature. North-west Norway's climate, for example, is moderated by the effects of the warm Gulf Stream.

The climate will have a bearing on the clothes you bring along. Insulation works on the principle of trapped air, so several layers of thin clothing are warmer than only one thick layer (and easier to dry where drying is difficult) and you'll have much more flexibility if the weather suddenly turns warm on you. Just be prepared for rain and cool weather at any time of year.

How Long?

The amount of time you spend in Europe is entirely up to you and your bank account. Travel in the Baltic states is still relatively cheap. Expenses are high in Scandinavia: your budget will be severely stressed if you visit Iceland or the Faroe Islands but it might be some consolation to know that Denmark is the cheapest of the Scandinavian countries. The more time you spend in the one place, the lower your daily expenses are likely to be as you get to know your way around. See the Money section that follows for an indication of expenses.

If you have a rail pass, you'll have to stay on the move to make the best use of it. Flexipass schemes are available, as well as extensions on transport like international ferries (especially in the Baltic Sea) and other discounts. Even so, you should be able to save money by timing your arrivals and departures so that you sleep on the train. See Move or Stay? in the following section. Allow extra travelling time if you wish to visit islands such as the Lofotens in north-west Norway, the Baltic islands of Gotland or Öland in Sweden, the Faroes, or even Iceland.

What Kind of Trip?

Travelling Companions Travelling alone is not a problem in Europe, if that's what you want to do. Because the region is well developed and relatively safe, you don't really need the support of a team.

If you decide to travel with others, keep in mind that travel can put relationships to the test as few experiences can. You won't find out until you try, but make sure you agree on itineraries and routines beforehand.

If travel is a good way of testing a friendship, it's also a great way of meeting new people. Hitchhiking will introduce you to many of the locals, and youth hostels and camping grounds are good places to meet fellow travellers. Even if you're travelling alone, you need never be lonely.

The Getting Around chapters have information on organised tours with groups. The young, the elderly and the inexperienced tend to appreciate these tours because they take the daily hassles and uncertainties out of travel. The longer tours, however, can become experiments in social cohesion and frictions can develop.

Move or Stay? 'If this is Thursday, it must

be Helsinki.' Though often ridiculed, the mad dash that crams six countries into a month does have its merits. If you've never visited Europe, you won't know which areas you'll like, and a quick 'scouting tour' can give an overview of your options. With a rail pass offering unlimited travel in a set period of time, why not do just this?

If you do know where you want to go, or find a place you like, you might like to stay for a while. Discover some of the lesser known sights, make a few local friends and settle in to a different way of life.

With your own transport, or buying train and bus tickets as you go along, you can stay in a place long enough to get a feel for it and then move on. You'll probably finish where you started, but rather than follow the same itinerary back, take a different route and see twice as much – or better still, make it a circuit and keep your options open.

Working Holiday European countries aren't keen to hand out jobs to foreigners. Officially, an EC (European Community) citizen is allowed to work in any other EC country, but the paperwork isn't always straightforward for longer term employment and can be offputting. Other country/nationality combinations require special work permits that can be almost impossible to arrange, especially for temporary work. That doesn't prevent enterprising travellers from topping up their funds occasionally, and they don't always have to do this illegally either. Denmark is the best place for trying to find work in Scandinavia.

Your national student exchange organisation may be able to arrange temporary work permits to several countries through special programmes. For more details on working as a foreigner, see Work in the Facts for the Visitor sections of the individual country chapters.

If you have a parent or grandparent who was born in an EC country, you may have certain rights within that country and other EC countries that you didn't know about. Get in touch with that country's embassy and ask about dual citizenship and work permits – if you are eligible for citizenship, also ask about any obligations, such as military service. Not all countries allow dual citizenship, so a work permit may be all you can get. Ireland is particularly easygoing about granting citizenship to people with Irish ancestry, and with an Irish passport, the EC is your oyster.

If you do find a temporary job, the pay is likely to be less than that offered to locals. The only exceptions appear to be jobs teaching English, but these are hard to come by. Other typical tourist jobs (for instance working in fish-processing factories or washing dishes at ski resorts) often come with board and lodging. The pay is little more than pocket money, but you could have a good time partying with other travellers. The following paperbacks from UK publisher Vacation Work give good practical advice on a wide range of issues: *Work Your Way Around the World* by Susan Griffith and *The Au Pair and Nanny's Guide to Working Abroad* by Susan Griffith and Sharon Legg. If you are planning a working holiday in Europe, *Transitions Abroad* (USA) and *New Traveller* (Australia) are useful periodicals.

If you play an instrument or have other artistic talents, you could try busking (street entertainment). It's fairly common in many major cities. In Finland you'll need to get permission from the relevant city or municipality. In Denmark acoustic music is allowed in pedestrian streets and squares between 7 am and 10 pm daily. Most other Scandinavian countries require municipal permits that can be hard to obtain. Talk to other buskers first.

Selling goods on the street is generally frowned upon and can be tantamount (as it is in Finland) to vagrancy apart from at flea markets. It's also a hard way to make money if you're not selling something special.

What to Bring
Bringing as little as possible is the best policy. It's very easy to find almost anything you need along the way and, since you'll probably buy things as you go, it's better to start with too little rather than too much.

Keep in mind that because of the value-added tax (VAT) and the overall high price of goods, most people are not going to want to pick up too many items in Scandinavia.

A backpack is still the most popular method of carrying gear as it is convenient and the only way to go if you have to do any walking. On the debit side, a backpack is awkward to load on and off buses and trains, it doesn't offer too much protection for your valuables, the straps tend to get caught on things and some airlines may refuse liability if the pack is damaged or broken into.

Travelpacks, a combination of backpack and shoulder bag, have become very popular. The backpack straps zip away inside the pack when they are not needed so you almost have the best of both worlds. Some packs have sophisticated shoulder strap adjustment systems and can be carried comfortably even on long hikes. Packs are always much easier to carry than a bag. Another alternative is a large, soft zip bag with a wide shoulder strap so it can be carried with relative ease. Small padlocks on your pack can help deter thieves. Forget suitcases unless you're travelling in style. Baggage lockers are most common at railway stations (sometimes left-luggage desks will accept items too large for a locker). Large bus stations and ferry terminals also provide lockers. This is useful security if your youth hostel provides little.

As for clothes, begin light and buy local clothes that take your fancy as you go along. Remember that wearing layers of clothing will help you keep a comfortable temperature in the Scandinavian and Baltic countries. Clothing to bring from home could include:

• underwear and swimming gear
• a pair of jeans and maybe a pair of shorts
• a few T-shirts and shirts
• a warm jumper (sweater)
• a solid pair of walking shoes
• sandals or thongs for showers
• a coat or jacket

See also the following Appearances & Conduct section. Bearing in mind that you can buy virtually anything on the spot, you could also consider bringing the following:

• tent and sleeping bag
• sleeping sheet including pillow cover
• medical and sewing kit
• padlock
• Swiss Army knife
• raincoat or waterproof jacket
• soap and towel
• toothpaste and toothbrush
• emergency supply of toilet paper
• elastic clothesline

Bringing a tent and a sleeping bag is vital if you want to save money by camping. Even if you're not camping a sleeping bag is still pretty essential. It can double as a cushion on hard train-seats, a seat for long waits at bus or railway stations, and a bedspread in cold hotels. A cheaper form of accommodation in the Faroe Islands is actually called sleeping-bag accommodation.

A sleeping sheet with pillow cover is necessary if you plan to stay in youth hostels – you'll have to hire or purchase them if you don't bring your own. In any case, a sheet that fits into your sleeping bag is easier to wash than the bag; make sure the sheet has a built-in pillow cover. You can make one of these sleeping sheets yourself out of old sheets or buy one from your youth hostel association. A tea towel and bath towel will also be handy if you're staying in youth hostels.

A padlock is useful for locking your bag to a train or bus luggage rack, and may also be needed to secure your youth hostel locker or for locking your room itself in some of the seedy, cheap hotels in Estonia, Latvia or Lithuania. A Swiss Army knife is useful for all sorts of things (any pocket knife is fine, so long as it includes a bottle opener and a strong corkscrew). You could need waterproof gear at any time of the year.

Soap, toothpaste and toilet paper are readily obtainable almost anywhere, but you'll need your own supply of paper in many public toilets and camping-ground amenity blocks. When using public toilets, have some small change handy; you may be charged a small fee. Tampons are available at pharmacies and supermarkets in all but the most remote places. In the Baltic states good soap, tampons and other toiletries which Westerners are used to may be available in only a few shops, so it's worth taking a supply to keep you going initially. Similarly, pharmacies in these countries tend to be poorly stocked with Western products. Condoms are widely available.

Optional items include a compass (to help orient yourself in large cities), a torch (flashlight), an alarm clock or a watch with an alarm function, an adapter plug for electrical appliances (such as a cup water heater to save on buying expensive tea and coffee and to make your own when your hotel has no open café as may happen in Estonia, Latvia or Lithuania), a universal bath/sink plug (do take one if travelling in the Baltic states), sunglasses and a few clothes pegs. During city sightseeing, a small daypack is better than a shoulder bag for deterring snatch thieves (see the Dangers & Annoyances section).

There are two final considerations. The secret of successful packing is using plastic carry bags or garbage bags inside your backpack, as they not only keep things separate and clean but dry too if the pack gets soaked. Airlines do lose luggage from time to time – you've got a much better chance of it not being yours if it is tagged with your name and address *inside* the bag as well as outside. Outside tags can always fall off or be removed.

Appearances & Conduct

Europeans are usually tolerant of eccentric fashions and behaviour, but attention to your appearance will help. Dress standards are fairly informal in northern Europe.

By all means dress casually, but keep it clean, and ensure sufficient body cover (trousers or knee-length dress) if your sightseeing includes churches. Wearing shorts away from the beach or on walking trails is not very common among men in Europe. Some nightclubs and fancy restaurants may refuse entry to anyone wearing jeans; men

might consider packing a tie as well, just in case. For more information on female dress codes, see Female Travellers in the Special Needs section. In Estonia, Lithuania, and Latvia you can get away with wearing jeans (provided they're clean) and sneakers (trainers) and, for men, no tie is needed in even the most select restaurants. You might feel uncomfortable wearing a T-shirt though.

Europeans have 'been there, done that' with hair length. The process has come full circle, and long hair appears to be making a bit of a comeback among men. Nevertheless, the 'long hair equals despicable hippy' syndrome still survives in out-of-the-way places, especially with unkempt and greasy hair.

Most border guards and immigration officials are too professional to judge people entirely by their appearance, but there are always the ambitious types who think they are on to a drug smuggling ring when they spot a 'hippy'. Officials are always paranoid about potential vagrants who have no means of support. This can be particularly true of the police in rural areas, though perhaps not so much in northern Europe. First impressions do count, and you'll find life easier if you're well presented when dealing with officialdom.

Nude bathing is usually limited to restricted beach areas, but topless bathing is very common in many parts of Europe – in Scandinavia, particularly on the beaches of Denmark, it can seem *de rigueur*. However, women should be wary of topless bathing; the rule is, if nobody else seems to be doing it, don't.

Europeans shake hands and even kiss when they greet one another. At least get into the habit of shaking hands with virtually everyone you meet. It's an important ritual.

It is customary in many countries to greet the owner, bartender or shopkeeper when you enter a shop, quite bar or café and to say goodbye when you leave.

The Top 10 Sights

There is so much to see in Europe, that compiling a top 10 is almost impossible. But we asked the authors of this book to list their personal highlights, and the results are as follows:

1. Geirangerfjord, Norway's western fjords
2. Frederiksborg Castle, Hillerød, Denmark
3. M vatn, Iceland
4. Gamla Stan, Stockholm
5. Lofoten islands, north-west Norway
6. Bygdøy Viking Ship Museum, Oslo
7. Karelia and Saimaa lakes, Finland
8. The Old Town in Tallinn, Estonia
9. The Old Town in Vilnius, Lithuania
10. Abisko national park, Sweden

The Bottom 10 Sights

The writers were also asked to list the 10 worst sights and came up with the following:

1. Göna Lund Tivoli, Stockholm
2. Santa Claus' house, Rovaniemi, Finland
3. The Little Mermaid, Copenhagen
4. Metro paintings, Stockholm
5. Norwegian beaches
6. Seal clubbing display at Polar Museum
7. Legoland without kids
8. Blue Lagoon, Iceland
9. The Soviet-era suburbs of any sizeable town in Estonia, Latvia or Lithuania
10. Any place with so many tour buses that you can't see the attraction

Other nominations included high prices, the weather and drunken Scandinavian tourists bingeing when they can get tax-free alcohol. Any of these could leave you feeling that you've wasted your time.

PASSPORT & VISAS
Passport

Your most important travel document is a passport, which should remain valid until · well after your trip. If it's just about to expire, renew it before you go – having it done by your embassy in Stockholm (or wherever) could be tedious and inconvenient. Some countries insist that your passport remain valid for a specified minimum period (usually three months) after your date of entry; even if this isn't insisted on, expect questions from immigration officials if it's due to expire in a matter of days.

If you don't have a passport, you'll have to apply for one, which can be an involved process. A renewal or application can take anything from a few days to several months, depending on many factors, so don't leave it till the last minute; it can sometimes be speeded up with a good excuse, though this may attract a higher fee. Bureaucracy usually grinds faster if you do everything in person at the actual passport issuing office if possible, rather than relying on the mail or agents. Ask first what you need to bring: passport photos, birth certificate, population register extract, signed statements, exact payment in cash, whatever.

Australian citizens can apply at a post office or the passport office in their state capital; Britons can get application forms from travel agents and major post offices, and the passport is issued by the regional passport office; Canadians can apply at regional passport offices; New Zealanders can apply at any district office of the Department of Internal Affairs; US citizens must apply in person (but may usually renew by mail) at a US Passport Agency office or some courthouses and post offices.

Once you start travelling, carry your passport at all times and guard it carefully. The locals in some countries are required by law to carry personal identification, and the same applies to foreigners. Camping grounds and hotels sometimes insist that you hand over your passport for the duration of your stay – very inconvenient, since you won't be able to cash travellers' cheques or arrange visas. They tend to be a bit more flexible about this if you pay in advance, but a Camping Carnet usually solves the problem (see the Documents section).

See Theft in the Dangers & Annoyances section for advice about photocopying your passport and other important documents.

Europeans Citizens of many European countries don't always need a valid passport to travel within the region. A national identity card or something like the British Visitor's Passport may be sufficient; this can often work out cheaper and usually involves less paperwork and processing time. An expired passport may be all right, too. An EC citizen travelling to another EC country will generally face the fewest problems. It's very important if you want to exercise any of these options, check with your travel agent or the embassies of the countries you plan to visit.

Visas

A visa is a stamp in your passport permitting you to enter the country in question and stay for a specified period of time. There's a wide variety including tourist, transit and business visas. Transit visas are usually cheaper than tourist or business visas, but only allow a very short stay of one or two days and can be difficult to extend.

Readers of this book will have little to do with visas unless they're going to Estonia, Latvia or Lithuania (see those country chapters for more information). With a valid passport they'll be able to visit most European countries for up to three (sometimes even six) months, provided they have some sort of onward or return ticket and/or 'sufficient means of support' (money). Except at international airports, it's unlikely that immigration officials will give you and your passport more than a cursory glance if you look OK (see the Appearances & Conduct section).

This is likely to become even more relaxed: the Schengen accord signed by eight of the 12 EC countries (the exceptions are the UK, Ireland, Denmark and Greece) aims to abolish passport controls within the EC altogether. Border procedures between EC and non-EC countries remain a bit more thorough.

There are a few important exceptions to these easy visa rules. Holders of diplomatic or official passports face different requirements from ordinary passport holders, and should check with the embassies of the countries they wish to visit. South Africans have

						Visas (Country of Origin)				
	Aust	Can	HK	Ire	NZ	Sing	S Afr	UK	USA
Scandinavia									
Denmark (Faroe Islands)	–	–	✓	–	–	–	✓	–	–
Finland	–	–	✓	–	–	–	✓	–	–
Iceland	–	–	–	–	–	–	✓	–	–
Norway	–	–	–	–	–	–	✓	–	–
Sweden	–	–	–	–	–	–	✓	–	–
Baltic States									
*Estonia	✓	✓	✓	✓	✓	✓	✓	✓	✓
*Latvia	✓	✓	✓	✓	✓	✓	✓	✓	✓
*Lithuania	✓	✓	✓	✓	✓	✓	✓	–	✓

✓ Tourist visa required
Visas for Estonia, Latvia or Lithuania are also good for two days in each of the other * countries.

little joy travelling on their 'Green Mamba', though restrictions may gradually be eased.

Hong Kong residents may need visas to several countries depending on their (British) passport endorsements. Australians will need a visa to visit France – it may not be checked when entering the country overland, but major problems can arise if it is requested on departure and can't be shown.

Although European countries are tolerant of the nationalities they allow in, it pays to beware of 'unpopular' passport markings if you do any further travelling. South Africans have had trouble in the past getting in to Scandinavia; visa stamps from Cuba, Vietnam or North Korea could cause delays at some borders while reference lists are consulted. 'Unpopular' countries will often provide a loose-leaf visa if you ask for one.

Visa requirements can change (and this applies particularly to the Baltic states). Always check with the individual embassies or a reputable travel agent well before travelling. In most cases, visas are available on the spot at the border, but it pays to check that too. It's generally easier to get your visas as you go along, rather than arranging them all beforehand. Carry plenty of spare passport photos (you'll need up to four every time you apply for a visa). The previous chart lists visa requirements for some nationalities.

DOCUMENTS
Apart from your passport there are a number of documents worth considering.

International Health Certificate
You'll need this yellow booklet only if you're coming into the region from areas, such as Africa and South America, where cholera or yellow fever are prevalent – see Immunisation in the Health section for more details. Europe is free of such diseases.

International Driving Permit (IDP)
If you hold a non-European driving licence and plan to drive in the region, obtain one of these permits from your local automobile association before you leave; you'll need a passport photo and a valid licence. They are usually inexpensive and valid for one year only. An IDP helps Europeans make sense of your unfamiliar local licence (make sure you take it with you) and can make life much simpler, especially for renting cars and motorbikes.

While you're at it, ask your automobile association for a Card of Introduction. This entitles you to services offered by sister organisations in Europe, usually free of charge (touring maps and information, help with breakdowns, technical and legal advice etc). See the introductory Getting Around chapter for more details.

Camping Carnet
Your local automobile association also issues a Camping Carnet, which is basically a camping ground identification. Carnets are also issued by your local camping federation, and sometimes on the spot at camping grounds. They incorporate third party insurance for damage you may cause, and many camping grounds offer a small discount if you sign in with one. Some hostels and hotels also accept carnets for signing-in purposes, but won't give discounts.

International Youth Hostel Card
An International Youth Hostel (IYHF) card is useful if you're staying at youth hostels. Some European hostels don't require that you be a Youth Hostel Association (YHA) member, but often charge less if you have a card. Many youth hostels will issue one on the spot, though this costs a bit more than getting it in your home country.

Student & Youth Cards
The most useful of these is the International Student Identity Card (ISIC), a plastic identification card with your photograph. It can perform all sorts of wonders, particularly attracting discounts on many forms of transport including airlines and local public transport. Even if you have your own transport, the card will soon pay for itself through cheap or free admission to museums and sights, and cheap meals in some student res-

taurants – a worthwhile way of cutting costs in the expensive Scandinavian countries.

It's no surprise that there is a worldwide industry in fake student cards, and many places now stipulate a maximum age for student discounts or, more simply, they've substituted a youth discount for a student discount. If you're aged under 26 but not a student, you can apply for a Federation of International Youth Travel Organisations (FIYTO) card which gives much the same discounts as an ISIC.

Both types of card are issued by student unions or 'alternative-style' travel agencies. They don't automatically entitle you to discounts, and some companies and institutions refuse to recognise them altogether. However, you won't find out until you flash the card.

MONEY

Bring as much of this fine stuff as you can. You will generally find that US dollars, Deutschmarks, pounds sterling, and French and Swiss francs are easily exchanged. But you may well decide that other currencies suit your purposes better. You lose out through commissions and customer exchange rates every time you change money, so if you only visit Finland, for example, you may be better off buying markka straight away if your bank at home can provide them.

All Scandinavian currencies are fully convertible. In the Baltic states the rouble, which was being used at the time of writing, isn't; Estonia's kroon is, however. Latvia and Lithuania also planned to switch to convertible currencies in 1992.

In general, you may have trouble exchanging some of the more obscure currencies in small banks in northern Europe, while currencies of countries with high inflation face unfavourable exchange rates. Be aware that banks are closed on public holidays which are listed in the individual country chapters. However, most airports, central railway stations, some fancy hotels and many border posts have banking facilities outside working hours, sometimes open on a 24-hour basis. Post offices in Europe often provide banking service; they tend to be open longer hours, and outnumber banks in more remote places.

If you visit several countries, the constant currency conversions can drive you up the wall. Buy a cheap pocket calculator, cut out the list of exchange rates from a newspaper, and stick it to the back of the calculator for easy reference. The best exchange rates are usually offered at banks. *Bureaux de change* usually (but not always) offer worse rates or charge higher commissions. Hotels are almost always the worst places to change money. American Express and Thomas Cook offices usually do not charge commission for changing their own cheques but they may offer a less favourable exchange rate.

At the time of writing Estonia, Latvia, and Lithuania were on the verge of switching over to their own currencies from combinations of the Soviet rouble and the US dollar, a confusing situation with strange effects on prices. See the individual country chapters.

How Much Money?

Travelling in Europe is seldom cheap and you don't necessarily get value for money but it also attracts its fair share of people whose surname isn't Rockefeller who manage to travel quite well without spending a fortune.

The secret is cheap accommodation. Scandinavian Europe has a highly developed network of camping grounds, some of them quite luxurious, and they're great places to meet people. The youth hostel network, too, is well developed, and used equally by all age groups. In the Baltic states, however, camping and youth hostels are not well developed.

Other money-saving strategies include using a student card, which offers worthwhile discounts (see the Documents section); various rail and public transport passes (see the Getting Around chapter); applying for consumer tax rebates on large purchases (see Consumer Taxes in the Facts for the Visitor section of the individual countries); and, generally, following the advice in this book on food and accommodation.

Your budget depends upon how you live and travel. If you're moving around fast, going to lots of places, spending time in the big cities, then your day-to-day living costs are going to be quite high. If you stay in one place and get to know your way around, costs are likely to come down. Hitchhiking, preparing your own meals (self-catering) and avoiding alcohol will also help you save money.

Including transport, but not private motorised transport, your daily expenses could be around US$30 a day if you're on a rock-bottom budget in Scandinavia. This means camping or staying in hostels, eating as economically as possible and using a transport pass. In Estonia, Latvia and Lithuania using rock-bottom priced hotels you could get by on US$10 a day in 1992, but things are likely to get more expensive as economic reform takes effect.

Travelling on a moderate budget you should be able to manage on US$50 to US$75 a day. This would allow you to stay at cheap hotels, guesthouses or bed & breakfasts (B&Bs). You could afford meals in economical restaurants and even a few beers.

Tipping

In Europe tipping is much less prevalent than in North America, but much more so than in Australia, New Zealand or Asia. In many countries it's common for a service charge to be added to restaurant or hotel bills, in which case no tipping is necessary. In others simply rounding up the bill is sufficient. See the individual country chapters for more details.

Cash

Nothing beats cash for convenience...or risk. If you lose it, it's gone forever and very few travel insurers will come to your rescue.

But it's still a good idea to bring some local currency in cash, if only to tide you over until you get to an exchange facility. The equivalent of, say, US$100 should usually be enough. Some extra cash in an easily exchanged currency is a good idea,

too. Often it is much easier to change just a few dollars when leaving a country for example, in cash rather than cheques, and it's more economical.

Remember that banks will always accept paper money but very rarely coins in currencies other than their own. Before you leave one country for the next, spend your last coins on a cup of coffee, fuel if travelling by car, whatever. In Estonia and Latvia, cash and credit cards are the only viable forms of money at the time of writing, although travellers" cheques may become easier to exchange as economic reforms take effect.

Travellers' Cheques

American Express, Visa or Thomas Cook travellers' cheques are probably the best to carry because of their wide acceptance and 'instant replacement' policies. The main idea of carrying cheques rather than cash is the protection they offer from theft, but it doesn't do a lot of good if you have to go back home first to get the refund. Ask about local representatives and telephone hotline numbers when you buy your cheques.

Keeping a record of the cheque numbers and the initial purchase details is vital when it comes to replacing lost cheques. Without this you may well find that 'instant' is a very long time indeed. You also need to keep a record of which cheques you have cashed. Keep these details separate from the cheques themselves. If you're going to less touristy places, it's worth sticking to American Express since small local banks may not always accept other brands. American Express has offices in most of the major cities.

Cheques are available in various currencies. American Express, for instance, offers US dollars, pounds sterling, Deutschmarks, French and Swiss francs, Japanese yen and Canadian dollars. Unless you live in the USA, there's little point in using US$ cheques in Europe, since you'll lose on the exchange rate when you buy the cheques as well as every time you cash one in. The trick is to ensure that you only convert currencies once, not twice. You pay for the cheques in two ways when you buy them; not only does the vendor make a margin on the exchange rate but there is also a commission on the sale, usually 1%.

When you change cheques don't look at just the exchange rate, ask about fees and commissions as well. Some places charge a per-cheque service fee, so changing US$100 in $20 cheques can be more expensive than changing a single US$100 cheque. Other places charge a flat transaction fee instead, or a percentage of the total amount, regardless of the number of cheques and you might want to take advantage of this by changing a few small cheques at once. Some banks charge fees to cash some brands of travellers' cheques but not others. In most countries these days, the exchange rate for travellers' cheques is slightly better than the exchange rate for cash but it's often better to settle for a worse exchange rate if it's balanced by lower fees or commissions.

Take most of the cheques in large denominations, say US$100s or £100s. It's only at the very end of a stay that you may want to change a US$20 or US$10 cheque just to get you through the last day or two.

Travellers' cheques were very difficult to get rid of in Estonia, Latvia and (less so) Lithuania as this book was being researched, but that may be remedied by the introduction of their own currencies. Their embassies in other countries may be able to advise you.

International Transfers

If you run out of money or need more for whatever reason, you can instruct your bank back home to send you a draft. Make sure you specify the city, the bank and the branch you want your money to be directed to. If you don't know a bank to transfer money to, ask your bank to tell you where a suitable one is and make sure you get all the details correct.

The whole procedure will be easier if you've authorised someone back home to access your account. Also, a transfer to a tiny bank in an isolated village in the Lofoten islands is obviously going to be more difficult than to a head office in Oslo. If you have

the choice, find a large bank and ask for the international division.

Money sent by telegraphic transfer (which usually involves costs of US$20 or more, but ask) should reach you in within a week; by mail, allow at least two weeks. When it gets there, it will most likely be converted into local currency – you can take it as it is or buy travellers' cheques.

You can also transfer money by American Express or Thomas Cook. Americans can also use Western Union although they have fewer offices in Europe to collect from. If you have an American Express card you can cash up to US$1000 worth of personal cheques at American Express offices in any 21-day period.

Credit Cards & ATMs

Credit Card A credit card can be an ideal travelling companion. If you're not familiar with credit cards, ask your bank to explain the workings and relative merits of credit, credit/debit, debit and charge cards. Make sure you know what to do in case of theft (obtain telephone hotline numbers etc).

With a credit card you can put many things (like airline tickets) on your account and save carrying so much cash with you. Another major advantage is that they allow you to withdraw cash at selected banks or to draw money from automated teller machines (ATMs).

With a credit card you don't have money tied up in travellers' cheques in a currency that might be diving, you don't pay commission charges or transaction fees, you don't have cash or cheques to lose (though you could, of course, lose your card), you can get money after hours and on weekends, and the exchange rate is at a better interbank rate than that offered for travellers' cheques or cash exchanges.

When using your credit card for purchases, bear in mind that it can take some time to process your credit-card bills back home and that you will be charged the going exchange rate at the time your bank processes your bills. This exchange rate may be substantially different from what it was at the time of your purchase.

The major drawback of credit and credit/debit cards like Visa and MasterCard is that they have a credit limit based on your regular income, and this limit is usually too low to cover major expenses such as long-term car hire or long-distance airline tickets. You can get around this by leaving your card in credit before embarking on your trip. Other disadvantages are that interest is charged on outstanding accounts, either immediately or after a set period (always immediately on cash advances), and that the card can be very difficult to replace if lost abroad.

One problem that can arise with credit cards is that you run out of credit even though you're sure that you haven't reached your credit limit. This is because of authorisations that haven't been cancelled. What happens is that when you leave an imprint of your credit card as security with your hotel or car-rental agency, they can contact your card agency and ask that a certain amount of your credit be set aside ('authorised') to cover your expected bill. If the eventual bill is lower and the hotel or rental agency forgets to cancel its authorisation with your card agency, you won't be able to delve into the remaining portion of the credit that was set aside. Contact your card company if you think this may have happened.

A final word of warning: fraudulent shopkeepers have been known to make several charge slip imprints with credit cards rather than the single one authorised by the customer. Always check your credit-card statements against your receipts.

ATMs Though still not as widespread in Europe as they are in other parts of the world, ATMs are now linked up internationally in many countries (ask your bank for details) and you can use your card abroad as you do at home. But ATMs aren't fail-safe, especially if the card was issued outside Europe, and you may be better off withdrawing cash at a bank counter. If an ATM abroad swallows your card it can be a major headache.

Credit cards usually aren't hooked up to ATM networks unless you specifically ask your bank to do this and request a personal identification number (PIN). You will need to do this well in advance of your trip. You should also ask which ATMs abroad will accept your particular card. Note that many European ATMs won't accept PIN numbers of more than four digits.

Cash cards, which you use at home to withdraw money directly from your bank account or savings account, are slowly becoming more widely linked abroad, so ask your bank at home for advice.

Money withdrawn from an ATM using your credit card will immediately attract interest. Again, you can get around this by leaving the card in credit when you depart, or by having somebody at home pay money into the card account from time to time.

Charge Cards Charge cards like American Express and Diners Club have offices in most countries, and will generally replace a lost card within 24 hours. That's because they treat you as a customer of the company, rather than of the bank that issued the card. In theory, the credit they offer is unlimited and they don't charge interest on outstanding accounts, but they do charge fees for joining and annual membership, and payment is due in full within a few days of the account statement date. Charge cards can also be hooked up to ATM networks on request. Their major drawback is that they're not widely accepted beyond the beaten track of mainstream travel.

Credit and credit/debit cards like Visa and MasterCard are more widely accepted because they tend to charge lower commissions to merchants.

Which Card? Europe has only recently embraced credit cards in a major way, and quite a few shops, restaurants and service stations may still only accept cash. Visa and MasterCard are the most popular cards. MasterCard is also known as Access in the UK and is linked to Europe's extensive

Eurocard system, making it a very convenient card to carry.

To overcome potential problems, it's a good idea to travel with a combination of cards, for instance, an American Express or Diners Club as well as a Visa or MasterCard. Better still, take a credit card and travellers' cheques so that you have something to fall back on if an ATM swallows your card for some obscure reason or the banks in the area don't accept your brand.

Credit cards are still in their infancy in the Baltic states, but take any major cards you have as their use is increasing quite fast.

Eurocheques

There are even more ways of carrying money or obtaining cash. While countries like the USA, Canada and Australia went from unguaranteed personal cheques straight to electronic banking in the form of credit cards and ATM cash cards, Europe replaced bouncing personal cheques with cheques guaranteed to a certain limit.

The most popular of these is the Eurocheque system. To get Eurocheques, you need a European bank account. Depending on the bank it can take at least two weeks to apply for the cheques, which may be too long for most visitors. It's a useful system, however.

Throughout Europe, when paying for something in a shop or withdrawing cash from a bank or post office, you write out a cheque (up to its maximum limit, otherwise simply write out two or more cheques) and show the accompanying guarantee card with your signature and registration number. You may also have to show your passport. Once the shopkeeper or bank clerk has checked the cheque's signature with that on the card and copied your registration number onto the cheque, it's guaranteed by the issuing bank, which will deduct the amount from your account when the paperwork comes through. The card can double as an ATM card, and should obviously be kept separate from the cheques for safety.

COMMUNICATIONS & MEDIA
Post

Details of the main post offices are given in the city information sections of the individual country chapters. From major European centres air mail typically takes about a week to North American or Australasian destinations. Postage costs do vary from country to country but postal services are efficient in Scandinavian countries. You can collect mail from post office poste-restante sections. Delivery time for mail to or from the Baltic states can be very erratic – have your incoming mail sent instead to Finland or another nearby Western European country.

Ask people writing to you to print your name clearly and underline your surname and write it in capital letters. When collecting mail you may need your passport for identification. If an expected letter is not waiting for you, ask to check under your given name as letters do get misfiled. Unless the sender specifies otherwise, mail will always be sent to a city's main post office. The lines of travellers collecting mail are favourite meeting points in many European cities.

You can also have mail (but not parcels) sent to you at American Express offices so long as you have an American Express card or travellers' cheques. When you buy Amex travellers' cheques you can ask for a booklet listing all their office addresses worldwide.

Telephone

The telephone system in Europe generally works very well, though services are somewhat more primitive in the Baltic states.. You can ring abroad from most phone booths if you have sufficient coins; otherwise, use the phone cards that are becoming increasingly popular, or ring from a booth inside a post office or telephone centre and settle your bill at the counter – if you ring from a hotel room, the bill can be astronomical. Reverse-charge (collect) calls are often possible, but not always – for a start, you'll have to be able to communicate with the local operator, who might not always speak English. From many countries, however, you can dial direct to your home operator, which solves the problem. See the individual country chapters and the Telephones appendix in the back of this book for more details.

Newspapers & Magazines

If you want to keep up with the news in English, you can get the surprisingly interesting *International Herald Tribune* or the colourful but very superficial *USA Today* in large towns in Scandinavia. The British *Guardian* and *Financial Times* are also produced in widely available European editions. Other British papers are often available but are expensive and likely to be out-of-date (for example, Western newspapers three or four days old are on sale at Tallinn's Hotel Palace). In the newsmagazine category *Time* and *Newsweek* are widely available in Scandinavia but not in the Baltic states.

Radio & TV

The BBC World Service can be found in Scandinavian countries on short wave at 6195 kHz, 9410 kHz, 12095 kHz, 15070 kHz and 15575 kHz and other frequencies depending on where you are and the time of day. Voice of America (VOA) can usually be found on 1197 kHz. There are also numerous English-language broadcasts on local radio stations.

Cable and satellite TV has spread across Europe with much more gusto than radio. 'Sky TV' can be found in better hotels all over Europe, as can CNN (Cable News Network) and other networks.

ELECTRICITY

By all means bring along the electrical appliances that you feel you can't live without. If they're battery operated, so much the better, but hotels almost always have power points, and these are also fairly widespread in hostels and camping grounds. Voltage and plug design will be your main problems.

Voltage & Cycle

Most of Europe including the Baltic states runs on 220 V, 50 Hz AC. In the mid-1990s, the EC should become standardised at 230 V. Check the voltage and cycle (usually 50 Hz) used in your home country. Most appliances that are set up for 220 V will handle 240 V quite happily without modifications (and vice versa); the same goes for 110 V and 125 V combinations. It's always preferable to adjust your appliance to the exact voltage if you can (some modern battery chargers and radios will do this automatically). Just don't mix 110/125 and 220/240 V without a transformer (which will be built in if the appliance can be adjusted).

Several countries outside Europe (the USA and Canada for instance) have 60 Hz AC, which will affect the speed of electric motors even after the voltage has been adjusted to European values, so record players and tape recorders (where motor speed is all-important) will be useless. But things such as electric razors, hair driers, irons and radios will be fine.

If you want to record or buy video tapes to play back home, you won't get a picture if the image registration systems are different. Europe generally uses PAL (France, SECAM), which is incompatible with the North American and Japanese NTSC system. Australia also uses PAL.

Plugs & Sockets

Britain, Ireland and Malta use a design with three flat pins – two for current and one for earth. The rest of Europe uses two round pins. Many Continental plugs and some sockets don't have provision for earth since most local home appliances are double insulated; when provided, earth usually consists of two contact points along the edge. If your plugs are of a different design, you'll need an adapter. Get one before you leave, since the adapters available in Europe usually go the other way. See also the individual country chapters.

HEALTH

Europe is a healthy place and your main risks are likely to be sunburn, foot blisters, insect bites or upset stomachs from eating and drinking too much. Travel health depends on your predeparture preparations and fitness, your day-to-day health care while travelling and how you handle any medical problem or emergency that does develop. If you're reasonably fit, the only things to organise before departure are a visit to your dentist and travel insurance with good medical cover (see Predeparture Preparations).

Travel Health Guides
There are a number of books on travel health, most of them geared towards the tropics where health is a major issue. Worth considering are:

Travellers' Health, Dr Richard Dawood, Oxford University Press. It's a comprehensive, easy to read, authoritative and also highly recommended, although it's rather large to lug around.
Travel with Children, Maureen Wheeler, Lonely Planet Publications. This includes basic advice on travel health for younger children.

Predeparture Preparations
Health Insurance A travel insurance policy to cover theft, loss and medical problems is a must. There is a wide variety of policies and your travel agent will have recommendations. The international student travel policies handled by STA or other student travel organisations are usually good value. Some policies offer lower and higher medical expenses options – go as high as you can afford, especially if you're visiting any of the Scandinavian countries. Check the small print:

- Some policies specifically exclude 'dangerous activities' which can include scuba diving, motorcycling, skiing, mountaineering, and even trekking. If such activities are on your agenda, you don't want that sort of policy.
- You may prefer a policy that pays doctors or hospitals direct rather than you having to pay on the spot and claim later. If you have to claim later, make sure you keep all documentation. Some policies ask you to call back (reverse charges) to a centre in your home country where an immediate assessment of your problem is made.
- Check if the policy covers ambulances or helicopter rescue, and an emergency flight home. If you have to stretch out, you will need two seats and somebody has to pay for them.

Citizens of EC countries are covered for emergency medical treatment throughout the EC on presentation of an E111 form. Enquire about this at your national health service or travel agent well in advance. Similar reciprocal arrangements exist between the Nordic countries. Australian Medicare covers emergency treatment in Italy, Malta, the Netherlands, Sweden and the UK.

You may still have to pay on the spot but you'll be able to reclaim these expenses back home (keep all documentation). However, travel insurance is still advisable because of the flexibility it offers in where and how you're treated, as well as covering expenses for ambulance and repatriation.

Medical Kit A small, straightforward medical kit is a wise thing to carry. A possible kit list includes:

- Aspirin or Panadol – for pain or fever
- Antihistamines – useful as a decongestant for colds, allergies, to ease the itch from insect bites or stings or to help prevent motion sickness
- Kaolin preparation (Pepto-Bismol), Imodium or Lomotil – for possible stomach upsets in southern Europe
- Antiseptic, Mercurochrome and antibiotic powder or similar 'dry' spray – for cuts and grazes
- Calamine lotion – to ease irritation from bites or stings
- Bandages and Band-aids – for minor injuries.
- Scissors, tweezers and a thermometer (note that mercury thermometers are prohibited by airlines)
- Insect repellent, sunscreen, suntan lotion, chapstick, perhaps water purification tablets

When buying medicines over the counter make sure that correct storage conditions have been followed and that the expiry date has not passed. If you're travelling in the Baltic States, bring condoms and a broad spectrum antibiotic, sterile syringes (in case you need an injection), as well as any medicines you think you'll need on the trip – even aspirin.

Health Preparations If you wear glasses or contact lenses, take a spare pair and your prescription. Losing your glasses can be a real problem, but you can usually get new spectacles made up quickly, cheaply and competently.

If you require a particular medication, take an adequate supply, as it may not always be available in out-of-the-way places. The same applies for women's specific oral contraceptive. Take prescriptions, with the generic rather than the brand name (which may not be locally available), as it will be easier to obtain replacements.

It's a good idea to have a prescription and a letter from your doctor to show you legally use the medication – it's surprising how often over-the-counter drugs from one place are illegal without a prescription or even banned in another place. Keep the medication in its original container. If you're carrying a syringe for some reason also have a letter of explanation from your doctor.

A Medic Alert tag is a good idea if your medical condition is not always easily recognisable (heart trouble, diabetes, asthma, allergic reactions to antibiotics, etc).

Immunisations In Europe (including the Baltic states) jabs are not necessary, but they may be an entry requirement if you're coming from an infected area – yellow fever and cholera are the most likely requirements. If you're going to Europe with stopovers in Asia, Africa or Latin America, check with your travel agent or with the embassies of the countries you plan to visit.

There are, however, a few routine vaccinations that are recommended whether you're travelling or not, and this Health section assumes that you've had them: polio (usually administered during childhood), tetanus and diphtheria (usually administered together during childhood, with a booster shot every 10 years), and sometimes measles. See your physician or nearest health agency about these.

All vaccinations should be recorded on an International Health Certificate, which is available from your physician or government health department. Don't leave having the vaccinations till the last minute, since they may have to be spread over a period of time.

Basic Rules

Food Stomach upsets are probably a more likely travel-health problem in the Baltic states than in Scandinavian countries but most of these upsets will be relatively minor. Don't become paranoid: trying the local food is part of the experience of travel after all, although some of the traditional Icelandic food such as putrefied shark's meat *(hákarl)* doesn't sound very appetising.

Mushroom-picking is a favourite pastime in Europe especially as autumn approaches, but make sure you don't eat any mushrooms that haven't been positively identified as safe.

Salad vegetables and fruit should be safe throughout Western Europe, but elsewhere they should be washed with purified water or peeled where possible. Even though tap water in the Baltic states isn't always advisable to drink, cases of travellers getting ill after eating salads or other foods that may have been washed in it, are rare.

Ice cream is usually OK, but beware of that sold by street vendors, and of all ice cream that has melted and been refrozen. Take great care with fish or shellfish (for instance, cooked mussels that haven't opened properly can be dangerous), and avoid undercooked meat. If a place looks clean and well run and if the vendor also looks clean and healthy, then the food is probably safe. In general, places that are packed with travellers or locals will be fine. Be careful with food that has been cooked and left to go cold.

Nutrition If you don't vary your diet, and are travelling hard and fast and therefore missing meals, or you simply lose your appetite, you can soon start to lose weight and place your health at risk, just as you could at home.

If you rely on fast foods, you'll get plenty of fats and carbohydrates but little else. Remember that overcooked food loses much of its nutritional value. If your diet isn't well balanced, it's a good idea to take vitamin and iron pills. Fruit and vegetables are good sources of vitamin, but also are very expensive in Scandinavia where they're not often served in large quantities; taking vitamin supplements may be a good idea.

Water Tap water is almost always safe to drink in Scandinavia, but may be dubious in the Baltic states, where it smells distinctly unwholesome in some places. Some Baltic locals say they boil tap water before drinking it; others don't. It's a matter of taking local advice in each place you come to, and exercising care: even if locals can drink the stuff happily, you might not be able to since you won't have built up any immunity to whatever organisms it might contain. If in doubt, stick to mineral water (widely available and cheap), tea etc, or boil the tap water (an electric water-heating element is a useful item of luggage for this reason).

Throughout Scandinavian and Baltic Europe always be wary of drinking natural water. The burbling stream may look crystal clear and very inviting, but before drinking from it you want to be absolutely sure there are no people or cattle upstream; take particular care in Iceland, the Faroe Islands, and the Baltic States.

Water Purification This section is only relevant if you're going to spend some time in the Baltic states, or on extended hikes anywhere you'll have to rely on natural water.

The simplest way of purifying water is to boil it thoroughly. Technically this means boiling for 10 minutes, something which happens very rarely! Remember that at high altitude water boils at lower temperature, so germs are less likely to be killed.

Simple filtering will not remove all dangerous organisms, so if you cannot boil water it should be treated chemically. Chlorine tablets (Puritabs, Steritabs or other brand names) will kill many but not all pathogens. Iodine is very effective for purifying water and is available in tablet form (such as Potable Aqua), but follow the directions carefully and remember that too much iodine can be harmful.

If you can't find tablets, tincture of iodine (2%) or iodine crystals can be used. Two drops of tincture of iodine per litre or quart of clear water is the recommended dosage; the treated water should be left to stand for 30 minutes before drinking. Iodine crystals can also be used to purify water but this is a more complicated process, as you have to prepare a saturated iodine solution first. Iodine loses its effectiveness if exposed to air or damp so keep it in a tightly sealed container. Flavoured powder will disguise the taste of treated water and is a good idea if you are travelling with children.

Everyday Health A normal body temperature is 98.6°F or 37°C; more than 2°C higher is a high fever. A normal adult pulse rate is 60 to 80 beats a minute (children 80 to 100, babies 100 to 140). You should know how to take a temperature and a pulse rate. As a general rule the pulse increases by about 20 beats a minute for each °C rise in fever.

Respiration rate is also an indicator of illness. Count the number of breaths per minute: between 12 and 20 is normal for adults and older children (up to 30 for younger children, 40 for babies). People with a high fever or serious respiratory illness (such as pneumonia) breathe more quickly than normal. More than 40 shallow breaths a minute usually means pneumonia.

Many health problems can be avoided by taking care of yourself. Avoid climatic extremes: keep out of the sun when it's hot, dress warmly when it's cold. Minimise insect bites by covering bare skin when insects are around, or by using insect repellents.

Medical Treatment
Local pharmacies or neighbourhood medical centres are good places to visit if you have a small medical problem and can explain what it is. Hospital casualty wards will help if it's more serious, and will tell you if it's not. Major hospitals and emergency numbers are indicated on the maps in this book or mentioned in the text. Tourist offices and hotels can put you on to a doctor or dentist; your embassy will probably know one who speaks your language.

In an emergency whilst travelling in the Baltic states, seek help initially at your hotel. The bigger hotels may have a doctor on call. There are a few expensive medical and dental services aimed primarily at foreigners. They often advertise in the top hotels. If things are really serious, be prepared to fly out.

Climatic & Geographical Considerations
Sunburn Anywhere on water, sand, ice or snow, you can get sunburnt surprisingly quickly, even through cloud. Use a sunscreen and take extra care to cover areas that don't normally see sun – eg your feet. A hat provides added protection, and it may be a good idea to use zinc cream or some other barrier cream for your nose and lips. Calamine lotion is good for mild sunburn.

Remember that too much sunlight, whether it's direct or reflected (glare), can damage your eyes. If your plans include being near water, sand, ice or snow, then good sunglasses are doubly important. Make sure they're treated to absorb ultraviolet radiation; if not, they'll do more harm than good as they dilate your pupils and make it easier for ultraviolet light to damage the retina.

Cold Too much cold is just as dangerous as too much heat, particularly if it leads to hypothermia. Cold combined with wind and moisture (ie soaking rain) is particularly risky. If you are trekking at high altitudes or in a cool, wet environment, be prepared.

Hypothermia occurs when the body loses heat faster than it can produce it and the core temperature of the body falls. It is surprisingly easy to progress from very cold to dangerously cold through a combination of wind, wet clothing, fatigue and hunger, even if the air temperature is above freezing. It is best to dress in layers – silk, wool and some of the new artificial fibres are all good insulating materials. A hat is important, as most heat is lost through the head. A strong, waterproof outer layer is essential, as keeping dry is vital. Carry basic supplies, including food that contains simple sugars to generate heat quickly, and lots of fluid to drink.

Symptoms of hypothermia are exhaustion, numb skin (particularly toes and fingers), shivering, slurred speech, irrational or violent behaviour, lethargy, stumbling, dizzy spells, muscle cramps and violent bursts of energy. Irrationality may take the form of sufferers claiming that they are warm and trying to take off their clothes.

To treat hypothermia, first get the patient out of the wind and/or rain, remove their clothing if it's wet and replace it with dry, warm clothing. Give them hot nonalcoholic liquids and some high-kilojoule, easily digestible food. This should be enough for the early stages of hypothermia, but if it has gone further it may be necessary to place victims in warm sleeping bags and get in with them. Do not rub patients, place them near a fire or remove their wet clothes in the wind. If possible, place a sufferer in a warm, but not hot, bath.

Motion Sickness Eating lightly before and during a trip will reduce the chances of motion sickness. If you are prone to motion sickness, try to find a place that minimises disturbance – near the wing on aircraft, close to midships on boats, near the centre on buses. Fresh air and looking at a steady reference point like the horizon usually help, whereas reading or cigarette smoke don't. Commercial antimotion-sickness preparations, which can cause drowsiness, have to be taken before the trip commences; when you're feeling sick it's too late. Ginger is a natural preventative and is available in capsule form.

Diseases of Insanitation
Diarrhoea A change of water, food or climate can all cause the runs; diarrhoea caused by contaminated food or water is more serious. Despite all your precautions, you may still have a bout of mild travellers' diarrhoea if you travel beyond the relatively safe confines of Western Europe, but a few rushed toilet trips with no other symptoms is not indicative of a serious problem.

Moderate diarrhoea, involving half-a-dozen loose bowel movements in a day, is more of a nuisance. Dehydration is the main danger with any diarrhoea, particularly for children, so fluid replenishment is the number one treatment. Weak black tea with a little sugar, soda water, or soft drinks allowed to go flat and diluted by 50% with water are all good.

With any diarrhoea more severe than this, go straight to the casualty ward of the nearest hospital and have yourself checked. You may need a rehydrating solution to replace minerals and salts. Stick to a bland diet as you recover.

If you're going to Iceland and the Faroes or even on a short tour from the Baltic states to St Petersburg in Russia, you'll want to know about *Giardia lamblia* (an intestinal parasite which causes giardiasis, commonly known as giardia or 'beaver fever'). Get your physician to explain it in more detail. As previously mentioned, water purification tablets can be a good idea in these more remote areas and in the Baltic states (see also Health in the individual country chapters).

Viral Gastroenteritis This is caused not by bacteria but, as the name suggests, by a virus. It is characterised by stomach cramps, diarrhoea, and sometimes by vomiting and a slight fever. All you can do is rest and drink lots of fluids.

Worms These parasites are most common in rural areas outside Europe and a stool test when you return home is not a bad idea. They can be present on unwashed vegetables or in undercooked meat and you can pick them up through your skin by walking in bare feet. Infestations may not show up for some time, and, although they are generally not serious, if left untreated they can cause severe health problems. A stool test is necessary to pinpoint the problem, and medication is often available over the counter.

Diseases Spread by People & Animals
Rabies Though rare in Europe, and usually dealt with swiftly and decisively by the authorities, rabies is found in many countries including Denmark and is caused by a bite or scratch by an infected animal. Dogs are a noted carrier, but cats, foxes and bats can also be affected. Any bite, scratch or even lick from a mammal should be cleaned immediately and thoroughly. Scrub with soap and running water, and then clean with an alcohol solution. If there is any possibility that the animal is infected, particularly if it froths at the mouth and behaves strangely, medical help should be sought immediately. Even if it is not rabid, all bites should be treated seriously as they can become infected or can result in tetanus.

Tuberculosis (TB) Although this disease is widespread in many developing countries and used to be a scourge in Europe, it is not a serious risk to healthy travellers. Young children are more susceptible than adults and vaccination is a sensible precaution for children under 12 travelling in endemic areas. TB is commonly spread by coughing (droplet infection), or by eating or drinking unpasteurised dairy products from infected cows. Milk that has been boiled is safe to drink; the souring of milk to make yoghurt or cheese also kills the bacilli.

Sexually Transmitted Diseases (STDs) Sexual contact with an infected sexual partner spreads these diseases. Although abstinence is the only 100% preventative, using condoms is also effective. Gonorrhoea and syphilis are the most common sexually transmitted disease: sores, blisters or rashes around the genitals, discharges, or pain when urinating are common symptoms. Symptoms may be less marked or not observed at all in women. Syphilis symptoms eventually disappear completely but the disease continues and can cause severe problems in later years. Antibiotics are used to treat gonorrhoea and syphilis.

There are numerous other STDs. For most of them effective treatment is available. STD clinics are widespread in Europe. Don't be shy about visiting them if you think you may have contracted something. However, there is no cure for herpes.

HIV/AIDS has become a considerable problem in Europe. HIV, the human immunodeficiency virus, may develop into aids, acquired immune deficiency syndrome. Always practising safe sex using condoms is the most effective preventative; it is impossible to detect the sero-positivity (HIV positive status) of an otherwise healthy-looking person. HIV/AIDS can also be spread through infected blood transfusions; most developing countries cannot afford to screen blood used for transfusions.

It can also be spread by dirty needles – vaccinations, acupuncture, ear or nose piercing and tattooing can potentially be as dangerous as intravenous drug use if the equipment is not clean. If you do need an injection outside Western Europe, it may be a good idea to buy a new syringe from a pharmacy and ask the doctor to use it.

Cuts, Bites & Stings

Treat any cut with an antiseptic solution and Mercurochrome. Where possible avoid bandages and Band-aids, which can keep wounds wet.

Bee and wasp stings are usually painful rather than dangerous. Calamine lotion will give relief or ice packs will reduce the pain and swelling. There are some spiders with dangerous bites (rare in Europe) but antivenenes are usually available. Midges, small blood-sucking flies related to mosquitoes, are common in Arctic regions during summer.

Mosquitoes Mosquitoes, as well as being a nuisance, can almost drive you insane during the summer months in northern Europe – Finland, with its many lakes, is particularly notorious. The subsoil in much of Scandinavia remains frozen throughout the year (the so-called permafrost), and when snow and ice begin to melt in spring the water can't sink away, thus turning the countryside into one huge swamp. This is an ideal breeding ground for billions of hyperactive insects

that only have three months in which to do their thing.

Early summer is the worst period, and hikers will have to cover exposed skin and may even need special mosquito hats with netting to screen their faces. Seek local advice, as regular mosquito repellents and coils are hardly effective against the ravenous hordes that home in on you 24 hours a day. A mosquito-proof tent is absolutely essential at night. Fortunately, mosquito-borne diseases such as malaria are unknown in this part of the world, and the main risks are mental (people have been driven literally insane by the incessant buzzing and itching).

Most people get used to mosquito bites after a few days as their bodies adjust and the itching and swelling become less severe. An antihistamine cream should help alleviate the symptoms.

Snakes Snakes tend to keep a very low profile, but to minimise your chances of being bitten always wear boots, socks and long trousers when walking through undergrowth where snakes may be present. Tramp heavily and they'll usually slither away before you come near. Don't put your hands into holes and crevices, and be careful when collecting firewood.

Snake bites do not cause instantaneous death and antivenenes are usually available. Keep the victim calm and still, wrap the bitten limb tightly, as you would for a sprained ankle, and then attach a splint to immobilise it. Then seek medical help, if possible with the dead snake for identification. Don't attempt to catch the snake if there is even a remote possibility of being bitten again. Tourniquets and sucking out the poison are now comprehensively discredited.

Lice All lice cause itching and discomfort. They make themselves at home in your hair (head lice), your clothing (body lice) or in your pubic hair (crabs). You catch lice through direct contact with infected people or by sharing combs, clothing and the like. Powder or shampoo treatment will kill the lice, and infected clothing should then be washed in very hot water.

Women's Health
Some women experience irregular periods when travelling due to the upset in routine. Don't forget to take time zones into account if you're taking the pill. If you have intestinal problems, the pill may not be absorbed. Ask your physician about any of these concerns.

Gynaecological Problems Yeast infections, characterised by a rash, itch and discharge, can be treated with a vinegar or even lemon-juice douche or with yoghurt. Nystatin suppositories are the usual medical prescription for thrush. Trichomonas is a more serious infection; symptoms are a discharge and a burning sensation when urinating. Flagyl is the prescribed drug for trichomonas. If a vinegar-water douche is not effective, medical attention should be sought. With all of these infections male sexual partners must also be treated.

WOMEN TRAVELLERS
Women often travel alone or with other women in Europe. While this is usually quite safe, women do tend to attract more unwanted attention than men. Common sense is the best guide to dealing with potentially dangerous situations like hitchhiking, walking alone at night etc. In the former Soviet republics of Estonia, Latvia and Lithuania, prostitution is still rife in some tourist hotels (more rarely in the new ones run by Western companies): a woman sitting alone in a lobby, corridor or café might be propositioned.

The best advice is to act confidently, know where you're going and avoid problem areas. Recommended reading is the *Handbook for Women Travellers* by M & G Ross published by Judy Piatkus Publishers (London). See also Facts for the Visitor in the Scandinavian country chapters of this book.

DANGERS & ANNOYANCES
Europe is as safe or unsafe as any other developed part of the world. If you can handle Toronto, Sydney or Hong Kong, you'll have little trouble dealing with the less pleasant aspects of Europe.

Theft
As a traveller, you're often fairly vulnerable and when you do lose things it can be a real hassle. Theft is more of a problem in the Baltic states (see the Estonia Facts for the Visitor section for more details) than in Scandinavian countries and it's not primarily fellow travellers you have to be wary of. The most important things to guard are your passport, papers, tickets and money. It's best to carry these next to your skin or in a sturdy leather pouch on your belt at all times. Railway station lockers or luggage storage counters are useful places to store your luggage (but not valuables) while you get your bearings in a new town. Be very suspicious about people who offer to help you operate your locker. You should carry your own padlock for hostel lockers.

You can further lessen the risks by being careful of snatch thieves. Cameras or shoulder bags are great for these people, who sometimes operate from motorcycles or scooters and expertly slash the strap before you have a chance to react. A small daypack is better, but watch your rear. Pickpockets are most active in dense crowds, especially in busy railway stations and peak-hour public transport. A common ploy is for one person to distract you while another zips through your pockets. Beware of gangs of dishevelled-looking kids, waving newspapers and demanding attention. In the blink of an eye a wallet or camera can go missing.

Be careful even in hotels; don't leave valuables lying around in your room. Also be wary of sudden friendships as you never know what the 'new friend' may be after. Some of the prostitutes working in tourist hotels in the Baltic states rob their customers.

Parked cars are prime targets for petty criminals in most cities, and cars with foreign number plates or rental company stickers are in particular danger. Cover up the Avis or Hertz stickers with local football club stickers, or something, leave a local newspaper on the seat and generally try to make it look like a local car. Don't ever leave valuables in the car – remove all luggage overnight, even (some would say especially) if it's in a parking garage. In some places even freeway service centres have become unsafe territory: in the time it takes to drink a cup of coffee your car can be broken into and its contents cleared out. In case of theft or loss, always report the incident to the police and ask for a statement, or your travel insurance won't pay out.

There is a variety of other ways of losing things apart from straightforward theft and robbery. Over the years, Lonely Planet has received letters from unfortunate travellers who have been the victims of just about every scam imaginable. Two favourites have been airline-ticket rackets and 'bargain' antiques. Gambling rackets (such as the one where an operator shuffles matchboxes, one of them containing the token, amid a cheering crowd of helpers), travellers' cheques deals and guaranteeing loans are scams on which unfortunate or foolish travellers have lost their shirts. Just keep your wits about you.

Photocopies The loss of your passport is a real hassle but it can be made a little easier if, somewhere else, you've got a record of its number and issue date, or even better, photocopies of the relevant data pages. A photocopy of your birth certificate can also be useful.

While you're compiling that information, add the serial numbers of your travellers' cheques (cross them off as you cash them in) and photocopies of your credit cards, airline ticket and other travel documents. Keep all this emergency material totally separate from your passport, cheques and other cash, and leave extra copies with someone reliable at home. Add some emergency money, say US$50, to this separate stash as well. If you do lose your passport, notify the police immediately to get a statement and contact your nearest consulate.

Drugs

Always treat drugs with a great deal of caution. There is a fair bit of dope available in the region, sometimes quite openly, but that doesn't mean it's legal. Even a little harmless hashish can cause a lot of trouble. Also, as soon as you try to export it or start messing with heavier stuff the authorities will land on top of you.

Authorities in the Netherlands and Denmark unofficially tolerate 'soft' drugs so that police can concentrate on the harder stuff. But whatever you may have heard, it's still illegal there, despite the proliferation of 'coffee shops' and discos with 'house dealers' that sell hash and grass, complete with price lists and choice of brands. Getting caught with a small amount for personal use in those countries might earn you no more than an angry rap over the knuckles, but could make life very difficult if you're already in trouble for something else. Larger amounts (the distinction is murky) put you in the much more serious 'dealer' category. Authorities in surrounding countries often take a dim view of such tolerance, and may well single you out for special attention at the border.

Don't bother bringing drugs home with you either. With 'suspect' stamps (including Amsterdam Airport) in your passport, energetic customs officials could well decide to take a closer look.

WORK

For details of working holidays see What Kind of Trip earlier in this chapter. Also see Work in the Facts for the Visitor sections of the individual country chapters for details of finding work in the Scandinavian countries.

ACTIVITIES

Europe offers countless opportunities to indulge in activities other than sightseeing. The varied geography and climate of Scandinavian and Baltic Europe allow the full range of outdoor pursuits: windsurfing, skiing, fishing, trekking, cycling, mountaineering – you name it. If your interests are more cerebral, you can enlist in courses on anything from language to alternative medicine. For more information see the individual country chapters.

Windsurfing

The beaches of Denmark in particular attract crowds in summer and of the many water sports on offer in Europe, windsurfing could well be the most popular after swimming and fishing. Its growth has been explosive in recent years in Scandinavia. If you haven't visited Europe in the past decade, you'll be surprised at the transformation that the 'poor people's sailing boats' have caused to the weekend appearance of lakes and coastal resorts. Wetsuits enable the keener windsurfers to continue their sport throughout the colder months. It's easy to rent sailboards in many tourist centres, and courses are usually on offer for beginners.

Skiing

Scandinavia is famous for winter sports and, in winter, snow skiing is the activity many Europeans prefer. Many people still opt for downhill skiing, though cross-country or nordic skiing has become very popular – skiing in Scandinavia is usually cross-country, with some of the world's best trails.

Alpine or downhill skiing is quite expensive due to the costs of ski lifts, accommodation and the après-ski drinking sessions. The hassle of bringing your own skis may not be worthwhile as equipment hire can be relatively cheap. As a rule, a skiing holiday in Europe will work out twice as expensive as a summer holiday of the same length. Cross-country skiing costs less than downhill skiing where you have to use ski lifts.

The skiing season generally lasts from early December to late March, though at higher altitudes, it may extend an extra month either way. Snow conditions can vary greatly from one year to another and from region to region, but January and February tend to be the best (and busiest) months. As well as visiting the ski resorts, you can ski day or night on tracks in some Scandinavian cities.

Hiking

Keen hikers could spend a lifetime exploring Europe's many exciting trails. There are national parks, nature reserves, and other interesting areas that may qualify as a trekker's paradise, depending on your preferences. In Scandinavia you can hike on well-marked trails (some complete with duration indicators, and food and accommodation available along the way) during the summer months. Guided treks are often available for those who aren't sure about their physical abilities or who simply don't know what to look for.

The European Rambling Association promotes long-distance walking, can help with maps and information, and is keen on environmental issues – contact Europäische Wandervereinigung eV (☎ 0681-39 00 70), Reichsstrasse 4, Saarbrücken, Germany. The UK-based Ramblers Holidays (☎ 0707-33 1133) offers hiking-oriented trips in Europe and elsewhere. Read the hiking information in the individual country chapters of this book and take your pick.

Cycling

Along with hiking, cycling is the best way to really get close to the scenery and the people, keeping yourself fit in the process.

Much of Europe is ideally suited to cycling. In the north-west, the flat terrain ensures that bicycles are a popular form of everyday transport, though rampant headwinds often spoil the fun. Popular cycling areas include much of Denmark, west Norway and the Lofoten islands. If you come from outside Europe, you can often bring your bicycle along on the plane for a surprisingly reasonable fee. Alternatively, this book lists many places where you can rent one (make sure it has plenty of gears if you plan anything serious). The minimum rental period in Scandinavia is generally one day, though rental agencies might take a dim view of rentals lasting more than a week.

See the Getting Around chapter and the individual country chapters for more information on bicycle touring, and for rental agencies and tips on places to visit.

Boating

Scandinavian Europe's many lakes, rivers and diverse coastlines offer a variety of boating options unmatched anywhere in the world. You can ride the rapids in a canoe in Finland or, during winter, take a trip on a Bosnian icebreaker; charter a yacht or hire a rowing boat or cruise the fjords or peaceful lake Mjøsa in Norway; cruise from Helsinki to Tallinn in Estonia or to St Petersburg in Russia – the possibilities are endless. The country chapters have more details.

Courses

Apart from learning new physical skills doing something like a diving or cross-country skiing course, you could enrich your mind in a variety of structured ways. Language courses are often available to foreigners through universities, folk high schools or private institutions, and these are justifiably popular since the best place to learn a language is in the country where it's spoken. But you can also take courses in art, literature, architecture, drama, music, cookery, alternative energy, photography, organic farming – you name it, and chances are there'll be a course somewhere that suits you.

In general, the best sources of information are the cultural institutes maintained by many European countries around the world, with the second-best bet being their embassies. Student exchange organisations, student travel agencies, and organisations like the YMCA/YWCA and the YHA can also put you on the right track. Ask about special holiday packages that include a course in something or other. In the Baltic states, Tartu and Vilnius universities are among the colleges offering summer language and cultural courses.

SPECIAL NEEDS

If you're a traveller with special requirements, national tourist offices can often provide information about facilities for particular groups. There are local organisations in Europe that cater for students, gays and lesbians, women travelling solo, disabled travellers and so on (see also the Facts for the Visitor sections of the country chapters).

Student Travellers

There are no specific problems facing students travelling in Europe apart from the obvious ones like shortage of money. You'll want to take advantage of money-saving opportunities open to students. Your local student travel agency is a great source of information on discounts and special deals for students and other young people – make it your first port of call, as it might help determine what you're going to do in the first place. Ask for any pamphlets and books that seem useful.

Travel with Children

Successful travel with young children can require some special effort. Don't try to overdo things; even for adults, packing too much into the time available can cause problems. Make sure the activities include the kids as well. Include children in the trip planning; if they've helped to work out where you will be going they will be much more interested when they get there. See Lonely Planet's *Travel with Children* by Maureen Wheeler for more information.

Disabled Travellers

If you have a physical disability, get in touch with the people at your national support organisation and ask about the countries you plan to visit; they can tell you about travelling independently or on a package tour. They often have complete libraries devoted to travel, and can put you in touch with travel agents who specialise in tours for the disabled. The British-based Royal Association for Disability and Rehabilitation (RADAR) publishes a useful guide called *Holidays and Travel Abroad: A Guide for Disabled People* which gives a good overview of facilities available to disabled travellers in Europe. Contact RADAR (☎ 071-637 5400) at 25 Mortimer St, London W1N 8AB.

Gay & Lesbian Travellers

Gays and lesbians can get in touch with the

relevant national organisations. This book lists several contact addresses and gay and lesbian venues in Europe, but your organisation should be able to provide you with much more comprehensive information. *The Spartacus Guide for Gay Men* published by Bruno Gmünder is a good international directory particularly for entertainment venues; it's best used in conjunction with listings in local newspapers. For lesbians, the international *Gaia's Guide* is recommended and lists local publications offering specific local information.

Senior Travellers

Senior citizens are entitled to many discounts in Europe on things like public transport, museum admission fees etc, provided they show proof of their age. In some cases they might need a special pass. The minimum qualifying age is generally from 60 to 65 for men, and from 55 to 65 for women. In your home country, a lower age may already entitle you to all sorts of interesting travel packages and discounts (on car rental, for instance) through organisations and travel agents that cater for senior travellers. Start hunting at your local senior citizens advice bureau. See the introductory Getting There & Away chapter for information about discounts.

Special Diets

If you have dietary restrictions – you're a vegetarian or you require kosher food, for example – tourist organisations may be able to advise you or provide lists of suitable restaurants. Some vegetarian restaurants are listed in this book. See also the Food section later in this chapter.

ACCOMMODATION

The cheapest places to stay in Europe are camping grounds, followed by hostels and student accommodation. Cheap hotels are virtually unknown in most of the northern half of Europe, but guesthouses, pensions, private rooms and B&Bs often present good value. (See the Accommodation sections of the Estonia, Latvia and Lithuania chapters

for specific details of accommodation in the Baltic states, where the situation has some unique features.) Self-catering flats and cottages are worth considering if you're with a group, especially if you plan to stay somewhere for a while.

The Facts for the Visitor sections of the individual country chapters give an overview of each of the accommodation options. During peak holiday periods, accommodation can be hard to find and unless you're camping it's advisable to book ahead. Even camp sites can often fill up, particularly popular big city ones.

Reservations

If you arrive in a country by air, there is often an airport hotel-booking desk, although it rarely covers the lower strata of hotels. Tourist offices often have extensive lists of accommodation, and the more helpful ones will go out of their way to find you something suitable. In most countries the fee for this service is very low and if accommodation is tight it can save you a lot of running around and phone calls. This is also an easy way to get around language problems. Agencies offering private rooms can be good value if you don't mind staying with a local family.

Sometimes people will come up to you on the street offering a private room or a hostel bed. This can be good or bad, there's no hard and fast rule – just make sure it's not way out in a suburb somewhere, and that you negotiate a clear price. As always, be wary when someone offers to carry your luggage: they might carry it right off.

Camping

Camping is immensely popular in most of Europe (Estonia, Latvia and Lithuania are exceptions) and is the cheapest form of accommodation. There's usually a charge per tent or site, per vehicle and per person. National tourist offices generally have booklets or brochures listing camp sites all over their country. See the Documents section for information on camping carnets.

Although some camp sites are commendably close to city centres in most cases they will be some distance out from the centre in larger cities. For this reason camping is most popular for people with their own vehicles. If you're on foot the money you save by camping can quickly be outweighed by the money you spend on commuting to and from a town centre. You also need a tent, sleeping bag, cooking equipment and other bits and pieces – easier to cart around if you have a vehicle.

Camping other than in designated camping grounds is difficult. The population density makes it hard to find a suitable spot to pitch a tent away from prying eyes. It is also illegal to camp without permission from the local authorities (the police or local council office) or from landowners (don't be shy about asking, since you may be pleasantly surprised by their response).

In some countries free camping is illegal on all but private land. This doesn't prevent hikers from occasionally pitching their tent for the night, and they'll usually get away with it if they keep a low profile (don't disturb the locals, don't build a fire or leave rubbish). At worst, they'll be woken up by the police and asked to move on. Beware of camping freelance near camping grounds. The right of common access applies in Scandinavian countries, but you need to follow each country's conventions as well as their laws. See the Facts for the Visitor sections of the individual country chapters for additional information.

Hostels & Youth Hostels

Hostels offer the cheapest roof over your head to be found in Europe. Most hostels are part of the national YHA (Youth Hostel Association), which is affiliated with the IYHF (International Youth Hostel Federation) but there are also some privately run hostels.

Technically you're supposed to be a member of the IYHF in order to use their hostels but you can often stay by simply paying an extra charge and this will often be set against future membership. Stay enough nights as a nonmember and you're automat-

ically a member. In Scandinavian countries, the hostels are geared for budget travellers of all ages, including families with kids, and have both dorms and private rooms. These hostels usually serve breakfast and/or have a group kitchen.

Some places may give IYHF members under 27 years of age priority if space is limited. To join the IYHF ask at any hostel or contact your national or local YHA office. The offices for each European country are covered in this book. National IYHF offices include:

Australia
Each state has its own Youth Hostel Association organisation. The National Administration Office is at Australian Youth Hostels Association, Level 3, 10 Mallett St, Camperdown NSW 2050 (☎ 02-565 1699)
Canada
Canadian Hostelling Association, 1600 James Naismith Drive, Suite 608, Gloucester, Ontario K1B 5N4 (☎ 613-748 5638)
England & Wales
Youth Hostels Association, Trevelyan House, 8 St Stephen's Hill, St Alban's, Herts AL1 2DY (☎ 0727-55215)
New Zealand
Youth Hostels Association of New Zealand, PO Box 436, Christchurch 1 (☎ 03-799 970)
Northern Ireland
Youth Hostels Association of Northern Ireland, 56 Bradbury Place, Belfast BT7 1RU (☎ 0232-324733)
Scotland
Scottish Youth Hostels Association, 7 Glebe Crescent, Stirling FK8 2JA (☎ 0785-51181)
USA
American Youth Hostels, PO Box 37613, Washington DC 200013-7613 (☎ 202-783 6161)

At a hostel you'll get a bed for the night, plus use of communal facilities which often include a kitchen where you can prepare your own meals. You are usually required to have a sleeping sheet, simply using your own sleeping bag is not permitted. If you don't have your own approved sleeping sheet you can usually hire one.

Hostels vary widely but the growing number of young people travelling and the increased competition from other forms of accommodation, particularly private 'backpacker hostels', have prompted many hostels to improve their facilities and cut back on rules and regulations. Increasingly hostels are open all day, curfews are disappearing and 'wardens' with a sergeant-major mentality are an endangered species. In some places, particularly Scandinavia and northern Europe you'll even find hostels with single and double rooms. Everywhere the trend has been towards smaller dormitories with just four to six beds.

The IYHF *Guide to Budget Accommodation* details hostels throughout Europe. There are other hostel guides available. Many hostels accept reservations by phone but usually not during peak periods; they'll often book you a place at your next destination for a small fee. You can also book hostels through national hostel offices. Popular hostels can be heavily booked in summer and limits may be placed on the number of nights you can stay.

Latvia and Lithuania so far have no youth hostels but Estonia has about a dozen, not (yet) affiliated to the IYHF. In late summer 1992 a new agency specialising in youth tourism, with hostels in the main Baltic cities and B&B places in several towns, made its appearance. Called BATS (Baltic Accommodation & Travel Service), its advertised prices were US$9 to US$11 a night. BATS (☎ 68 18 93) is at Sakala 11C, Tallinn, near the Hotel Palace.

The first BATS hostels opened in Tallinn, Riga, Vilnius and Kaunas. Initially it was uncertain whether they would be year-round or summer-only, or whether they would remain at the same addresses. You can telephone Helsinki 496 585 for the latest information, fax 44 92 16, or contact the Tallinn office.

Student Accommodation

Some university towns rent out student accommodation during holiday periods. These will often be single rooms and may have cooking facilities available. Enquire at the college or university, at student information services or at local tourist offices.

B&Bs, Guesthouses & Hotels

There's a huge range of accommodation above the hostel level. B&Bs, where you get a room and breakfast in a private home, are often the real bargains in this field. Private accommodation may go under the name of pensions, guesthouses and so on. Although the majority of B&Bs are simple affairs, there are more expensive ones where you will find attached bathrooms and other luxuries.

Above this level are hotels which at the bottom of the bracket may be no more expensive than B&Bs or guesthouses while at the other extreme they extend to luxury five-star hotels with price tags to match. Although categorisation varies from country to country, the hotels recommended in this book will usually range from no stars to one or two stars. In any town you'll generally find hotels clustered around the bus and railway station areas – always good places to start hunting.

Check your hotel room and the bathroom before you agree to take it, and make sure you know what it's going to cost – discounts are often available for longer stays. Also ask about breakfast, as it's sometimes included but other times you may be required to have it and to pay extra for it (which can be a real rip-off). If the sheets don't look clean, ask to have them changed right away. Check where the fire exits are.

If you think a hotel is too expensive, ask if they have anything cheaper. Often they may have tried to steer you into more expensive rooms. If you are with a group or plan to stay for a reasonable length of time, it's always worth trying to negotiate a special rate.

FOOD

Few regions in the world offer such a variety of cuisines in such a small area. Dishes can be completely different from one country to the next and sampling the local food is one of the most enjoyable aspects of travel.

The introductions to the country chapters contain details of local cuisine, and there are many suggestions on places to eat within the chapters. If you've tried several dishes and not found one to your taste, the best advice is to persevere – there will always be something to your taste. There often are alternatives, if you prefer – Chinese, Indian and the wide range of US-inspired fast-food places.

Restaurant prices vary enormously. In Scandinavia the cheapest places for a decent meal are often the self-service restaurants in department stores. Official student mensas or cafeterias are dirt cheap, but the food tends to be bland and it's not always clear whether you'll be allowed in if you're not a local student. Kiosks also sell cheap snacks that can be as much a part of the national cuisine as the fancy dishes.

Self-catering (buying your ingredients at a shop or market and preparing your own meals) can be a cheap and wholesome way of eating. Most campers and hostellers will end up preparing at least some of their meals

(Camping Gaz replacement canisters are widely available); hostels and student accommodation often have cooking facilities. Even if you don't cook, a lunch in a park with some crisp bread, local cheese and slivers of smoked fish or salami can be one of the recurring highlights of your trip.

Vegetarians are fairly well catered for in Scandinavia, less well in the Baltic states. Vegetarianism has taken off in a big way, though not everywhere to the same extent. Tourist offices can supply lists of vegetarian restaurants, and some are recommended in this book. Many standard restaurants have one or two vegetarian dishes, or at least a few items on the menu that don't contain meat. Some restaurants will prepare special diets if approached about this in advance and you can always ask the waiter to talk with the cook on your behalf. If all else fails, you'll have to put together your own meals from ingredients bought in shops and markets.

Getting There & Away

If you're heading for Scandinavian or Baltic countries from outside Europe, step one is still most likely to involve travel to/from Western Europe until travel to/from the former Soviet Union becomes less complicated.

If you're flying in these days of severe competition between the airlines, there are plenty of opportunities to find cheap tickets to a variety of 'gateway' cities like London, Athens, Frankfurt, Berlin or even Copenhagen which has one of the busiest airports in Europe.

Forget shipping, unless by 'shipping' you mean the many ferry services operating in the Baltic and North seas and in the Atlantic Ocean between Iceland and the Faroe Islands and the UK or Denmark. Only a handful of ships still carry passengers across the Atlantic. They don't sail often and passages are very expensive even compared with full-fare air tickets. See the Sea section of this chapter for more details.

Some travellers still arrive in Scandinavia or the Baltic states overland through what used to be the Soviet Union: Russia has borders with Norway, Finland, Estonia and Latvia; Belorussia borders Lithuania and Latvia. The trans-Siberian trains could well begin to carry more people to and from Europe as Russia opens up to tourism. See the following Train and Land sections for more details.

Whichever way you're travelling, make sure you take out travel insurance. This not only covers you for medical expenses and luggage theft or loss, but also for cancellation and delays in your travel arrangements (you might fall seriously ill two days before departure or something like that). It depends on your insurance and type of ticket, so ask both your insurer and your ticket-issuing agency to explain where you stand. Ticket loss is also covered by travel insurance. Make sure you have a separate record of all your ticket details – or better still, a photocopy (see Photocopies under Dangers & Annoyances in the introductory Facts for the Visitor chapter). Buy travel insurance as early as possible. If you buy it the week before you fly, you could find, for example, that you're not covered for delays to your flight caused by industrial action.

Paying for your ticket with a credit card often provides limited travel accident insurance. You may also be able to reclaim the payment if the operator doesn't deliver – in the UK, for instance, credit card providers are required by law to reimburse consumers if a company goes into liquidation and the amount in contention is over £100. Ask your credit card company what it will cover.

AIR

Remember always to reconfirm your onward or return booking by the specified time, usually 72 hours before departure on international flights. Otherwise there's a real risk that you'll turn up at the airport only to find that you've missed your flight because it was rescheduled or that you've been reclassified as a 'no show' (see the Air Travel Glossary), with all the problems that involves if your flight happens to be full.

Buying a Plane Ticket

The plane ticket will probably be the single most expensive item in your travel budget, and buying it can be an intimidating business. There is likely to be a multitude of airlines and travel agents hoping to separate you from your money, and it is always worth spending some time researching the current state of the market. Start early: some of the cheapest tickets have to be bought months in advance, and some popular flights sell out early.

Talk to other people who have travelled recently – they may be able to help stop you making some of the same old mistakes. Look at the ads in newspapers and magazines (don't forget the press of the ethnic group whose country you plan to visit), and watch for special offers.

Cheap tickets are available in two categories – official and unofficial. Official ones are advance purchase tickets, budget fares, youth fares, Apex, super-Apex or whatever other name the airlines care to tack on to them in order to fill seats.

Unofficial tickets are simply discounted tickets that the airlines release through selected travel agents. Don't go looking for discounted tickets straight from the airlines: they are only available through travel agents. Airlines can, however, supply information on routes and timetables, and their low-season, student and senior citizens' fares can be very competitive.

Return tickets usually work out cheaper

Air Travel Glossary

Apex Apex ('advance purchase excursion') is a discounted ticket which must be paid for in advance. There are penalties if you wish to change it.

Baggage Allowance This will be written on your ticket: usually one 20-kg item to go in the hold, plus one item of hand luggage.

Bucket Shop This is an unbonded travel agency specialising in discounted airline tickets.

Bumped Just because you have a confirmed seat doesn't mean you're going to get on the plane – see Overbooking.

Cancellation Penalties If you have to cancel or change an Apex ticket there are often heavy penalties involved – insurance can sometimes be taken out against these penalties. Some airlines impose penalties on regular tickets as well, particularly against 'no show' passengers (see No Shows).

Check In Airlines ask you to check in a certain time ahead of the flight departure (usually 1½ hours on international flights). If you fail to check in on time and the flight is overbooked, the airline can cancel your booking and give your seat to somebody else.

Confirmation Having a ticket written out with the flight and date you want doesn't mean you have a seat until the agent has checked with the airline that your status is 'OK' or confirmed. Meanwhile, you could just be 'on request'. It's also wise to reconfirm onward or return bookings directly with the airline 72 hours before departure (see Reconfirmation).

Discounted Tickets There are two types of discounted fares: officially discounted (see Promotional Fares) and unofficially discounted. The lowest prices often impose drawbacks like flying with unpopular airlines, inconvenient schedules, or unfavoured routes and connections. A discounted ticket can save you things other than money – you may be able to pay Apex prices without the associated Apex advance booking and other requirements. Discounted tickets only exist where there is fierce competition.

Full Fares Airlines traditionally offer 1st-class (coded F), business-class (coded J) and economy-class (coded Y) tickets. These days there are so many promotional and discounted fares available from the regular economy class that few passengers pay full economy fare.

Lost Tickets If you lose your airline ticket, an airline will usually treat it like a travellers' cheque and, after enquiries, issue you with another one. Legally, however, an airline is entitled to treat it like cash and if you lose it then it's gone forever. Take good care of your tickets.

No Shows No shows are passengers who fail to show up for their flight, sometimes due to unexpected delays or disasters, sometimes due to simply forgetting, sometimes because they made more than one booking and didn't bother to cancel the one they didn't want. Full fare passengers who fail to turn up are sometimes entitled to travel on a later flight. The rest of us are penalised (see Cancellation Penalties).

On Request An unconfirmed booking for a flight (see Confirmation) than two one-way tickets – often *much* cheaper (in some cases, a well-planned return ticket can even be cheaper than a single one-way). Beware that immigration officials often insist on return or onward tickets, and if you can't show either, you might be asked to provide proof of 'sufficient means of support', which means you have to show a lot of money.

Round-the-World (RTW) tickets have become very popular in recent years. The airline RTW tickets are often real bargains, and can work out to be no more expensive or even cheaper than an ordinary return ticket. Prices start at about UK£850, A$1800 or US$1300 depending on the season. The official airline RTW tickets are usually put together by a combination of two airlines,

---

Open Jaws This is a return ticket where you fly out to one place but return from another. If available, this can save you backtracking to your arrival point.

Overbooking Airlines hate to fly empty seats, and since every flight has some passengers who fail to show up (see No Shows), airlines often book more passengers than they have seats. Usually the excess passengers balance those who fail to show up but occasionally somebody gets bumped. If this happens, guess who it is most likely to be? The passengers who check in late.

Promotional Fares These are officially discounted fares like Apex fares which are available from travel agents or direct from the airline.

Reconfirmation At least 72 hours prior to departure time of an onward or return flight you must contact the airline and 'reconfirm' that you intend to be on the flight. If you don't do this the airline can delete your name from the passenger list and you could lose your seat. You don't have to reconfirm the first flight on your itinerary or if your stopover is less than 72 hours. It doesn't hurt to reconfirm more than once.

Restrictions Discounted tickets often have various restrictions on them – advance purchase is the most usual one (see Apex). Others are restrictions on the minimum and maximum period you must be away, such as a minimum of 14 days or a maximum of one year. See Cancellation Penalties.

Standby This is a discounted ticket where you only fly if there is a seat free at the last moment. Standby fares are usually only available on domestic routes.

Tickets Out An entry requirement for many countries is that you have an onward or return ticket – in other words, a ticket out of the country. If you're not sure what you intend to do next, the easiest solution is to buy the cheapest onward ticket to a neighbouring country or a ticket from a reliable airline which can later be refunded if you do not use it.

Transferred Tickets Airline tickets cannot be transferred from one person to another. Travellers sometimes try to sell the return half of their ticket, but officials can ask you to prove that you are the person named on the ticket. This is unlikely to happen on domestic flights, but on international flights, tickets may be compared with passports. Also, if you're flying on a transferred ticket and something goes wrong with the flight (hijack, crash), there will be no record of your presence on board.

Travel Agencies Travel agencies vary widely and you should ensure you use one that suits your needs. Some simply handle tours while full-service agencies handle everything from tours and tickets to car rental and hotel bookings. A good one will do all these things and can save you a lot of money, but if all you want is a ticket at the lowest possible price, then you really need an agency specialising in discounted tickets. A discounted ticket agency, however, may not be useful for other things, like hotel bookings.

Travel Periods Some officially discounted fares, Apex fares in particular, vary with the time of year. There is often a low (off-peak) season and a high (peak) season. Sometimes there's an intermediate or shoulder season as well. At peak times, when everyone wants to fly, not only will the officially discounted fares be higher but so will unofficially discounted fares, or there may simply be no discounted tickets available. Usually the fare depends on your outward flight – if you depart in the high season and return in the low season, you pay the high-season fare. ■

and permit you to fly anywhere you want on their route systems so long as you do not backtrack. Other restrictions are that you (usually) must book the first sector in advance and cancellation penalties then apply. There may be restrictions on how many stops you are permitted and usually the tickets are valid from 90 days up to a year. An alternative type of RTW ticket is one put together by a travel agent using a combination of discounted tickets.

Generally you can find discounted tickets at prices as low as or lower than the Apex or budget tickets. Phone around the travel agents for bargains. Find out the fare, the route, the duration of the journey, the stopovers allowed, and any restrictions on the ticket (see Restrictions in the Air Travel Glossary). Ask about cancellation penalties.

You may discover that those impossibly cheap flights are 'fully booked, but we have another one that costs a bit more...'. Or the flight is on an airline notorious for its poor safety standards and leaves you confined to the transit lounge in the world's least favourite airport in mid-journey for 14 hours. Or they claim only to have the last two seats available for that country for the whole of July, which they will hold for you for a maximum of two hours. Don't panic – keep ringing around.

If you are travelling from the USA or South-East Asia, or trying to get out of Europe from the UK, you will probably find that the cheapest flights are being advertised by obscure agencies whose names haven't yet reached the telephone directory. Many such firms are honest and solvent, but there are still a few rogues who will take your money and disappear, to reopen elsewhere a month or two later under a new name. If you feel suspicious about a firm, don't give them all the money at once – leave a deposit of 20% or so and pay the balance when you get the ticket. If they insist on cash in advance, go somewhere else or be prepared to take a very big risk. And once you have the ticket, ring the airline to confirm that you are actually booked on the flight.

You may decide to pay more than the rock-bottom fare by opting for the security of a better-known travel agent. Firms such as STA, which has offices worldwide, Council Travel in the USA or Travel CUTS in Canada offer good prices to most destinations, and are unlikely to disappear overnight leaving you clutching a receipt for a nonexistent ticket.

Use the fares quoted in this book as a guide only. They are approximate and based on the rates advertised by travel agents at the time of going to press, and are likely to have changed by the time you read this.

Travellers with Special Requirements
If you've broken a leg, are vegetarian, travelling in a wheelchair, taking the baby, terrified of flying, whatever – let the airline staff know as soon as possible so that they can make arrangements. Remind them when you reconfirm your booking (at least 72 hours before departure) and again when you check in at the airport. It may also be worth ringing round the airlines before you make your booking to find out how they can handle your particular needs.

Children aged under two years travel for 10% of the standard fare (or free, on some airlines) as long as they don't occupy a seat. They don't get a baggage allowance either. 'Skycots', baby food and diapers should be provided by the airline if requested in advance. Children aged between two and 12 years can usually occupy a seat for half to two-thirds of the full fare, and do get a baggage allowance.

To/From the USA
The North Atlantic is the world's busiest long-haul air corridor and the flight options are bewildering. The *New York Times*, the *LA Times*, the *Chicago Tribune* and the *San Francisco Chronicle Examiner* all produce weekly travel sections in which you'll find any number of travel agents' ads. Council Travel and STA have offices in major cities nationwide. Access International in New York offers discounts to Europe from 50 cities in the USA.

You should be able to fly from New York

to Copenhagen, Oslo or Stockholm return for US$500 to US$600 low season, US$700 to US$800 high season. A number of US airlines have recently begun flying to Scandinavia, so fares should remain competitive. If you fly with SAS you can usually travel 'open-jaws' even with its cheapest fares, allowing you to land in one Scandinavian capital and return to New York from another at no extra cost.

One-way fares can work out to about half this on a stand-by basis. Airhitch (☎ 212-864 2000) specialises in this sort of thing. It can get you a one-way fare to Europe for US$160/269/229 from the east coast/west coast/elsewhere in the USA.

An interesting alternative to the boring New York-London flight is offered by Icelandair (☎ 800-223 5500 toll free USA), which has competitive year-round fares to Luxembourg with a stopover in Iceland's capital, Reykjavík – a great way of spending a few days in Iceland.

Another option is a courier flight, where you accompany a parcel or some freight to be picked up at the other end. A return fare from New York to London costs around US$250/500 for low/high season or less (around US$100 more from the west coast). The drawbacks are that your stay in Europe may be limited to one or two weeks, that your luggage is usually restricted to hand luggage (the parcel or freight you carry comes out of your luggage allowance), and that you may have to be a resident and apply for an interview before they'll take you on.

Find out more about courier flights from Council Travel in New York (☎ 212- 661 1450) and Los Angeles (☎ 310-208 3551), Discount Travel International in New York (☎ 212-362 3636), and Way to Go in Los Angeles (☎ 213-466 1126) and San Francisco (☎ 415-292 7801). Call two or three months in advance, at the very beginning of the calendar month.

The *Travel Unlimited* newsletter, PO Box 1058, Allston, MA 02134, USA publishes details of the cheapest air fares and courier possibilities for destinations all over the world from the USA and other countries including the UK. It's a treasure trove of information. A single monthly issue costs US$5, and a year's subscription, US$25 (US$35 abroad).

To/From Canada

Travel CUTS has offices in all major cities. Scan the budget travel agents' ads in the *Toronto Globe & Mail*, the *Toronto Star* and the *Vancouver Province*.

See the previous To/From the USA section for general information on courier flights. For courier flights originating in Canada, contact FB On Board Courier Services (☎ 514-633 0740 in Toronto or Montreal, or ☎ 604-338 1366 in Vancouver). A courier return flight to London or Paris will set you back about C$350 from Toronto or Montreal, or C$425 from Vancouver.

To/From Australia

STA and Flight Centres International are major dealers in cheap air fares. Check the travel agents' ads in the Yellow Pages and ring around.

The Saturday travel sections of Sydney's *Sydney Morning Herald* and Melbourne's the *Age* newspapers have many ads offering cheap fares to Europe, though don't be surprised if they happen to be 'sold out' when you contact the agents; they're usually low-season fares with conditions attached on obscure airlines. With Australia's large ethnic populations, it pays to check special deals in the ethnic press; Olympic Airways sometimes has good deals to Athens.

Discounted return fares on mainstream airlines through a reputable agent like STA cost between A$1600 (low season) and A$2500 (high season). Flights to/from Perth are a couple of hundred dollars cheaper.

To/From New Zealand

As in Australia, STA and Flight Centres International are popular travel agents in New Zealand. Not surprisingly, the cheapest fares to Europe are routed through the USA, and a Round-the-World ticket can be cheaper than a return.

To/From Africa

Nairobi is probably the best place in Africa to buy tickets to Europe, thanks to the many bucket shops and strong competition between them. A typical one-way/return fare to London would be about US$550/800. Several West African countries such as Burkina Faso and The Gambia offer cheap charter flights to France, and charter fares from Morocco can be incredibly cheap if you're lucky enough to find a seat. If you are thinking of flying to Europe from Cairo, it's often cheaper to fly to Athens and to proceed with a budget bus or train from there.

To/From Asia

Hong Kong is the discount plane-ticket capital of Asia, and its bucket shops are at least as unreliable as those of other cities. Ask the advice of other travellers before buying a ticket. Many of the cheapest fares from South-East Asia to Europe are offered by Eastern European carriers. STA has branches in Hong Kong, Tokyo, Singapore, Bangkok and Kuala Lumpur.

To/from India, the cheapest flights tend to be with Eastern European carriers like LOT and Aeroflot, or with Middle Eastern airlines such as Syrian Arab Airlines and Iran Air. Bombay is the air transport hub, with many transit options to/from South-East Asia, but tickets are slightly cheaper in Delhi. Try Delhi Student Travel Services in the Imperial Hotel, Janpath.

From the UK

If you're looking for a cheap way out of Europe, London is Europe's major centre for discounted fares. The Trailfinders head office in west London is an amazing place complete with travel library, bookshop, visa service and immunisation centre. STA also has branches in the UK. Campus Travel is helpful and has many interesting deals. Ask at discount travel agencies about courier flights organised by Polo Express, Courier Travel Service and Shades International Travel. The listings magazines *Time Out* and *City Limits*, the Sunday papers, the *Evening Standard* and *Exchange & Mart* carry ads for cheap fares. Also look out for the free magazines widely available in London, especially *TNT* (recommended), *Southern Cross* and *Trailfinder* – start by looking outside the main railway stations.

Most British travel agents are registered with ABTA (Association of British Travel Agents). If you have paid for your flight to an ABTA-registered agent who then goes out of business, ABTA will guarantee a refund or an alternative. Unregistered bucket shops are riskier but sometimes cheaper.

The Globetrotters Club (BCM Roving, London WC1N 3XX) publishes a newsletter called *Globe* which covers obscure destinations and can help you find travelling companions.

In London, Trailfinders (☎ 071-937 5400) and STA (☎ 071-937 9921) can both give you tailor-made versions of open-jaw return tickets where you fly into one city and out of another. Your chosen cities needn't necessarily be in the same country.

If you are travelling alone it might be worth looking into courier flights. See the previous To/From the USA section. Polo Express (☎ 081-759 5383) in London has the most options within Europe. Routes are subject to change every six months and you are committed to returning on a set date, usually within two weeks, although one-way courier options do exist.

From Continental Europe

Although London is the currently the travel discount capital of Europe, there are several other European cities where you'll find a wide range of good deals. Athens is one of them: shop around the travel agents in the backstreets between Syntagma and Omonia squares. Amsterdam is another good centre for cheap tickets.

In the future, Berlin looks likely to become Scandinavian and Baltic Europe's new air hub including flights to/from Moscow, and it's worth looking for airfare bargains. Travel agencies offering cheap flights advertise in the *Reisen* classified section of *Zitty*. The best of these is Alternativ Tours (☎ 8 81 20 89), Wilmersdorfer Strasse 94 (U-Bahn: Adenauerplatz). It specialises in unpublished, discounted tickets to anywhere in the world.

From Germany Lufthansa has regular connections with the Baltic states, Belorussia, Ukraine, Moscow and St Petersburg in Russia – a return Frankfurt-Minsk fare, for instance, can be had from DM788. Lufthansa also flies Berlin-Prague/Budapest/Warsaw; there are many discount options. For other information on cheap flights from Germany, check with travel agencies. Individuals offering plane tickets they no longer require, at very cheap prices, advertise in the *Urlaub & Reisen (biete)* section of major city newspapers. An airport departure tax of DM6 is included in German ticket prices.

Across Europe many travel agents have ties with STA, where cheap tickets can be purchased. Outlets in important transport hubs include:

Voyages et Découvertes (☎ 1-42.61.00.01),
    21 Rue Cambon, Paris
SRID Reisen (☎ 069-43 01 91), Berger Strasse 118,
    Frankfurt
ISYTS (☎ 01-32 21 267), 2nd floor, 11 Nikis St,
    Syntagma Square, Athens

The Belgian newsletter for 'passionate travellers', *Farang* (☎ 019-69 98 23), La Rue 8, 4261 Braives, Belgium, deals with exotic destinations as does the French club, Aventure du Bout du Monde, (☎ 1-43.35.08.95), 11bis Rue Maison Dieu, 75014 Paris.

TRAIN

To/from central and eastern Asia, a train can work out more cheaply than flying depending on how much time and money you spend along the way. You can choose from four different routes, three of which (the trans-Siberian, trans-Mongolian and trans-Manchurian) follow the same route to/from Moscow across Siberia but have different eastern railheads. The fourth, the trans-Kazakhstan, runs between Moscow and Ürümqi (north-western China) across central Asia. Trains between Moscow and Vilnius, Riga, Tallinn or Helsinki provide connections with the region covered by this book. Prices can vary enormously, depending on where you buy the ticket and what is included – the prices quoted here are a rough indication only.

Planning a trans-Siberian trip can be a complicated business, with decisions to be made on where to get your tickets, where to stop over (and how to avoid extortionate Intourist accommodation prices when you do), and what kind of Russian visa to get (and how to get it). Lonely Planet's *USSR – a travel survival kit* has a wealth of detail on all these aspects including details of ticket outlets in numerous countries. One basic fact to remember is that with a transit visa, as opposed to a tourist visa, for Russia, you don't have to book and pay in advance for overpriced accommodation at stopovers.

The trans-Siberian takes 6½ days from Moscow via Khabarovsk to Nakhodka, from where there is a boat to Japan (Yokohama) or Hong Kong. The boats only run from May to September. The complete rail/boat journey from Moscow to Yokohama costs upwards of US$640 per person, for a 2nd-class sleeper in a four-berth cabin.

The trans-Mongolian passes through Mongolia to Beijing and takes about 5½ days. A 2nd-class sleeper in a four-berth compartment would cost upwards of US$530 in Moscow. In Europe, cheaper tickets can be purchased from some travel agents in Budapest or Warsaw. In Beijing, CITS sells the cheapest tickets, starting at US$150. Tickets take about a week to organise, but if you need to prebook accommodation in Russia (depending on your visa), Intourist takes about four weeks to organise this.

The trans-Manchurian passes through Manchuria to Beijing and takes six days, costing the same as the trans-Mongolian.

The trans-Kazakhstan runs via Alma Ata (Kazakhstan). CITS at the moment will not book the ticket in Beijing, so you'll have to travel to Ürümqi first, where the ticket to Moscow is about US$95.

There are countless travel options

between Moscow and the rest of Europe. Most people will opt for a train, usually to/from Berlin, Helsinki, Munich or Vienna.

In Berlin, Reisewelt at Charlottenstrasse 45 just off Unter den Linden is a good place to buy international train tickets or make reservations as it's not too crowded. Youth-fare international train tickets are available from the former Jugendtourist, Friedrich-strasse 79a (open weekdays from 10 am to 6 pm, Saturday from 9 am to noon).

SRS Studenten Reise Service, at Marien-strasse 23, (U and S-Bahn: Friedrichstrasse) offers flights at student (aged 34 or less) or youth (aged 25 or less) rates. It also sells the FIYTO youth and ISIC student cards (DM10 and one photo).

If you're heading to Continental Europe from the UK, there are eight major railway stations in London all connected by the underground tube. If your train goes via south-east England (to/from France, Belgium, Spain or Italy), Victoria is the station; to/from Harwich or Felixstowe (for Germany, the Netherlands and Scandinavia), Liverpool St is your station; to/from New-castle (for Scandinavia), King's Cross is your station. A new international terminal is being built at Waterloo for the service that will use the Channel Tunnel. British Rail has information centres at all its main stations.

For more details of trains (including information on boat-trains and ferry services to Scandinavian and Baltic Europe), see the Getting There & Away chapters of the individual countries. For information about rail passes, see the Getting Around chapter.

LAND

After the heady 1970s, the overland trail to/from Asia lost much of its popularity in the 1980s as the Islamic regime in Iran made life hard for travellers from certain countries, while the war in Afghanistan closed that country to all but the most foolhardy. Now that Iran is rediscovering the merits of tourism, the Asia route has begun to pick up again, though unsettled conditions in Afghanistan and southern Pakistan could

prevent the trickle of travellers turning into a flood for the time being.

A new overland route through what used to be the Soviet Union could become important over the next few years. At this stage the options are more or less confined to the trans-Siberian railway lines to/from Moscow (see the previous Train section), but other modes of transport are likely to become available beyond the Urals as the newly independent states open up to travellers.

Going to/from Africa will involve a Mediterranean ferry crossing (discounting the complicated Middle East route). Due to political problems in Africa (war between Morocco and the Polisario in the west, civil war in Sudan in the east) the most feasible Africa overland routes run through Algeria and its southern neighbours.

Travelling by private transport beyond Europe requires plenty of paperwork and other preparations. A detailed description is beyond the scope of this book, but the following Getting Around chapter tells you what's required within Scandinavian and Baltic Europe.

Bus

If you're already in Europe, it's generally cheaper to get to Scandinavian and Baltic Europe by bus than it is by train or plane, though some discount plane fares can work out cheaper. Long bus rides can be tedious, so bring along a good book. Some of the coaches are quite luxurious with WC, air-conditioning, stewards and snack bar.

National Express Eurolines, 52 Grosvenor Gardens, London SW1 (☎ 071-730 0202) has representatives across Europe (buses leave from Victoria Coach Station in London). Eurolines' European representatives include:

Eurolines/Budgetbus (☎ 020-627 51 51), Rokin 10, Amsterdam
Eurolines (☎ 1-43.54.11.99), 55 Rue Saint Jacques, Paris
Deutsche Touring GmbH (☎ 069-7 90 30), Am Römerhof 17, 6000 Frankfurt 90
Deutsche Touring (☎ 089-59 18 24), Arnulfstrasse 3, Munich

Lazzi Express (☎ 06-884 0840), Via Tagliamento 27R, Rome

These offices may also have information on other bus companies and deals. A convenient West Berlin travel agency handling bus tickets is Reisebüro Zoo, Hardenbergplatz 2 opposite Zoo Station.

Eurolines Capital Trippers offer a return ticket from London taking in two capital cities from £59. There are regular services to Scandinavia from the Netherlands – from Amsterdam to Copenhagen takes 12 hours and costs f115. Advance reservations may be necessary on international buses and travel agents should be able to tell you where to go for them. Return fares are notably cheaper than two one-ways.

Eurolines has a youth fare for those aged under 26, which saves around 10%. It also has a daily service from London to Frankfurt which costs £49/83 for an adult one-way/return. Eurolines buses also run from Frankfurt to Warsaw and Prague, and from Munich to Prague, Zagreb, Istanbul and Athens. There are many other connections.

Europabus is the motor coach system of the European railways and has the following information offices:

Brussels (☎ 02-217 66 60)
Frankfurt (☎ 069-7 90 30)
Gothenburg (☎ 031-718 200)
Rome (☎ 06-481 82 77)
Vienna (☎ 01-501 80)

Most buses to the Baltic states start from Poland, so you may find it easier when heading for the Baltics to start with a bus to Warsaw, which is reached by many services. However, buses from Warsaw to the Baltics can get heavily booked, so be prepared to take a train or fly if necessary. Also check up on likely delays at road borders before committing yourself to a bus.

Car & Motorbike

Drivers of cars and riders of motorbikes will need the vehicle's registration papers as well as liability insurance and, sometimes, an international driving permit in addition to their domestic licence.

Liability insurance is not available in advance for many out-of-the-way countries, but has to be bought when crossing the border. The cost and quality of such local insurance varies wildly, and you will find in some countries that you are effectively travelling uninsured.

Anyone who is planning to take their own vehicle to the Baltic states needs to check in advance what spare parts and petrol are likely to be available. Lead-free petrol is not on sale everywhere, and neither are parts for your car. See also the introductory Getting Around chapter for details of travel in Scandinavian and Baltic Europe.

Cycling

Cycling is a cheap, convenient, healthy, environmentally sound and above all a fun way of travelling. One note of caution: before you leave home, go over your bike with a fine-tooth comb and fill your repair kit with every imaginable spare. As with cars and motorbikes, you won't necessarily be able to buy that crucial gizmo for your machine when it breaks down somewhere in the back of beyond as the sun sets.

Bicycles can travel by air. You *can* take them to pieces and put them in a bike bag or box, but it's much easier simply to wheel your bike to the check-in desk, where it should be treated as a piece of baggage. You may have to remove the pedals and turn the handlebars sideways so that it takes up less space in the aircraft's hold; check all this with the airline well in advance, preferably before you pay for your ticket. See also the introductory Getting Around chapter and the Getting Around sections of the individual country chapters.

Hitching & Ride Services

Several European organisations can help you find a ride to/from the Scandinavian or Baltic countries. Besides hitchhiking, the cheapest way to get to northern Europe from elsewhere in Europe is as a paying passenger in a private car.

If you are leaving from Germany, or travelling within that country, such rides are arranged by Mitfahrzentrale agencies in many German cities. You pay a reservation fee to the agency and your share of petrol to the driver. The local tourist information office will be able to direct you to several such agencies, or you can check the entry 'Mitfahrzentrale' in the Yellow Pages phone book.

There are organisations offering ride services in a number of other European countries, including the following:

Austria
    Daungasse 1a, Vienna (☎ 01-408 2210)
Belgium
    Marché aux Herbes 27, Brussels
    (☎ 02-512 1015)
The Netherlands
    Nieuwezijds Voorburgwal 256, Amsterdam
    (☎ 020-620 5121)
Switzerland
    Leonhardstrasse 15, Zürich (☎ 01-261 68 93)

For more details of local conditions and laws, see the individual country chapters.

SEA

The following are some of the companies running ferry services to/from Scandinavian or Baltic Europe:

Bergen Line (☎ 212-986 2711), 505 Fifth Ave, New York, NY 10017, USA
Color Line (☎ 091-296 1313), Tyne Commission Quay, North Shields NE29 6EA, UK
Norway Line (☎ 091-296 1313), Tyne Commission Quay, Albert Edward Dock, North Shields NE29 6EA, UK
Sealink (Stena Line Ltd) (☎ 0233-647047),Charter House, Park St, Ashford, Kent TN24 8EX, UK
Scandinavian Seaways, 15 Hanover St, London W1R 9HG, UK (☎ 071-493 6696), with offices at the ports in Newcastle and Harwich
Smyril Line (☎ 97 96 22 44), Auktionsgade 13, 7730, Hanstholm, Denmark
United Baltic, Baltic Exchange Buildings, 21 Bury St, London EC3 (☎ 071-493 6696)

See the individual Getting There & Away sections of the country chapters for information about boat-trains or rail/ferry links within Scandinavian and Baltic Europe. See also the introductory Getting Around chapter for details of rail passes and their validity on state-owned and other ferries.

From Germany

Hamburg is 20 hours by car ferry from the English port of Harwich. Timetables vary according to the time of year, and may be affected by extremes in the weather, but sailings are at least twice weekly in either direction. Check with the Scandinavian Seaways information line on Hamburg 38 90 31 17.

The busy train, car and passenger ferry from Puttgarden to Rødbyhavn (the quickest way to Copenhagen) goes every half hour 24 hours a day, and takes one hour. If you're travelling by train, the cost of the ferry will be included in your ticket.

From Kiel, Stena Line runs ferries to a number of Scandinavian ports including Gothenburg (Sweden) and Bagenkop on the Danish island of Langeland. Color Line has a service to Oslo (Norway) from Kiel which takes around 20 hours. Baltic Express Line has a service from Kiel to Stockholm.

In eastern Germany, there are five large ferries in each direction daily all year between Trelleborg just south of Malmö (Sweden) near Copenhagen, and Sassnitz Hafen near Stralsund.

From April to October, ferries also run several times a week between the Danish island of Bornholm and Sassnitz. Services from Ustad to Mukran (near Sassnitz) are planned as are weekly services to Lithuania from Kiel and Gdynia (Poland).

Coming from Berlin there are two car-ferry trains a day between Berlin-Zoo Station and Copenhagen via Rostock. These trains connect with the international ferry service from Warnemünde to Gedser, Denmark. The ferry terminal is a few minutes' walk from Warnemünde railway station, and the crossing takes only two hours. There is also a ferry (from Rostock, not Warnemünde) once a week to Rønne on the Danish island of Bornholm. Departures are on Saturday evening at 9 pm, the crossing takes around 11 hours. There is at least one ferry departure every day from Rostock to Trelleborg, Sweden. See also the relevant Getting There & Away sections in the individual country chapters.

To/From the UK or the Netherlands

Until one looks at the ferry possibilities, it's easy to forget how close Scandinavia and the UK are to each other.

Scandinavian Seaways has daily sailings from Harwich (England) to Gothenburg (Sweden), from where Stockholm is a seven-hour bus ride. There are also ferry services from Newcastle (England) to Esbjerg (Denmark) and Gothenberg. The ferry, the *Smyril*, sails weekly from Scrabster in Scotland to Tórshavn in the Faroe Islands.

One of the most interesting possibilities of travelling to Scandinavia is the summer-only link between the Shetlands, Norway, the Faroes, Iceland, and Denmark. The agent is P&O (☎ 0224-571615), but the operator is the Smyril Line.

The Smyril boat operates from 3 June to 28 August. The sailing order is Denmark (Saturday), to the Faroes (Monday), to the Shetlands (Monday), to Norway (Tuesday), to the Shetlands (Wednesday), to the Faroes (Wednesday), to Iceland (Thursday), to the Faroes (Friday), to Denmark (Saturday) and so on. One-way couchette fares from Shetland to Norway are £38/50, to the Faroes £45/60, to Denmark £92/122, to Iceland £97/130 in the low/high season.

From Newcastle, the Norwegian Color Line (☎ 091-296 1313) operates ferries all year to Stavanger and Bergen in Norway. During summer, Scandinavian Seaways (☎ 091-296 0101) operates ferries to Esbjerg, Denmark and Gothenburg, Sweden.

Harwich is the other major British port linking southern England and Scandinavia. Scandinavian Seaways (☎ 0255-240240) has ferries to Esbjerg (Denmark) and Gothenburg (Sweden). In summer, ferries leave every two days.

Sealink (☎ 0255-243333) runs two ferries a day from Harwich to the Hook of Holland in the Netherlands from where you can head

north by land. Scandinavian Seaways (☎ 0255-240240) runs at least three services a week to Esbjerg and Hamburg, and at least two a week to Gothenburg.

P&O (☎ 0304-203388) also runs two ferries a day from Felixstowe to Zeebrugge in the Netherlands from where you can travel by bus or train to Scandinavian or Baltic Europe. The shortest cross-Channel routes (from Dover to Calais or from Folkestone to Boulogne) are the busiest.

There are cargo ships from the UK to Baltic ports but agents say they don't take passengers. See the other relevant Getting There & Away sections for more travel details.

To/From Russia

If you're travelling to/from the Baltic states or Scandinavia via Russia (for example between St Petersburg and Finland, Sweden and possibly Denmark or Norway), Morpasflot (the former Soviet Passenger Shipping Association) is the parent body for CIS passenger lines operating in the Baltic Sea. In addition to cruises it has scheduled international services that can be booked by individuals.

Generally, your travel agency (or you) must contact the separate lines or their agents. All have roughly the same list of representatives abroad, including:

Australia: CTC Cruises, 6th floor, Forum House, 35-43 Clarence St, Sydney, NSW 2000
Finland: OY Saimaa Lines (☎ 43-05-225, telex SAILS SF 123473), Keilaranta 6, 02150 Espoo (PO Box 12)
Hong Kong: Wallem Travel (☎ 528-6514), 46th floor Hopewell Centre, 183 Queen's Rd East, Wanchai
Japan: United Orient Shipping & Agency Co (telex 26336), New Aoyama Building W-21F, 1-1-1 Minami-Aoyama, Minato-ku, Tokyo 107
Sweden: Scansov Transport AB, Karlavägen 53, S-10246 Stockholm (Box 5937 sa)
UK: CTC Lines (☎ 071-930 5833), 1-3 Lower Regent St, London SW1Y 4NN. Other sales agents in London are Scandinavian Seaways (☎ 071-491 7256) and Scantours (☎ 071-839 2927).

USA: International Cruise Center (☎ 516-747-8880 or toll-free 800-221-3254), 250 Old Country Rd, Mineola, NY 11501

For current schedule information, consult the monthly *ABC Passenger Shipping Guide* (see the following Passenger Ships section for more details). For those who want to try and book in Moscow, Morpasflot's administrative headquarters (telex 411134) is at korpus 7, ulitsa Novoslobodskaya 14/19, Moscow 103030.

Passenger Ships

The days of earning your passage on a freighter to or from Europe have well and truly passed. Even if you have a mariner's ticket, a shipping company is unlikely to want to sign you up for a single trip.

Regular, long-distance passenger ships disappeared with the advent of cheap air travel, to be replaced by a small number of luxury cruise ships. The grand lady of them all, Cunard's *Queen Elizabeth 2*, sails between New York and Southampton 20 times a year; the trip takes five nights each way and a return ticket can be had from UK£1255, though there are also one-way and 'fly one way' deals. Your travel agent will have more details. The standard reference for passenger ships is the *ABC Passenger Shipping Guide* published by the Reed Travel Group (☎ 0582-60 0111), Church St, Dunstable, Bedfordshire LU5 4HB, UK.

A more adventurous (though not necessarily cheaper) alternative is as a paying passenger on a freighter. Freighters are far more numerous than cruise ships and there are many more routes from which to choose. With a bit of homework, you'll be able to sail between Europe and just about anywhere else in the world, with stopovers at exotic ports which you may never have heard of. The previously mentioned *ABC Shipping Guide* is a good source of information, or contact the Freighter Travel Club of America, 3524 Harts Lake Rd, Roy, WA 98580 – included in the US$18 yearly membership is a monthly bulletin, *Freighter Travel News*.

Passenger freighters typically carry six to 12 passengers (more than 12 would require a doctor on board), and, though less luxurious than dedicated cruise ships, give you a real taste of life at sea. Schedules tend to be flexible and costs vary, but seem to hover around US$95 a day; vehicles can often be included for an additional fee.

One of the better known passenger freighter operators is Polish Ocean Lines. Its popular Atlantic routing (weekly service) is Bremerhaven, Le Havre, Halifax, New York, Baltimore, Wilmington, New York, Le Havre, Rotterdam and Bremerhaven, which costs UK£1375 for the 28-day round voyage or US$1010 for New York-Le Havre one-way (prices per person in a double cabin). Contact Gdynia America Line (☎ 212-952 1280), 39 Broadway, 14th floor, New York, NY 10006.

DEPARTURE TAXES

Some countries charge you a small fee for the privilege of leaving from their airports. Some also charge port fees when leaving by ship. Such fees are usually included in the price of your ticket, but it pays to check this when purchasing your ticket. If not, you'll have to have the fee ready when you leave. Details of departure taxes are given in the individual country chapters.

WARNING

This chapter is particularly vulnerable to change – prices for international travel are volatile, routes are introduced and cancelled, schedules change, special deals come and go, and rules and visa requirements are amended.

Airlines and governments seem to take a perverse pleasure in making price structures and regulations as complicated as possible. You should check directly with the airline or travel agent to make sure you understand how a fare (and ticket you may buy) works.

In addition, the travel industry is highly

competitive and there are many lurks and perks. The upshot of this is that you should get opinions, quotes and advice from as many airlines and travel agents as possible before you part with your hard-earned cash. The details given in this chapter should be regarded as pointers and are not a substitute for careful, up-to-date research.

Getting Around

If you can adapt your activities to the time-tables, getting around in Scandinavian Europe is a hassle-free experience; public transport services are efficient with excellent connections. Travelling around Baltic Europe will not be quite so straightfoward.

If you're experiencing language difficulties (particularly in the Baltic states, where few ticket clerks speak in foreign tongues), you can simplify ticket-buying by writing your requirements on a slip of paper, using the 24-hour clock for departure times and Roman numerals for the month in the date. If you want a ticket on the 3.45 pm departure to Vilnius on 24 July, write 15.45 Vilnius 24/VII.

Another problem in Estonia, Latvia and Lithuania is knowing which ticket window to go to. Some windows are reserved for same-day tickets, some for advance bookings, some for other arcane purposes. So don't be put off if the first clerk you deal with shouts brusquely at you and turns away.

AIR

At the beginning of 1993 the skies over the EC were deregulated, ending the virtual monopoly of some airlines within their home countries. Though the details are still being worked out, the likely result will be a slight drop in fares and a great increase in the choice of airlines on which to fly.

The different classes of cheap air tickets mentioned in the introductory Getting There & Away chapter are also available on internal European routes, in this case within Scandinavian and Baltic countries. Across Europe many travel agents have ties with STA, where cheap tickets can be purchased and even altered free of charge (for the first change only). For longer journeys, you can sometimes find air fares that beat on-the-ground alternatives in terms of cost. Getting between airports and city centres is rarely a problem in Scandinavian or Baltic Europe thanks mainly to good bus services.

The main drawback with flying is that you can't see very much from the air. It's the best way to go if you're very pushed for time, but if you really want to tour properly do it at ground level. Air travel is best regarded as a means to get you to the starting point of your itinerary rather than as your main means of travel. If you start taking aeroplanes for relatively short hops it can be extremely expensive, but the Scandinavian domestic airlines do offer some enticing discounts.

Open-jaw returns, by which you can travel into one city and out of another, provide some measure of flexibility (see the Getting There & Away chapter).

Visitors who fly SAS to Scandinavia from Europe, North America or Asia can purchase tickets on a Visit Scandinavia Fare which allows one-way travel on direct flights between any two Scandinavian cities serviced by SAS for US$80. Tickets must be purchased in advance before arriving in Scandinavia and in conjunction with a return SAS international ticket. There's no limit on the number of US$80 tickets you can buy.

BUS
International Buses

Bus travel tends to take second place to getting around by train in most of Europe, though when it comes to Estonia, Latvia and Lithuania it's at least as efficient and a little more expensive than the train. In Scandinavia, the bus has the edge in terms of cost but is generally slower, less comfortable and more cramped. Eurolines Bus Circuits offers a variety of tours of cities, see also the introductory Getting There & Away chapter for more details. Tickets are valid for two months with no reductions for students or young people.

On ordinary return trips, youth fares cost around 10% less than the ordinary full fare. Onward or return journeys must be reserved prior to departure for all tickets.

Local Buses

Buses provide a viable alternative to the rail network in Scandinavian countries. Again, compared with trains in these countries, buses are usually slightly cheaper and slightly slower. Bus travel tends to be best for shorter hops such as getting round cities and reaching remote rural villages.

Buses are often the only option in regions where rail tracks fear to tread; these buses often connect with train services. Advance reservations are rarely necessary. Many city buses operate on a pay-in-advance and punch-your-ticket-in-the-slot system. The Nordturist rail ticket is valid on the local bus lines from Storlien to Trondheim and from Halden/Sarpsborg to Strömstad. In the Baltic states, however, buses are generally more frequent, quicker, and a bit more expensive than trains (though still very cheap). See the individual country chapters for more details.

TRAIN

Trains are a popular way of getting around for backpackers; they are good meeting places and in Scandinavia are comfortable, frequent, and generally on time. Also in the Scandinavian countries, European rail passes make travel affordable. Supplements and reservation costs are not covered by passes, and pass holders must always carry their passport on the train for identification purposes.

If you plan to travel extensively by train it might be worth getting hold of the *Thomas Cook European Timetable*, which gives a complete listing of schedules and indicates where supplements apply or where reservations are necessary. Updated monthly, it is available from Thomas Cook outlets worldwide.

Oslo, Stockholm, Helsinki and Copenhagen are all important hubs for international rail connections. See the relevant city sections for budget ticket agents.

Express Trains

Fast trains can be identified by the symbols EC (EuroCity) or IC (InterCity). Supplements can apply on fast trains and it is a good idea (sometimes essential) to make seat reservations at peak times and on certain lines.

In Estonia, Latvia and Lithuania there are no fast trains. The few that are classed 'quick' (Russian: *skoryy*) are just a bit slower than the others (*passazhirskiy* or *dizel*). To make up for this, trains (like buses) in these countries are still amazingly cheap at the time of writing. The 440-km trip from Tallinn to Riga may take 7½ hours but it'll only cost US$1 in a four-bunk couchette if you buy the ticket yourself from the station. (You might be asked to pay an extra few cents for bedding once on board.)

Overnight Trains

Overnight trains will usually offer a choice of couchette or sleeper if you don't fancy sleeping in your seat with somebody else's elbow in your ear. Reservations are advisable and in Scandinavia are often necessary as they are allocated on a first-come, first-served basis.

Couchettes are bunks numbering four (1st class) or six (2nd class) per compartment and are comfortable enough, if lacking a bit in privacy. A bunk costs a fixed price of around US$16 for international travel irrespective of the length of the journey except between Estonia, Latvia and Lithuania.

In Russian, the language used most in the Baltic states, a four-bunk couchette is called *kupeynyy* (compartmentalised) and regarded as 2nd-class. Third class is *platskartnyy* (literally 'reserved place'), which is six bunks partitioned, but not closed, off from each other. Kupeynyy and platskartnyy together make up 'hard-class' (*zhyostkiy*). *Obshchiy* or general class is unreserved bench-type seating.

Sleepers are the most comfortable option, offering beds for one or two passengers in 1st class, and two or three passengers in 2nd class. All sleepers in Norway, for example, are either for one person (1st class only) or two to three people (2nd class); there are no couchettes as previously described, however, the three-person 2nd-class compartments function the same way. An individual traveller can book a bed in one

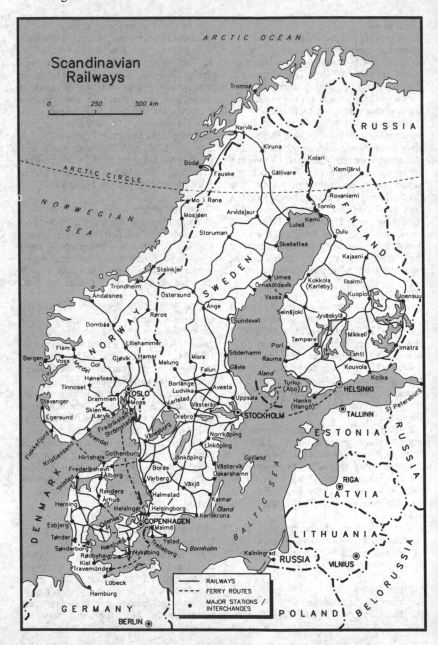

(100 Nkr), in which case they'll be booked into a compartment with two other people of the same sex. Denmark has six-person compartments (60 Dkr), as well as single and double cabins. Charges vary depending upon the journey but they tend to be significantly more expensive than couchettes. Couchettes but not sleepers are available on trains within Estonia, Latvia and Lithuania but sleepers may be available on trains to/from Moscow, St Petersburg, Warsaw or Berlin. In Russian, a sleeper is a *spalnyy vagon (SV)* also known as *myngkiy* (soft class).

Most long-distance trains, except those in the Baltic states, have a dining car or an attendant who wheels a drink and snack-laden trolley through carriages – prices tend to be steep. On overnight trains in the Baltic states be prepared to freeze or bake depending on whether the heating is on or not.

Security

People often tell horror stories about train journeys, ranging from whole carriages being gassed through the ventilation system by bandits and the occupants divested of their belongings, to individual travellers being drugged and robbed with the collusion of the railway staff. This sort of thing can happen, although it's not nearly as widespread as some people make out. In Scandinavia, however, travellers commonly leave their backpacks unattended at railway stations.

The overwhelming chances are that you will only have fond memories of being on the train. Nevertheless, it pays to take basic precautions. Don't leave your stuff unattended on the train, and lock compartment doors overnight. Some people make a point of leaving a window open to maintain a flow of fresh air.

Eurail Passes

These passes can only be bought by residents of non-European countries and generally are supposed to be purchased before arriving in Europe. However, Eurail passes can be purchased within Europe so long as your passport proves you've lived there for less

than six months, but the outlets at which you can buy the passes are limited. For example, Copenhagen is the only city in Denmark and Oslo is the only city in Norway where you can buy the Eurail passes (at the Eurail Aid counters at the main railway stations). It's all straightforward, the only thing travellers need to do is show their passport.

If you've lived in Europe for more than six months, however, you are eligible to buy an Inter-Rail pass which is a better buy. In the UK, French National Railways (☎ 071-493 9731), 179 Piccadilly, London, sells passes to non-Europeans who have been in Britain for less than six months.

Eurail passes are valid for unlimited travel on national railways and some private lines in Austria, Belgium, Denmark, Finland, France (including Monaco), Germany, Greece, Hungary, Italy, Luxembourg, the Netherlands, Norway, Portugal, Ireland, Spain, Sweden and Switzerland (including Liechtenstein). The UK is not covered nor are Estonia, Latvia and Lithuania.

Eurail is also valid for ferries between Ireland and France (but not between the UK and France), between Italy and Greece, and from Sweden to Finland, Denmark or Germany. In addition, reductions are given on steamer services in various countries.

Eurail passes offer reasonable value to people aged under 26. A Youthpass is valid for 2nd-class travel for one month (US$470, £294, 3450 Nkr or 3773 Dkr) or two months (US$640, £384, 4506 Nkr or 4928 Dkr). The Youth Flexipass, also for 2nd class, is valid for 15 days in two months (US$420 or £254).

A journey commencing after 7 pm counts as the next day's travel but there is no leeway beyond midnight at the end of a day's travel. The traveller must fill out (in ink) the relevant box in the calendar before starting a day's travel. Some people try to sneak extra days by 'forgetting' to fill in the box or using an erasable pen and hoping the ticket isn't stamped for that day. However, conductors are getting wise to such dodges and, if caught, you are liable to pay a fine of US$100 in local currency.

The corresponding passes for those aged

over 26 are available in 1st class only. The Flexipass (five versions) costs from US$280 (£168) for five days within 15 days up to US$610 (£366) for 14 days within one month.

The standard Eurail pass (also in five versions) costs from US$430 (£270) for 15 days' unlimited travel, up to US$680 for one month and the maximum pass (for three months) costs US$1150 (£726). Two or more people travelling together (a minimum of three people between 1 April and 30 September) can get good discounts on a Saverpass, which works like the standard Eurail pass.

In Scandinavia, the ScanRail and Nordturist passes are generally better deals than the Eurail pass, so this information will be of most interest to the traveller who is going to visit other parts of Europe too.

If you lose your Eurail card before you get to Europe you cannot claim a refund. If your pass is lost or stolen once you are in Europe you may apply for a duplicate, but only if the original pass was already validated and you can prove it by showing a validation slip. A police report is also necessary and a US$25 reissuance fee applies.

The catch with losing a Flexipass is that they assume you've been travelling every day since the validation (even if you haven't), so if your number of flexible days is equal to or is exceeded by the number of days since the pass was validated, you won't be able to claim anything at all.

There is at least one Eurail Aid office or counter (where duplicates are issued) in each country participating in the scheme; addresses are listed in the *Eurail Traveller's Guide* which comes with the pass.

Inter-Rail

Inter-Rail passes are available to residents of European countries. Terms and conditions vary slightly from country to country but in all cases it applies that travel is never free in the country of origin; there is only a discount of around 50%. Within the UK, Inter-Rail passes can only be purchased by people who have been resident in the UK for at least six months, and passport identification is required. Inter-Rail cards should be kept secure and treated like cash as you can make no claims in the event of loss or theft.

The normal Inter-Rail card is limited to travellers under 26 years of age and costs £180 for one month. Cards are valid for free 2nd-class rail travel in all countries covered by Eurail, plus Bulgaria, Czechoslovakia, Morocco, Poland, Romania, Turkey and the former Yugoslavia. The Baltic states are not included. If bought in Britain card is also valid for 34% to 50% discounts on train travel within the UK as well as 30% to 50% discounts on various ferry routes (many more than are covered by Eurail) and certain river and lake services. It also gives free travel (barring port tax) on shipping routes from Brindisi (Italy) to Patras (Greece).

There is also an Inter-Rail card for people aged 26 or over, imaginatively called the Inter-Rail 26+. This is nowhere near as good a deal. Not only are the costs higher (£180 for 15 days or £260 for one month), but the card is also more restricted: it is not valid in the UK or Spain and it attracts discounts on fewer ferry routes. On certain trips, though, it can still be very good value.

The national rail organisations of France, Italy, Portugal and Spain have indicated that they want to pull out of the Inter-Rail accord by the beginning of 1993, which would seriously undermine the attraction of an Inter-Rail pass. As this book went to press the issue was still under negotiation. One compromise being discussed was the charging of supplements to Inter-Rail pass holders travelling in these countries.

The Baltic states are expected to join the Inter-Rail system and Inter-Rail is keen that they join; check for the latest information when you buy your Inter-Rail pass.

Scandinavian Rail Passes

There are a number of rail passes valid in Scandinavia including Eurail (in all its forms) and Inter-Rail.

ScanRail Pass This is a flexible rail pass for travel in Norway, Denmark, Sweden and Finland and must be purchased before arrival in Scandinavia. There are three versions: for any four days within a 15-day period (US$145/179 for 2nd/1st class), any nine days within a 21-day period (US$239/299), and any 14 days within a one-month period (US$349/459). It's half-price for children aged between four and 12. The ScanRail pass cannot be bought or used by residents of Scandinavia.

The pass can be used on trains run by the Danish (DSB), Finnish (VR), Norwegian (NSB) and Swedish (SJ) state railways and also includes free travel on the following boat services:

Frederikshavn to Gothenburg (Stena Line)
Stockholm to Turku/Åbo (Silja Line)
DSB domestic ferry lines (Denmark)
Helsingør (Elsinore) to Helsingborg (SJ/DSB)
Rødbyhavn to Puttgarden (DB/DSB)
Gedser to Warnemünde (DR/DSB)
Trelleborg to Sassnitz (SJ/DR)

There's 50% discount if you're travelling on the following services:

Copenhagen to Malmö (DSØ Flyvebådene (hydrofoils)
Stockholm to Helsinki (Silja Line)
Copenhagen to Rønne (Bornholmstrafikken)
Rønne to Ystad (Bornholmstrafikken)
Bergen-Flåm-Bergen (Expressbåt)
Hjørring to Hirtshals (train)
Frederikshavn to Oslo (Stena Line)

Nordturist The Nordturist (North Tourist) card allows 21 days unlimited travel on state railways throughout Norway, Sweden, Denmark and Finland. It's sold at railway stations in these four countries and can only be purchased in Scandinavia. In Norway it costs around 1775/1320/890 Nkr (Norwegian kroner) for adult/youth/child in 2nd class, 2365/1775/1185 Nkr in 1st class. Buying the card in Denmark will cost around 1830/1380/915 Dkr (Danish kroner) in 2nd class, 2370/1830/1185 in 1st class. ('Youth' refers to those aged from 12 to 25 years, and 'child' to those aged from four to 11 years.)The card is valid on all routes that the ScanRail pass applies to. It's also valid on

the boats and other forms of transport including from:

Frederikshavn to Gothenburg (Stena Line)
Stockholm to Turku/Åbo (Silja Line)
DSB domestic ferry lines (Denmark)
Helsingør to Helsingborg (SJ/DSB)
Rødbyhavn to Puttgarden (DB/DSB)
Gedser to Warnemünde (DR/DSB)
Trelleborg to Sassnitz (SJ/DR, the Nordic sector only)
Kristiansand to Hirtshals (Color Lines)
Umeå to Vaasa (Wasa Line/Jakob Lines)
Copenhagen to Oslo (DFDS/Scandinavian Seaways)

The Nordturist pass attracts half-price fares on the following services:

Copenhagen to Malmö (DSØ Flyvebådene)
Stockholm to Helsinki (Silja Line)
Copenhagen to Rønne (Bornholmstrafikken)
Rønne to Ystad (Bornholmstrafikken)
Hjørring to Hirtshals (train)
Rønne to Ystad (Bornholmstrafikken)
Bodø/Fauske to Narvik (bus)
Narvik to Kirkenes (bus)

Whether the ScanRail pass or the Nordturist card works out better for individual travellers depends on how long they are going to be in Scandinavia, how quickly they are going to be moving around and, to a lesser degree, what the exchange rate is. As Nordturist is good for 21 days of travel within 21 days and the 21-day ScanRail pass is only good for nine days of travel, for someone moving around a lot, the Nordturist card will work out better even though it would cost about 10% more at current exchange rates.

EastRail

The EastRail pass is valid for 15 days of travel in Denmark, Poland, Hungary, Czechoslovakia and the eastern part of Germany. You can buy the pass in Denmark for 1300 Dkr.

Cheap Tickets

European rail passes are only worth buying if you plan to do a reasonable amount of travelling within a short period of time: Eurail itself reckons its passes only start saving you money if you travel over 2400 km within a two-week period – a long distance in Europe, equivalent to a one-way trip from London to the south of Spain, or not quite from London to Athens. Some people tend to overdo it and spend every night they can on the train, and end up too tired to enjoy the sightseeing the next day.

When weighing up options you should consider the cost of other cheap ticket deals. Travellers aged under 26 can pick up BIJ (Billet International de Jeunesse) tickets which cut fares by up to 50%. Unfortunately, you can't always bank on a substantial reduction.

Various agents issue BIJ tickets in Europe, including Eurotrain (☎ 071-730 3402), 52 Grosvenor Gardens, London SW1. Eurotrain also sells circular Explorer tickets for those aged under 26, allowing a different route for the return trip. British Rail International (☎ 071-834 2345) and Wasteels (☎ 071-834 7066) also sell BIJ tickets.

If you intend to travel extensively within one country it might be worth getting a national rail pass which allows unlimited travel in that country within a set period. All Western European countries offer their own version of this sort of deal, although to make them pay, you may have to travel even more slavishly to a tight schedule than with the pan-European passes. Details can be found in the Getting Around sections of the relevant countries. You need to plan ahead if you intend to take this option as some passes can only be purchased prior to arrival in the country concerned. Other passes that allow ticket discounts are the Rail Europe Family Card and the Rail Europe Senior Card, worth investigating for families or travellers aged over 60.

Though Estonia, Latvia and Lithuania are outside the Eurail and Inter-Rail networks in 1992 Eurotrain and Campus travel offices in the UK introduced a Baltic rail pass giving unlimited train travel in these three countries costing £13/18/25 for one/two/three weeks. Only ISIC holders and those aged under 26 were eligible.

TAXI

Taxis in Europe are generally an avoidable and ill-affordable luxury, and this is certainly the case in Scandinavia. Taxis are metered and rates are high (watch your savings ebb away) unless you share the fare; there are also supplements (depending on the country) for things like the time of day, the location from which you were picked up, and the presence in the cab of extra people.

Good bus, rail and, in Scandinavia, underground networks make the taking of taxis all but unnecessary, but if you need one in a hurry they can usually be found idling like a gang of street urchins by railway stations. By contrast, in Estonia, Latvia and Lithuania taxis are so cheap by Western standards that they can even be considered as possible intercity transport.

CAR & MOTORBIKE

Travelling in your own vehicle is the best way to get to those out-of-the-way places as it gives you the most flexibility. An added bonus is that, compared to when you're in North America or Australia, it is not necessary to spend very long on the road between places of interest. The independence you enjoy, however, does tend to insulate you to some extent from the local people. The exception is in city centres where it is generally worth ditching your trusty chariot and relying on public transport.

In Estonia, Latvia and Lithuania your Western vehicle will attract attention so take all the security precautions you can. Don't leave anything valuable in your parked car and try to use hotels with lock-up car parks.

Paperwork & Preparations

Proof of ownership of a private vehicle should always be carried (Vehicle Registration Document for UK-registered cars) when touring Europe. A British or other European driving licence is acceptable for driving throughout Europe. If you have any other type of licence, you should obtain an International Driving Permit from your motoring organisation (see Documents in the introductory Facts for the Visitor chapter).

The Estonian and Latvian tourist boards say that an International Driving Permit is needed by Western tourists driving to their countries. The same can be assumed for Lithuania. Take along your home-country licence too. In any case the more documents the better when you're dealing with post-Soviet bureaucrats.

Third party motor insurance is a minimum requirement in most of Europe but is not compulsory in Estonia, Latvia or Lithuania, so it's highly advisable to take out a comprehensive policy if you're driving in the Baltic states. If you have difficulty getting cover for travel in these countries by mainstream motor insurers, try Black Sea & Baltic General Insurance (☎ 071-709 9202) of 65 Fenchurch St, London EC3M 4EY.

Most UK motor insurance policies automatically provide comprehensive cover for EC countries and some others. Get your insurer to issue a Green Card (which may cost extra), an internationally recognised proof of insurance, and check that it lists all the countries you intend to visit. Though seldom checked at borders, a Green Card is compulsory, and you'll need it if you're involved in an accident. Also ask your insurer for a European Accident Statement form, which can simplify things if the worst comes to the worst. Never sign statements you can't read or understand – insist on a translation and sign *that* if it's acceptable.

If you want to insure a vehicle you've just purchased and have a good insurance record, you might be eligible for considerable premium discounts if you can show a letter to this effect from your insurance company back home.

Taking out a European breakdown assistance policy is a good investment, such as the AA Five Star Service or the RAC Eurocover Motoring Assistance. Ask your motoring organisation for a Card of Introduction, which entitles you to free services offered by sister organisations around Europe (see Documents in the Facts for the Visitor chapter).

Every vehicle travelling across borders should display a nationality plate of its country of registration. A warning triangle (to be used in the event of breakdown) is compulsory almost everywhere. Recommended accessories are a first-aid kit, a spare bulb kit and a fire extinguisher. Contact the RAC (☎ 081-686 0088) or the AA (☎ 0256-20123) in the UK for more information.

Road Rules

You'll drive on the right in all the northern European countries. Vehicles brought over to Continental Europe from the UK should have their headlights adjusted to avoid blinding oncoming traffic at night (a simple solution on older headlight lenses is to cover up the triangular section of the lens with tape). Priority is usually given to traffic approaching from the right in countries that drive on the right-hand side. The British RAC annually brings out its *European Motoring Guide* (paperback) which gives an excellent summary of regulations in each country, including parking rules. Motoring organisations in other countries have similar publications.

Take care with speed limits as they vary significantly from country to country. You may be surprised at the apparent disregard of traffic regulations in some places but as a visitor it is always best to err on the side of caution. Many motoring infringements are subject to an on-the-spot fine. Denmark has on-the-spot fines for all offences. Always ask for a receipt if you're fined.

Scandinavian countries are particularly strict with drink-driving regulations: in some places and in Estonia, Latvia and Lithuania only a zero blood-alcohol level is tolerated, so don't drive after drinking at all.

Roads

Conditions and types of roads vary across Europe but it is possible to make some generalisations. The fastest routes are four or six-lane dual carriageways, ie two or three lanes either side (motorway). These tend to skirt cities and plough though the countryside in straight lines, often avoiding the most scenic parts. Some of these roads incur tolls, which are often quite hefty, but there will always be an alternative route you can take.

Motorways and other primary routes are universally in good condition.

Road surfaces on minor routes are not so reliable in some countries although normally they will be more than adequate. These roads are narrower and progress is generally much slower. To compensate you can expect much better scenery and plenty of interesting villages along the way. Main roads in the Baltic states are good enough. They may have a few more bumps than those in Scandinavia, but they also have little traffic.

Rental

Renting a car is a very expensive within Scandinavian countries (see the individual country chapters for details). The variety of special deals and terms and conditions attached to car rental can be mind-boggling. However, there are a few pointers that can help you through. The multinationals – Hertz, Avis, Budget Car, and Europe's largest rental agency, Europcar – will give you a reliable service and good standard of vehicle. Usually you will have the option of returning the car to a different outlet at the end of the rental period. Try to avoid airport outlets as they tend to charge higher fees.

Unfortunately, if you walk into an office and ask for a car on the spot you will pay over the odds, even allowing for special weekend deals. If you want an on-the-spot deal like this, look to national or local firms which can often undercut the big operators by up to 40%. Nevertheless, you need to be wary of the neighbourhood cowboy who will take your money and point you towards some clapped-out wreck. Additionally, the rental agreement you sign might be bad news if you have an accident or the car is stolen – a cause for concern if you can't even read what you sign (ask for a translation and sign that).

If you plan ahead, the multinationals might have the deal for you. Prebooked and prepaid rates are always cheaper, and there are fly/drive combinations and other programmes that are worth looking into. SAS often offers cheaper car rentals to its international passengers. No matter where you rent, make sure you understand what is included in the price (unlimited km, tax, insurance, collision damage waiver etc) and what your liabilities are. The minimum rental age is either 21 or 23, and you'll often need a credit card.

It is possible to rent cars in Estonia, Latvia and Lithuania. Tallinn offers more possibilities than anywhere else but the cheaper vehicles may be fully booked. Some Finnish or Swedish car-hire firms will apparently let you take their cars to the Baltic states, which is well worth looking into. If renting a car on the spot in Estonia, Latvia or Lithuania, pay special attention to the insurance provisions. You may be able to limit your liability by paying a few extra dollars.

Motorbike and moped rental is common in some countries, but it is all too common to see inexperienced riders leap on bikes and very quickly fall off them again at the expense of nasty gravel rashes on arms and legs.

Purchase

The purchase of vehicles in some European countries is illegal for nonresidents of that country. The UK is probably the best place to buy: second-hand prices are good and, whether buying privately or from a dealer, the absence of language difficulties will help you establish exactly what you are getting for your money and what guarantees you can expect in the event of a breakdown. Bear in mind you will be getting a left-hand drive (ie steering wheel on the right) car in the UK. If you want right-hand drive and can afford to buy new, prices are low in Belgium, the Netherlands and Luxembourg. Paperwork can be tricky wherever you buy, and many countries have compulsory road worthiness checks on older vehicles.

Camper Van

A popular way to tour round Europe is for three or four people to band together to buy or rent a camper van. London is the usual embarkation point. Look at the adverts in London's free magazine *TNT* if you wish to form or join a group. *TNT* is also a good source for purchasing a van, as is *Loot* newspaper and the Van Market in Market Rd, London N7 (near Caledonian Rd tube station) where private vendors congregate on a daily basis. Some second-hand dealers offer a 'buy-back' scheme for when you return from Europe, but buying and re-selling privately should be more advantageous if you have the time.

Camper vans usually feature a fixed high-top or elevating roof and between two and five bunk beds. Aside from the essential camping-gas cooker, professional conversions may include a sink, fridge and built-in cupboards. You will need to spend at least £1000 to £1500 (US$1800 to US$2700) for something reliable enough to get you around Europe. The most common camper van is the VW based on the 1600 cc or 2000 cc Transporter. It has a deserved reputation for reliability and durability, and the additional advantage that spares are widely available throughout Europe. Ford and Bedford camper vans are slightly roomier despite returning a similar fuel consumption to the VW of approximately nine km per litre (25 miles per gallon).

The main advantage of getting around in a camper van is flexibility: with transportation, eating and sleeping requirements all taken care of in one unit, you are tied to nobody's timetable but your own. You don't always need to rely on camping grounds, either. Discreet free camping is not overly encouraged in some countries but it is rarely a problem; however, you may be moved on by the police occasionally in built-up areas. The golden rule is to act responsibly. Don't stop where you will be a nuisance to other road users and don't damage the countryside or leave litter. Autobahn rest areas are ideal, if not very pleasant, stopover sites.

Camper vanning can work out to be very cheap: a group which predominantly free-camps and self-caters in the van, can get by on spending US$30 per person per day. When planning your budget, remember to set some money aside for emergency repairs.

The main disadvantage of camper vanning is that you are in a confined space for much of the time. Four adults in a small van can soon get on each other's nerves, particularly if the group has been formed at short notice. It is not unknown for van members to split up and go their separate ways once in Europe. Tensions can be minimised if you agree on itineraries and daily routines before setting off. When planning your trip, bear in mind that travelling around 250 km a day is the maximum with which most people feel comfortable in Europe.

Another disadvantage of camper vans is that they're expensive to buy in spring and difficult to sell in autumn. As an alternative, consider a car and tent.

Motorcycle Touring

Europe is made for motorcycle touring, with winding roads of good quality, stunning scenery to stimulate the senses, and an active motorcycling scene. Just make sure your rain gear is up to scratch.

The motorcycle often puts you at a psychological advantage with the locals, and elderly people will sometimes come up and chat enthusiastically about the bikes they used to own. Sometimes, though, it can have an adverse effect due to the *Easy Rider* image, but motorcyclists so affected often have themselves to blame for living up to this image.

The wearing of crash helmets for rider and passenger is compulsory everywhere in Europe nowadays. Using headlights during the day is recommended and is compulsory in Scandinavia.

Motorcycles can sometimes be parked on pavements (sidewalks) as long as they don't obstruct pedestrians – a great advantage over other forms of motorised transport – but check as this is against the law in parts of Scandinavia. Another advantage of travelling by motorcycle is that you very rarely have to book ahead with ferries. Unless you're very unlucky, you can turn up an hour before departure, buy the ticket and they'll usually be able to squeeze you in.

Anyone considering a motorcycle tour from the UK might benefit from joining the International Motorcyclists Tour Club (£14 a year plus a £2 joining fee). It organises

European (and worldwide) biking jaunts, and members regularly meet to swap information. Contact Ken Brady, Membership Secretary, Cornerways, Chapel Rd, Swanmore, Southampton, SO3 2QA UK.

Fuel

Fuel prices can vary enormously from country to country, so considerable savings may be be made by filling up in the right place. Prices also sometimes bear little relation to the general cost of living in each country. The relative cost of unleaded, super (premium) and diesel is fairly consistent in each country.

Estonia, Latvia and Lithuania, still largely dependent on the CIS for fuel supplies, are a special case. Unleaded petrol is not widely available in the Baltic states and fuel supplies are erratic: they were adequate at the time of writing but had been drastically short only a few weeks previously. Even when there is plenty of petrol, long queues may still form at filling stations because only one pump is operating or the cashier had gone to lunch or people are filling cans ready for the next shortage. You too should carry a large can and keep it filled.

Petrol in the Baltic states generally comes in four grades: 76, 93, 95 and 98 octane (none of them lead-free), marked A-76 or AI-76 etc on pumps. But the best available is usually 93, lower than is good for most of the older Western engines. The saving grace for foreigners (and anyone else who can afford around US$0.70 a litre against the normal price of US$0.20 or so at the time of writing) is the handful of Western-run and Western-supplied petrol stations that have opened up in main cities and on main roads in the last couple of years.

With a canister to fill for back-up fuel, you can get most or all of the petrol you need from these. They have reliable supplies, no queues and better fuel (up to 99 octane, and usually unleaded too).

Other Equipment

In Estonia, Latvia and Lithuania it's advisable to take along a supply of oil and a few spare parts as these are in extremely short supply for Western vehicles. If you break down on the open road, the best thing to do is flag down a passing motorist and get a tow to the nearest garage.

BICYCLE

Cycling as a means of getting around is gaining in popularity, but contemplating a tour of Europe on a bike is rather daunting. One organisation that can help is the Cyclists' Touring Club (☎ 0483-417 217), Cotterell House, 69 Meadrow, Godalming, Surrey GU7 3HS, UK. It can supply information to members on cycling conditions in Europe as well as detailed routes, itineraries and cheap insurance. Membership costs £24 a year or £12 for people aged under 18.

A worthwhile book is *Europe by Bike* by Karen & Terry Whitehall (paperback), available in the USA or at selected outlets in the UK. It has good descriptions of 18 cycling tours of up to 19 days' duration, although city information should be taken with a pinch of salt.

A primary consideration on a cycling tour is to travel light, but you should take a few tools and spares including a puncture-repair kit and a spare inner tube. Panniers are essential to balance your possessions on either side of the bike frame. A bike helmet is also a very good idea. Take a good bike lock and always use it when you leave your machine unattended.

Seasoned cyclists can average 80 km a day but there's no point in overdoing it. The slower you travel, the more locals you're likely to meet. If you get weary of pedalling or simply want to skip a boring section, you can put your feet up on the train. On slower trains, bikes can usually be taken on board as luggage, subject to a small supplementary fee. Fast trains (IC, EC etc) can rarely accommodate bikes: they need to be sent as registered luggage and may end up on a different train to the one you take (the cost varies).

For more information on cycling, see the Activities sections in the introductory Facts for the Visitor chapter and in the individual country chapters.

Rental

Cycling doesn't have to be an endurance test, it can be a relaxing (and quiet) means of exploring the countryside. It is easy to rent bikes throughout Europe on a half-daily, daily or weekly basis. Often it is possible to return the machine at a different outlet so you don't have to double back. Many railway stations have bike rental counters, some of which are open 24 hours a day. See the various country chapters for more details.

HITCHING

Hitching can be the most rewarding and frustrating way of getting around in Europe. Rewarding, because it makes you meet and interact with the locals, and forces you into unplanned detours that may yield unexpected, off-the-beaten-track treasures. It's frustrating, because you may get stuck on the side of the road to nowhere with nowhere (or nowhere cheap) to stay.

Hitchhikers can end up making good time but obviously your plans need to be flexible in case a trick of the light makes you appear invisible to passing motorists. A man and woman travelling together is probably the best combination. Two or more men must expect some delays; two women together could make good time and will be reasonably safe. A woman hitching on her own is taking a risk.

Don't try to hitch from city centres: take public transport to suburban exit routes. Hitching is usually illegal on motorways; stand on the slip roads, or approach drivers at petrol stations and truck stops. Look presentable and cheerful and make a cardboard sign indicating your intended destination in the local language. Never hitch where drivers can't stop in good time or without causing an obstruction. At dusk, give up and think about finding somewhere to stay.

Dedicated hitchers may wish to invest in *Europe – a Manual for Hitch-hikers* by Simon Calder (paperback), even though it's getting a bit ancient by now. It is sometimes possible to arrange a lift in advance: scan student notice boards in colleges, or contact car-sharing agencies. Such agencies are particularly popular in France (Allostop-Provoya) and Germany (Mitfahrzentrale).

Although many travellers hitch rides in Europe, it is not a totally safe way of getting around. Just because we explain how it works doesn't mean we recommend it.

WALKING

Many city centres are compact enough to enable major tourist sights to be seen on a walking tour, but walking really comes into its own in rural areas. Hikes are an excellent way to leave behind the wail of car horns and the opaque logic of train schedules. See also the Activities section in the introductory Facts for the Visitor chapter, as well as the individual country chapters.

BOAT

Ferries

Several ferry companies compete on all the main ferry routes in the Baltic, North and Norwegian seas and the Atlantic Ocean. The resulting service is comprehensive but complicated. The same ferry company can have a whole host of different prices for the same route depending upon the time of day or year, the validity of the ticket, or the length of your vehicle. It is worth planning (and booking) ahead where possible as there may be special reductions on off-peak crossings.

Stena Line (which owns Sealink) is the largest ferry company in the world and services British and Scandinavian routes. Rail pass holders are entitled to discounts or free travel on some of the previously mentioned routes.

The already dense traffic in the Baltic Sea between Scandinavia and Germany and Poland has been swelled by new services to the Baltic states and Russia, and the emergence of a Baltic circle summer cruises. Food is often expensive on ferries so it is worth bringing your own when possible. It is also worth knowing that if you take your vehicle on board you are usually denied access to it during the voyage. For further information, see the Getting There & Away sections of the individual country chapters.

Steamers

Europe's main lakes and rivers, including the Saimaa lakes in Finland, are serviced by steamers and, not surprisingly, schedules are more extensive in the summer months. Rail pass holders are entitled to some discounts (see the earlier Train section). Consider extended boat trips as relaxing and scenic excursions; if you view them merely as a functional means of transport, they can be grotesquely expensive.

TOURS

Young people who like travelling in a group with like-minded revellers may consider joining one of the youth-oriented tour buses offering trips based on hotel or camping accommodation. In London, Contiki (☎ 081-290 6422) offers a variety of tours starting from 14 days for £420 (plus food fund). Group camping tours with Tracks (☎ 071-937 3028) can work out slightly cheaper.

Top Deck (☎ 071-370 6487) has the added novelty of offering tours where you travel and sleep in a converted double-decker bus. Student or youth travel agencies in other countries have similar deals.

For people aged over 60, Saga Holidays (☎ 0800-300 500), Saga Building, Middelburg Square, Folkstone, Kent CT20 1AZ, UK, offers holidays ranging from cheap coach tours to luxury cruises. Saga also operates in the USA (☎ 617-451 6808), 120 Boyleston St, Boston, MA 02116; and Australia (☎ 02-957 4222), Level 4, 20 Alfred St, Milsons Point, Sydney 2061. See also the Special Needs section of the introductory Facts for the Visitors chapter.

National tourist offices in most countries offer organised trips to points of interest. These may range from two-hour city tours to several-day circular excursions. They often are more expensive than going it alone, but are sometimes worth it if you are pressed for time. A short city tour will give you a quick overview of the place and can be a good way to begin your visit. See the individual country chapters for more details of tours.

Denmark

The smallest and most southern of the Scandinavian countries, Denmark (Danmark) is an interesting mix of lively cities and pastoral farmland. The country abounds with medieval churches, Renaissance castles and tidy 18th century fishing villages. Copenhagen, Scandinavia's largest and most cosmopolitan capital, has top museums and a spirited music scene.

Denmark's historic treasures include 2000-year-old 'bog people', Neolithic dolmens and Viking ruins. Denmark has wonderful white sand beaches, Scandinavia's warmest waters and scores of unspoiled islands to explore.

Despite gentle hills here and there, Denmark is largely flat which, combined with an extensive network of cycle routes, makes it a great place to explore by bike.

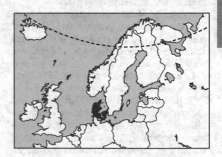

Facts about the Country

HISTORY

Present-day Denmark traces its linguistic and cultural roots back to when the region was settled by the Danes, a tribe that may have migrated south from Sweden around 500 AD. In the late 9th century, warriors led by the Viking chieftain Hardegon conquered the Jutland peninsula. The Danish monarchy (which claims to be the world's oldest) dates back to Hardegon's son, Gorm the Old, who established his reign in the early 10th century. Gorm's son, Harald Bluetooth, completed the conquest over the Danes who were also converted to Christianity. Succeeding Danish kings went on to invade England and conquer most of the Baltic region.

In 1397 the Danish queen Margrethe I established a union between Denmark, Norway and Sweden to counter the influence of the powerful Hanseatic League which had come to dominate the region's trade. Sweden withdrew from the union in 1523 and over the next few hundred years Denmark and Sweden had numerous border skirmishes and fully fledged war, largely over control of the Baltic Sea. Norway remained under Danish rule until 1814.

In the 16th century the Reformation swept through the country amidst church burnings and civil warfare. The fighting ended in 1536 with the ousting of the powerful Catholic church and the establishment of a Danish Lutheran church headed by the monarchy.

Denmark's golden age was under Christian IV (1588-1648) with Renaissance cities, castles and fortresses flourishing throughout his kingdom. A wealthy upper class prospered during his reign and many of Denmark's most lavish mansions and palaces were built during that period. In the 1650s, however, Denmark lost Skåne and its other territories on the Swedish mainland.

Literature, the arts, philosophy and populist ideas flourished in Europe of the 1830s and the events of 1848, 'The Year of Revolutions', helped inspire a democratic movement in Denmark that led to the adoption of a constitution on 5 June 1849. As a result, King Frederik VII was forced to relinquish most of his political power to an elected parliament and in doing so became Denmark's first constitutional monarch.

Denmark's involvement in a series of

failed military campaigns resulted in a steady decline of its borders, culminating with the ceding of the Schleswig and Holstein regions to Germany in 1864.

By the end of the 19th century, large landowners had lost ground to farmers' cooperatives and the country's government shifted from a conservative to a liberal one with a socialist bent.

Denmark remained neutral in WW I and also declared its neutrality at the outbreak of WW II. Still, on 9 April 1940 an unfortified Denmark faced either a quick surrender or a full-scale invasion by German troops massed along its border. The Danish government settled for the former, in return for an assurance that the Nazis would allow the Danes a degree of autonomy. For three years the Danes managed to walk a thin line, basically running their own internal affairs but doing so under Nazi supervision, until in August 1943 the Germans took outright control. The Danish Resistance movement mushroomed and 7000 Jewish Danes were quickly smuggled into neutral Sweden. In 1944 Iceland, under Danish rule since 1380, declared itself an independent republic.

Though the island of Bornholm was heavily bombarded by Soviet forces, the rest of Denmark emerged from WW II relatively unscathed. Denmark joined NATO in 1949 and the European Community (EC) in 1973.

Under the leadership of the social democrats a comprehensive social welfare state was established in the postwar period. Though a tax revolt in the 1980s led to some revisions, Denmark still provides its citizens with cradle-to-grave securities.

GEOGRAPHY

Denmark is a small country with a land area of 42,930 sq km, mostly on the Jutland peninsula. In addition there are nearly 500 islands, 100 of which are inhabited. Copenhagen is on Zealand, the largest island.

Most of Denmark is a lowland of fertile farms, rolling hills, beech woods and heather-covered moors. The highest elevation is a mere 173 metres. Except for its land border with Germany, Denmark is surrounded by the North and Baltic seas.

GOVERNMENT

Denmark is a constitutional monarchy. Queen Margrethe II has been on the throne since 1972 but legislative powers rest with the Folketing which is the elected parliament. The social democrats, conservatives, liberals and socialists form the four main political parties, though in recent times there have been close to a dozen parties represented in the 179-seat parliament. The government has been headed by prime minister Poul Schlüter since 1982.

In December 1991 the heads of state of the European Community agreed upon terms of a European economic and political union, known as the Maastricht Treaty, which was then brought back to each country for ratification. When the treaty was voted on in the Danish Folketing, 75% of the legislators voted in its favour. However as the vote was short of the five-sixths parliamentary majority required for ratification, a national referendum was held in June 1992. The referendum, which was preceded by a heated national debate, brought out 82% of Denmark's voters. By a margin of 51% to 49%, Danes voted against ratification, casting doubts over the future of European unity.

Danes have long-held reservations about the march towards European unity and the impact it could have on their national identity. Denmark has a steadfast tradition of participatory local government and many citizens felt threatened by terms of the agreement that called for a common defence policy and the development of a European parliament and court of justice. There were also concerns that the European union might undermine the nation's strong social legislation and environmental laws, as well as worries of being dominated by a powerful neighbouring Germany.

ECONOMY

Spurred in part by a highly efficient agricultural sector, Denmark has one of the world's

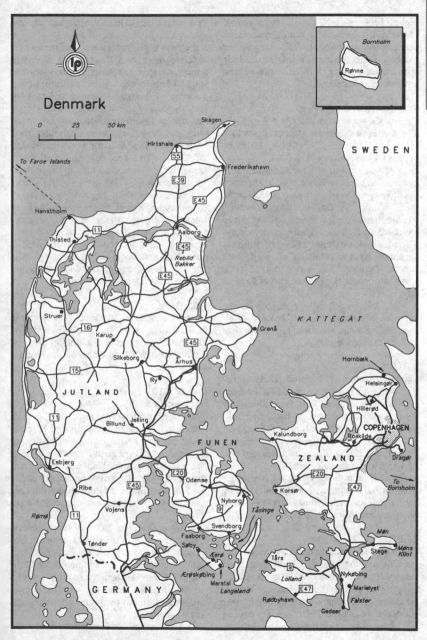

highest per capita GNPs and a high standard of living. It's the world's leading exporter of canned meat and boasts the EC's largest fish catches. Other important exports include butter, cheese, beer, furniture, electronics, silverware and porcelain.

POPULATION & PEOPLE

Denmark's population is about 5.1 million. The four largest cities are Copenhagen (1.3 million), Århus (265,000), Odense (175,000) and Aalborg (155,000).

In part as a result of a racial mixture that occurred in the New Stone Age, and subsequent integration of European populations, there is no pure Danish type. However, Nordic characteristics, including blonde hair and blue eyes, are certainly predominant. There's a well-established German minority in south Jutland totalling about 45,000 people. Denmark also has about 150,000 aliens, the majority of whom live in Copenhagen.

More than two-thirds of all Danes have a surname ending in 'sen', with Jensens, Nielsens and Hansens accounting for more than 20% of the population.

ARTS

Famed Danish writers include Hans Christian Andersen, whose fairy tales have been translated into more languages than any other book has been except the Bible; religious philosopher Søren Kierkegaard, whose writings were a forerunner of existentialism; and Karen Blixen, who penned *Out of Africa* and *Babette's Feast*.

On a different front, Denmark is a leader in industrial design, with a style marked by cool, clean lines applied to everything from architecture to furniture and silverwork.

CULTURE

Danes pride themselves on being thoroughly modern, and the wearing of folk costumes, the celebration of traditional festivals and the clinging to old-fashioned customs is less prevalent in Denmark than in most other European countries. There are, of course, traditional aspects of the Danish life style that aren't immediately apparent at first glance.

Perhaps nothing captures the Danish perspective more than the concept of *hygge* which, roughly translated, means cosy and snug. It implies shutting out the turmoil and troubles of the outside world and striving instead for a warm intimate mood. Hygge affects how Danes approach many aspects of their personal lives, from designing their homes to a fondness for small cafés and pubs. There's no greater compliment that a Dane can give their host than to thank them for a cosy evening.

Visitors will find Danes to be relaxed, casual and not given to extremes. They are tolerant of different life styles and quite carefree about dress. Swimsuits are optional at many beaches, and tops are not required at any. The national sport is soccer, while cycling, rowing, sailing and windsurfing are other popular Danish pastimes.

RELIGION

More than 90% of all Danes belong to the state-supported National Church of Denmark, an Evangelical Lutheran denomination, though fewer than 5% are regular church-goers.

LANGUAGE

Introduction

The Danish language belongs, together with Swedish, Norwegian, Icelandic and Faroese, to the northern branch of the Germanic language group. Consequently, written Danish bears a strong resemblance to these languages. Spoken Danish on the other hand has evolved in a different direction, introducing sounds and pronunciation not found elsewhere.

Grammatically it has the same general rules and syntax as the other Germanic languages of Scandinavia. The nouns have two genders: masculine, *en*, and neuter, *et*. Definite articles are suffixed to the noun: *-en* and *-et* for singular nouns, and *-ne* (indefinite) and *-ene* (definite) for plural nouns regardless of gender.

Danish has a polite form of address, using

the personal pronouns *De* and *Dem*. The translations in this chapter are mostly in the familiar form using *du* and *deg*, except where it is appropriate and/or wise to use the formal form. In general, use the formal form when speaking to senior citizens and officials, and the familiar form the rest of the time.

Danish is a minor language and many Danes speak English. However, an effort to at least learn the basics, such as memorising the words for 'thank you', 'goodbye', 'hello' and 'I'm sorry', will be appreciated. With an increased command of the language, you will be rewarded by gaining a greater insight into Denmark and the Danes.

Pronunciation

You will find Danish a difficult language to speak or understand. Consonants are drawled, swallowed and even omitted completely, creating, in conjunction with vowels, the peculiarity of the glottal stop or *stød*. Its sound is rather as a Cockney would say 'bottle'. Stress is usually placed on the first syllable or on the first letter of the word. In general though, the best advice is to listen and learn. Good luck.

Vowels

a	a long flat 'a' as in 'father'
a, œ	a long sharp 'a' as in 'act'
u(n), å, & o	a long rounded 'a' as in 'walk'
e(g)	as in 'eye'
e, i	a short flat 'e' as in the Italian *che*
i	a long sharp 'e' as in 'see'
œ	a long flat 'e' as in 'bet'
ø	an 'er' sound similar to 'fern', the French *deux* and the German *schön*
o, u	a long 'o' as in 'zoo'
o	a short 'o' as in 'pot'
o(v)	somewhat shorter sound than 'out' or 'vow'
o(r)	with less emphasis on the 'r', as in 'more'
u	as in 'pull'
y	a long sharp 'u' as in the German *über*

Semiconsonants

w	similar to the 'wh' in 'what'
j	as in 'yet'

Consonants

sj	as in 'ship'
ch	a sharper sound than the 'ch' in 'cheque'
c	as in 'cell'
(o)d	a flat 'dh' sound, like the 'th' in 'these'
ng	as in 'sing'
g	a hard 'g' as in 'get', if followed by a vowel
h	as in 'horse'
k	as the 'c' in 'cat'
b	as in 'box'
r	a rolling 'r' abruptly cut short

All other consonants are pronounced as in English.

Greetings & Civilities

Hello./Goodbye.	*Hallo./Farvel.*
Yes./No.	*Ja./Nej.*
Please.	*Må jeg bede. Værsgo.*
Thank you.	*Tak.*
That's fine. You're welcome.	*Det er i orden. Selv tak.*
Excuse me.	*Undskyld.*
May I? Do you mind?	*Må jeg? Tillader De?*
Sorry. (excuse me, forgive me)	*Undskyld. Beklager.*
Do you speak English?	*Taler De engelsk?*
Does anyone speak English?	*Er det nogen som taler engelsk?*
I (don't) understand.	*Jeg forstår (ikke).*
How much is it ...?	*Hvor meget koster det ...?*

Signs

Camping Ground	*Campingplads*
Entrance	*Indgang*
Exit	*Udgang*
Guesthouse	*Gjæstgiveri*

DENMARK

Inn	*Kro*
No Entry	*Ingen Adgang*
No Smoking	*Ikke-Rygere*
Open/Closed	*Åben/Lukket*
Police	*Politi*
Police Station	*Politistation*
Prohibited	*Forbudt*
Railway Station	*Jernbanesta-tion/Banegård*
Toilets	*Toiletter*
Youth Hostel	*Vandrerhjem*

Getting Around

What time does ... leave/arrive?	*Hvornår går/ ankommer ...?*
the boat	*båden*
the bus (city)	*bussen*
the bus (intercity)	*rutebilen*
the train	*toget*
the tram	*sporvognen*

I would like ...	*Jeg vil gerne have ...*
a one-way ticket	*en enkeltbillet*
a return ticket	*en tur-retur billet*
1st class	*første klasse*
2nd class	*anden klasse*

Where is ...?	*Hvor er ...?*
I want to go to ...	*Jeg ønsker at komme til ...*
Can you show me (on the map)?	*Kunne de vise mig (på kortet)?*

far/near	*fjern/nær*
Go straight ahead.	*Gå ligefrem.*
Turn left ...	*Drej tel venstre ...*
Turn right ...	*Drej til højre ...*

Around Town

I'm looking for ...	*Jeg søger efter ...*
a bank	*en bank*
the city centre	*centrum*
the ... embassy	*den ... ambassade*
my hotel	*mit hotel*
the market	*markedet*
the museum	*museet*
the police	*politiet*
the post office	*postkontoret*
a public toilet	*et offentligt toilet*
the telephone centre	*telefoncentralen*

the tourist informa-tion office	*turistinformationen*

beach	*strand*
castle	*slot*
cathedral	*katedral, domkirke*
church	*kirke*
main square	*hovedtorv, torvet*
monastery	*kloster*
mosque	*moské*
old city	*gamle byen*
palace	*palads*
ruins	*ruiner*
synagogue	*synagoge*

Accommodation

Where is a cheap hotel?	*Hvor er et billig hotel?*
What is the address?	*Hvad er adressen?*
Could you write the address, please?	*Kunne De være så venlig at skrive ned adressen?*

At the Hotel

Do you have any rooms available?	*Har I ledige værelser?*

I would like ...	*Jeg ønsker ...*
a single room	*et enkeltværelse*
a double room	*et dobbeltværelse*
a room with a bath-room	*et værelse med bad*
to share a dorm	*plads i en sovesal*
a bed	*en seng*

How much is it per night/per person?	*Hvor meget koster det per nat/per person?*
Can I see it?	*Må jeg få se værelset?*
Where is the bath-room?	*Hvor er toiletet?*

Food

breakfast	*morgenmad*
lunch	*frokost*
dinner	*middag*

I would like the set lunch, please.	*Jeg tager dagens ret, tak.*

Is service included in the bill?	*Er service inkluderet i regningen?*	November	*november*
		December	*december*
I am a vegetarian.	*Jeg er vegetarianer.*		

Numbers

		0	*nul*
At the Chemist		1	*en*
I need medication for ...	*Jeg behøver et medikament imod ...*	2	*to*
		3	*tre*
		4	*fire*
I have a prescription.	*Jeg har en recept.*	5	*fem*
		6	*seks*
At the Dentist		7	*syv*
I have a toothache.	*Jeg har tandpine.*	8	*otte*
I've lost a filling.	*Jeg har tabt en plombe.*	9	*ni*
		10	*ti*
I've broken a tooth.	*Jeg har brækket en tand.*	11	*elleve*
		12	*tolv*
My gums hurt.	*Mit tandkød gør ondt.*	13	*tretten*
		20	*tyve*
I don't want it extracted.	*Jeg vil ikke have den trukket.*	21	*enogtyve*
		30	*tredive*
Please give me an anaesthetic.	*Må jeg få en lokal bedøvelse?*	40	*fyrre*
		50	*halvtreds*
		60	*tres*
Time & Dates		70	*halvfjerds*
What time is it?	*Hvad er klokken?*	80	*firs*
		90	*halvfems*
today	*i dag*	100	*hundrede*
tomorrow	*i morgen*	1000	*tusind*
in the morning	*om morgenen*	one million	*en million*
in the evening	*om aftenen*		

Health

Monday	*mandag*	I'm ...	*Jeg er ...*
Tuesday	*tirsdag*	diabetic	*diabetiker*
Wednesday	*onsdag*	epileptic	*epileptisk*
Thursday	*torsdag*	asthmatic	*astmatisk*
Friday	*fredag*		
Saturday	*lørdag*	I'm allergic to ...	*Jeg er allergisk for imod ...*
Sunday	*søndag*		
		antibiotics	*antibiotikum*
January	*januar*	penicillin	*penicillin*
February	*februar*		
March	*marts*	antiseptic	*antiseptisk*
April	*april*	aspirin	*aspirin*
May	*maj*	condoms	*kondomer*
June	*juni*	contraceptive	*præventiv*
July	*juli*	medicine	*medicin*
August	*august*	nausea	*kvalme*
September	*september*	sunblock cream	*solcreme*
October	*oktober*	tampons	*tamponer*

DENMARK

Emergencies

Help!	*Hjælp!*
Call a doctor!	*Ring efter en læge!*
Call the police!	*Ring efter politiet!*
Go away!	*Forsvind!*

Facts for the Visitor

VISAS & EMBASSIES

Citizens of the USA, Canada, Australia and New Zealand need a valid passport to enter Denmark, but don't need a visa for stays of less than three months.

Danish Embassies

Embassies include:

Australia
Royal Danish Embassy, 15 Hunter St, Yarralumla, ACT 2600 (☎ 06-2732195)
Canada
Royal Danish Embassy, 85 Range Road, Apt 702, Ottawa, Ontario K1N8J6 (☎ 613-234-0704)
Germany
Königliche Dänische Botschaft, Pfälzer Strasse 13, 5300 Bonn 1 (☎ 0228-72 99 10)
New Zealand
Contact the embassy in Australia
UK
Royal Danish Embassy, 55 Sloane St, London SW1X 9SR (☎ 071-235 1255)
USA
Royal Danish Embassy, 3200 Whitehaven St NW, Washington DC 20008 (☎ 202-234-4300)

Foreign Embassies in Denmark

Foreign embassies include:

Australia
Kristianiagade 21, Copenhagen (☎ 35 26 22 44)
Canada
Kristen Bernikows Gade 1, Copenhagen (☎ 33 12 22 99)
Germany
Stockholmsgade 57, Copenhagen (☎ 35 26 16 22)
New Zealand
Contact the British embassy
UK
Kastelsvej 40, Copenhagen (☎ 35 26 46 00)
USA
Dag Hammarskjölds Allé 24, Copenhagen (☎ 31 42 31 44)

DOCUMENTS

A youth hostel association card will get you lower hostel rates and showing a student identity card will often get you a discount on museum fees.

CUSTOMS

One litre of hard liquor or two litres of wine, 10 litres of beer and 200 cigarettes can be brought into Denmark duty free.

MONEY

All common travellers' cheques are accepted in Denmark. Fees for changing money are 30 kr for any number of travellers' cheques at Sparebanken and Jyske banks, two major nationwide chains. Den Danske Bank, the nation's largest bank and the one usually found at airports and ferry terminals, charges an outrageous 20 kr per cheque, with a 40 kr minimum. All three banks charge 20 kr to exchange foreign currencies of any amount.

Travellers' cheques command a better exchange rate than cash by about 1%. Visa, Eurocard, MasterCard, American Express and Diners Club credit cards are widely accepted throughout Denmark.

Currency

The Danish krone, which is linked to the European Currency unit, is most often written DKK in international money markets, Dkr in Northern Europe and kr within Denmark.

The Danish krone is divided into 100 øre. There are 25 øre, 50 øre, one krone, five kroner, 10 kroner and 20-kroner coins. Notes come in 50, 100, 500 and 1000-kroner denominations.

Exchange Rates

The following currencies convert at these approximate rates:

1 Fmk	=	0.71 Dkr
1 Ikr	=	10.40 Dkr
1 Nkr	=	1.02 Dkr
1 Skr	=	0.94 Dkr
A$1	=	4.07 Dkr

C$1	=	4.56 Dkr
DM1	=	3.86 Dkr
NZ$1	=	3.09 Dkr
UK£1	=	9.69 Dkr
US$1	=	5.69 Dkr

Costs

Costs in Denmark are not exorbitant, at least by Scandinavian standards, but nothing's cheap either – partly due to the 25% value-added tax (VAT), called *moms* in Danish, included in every price.

Your costs will depend on how you travel. In terms of basic expenses, if you camp or stay in hostels and prepare your own meals you might get by on 125 kr a day. If you stay in modest hotels and eat at inexpensive restaurants, expect to spend about 350 kr a day if you're doubling up, 450 kr if you're travelling alone.

To this you need to add local transport (about 10 kr a ride), admission fees (top sights often cost about 30 kr), entertainment and incidentals. Long-distance transport is reasonably priced and it helps that Denmark is small. The most expensive train ticket possible between any two points costs just 231 kr.

Tipping

Restaurant bills and taxi fares have service charges already added in. Though further tipping is unnecessary, rounding up the restaurant bill is not uncommon.

Consumer Taxes

Foreign visitors can get a refund of the 25% VAT, less a handling fee, for goods costing more than 600 kr (4700 kr for EC citizens) purchased at stores participating in the Danish Tax-Free plan. Present the tax-free receipt to customs authorities at your departure point to get the refund, which is generally provided on the spot to non-EC citizens and by cheque after returning home to EC citizens.

CLIMATE & WHEN TO GO

Considering its northern latitude, Denmark has a fairly mild climate. May and June can be a delightful time to visit: the earth is a rich green accented with fields of yellow mustard flowers *(sennepsblomster)*, the weather is generally warm and comfortable, and you'll beat the rush of tourists. While autumn can also be pleasant, it's not nearly as scenic as the rural landscape has largely turned to brown and the air quality suffers as many Danish farmers burn crop waste in the fields.

July and August is the peak tourist season and the time for open-air concerts, lots of street activity and basking on the beach. Other bonuses for travellers during midsummer are longer hours at museums and other sightseeing attractions and potential savings on accommodation, as many hotels drop their rates.

WHAT TO BRING

If you visit Denmark during the warm season you can travel light. Unless you plan on fine dining there's little need to bring dressy clothing. If you're using youth hostels, bringing your own sleeping sheet will save a lot.

SUGGESTED ITINERARIES

Depending on the length of your stay you might like to see and do the following:

Two days
    Copenhagen – get a Copenhagen card and explore the city
One week
    Copenhagen, North Zealand's castles and beaches, Roskilde, Ærø
Two weeks
    Sights listed above plus Odense, Århus, Skagen, Ribe and other Jutland sights of interest (or Bornholm)
One month
    As above plus Bornholm, south Funen (including Faaborg and the islands of Tåsinge and Langeland), Møn and Falster islands
Two months
    As above but at a slower pace, possibly much of it by bicycle

TOURIST OFFICES
Local Tourist Offices

Brochures about all parts of Denmark are

available at the main tourist office: Danish Tourist Board (☎ 33 11 13 25), Bernstorffsgade 1, 1577 Copenhagen V. Virtually every good-sized town in Denmark has a tourist office, most often found in the town hall *(rådhus)* or elsewhere on the central square *(torvet)*.

Tourist Offices Abroad

Danish tourist offices abroad include:

Canada
Danish Tourist Board, PO Box 115, Station N, Toronto, ONT M8V 3S4 (☎ 416-823 9620)
Germany
Dänisches Fremdenverkehrsamt, Glockengiesserwall 2, Box 101329, 2000 Hamburg 1 (☎ 040-32 78 03)
Norway
Danmarks Turistkontor, Tollbugata 27, Boks 406 sentrum, 0103 Oslo (☎ 22 41 17 76)
Sweden
Danska Turistbyrån, Riddargatan 7, 114 85 Stockholm (☎ 08-662 05 80)
UK
Danish Tourist Board, PO Box 2LT London W1A 2LT (☎ 071-734 2637)
USA
Danish Tourist Board, 655 Third Ave, New York, NY 10017 (☎ 212-949 2333)

USEFUL ORGANISATIONS

Danmarks Vandrerhjem (☎ 31 31 36 12), Vesterbrogade 39, 1620 Copenhagen V, sells international youth hostel cards and produces a handy booklet in English detailing all hostels in Denmark.

For gay issues, contact the National Organization for Gay Men & Women (☎ 33 13 19 48), Knabrostræde 3, 1210 Copenhagen K.

The Danish Tourist Board distributes the free and comprehensive book *Access in Denmark – a Travel Guide for the Disabled.* For specific questions, disabled travellers can contact Dansk Handicap Forbund (☎ 31 29 35 55), Kollektivhuset, Hans Knudsens Plads 1A, 2100 Copenhagen.

Kilroy Travels, formerly DIS Rejser, specialises in youth travel and has offices in Copenhagen, Århus and Odense. The addresses and phone numbers are Skindergade 28 (☎ 33 11 00 44) in Copenhagen,

Fredensgade 40 (☎ 86 20 11 44) in Århus and Pantheonsgade 7 (☎ 66 17 77 80) in Odense.

The main motoring organisation is the Federation of Danish Motorists (FDM), or Forenede Danske Motorejere (☎ 45 93 08 00), Firskovej 32, 2800 Lyngby.

Danes Worldwide Archives (☎ 98 12 57 93), Postboks 1731, 9100 Aalborg, helps people of Danish descent trace their roots.If you want to get together with a Danish family, both the Århus and Odense tourist offices have 'Meet the Danes' programmes that link up people with similar interests.

BUSINESS HOURS & HOLIDAYS

Office hours are generally from 9 am to 4 pm Monday to Friday. Most banks are open from 9.30 am to 4 pm weekdays and to 6 pm on Thursdays, though banks at international ports and at Copenhagen's Central Station are open longer hours and on weekends. Most stores are open to 5.30 pm weekdays and to 2 pm on Saturdays.

Summer holidays for schoolchildren begin around 20 June and end around 10 August. Many Danes go on holiday during the first three weeks of July. Public holidays observed in Denmark are:

New Year's Day, 1 January
Maundy Thursday, the Thursday before Easter
Good Friday, the Friday before Easter
Easter Day
Easter Monday, the day after Easter
Common Prayer's Day, the fourth Friday after Easter
Ascension Day, the 40th day after Easter
Whit Sunday, the seventh Sunday after Easter
Whit Monday, the seventh Monday after Easter
Constitution Day, 5 June
Christmas Eve, 24 December (from noon)
Christmas Day, 25 December
Boxing Day, 26 December

CULTURAL EVENTS

Beginning with Midsummer's Eve bonfires in late June, Denmark is buzzing with outdoor activity throughout the summer. The main attractions are the dozens of music festivals which run almost nonstop.

The acclaimed 10-day Copenhagen Jazz Festival is held in early July, with outdoor concerts and numerous performances in clubs around the city. Roskilde has a Woodstock-style rock festival around the last weekend of June; a single admission fee includes tent space and all concerts.

There are folk festivals in Skagen and mid-Funen around early July, a jazz festival in Femø during the first weekend in August, and a folk and jazz festival in Tønder in late August. Tønder is a particularly pleasant scene, with amateur and professional musicians jamming together on the cobbled streets of the old town between concerts. For a complete list of music festivals contact Dansk Musik Information Center (☎ 33 11 20 66), Gråbrødretorv 16, 1154 Copenhagen K.

The nine-day Århus Festival, beginning on the first Saturday in September, is the nation's largest cultural event with classical concerts, theatre and numerous goings-on around the city.

POST & TELECOMMUNICATIONS

Most post offices are open from 9 am to 6 pm weekdays and to noon on Saturdays. You can receive mail at poste restante at any post office in Denmark. It costs 3.50 kr to mail a postcard or letter weighing up to 20 grams to Western Europe, 4.75 kr to other countries. International mail sent from Copenhagen is generally out of the country in 24 hours.

It costs one krone to make a local call at public phones and you must dial all eight numbers. Depending on the time of day, you usually get one or two minutes before you need to insert another krone.

You get twice as much calling time for your money on domestic calls made between 7.30 pm and 8 am daily and all day on Sundays. If you're going to be making many calls, consider buying a plastic *telekort* card (20 kr), which is used in special card phones and works out cheaper than pumping in coins. The card can be bought at post offices and at many kiosks.

The telephone country code for calling Denmark from abroad is 45. To make international calls from Denmark dial 009 and then the country code for the country you're calling. There are no area telephone codes within Denmark.

TIME

Time in Denmark is normally one hour ahead of GMT/UTC, the same as in neighbouring European countries. When it's noon in Denmark, it's 11 am in London, 6 am in New York and Toronto, 3 am in San Francisco, 9 pm in Sydney and 11 pm in Auckland.

Clocks are moved forward one hour for daylight-saving time from late March to late September. Denmark uses the 24-hour clock and all timetables and business hours are posted accordingly.

ELECTRICITY

The electric current is 220 volts, 50 Hz, and plugs have two round pins.

LAUNDRY

Laundrettes (*møntvaskeri*) are much easier to find in Denmark than in other Scandinavian countries. Not only can you find them in cities and towns, but youth hostels and camping grounds often have coin-operated machines as well. The cost to wash and dry a load of clothes is generally around 40 kr.

WEIGHTS & MEASURES

Denmark uses the metric system. Fruit is often sold by the piece (*stykke*), abbreviated 'stk'. Decimals are indicated by commas and thousands by points.

BOOKS & MAPS

Most tourist offices have fairly good city maps that often as not show bus routes. If you're renting a car, you can usually pick up a suitable Denmark road map free from the rental agency.

The Danish Tourist Board also has a free national road map that's quite good for most uses, while the most detailed map of Denmark is published by the Danish company Kort og Matrikelstyrelsen and can be bought in Danish bookshops for 119 kr.

For hiking trails in scenic regions, walk into any library and ask for the free Skov og Naturstyrelsen (Forest & Nature bureau) brochures, which are detailed sketch maps to areas of unique natural beauty. There are maps to Dyrehave (north of Copenhagen), Rebild Bakker national park and Skagen, among others.

We recommend some of the following books as background reading:

Denmark: A Modern History (hardback) by W Glyn Jones is one of the more comprehensive accounts of contemporary Danish society.
Drive Around Denmark (hardback) by Robert Spark has ideas on auto routes, itineraries and what to see along the way.
Danmark (hardback) by Robert Trojaborg is a beautiful four-colour, coffee-table-style pictorial of the entire country.
Facts About Denmark (Ministry of Foreign Affairs) provides a readable history, with statistics and cultural background.

The much acclaimed *Pelle the Conqueror* by Martin Andersen Nexø is an intriguing novel about the harsh reality of life as an immigrant in 19th century Denmark. Works by Karen Blixen (written under the pen name Isak Dinesen), Denmark's best-known modern writer, are widely available in English. There's also an avalanche of books by and about Hans Christian Andersen.

MEDIA

Denmark has 46 daily newspapers, the largest of which is *Politiken*. None are in English but the *International Herald Tribune* and other English-language newspapers and magazines are readily available at railway station kiosks in larger towns.

You can hear the news in English at 8.10 am Monday to Friday on Radio Denmark's Programme 1 (90.8 FM in Copenhagen, 88.1 FM in Århus). British and US programmes are common on Danish TV and are usually presented in English with Danish subtitles.

FILM & PHOTOGRAPHY

Print and slide films are readily available in major cities. A 24-exposure roll of Kodacolor Gold 100 will cost about 50 kr to buy, 120 kr to develop and print. A 36-expo-

sure roll of Kodachrome 64 with processing costs about 120 kr.

HEALTH

No unusual precautions are needed. Visitors whose countries have reciprocal agreements with Denmark are covered by the national health insurance programme. All visitors, however, receive free hospital treatment in the event of a sudden illness or accident. For more health information, see the Facts for the Visitor chapter at the start of this book.

WOMEN TRAVELLERS

Denmark is by and large a safe country and travelling presents no unusual hassles for women. For women's issues, contact Kvindehuset (☎ 33 14 28 04), Gothersgade 37, 1123 Copenhagen K.

WORK

Denmark has a double-digit percentage of unemployment and the job situation is bleak for those who are not Danes, doubly so for those who don't speak Danish. Citizens of other Scandinavian countries, however, have the right to reside and work in Denmark.

For citizens of EC countries, it's legal to look for work in Denmark and it's fairly straightforward to get a residency permit if you can find work. Citizens of other countries are required to get a work permit in their home country before entering Denmark.

This requires first securing a job offer and then applying for a work and residence permit while you're still in your home country (or in a country where you've had legal residency for at least six months). You can enter Denmark only after the permit has been granted. Currently these permits are extraordinarily rare for anyone without a specialised skill.

ACTIVITIES
Cycling

Denmark is a bicycle-friendly country, with plenty of long-distance cycling routes: around Bornholm, Ærø and the Old Military Road (Haervejen) through central Jutland are among the most popular.

The Danish Tourist Board has a free cycling map which shows youth hostels and camping grounds along the routes and has information on packaged cycling holidays. To purchase even more detailed cycling maps, contact the Dansk Cyklist Forbund (☎ 33 32 31 21), Rømersgade 7, 1362 Copenhagen K. It also publishes a book with a list of 218 farmers who provide cyclists with a place to pitch a tent for only 10 kr a night.

Folk High Schools

Scandinavia's unique *folkehøjskole*, literally 'folk high school' (the 'high' meaning institute of higher learning), provides a liberal education within a communal living environment. Folk high schools got their start in Denmark, inspired by philosopher Nikolai Grundtvig's concept of 'enlightenment for life'. The curriculum varies among schools but includes such things as drama, Danish culture, peace studies and organic farming. People aged 19 and older can enrol and there are no entrance exams and no degrees. For a catalogue of the nearly 100 schools, write to Højskolernes Sekretariat, Farvergade 27G, 1463 Copenhagen K.

While most schools teach in Danish only, at the International People's College (☎ 49 21 33 61), Montebello Allé 1, 3000 Helsingør, students and teachers come from around the world and instruction is in English. The fees are quite reasonable as they're subsidised by the Danish government. Eight-week courses cost 9500 kr including all meals, accommodation, tuition and outings.

HIGHLIGHTS
Castles

Denmark is full of castles, some with turrets and towers, some with dungeons and others just misnamed manor houses. The most strikingly set is **Egeslov Castle**, surrounded by a moat and expansive formal gardens in the Funen countryside. For the most elaborately decorated Renaissance interior, **Frederiksborg Castle** in Hillerød is unequalled. In Copenhagen the king of

castles is **Rosenborg**, where the dazzling crown jewels are on display.

Historic Towns

Half-timbered houses, cobblestone streets and ancient churches are thick on the ground in Denmark, but a few places are singularly unique. **Ribe**, the oldest town in Denmark, has an exquisite historic centre encircling a 12th century cathedral.

The tiny fortress island of **Christiansø**, off the coast of Bornholm, retains its ramparts and 17th century buildings, with almost no trace of the 20th century. And **Ærøskøbing** on the island of Ærø has a town centre with 18th century terrace houses that's arguably the most picturesque in Denmark.

Museums

Denmark has a number of open-air folk museums with period buildings. The most impressive is **Den Gamle By** in Århus, which is set up as a provincial town, while the folk museum in Odense has the most engaging natural setting.

The best preserved bog people – intact Iron Age bodies found preserved in peat bogs – are at the **Silkeborg Museum** in Silkeborg and the **Moesgård Prehistoric Museum** in Århus. In Zealand, top art museums are **Ny Carlsberg Glyptotek** in Copenhagen and **Louisiana** in Humlebæk.

Viking Age Sites

The Danish countryside holds a number of Viking Age sites, including three Viking **fortresses** dating back to approximately 980 AD. Their circular earthen-work walls remain intact and surround the faint remains of house sites where timbered stave-style structures once stood. Two are in Jutland: the **Aggersborg fortress** at Aggersund and the **Fyrkat fortress** at Hobro. The third and most easily visited is **Trelleborg fortress** in Zealand, six km outside Slagelse.

There are reconstructed Viking Age **ships** on display at the **Vikingeskibshallen** in Roskilde and the **Bangsbo Museum** outside Frederikshavn.

The impressive **Lindholm Høje** outside

Aalborg contains the most Viking Age and Iron Age **graves** in Scandinavia.

In the summer, a number of towns throughout Denmark hold Viking period festivals and open-air Viking plays. There are also a few sailing ships built in the traditional Viking style that provide cruises. The Roskilde University Extension Service (☎ 42 36 18 12) offers a two-day cruise on the Roskilde fjord in one of their Viking-style ships which includes meals and overnighting in tents for 900 kr.

ACCOMMODATION
Camping & Cabins
Denmark's 500 camping grounds charge from 35 to 40 kr per person to pitch a tent. A camping carnet is required (for 6 kr a night or 24 kr for the season) and can be picked up at any camping ground.

Many camping grounds rent cabins that sleep four to six people and cost from 150 kr a day, 900 kr a week. Though cabins often have cooking facilities, bedding is rarely provided so you'll need your own sleeping bag.

Camping is regulated in Denmark and only allowed in camping grounds or on private land with the owner's permission. While it may seem tempting, camping in a car along the beach or in a parking lot is prohibited and can result in an immediate fine. Tourist office maps show camping sites and the tourist office provides a brochure listing the locations of camping grounds throughout Denmark.

Hostels
Most of Denmark's 106 hostels (*vandrerhjem*) have private rooms in addition to dormitory rooms, making hostels a good alternative to hotels. Dorm beds cost from 53 to 79 kr, while private rooms range from 110 to 160 kr for singles, 152 to 212 kr for doubles, plus 40 to 50 kr for each additional person. Priority for private rooms is generally given to families with children, however, these rooms aren't so difficult to book as most hostels are comprised of many small rooms.

Rates are set by the hostel association and are based upon the category of the room – in the A category, rooms have one to six beds and private bathrooms, whereas in the lower-end C category, rooms are straightforward dormitory-style with more than six beds.

Blankets and pillows are provided at all hostels but if you don't bring your own sheets you'll have to hire them for around 35 kr. Sleeping bags are not allowed.

Travellers without an international hostel card can buy one in Denmark for 112 kr or pay 22 kr extra a night. Most Danish road maps show hostels, and routes to the hostels from railway stations and ferry terminals are usually well signposted. During the summer, hostels in popular locales can be booked out in advance and it's always a good idea to call ahead for reservations. Outside Copenhagen, check-in is generally between 4 and 9 pm, and the reception office is usually closed (and the phone not answered) between noon and 4 pm. Therefore if you want to make reservations for the same day, it's a good idea to call before noon.

While generally not as busy in spring and autumn, hostels can get crowded with children on school outings and most hostels require individuals to make advance reservations from 1 September to 15 May. Almost all Danish hostels close in winter for any time from a few weeks to several months.

You can pick up a free 150-page pocket guide from tourist offices or the hostel association that gives information on each hostel, including such things as which have laundry facilities, bicycle rentals and wheelchair-accessible rooms.

All Danish hostels provide an all-you-can-eat breakfast for 38 kr or less and many provide lunch (50 kr maximum) and dinner (60 kr maximum). Except for the Bellahøj hostel in Copenhagen, hostels also have guest kitchens with pots and pans where you can cook your own food.

In addition to the 106 IYHF-associated vandrerhjem, hostel-type accommodation is provided seasonally in Copenhagen by the municipality and by the YMCA (KFUM) and YWCA (KFUK). Copenhagen also has a couple of privately owned facilities that offer cheap dormitory-style accommodation.

Hotels

Hotels are found in the centre of all major towns, with the bottom end averaging around 250/375 kr for singles/doubles. Though the cheapest places tend to be spartan, they're rarely seedy or unsafe. *Kro*, a name that implies country inn but is more commonly the Danish version of a motel, are common along major motorways near the outskirts of town and are generally cheaper than hotels by about a third. Both usually include an all-you-can-eat breakfast which varies from bread, cheese and coffee to a generous buffet.

Rates listed in this chapter include all taxes and unless otherwise noted are for rooms with shared baths in the hall, which are quite standard in Denmark. Most hotels charge about 100 kr more for a room with its own toilet and shower. Many hotels have reduced rates in summer, when business travel is light, and on weekends all year round.

Countryside Holidays

If you'd like to be in the country, there are several farmhouse holiday programmes that book stays on Danish farms for around 150 kr a person a day (half-price for children under 12 years), generally with a three-day minimum. You can also book self-contained flats for about 1800 kr a week for up to six people. Nationwide bookings can be made through Horsens Turistbureau (☎ 75 62 38 22), Sondergade 26, 8700 Horsens, or Varde Turistkonger (☎ 75 22 32 22), Torvet 5, 6800 Varde.

FOOD

Nothing epitomises Danish food more than *smørrebrød* (literally 'buttered bread'), an open-faced sandwich that ranges from very basic fare to elaborate sculpture-like creations. Though it's served in most restaurants at lunch time, it's cheapest at bakeries or at specialised smørrebrød takeaway shops found near railway stations and office buildings.

The rich pastry known worldwide as 'Danish' is called *wienerbrød* in Denmark, and nearly every second street corner has a bakery with mouth-watering varieties for about 7 kr. For a cheap munch, stop at one of the ubiquitous *pølsemandens*, the wheeled carts which sell a variety of frankfurters from 10 to 15 kr.

The cheapest restaurant food is generally pizza and pasta; you can usually eat your fill for about 35 kr at lunch, 50 kr at dinner. Danish food, which relies heavily on fish, meat and potatoes, generally costs double that. *Dagens ret*, which means daily special, is usually the best deal on the menu, while the *børn* menu is for children. Larger cities usually have restaurants featuring vegetarian dishes, cafés commonly serve a variety of salads, and vegetarians can often find something suitable at the smørrebrød counter.

DRINKS

Beer, wine and spirits can be purchased at grocery stores during normal shopping hours and prices are quite reasonable compared to those in other Scandinavian countries. The minimum legal age for purchasing all alcoholic beverages is 18 years.

ENTERTAINMENT

Denmark's cities have some of the most active nightlife in Europe. Jazz and blues are alive and well. Live music wafts through numerous side-street cafés, especially in the university cities of Copenhagen, Århus and Odense. Little begins before 10 pm or ends before 3 am. Most towns have movie theatres showing first-run English-language films (from 30 to 50 kr), subtitled in Danish.

THINGS TO BUY

Silverwork, ceramics and hand-blown glass – all in the sleek style that typifies Danish design – are popular though not inexpensive purchases. Danish amber, which washes up on Jutland's west coast beaches, makes wonderful jewellery and prices are reasonable.

Getting There & Away

AIR

Scandinavian Airlines (SAS) is the carrier linking Scandinavian countries. SAS often offers discounted domestic air fares and cheaper car rentals to its international passengers.

Aer Lingus, Air France, Alitalia, British Airways, Canadian Airlines, Delta, Icelandair, Finnair, Japan Air Lines, KLM, LOT, Lufthansa, Northwest Airlines, Olympic Airways, TAP Air Portugal, Sabena, Singapore Airlines, Sterling Air, Swissair, TWA, Varig and Thai International all fly into Copenhagen.

LAND
To/From Germany

The E45 is the main route between Germany and Denmark's Jutland peninsula. There are daily buses as well as three railway lines linking the two countries; 2nd-class trains from Copenhagen to Frankfurt cost 839 kr (550 kr for those aged under 26 years). See also the introductory Getting There & Away chapter and Copenhagen, Getting There & Away.

To/From Norway

The 2nd-class rail fare from Copenhagen to Oslo (via Sweden) is 599 kr (350 kr for those aged under 26). There are a couple of daily buses to Oslo from Copenhagen (470 kr), Esbjerg (437 kr) and Aalborg (315 kr).

To/From Sweden

Despite the waters of the Øresund which separate Denmark and Sweden, there is bus and train travel via the several types of ferry which shuttle between Helsingør and Helsingborg.

Buses from Copenhagen's Central Station run almost hourly to Helsingborg (1¾ hours, 55 kr). A 2nd-class rail fare from Copenhagen is 286 kr (225 kr, if aged under 26) to Gothenburg and 493 kr (375 kr under 26) to Stockholm.

SEA
To/From Germany

Ferries run from Rømø to Sylt (one hour, 16 kr), Faaborg to Gelting (two hours, 40 kr), Langeland to Kiel (2½ hours, 30 kr), Rødbyhavn to Puttgarden (one hour, 40 kr), Rønne to Sassnitz (four hours, 120 kr), Gedser to Warnemünde (two hours, 50 kr) and Gedser to Rostock (two hours, 25 kr). Fares are given for midsummer travel and some of the ferries lower their fares in the off season. See also the relevant Getting There & Away sections.

To/From Norway

A daily overnight ferry goes from Copenhagen to Oslo. Ferries also run between Hirtshals and Kristiansand and from Frederikshavn to Oslo, Moss and Larvik. For more details see also the relevant Getting There & Away sections.

To/From Sweden

The cheapest ferry to Sweden is the shuttle between Helsingør and Helsingborg (25 minutes, 21 kr), if you're travelling by train it's part of your rail ticket. Ferries leave from opposite the Helsingør railway station on an average of every 10 minutes during the day and once an hour through the night. Ferry passage for a motorcycle and up to two riders costs 100 kr; a car with up to five people costs 280 kr.

Ferries go from Rønne on Bornholm to Ystad in Sweden (2½ hours, 98 kr), from Dragør to Limhamn (one hour, 35 kr), Frederikshavn to Gothenburg (three hours, 90 kr) and from Grenå to Halmstad or Varberg (four hours, 130 kr). There are also hydrofoils (Flyvebådene) from Copenhagen to Malmö which leave hourly, take 45 minutes and cost 39 kr. See also the relevant Getting There & Away sections in this chapter.

To/From the Faroe Islands

The Smyril Line (☎ 97 96 22 44 Hanstholm) runs weekly ferries from Hanstholm to Tórshavn in the Faroe Islands from around 1 June to the end of August. The boat leaves

Hanstholm on Saturdays at 8 pm and arrives in Tórshavn on Mondays at 6 am.

The cheapest fares are for a couchette, which costs 1040 kr for the first three and last four sailings of the season and costs 1390 kr in high season. Four-person cabins are only 100 kr a person more, and two-person cabins begin at 1570/2090 kr a person in the low/high season. Students are entitled to a 25% discount on fares for couchettes and four-person cabins. You can bring a bicycle along for just 60 to 80 kr more.

Scandinavian Seaways (☎ 75 12 48 00) sails from Esbjerg to Tórshavn from mid-June to mid-August, with departures on Mondays at 7 pm. The ferry arrives in Tórshavn at 6 am on Wednesdays. The fares for the first two and last two crossings of the season are 990 kr for a couchette (1690 kr return), 1350 kr (2390 kr return) in the mid-season. Add 20% for an economy cabin or 60% for a two-berth cabin, while single cabins are almost double the fare of a couchette. There are sometimes special youth fares for those under aged 26 for as low as 695 kr one way, 995 kr return.

To/From Iceland

The Smyril Line sails from Hanstholm to Seyðisfjörður (Iceland) via Tórshavn in the Faroe Islands, once a week from early June to late August. The trip requires disembarking for two days in Tórshavn while the boat makes a side trip to the Shetland Islands and Bergen (Norway) before returning to continue its journey to Iceland.

The ferry leaves Hanstholm at 8 pm on Saturdays, arrives at Tórshavn at 6 am on Mondays and then leaves Tórshavn at 5 pm on Wednesdays, arriving in Iceland at noon the next day. The cheapest fares between Denmark and Iceland are those for a couchette, which cost 1550/2060 kr in the low/high season. Cabins are also available and students qualify for a discount.

To/From the UK

Scandinavian Seaways sails from Esbjerg to Harwich in England at least three times a week all year round, usually at 6 pm (20 hours, from 780 to 1145 kr); and to Newcastle on Thursday and Saturday evenings from mid-June to mid-August (20 hours, 1145 kr).

Getting Around

AIR

Danair, a subsidiary of SAS, connects Copenhagen with the Jutland cities of Århus, Aalborg, Billund, Esbjerg, Karup, Sønderborg and Vojens; with Odense on the island of Funen; and Rønne on Bornholm. The one-way fare from Copenhagen is 575 kr to Århus, Odense and Rønne, from 655 to 680 kr to the other destinations. If you travel on specified flights from Monday to Friday, and stay over at least two nights, the return fare is the same price as the normal one-way fare. This is a good deal as many of the discounted flights are simply midday flights that are inconvenient for businesspeople but work out fine for travellers. On weekends there's a return fare that's about 75% of the regular return fare, with additional discounts for accompanying family members. Travellers aged under 26 years or over 60 are eligible for stand-by fares of 350 kr on domestic flights.

BUS

All large cities and towns have a local bus system and most places are also served by regional buses which often connect with trains. There are only a few long-distance bus routes, including from Copenhagen to Aalborg and Århus. Travelling by bus on both these routes is about 25% cheaper than standard train fares, though comparable to midweek train fares.

TRAIN

With the exception of a few short private lines, the Danish State Railways (DSB) runs all train services in Denmark. Rail passes, which are good on DSB ferries and trains, are generally not valid on the private lines.

There are two types of long-distance trains and ticket prices are the same on both. The new, sleek intercity (IC) trains have ultra-modern comforts and 1st and 2nd-class cars. IC trains generally require reservations. Reservations are not needed, however, if you board an IC train after 8 pm or on IC trains that depart from Aalborg to Frederikshavn. Inter-regional (IR) trains are older, a bit slower, solely 2nd-class, and don't require reservations except for the three weekend IR trains that go on the ferry between Zealand and Funen. While usually you'll be fine taking your chances on IR trains, you might want to consider reservations during rush hour to be assured of a seat. Regardless of distance, reservation fees are 30 kr (60 kr for 1st class) for IC trains and 20 kr for IR trains. None of the rail passes cover the reservation fees.

Sleepers are available on overnight trains between Copenhagen and Frederikshavn, Esbjerg and Struer. The cost per person is 60 kr in a six-person compartment, 160 kr in a two-person cabin, or 300 kr in a private cabin, all in addition to the usual train fare.

Standard 2nd-class fares work out to about 1 kr per km. Travel of more than 100 km on Tuesdays, Wednesdays, Thursdays and Saturdays gets an automatic 20% discount.

Children aged from four to 11 years pay half the adult fare, while those aged from 12 to 17 pay 75% of the adult fare. Three or more adults travelling together are entitled to either a 20% discount or to travel 1st class for standard 2nd-class fares any day of the week – ask for the *grupper* rate. People aged 65 and older are entitled to a 20% discount on regular fares, as well as an additional 20% off on the discounted weekday and Saturday fares.

In general, travelling in 2nd class is quite comfortable and there's no need to pay the 50% surcharge for 1st class.

TAXI

Taxis are available throughout Denmark. The fare is typically 12 kr at flagfall and from 8 to 10 kr per km. If you call for a taxi, the meter isn't started until you're picked up.

CAR & MOTORBIKE

Denmark is a pleasant country for driving around. Roads are in good condition, almost invariably well signposted and overall traffic is surprisingly manageable, even in major cities including Copenhagen, rush hours excepted.

Access to and from motorways is made easy in Denmark as roads leading out of city and town centres are sensibly named for the main city to which they're routed. For instance, the road leading out of Odense to Faaborg is Faaborgvej, the road leading to Nyborg is Nyborgvej, and so on.

In Denmark you drive on the right-hand side of the road, seat belt use is mandatory (provided the car is fitted with seat belts) and all drivers are required to carry a warning triangle. Speed limits range from 50 km/h in towns to 110 km/h on expressways though Danes rarely go so slowly. Cars and motorbikes must have their headlights on at all times. It's a good idea for visitors to carry a Green Card.

The authorities are very strict about drunken driving. It's illegal to drive with a blood alcohol concentration of 0.08% or greater, and driving under the influence will subject drivers to stiff penalties and a possible prison sentence.

One litre of unleaded petrol costs about 5.5 kr, a litre of super petrol costs about 5.8 kr and a litre of a diesel fuel costs about 4.5 kr. You'll find the best prices at stations along motorways, which sometimes stage little price wars.

To park in the street in city centres you usually have to buy a ticket from a pavement machine (*billetautomat*). The billetautomat has an LCD read-out showing the current time and as you insert coins the time advances. Put in enough money to advance the read-out to the time you desire and then push the button to eject the ticket from the machine. Place the ticket, which shows the exact time you've paid for, face up inside the windscreen. The cost is generally from 4 to

16 kr an hour. Unless otherwise posted, street parking is usually free from 6 pm to 8 am, after 2 pm on Saturdays and all day on Sundays.

In smaller towns, which are delightfully free of coin-hungry billetautomats, street parking is free within the time limits posted. You will, however, need a windscreen parking disk (free from some tourist offices and petrol stations) which you set at the time you park. For parking purposes, motorbikes are treated like cars and cannot be parked on the pavement. *Parkering forbudt* means 'no parking'.

Denmark's extensive network of ferries carries motor vehicles for reasonable rates. Though fares vary, as a rule of thumb, domestic fares for cars average three times the passenger rate. The ferry timetable available from the tourist office lists fares and phone numbers for all ferries serving Denmark, and it's always a good idea to call ahead and make a reservation.

As for car rentals, you'll generally get the best deal by booking through an international rental agency before you arrive in Denmark. Otherwise rates for the cheapest cars, including VAT and unlimited km, begin at about 450 kr a day with Europcar/Inter-Rent or Pitzner, though Europcar often drops its rates to about 315 kr a day for rentals of three days or more. Many companies have good weekend deals. Hertz, for instance, which has offices throughout Denmark, has a weekend rate that includes unlimited km, VAT and insurance for 910 kr and allows you to keep the car from 4 pm Friday to 9 am Monday.

BICYCLE

Cycling is a practical way to get around Denmark. There are extensive bike paths linking towns throughout the country and bike lanes along the streets of most city centres. You can rent bikes in most towns from 35 to 50 kr a day and it's possible to take them on trains and ferries. On trains, the charge is 40 kr for journeys of more than 100 km and reservations should be made at least three hours in advance. Contact Dansk Cyklist Forbund, the Danish cycle federation at Rømersgade 7, 1362 Copenhagen K, for details and maps.

HITCHING

Hitching in Denmark is quite rare, generally not very good, and is illegal on motorways.

BOAT

An extensive network of ferries links Denmark's main islands as well as most of the smaller populated ones. Generally where there's not a bridge, there's a ferry. Pick up a free ferry timetable at tourist offices.

TOURS

Denmark is so small and public transport systems so extensive that organised tours are not so common. DSB (☎ 33 14 17 01) does offer one-day self-guided tours from Copenhagen to the Louisiana art museum (77 kr), Legoland (310 kr for adults, 155 kr for children) and south Sweden (150 kr). Some local tourist offices offer walking tours of their towns, and occasionally provide more extensive city tours.

Copenhagen

Copenhagen (Danish: København) is Scandinavia's largest and liveliest city, with a population of 1.3 million. Founded in 1167, it became the capital of Denmark in the early 15th century.

Copenhagen is largely a low-rise city, with block after block of historic six-storey buildings. Church steeples add nice punctuation to the skyline and only a couple of modern hotels burst up to mar the scene.

The city has an active nightlife which rolls into the early hours of the morning, and for sightseers there's a treasure trove of museums, castles and old churches to explore.

For a big city, Copenhagen is easy enough to get around. The central area is largely reserved for foot traffic, making it good for

DENMARK

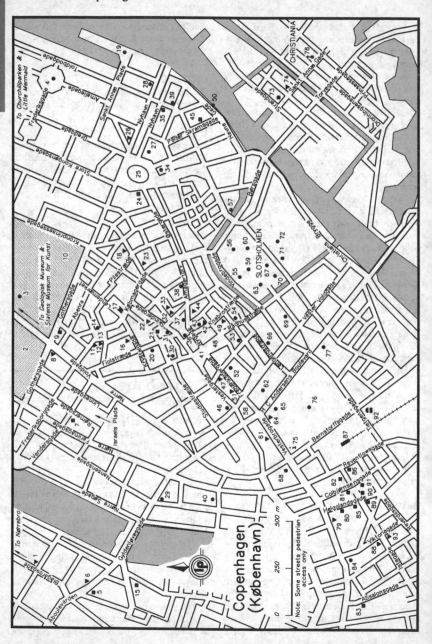

Copenhagen
(København)

0   250   500 m

Note: Some streets pedestrian
access only

■ PLACES TO STAY

5	Hotel Sankt Jørgen
7	Hotel Jørgensen
9	KFUM's Soldaterhjem & Hotel
15	Hotel Cab-Inn Scandinavia
21	Inter-Rail Point
24	Hotel d'Angleterre
35	Sømandshjemmet Bethel
45	Søfolkenes Mindehotel
73	Guesthouse
80	Missionshotellet Hebron
81	Hotel du Nord
82	Missionshotellet Nebo
83	City Public Hostel
85	Selandia Hotel
86	Copenhagen Backpacker
89	Hotel Centrum
90	Absalon Hotel
91	Saga Hotel

▼ PLACES TO EAT

1	Solsikken
6	Mexicali
8	Møi Chiang
11	Jensen's Bøfhus
12	Klaptræet
16	Krystal Café
18	Wessels Kro
22	Det Lille Apotek
23	Café Sommersho
26	Nyhavns Færgekro
32	Peder Oxe
33	Pasta Basta
42	Café Sorgenfri
44	Café de Paris
47	American Deep Pan Pizza
49	RizRaz
51	Shawarma Grill House
61	Scala
64	Rådhusarkaden
74	Café Wilder
79	ThSørensen Smørrebrød
88	Restaurant Shezan
93	Indus Restaurant

OTHER

2	Botanical Gardens
3	Rosenborg Slot
4	Amalienborg Palace
10	Kongens Have
13	Kultorvet
14	Library
17	Rundetårn
19	Boats to Oslo/Bornholm
20	University Library
25	Kongens Nytorv
27	Charlottenborg
28	Hans Christian Andersen Museum
29	Europcar/InterRent
30	Vor Frue Kirke
31	Kilroy Travels
34	Royal Theatre
36	Transalpino
37	GAD Bookshop
38	American Express
39	Laundrette
40	Petrol Station
41	Gammel Torv
43	Pan Club
46	Boghallen Bookshop
48	Nytorv
50	Boats to Malmö
52	Lade's Kælder
53	Drop-In
54	Use It
55	Thorvaldsens Museum
56	Ruins of Absalon's Fortress
57	Netto Bådene Boats
58	Rådhuspladsen
59	Royal Reception Chambers
60	Folketinget (Parliament)
62	Rådhus (City Hall)
63	Christiansborg Palace
65	Louis Tussaud's Wax Museum
66	Rådhuskroen
67	Teatermuseet
68	SAS Ticket Office
69	Nationalmuseet
70	Museum of Royal Coaches
71	Tøjhusmuseet (Royal Arsenal)
72	Royal Library
75	Tourist Office
76	Tivoli
77	Ny Carlsberg Glyptotek
78	Vor Frelsers Kirke
84	Danmarks Vandrerhjem
87	Central Station
92	Main Post Office

strolling in, while the main roads have cycle lanes for those who prefer to move at a faster pace.

Orientation

The main railway station, Central Station (Danish: Hovedbanegården or København

H), is flanked on the west by the main hotel zone and on the east by Tivoli amusement park. At the northern corner of Tivoli is Rådhuspladsen, the central city square and the main city bus transit point.

Strøget, 'the world's longest pedestrian mall', runs through the city centre between Rådhuspladsen and Kongens Nytorv, the square at the head of the Nyhavn canal. Strøget is made up of five continuous streets: Frederiksberggade, Nygade, Vimmelskaftet, Amagertorv and Østergade. Pedestrian walkways run north from Strøget in a triangular pattern to the Latin Quarter, a student haunt.

Information

Tourist Offices The Danish Tourist Board (☎ 33 11 13 25), at Bernstorffsgade 1 just north of the railway station, distributes the comprehensive *Copenhagen This Week* and maps and brochures for all Denmark. It's open from 9 am to 6 pm daily from 1 June to mid-September; to 5 pm weekdays, 2 pm Saturdays and 1 pm Sundays in May; and to 5 pm weekdays and noon on Saturdays the rest of the year.

Use It (☎ 33 15 65 18), Rådhusstræde 13, is an alternative information centre catering to young low-budget travellers. They book rooms, store luggage, provide information on everything from hitching to nightlife, and have good city maps and a useful general guide *Playtime* – all free. Opening hours are from 9 am to 7 pm daily from mid-June to mid-September, from 10 am to 4 pm weekdays the rest of the year.

Copenhagen Card The Copenhagen card allows unlimited travel on buses and trains around Copenhagen and North Zealand, free admission to virtually all of the region's museums and attractions, and 50% off ferry fares to and from Sweden. The card costs 120/200/250 kr (half-price for children aged between five and 11 years) for one/two/three days, is sold at Central Station, the tourist office and some hotels. The card can be a bargain if you plan on doing lots of sightseeing.

Money American Express (☎ 33 12 23 01), whose sole Denmark office is on Strøget at Amagertorv 18, cashes all major travellers' cheques free of commission. It's open from 9 am to 5 pm weekdays, until noon on Saturdays.

Banks, which charge transaction fees, are found on nearly every second corner in the city centre. The bank at Central Station is open from 6.45 am to 10 pm daily (9 pm in winter), though there's a 25% surcharge on all transactions after 4 pm. The airport bank is open from 6.30 am to 10 pm daily.

Post & Telecommunications Pick up poste restante mail at the main post office, Tietgensgade 37, from 10 am to 6 pm weekdays, 9 am to 1 pm on Saturdays. The post office in Central Station is open from 8 am to 10 pm weekdays, 9 am to 4 pm on Saturdays, 10 am to 5 pm on Sundays. You can make international phone calls and send fax and telegrams from 8 am to 10 pm weekdays, 9 am to 9 pm weekends, at the Telecom Center above the Central Station post office.

Foreign Embassies For details see Denmark, Facts for the Visitor.

Travel Agencies Kilroy Travel (☎ 33 11 00 44) at Skindergade 28 and nearby Transalpino (☎ 33 14 46 33) at Skoubogade 6 specialise in discount, student and youth travel.

Laundry Laundrettes (look for the word *møntvask*) are not terribly difficult to find around the city. There's one next to the Saga Hotel, Colbjørnsensgade 18, and another near Nyhavn at Herluf Trolles gade 19. Hours are from 6 am to 10 pm daily and the cost is 25 kr to wash, about 15 kr to dry.

Bookshops GAD, on Strøget at Vimmelskaftet 32, and Boghallen, at Rådhuspladsen 37, both have good selections of English-language books, travel guides and maps. You can read international newspapers at the main public library, Kultorvet 2.

Emergency Dial 112 for police or an ambulance. Several city hospitals have 24-hour emergency wards; the most central is at Rigshospitalet (☎ 31 39 66 33), Blegdamsvej 9. Private doctor visits (☎ 33 93 63 00 for referrals) usually cost from 200 to 350 kr.

Things to See
No visit to Copenhagen is complete without a visit to Tivoli and a stroll down Strøget. The best museum is Ny Carlsberg Glyptotek and, if you're into modern art, don't miss visiting the Louisiana museum in Humlebæk.

Walking Tour Taking a half-day's walk from the Rådhus (city hall) to the Little Mermaid is a good way to get oriented and take in some of the city's central sights.

The **Rådhus** building itself is worth a glance. You can take a free look at the theatre-like interior or, for 10 kr, walk 300 steps to the top of its tower at 10 am, noon or 2 pm.

From the Rådhus walk down Strøget, which after a couple of blocks cuts between two squares, Gammel Torv and Nytorv. The water fountain at **Gammel Torv** marks what was once the old city's central market. Pedlars still sell jewellery, flowers and fruit; the square is one of Copenhagen's most popular hang-outs.

At the end of the Strøget mall you'll reach Kongens Nytorv, a square circled by gracious old buildings including the **Royal Theatre**, home to the Royal Danish Ballet, and **Charlottenborg**, a 17th century Dutch Baroque palace that houses the Royal Academy of Arts. The academy's rear building has changing exhibits of contemporary art and architecture and is open from 10 am to 5 pm daily, usually charging a fee of 20 kr.

On the east side of Kongens Nytorv is picturesque **Nyhavn** canal, dug 300 years ago to allow traders to bring their wares into the heart of the city. Long a haunt for sailors and writers, Nyhavn is today half-salty, half-gentrified, with a line of trendy pavement cafés and restored gabled townhouses.

One of them, Nyhavn 69, has been turned into a museum dedicated to Hans Christian Andersen, who lived next door in the adjacent townhouse for 19 years.

From the north side of Nyhavn, head north on Toldbodgade, turn right on Sankt Annæ Plads and then turn left to continue walking north along the waterfront. When you reach the fountain, turn inland to get to **Amalienborg Palace**, home of the royal family since 1794. The palace's four nearly identical Rococo mansions surround a central square that's the scene of a colourful noontime changing of the guard when the queen is in residence.

Continue down Amaliegade to Churchillparken, where you'll find **Frihedsmuseet**, which depicts the history of Danish Resistance against Nazi occupation. The museum is free and open from 10 am to 4 pm Tuesday to Saturday, to 5 pm on Sundays, with slightly shorter hours in the off season.

Taking a 10-minute walk up past the immense **Gefion Fountain** and through the park will lead you to the statue of the famed **Little Mermaid** (Den Lille Havfrue), a diminutive bronze with an industrial harbour backdrop that disappoints all but the most steadfast Hans Christian Andersen fans.

From the Little Mermaid continue on the road inland (west). In just a few minutes you'll reach steps leading down to a wooden bridge that crosses a moat into an interesting 17th century citadel called the **Kastellet**. It's a short walk south through the Kastellet, where a second bridge spans the moat and leads back into Churchillparken. From the park, turn right onto Esplanaden to Store Kongensgade, where you can catch bus No 6 back to the Rådhus.

Latin Quarter With its cafés and second-hand bookshops, the area north of Strøget surrounding the old university is a good place for ambling around.

Ascend the stairs of the **University Library** (you enter from Fiolstræde) to see one quirky remnant of the 1807 British bombardment of Copenhagen: a cannonball in five fragments and the target it hit, a book titled *Defensor Pacis* (Defender of Peace).

Opposite the university is **Vor Frue Kirke**, Copenhagen's neoclassical cathedral. With its high vaulted ceilings and columns it seems as much museum as church – all quite apropos as it's also the showcase for the most acclaimed works of Bertel Thorvaldsen, his statues of Christ and the 12 apostles. The cathedral is open free from 9 am to 5 pm, with shorter Sunday hours.

At the north side of the Latin Quarter is **Kultorvet**, a lively place where on sunny days you'll almost surely find impromptu street entertainment, as well as beer gardens, flower stalls and produce stands.

Rundetårn This round tower, at Købmagergade 52, is the best vantage point for viewing the old city's red-tiled rooftops and abundant church spires. Built by Christian IV in 1642 as an astronomical observatory, it still is used as such in winter. Halfway up the 209-metre spiral walkway is a hall with art exhibits worth a visit. It's open from 10 am to 8 pm daily in summer (on Sundays from noon), to 4 pm in winter. Admission is 12 kr.

Rosenborg Slot This 17th century castle, built by Christian IV in Dutch Renaissance style, is a repository of regalia. The main attraction is the dazzling collection of crown jewels which include Christian IV's crown, the jewel-studded sword of Christian III and Queen Margrethe II's emeralds and pearls. It's open from 10 am to 4 pm daily from June to August and from 11 am to 3 pm the rest of the year, though in midwinter it's closed on Mondays. Admission costs 30 kr.

Gardens The green stretch of gardens along Øster Voldgade offers a refuge from the city traffic. **Kongens Have**, the large public park behind Rosenborg Slot, is a popular picnic spot and the site of a free marionette theatre on summer afternoons.

The **Botanical Gardens** on the west side of Rosenborg Slot have fragrant trails amidst arbours, terraces and ponds, open free from 8.30 am to 6 pm. Also in the grounds is the **Palmehus**, a large walk-through glasshouse with tropical plants, open from 10 am to 3

pm. One entrance to the gardens is at the intersection of Gothersgade and Voldgade and the other is off Øster Farimagsgade.

Statens Museum for Kunst Denmark's national gallery, Statens Museum for Kunst, at Sølvgade 48, contains a good fine-arts collection by 19th century Danish masters, such as Jens Juel and C W Eckersberg, and works by European artists including Matisse, Picasso and Munch. Hours are from 10 am to 4.30 pm Tuesday to Sunday. Admission costs 20 kr.

Slotsholmen On an island separated from the city centre by a moat-like canal, Slotsholmen is the site of **Christiansborg Palace** and the seat of Denmark's national government. Of the numerous sites to explore, grandest is the **Royal Reception Chambers**, the ornate Renaissance hall where the queen entertains heads of state. Tours with commentary in English (25 kr) are at 11 am and 1 and 3 pm except Mondays in summer, and less frequent in winter.

The **Ruins of Absalon's Fortress**, the excavated foundations of the original castle built by Bishop Absalon in 1167, are in the basement below the present palace tower and can be explored for 12 kr from 9.30 am to 3.30 pm daily (closed Saturdays and Mondays from October to April).

During summer when the **Folketing** (Parliament) is in recess, free tours of the assembly chambers are given hourly in Danish from 10 am to 4 pm.

At **Thorvaldsens Museum** (enter from Vindebrogade) there are statues by the famed Danish sculptor who was heavily influenced by Greek and Roman mythology. It's open free from 10 am to 5 pm Tuesday to Sunday.

The **Royal Library**, which dates from the 17th century and has lovely flower gardens at the front, is open to 7 pm from Monday to Saturday. Hans Christian Andersen applied for work here in 1834 'to be freed from the heavy burden of having to write in order to live'. His unsuccessful application and many of his original manuscripts are now part of the archives.

Next door at **Tøjhusmuseet**, the royal arsenal built in 1600, there's an impressive collection of hand weapons and old armour and a huge hall filled with historic cannons. Hours are from 10 am to 4 pm Tuesday to Sunday, afternoons only in winter. Admission costs 20 kr.

At the **Museum of Royal Coaches** the coaches used for regal events can be viewed from 2 to 4 pm weekends for 10 kr. The **Teatermuseet**, which houses the royal stage dating from 1766 and has exhibits on Danish theatre history, is open from 2 to 4 pm Wednesdays and noon to 4 pm on Sundays. Admission costs 20 kr.

Nationalmuseet The National Museum, at Ny Vestergade 10, holds Danish artefacts from the Palaeolithic period through to the 1830s, including Viking weaponry and impressive Bronze Age, Iron Age and runestone collections. There's also a noteworthy coin collection, Egyptian mummies and Grecian urns. The museum is open from 10 am to 5 pm Tuesday to Sunday, admission costs 20 kr.

Christianshavn Christianshavn was established by King Christian IV in the early 1600s as a commercial centre and military buffer for the expanding city of Copenhagen. Still surrounded by ramparts and cut by canals, Christianshavn today is a mix of renovated period warehouses and newer apartment buildings.

In 1971 an abandoned military camp on the east side of Christianshavn was taken over by squatters who proclaimed it the 'free state' of **Christiania**, subject to their own laws. Bowing to public pressure the government eventually agreed to allow the community to continue as a 'social experiment'. About 1000 people settled into Christiania, starting their own collective businesses, schools and recycling programme.

Along with progressive happenings, Christiania also became a magnet for runaways and junkies. Hard drugs have since been outlawed. Visitors are welcome to stroll car-free Christiania, though large dogs may intimidate some free spirits. Photography is frowned upon, and outright forbidden on Pusherstreet where hashish is openly (though not legally) smoked and sold.

A few minutes' walk from Christiania is the 17th century **Vor Frelsers Kirke**, on Sankt Annæ Gade, which has an elaborately carved pipe organ and a Baroque altar with cherubs and angels. For a panoramic city view, make the dizzying 400-step ascent up the church's 95-metre spiral tower. The last 160 steps run along the outside rim, narrowing to the point where they literally disappear at the top. Entrance is free to the church, 10 kr to the tower which is open from 9 am to 4.30 pm (from noon on Sundays) in summer, earlier closings in winter.

To get to Christianshavn, walk over the bridge from the north-east side of Slotsholmen or take bus No 8 from Rådhuspladsen.

Tivoli Right in the heart of the city, Tivoli, Copenhagen's century-old amusement park, is a mishmash of gardens, food pavilions, amusement rides, carnival games and stage shows that can be surprisingly tantalising, particularly in the evening. Fireworks light up the skies shortly before midnight on Wednesdays, Fridays and Saturdays. It's open late-April to mid-September from 10 am to midnight daily. Admission is 33 kr.

Ny Carlsberg Glyptotek This museum, housed in a grand period building on HC Andersen Boulevard near Tivoli, has an exceptional collection of Greek, Egyptian, Etruscan and Roman ancient art and paintings by Gauguin, Monet and Van Gogh. It's open daily except Mondays, 10 am to 4 pm from 1 May to 31 August, noon to 3 pm Tuesday to Saturday and 10 am to 4 pm on Sundays the rest of the year. Admission is free on Wednesdays and Sundays, but otherwise it's 15 kr.

Holographic World This exhibit of life-like holographic images, in the same building as the tourist office, will appeal to hologram fanatics but probably not seem worth the 32 kr admission fee to others. It's open from 10 am to 6 pm daily, to midnight in summer.

Louis Tussaud's Wax Museum At HC Andersens Boulevard 22, these wax figure exhibits with an emphasis on great Danes are spruced up with a few lively holograms. It's open from 10 am to 11 pm in summer, to 4.30 pm in winter. Admission is a hefty 42 kr.

Zoo The Copenhagen Zoo, in the Frederiksberg area, has the standard collection of caged creatures, including elephants, lions and giraffes. Bus No 28 stops outside the gate. Admission is 45 kr.

Other Museums It could take weeks to fully explore all of Copenhagen's museums, which cover practically every special interest: Danish architecture, working-class cultural history, Copenhagen's history, geology, toys, tobacco & pipes, post & telegraph, European musical instruments, the drawings of humourist Storm P, the silver design of Georg Jensen and more. *Copenhagen This Week* has a complete list with addresses, hours and admission fees.

Dragør If Copenhagen begins to feel crowded, consider an afternoon excursion to Dragør, a quiet maritime town on the island of Amager, a few km south of the airport. In the early 1550s King Christian II allowed Dutch farmers to settle in Amager to provide his court with flowers and produce, and Dragør still retains a bit of Dutch flavour.

Along the waterfront are fish shops, smokehouses, a sizeable fishing fleet and the Dragør Museum, a half-timbered house holding ship models and period furnishings. The winding cobblestone streets leading up from the harbour are lined with the thatch-roofed, mustard-coloured houses that comprise the old town. Take bus No 30 or 33 (13.50 kr) from Rådhuspladsen, a 35-minute ride. Ferries to Sweden also leave from Dragør; see Denmark, Getting There & Away.

Klampenborg Klampenborg, only 20 minutes from Central Station on the S-train's line C, is a favourite spot for people from Copenhagen on family outings.

A 10-minute walk west from Klampenborg station is **Bakken**, the world's oldest amusement park. A blue-collar version of Tivoli, it's a honky-tonk carnival of bumper cars, slot machines and beer halls. It's open from 2 pm to midnight daily from late March to late August. Entry is free.

Bakken is at the southern edge of **Dyrehave**, a huge woodland of beech trees and meadows crossed with walking and cycling trails. Dyrehave was established as a royal hunting ground in 1669 and has evolved into the capital's most popular picnicking area. At its centre, two km north of Bakken, is the old manor house **Eremitagen**, a good vantage point for spotting herds of grazing deer.

A couple of hundred metres east of Klampenborg station is **Bellevue beach**, a sandy strand that gets packed with sunbathers in summer.

Frilandsmuseet Frilandsmuseet is a sprawling open-air museum of old countryside dwellings, workshops and barns in the town of Lyngby. The museum, at Kongevejen 100, is a 10-minute signposted walk from Sorgenfri station which is 25 minutes from Central Station on the S-train's line L or B. Opening hours are from 10 am to 5 pm in spring and summer, to 3 pm in autumn, closed Mondays and during winter. Admission is 20 kr.

Louisiana, Museum of Modern Art Louisiana, Denmark's best modern art museum, is on a seaside knoll in a strikingly modernistic building with sculpture-laden grounds. In addition to the permanent collection, the museum has top-notch changing exhibits. It's a fascinating place to visit even if you're not passionate about modern art. The museum is a 10-minute signposted walk down Strandvej from Humlebæk station, a 35-minute train ride from Copenhagen. It's open daily from 10 am to 5 pm. Admission costs 42 kr.

Organised Tours

Brewery Visits Both Tuborg and Carlsberg breweries offer weekday tours, ending with free brew to drink. Carlsberg, at Elephant Gate, Ny Carlsbergvej 140 (by bus No 6 westbound), has tours at 11 am and 2 pm. The tours at Tuborg, Strandvejen 54 in Hellerup (by bus No 6 northbound), are at 10 am and 12.30 and 2.30 pm.

Sightseeing Bus From 1 June to 1 September the city operates a sightseeing bus which runs every 30 minutes between 10 am and 4.30 pm. It takes a circular route from the Rådhus, stopping at the National Museum, Kongens Nytorv, Amalienborg Palace, Churchillparken, the Little Mermaid and Rosenborg Slot. You can get on and off as often as you want within 24 hours for 20 kr.

Canal Tours For a different angle on the city, hop onto one of the boat tours that wind through Copenhagen's canals from early May to late September. Though most of the passengers are usually Danes, multilingual guides give a lively commentary in English as well. The biggest company, Canal Tours Copenhagen, leaves from the head of Nyhavn and charges 36 kr, but the best deal is with Netto-Bådene, which has a 50-minute guided tour that includes Nyhavn, the Little Mermaid, Christianshavn and the Christiansborg Slot canals for only 15 kr. Netto-Bådene boats leave from Holmens Kirke, opposite the stock exchange, on the hour between 10 am and 5 pm and also pick up passengers on the south side of Nyhavn.

Canal boats also make a fine traffic-free alternative for getting to some of Copenhagen's waterfront sites, including the Little Mermaid and Christianshavn. Canal Tours Copenhagen charges 30 kr for a one-day pass on its green-route 'water taxi'. The boats leave Nyhavn every 30 minutes from 10.15 am to 4.45 pm (until 5.45 pm in July and August) and make eight stops, allowing you to get on and off as you like.

Festivals

The Copenhagen Jazz Festival is the biggest event of the year, with 10 days of music in early July. The festival presents a wide range of Danish and international jazz, blues and fusion music. All in all there's a cornucopia of more than 400 indoor and outdoor concerts, with music wafting out of practically every public square, park, pub and café from Strøget to Tivoli. For information, contact the festival office (☎ 33 93 20 13).

Places to Stay

The *værelseanvisning* counter at the tourist office, at Bernstorffsgade 1, books rooms in private homes for 150/250 kr for singles/doubles. It also books unfilled hotel rooms, usually at discount rates, though this is purely based on a supply-and-demand situation. When it's not busy, rooms without bath go from about 250/350 kr at hotels like the Centrum or Absalon – though if there's something like a large convention in town it's back to standard rates. The counter is open from 9 am to midnight daily from late April to late September and from 9 am to 5 pm Monday to Saturday (to noon on Saturdays in midwinter) the rest of the year. The booking fee is 13 kr per person.

Use It, Rådhusstræde 13, books private rooms for about 130/200 kr (no booking fee), keeps tabs on which hostel beds are available, and is a good source of information for subletting student housing and other long-term accommodation.

Camping *Bellahøj-Camping* (☎ 31 10 11 50), near the Bellahøj youth hostel, is open from 1 June to 31 August. From Rådhuspladsen take bus No 2 to the Bellahøj stop.

Absalon Camping (☎ 31 41 06 00), which is open all year round, is nine km west of the city centre at Korsdalsvej 132 near Brøndbyøster station on the S-train's line B.

IYHF Hostels Copenhagen has two IYHF hostels, each about five km from the city centre. The Bellahøj hostel is open all year round except from 20 November to 20 December, while the Amager hostel closes for the holidays from 20 December to 2 January. Both hostels have laundry facilities but only the Amager hostel has a guest kitchen. They generally fill early in the summer and it's worth calling ahead for reservations.

The more convenient *Bellahøj Vandrerhjem* (☎ 31 28 97 15), Herbergvejen 8, has 296 dorm beds (53 kr), 14 family rooms and 24-hour reception. From Rådhuspladsen you can take bus No 2-Brønshøj and get off at Fuglsangs Allé.

The newer, Orwellian *Copenhagen Youth Hostel* (☎ 32 52 29 08), in Amager just off the E20, is Europe's largest hostel with 528 beds (59 kr) in cell-like two-bed and five-bed rooms. Check-in time is from 1 pm. From Central Station take bus No 16-Vigerslev, change at Mozarts Plads to bus No 37-Holmens Bro and get off at Vejlands Allé. Until 5 pm weekdays bus No 46 runs from Central Station directly to the hostel.

Other Hostels Even when the IYHF hostels are full you can nearly always find a bed at one of the private or city-sponsored hostels in summer. Though they tend to be more of a crash-pad scene, they're also more central.

The city-run 452-bed *Sleep-In* (☎ 31 26 50 59), Per Henrik Lings Allé 6, is a big divided hall buzzing with activity. It's open from mid-June to 31 August and costs 80 kr with breakfast. Reception is open 24 hours. Use your own sleeping bag or hire linen there. From Rådhuspladsen take bus No 1-Ordrup or No 6-Klampenborg and get off at Idrætsparken. When Sleep-In is full, *Sleep Flat* (☎ 31 26 50 59) opens with another 320 beds at Blegdamsvej 132A.

City Public Hostel (☎ 31 31 20 70), on Vesterbro Ungdomsgård, at Absalonsgade 8, has 200 beds in rooms for six to 24 people. It's rather cheerless, but clean and close to Central Station: walk 10 minutes west from the station along Vesterbrogade. It's open from early May to late August, has 24-hour reception and costs 100 kr with breakfast.

The YMCA/YWCA (KFUM/KFUK) operates two summer *Inter-Rail Points* which provide dorm beds to travellers of both sexes. The facility at Store Kannikestræde 19 (☎ 33 11 30 31) has a great central

location and is open from 1 July to 15 August. A second Inter-Rail Point (☎ 31 31 15 74) at Valdemarsgade 15 is open from mid-July to mid-August. Both places charge 55 kr, provide breakfast for 20 kr, and fill up early. Reception hours are from 8 am to noon and from 2 pm to 12.30 am daily.

You couldn't be more in the middle of things than at *Copenhagen Backpacker* (☎ 31 22 99 31), Reventlowsgade 16, a private flat with six rooms and 22 beds behind Central Station. Dormitory-style beds in a casual setting, free of curfews and rules, cost 75 kr. There are kitchen privileges, a washer and dryer is available (25 kr), and sleeping bags are OK to use or you can hire sheets for 25 kr. The biggest drawback is that there's only one shower and toilet, though there are plans to expand to another floor so that may change.

Guesthouses Schoolteacher Gitte Kongstad (☎ 31 57 24 66) runs a small guesthouse in a restored 1782 warehouse at Sankt Annæ Gade 1B in Christianshavn, just over the bridge from Christiansborg Slot. Rooms are homy with beam ceilings, wooden floors and TV, and are excellent value at 200/250 kr for singles/doubles. There's an extra 25-kr charge for stays of just one night. Gitte runs a small guesthouse-booking service and, if her place is full, she can usually find you another room at the same rates.

Hotels The following hotel accommodation is listed according to location.

Around Central Station Copenhagen's main sleeping quarter (and red-light district) is along the west side of Central Station where rows of six-storey turn-of-the-century buildings house one hotel after the other. Rates given are for rooms without private baths, but include breakfast.

Missionshotellet Hebron (☎ 31 31 69 06), Helgolandsgade 4, is a quiet hotel popular with businesspeople. Best value are the standard rooms at 370/480 kr (330/390 kr on weekends and in midsummer), nearly as cosy as the more expensive renovated rooms.

The *Missionshotellet Nebo* (☎ 31 21 12 17), Istedgade 6, is similarly comfortable and costs 340/560 kr, with rates of 290/490 kr from late June to early August.

The *Hotel Centrum* (☎ 31 31 31 11), Helgolandsgade 14, has small, straightforward rooms for 340/550 kr. When the hotel's not busy rates are often negotiable.

Hotel du Nord (☎ 31 31 77 50), Colbjørnsensgade 14, is a small tidy hotel with comfortable rooms, mostly with TV, for 375/550 kr. Courtyard rooms are larger and quieter than streetside ones.

The popular *Selandia Hotel* (☎ 31 31 46 10), Helgolandsgade 12, is small and personable, with pleasant rooms for 390/540 kr.

At the *Absalon Hotel* (☎ 31 24 22 11), Helgolandsgade 15, the cheaper rooms (400/500 kr) are faded and the shared toilets a bit grubby, but otherwise it's adequate and includes one of the best hotel breakfasts.

The two cheapest places in the area, *Turisthotellet* and *Saga Hotel*, both have rooms for around 300/400 kr though they're on the down-and-out side.

Elsewhere in Copenhagen Despite its name, *KFUM Soldaterhjem & Hotel* (☎ 33 15 40 40) is not really a hotel, but rather 10 simple rooms atop a soldiers' recreational facility, opposite the Rosenborg barracks at Gothersgade 115. When it's not full of soldiers and visiting family members, tourists can rent the rooms for 175/290 kr.

The *Hotel Jørgensen* (☎ 33 13 81 86), at Rømersgade 11 near Nørreport station, is popular with gay travellers. Room rates start at 250/400 kr and in summer it also has dorms for 85 kr. All prices include an excellent breakfast.

Sømandshjemmet Bethel (☎ 33 13 03 70), Nyhavn 22, has good-sized rooms, private showers and unbeatable views of Nyhavn harbour. Ask for a corner room. Rates are 390/560 kr, though when things are slow you should be able to get seamen's rates, which are 10% lower.

Søfolkenes Mindehotel (☎ 33 13 48 82), Peder Skramsgade 19, a couple blocks south of Nyhavn, has a Salvation Army ambience

but offers Copenhagen's cheapest standard hotel rates at 215/380 kr. *Hotel Sankt Jørgen* (☎ 35 37 15 11) at Julius Thomsens Gade 22 is spotless, family-run, and pleasantly old fashioned. There are 18 comfortable and spacious double rooms for 450 kr and two rather cramped single rooms for 350 kr. Toilets and showers are in the hall. It's about a 20-minute walk from the centre.

The newly constructed *Hotel Cab-Inn Scandinavia* (☎ 35 36 11 11), Vodroffsvej 55-57, has 201 sleekly compact rooms that resemble cabins in a cruise ship. Though small, they're quite comfortable, with amenities like remote cable TV, telephones, air-con and private bathrooms with showers. Rates are 385/465 kr for singles/doubles and there's basement parking for 30 kr a day. As it's a popular place, reservations are suggested though if it's full, the sister hotel *Cab-Inn Copenhagen* (☎ 31 21 04 00) at Danasvej 32-34 charges the same rates and is just a few blocks away.

Copenhagen also has many up-market hotels with rates beginning around 1000 kr, all listed in the standard hotel brochures available from the tourist office. For the ultimate splurge, the city's grandest hotel is the *Hotel d'Angleterre* (☎ 33 12 00 95), at Kongens Nytorv 34, which has chandeliers, marble floors, old-world charm and a history that goes back to the 17th century. The d'Angleterre has Copenhagen's grandest rates as well, beginning at 1750/1900 kr for singles/doubles.

Places to Eat
Around Central Station Central Station has a supermarket open daily to midnight, a bakery with good breads and pastries open to 9 pm and several fast-food eateries. Of the four DSB restaurants in the station, the cheapest is *Spise Hjørnet*, open to 10 pm, which serves up a filling if unexciting daily special for 32 kr weekdays, 43 kr on weekends.

More appealing is *Restaurant Bistro* with a full Danish buffet from 11.30 am to 9.30 pm for 125 kr, or a more limited selection for 69 kr. There's a good-value fruit stand outside the station opposite the main post office.

ThSørensen, Vesterbrogade 15, has an elaborate window display with nearly 100 different smørrebrød creations sold as takeaways. Even if you're not hungry it's worth going by just to see what can be done with a lowly slice of bread. It's open from 8 am to 7 pm on weekdays, 10 am to 4 pm on Saturdays.

Restaurant Shezan and *Indus Restaurant*, both on the corner of Viktoriagade and Istedgade, serve Pakistani food from 11 am to 11.30 pm daily. Prices are similar at each place: vegetarian dishes with rice from 50 kr, curries from 60 kr. The food's a bit more authentic at the popular Shezan, the atmosphere's better and less smoky at Indus.

Hercegovina, inside Tivoli, is a fun place for a splurge. After 9 pm a buffet of Yugoslav specialities with a half bottle of wine costs 99 kr. If you dine on the balcony you can watch Tivoli's pantomime ballet perform below.

Scala, on Vesterbrogade opposite Tivoli, is a multi-storied building full of fast-food eateries, restaurants and a cinema. There's a wide range of food, though much of it's lacklustre. Best bets are *Strecker's*, which has sandwiches for 25 kr; *Frisk*, with pasta dishes for about 45kr; *City Rock Café*, where a big burger-and-fries plate costs 55 kr; and *Croissanteri* for sandwiches and beer.

Rådusarkaden, an indoor shopping centre on Vesterbrogade near the Rådhus, has an Irma grocery store and the *Conditori Hans Christian Andersen* which has good sandwiches, pastries and coffee as well as plenty of café tables.

Strøget & Around Strøget has an abundance of cheap eateries including hot-dog, hamburger and ice-cream stands and numerous hole-in-the-wall kebab joints with felafels and shish kebabs for around 25 kr. One of the best is *Shawarma Grill House* at the west end of Strøget and a two-minute walk from Rådhuspladsen. It's a friendly spot, has a sit-down counter, and is open from 11 am to 11 pm.

For night owls the popular *Pasta Basta*, Valkendorfsgade 22, is open to 3 am (to 5 am weekends) and has a self-service table of cold pasta dishes and salads for 69 kr. *American Deep Pan Pizza*, Frederiksberggade 22, has a pizza buffet which includes an all-you-can-eat fresh salad bar for 49 to 69 kr depending on the season.

Café de Paris, at Strøget at Vimmelskaftet 39, has a good-value pizza and salad special for 39 kr. In the same arcade is *Firenze* with Italian food and *Hana Kyoto* with Japanese food; both places have moderate prices.

At *RizRaz*, just south of Strøget at Kompagnistræde 20, you can feast on a superb Mediterranean-style vegetarian buffet including salads, felafels and pizza for only 39 kr from 11.30 am to 5 pm, 59 kr to 11 pm. It's open daily and accepts credit cards.

Café Sorgenfri, Brolæggerstræde 8, is a smoky corner restaurant and pub with good cheap Danish food. Traditional cold dishes cost about 40 kr, hot dishes about 50 kr. The roast pork is a speciality and a full plate of traditional Danish foods costs 90 kr. It's open from 10 am to 9 pm.

For fine dining there's *Peder Oxe* at Gråbrødre Torv, just north of Strøget, which is housed in an older building with a traditional ambience. It specialises in meat dishes, with selections from a salad bar, for 140 kr. It's open from 11.30 am to midnight.

In & Around the Latin Quarter *Jensen's Bøfhus*, Kultorvet 15, has a good lunch deal of a steak and baked potato served from 11.30 am to 3.30 pm for 39 kr. At dinner time a similar meal plus selections from a salad bar is 84 kr.

Next door, *Klaptræet*, a 2nd-floor café at Kultorvet 13, is a student hang-out with sandwiches and hot dishes such as enchiladas or chilli con carne for under 50 kr. It's open daily from 11 am to 11 pm.

Det Lille Apotek, Store Kannikestræde 15, serves a nice Danish lunch plate that includes pickled herring, fish fillet, roast beef, roast pork with red cabbage, pâté, cheese and bread for 80 kr from 11 am to 5 pm. A smaller plate with fewer selections costs 60 kr. *Café Sommersko*, Kronprinsensgade 6, open from 9 am to midnight daily, draws a high-energy university crowd and has a varied menu with lasagne, chilli con carne or quiche with salad for about 50 kr. *Wessels Kro*, a small pub at Sværtegade 7, serves 500 grams of beef with baked potato and salad for 48 kr from 5 to 10 pm on Wednesdays, Saturdays and Sundays.

Krystal Café, an inviting jazz café on Krystalgade, offers snacks such as gazpacho or Greek salad for 25 kr.

Mei Chiang, Gothersgade 129, a fine Chinese restaurant opposite the entrance to the Botanical Gardens, has 10 lunch specials for 35 to 45 kr from 11 am to 4 pm daily. Dinner costs about double that.

Westside The area around where Nørrebrogade and Blågårdsgade meet has a lively ethnic mix of Middle Eastern and Asian peoples and food. This neighbourhood, part of the suburb of Nørrebro, has become quite trendy as a place to go in the evening for both food and entertainment and has a growing number of small cafés as well as Turkish, Pakistani, Egyptian, Indian and Italian eateries.

Quattro Fontane, Guldbergsgade 3, has excellent Italian food at reasonable prices. Pizza and pasta cost from 40 to 50 kr, meat dishes cost around 70 kr. It's open for dinner only, from 4 to 11.30 pm daily. To avoid a long wait for a table, it's best to arrive before 7 pm.

Kashmir, at Nørrebrogade 35, and open to 11.30 pm daily, has authentic Indian food and atmosphere. The lunch special, which is served from 11 am to 2.30 pm daily, is particularly good value at around 50 kr.

Mexicali, Åboulevard 12, has Mexican vegetarian dishes for 70 kr and meat dishes for 80 to 90 kr. Hours are from 5 pm to midnight daily.

Floras, a mellow jazz café at Blågårdsgade 29, is a good place for espresso and cheesecake or light meals such as ratatouille or African stew for 35 kr. There's usually live jazz on Sunday afternoons.

Solsikken, Blågårdsgade 33, is an excellent health-food store with produce, bakery, wine and crystal sections.

Elsewhere in Copenhagen For a thoroughly Danish experience, don't miss the herring buffet at *Nyhavns Færgekro*, an old atmospheric restaurant right on the canal at Nyhavn 5. There are 10 different kinds of herring including baked, marinated, rollmops and whole smoked fish, with condiments to sprinkle on top and bread and boiled potatoes to round out the meal. The all-you-can-eat buffet costs 65 kr and is available from 11 am to 4 pm daily. If you're not a herring lover, there's also a variety of smørrebrød for 19 to 52 kr each. If you're in Christianshavn, *Café Wilder*, Wildersgade 56, is a pleasant neighbourhood eatery serving Danish-style deli foods and sandwiches at honest prices. It opens around 10 am on weekdays and noon on weekends and closes around 2 am. Christiania has a few places to eat, the best being *Spiseloppen*, which is open from 5 to 11 pm Tuesday to Sunday. It's on the 3rd floor of Gallopperiet, the first building on the right after entering Christiania.

The main city produce market is at Israels Plads, a few minutes' walk west of Nørreport station. Stalls are set up from Monday to Friday to 5 pm and on Saturdays, when it also doubles as a flea market, to 2 pm.

Entertainment
Copenhagen is a 24-hour party city. For free entertainment simply stroll along Strøget, especially between Nytorv and Hobjro Plads, which is a bit like an impromptu three-ring circus of musicians, jugglers, dancers and other street performers.

Throughout the summer, numerous free concerts are held in city parks and squares. The biggest of these concerts are those sponsored by the city breweries on Saturday or Sunday afternoons from June to August at Amager Strandpark, reached via bus No 12 or 13. The music is rock or jazz, usually top Danish groups play, and each summer there's at least one big-name concert given by the likes of BB King. Bring your own food, but the custom is to buy drinks at the concerts as it helps offset the costs.

Copenhagen has scores of backstreet cafés with live music. Entry is generally free on weeknights, while there's usually a cover charge of 20 to 50 kr on weekends.

The three following cafés are just a few minutes east of the Rådhus: *Rådhuskroen*, Løngangstræde 21, a hot spot for jazz and blues bands from 10 pm to 4 am nightly; *Drop-In*, on the corner of Hestemøllestræde and Kompagnistræde, with live blues from midnight to 4 am weekends; and *Lade's Kælder*, Kattesundet 6, an Irish pub with blues and other music from about 10 pm nightly.

Huset, Rådhusstræde 13, the home of Use It and the site of the first 1960s squatters settlement, is now an alternative cultural centre with cafés, live music, a disco, cinema, theatre and galleries. Another up-and-coming entertainment scene is at Nørrebro. *Bananrepublikken*, Nørrebrogade 13, is one of the hottest spots, featuring live music from 'around the equator' such as salsa, calypso and flamenco on Thursdays and Saturdays, with a 40-kr cover charge. Two other happening places are *Cafe Cikaden*, Griffenfeldsgade 35, and *Cafeen Funke* at Sankt Hans Torv. For a rundown on Copenhagen's music scene, pick up a copy of *Neon Guiden* at cafés or the tourist office.

There are about 20 screens showing first-release movies in the cinemas along Vesterbrogade between Central Station and Rådhuspladsen. *Det Danske Filminstitut* (☎ 31 57 65 00), at Store Søndervoldstræde in Christianshavn, has free screenings of Danish films with English subtitles at 1 and 3 pm from Monday to Thursday in summer.

Gay Scene Copenhagen has more than a dozen gay bars and clubs. The heart of the gay scene is the *Pan Club*, Knabrostræde 3, a café and disco open to at least 3 am daily. Thursdays here are for women only.

Things to Buy

Copenhagen's main shopping street is Strøget and if money's not a factor you can buy anything you want there, including top-quality amber and Danish silver, china and glass.

Getting There & Away

Air Copenhagen's modern international airport is in Kastrup, 10 km south-east of the city centre. Most airline offices are north of Central Station near the intersection of Vester Farimagsgade and Vesterbrogade. The SAS ticket office (☎ 33 15 48 77), in the SAS Royal Hotel, is open weekdays to 5.30 pm.

Bus Buses to Bornholm (Denmark) and to Ystad and Malmö (Sweden) leave from Bernstorffsgade in front of Central Station, while buses to the Swedish cities of Halmsted and Kristianstad leave from Kastrup airport. Buses to Århus (☎ 86 78 48 88) leave from Valby station and buses to Aalborg (☎ 31 57 47 11) leave from the Herlev station. Both buses require reservations.

Train All long-distance trains arrive and depart from Central Station. Trains to Funen and Jutland leave on the hour from 6 am (7 am Sundays) to 8 pm (9 pm Fridays and Sundays). Central Station is a huge complex with lockers, eateries and a summer Inter-Rail Centre where travellers with rail passes can shower for 10 kr and cook food and store packs free.

Car & Motorbike The main highways into Copenhagen are the E20 from Jutland and Funen, the E47 from Helsingør and Sweden. If you're coming from the north on the E47, exit onto Lyngbyvej (route 19) and continue south to get into the heart of the city.

Hitching If you want to try your luck at hitching it's best to start outside the city centre. For rides north, take bus No 6 to Vibenhus Runddel. If you're heading towards Funen, take the S-train's line A to Ellebjerg. Use It has a free message board that attempts to link up drivers and riders. Car-Pool Inter Stop (☎ 31 23 24 40), Vesterbrodgade 54, provides a similar service but charges riders a fee: rides to Amsterdam, for instance, cost 80 kr for the service plus 160 kr to the driver for petrol.

Boat The Oslo ferry departs at 5 pm daily and the Bornholm ferry departs at 11.30 pm nightly. Both leave from Kvæsthusbroen, north of Nyhavn. Take bus No 6 or 9. Boats to Malmö leave from Havnegade on Nyhavn's south side; take bus No 41. See also the Denmark Getting There & Away section.

Getting Around
To/From the Airport The airport is 15 minutes and about 100 kr from the city centre by taxi. The SAS airport bus makes frequent, though sometimes packed, runs from Central Station for 28 kr. You could also take local bus No 32 from Rådhuspladsen, which stops in front of the terminal opposite the SAS bus stand.

Bus & Train Copenhagen has a extensive public transit system consisting of a metro rail network called S-train, whose six main lines pass through Central Station (København H), and a vast bus system, whose main terminus is nearby at Rådhuspladsen.

Buses and trains use a common fare system based on the number of zones you pass through. The basic fare of 9 kr for up to two zones covers most city runs and allows transfers between buses and trains on a single ticket as long as they're made within an hour. Third and subsequent zones cost 4.50 kr more with a maximum fare of 36 kr for travel throughout North Zealand.

On buses, fares are paid to the driver when you board, while on S-trains tickets are purchased at the station and then punched in the yellow timeclock on the platform. You can also buy a Yellow Card, good for 10 rides in up to three zones for 80 kr, or get a 24-hour ticket, good for unlimited travel in all zones for 65 kr. S-trains run from 5 am (6 am on Sundays) to about 12.30 am, which is also the cut-off for most buses – though buses continue to run through the night on a few main routes.

Taxi Taxis with signs saying *'fri'* can be flagged down or you can call 31 35 35 35. The cost is 12 kr at flagfall plus 8 kr per km (10 kr after 6 pm and on Saturdays, Sundays and holidays). Most taxis accept credit cards.

Car & Motorbike With the exception of the weekday-morning rush hour, when traffic can bottleneck coming into the city (and vice versa around 5 pm), traffic is usually manageable. Getting around by car is not problematic other than for the usual challenges of finding an empty parking space in the most popular places. To explore sights in the centre of the city, you're best off on foot or using public transport, but a car is quite convenient for reaching suburban sights. For kerbside parking, buy a ticket from a pavement billetautomat and place it inside the windscreen. Search out a blue or green zone where parking costs 4 to 6 kr an hour; in red zones it's a steep 15 kr. Parking fees must be paid from 8 am to 6 pm weekdays in all zones and from 8 am to 2 pm on Saturdays and Sundays in yellow and blue zones. Overnight kerbside parking is generally free and finding a space, even in the hotel district, is not usually a problem.

Bicycle You can rent bicycles for around 50 kr a day, plus a 200 kr deposit, at various spots around the city including DSB Cykelcenter, outside Central Station on Reventlowsgade, and at the Østerport and Klampenborg stations. Except during weekday rush hours, you can carry bikes on S-trains for 16 kr. If you're travelling with a bike be careful, as expensive bikes are hot targets for 'rip-offs' on Copenhagen streets.

Around Zealand

There are a number of places around Zealand (Danish: Sjælland) that make for interesting excursions from Copenhagen. Northern

Zealand has sandy beaches and castles, while a trip to the southern islands of Møn and Falster will take you farther off the beaten path.

NORTH ZEALAND

Considering its proximity to Copenhagen, the northern part of Zealand is surprisingly rural, with small farms, wheat fields and beech woodlands. It also has fine beaches and some notable historic sights.

One of the most popular day trips from Copenhagen is a loop tour taking in Frederiksborg Castle in Hillerød and Kronborg Castle in Helsingør, with a stop at Fredensborg Palace in between. With an early start you might even have time to continue on to one of the north shore beaches or stop off at the Louisiana modern art museum in Humlebæk on the way back to the city.

If you're driving between Helsingør and Copenhagen ignore the motorway and take the coastal road, Strandvej (route 152), which is far more scenic.

Hillerød

Hillerød, 30 km north of Copenhagen, is the site of Frederiksborg Slot, a Dutch Renaissance castle spread across three islands. The oldest part of the castle dates from Frederik II's time, though most of the present structure was built by his son Christian IV in the early 1600s. After parts of the castle were ravaged by fire in 1859, Carlsberg beer baron JC Jacobsen spearheaded a drive to restore the castle and make it a national museum.

The sprawling castle has a magnificent interior with gilded ceilings, wall-sized tapestries, royal paintings and antiques. The richly embellished Knights Hall (Riddershalen) and the coronation chapel where Danish monarchs were crowned between 1671 and 1840 alone are worth the 30 kr admission fee. It's open daily from 10 am to 5 pm from May to September, to 3 or 4 pm from October to April.

Getting There & Away The S-train (A & E lines) runs every 10 minutes from Copenhagen to Hillerød (36 kr), a 40-minute ride.

From Hillerød station walk down Jernbanevej to Torvet and then along the lake to the castle, about 15 minutes in all, or take bus No 701.

Fredensborg Palace

Fredensborg, the royal family's residence during part of summer, is an 18th century Italianate mansion in the midst of formal gardens. Though it's not a must to see, if the queen is in residence you might want to stop to catch the midday changing of the guard.

The wooded grounds, on the edge of Denmark's second largest lake, make for serene strolling and are open to the public all year round. The palace interior can only be visited during July (from 1 to 5 pm, for 8 kr).

Getting There & Away Fredensborg is midway on the railway line between Hillerød and Helsingør. Go left out of Fredensborg station and turn right onto the main road which runs through town to the palace, a km away.

Helsingør (Elsinore)

Helsingør is a busy port town, with ferries shuttling to and from Sweden 24 hours a day. The tourist office is in Kulturhuset, opposite the railway station.

Helsingør's top sight is Kronborg Castle, made famous as the Elsinore Castle in Shakespeare's *Hamlet*. Actually, Kronborg's primary function was not as a royal residence but rather as a grandiose tollhouse, wresting taxes from ships passing through the narrow Øresund for more than 400 years. The castle is open from 10.30 am to 5 pm in summer, 11 am to 3 pm in winter. You can cross the moat and walk around the courtyard for free, enter the chapel and tour the dungeons for 10 kr or see the whole shebang including the royal apartments, banquet hall and maritime museum for 34 kr.

The castle is on the north side of the harbour and the best way to get there is to walk past the tourist office up Brostræde and along Sankt Anna Gade. This route will take you through the medieval quarter and past the old cathedral, Sankt Olai Kirke; the city

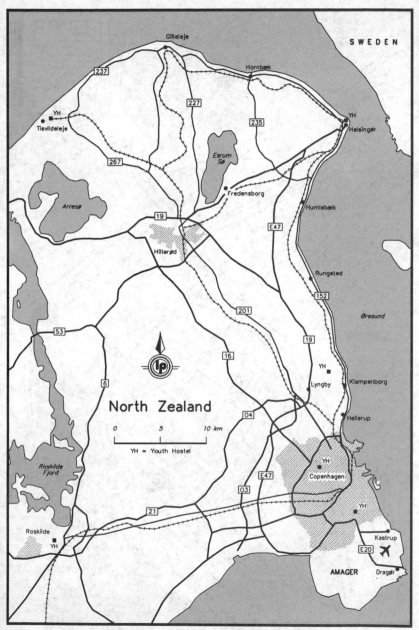

SWEDEN

Gilleleje

Hornbæk

237

227

YH
Tisvildeleje

235

YH
Helsingør

267

Esrum
Sø

Arresø

Fredensborg

Humlebæk

19

E47

Hillerød

Rungsted

152

201

Øresund

53

19

16

YH

6

Lyngby

Klampenborg

North Zealand

04

Hellerup

0   5   10 km

YH = Youth Hostel

YH
Copenhagen

Roskilde
Fjord

E47

YH

03

Roskilde

21

YH

Kastrup

E20

AMAGER Dragør

DENMARK

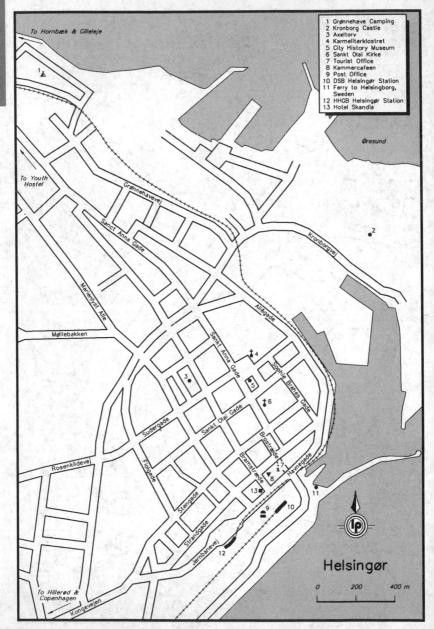

1 Grønnehave Camping
2 Kronborg Castle
3 Axeltorv
4 Karmeliterklostret
5 City History Museum
6 Sankt Olai Kirke
7 Tourist Office
8 Kammercafeen
9 Post Office
10 DSB Helsingør Station
11 Ferry to Helsingborg, Sweden
12 HHGB Helsingør Station
13 Hotel Skandia

To Hornbæk & Gilleleje

Øresund

To Youth Hostel

Grønnehavevej

Sanct Anna Gade

Kronborgvej

Marienlyst Allé

Møllebakken

Allégade

Sankt Anna Gade

Sophie Brahes Gade

Sudergade

Sankt Olai Gade

Rosenkildevej

Folagade

Brostræde

Bramstræde

Havnegade

Stengade

Strandgade

Jernbanevej

To Hillerød & Copenhagen

Kongevejen

Helsingør

0   200   400 m

history museum; and Karmeliterklostret, one of Scandinavia's best preserved medieval monasteries.

Places to Stay & Eat *Helsingør Youth Hostel* (☎ 49 21 16 40), Nedre Strandvej 24, is two km north-west of the centre at an old coastal manor house. The 200-bed hostel is open all year round except December and January; dorm beds cost from 59 to 79 kr. The beachside *Grønnehave Camping*, Sundtoldvej 9, is east of the hostel.

The tourist office books rooms in private homes for 170/270 kr for singles/doubles. The cheapest in-town hotel is *Hotel Skandia* (☎ 49 21 09 02), Bramstræde 1, with rooms from 300/500 kr.

Kammercafeen, in the old customs house behind the tourist office, has reasonably priced sandwiches. Or head for Axeltorv square, four blocks north-west of the railway station, which has beer gardens and a handful of eateries.

Getting There & Away Trains from Hillerød (30 minutes, 27 kr) run twice hourly on weekdays, once an hour on weekends. Trains from Copenhagen run at least twice hourly (50 minutes, 36 kr). For information on ferries to Helsingborg (25 minutes, 21 kr) see Denmark, Getting There & Away.

Zealand's North Coast

The north coast of Zealand has a handful of small maritime towns which date back to the 1500s. Along their backstreets you'll find half-timbered thatch-roofed houses and tidy flower gardens. Though the towns have only a few thousand winter residents, in summer the population swells with throngs of swimmers, sunbathers and windsurfers.

Hornbæk has the best beach on the north coast, a vast expanse of soft white sands that run the entire length of the town. From the railway station, it's a five-minute walk directly down Havnevej to the harbour. Climb the dunes to the left and you're on the beach.

Zealand's northernmost town, **Gilleleje**, has the island's largest fishing port with a

lively morning fish auction, a smokehouse (a whole smoked herring costs 6 kr and makes a tasty snack) and dockside fish markets.

Tisvildeleje is a pleasant old seaside village with a broad stretch of sandy beach backed by low dunes. At the back of the beach is **Tisvilde Hegn**, a windswept forest of twisted trees and heather-covered hills with good walking paths.

Places to Stay There are camping grounds at Hornbæk and Gilleleje. There's a 272-bed *youth hostel* (☎ 42 30 98 50) in the new Sankt Helene Holiday Centre at Bygmarken 30 in the middle of Tisvildeleje, which is open all year round. The tourist offices in Hornbæk and Gilleleje book double rooms in private homes for about 200 kr and there are 'room for rent' signs along the beach road in Hornbæk.

Getting There & Away Trains from Hillerød run to Gilleleje and to Tisvildeleje (22.50 kr), but there's no rail link between the two. Trains from Helsingør go to Hornbæk (13.50 kr) and on to Gilleleje (27 kr) twice an hour on weekdays, once hourly on weekends. The north coast towns are also linked by bus. The bus from Helsingør station to Hornbæk leaves at 25 minutes past the hour and the trip takes about 30 minutes.

ROSKILDE

Roskilde, Denmark's first capital, was a thriving trade centre throughout the Middle Ages. It was also the site of Zealand's first Christian church, which was built by Viking king Harald Bluetooth in 980 AD. As it was the centre of Danish Catholicism, Roskilde's population shrank radically after the Reformation. Today it's a likeable, low-profile town.

You can easily walk to the main sights. The cathedral is on Torvet, 10 minutes north-west of the railway station: cut diagonally across the old churchyard and go left along Algade. The harbourside Viking ship museum is north of the cathedral, a pleasant 15-minute stroll through city parks.

Northern Europe's largest music festival

DENMARK

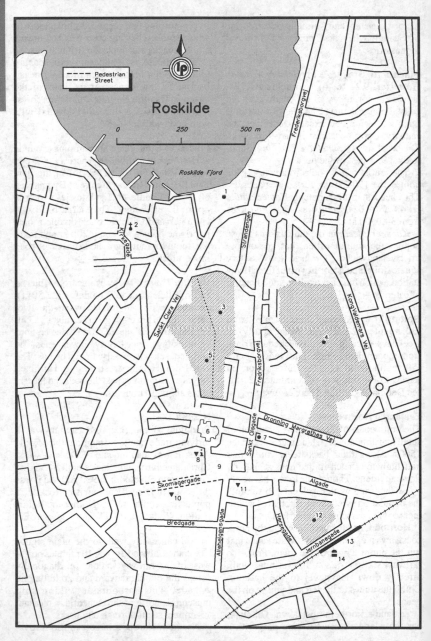

Roskilde

Pedestrian
Street

Roskilde Fjord

0   250   500 m

1	Vikingeskibshallen
2	Jørgensbjerg Church
3	Roskilde Park
4	Folkeparken
5	Site of Medieval Town
6	Roskilde Domkirke
7	Roskilde Museum
8	Tourist Office & Raadhus-Kælderen
9	Torvet
10	S Supermarket
11	Bakery
12	Old Churchyard
13	Railway Station
14	Post Office

rocks Roskilde each summer, usually during the last weekend in June.

Things to See

Though most of Roskilde's medieval buildings have vanished in fires over the centuries, the imposing cathedral **Roskilde Domkirke** still dominates the city centre. Started in 1170 by Bishop Absalon, the cathedral has been rebuilt and added onto so many times that it represents a millennium of Danish church architectural styles.

The cathedral has tall spires, a splendid interior and the crypts of 37 Danish kings and queens. Some of the crypts are spectacularly embellished and guarded by marble statues of knights and women in mourning, while others are simple coffins. There's something quite awesome about being able to stand next to the bones of so many of Scandinavia's most powerful historical figures.

If you're there on the hour, check out the 16th century clock above the entrance, where a tiny St George on horseback marks the hour by slaying a yelping dragon. In summer, the cathedral is open from 9 am to 5.45 pm, from 12.30 pm on Sundays, and costs 3 kr. Winter hours are a bit shorter. It's not unusual for the cathedral to be closed on Saturdays for weddings and occasionally on other days for funerals. You can check in advance by

calling the Roskilde tourist office (☎ 42 35 27 00).

From the north side of the cathedral, you can walk across a field where wildflowers seasonally blanket the unexcavated remains of Roskilde's original medieval town, and can continue through a green belt all the way down to **Vikingeskibshallen**, the Viking ship museum. This well-presented museum contains five reconstructed Viking ships, (circa 1000 AD) that were excavated from the bottom of Roskilde fjord in 1962 and brought to shore in thousands of fragments. The museum is open from 9 am to 5 pm daily from April to October, 10 am to 4 pm in winter. Admission costs 28 kr.

From the museum, a five-minute walk west along the harbour will bring you to the **Sankt Jørgensbjerg quarter**, where the cobbled walkway Kirkegade leads through a neighbourhood of old straw-roofed houses and into the courtyard of an 11th century church.

Back near Torvet, the **Roskilde Museum** (5 kr), Sankt Olsgade 18, is a reasonably interesting local museum with old bones, pottery and archaeological finds.

Eight km south-west of Roskilde in Lejre is the **Historical-Archaeological Experimental Centre**, which aims to study the distant past. Part of the centre is a reconstructed Iron Age village in which Danish families can spend their summer holidays living on site as 'prehistoric families' using technology from that period. It's not as riveting as it sounds but if you're curious, it's a short train ride from Roskilde to Lejre station where bus No 233 will take you to the centre. However, admission costs a hefty 40 kr. The centre is open from 10 am to 5 pm daily from May to late September.

Places to Stay & Eat

Most travellers visit Roskilde on a day trip, but should you want to stay, the tourist office at Torvet books rooms in private homes at 110/220 kr for singles/doubles. *Roskilde Youth Hostel* (☎ 42 35 21 84) is at Hørhusene 61, three km from the city centre by bus No 601 or 604.

There's a cheap cafeteria above *S Supermarket* on Skomagergade near Torvet, and a bakery at Algade 6 with good cinnamon rolls and inexpensive sandwiches. For a treat, there's the atmospheric *Raadhus-Kælderen* in the town hall dating from around 1430. You can have a tasty fish meal for 58 kr from 11 am to 5 pm, 130 kr in the evening. There's a produce market at Torvet on Wednesdays and Saturdays from 9 am to 2 pm.

Getting There & Away
Trains from Copenhagen to Roskilde are frequent (25 minutes, 36 kr). If you're continuing to Odense the same day you can stop over for free. There are lockers at the railway station. From Copenhagen by car, route 21 leads to Roskilde. Upon approaching the city, exit onto route 156, which leads into the centre. You might be able to find parking north of the railway station, but if not, there's plenty of parking down by the Vikingeskibshallen.

MØN, FALSTER & LOLLAND
The three main islands south of Zealand – Møn, Falster and Lolland – are all connected with Zealand by bridges. Møn is known for its spectacular white chalk sea cliffs and Falster has fine white sand beaches. Lolland, the largest and least interesting island, has a handful of scattered sights that are only worth exploring if you have your own transport. All three islands are predominately rural and, except for Møn's rolling hills, the terrain is largely flat and monotonous.

Møn
The main town on Møn, **Stege**, has a church with **medieval frescoes** worth seeing, but the real lure is at **Møns Klint** across the island.

The chalk cliffs at Møns Klint were created 5000 years ago when the calcareous deposits from eons of seashells were uplifted from the ocean floor. The gleaming white cliffs rise sharply 128 metres above an azure sea, presenting one of the most striking landscapes in Denmark.

Møns Klint is a popular destination for Danish tourists. The park contains a cafeteria, a couple of souvenir shops, and picnic grounds in the woods above the cliffs, but none of this detracts from the cliffs themselves.

You can walk down the cliffs to the beach and back up again in about 30 minutes, or go along the shoreline in either direction and then loop back up through a thick forest of beech trees for a hearty walk. Either way, start on the path directly below the cafeteria – it's a quick route to the most scenic stretch of the cliffs.

With time on your hands, Møn would be a fine island to explore more thoroughly. The scenery is rustic, the pace slow and there are prehistoric dolmens and passage graves as well as some good beaches, but the island lacks a rail system and the bus service is sketchy.

Places to Stay & Eat *Camping Møns Klint*, opposite the hostel, is open from April to 1 November. *Møns Klint Youth Hostel* (☎ 55 81 20 30), in a former lakeside hotel three km from the cliffs, is open from April to mid-September.

Hotel Store Klint (☎ 55 81 90 08), a small hotel at the cliffs, costs 300/450 kr for singles/doubles. You can get meals at the cafeterias at the cliffs and camping ground, or pick up supplies at *Land & By* natural-food store in Stege.

Getting There & Away From Copenhagen take the train to Vordingborg (1½ hours, 75 kr) from where it's a 45-minute (28 kr) bus ride to Stege. From late June to August, buses make the 35-minute run (14 kr) from Stege to Møns Klint five times a day; the first service is at 9.10 am and the last at 3.10 pm. The bus stops at the camping ground en route.

Falster
The east coast of Falster is lined with white sandy beaches that are a magnet for German and Danish holiday-makers.

The most glorious stretch is at **Marielyst**,

a lively beach resort. Though Marielyst draws crowds in summer, the beach runs on for many km and there's easy access to its entire length so you'll never need to feel crowded. A bike trail runs on top of the dunes the whole way, which makes it easy to get around even if you're staying at one of the camping grounds a few km out of the town centre. Bikes can be rented from Statoil Servicenter for 30 kr a day.

Places to Stay Falster's only *youth hostel* (☎ 54 85 66 99) is in Nykøbing, one km east of the railway station opposite the zoo.

Marielyst's most central camping ground is *Smedegårdens*, right in town two minutes from the beach. It's open from 1 June to mid-September. The nearby *Hotel Marielyst Strand* (☎ 54 13 68 88) charges 275/350 kr for singles/doubles, 100 kr more for a room with a private bath.

The Marielyst tourist office, which is open from Monday to Saturday, books a few rooms in private homes for 130/250 kr singles/doubles.

Places to Eat Marielyst is filled with cafés, hot-dog stands and ice-cream shops. A good alternative to junk food is offered by *Schous Kød*, 200 metres down Bøtøvej, which sells cooked meats and deli foods by the piece to take away and has a little fruit & vegetable stand next door. There's a good bakery 50 metres west of the tourist office that's open daily from 6 am to 5 pm.

Getting There & Away Trains leave Copenhagen hourly for Gedser at the southern tip of Falster, stopping in Nykøbing (two hours, 95 kr) from where it's a 20-minute bus ride to Marielyst. If you want to do the last leg to Marielyst by bicycle, DSB rents bikes at the Nykøbing railway station. In summer there are daily ferries from Gedser to Warnemünde and Rostock in Germany. Each trip takes about two hours and costs 25 kr.

Bornholm

Bornholm, 200 km east of Copenhagen, is a delightful slow-paced island that makes for a nice getaway. The centre of the island is a mixture of wheat fields and forests, the coast is dotted with small fishing villages, and there's a scattering of half-timbered houses throughout. The northern part of Bornholm has sea cliffs and a rocky shoreline, while the south coast has long stretches of powdery white sands.

Unique among Bornholm's sights are its four 12th century round churches, with two-metre-thick whitewashed walls and black conical roofs. Each was designed not only as a place of worship but also as a fortress against enemy attacks, with an upper storey that served as a shooting gallery. All four churches are still used for Sunday services and are otherwise open to visitors from Monday to Saturday.

Be sure to try Bornholm's smoked herring, *bornholmers*, and Christiansø's spiced herring, considered the best in Denmark.

Getting There & Away

Air Danair (☎ 32 32 68 28) has several flights a day between Copenhagen and Rønne. If you fly on certain weekday flights (such as the 1 pm flight from Copenhagen) the cost is 575 kr return, which is otherwise the standard one-way fare.

Bus & Ferry Bornholmstrafikken (☎ 33 13 18 66) operates a ferry from Copenhagen to Rønne which leaves at 11.30 pm daily, takes seven hours and costs 168 kr. Add 55 kr for a dorm bunk, 262 kr for a double cabin, or spread out your sleeping bag in the TV lounge for no charge.

In midsummer there's also a daytime ferry daily except Wednesdays that leaves Copenhagen at 8 am and returns from Rønne at 3 pm. It costs 47 kr to take a bicycle, 172 kr for a motorcycle and 344 kr for a car up to

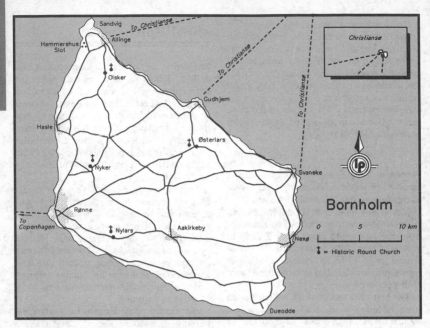

six metres in length. Bornholmstrafikken also operates at least two ferries a day from Ystad (Sweden) to Rønne (2½ hours, 98 kr).

Pilen (☎ 33 32 12 60) provides transport from Copenhagen to Bornholm via its hydrofoil to Malmö (Sweden), followed by bus and ferry connections to Rønne. The whole package takes about 4¾ hours and leaves a few times a day, with the first departure at 8.50 am. The cost is 129 kr in the off season, 159 kr from late June to mid-August. From mid-June to mid-August Pilen also operates daily services from Copenhagen to Allinge for 159 kr. Both Pilen and Bornholmstrafikken accept credit cards.

A third option is bus No 866 (☎ 44 68 44 00) which goes from Copenhagen's Central Station to Ystad, where it connects with the ferry to Rønne. The service runs at least twice daily, takes 5½ hours and costs 160 kr. There are also ferries to Bornholm from Simrishamn (Sweden) and Sassnitz (Germany).

Getting Around

Bus Bornholms Amts Trafikselskab (known as BAT) operates a good, inexpensive bus service around the island. Fares, which are based on a zone system, cost 7 kr per zone, with the maximum fare set at 10 zones. The cheapest deal is to buy a bus pass called 'RaBATkort' from the bus driver for 56 kr, which is good for 10 zones of travel and can be used for multiple rides and by more than one person. Buses operate all year round, but schedules are less frequent in winter.

In summer, bus No 7 leaves from the Rønne ferry terminal every two hours during the day and goes anticlockwise around the island, stopping at Dueodde beach and all major coastal villages before terminating at Hammershus. Other buses make direct runs from Rønne to Nexø, Svaneke, Gudhjem and Sandvig.

Bicycle Cycling is a fine option, as Bornholm is crisscrossed with bike trails, many of which have been built over former rail routes. Bicycles can be rented around the island for about 50 kr a day.

RØNNE

Rønne (population 12,000) is Bornholm's largest town. There are a couple of local museums and older neighbourhoods you could explore, but Rønne is more of a watering hole and shopping locale for Swedes on day trips than a sightseeing destination.

The tourist office, at Munch Petersensvej 4, a few minutes from the harbour, has information on all Bornholm. It's open from 7 am to at least 10.30 pm daily from 1 June to mid-September, and from 9 am to 5 pm weekdays and noon to 3 pm on Saturdays in the off season.

The attractive round church **Nylars Rundkirke**, built in 1150 and decorated with 13th century frescoes, is only a 15-minute ride from Rønne on bus No 2. It's open until 5 pm from Monday to Saturday and there's no admission fee.

Places to Stay & Eat

Rønne Youth Hostel (☎ 56 95 13 40) at Søndre Allé 22 is out towards the airport, a 10-minute bus ride plus a one-km walk. The 160-bed hostel has 15 family rooms and is open from late March until 1 November. *Galløkken Camping*, at Strandvegen 4, is about a km south of the hostel. The tourist office books private rooms for 100 kr a person.

There's a konditori opposite the central bus stop on Snellemark, a cafeteria in the nearby *Kvickly* supermarket and many restaurants of the fast-food variety at Store Torv. *Restaurant Perronen*, opposite the tourist office, has an adequate salad bar for 35 kr, 50 kr with lasagne.

DUEODDE

Dueodde is a vast stretch of white sand beach backed by woodlands and dunes. There's no village, just a bus stop with a single hotel, a pricey café and a couple of ice-cream kiosks. Dueodde is a true beach-bum hang-out. The only 'sight' is a lighthouse a short walk west along the beach.

Places to Stay & Eat

The beachside *Dueodde Youth Hostel & Campground* (☎ 56 48 81 19), open from 1 May to 1 October, is a 10-minute walk east of the bus stop. Rooms at *Dueodde Badehotel* (☎ 56 48 86 49) start at 390 kr. Bring your own supplies, or eat meals at the hostel.

SVANEKE

Svaneke is a quaint harbourfront town that has won international awards for the preservation of its historic buildings.

Places to Stay & Eat

Svaneke has two camping grounds: one near the youth hostel and another on the coast at the north side of the village. The *Svaneke Youth Hostel* (☎ 56 49 62 42) is about one km south of the centre, at Reberbanevej 5. The tourist office at Storegade 24, two blocks north of Torv, books rooms in private homes.

There's a pizza parlour, bakery and grocery store at the central square and more expensive restaurants along the harbour.

GUDHJEM

Gudhjem is a pretty seaside village with half-timbered houses and sloping streets. The shoreline is rocky, though sunbathers will find a small beach at Melsted, one km south. A bike path leads inland four km south from Gudhjem to **Østerlars Rundkirke**, the most impressive of the island's round churches. Bus No 9 also goes by the church. Climb the heather-covered hill behind the hostel for a good view of the town. At the dockside Glasrøgeri you can watch glass being hand blown.

Gudhjem's harbour was, incidentally, one of the settings for the filming of Bornholm novelist Martin Andersen Nexø's *Pelle the Conqueror*. The Oscar-winning film tells the story of the harsh life experienced by Swedish immigrants in the 'promised land' of Bornholm in the late 19th century.

Places to Stay & Eat

The nearest camping ground is *Sletten Camping*, a 15-minute walk south of the village. *Gudhjem Youth Hostel* (☎ 56 48 50 35), at the harbourside bus stop, has the usual 59-kr dorms as well as rooms in private homes for 200 kr a double. The hostel serves up a hearty dinner for just 40 kr.

The fish market by the bus stop sells shrimp and fried fish by the piece and has picnic tables out the front. *Gudhjem Røgeri*, a waterfront smokehouse, sells fish and salads deli-style and doubles as a pizzeria and popular bar featuring live folk music nightly.

SANDVIG

Bornholm's best known sight is **Hammershus Slot**, three km south of Sandvig. These impressive 13th century castle ruins, dramatically perched on top of a sea cliff, are the largest in Scandinavia. There's an hourly bus to the ruins, but the best way to get there from Sandvig is via footpaths through the heather-covered hills of Hammeren – a wonderful hour's hike. The trail begins down by the camping ground.

Sandvig itself is a quiet village with older houses, well-tended flower gardens and a nice sandy beach right in town.

Places to Stay & Eat

Sandvig Familie Camping is on the north side of town. *Sandvig Youth Hostel* (☎ 56 48 03 62), open from 1 June to 1 October, is midway between Hammershus and Sandvig. The old-fashioned *Alexandersens Hotel* (☎ 56 48 20 30), below the bus stop, costs 325/550kr for singles/doubles during peak season, and there are also a number of moderately priced pensions in the area. There's a cafeteria by the beach and restaurants near the camping ground.

CHRISTIANSØ

Tiny Christiansø is a charmingly preserved 17th century fortress island an hour's sail north-east of Bornholm. A seasonal fishing hamlet since the Middle Ages, Christiansø fell briefly into Swedish hands in 1658, after which Christian V decided to turn the island into an invincible naval fortress. Bastions and barracks were built; a church, school and prison followed.

By the 1850s the island was no longer needed as a forward base against Sweden and the navy withdrew. Soldiers who wanted to stay on as fishermen were allowed to live as free tenants in the old cottages. Their offspring, and a few latter-day fisherfolk and artists, currently comprise Christiansø's 140 residents. The entire island is an unspoiled reserve – there are no cats or dogs, no cars, and no modern buildings.

Christiansø is connected to a smaller island, Frederiksø, by a footbridge. There's a **local history museum** in Frederiksø's **tower** and a great 360-degree view from the Christiansø **lighthouse**. Otherwise the main activity is walking the footpaths along the fortified walls and batteries. There are skerries with nesting sea birds and a secluded swimming cove on Christiansø's east side.

Places to Stay & Eat

Camping is allowed in a field at the Duchess Battery from June to August and costs 25 kr. *Christiansø Gæstgiveriet* (☎ 56 46 20 15), the island's only inn, has four rooms with shared bath for 250/350 kr a single/double including breakfast. There's a restaurant at the inn, a small grocery store and a snack shop.

Getting There & Away

Boats sail to Christiansø from Allinge and Gudhjem daily from 1 May to 30 September, while the mailboat from Svaneke makes the trip all year round. All boats charge 110 kr return on a day trip; it's 180 kr open return.

Funen

Funen (Fyn) is Denmark's garden island. It's largely rural and green, with rolling woodlands, pastures, wheat fields and lots of old farmhouses. During May, the landscape is ablaze with solid patches of yellow mustard flowers.

The main railway line from Copenhagen runs straight through Odense, Funen's main city, and westward to Jutland, but it would be a shame to zip through without stopping to explore some of the unspoiled islands in the South Funen archipelago. Svendborg and Faaborg are the main jumping-off points to Ærø, the most popular island.

Store Bælt (Great Belt), the channel that separates Zealand and Funen, can only be crossed by boat. The IC trains roll right onto the ferries, whereas on most IR trains you walk onto the boat and then off onto a waiting train upon reaching the other side of the channel.

A massive project is underway to build both a 20-km vehicle bridge and an undersea railroad tunnel which will eventually link the islands at Korsør and Nyborg, two otherwise forgettable industrial ports. In the meantime automobiles must travel by ferry between the two ports. The ferry operated by Vognmandsruten (☎ 53 57 02 04) has the cheapest fares, runs about 20 times a day, takes a little over an hour and charges 175 kr for a car.

ODENSE

Denmark's third largest city makes much ado about being the birthplace of Hans Christian Andersen though in actuality, after a fairly unhappy childhood, Hans got out of Odense as fast as he could. Nonetheless, Odense is an affable university city with lots of bike lanes and pedestrian streets, an intercsting cathedral and a number of worthy museums.

Orientation & Information

The tourist office (☎ 66 12 75 20), at the Rådhus, is a 15-minute walk from the railway station, south on Jernbanegade and north-east (left) on Vestergade. It's open from 9 am to 7 pm (on Sundays from 11 am) daily in summer, and from 9 am to 5 pm weekdays and 10 am to 1 pm Saturdays, in the off season.

The cathedral and public library are on Klosterbakken, two minutes from the tourist office, and most of the city sights are within walking distance. The central bus transit point is in front of the cathedral.

Things to See

The east side of the city centre has some of Odense's oldest buildings. **Vor Frue Kirke**, Odense's oldest church, dates back to the 13th century and is open from 10 am to 3 pm.

Around the corner, **Møntergården**, a city museum at Overgade 48, has displays of Odense's history dating back to the Viking Age and a number of 16th and 17th century half-timbered houses that you can walk through. It's open daily from 10 am to 4 pm and admission is 15 kr.

You can make a pleasant loop from the city centre by strolling down Nedergade, a cobblestone street with leaning half-timbered houses and antique shops, and returning via Overgade.

The museum **HC Andersens Hus**, at Hans Jensens Stræde 39, depicts Andersen's life story through his memorabilia and books, though the presentation doesn't match up to the author's rich imagination. It is open daily from 1 June to 31 August from 9 am to 6 pm, in spring and autumn from 10 am to 5 pm, and in winter from 10 am to 3 pm. Admission costs 20 kr for adults and 10 kr for children.

At Munkemøllestræde 3, **HC Andersens Barndomshjem** has a couple of rooms of exhibits in the small house where Hans grew up. It's open from 10 am to 5 pm April to September and from noon to 3 pm October to March. Admission costs 5 kr.

Sankt Knuds Kirke Odense's 12th century Gothic cathedral has an ornate gilded altar dating from 1520, but the cathedral's real intrigue lies in the basement where you'll find a glass case containing the 900-year-old skeleton of King Knud II.

A few metres from the coffin, stairs lead down to the remains of St Alban's church. In 1086 Knud II fled into St Alban's and was killed at the altar by farmers in a tax revolt. Though less than saintly, in 1101 Knud was canonised Knud the Holy by the pope in a

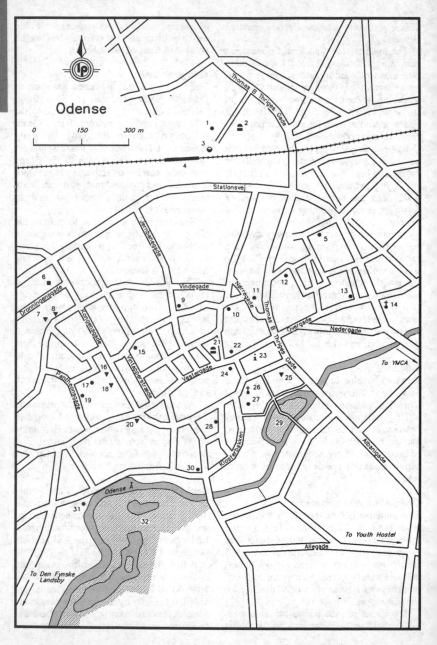

Odense

0   150   300 m

Thomas B Thriges Gade

Stationsvej

Jernbanegade

Vindegade

Dronningensgade

Kongensgade

Nørregade

Thomas B Thriges Gade

Overgade

Nedergade

To YMCA

Vintapperstræde

Pantheonsgade

Vestergade

Albanigade

Klosterbakken

Odense Å

To Youth Hostel

Allégade

To Den Fynske
Landsby

1	Jernbanemuseet
2	Main Post Office
3	Regional Bus Terminal
4	Railway Station
5	Carl Nielsen Museet
6	Hotel Kahema
7	Pizza Express
8	Jazzhus Kabyssen
9	Fyns Kunstmuseum
10	Naturkost
11	Boogies
12	HC Andersens Hus
13	Møntergården Museum
14	Vor Frue Kirke
15	Irma Supermarket
16	Burger King
17	Brandts Klædefabrik
18	McDonald's
19	Cotton Club
20	Akropolis
21	Post Office
22	Raadhus Bageriet
23	Tourist Office/Rådhus
24	Den Danske Bank
25	Mekong Restaurant
26	Sankt Knuds Kirke
27	Library
28	HC Andersens Barndomshjem
29	HC Andersen Haven
30	Cykel Centret
31	Boat Dock
32	Munke Mose

move to secure the church in Denmark. The cathedral is free and open daily except Sundays from 10 am to 4 pm.

Den Fynske Landsby This is a delightful open-air museum whose furnished period buildings are authentically laid out like a small country village, complete with barnyard animals, a duck pond, apple trees and flower gardens. It's open daily between 1 April and mid-October from 10 am to 4 pm, until 7.30 pm in summer. Admission is 20 kr.

The museum is in a green zone four km south of the city centre; bus Nos 25 and 26 stop in front. In summer you can take a boat from Munke Mose down the river to Erik Bøghus Sti, from where it's a refreshing 15-minute woodland walk along the river to Den Fynske Landsby.

Fyns Kunstmuseum The stately Graeco-Roman building at Jernbanegade 13 contains a quality collection of Danish art, from paintings of the old masters to abstract contemporary works. It's open from 10 am to 4 pm daily for 15 kr, free on Wednesdays from 7 to 10 pm.

Carl Nielsen Museet This museum, in the concert hall at Claus Bergs Gade 11, details the career of Odense's native son, Carl Nielsen, Denmark's best known composer, and displays the works by his wife, sculptor Anne Marie Brodersen. Hours are from 10 am to 4 pm daily. Admission costs 15 kr.

Jernbanemuseet Railway buffs shouldn't miss the 19th century locomotives at the rail museum, just behind the railway station. Hours are from 10 am to 4 pm daily (in winter to 1 pm). Admission costs 15 kr, but is free if you're travelling with a Nordturist rail pass.

Brandts Klædefabrik The former textile mill on Brandts Passage has been converted into a cultural centre with a photography and modern art museum, both featuring changing exhibits, and a museum of graphics and printing. The museums are open from Tuesday to Sunday from 10 am to 5 pm. Entry to all three costs 40 kr or you can buy separate tickets. The amphitheatre out the back is a popular gathering place and a venue for free summer concerts.

Places to Stay

DCU Camping, Odensevej 102, is out by the open-air museum (take bus No 26 or take the train to Fruens Bøge). *Odense Youth Hostel* (☎ 66 13 04 25) is at Kragsbjergvej 121, two km south-east of the city centre via bus No 62 or 63. The 168-bed hostel occupies a former manor house, charges 59 kr for a dorm bed and is open from mid-February to the end of November. *YMCA Inter-Rail Point* (☎ 66 14 23 14), Rødegårdsvej 91, open from mid-June to mid-August only, has bed space for 50 kr.

The tourist office books rooms in private

homes at 100/200 kr for singles/doubles. The 14-room *Hotel Kahema* (☎ 66 12 28 21), at Dronningensgade 5, a 10-minute walk from the station, is a comfortable family-run inn on a quiet street. Rooms cost 220/350 kr including breakfast and there's free parking nearby.

Motel Næsbylund (☎ 66 18 00 39), at Bogensevej 105 three km north of the centre, offers 'discount rooms' to Inter-Railers for 100 kr per person with a two-person minimum; bring sheets or hire linen.

Places to Eat

There are numerous restaurants and cafés along Kongensgade and Vestergade, many of which chalk up daily specials. Bakeries and cheap fast food are easy to find all around the city. *Akropolis*, on the corner of Vestergade and Kongensgade, has Greek food from about 35 kr at lunch, 60 kr at dinner. It's open daily from 11 am to 10 pm.

Café Biografen at Brandts Klædefabrik is a student haunt with pastries, coffees, light meals and beer at reasonable prices. It's open from 11 am to at least midnight daily. *Birdy's Café*, Nørregade 21 (at Boogies – see the following Entertainment section), attracts a similar crowd and has Mexican food. Nachos or quesadillas cost about 40 kr, while enchilada with rice and salad costs 55 kr. It's open from 6 pm to around 2 am Monday to Saturday.

One of the best food deals in Odense is at *Jazzhus Kabyssen*, Vindegade 65, a friendly neighbourhood pub. It offers some terrific buffets with hot and cold Danish dishes. From Tuesday to Friday from 11.30 am to 4 pm the buffet costs 29 kr and you can get a glass of beer for only 10 kr. On Fridays and Saturdays from 5 to 9 pm there's a more elaborate dinner spread for 39 kr, which is also featured on Saturdays from noon to 3 pm when it's accompanied by live jazz.

The best and cheapest pizza is at *Pizza Express*, Vindegade 73, open from 5 to 11 pm, for takeaways only.

Raadhus Bageriet, opposite the tourist office, has big sandwiches made with wholegrain bread for 13 to 17 kr. *Mekong*, at Albanitorv 3, has moderately priced Vietnamese food. There's a health-food store, *Naturkost*, at Gravene 8.

Entertainment

The *Cotton Club*, Pantheonsgade 5, is a good place to hear Danish jazz. University students often hang out at *Boogies*, a dance spot at Nørregade 21, open from 10 pm to 5 am. The outdoor cafés on Vintapperstræde are good for a quiet evening drink.

Getting There & Away

Odense is on the main railway line between Copenhagen (2½ hours, 130 kr) and Århus (1¾ hours, 118 kr). Regional buses leave from the rear of the railway station. Odense is just north of the E20 and access from the highway is clearly marked. Route 43 connects Odense with Faaborg, while route 9 connects Odense with Svendborg.

Getting Around

In Odense you board city buses at the back and pay the driver when you get off. The fare is 9 kr, or 10 kr if you require a transfer. You can buy a 24-hour bus pass at the tourist office for 25 kr, or a pass which allows two days' bus travel and museum admissions for 70 kr (35 kr in winter).

Outside rush hour, driving in Odense is not difficult, though many of the central sights are on pedestrian streets and it's best to park your car and explore on foot. Near the city centre, parking is largely metered, with a fee of 1 kr per 15 minutes from 9 am to 5 pm weekdays and to noon on Saturdays. Outside those hours it's free. There are parking lots near the west side of the Rådhus and north of Brandts Passage.

You can rent bikes from Cykel Centret (☎ 66 13 88 94), Klaregade 29. Hours are from 9.30 am to 5.30 pm weekdays, 10 am to 1pm on Saturdays.

EGESKOV CASTLE

Egeskov Castle is a gem of a Renaissance castle complete with moat and drawbridge. Egeskov, literally 'oak forest', was built in 1554 in the middle of a small lake on top of a foundation of thousands of upright oak trunks. The expansive grounds include century-old privet hedges, free-roaming peacocks, topiary and English gardens.

However, not all is formal – laugh your way through the a-maze-ing bamboo grass labyrinth, dreamed up a few years back by the Danish poet-artist Piet Hein.

The castle is open from May to September from 10 am to 5 pm daily, the grounds to 6 pm in summer. Admission to the grounds and an antique auto museum is 40 kr. The castle is most impressive from the outside – the interior is mostly Victorian furnishings, guns, and hunting trophies of rare beasts, and costs 40 kr extra.

Getting There & Away

Egeskov Castle is three km west of Kvændrup on route 8. From Odense take the Svendborg-bound train or bus No 800 to Kvændrup (about 40 minutes, 35 kr). From there you can take bus No 920, which runs between Faaborg and Nyborg, to the castle.

FAABORG

In the 17th century, Faaborg was a bustling harbour town with one of Denmark's largest fleets. Home to only 6000 people today, Faaborg retains many vestiges of that previous era and its picturesque cobbled streets and old half-timbered houses make for delightful walking. Pick up a free walking-tour map from the tourist office at Havnegade 2.

There are two fine museums: **Den Gamle Gaard**, at Holkegade 1, an old merchant's house with period furnishings; and **Faaborg Museum**, a former winery at Grønnegade 75 which contains Denmark's best collection of Funen art. Den Gamle Gaard is open daily from mid-May to mid-September from 10.30 am to 4.30 pm and admission costs 15 kr. The Faaborg Museum is open daily from March to November. Summer hours are from 10 am to 5 pm and admission costs 20 kr.

If you have more time, the countryside north of Faaborg is worth exploring, as are the small rural islands of Avernakø, Lyø and

Bjørnø. Bikes can be rented at the harbour for 40 kr a day.

Places to Stay & Eat

Holms Camping is on Odensevej, one km north of the town centre. The tourist office books private rooms from 100 kr a person. The 81-bed *Faaborg Youth Hostel* (☎ 62 61 12 03) is in a half-timbered building at Grønnegade 71, opposite Faaborg Museum. *Hotel Strandgade* (☎ 62 61 20 12), near Torvet at Strandgade 2, has pleasant rooms with bath (but no breakfast) for 225/350 kr for singles/doubles.

China House, Strandgade 4, has lunches for 40 kr to 4 pm and the atmospheric *Tre Kroner* at Torvet sometimes has daily specials for not much more. *Cafe Mouritz*, Østergade 27, has vegetarian dishes, cappuccino and home-made cakes at good prices.

Getting There & Away

Faaborg has no rail service. Buses from Odense cost 40 kr, take 1¼ hours and run at least hourly. Getting to Faaborg by car is straightforward. From the north, simply follow route 43, which is called Odensevej as it enters the town. There's free parking at Torvet and down by the harbour.

There are numerous daily ferries to the nearby islands of Avernakø and Lyø (35 kr return, bicycle 15 kr), and a passenger boat to Bjørnø. Ferries leave Faaborg daily for Ærø and for Gelting in Germany.

SVENDBORG

South Funen's largest municipality and a transit point for travel between Odense and Ærø, Svendborg itself is a rather ordinary town and there's little reason to linger. The railway station is two blocks uphill from the dock.

More appealing is the island of **Tåsinge**, just over the bridge from Svendborg, with its charming harbourside village of Troense and the nearby 17th century castle **Valdemars Slot**, whose grounds and white sand beach are open free 24 hours a day. In addition to bus service, the MS *Helge* ferries from

Svendborg to Troense and Valdemars Slot (25 kr) every few hours in summer.

Places to Stay & Eat
In a renovated 19th century iron foundry, the *Svendborg Youth Hostel* (☎ 62 21 66 99) is at Vestergade 45 in the centre of town. *Hotel Ærø* (☎ 62 21 07 60), with 13 rooms at 200/375 kr for singles/doubles, is opposite the Ærø ferry dock as are a couple of moderately priced restaurants, *Svendborgsund* with Danish and beef dishes and the *Bella Italia* pizzeria. There are four camping grounds on Tåsinge.

Getting There & Away
Trains leave Odense for Svendborg at 13 minutes past the hour; the trip takes one hour and costs 41 kr. Ferries to Ærøskøbing depart five times a day; the last crossing is at 9 pm.

LANGELAND
The long, narrow island of Langeland, connected by bridge to Funen via Tåsinge, has good beaches and cycling and some of Denmark's best bird-watching. For beaches head for **Ristinge** or the northern tip of the island. For bird-watching there's a sighting tower at **Tryggelev Nor** and a sanctuary at **Gulstav Bog** at the island's southern tip.

Langeland's top sight is the salmon-coloured **medieval castle** at Tranekær, scenically set above a lake with swans and herons. The castle is the private residence of a countess, but the grounds are open free to the public daily.

Places to Stay & Eat
There are seven camping grounds scattered around the island. Langeland's only *youth hostel* (☎ 62 51 18 30) is at Engdraget 11 in Rudkøbing. *Hotel Rudkøbing* (☎ 62 51 36 18), at the Rudkøbing ferry dock, costs 250/400 kr for singles/doubles.

Getting There & Away
Buses make the 25-minute run from Svendborg to Rudkøbing at least hourly; most connect onwards to Tranekær. There are multiple daily ferries from Rudkøbing to

Marstal in Ærø; from Spodsbjerg to Tårs in Lolland (hourly, 38 kr); and from Bagenkop to Kiel in Germany (25 kr).

ÆRØ
Well off the beaten track, Ærø is an idyllic island with small fishing villages, rolling hills and patchwork farms. It's a great place to tour by bicycle – the country roads are enhanced by **thatched houses** and old **windmills**, and the island has ancient passage graves and dolmens to explore.

Ærø's three main towns – Ærøskøbing, Marstal and Søby – each have ferry connections, places to stay and a tourist office.

Ærøskøbing, a prosperous merchants' town in the late 1600s, has been preserved in its entirety. Its narrow cobblestone streets are tightly lined with 17th and 18th century houses, many of them gently listing half-timbered affairs with handblown glass windows, decorative doorways and streetside hollyhocks. In keeping with the town's nature, sights are low-key.

The main attraction is **Flaskeskibssamlingen**, at Smedegade 22, where Bottle Peter's lifetime work of 1700 ships-in-a-bottle and other local folk art are displayed in the former poorhouse. It's open daily from 9 am to 4 pm. Admission costs 10 kr. There are also two local history museums full of antiques and period furnishings.

Søby has a shipyard, which is the island's biggest employer, a sizeable fishing fleet and a popular yacht harbour. Five km beyond Søby, at Ærø's northern tip, there's a pebble beach with clear water and a stone lighthouse with a view.

Marstal, on the south-eastern end of the island, is the most modern-looking place on the island though it too has a nautical character with a maritime museum, shipyard and yacht harbour, and a reasonably good beach on the south side of town.

Store Rise is the site of **Tingstedet**, a Neolithic Age passage grave in a field behind the village's attractive 12th century **church**. A few km to the south is **Risemark Strand**, the best of Ærø's few sandy beaches.

Places to Stay

There are camping grounds at Søby, Ærøskøbing and Marstal. The tourist offices maintain a list of islanders who rent out rooms in their homes for 100/175 kr for singles/doubles.

There's a *youth hostel* (☎ 62 52 10 44), in Ærøskøbing just a km from the centre on the road to Marstal, open from 1 April to 30 September, and another in the centre of Marstal (☎ 62 53 10 64) at Færgestræde 29, open from 1 May to 31 August.

In Ærøskøbing, the cosy *Det Lille Hotel* (☎ 62 52 23 00), Smedegade 33, and the historic *Hotel Ærøhus* (☎ 62 52 10 03), Vestergade 38, both have nice rooms for 225/370 kr. In Marstal, *Hotel Marstal* (☎ 62 53 13 52) at Dronningestræde 1A, near the harbour, has 10 rooms for 195/310 kr singles/doubles.

An alternative place to stay is *Biokol* (☎ 62 53 18 12), 5960 Marstal, a small organic farm commune in Kragnæs, a few km west of Marstal, which allows travellers to stay in exchange for work on the farm.

Places to Eat

All three towns have a bakery, restaurants and food stores. In Ærøskøbing on Vestergade, 50 metres up from the dock, there's a fast-food café, a small grocery store and the moderately priced *Phønix* which serves Danish food, lasagne and fish and chips. The fish fillet and potatoes on the snacks menu at the *Hotel Ærøhus* makes for a full meal at 50 kr. Biokol commune sells organic vegetables at Torvet on Friday afternoons.

At Marstal's harbour, there's a small food store and the *Færgehavnen's Grill* with inexpensive fish and chips and pitta sandwiches.

For something more substantial, *Hotel Marstal* has half a chicken with salad for 50 kr and a daily special for 75 kr.

Getting There & Away

There are year-round car ferries to Søby from Faaborg, to Ærøskøbing from Svendborg, and to Marstal from Rudkøbing. All run about five times a day, take about an hour and charge 38 kr a person, 13 kr for a bike, 75 kr for a car. It's a good idea to make reservations

if you're going over with a car, particularly on weekends and in midsummer. The phone numbers are: 62 61 14 88 in Faaborg, 62 52 10 18 in Svendborg, 62 53 17 22 in Rudkøbing.

There's also a summer ferry (☎ 62 58 17 17) between Søby and Mommark which has the same fares but operates four times a day in midsummer, a couple of times daily in spring and early autumn, and weekends only in October.

Getting Around

Buses run from Søby to Marstal via Ærøskøbing almost hourly on weekdays, half as frequently on weekends. A pass for unlimited one-day travel costs 42 kr.

You can rent bikes for 35 kr a day at the youth hostel and camping ground in Ærøskøbing, the Marstal tourist office, and the cycle shop at Langebro 4 in Søby. The tourist office has a free cycling map.

Jutland

The Jutland (Danish: Jylland) peninsula, the only part of Denmark connected to the European mainland, was originally settled by the Jutes, a Germanic tribe whose forays included invading England in the 5th century. Jutland's southern boundary has been a fluid one, last drawn in 1920 when Germany relinquished its holdings in Sønderjylland.

Jutland's west coast has endless stretches of windswept sandy beaches, often a good km wide and packed down hard enough for you to drive cars on. Most of the main cities, including Århus and Aalborg, are along the more sheltered east coast.

The northern end of Jutland is largely sand dunes and heathland, while southern Jutland is dominated by moors and marshes. Though parts of the interior are forested, most of Jutland is level farmland whose fields are a brilliant green in spring and a monotonous brown in autumn.

DENMARK

ÅRHUS

On the centre of Jutland's east coast, Århus has been an important trade centre and seaport since Viking times. It is Denmark's second largest city, with just over a quarter of a million residents.

The cultural centre of Jutland, Århus is a lively university city with more than 40,000 students. It has one of Denmark's best music and entertainment scenes, a well-preserved historic quarter and plenty to see and do, ranging from good museums and old churches in the centre to woodland trails and beaches along the city's outskirts.

Orientation

Århus is fairly compact and easy to get around. The railway station is at the south side of the city centre. The pedestrian shopping streets (malls) of Søndergade and Sankt Clements Torv lead to the cathedral in the heart of the old city. The small streets around the cathedral are filled with cafés, pubs and restaurants.

Information

Tourist Office The tourist office (☎ 86 12 16 00), in the Rådhus on Park Allé, is open from 9 am to at least 7 pm daily from late June to mid-September, and from 9.30 am to 4.30 pm weekdays and 10 am to 1 pm Saturdays the rest of the year. Pick up a free map of the city and the handy guide *Århus This Week*.

Money There's a bank at the front of the railway station and many more along Søndergade.

Post & Telecommunications The main post & telegraph office is beside the railway station. It's open from 9 am to 5.30 pm weekdays, to noon Saturdays.

Emergency Dial 112 for police or ambulance and 86 15 73 11 for referrals to a doctor. Århus Kommunehospital on Nørrebrogade has a 24-hour emergency ward.

Meet the Danes The tourist office can arrange for foreign travellers to meet with a

Danish family in their home for tea and conversation. Because they try to match

■	PLACES TO STAY
19	Århus Sømandshjem
25	Park Hotel
35	Ansgar Missions Hotel
40	Eriksens Hotel

▼	PLACES TO EAT
4	Kulturgyngen/Musikcafeen
5	Gallorant Kif-Kif
6	Hornitos
8	Naturkost
11	Huset
21	Colosseum Restaurant
22	Bakery/Supermarket
23	McDonald's
28	Jensen's Bøfhus
30	China Town
34	Supermarket
37	Loft Konditori
38	Hollywood Café
39	Sundhedskost
41	Fruit Stand

	OTHER
1	University
2	Århus Kommunehospital
3	Århus Kunstmuseum
7	Laundrette
9	Den Gamle By
10	Vor Frue Kirke
12	Library
13	Unibank/Vikinge-Museet
14	Århus Domkirke
15	Besættelses-Museet/Kvindemuseet
16	Glazzhuset
17	Århus Teater
18	Fatter Eskil
20	Kalundborg Ferry
24	GAD Bookstore
26	Musikhuset Århus
27	Tourist Office/Rådhus
29	Asmussen Cykler
31	Kilroy Travels
32	InterRent Car Rental
33	Bus Station
36	SAS Ticket Office
42	Railway Station
43	Post & Telegraph Office

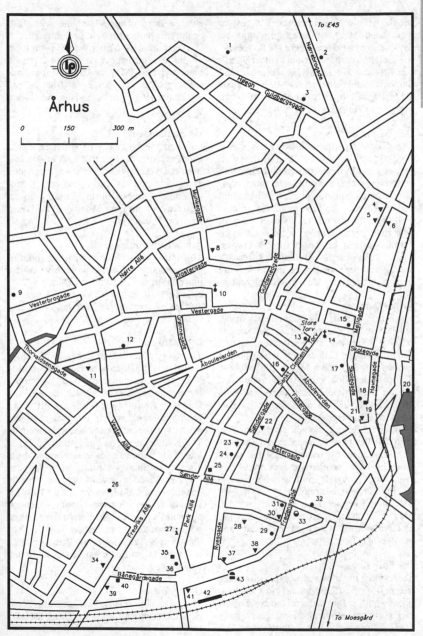

people with similar interests, it's best to request the 'Meet the Danes' programme a day or two in advance. There are no fees.

Foreign students who want to meet Danish students can do so at the International Student Centre (☎ 86 16 28 90), Niels Juels Gade 84. It's open from 9 am to 3 pm Monday to Thursday, to 2 pm on Fridays.

Den Gamle By

Den Gamle By (the Old Town) is a fine open-air museum with 70 half-timbered houses brought here from around Denmark and reconstructed as a provincial town, complete with a functioning bakery, silversmith and bookbinder. On Viborgvej, a 20-minute walk from the city centre, it's open daily all year round, from 9 am to 6 pm in summer. Admission is 35 kr, though after hours you can walk through the old streets for free. It's a delightful time to stroll as the crowds are gone and the light is ideal for photography.

Århus Domkirke

The Århus cathedral is Denmark's longest, with a nave that spans nearly 100 metres. The original Romanesque chapel at the east end dates back to the 12th century, while most of the rest of the church is 15th century Gothic. The cathedral, like other Danish churches, was in olden times richly decorated with frescoes which served to convey biblical parables to illiterate peasants.

After the Reformation church authorities, who felt the frescoes represented Catholicism, had them all whitewashed but many have now been uncovered and restored. They range from fairy-tale paintings of St George slaying a dragon to tormented scenes of hell. The church is open from 9.30 am to 4 pm May to September, from 10 am to 3 pm October to April. It's closed on Sundays and admission is free.

Vor Frue Kirke

This church has a carved wooden altarpiece dating from the 1530s, but far more interesting is what's in its basement: the crypt of the city's original cathedral, dating from around 1060. Enter via stairs beneath the altar. You

enter a third chapel, this one with 16th century frescoes, through the courtyard.

The church, off Vestergade, is open from 10 am to 4 pm weekdays and to 2 pm on Saturdays from May to August. From September to April it's open from 10 am to 2 pm weekdays, to noon on Saturdays. Admission is free.

Vikinge-Museet

Pop into the basement of Unibank, Sankt Clements Torv 6, for a free look at artefacts from the Viking village that was excavated at this site in 1964 during the bank's construction. It's open during banking hours: 9.30 am to 4 pm from Monday to Friday, to 6 pm on Thursdays.

Århus Kunstmuseum

This museum, at Vennelystparken south of the university, has a comprehensive collection of 19th and 20th century Danish art. It's open from 10 am to 5 pm Tuesday to Sunday. Admission costs 30 kr. Take bus No 1, 2, 3 or 6 to Nørreport.

Other Museums

The old city hall at Domkirkeplads 5, which served as the Gestapo headquarters during WW II, now contains two museums: **Besættelses-Museet**, which details the Danish Resistance movement, and **Kvindemuseet**, which features changing exhibits on the culture and history of women. The Kvindemuseet is open from 10 am to 5pm daily June to mid-September, to 4 pm Tuesday to Sunday for the rest of the year. The Resistance museum has more sporadic opening hours. Both places charge 10 kr for admission. **Brandværnsmuseet**, which has the world's largest collection of fire engines, is in a warehouse at Dalgas Ave 56. The university's **Naturhistorisk Museum** has a collection of stuffed creatures from around the world.

Moesgård

The Moesgård woods, five km south of the city centre, make for an absorbing half-day outing. The main focal point is the

Moesgård Prehistoric Museum with quality displays from the Stone Age to the Viking Age, including a roomful of **rune stones**. The most unique exhibit is the 2000-year-old **Grauballe man**, found preserved in a nearby bog in 1952. The dehydrated, leathery body is amazingly intact, right down to its red hair and fingernails. The museum is open from 10 am to 5 pm daily from 1 April to late October, to 4 pm Tuesday to Sunday the rest of the year. Admission costs 25 kr.

An enjoyable trail dubbed the 'prehistoric trackway' leads from behind the museum through fields of grazing sheep and beech woods down to Århus' best sandy beach. The trail, marked by red-dotted stones, passes reconstructed historic sights including a **dolmen, burial cists** and an **Iron Age house**. Pick up a trail-guide booklet at the museum. You can walk one way and catch a bus from the beach back to town, or do the trail round trip as a five-km loop. Bus No 6 from Århus railway station terminates at the museum, and bus No 19 at Moesgård beach; both buses run twice an hour.

Ceres Brewery

Tours of the Ceres Brewery are given at 9 am Tuesdays and Thursdays and 2 pm Wednesdays from late June to early August. Pick up free passes at the tourist office – the tours are quite popular so it's best to get the passes a day or two in advance.

Sightseeing Tour

A guided 2½-hour public bus tour leaves from the tourist office at 10 am daily from late June to the end of August giving a glimpse of the main city sights. The 35-kr tour is a good deal as it includes entry into Den Gamle By and also leaves you with a 24-hour bus pass.

Places to Stay

Camping The nearest camping ground is *Camping Blommehaven* in the Marselisborg woods, six km south of Århus station on bus No 19 or 6. It's open from mid-April to mid-September.

Hostel & Rooms *Århus Youth Hostel* (☎ 86 16 72 98), Marienlundsvej 10, is in a renovated 1850s dance hall in the Risskov woods, four km north of the city centre. Take bus No 6 or 9. The tourist office books rooms in private homes for 110 kr a person, plus a 25-kr booking fee.

Hotels *Eriksens Hotel* (☎ 86 13 62 96), Banegårdsgade 6, a pleasant family-run hotel a few minutes from the railway station, costs 235/350 kr for singles/doubles. Breakfast costs 30 kr extra.

The 14-room *Park Hotel* (☎ 86 12 32 31), at Sønder Allé 3 on the corner of a busy intersection, has simple rooms for 235/350 kr (no breakfast). If you're coming off the ferry, the *Århus Sømandshjem* (☎ 86 12 15 99), at Havnegade 20 opposite the harbour, is not only a convenient place to stay but has some of the better bargains in Århus. Renovated rooms with private baths, which are small but quite comfortable, cost 295/450 kr for singles/doubles. Less stylish rooms with shared bath cost 195/330 kr. Both include breakfast. Or, request an 'Inter-Rail discount' for a spartan unrenovated room at 100 kr a single (no breakfast), plus 25 kr if you need sheets. For something more up-market, the best value is the central and traditional *Ansgar Missions Hotel* (☎ 86 12 41 22), at Banegårdsplads 14. Rates, which include breakfast, are 275 kr for a single room with a shared bath, from 380/495 kr for singles/doubles with a private bath. Ask for one of the rooms in the rear wing; these are marginally more expensive but are very comfortable and quiet and have pleasant décor, cable TV and deep bathtubs. There's guest parking for 15 kr a day.

Places to Eat

The narrow streets of the old quarter north of the cathedral are thick with cafés serving Danish, Middle Eastern, Mexican and other ethnic foods at moderate prices. It's pure Italy and savoury chow at the *Colosseum*, Skolegade 33. Large cheese pizzas cost 33 kr, pasta dishes start at 55 kr and there's also a salad bar. It's open from 5 to 11 pm daily.

The countercultural *Kulturgyngen* at Mejlgade 53, open from 10 am to 4 pm and 6 to 9 pm except Sundays, serves hearty portions of good food, offering one vegetarian and one fish or meat dinner nightly for 40 to 50 kr.

Nearby, the cosy *Gallorant Kif-Kif*, Mejlgade 41, has crêpes with salad and hummus and other Turkish dishes from 45 to 70 kr. *Hornitos*, at the end of the courtyard at Mejlgade 46B, has inexpensive takeaway Chilean empanadas (meat pies) and is open from 9 am to 5 pm weekdays. The railway station has a supermarket open to midnight daily and a few fast-food restaurants. There's a fruit stand in front of the station and a good bakery, *Loft Konditori*, across the street. A few minutes away *Jensen's Bøfhus*, Rosenkrantzgade 23, has a salad bar for 29 kr and a steak-and-potato deal for 39 kr at lunch time.

Also near the station is *Hollywood Café*, Banegårdsgade 47, which has salads, pastas and deli dishes for under 50 kr. If you want to hang around for a while, there's a pool table, darts and a bar. It's open from 11 am to midnight.

China Town, at Fredensgade 46 opposite the bus station, has 10 daily lunch specials until 4 pm for around 50 kr, and a rather fine-dining atmosphere. It's open from noon to 11 pm daily.

The outdoor café at *Huset*, Vester Allé 15, has good salads and sandwiches from noon, and vegetarian and fish meals for 40 to 60 kr from 5 to 8 pm. It's open from Monday to Friday only. *Naturkost* at Gammel Munkegade 4 and *Sundhedskost* at Frederiks Allé 49 are full-service health-food stores.

Entertainment

Much of Århus' vibrant music scene is centred around backstreet cafés. *Fatter Eskil*, Skolegade 25, has good blues from 10 pm most nights and a cover charge of only 15 to 25 kr. The more trendy *Glazzhuset*, on Åboulevarden, features top jazz performers.

Pan Café, a gay and lesbian disco, at Jægergårdsgade 42 south of the railway station, is open from 10 pm to at least 3 am Wednesday to Saturday. Thursdays are for women only.

Musikcafeen, Mejlgade 53, is an alternative scene with folk, jazz and reggae. There's always something happening at *Huset*, Vester Allé 15, a good-energy cultural centre with rock and jazz concerts, movies and workshops. There are sometimes free performances in the foyer of *Musikhuset Århus*, the city concert hall.

Ugen Ud and *Århus This Week* list current happenings in detail. The nine-day Århus Festival in early September turns the city into a stage for nonstop revelry with jazz, rock, nordic folk, classical music, theatre and dance.

Getting There & Away

Air The airport is in Tirstrup, 44 km northeast of Århus. There are direct flights from Copenhagen, London and Oslo. The airport bus to Århus railway station costs 45 kr.

Bus Express buses (☎ 86 78 48 88) run a few times daily between Århus and Copenhagen's Valby station via a channel crossing at Ebeltoft. They take 4½ hours and cost 130 kr. There's also a faster catamaran/bus service (☎ 86 18 10 11) from Århus harbour to Copenhagen via Kalundborg that takes about three hours and costs 160 kr.

Train Trains to Århus, via Odense, leave Copenhagen on the hour from at least 7 am to 8 pm daily (4¼ hours, 201 kr).

Car & Motorbike The main highways entering Århus are the E45 from the north and south and route 15 from the west. The E45 curves around the western edge of a city as a ring road. There are a number of turn-offs from the ring road into the city, including Åhavevej from the south and Randersvej from the north.

Boat DSB car ferries (☎ 86 13 17 00) sail an average of six times a day between Århus and Kalundborg. They take three hours and cost from 83 to 104 kr for passengers, 235 kr for a car. Cittiships (☎ 86 18 10 11) runs a hydrofoil two to three times a day on the same route for 120 kr, taking 1¼ hours.

Getting Around

City bus tickets are bought from a machine in the back of the bus for 12 kr and are good for unlimited rides within the time period stamped on the ticket, which is about two hours. You can also buy a 24-hour pass at newsstands for travel in Århus and Viborg counties (75 kr) or in Århus municipality alone (35 kr).

A car is quite convenient for getting to sights such as Moesgård on the outskirts of the city, though the city centre is best explored on foot. Århus has numerous billetautomats (parking meters) along its streets.

Parking generally costs 1 kr per seven minutes, with a three-hour maximum, between 8 am and 6 pm from Monday to Thursday, to 8 pm on Fridays and to 2 pm on Saturdays. Outside those hours you can park free of charge, but be sure to put money in the meter or get out to your car by 8 am (except on Sundays) or you'll risk a 400-kr fine.

You can rent bicycles at Asmussen Cykler, Fredensgade 54, near the bus station.

JELLING

Jelling is a sleepy rural town with one of Denmark's most important historic sites – the Jelling **church**. Inside the small white-washed church are 12th century **frescoes** and outside the door are two **rune stones**.

The smaller stone was erected in the early 900s by King Gorm the Old, Denmark's first king, in honour of his wife. The larger one, raised by Harald Bluetooth and dubbed 'Denmark's baptismal certificate', is adorned with the oldest representation of Christ found in Scandinavia and reads:

Harald king bade this be ordained for Gorm his father and Thyra his mother, the Harald who won for himself all Denmark and Norway and made the Danes Christians.

Two huge burial mounds flank the church;

the one on the north side is speculated to be King Gorm's and the other, his wife's.

Jelling makes a good two-hour side trip off the Odense-Århus run. Change trains at Vejle for the 15-minute ride to Jelling. The church is 100 metres straight up Stationsvej from the Jelling railway station.

THE LAKE DISTRICT

The Danish Lake District, the closest thing Denmark has to hill country, is a popular 'active holiday' spot for Danes, with good canoeing, biking and hiking. The scenery is pretty, but placid and pastoral rather than stunning. The district contains the Gudenå, Denmark's longest river; Mossø, Jutland's largest lake; and Yding Skovhøj, Denmark's highest point – none of which are terribly long, large or high.

Silkeborg

Silkeborg, the Lake District's biggest town, has a rather bland and modern town centre though it's bordered by green areas and waterways.

Things to See & Do There are some worth-while exhibits at the **Silkeborg Museum** on Hovedgårdsvej. Its main attraction is the **Tollund Man** who was executed in 200 BC and whose body, complete with the rope still around his neck, was discovered in a nearby bog in 1950. The face is so well preserved you can count the wrinkles in his forehead. Museum hours are from 10 am to 5 pm daily from mid-April to mid-October, and from noon to 4 pm on Wednesdays, Saturdays, and Sundays in winter. Admission costs 20 kr.

The **Silkeborg Kunstmuseum**, on Gudenåvej one km south of the town centre, features the works of native son Asger Jorn and other modern artists. Hours are from 10 am to 5 pm, closed Mondays. Admission costs 20 kr.

On Saturdays there's a produce and flower **market** at Torvet.

To get to **Nordskoven**, a beech forest with hiking and bike trails, simply walk over the old railway bridge down by the hostel. You can rent bicycles at Cyclecompagniet at Vestergade 18, and canoes at Slusekiosken at the harbour.

Places to Stay & Eat The nearest camping ground is *Indelukket Camping*, one km south of the art museum. *Silkeborg Youth Hostel* (☎ 86 82 36 42) has a scenic riverbank location at Åhavevej 55, a 10-minute walk east of the railway station. Dorm beds cost from 59 to 69 kr, double rooms 152 to 192 kr. The hostel has free parking and can arrange bicycle hire. The tourist office at Torvet maintains a list of rooms in private homes that cost from 100 to 125 kr for singles, 175 to 225 kr for doubles. For 25 kr the tourist office will book the rooms, or you can call the places yourself.

There's a bakery, a health-food store and several drinking holes and restaurants on Nygade. The best is *Dengoe fe*, Nygade 18, with delicious wholesome vegetarian, fish and chicken dishes for 50 to 70 kr. Out the back, *Music Værkstedet* has live rock, jazz and blues on weekends. *Føtex* supermarket at Torvet has a cafeteria with a daily special for 30 kr and a bakery.

Getting There & Away Hourly trains connect Silkeborg with Skanderborg (30 minutes, 30 kr) and Århus (45 minutes, 47 kr) via Ry.

Ry

A smaller town in a more rural setting than Silkeborg, Ry is a good place from which to base your exploration of the Lake District.

Things to See & Do The Lake District's most visited spot is the whimsically named **Himmelbjerget** (Sky Mountain) which, at just 147 metres, is one of Denmark's highest hills. It can be reached via a nice six-km hike from Ry, or by bus or boat. From the hilltop **tower** (where admission costs 3 kr) there's a windy 360-degree view of the lakes and surrounding countryside.

Another good half-day outing is to cycle from Ry to **Boes**, a tiny hamlet with picturesque thatched houses and bounteous flower gardens. There's even a rustic kro (inn)

where you can have lunch. From there continue across the Danish countryside to **Om Kloster**, the ruins of a medieval monastery (open from 9 am to 5 pm, closed Mondays, 20 kr), where glass-topped tombs reveal the 750-year-old bones of Bishop Elafsen of Århus and many of his abbots. The whole trip from Ry and back is 18 km.

Ry Cykel, Skanderborgvej 19, rents bikes for 45 kr a day. If you want to explore the lakes in the district, Ry Kanofart, Kyhnsvej 20, rents canoes for 40 kr an hour.

Places to Stay & Eat There's a camping ground in town on Søndre Ege. *Ry Youth Hostel* (☎ 86 89 14 07) is at a bathing lake at Randersvej 88. To get there from the railway station cross the tracks, turn left and go 2.5 km, or take bus No 104.

The tourist office, at the railway station, books private rooms for 100 kr a person. The best place to eat is *Alberto*, Randersvej 1, a popular gathering spot with tasty vegetarian dishes, chicken and chilli con carne for around 50 kr. The butcher shop opposite the railway station has takeaway sandwiches.

Getting There & Away Hourly trains connect Ry with Silkeborg (20 minutes, 24 kr) and Århus (30 minutes, 35 kr).

AALBORG

Jutland's second largest city, Aalborg is an industrial and trade centre, well known to bar hoppers as the leading producer of aquavit. Linked by bridge and tunnel, Aalborg spreads across both sides of the Limfjord, the long body of water that cuts Jutland in two.

Though it's skipped over by most travellers Aalborg has a few worthwhile sites, the paramount attraction being Lindholm Høje, Denmark's largest Viking burial ground.

Orientation & Information

The town centre is a 10-minute walk from the railway and bus stations, north down Boulevarden. The tourist office, at Østerågade 8, is open from 9 am to 4 pm weekdays, to noon on Saturdays, with slightly longer hours in summer. Danes Worldwide

Archives, behind Vor Frue Kirke, helps foreigners of Danish descent trace their roots.

Things to See

Old Town The whitewashed **Buldolfi Domkirke** marks the centre of the old town. On the cathedral's east side is the **Aalborg Historiske Museum** with interesting excavated artefacts, the requisite Renaissance furnishings and a fine collection of ancient **Danish coins**. It's open from 10 am to 5 pm Tuesday to Sunday. Admission costs 10 kr.

The alley between the museum and church leads to the rambling **Monastery of the Holy Ghost** which dates back to 1431 (you can visit it on a tour arranged through the tourist office). West of the cathedral on Østerågade are three noteworthy historic buildings: the **old town hall** (circa 1539), the five-storey **Jens Bangs Stenhus** (circa 1624) and **Jørgen Olufsens House** (circa 1616), the latter at Østeragade 25.

In addition, the half-timbered neighbourhoods around **Vor Frue Kirke** are worth exploring, particularly the cobbled Hjelmerstald. **Aalborghus Slot** is more administrative office than castle, but you can walk in the grounds free.

Nordjyllands Kunstmuseum This regional art museum, at Kong Christian Allé 50 in a marble building designed by Finnish architect Alvar Aalto, has a fine collection of Danish modern art. Opening hours are from 10 am to 5 pm and it's closed on Mondays for most of the year. Admission costs 20 kr.

To get there, take the tunnel beneath the railway station which emerges into a park with statues of nudes and water fountains. Go directly through the park, cross Vesterbro and continue through a wooded area to the museum, a 10-minute walk in all.

Aalborg Tower The hill behind the museum has an ungainly tower offering a panoramic view of the city's steeples and smokestacks (15 kr). The tower sits on the edge of an expansive wooded area, **Mølleparken**, which has walking trails, views and a zoo.

Lindholm Høje On a hilltop pasture overlooking the city, Lindholm Høje is the site of 682 graves from the Iron Age and Viking Age. Many of the **Viking graves** are marked by stones placed in an oval ship shape, with two larger end stones as stem and stern. There's something almost spiritual about the site. Open free from dawn to dusk, it's 15 minutes from Aalborg on bus No 6. Cross the fence 50 metres beyond the bus stop and you're in the burial field.

A new museum which depicts the site's history is at the opposite side of the field. The museum is open from 10 am to 7 pm daily from June to August and to 5 pm daily except Monday the rest of the year. Admission costs 20 kr.

Places to Stay

Aalborg Youth Hostel (☎ 98 11 60 44), at Skydebanevej 50 at the marina four km from the centre, is reached by bus No 8. *Strandparken Camping* is about 500 metres before the hostel. The tourist office books rooms in private homes for 100 kr a person, plus a booking fee of 20 kr.

The *Turist Hotel* (☎ 98 13 22 00), above a bar at Prinsensgade 36, has straightforward rooms at 285/395 kr for singles/doubles (no breakfast). Rooms at the *Hotel Ansgar* (☎ 98 13 37 33), Prinsensgade 14, start at 350/500 kr and are pleasant with TV etc, though most are on the small side.

The traditional *Park Hotel* (☎ 98 12 31 33), Boulevarden 41, has comfortable rooms with private bath, TV and standard rates from 560/650 kr with a discount of about 100 kr from June to August.

Places to Eat

You'll find two-course meals for 60 kr at lunch and 90 kr at dinner along Jomfru Ane Gade, a boisterous pedestrian street lined with restaurants, pavement cafés and discos.

Romeo & Julie, a pleasant pizzeria at Ved Stranden 5, has an all-you-can-eat buffet of pizza, lasagne and salad for 59 kr from 11.30 am to 4 pm daily. *Skibsted's Fish Market*, Algade 23, has takeaway salmonburgers and fresh fish and chips (request 'no remoulade'

DENMARK

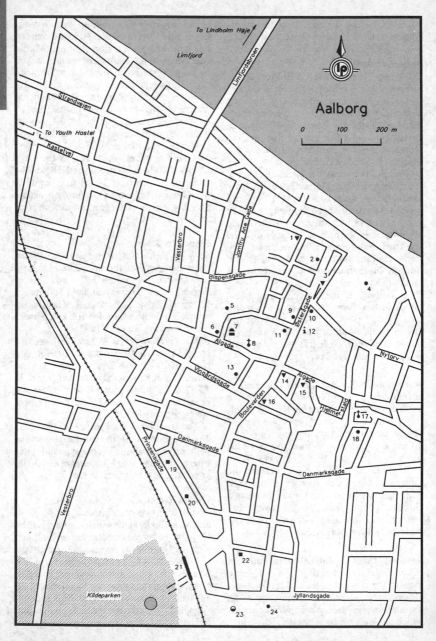

1	Romeo & Julie
2	Jørgen Olufsens House
3	Burger King
4	Aalborghus Slot
5	Monastery of the Holy Ghost
6	Aalborg Historiske Museum
7	Post Office
8	Buldolfi Domkirke
9	Jens Bangs Stenhus
10	Bank
11	Old Town Hall
12	Tourist Office
13	Brugsen Supermark
14	Skibsted's Fish Market
15	Café Underground
16	Bakery
17	Vor Frue Kirke
18	Danes Worldwide Archives
19	Turist Hotel
20	Hotel Ansgar
21	Railway Station
22	Park Hotel
23	Bus Station
24	Europcar Car Rental

unless you want it drenched in mayonnaise) for under 20 kr.

Café Underground, Algade 21, has natural ice cream, espresso and sandwiches. Cap off the night with a glass of wine (20 kr) at the romantic *Duus Vinkjælder*, a candle-lit 300-year-old wine cellar in the Jens Bangs Stenhus – surprisingly, it has good cheap eats as well.

Getting There & Away
Trains run hourly to Århus (1½ hours, 95 kr) and every two hours to Frederikshavn (one hour, 53 kr). Express buses (☎ 98 16 09 99 for reservations) run daily to Copenhagen (six hours, 165 kr). The E45 bypasses the city centre, tunnelling under the Limfjord, whereas the connecting route 180 leads into the centre. To get to Lindholm Høje or points north from the centre of Aalborg, take route 180 (Vesterbro) which crosses the Limfjord by bridge.

Getting Around
City buses leave from Østerågade and

Nytorv, near Burger King. The bus fare is 10 kr. The Aalborg Pass, which is valid for two days and costs 60 kr (30 kr from October to March), allows free transport on city buses, free parking in a parking garage and free or discounted admission to most of the city museums.

Other than for a few one-way streets that may have you driving in circles a bit, Aalborg is easy to get around by car. The city has free street parking along many of its back streets, as well as metered parking in the centre. If you're unable to find a parking space, there's a large parking garage at Ved Stranden 11 at the north end of Østerågade.

REBILD BAKKER NATIONAL PARK
If you're ready for a break in the countryside, Rebild Bakker national park is a good destination. It was founded in 1912 by Danish-Americans and is best known for its crowded US-style 4 July celebration.

Though there's a Lincoln log cabin and a few souvenir shops near the centre, the rest of the park is an unspoiled area of rolling hills and heathland. A delightful four-km trail begins in a sheep meadow just up from the parking lot, and numerous other trails crisscross the park and the adjacent **Rold Skov** forest.

Places to Stay & Eat
The thatch-roofed *Rebild Youth Hostel* (☎ 98 39 13 40) is next to the park entrance, and *Safari Camping* is nearby at Rebildvej 17A. You can take meals at the hostel or the park cafeterias.

Getting There & Away
From Aalborg, all Århus-bound trains stop in Skørping (16 minutes, 24 kr), from where it's a three-km bus ride to Rebild. Buses run between Aalborg and Rebild (45 minutes, 40 kr) via Skørping 12 times daily on weekdays, four times daily on weekends.

FREDERIKSHAVN
Frederikshavn is a major ferry town with a busy industrial port. There are a couple of local museums, but overall the town is not

terribly appealing and most travellers just pass right through. If you're waiting for a train, you might want to climb the nearby whitewashed **gun tower** (10 kr), a remnant of the 17th century citadel that once protected the port.

An overhead walkway leads from the ferry terminal to the tourist office. The railway station and adjacent bus terminal are a 10-minute walk to the north.

Bangsbo Museum

Bangsbomuseet, three km south of Frederikshavn centre, is an old country estate set in a deer park. There is a mishmash of collections. The manor house holds local history exhibits, paintings, Victorian furniture, antique dolls, and a peculiar collection of jewellery and ornaments woven from human hair.

The farm buildings have old ship figureheads, war paraphernalia and exhibits featuring the Danish resistance to German occupation. The museum's most intriguing exhibit is the **Ellingå ship**, the reconstructed remains of a 12th century Viking-style merchant ship that was dug up from a stream bed five km north of Frederikshavn. The museum's open from 10 am to 5 pm daily (closed on Mondays from November to March). Admission is 20 kr. To get there, take bus No 1 or 2 which stops near the entrance to the estate, from where it's an enjoyable 500-metre walk through the woods to the museum.

Places to Stay & Eat

Frederikshavn Youth Hostel (☎ 98 42 14 75), at Buhlsvej 6 two km north of the ferry terminal, has friendly staff, 53-kr dorms, and double rooms with bath for 152 kr. The central *Sømandshjemmet* (☎ 98 42 09 77), Tordenskjoldsgade 15B, has cheery rooms, and even TV for 265/415 kr singles/doubles.

The two grocery stores on Havnegade behind the tourist office have cafeterias, and there are pizzerias on Havnegade and Lodsgade, one street to the north. Havne Super, a supermarket at the ferry harbour, is open from 8 am to 10 pm daily.

Getting There & Away

Bus & Train Frederikshavn is the northern terminus of the DSB rail line. Trains run every two hours south to Aalborg (53 kr) and on to Copenhagen (231 kr). Nordjyllands Trafikselskab (NT) has both a train (40 minutes) and bus service (one hour) north to Skagen (30 kr), with the last departure by bus at 11.15 pm daily except Sundays. NT sells a clip-ticket (*klippekort*) for 70 kr that's good for 100-kr worth of travel and several people can clip the same card.

Boat Stena Line (☎ 98 42 43 66) runs ferries from Frederikshavn to Gothenburg in Sweden, six to eight times daily (three hours, 90 kr); daily to Moss in Norway (seven hours, from 140 to 350 kr); and to Oslo daily in summer and five or six times a week in winter (nine hours, from 190 to 410 kr).

The Larvik Line (☎ 98 42 14 00) has daily ferries to Larvik in Norway (six hours, from 210 to 340 kr). The lowest prices are for off-season weekdays, while the highest are for summer weekends. The cost to take a car on the ferries is roughly twice that of a standard passenger fare.

SKAGEN

A fishing port for centuries, Skagen's luminous heath-and-dune landscape was discovered in the mid-1800s by artists and in more recent times by summering urbanites.

The town's older neighbourhoods are filled with distinctive yellow-washed houses, each roofed with red tiles edged with white lines. Skagen is half arty, half touristy with a mix of galleries, souvenir shops and ice-cream parlours. The peninsula is lined with fine beaches, including a sandy stretch on the east end of Østre Strandvej, a 15-minute walk from the town centre.

Orientation & Information

Sankt Laurentii Vej, Skagen's main street, runs almost the entire length of the long thin town, never more than five minutes from the waterfront. The tourist office is in the railway/bus station at Sankt Laurentii Vej 22. Summer opening hours are 9 am to 6 pm daily, while the rest of the year it's open to 4 pm weekdays.

Things to See

Grenen Denmark's northernmost point is the long curving sweep of sand at Grenen, three km north-east of Skagen. From the end of route 40 it's a 30-minute walk out along the vast beach to the very tip where the waters of Kattegat and Skagerrak clash and you can put one foot in each sea.

Skagens Museum This first-rate museum, Brøndumsvej 4, displays the paintings of PS Krøyer, Michael & Anna Ancher and other artists who flocked to Skagen between 1830 and 1930 to 'paint the light'. Opening hours are 10 am to 5 or 6 pm daily from May to September, with shorter hours in the off season. Admission costs 25 kr.

Skagen Fortidsminder Evocatively presented, this open-air museum depicts Skagen's maritime history and includes the homes of fisherfolk and a picturesque old windmill. It's a 15-minute walk from the railway station, west down Sankt Laurentii Vej, then south on Vesterled. Hours are 10 am to 5 pm daily from May to September, weekdays to 4 pm in March, April, October, and November. Admission costs 20 kr.

Tilsandede Kirke This whitewashed medieval church tower still rises up above the sand dunes that buried the church and surrounding farms in the late 1700s. The tower, in a nature reserve, is five km south of Skagen and well signposted from route 40. By bike, take Gammel Landevej from Skagen. The tower interior is open 11 am to 5 pm from June to August. Admission costs 7 kr.

Råbjerg Mile Denmark's largest expanse of shifting dunes, these undulating 40-metre hills are the ultimate sandpit, almost large enough to disappear in and good fun to explore. Råbjerg Mile is 16 km south of Skagen, off route 40 on the road to Kandestederne. From the end of June to early

August, buses run six times a day from Skagen station (25 minutes, 15 kr).

Places to Stay

There are two summer camping grounds 1.5 km north-east of Skagen's centre. The best is *Grenen Camping* (☎ 98 44 25 46), which has a fine seaside location, friendly managers, some semi-private tent sites, and pleasant new four-bunk huts with heaters and refrigerators for 125 kr plus 40 kr a person.

The popular *Gammel Skagen Youth Hostel* (☎ 98 44 13 56) is at 32 Højensvej in Gammel Skagen, a summer cottage community four km north-west of Skagen's centre. Call ahead for reservations. Buses from Hirtshals and Frederikshavn stop out the front. The tourist office books private rooms for 100/200 kr singles/doubles, plus a 20-kr booking fee.

The following places all have bright, cosy rooms: *Skagen Sømandshjem* (☎ 98 44 21 10) near the harbour at Østre Strandvej 2 (210/400kr), the 12-room *Marienlund Badepension* (☎ 98 44 13 20) at Fabriciusvej 8 on the older west side of town near Fortidsminder (210/400 kr), and *Clausens Hotel* (☎ 98 45 01 66) across from the railway station (395/495 kr). All prices include breakfast and are for rooms with shared bathrooms.

Places to Eat

Moderately priced restaurants are few. There are three pizzerias on Havnevej, the nearby *Sømandshjem* hotel has an inexpensive cafeteria, and there are some bakeries on Sankt Laurentii Vej, the best being *Krages Bageri* at No 104 with sinful cinnamon rolls. There's a grocery store on Sankt Laurentii Vej, a two-minute walk west of the tourist office.

Getting There & Away

Either a bus or a train leaves Skagen station for Frederikshavn (30 kr) about once an hour. The seasonal Skagerakkeren bus runs seven times daily between Hirtshals and Skagen (1½ hours, 25 kr) from late June to early August.

DENMARK

Getting Around
Cycling is the best option for getting around. Both camping grounds rent bicycles (40 kr), as does the youth hostel and the cycle shop at Sankt Laurentii Vej 15 (50 kr). In summer, buses run from Skagen station to Grenen about once an hour (10 kr). Taxis, available at the railway station, charge about 30 kr to Grenen.

HIRTSHALS
Hirtshals gets its character from its commercial fishing harbour and ferry terminal. The main street is lined with supermarkets catering to Norwegian shoppers who pile off the ferries to load up with relatively cheap Danish meats and groceries.

Though it's not a town that invites lingering in, at least the hostel and camping ground are on the more scenic western side, where there are coastal cliffs and a lighthouse. If you want beaches and dunes, there's a magnificent unspoiled stretch at **Tornby Strand**, five km to the south.

Places to Stay & Eat
Hirtshals Youth Hostel (☎ 98 94 12 48) at Kystvejen 53, a km from the railway station, is open from March to November. *Hirtshals Camping* is nearby at Kystvejen 6. *Svenka Sjömanskyrkan* (☎ 98 94 17 66), the Swedish church near the railway station, has beds for 85 kr and a curfew at 9 pm. There are cafés and a bakery along Hjørringgade.

In Tornby Strand *Munch Badepension* (☎ 98 97 71 15), right on the beach at the end of Tornby Strandvej, has a handful of rustic rooms with dune views from 150/225 kr for singles/doubles, a food store and a restaurant.

Getting There & Away
Train Hirtshals' main railway station is 500 metres south of the ferry terminal, but trains connecting with ferry services terminate at the harbour. The railway, which is operated by a private company, connects Hirtshals with Hjørring, 20 minutes to the south. Trains run at least hourly, with the last departure from Hjørring at 11.13 pm. The fare is

15 kr. From Hjørring you can take a DSB train to Aalborg (35 kr) or Frederikshavn (30 kr). From late June to early August there's a bus from Hirtshals station to Hjørring which stops at Tornby Strand six times a day.

Boat The Color Line (☎ 98 94 19 66) runs year-round ferries to the Norwegian ports of Oslo (at 10 am daily in summer, 8½ hours, from 270 to 310 kr) and Kristiansand (four times daily in summer, 4½ hours, from 218 to 308 kr). There's no Monday sailing to Oslo from mid-August to mid-June. The cost for transporting a car is roughly 125% the cost of a passenger ticket.

ESBJERG
Esbjerg was established as a port in 1868 following the loss of the Schleswig and Holstein regions to Germany. It's now Denmark's fifth largest city, the centre of Denmark's North Sea oil activities and the country's largest fishing harbour. Though it has its fair share of turn-of-the-century buildings, Esbjerg lacks the intrigue found in the medieval quarters of other Danish cities and isn't on the itinerary of most travellers unless they're heading to or from the UK.

Orientation & Information
The tourist office (open from 9 am to 5 pm weekdays, to noon Saturdays), post office and a bank are at Torvet, the city square where Skolegade and Torvegade intersect. The railway and bus stations are about 300 metres east of Torvet, the ferry terminal is one km south. Trains that meet the ferries continue down to the harbour.

Things to See
The **Fiskeri og Søfartsmuseet**, at Tarphagevej north of the harbour, has an aquarium, an outdoor seal pool (feedings at 11 am and 2.30 pm) and an exhibit of fishing paraphernalia. Opening hours are from 10 am to 4 pm daily, to 6 pm in summer. Admission costs 30 kr. Take bus No 22, 23 or 30. There are also a few **local museums** in town that could be explored if you're waiting for

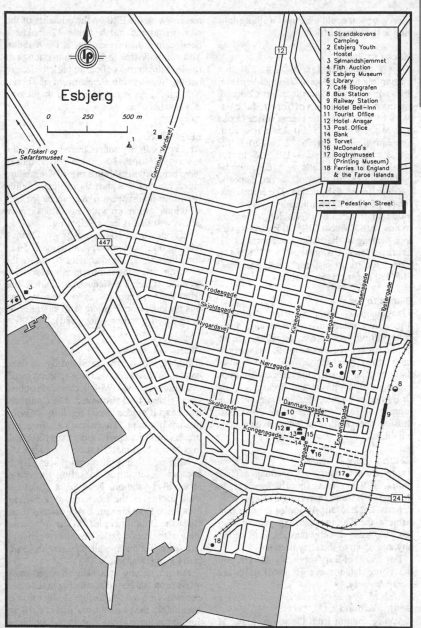

Esbjerg

0   250   500 m

To Fiskeri og
Søfartsmuseet

To Fiskeri og
Søfartsmuseet

1 Strandskovens
   Camping
2 Esbjerg Youth
   Hostel
3 Sømandshjemmet
4 Fish Auction
5 Esbjerg Museum
6 Library
7 Café Biografen
8 Bus Station
9 Railway Station
10 Hotel Bell-Inn
11 Tourist Office
12 Hotel Ansgar
13 Post Office
14 Bank
15 Torvet
16 McDonald's
17 Bogtrymuseet
   (Printing Museum)
18 Ferries to England
   & the Faroe Islands

= = = Pedestrian Street

Gammel Vardevej

Frodesgade
Skjoldsgade
Nygardsvej
Kirkegade
Torvegade
Finsensgade
Østergade
Nørregade
Skolegade
Danmarksgade
Kongensgade
Englandsgade
Torvegade

a ferry, or you could pick up a walking-tour map at the tourist office.

Places to Stay
Esbjerg Youth Hostel (☎ 75 12 42 58), in a former folk high school at Gammel Vardevej 80, and the nearby *Strandskovens Camping* are three km north-west of Torvet. Take bus No 9 or 31 (8 kr). The tourist office books private rooms for 90 kr a person. *Sømandshjemmet* (☎ 75 12 06 88) is the city's cheapest hotel at 195/315 kr for singles/doubles but it's at a commercial harbour three km west of Torvet, opposite the odoriferous fish auction. The *Hotel Bell-Inn* (☎ 75 12 01 22), Skolegade 45, is the best value in the centre of Esbjerg. Pleasant rooms with TV cost 310/450 kr and there's free parking at the back. The rooms at the nearby *Hotel Ansgar* (☎ 75 12 82 44), Skolegade 36, are also comfortable and cost 305/430 kr for singles/doubles.

Places to Eat
Kongensgade, the pedestrian street off Torvet, has restaurants, a *McDonald's* and a bakery. *Biblioteks Cafeen*, the cafeteria in the public library at Nørregade 19, has surprisingly good inexpensive food – the 30-kr daily special usually includes a generous green salad. Opposite the library is *Café Biografen*, a popular student hang-out with more good food and one of the city's best music scenes. Both restaurants have vegetarian dishes.

Getting There & Away
Trains from Esbjerg to Copenhagen (five hours, 189 kr) leave hourly on average during the day, and an overnight sleeper train departs at 12.26 am. If you're driving into Esbjerg, the E20, the main expressway from the east, leads directly into the heart of the city and down to the ferry harbour.

For details of ferry services to the UK and the Faroe Islands see Denmark, Getting There & Away.

Getting Around
If you're coming from the south, route 24

merges with the E20 on the outskirts of the city. From the north, route 12 makes a beeline into the city ending at the harbour. You can park free in Torvet long enough to run into the tourist office. To park for longer periods try the side streets north of Torvet; Nørregade, the street in front of the library, is a good choice.

LEGOLAND
At Legoland, a popular theme park in the town of **Billund**, 30 million plastic blocks have been arranged into a world of miniature cities, Lego pirates and safari animals. While it will no doubt seem like a mecca for kids who have grown up with Lego blocks, most adults will find it less fascinating.

It's open from 10 am to 8 or 9 pm from 1 May to mid-September. Admission is 50 kr for adults, 25 kr for kids; it's free during the evening after the amusement rides have stopped. There's a frequent 25-minute bus from Vejle to Legoland, as well as an express bus package from Esbjerg (100 kr adults, 50 kr children, admission included).

RIBE
Ribe, the oldest town in Scandinavia, dates back to 869 AD and was an important medieval trading centre. With its crooked cobbled streets and **half-timbered 16th century houses**, it's like stepping into a living history museum. The entire old town is a preservation zone, with more than 100 buildings in the National Trust.

Ribe is a tightly clustered place, easy to explore. Everything, including the hostel and railway station, is within a 10-minute walk of Torvet, the town square dominated by a huge Romanesque **cathedral**. You can climb the church steeple (5 kr) for a towering view of the countryside. The streets radiating out from Torvet are all picturesque, especially Puggårdsgade.

For 15 kr you can visit all three **town museums** and see such enticing items as the executioner's axe. A costumed night watchman makes the rounds from Torvet at 10 pm during the tourist season and you can follow him as he sings his way through the old streets – touristy but fun and free.

Places to Stay & Eat

The 120-bed *Ribe Youth Hostel* (☎ 75 42 06 20) is at Sankt Pedersgade 16. The tourist office at Torvet has a list of private rooms. Three in-town taverns rent 2nd-storey rooms: *Weis Stue* at Torvet, *Backhaus* at Grydergade 12 and *Hotel Sønderjylland* at Sønderportsgade 22 – all charge 200/400 kr for singles/doubles including breakfast. The atmospheric *Weis Stue*, a leaning half-timbered tavern with wooden-plank tables, has Danish meals for 60 to 95 kr at lunch time.

Getting There & Away

Trains from Esbjerg to Ribe take 40 minutes and cost 30 kr.

RØMØ

The island of Rømø lies off the coast midway between the historic towns of Ribe and Tønder and is a mere 30-minute drive from either. It's connected to the Jutland mainland by a 10-km causeway that passes over a scenic marshland with grazing sheep and wading waterbirds.

Rømø is a windsurfing haven whose western side is lined with expansive sandy beaches that attract scores of German tourists. Despite the caravan parking lots and eyesore-design of a couple of the tourist centres, most of Rømø is a rural scene with straw-roofed houses, open spaces and the scent of the sea heavy in the air. Among the sights, there's an **old church** with interesting gravestones on the main road in the village of Kirkeby, and a small **sea captain's museum** on the north side of the island.

The inland section of this flat island, which is 17 km long and five km wide, has heathered moors and gentle wooded areas which offer some fine hiking. In the summer, seal-watching cruises go out each afternoon to view the seal colonies that frequent the banks off the western coast.

Places to Stay & Eat

There are a few *camping grounds* on Rømø,

including one near the youth hostel and another on the west coast beach at Lakolk. The 91-bed *Rømø Youth Hostel* (☎ 74 75 51 88), on the south-eastern side of the island near Havneby, is in a delightful traditional building with a thatched roof. It's open from 15 March to 1 November and has dorm beds for 59 kr and doubles from 152 kr. *Frisk Super* on Vestergade in Havneby is a good place to pick up groceries and fresh bakery items including good chocolate-chip scones.

Getting There & Away

Rømø is 14 km west of the town of Skærbæk and route 11. Buses run from Skærbæk to Havneby (35 minutes, 7 kr) numerous times a day. From Skærbæk there's train service to Ribe, Tønder and Esbjerg about once an hour. Car ferries connect Havneby with Germany's island of Sylt (one hour, 16 kr) four to eight times a day.

Getting Around

Rømø is ideal for cycling. You can rent bikes at a few places, but the best deal is from Robert Christensen, at Håndværkervej 17 in Havneby, who charges 25 kr a day, 100 kr a week. In summer a limited bus service connects villages on the island.

TØNDER

Tønder is another historic southern town that retains a few curving cobblestone streets with half-timbered houses. Its high point is during the last weekend of August when the Tønder Festival (☎ 74 72 46 10), one of Denmark's largest, brings a multitude of international and Danish folk musicians to town for more than 40 concerts.

The **Tønder Museum** has regional historic objects including a collection of Tønder lace, which was once considered some of the world's finest, as well as furniture and wall tiles. The adjacent **South Jutland Art Museum** features Danish surrealist and modern art. Both museums are at Kongevej 55, a 10-minute walk east of the station, and are open from 10 am to 5 pm May to October, 1 to 5 pm in winter, closed on Mondays. Admission is 10 kr.

Places to Stay

The *Tønder Youth Hostel* (☎ 74 72 35 00), Sønderport 4, is on the east side of the town centre, about a 15-minute walk from the railway station. It's in a nondescript modern building, but the rooms are comfortable. Rates are 69 kr for a dorm bed and 150/192 kr for singles/doubles, the latter with private baths. There's a *camping ground* just beyond the hostel at Holmevej 2.

Places to Eat

Choices are limited and many people simply drive south to Germany where food is cheaper. In the town centre, *Pizzeria Italiano* at Østergade 40 has a nice atmosphere and good pizza and pasta dishes for around 60 kr. There's a market selling produce and cheese at Torvet on Tuesday and Friday mornings. The *Kvickly* grocery store has a cafeteria with fish and chips and similar dishes for around 40 kr, but it's a bit out of the way – one km west of the town centre on Plantagevej 38.

Getting There & Away

Tønder is on route 11, four km north of the German border. Trains run hourly on weekdays and slightly less frequently on weekends from Ribe (50 minutes, 41 kr) and Esbjerg (1½ hours, 59 kr).

Faroe Islands

The 18 Faroe Islands (Føroyar), which form an independent nation within the Kingdom of Denmark, lie midway between Iceland and the Shetland Islands but remain little known to outsiders. Here the forces of nature, the old Norse culture and today's technology combine to create a slice of modern Europe superimposed on a stunning traditional backdrop.

Apart from distressing news about the traditional (and abominable) *grindadráp* (pilot whale slaughters), these North Atlantic islands seem to get very little press. Visitors aren't normally prepared for the undeniable beauty of the landscape.

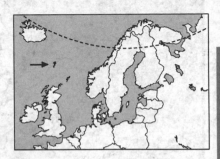

Facts about the Country

HISTORY

The first Norse people (farmers and pastoralists) arrived in the uninhabited Faroes in the early 9th century from southern Norway and the Orkneys.

From early on, the government of these islands lay in the hands of the Alting parliamentary body. With the Kalmar Union of 1397, in which Norway and Denmark merged politically, the Faroes became a Danish province. After 1380, parliamentary procedures ceased, the Alting became simply a royal court and the legislative body was renamed Løgting. In 1535, Denmark imposed the religious influences of the protestant Lutheran church.

During the 19th century, Denmark increasingly dominated the Faroes. In 1849, the Danish Rigsdag officially incorporated the Faroes into Denmark. During WW II, the British occupied the islands in order to secure the strategic North Atlantic shipping lanes and prevent German occupation.

On 23 March 1948, the *Act on Faroese Home Rule* was passed and the Faroes' official status was changed from 'county of Denmark' to 'self-governing community within the Kingdom of Denmark'. When Denmark joined the EEC, the Faroes refused to follow due to the locally hot issue of fishing rights. The Faroes maintain their claim to a 200-mile exclusion limit.

GEOGRAPHY & ECONOMY

The Faroe Islands lie about midway between Iceland and Scotland (300 km away) and cover 1399 sq km. The economy is based almost entirely upon fishing and fish processing.

POPULATION & PEOPLE

Around 49,000 people live in the Faroes: 15,000 of them in the capital, Tórshavn and 5000 more in Klaksvík.

LANGUAGE

Faroese is a Germanic language derived from old Norse and significantly influenced by Gaelic. It is related most closely to Icelandic and some Norwegian dialects.

In 1890 a standard written version of Faroese, Føroyskt, was made official and given equal status with Danish in public and government affairs.

Pronunciation

In most cases, Faroese words are stressed on the first syllable. Grammar is very similar to

FAROE ISLANDS

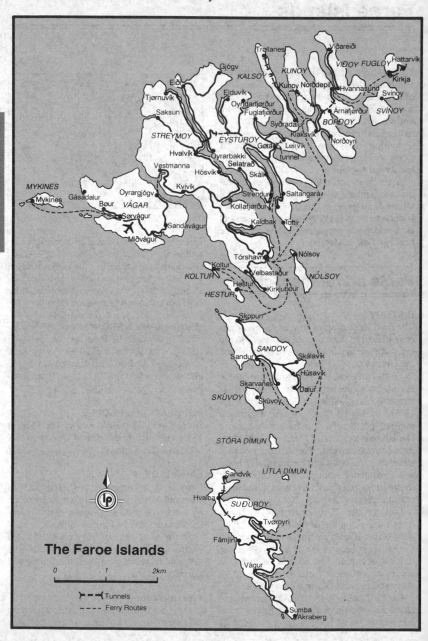

The Faroe Islands

0   1   2km

>--< Tunnels
---- Ferry Routes

that of Icelandic but pronunciation is another matter entirely. A lot of Icelandic, Danish, and even Gaelic influences come in to play. For example, Eysturoy's village Eiði is inexplicably pronounced 'OY-yeh'. The nearby village of Gjógv is referred to as 'Jag'. The capital, Tórshavn, gets the more or less Danish pronunciation, 'TORSH-hown'.

Quite a few Faroese people speak at least some English. Everyone speaks Danish and can handle Norwegian and Swedish as well.

Greetings & Civilities

Hello.	*Ey, Hallo, Goðan dag.*
Good morning.	*Goðan morgun*
Goodbye.	*Bay-bay/Farvael.*
How's it going?	*Hvussu gongur ta tað?*
What is your name?	*Hvussu eitar tú?*
Please.	*Ger so vael.*
Thank you.	*Takk fyri.*
Thank you very much.	*Stóra tøkk.*
Welcome.	*Vaelkomin.*
Excuse me.	*Orsaka.*

Useful Phrases

Do you speak English?
  Tala tygum enskt?
What would you like?
  Hvat vilja tygum hava?
What time is it?
  Hvat er klokkan?
It is ... minutes to/past ...
  Klokka er ... Minuttier i/yvir ...
How much is this?
  Hvussu nógv kostar tað?
Where is the ...?
  Hvar er ...?

Useful Words

bus	*bussur*
boat	*bátur*
plane	*flogfar*
bank	*banki*
post office	*posthús*
youth hostel	*ferðafuglaheim*
supermarket	*keypsamtøkan*
restaurant	*matstova*

cafe	*kaffistova*
tourist office	*ferðaskrivstova*
road	*vegur*
street	*gøta*
village	*bygd*
map	*vegakort*
rucksack	*ryggsekkur*

Geographical Features

bay	*vágur*
bird cliffs	*fuglaberg*
coast	*strond*
harbour	*havn*
island	*oy/oyggj*
lake	*vatn*
mountain	*fjall*
mountain pass	*fjalladskarð*
ravine	*gjógv*
river or stream	*á*
slope	*brekka*
valley	*dalur*

Food & Drink

bread	*breið*
butter	*smör*
cheese	*ostur*
chocolate	*sukurlátu*
egg	*egg*
fish	*fiskur*
fruit	*frukt*
lamb	*lamb*
meat	*kjót*
milk	*mjólk*
mutton	*seyðakjöt*
pork	*grisur*
potato	*jördepli*
salmon	*laksur*
sausage	*pýlsa*
sugar	*sukur*

Days & Months

Sunday	*sunnudag*
Monday	*mánadag*
Tuesday	*týsdag*
Wednesday	*mikudag*
Thursday	*hósdag*
Friday	*friggjadag*
Saturday	*leygardag*

FAROE ISLANDS

January	*januar*
February	*februar*
March	*mars*
April	*april*
May	*mai*
June	*juni*
July	*juli*
August	*august*
September	*september*
October	*oktober*
November	*november*
December	*desember*

Numbers

1	*eitt*
2	*tvey*
3	*tr*
4	*f ra*
5	*fimm*
6	*seks*
7	*sjey*
8	*átta*
9	*níggju*
10	*tíggju*
11	*ellivu*
12	*tólv*
13	*trettan*
14	*fjúrtan*
15	*fimtan*
16	*sekstan*
17	*seytjan*
18	*átjan*
19	*njan*
20	*tjúgu*
21	*ein og tjúgu*
30	*tredivu*
40	*fjøriti*
50	*hálvtr s*
60	*tr s*
70	*hálvfjers*
80	*f rs*
90	*hálvfems*
100	*hundra*
101	*hundra og eitt*
121	*hundra ein og tjúgu*
200	*tvey hundra*
1000	*túsund*

Facts for the Visitor

VISAS & EMBASSIES
Citizens of Western European countries, the USA, Canada, Australia and New Zealand need only a valid passport to visit the Faroes which are represented abroad by Danish embassies and consulates.

CUSTOMS
Visitors over 18 years of age may import 200 cigarettes, 50 cigars, or 250 grams of tobacco. Alcohol is strictly and puritanically controlled in the Faroes. Those over 20 years of age may bring in a litre of wine, a litre of spirits (from 22 to 60% proof), and two litres of beer (less than 4.6%). Two additional litres of spirits may be imported upon payment of duties. Non-recyclable containers are forbidden and animals may not be brought in.

MONEY
Although the Faroes issue their own currency, the Faroese króna (Fkr) is tied to the Danish krone (Dkr) and the two are used interchangeably throughout the Kingdom of Denmark. Foreign currency may be exchanged at any Faroese bank during regular hours: from 9.30 am to 4 pm Monday to Friday and until 6 pm on Thursdays. The exchange bank at the Vágar airport is open during regular banking hours and for arriving international flights. Normally a small commission is charged for exchange services. Outside banking hours, hotels normally exchange money as do tourist information offices and travel agencies. All brands of travellers' cheques and major currencies are accepted. Postal cheques may be exchanged at post offices in larger towns.

Currency
One króna is equal to 100 øre. Notes come in denominations of 20, 50, 100, 500, and 1000 krónur. Coins (all Danish) include five, 10, and 25 øre and one, five, and 10 kroner.

Exchange Rates

See the Denmark chapter for the Danish krone's rates.

Costs

The average price of a single hotel room is about 551 Dkr. Tipping is not required.

CLIMATE & WHEN TO GO

Rain in some form can be expected 280 days of the year. Fortunately, weather is somewhat localised. When timing your excursions, tune to Útvarp Føroya radio for weather information in English at 8.05 am. The best season to visit is from June to August. See the Iceland chapter for what to bring.

SUGGESTED ITINERARIES

Depending on the length of your stay you might like to see and do the following:

Two days
    Tórshavn and another village like Eiði, Gyógv, Kirkjubøur, Dyndarfjørður or Tjørnuvík
One week
    As above plus Viddy and Fugloy
Two weeks
    As above plus Mykines and Suðuroy

TOURIST OFFICES

For local tourist offices see Tours in the Getting Around section of this chapter and under Tórshavn, Information. Overseas representatives include:

Denmark
    Faerøernes Repraesentationskontor
    (☎ 33-140866), Højbroplads 7,
    DK-1200 Copenhagen
    Danish Tourism Board, HC Andersens
    Boulevard 22, DK-1553 Copenhagen
    Green Tours, Kultorvet 7, DK-1175 Copenhagen
    Føroyahúsið (Faroes House),Vesterbrogade 18 mezz, DK-1620 Copenhagen
UK
    Faroese Commercial Attaché (☎ 244-592777), 150 Market St, Aberdeen, Scotland AB1 2PP

BUSINESS HOURS & HOLIDAYS

Village post offices often close for a one to three-hour lunch break. Banking hours are between 9 am and 4 pm on weekdays; banks stay open until 6 pm on Thursdays.

Faroese Public Holidays

The Faroese observe the following holidays:

New Year's Day, 1 January
Epiphany, 6 January
Gregorius' Day, March
Maundy Thursday
Good Friday
Easter Day
Easter Monday
Flag Day, 25 April
Labour Day, 1 May
Common Prayer's Day, 11 May
Ascension Day, 11 May
Whit Sunday, June
Whit Monday, June
Constitution Day, 5 June
Ólavsøka (Faroese National Day), 28-29 July
All Saints' Day, 1 November
Christmas Eve, 24 December
Christmas Day, 25 December
Boxing Day, 26 December
New Year's Eve, 31 December (afternoon only)

POST & TELECOMMUNICATIONS

The postal service, Postverk Føroya, has post offices in most towns and villages. The central post office in Tórshavn is open Monday to Friday from 9 am to 5 pm and on Saturdays between 10 am and noon. Poste restante services are available in Tórshavn.

Overseas telephone calls may be booked at the central telephone office at Tinghúsvegur 76, Tórshavn. It's open Monday to Friday from 8 am to 9 pm and weekends 8 am to 2 pm.

TIME

From 25 October to 24 March, the Faroes are on Iceland time. The rest of the year, they're one hour behind London (GMT/UTC), five hours ahead of New York, eight hours ahead of Los Angeles and 10 hours behind Sydney.

ELECTRICITY

The electric current is 220 volts, 50 Hz, and plugs have two round pins.

MAPS

The Dansk Geodaetisk Institut publishes

topographic sheets at a scale of 1:100,000 which cover the Faroe Islands (Danish: Faerøerne) in two sheets. They cost 33 Dkr each and are available at tourist offices and bookshops in the Faroes and some places in Denmark.

WORK

Most jobs are in the fishing industry and nearly every town has a cannery and a harbour full of fishing boats.

Citizens of Scandinavian countries need only turn up at a plant and, if work is available, they can start immediately. Although Denmark is in the EC the Faroes are not, so EC citizens and others must obtain official permission to work. They must first secure a job then apply to the police in Tórshavn for a work permit. Expect delays unless the potential employer can convey a sense of urgency to the powers that be. Most canneries do not provide accommodation for workers. 'Illegals' are beyond protection of the law and may be exploited by unscrupulous employers.

ACCOMMODATION

The average price of a double hotel room will be around US$110. Alternatively, there are *sjómansheimið* (seamen's homes) in Tórshavn and Klaksvík. They were established by the Danish Lutheran church as safe lodging for sailors and fishermen. Strict Christianity is enforced – no alcohol or carousing – and there are formal prayers every morning. There's a cafeteria which serves à la carte meals and *smørrebrød* (open-face sandwiches) all day, and full meals for several hours in the evening. Doubles cost around 435/319 Dkr with/without bath.

There are also several *gistiheimilið* (guesthouses) and *ferðafuglaheim* (youth hostels) belonging to the Danish Youth Hostels Association. Rates range from 45 to 64 Dkr for members and 55 to 70 Dkr for nonmembers. There are youth hostels in Tórshavn (on Streymoy island), in Gjógv (☎ 23175) and Oyndarfjørður (☎ 44522) on Eysturoy, and

at Klaksvík (☎ 55403) and Norðdepil (☎ 52021) on Borðoy.

Those with webbed feet can try camping. There is a formal camping ground in Tórshavn and bush camping is possible anywhere but obtain permission before setting up in a farmer's sheep pasture. Also, take care not to trample hayfields and close any gates you may open when you're crossing private land.

Getting There & Away

AIR

Although Icelandair flies to the Faroes from the mainland, it takes a roundabout route through Reykjavík. A better option is to fly Danair or Atlantic Airways from Copenhagen. The price structure of both lines is similar: the discounted 'green price' return fare Copenhagen to Vágar is 1990 Dkr in low season and 2150 Dkr in the high season (from 11 June to 20 August). To qualify, you must stay a minimum of 14 days and maximum of 28 days. The non-discounted fare is 3020 Dkr.

SEA

Smyril Line's *Norrøna* operates from mid-May to mid-September. It sails from Hanstholm in Denmark (passengers are provided with inexpensive transport from Copenhagen on the day of departure) on Saturdays and arrives in Tórshavn on Monday morning.

Iceland-bound passengers must disembark while the ship continues back to Lerwick in the Shetland Islands, arriving Monday night. On Tuesday night the ferry's in Bergen, Norway. It arrives back in Tórshavn on Wednesdays, collects Iceland passengers, and sails overnight to Seyðisfjörður. It returns to Tórshavn on Friday morning, and continues to Hanstholm (Denmark) for another circuit. Iceland passengers must spend two days in the Faroes while the ship sails to the Shetland Islands and Norway. See also the introductory Getting There & Away chapter.

For more time in the Faroes, you'll have to break the journey and pay for two sectors. The normal deck fare from Hanstholm to Tórshavn (including a couchette or sleeper) is 1090 Dkr. Discounts apply for student-card holders.

There's a left-luggage service primarily for the benefit of Smyril Line stopover passengers at Kioskin á Steinatúni at the corner of Winthers Gøta and Niels Finsensgøta in central Tórshavn. It's open Monday to Friday from 7 am to 11 pm, Saturdays from 9 am to 11 pm, and Sundays from 2 to 11 pm. They charge 9 Dkr a day for a maximum of three days.

Transporting vehicles up to five metres long costs 75% of the deck-class passenger fare. Above deck class, there are three classes of cabins and a luxury suite. The ship also has a bar, cafeteria, restaurant, disco, casino and duty-free shops. For further information, contact Smyril Line (☎ 97 96 22 44), Auktiongade 13, 7730 Hanstholm, Denmark.

The DFDS Scandinavian Seaways' ship MS *Winston Churchill* operates between Esbjerg in Denmark and Tórshavn from mid-June to mid-August. It leaves Esbjerg on Mondays at 7 pm and Tórshavn on Wednesdays at 9 am. Prices and services are similar to those on Smyril Line.

The company's address is DFDS Scandinavian Seaways (☎ 298-11511 Tórshavn), Winthers Gøta 3, PO Box 28, FR-100 Tórshavn, Faroe Islands.

Faroe Ship Cargo & Passenger Line operates between Fredericia (Denmark) and Copenhagen (Denmark), Lysekil (Sweden), Stavanger (Norway) and Tórshavn weekly throughout the year. Contact them at Eystara Bryggja (☎ 298-11225), PO Box 47, FR-100 Tórshavn, Faroe Islands.

UK passengers can take Strandfaraskip Landsins' ferry, the *Smyril*, sailing weekly from Scrabster (Scotland) to Tórshavn. For information contact: Strandfaraskip Landsins (☎ 298-14550), Yvri við Strønd 6, Postbox 88, FR 110, Tórshavn, Faroe Islands.

Getting Around

Remember that in the Faroes, the weather has the final say on whether transport services will actually run.

AIR

The Faroes have only one airport, the international terminal on Vágar, so inter-island air travel is by helicopter (*tyrlan*, pronounced 'TOOR-lan'). Several times weekly, helicopters connect Tórshavn with the islands of Koltur, Skúvoy, Stóra Dímun and Klaksvík. There are also routes from Vágar to Mykines and Gásadalur and from Klaksvík to Svínoy and Fugloy.

Like the ferry system, helicopter services are operated by Strandfaraskip Landsins Tyrluavgreiðslan (see the Getting There & Away section). The Tórshavn heliport is 500 metres north of the camping ground.

The Faroes international air terminal is on Vágar, a bus ride, ferry ride and another bus ride from Tórshavn. There's a through bus to the airport leaving three hours prior to flight departures (there's also one from Klaksvík). For information and bookings, phone 12626 or make arrangements at the tourist office.

BUS

The Bygdaleiðir intercity bus service is excellent. It follows a strict and convenient schedule and, when combined with the ferry services, has links with virtually every corner of the country, including some fairly remote outposts like Akraberg on Suðuroy, Dalur on Sandoy, and Bøur on Vágar. (See also the helpful map *Ferðakort* available from Samferðsluskrivstovan (☎ 14366), RC Effersøesgøta 1, 3800 Tórshavn.) Bus fares are steep but visitors can minimise costs by purchasing the Bygdaleiðir Ferðamannakort which allows 14-days unlimited travel on intercity buses for 280 Dkr. Passes are available at tourist offices, at the Auto and Bíl taxi stands, and at LFÚ-Ferðir (Student Travel office) in Tórshavn.

CAR & MOTORBIKE

There are few unsurfaced roads and most islands are connected to Tórshavn by car-ferry. The greatest hazards are fog, sheep and precipitous drop-offs. Some of the numerous tunnels, especially those in the north-eastern islands, are wide enough for only one vehicle to pass but there are bays every few hundred metres. If they are marked 'V', you have to pull in and allow the other car to pass. If they are marked 'M', the other car has to give way.

Be alert in heavy fog, motorists must take financial responsibility for anything they hit. The speed limit on open highways is 80 km/h and 50 km/h through villages. Seat belt use is compulsory. In Tórshavn, you must place a parking disc in the front window set at the time you parked your car. These discs are available free at the tourist office and at local banks. Legal parking spaces are marked with a P followed by a number and the word *'tíma'*, indicating the length of time you're permitted to park there.

Rental agencies tack on Collision Damage Waiver (CDW) but with your own vehicle, you'll need proof of third party insurance or be required to purchase it from the customs department upon entering the country.

Car Rental

You must be at least 20 years old to rent a car. It's expensive but there's no per km charge and the daily rate decreases the longer you keep the car. For a sedan, the first day will cost between 290 and 350 Dkr while the seventh day will be only 203 Dkr or so. A deposit of around 870 Dkr is required against liability; tax and petrol are not included. Car rental outlets include:

Bilverkstaðið (☎ 13375), Eyðbjørn Hansen, Varðagøta 75, Tórshavn
Car Hire Á Heygnum Mikla (☎ 16190), Á Heygnum Mikla, FR-110, Tórshavn
Wenzel Petersen (☎ 13873 Tórshavn or 32765 Vágar Airport), Oyggjarvegur, Tórshavn
Inter-Rent Norrøna (☎ 15354), Vegurin Langi, Hoyvík

BICYCLE

Although there are lots of steep hills and tunnels as well as wind and rain, the Faroes are better than Iceland for cycling: the highways are surfaced and you don't have to contend with sandstorms and gravel-tearing motorists. Don't take Faroese cycling too lightly though; warm, windproof and waterproof clothing is essential. If the weather gets too wretched, remember that buses accept bicycles as luggage.

When riding through tunnels, use a good light both front and back which can be seen several km away. Under certain conditions, toxic gases can be trapped in congested tunnels so get through them as quickly as possible. Hills are steep, highways are wet and drop-offs severe so check your brakes carefully. Bicycles can be hired from:

André Andréson (☎ 11829), Varðagøta 9, Tórshavn
Thomas Dam(☎ 11403), Niels Finsensgøta 4, Tórshavn
John W Thomsen (☎ 55858), Nólsoyar Pállsgøta, Klaksvík

These places charge 45 Dkr a day for the first two days, 35 Dkr for the third day, and 25 Dkr for each day thereafter.

BOAT

All islands except the Dímuns are connected by ferry. Some ferries take automobiles and others carry only passengers. Students, children under 13 years and people over 65 receive a 20% to 50% discount. Some ferry trips, especially those to Mykines, Svínoy and Fugloy, through open seas in small boats are frequently cancelled because of the weather. Keep plans as flexible as possible.

TOURS

Tours and bookings are available from the following organisations:

LFÚ-Ferðir (☎ 15037), Dokta RA Jacobsensgøta 16, FR-100 Tórshavn
Tora Tourist Traffic (☎ 15505), Niels Finsensgøta 21, FR-100 Tórshavn
Arctic Adventure, 37 Aaboulevard, DK-1960 Copenhagen, Denmark

Green Tours, Kultorvet 7,
   DK-1175 Copenhagen, Denmark
Skandinavisches Reisebüro GMBH,
   Kurfürstendamm 206, D-1000 Berlin 15,
   Germany

Tórshavn

Despite being the capital and largest community of the Faroes, Tórshavn is not a typically vibrant European city but has picturesque charm. A stroll around Tinganes, the small peninsular headland where the town began nearly a thousand years ago, will endear this quiet and rainy little place to most people.

Orientation

Tórshavn is easy to walk around. The older section surrounds the two harbours, which are separated by the historical Tinganes peninsula. The eastern harbour is the ferry terminal and the western harbour is for commerce. The modern centre, uphill from the harbours, contains most of the shops, restaurants and services. The SMS Centre on RC Effersøesgøta is an indoor shopping mall.

Information

Tourist Office The tourist office, Faroe Islands Tourist Board, is at Reynagøta 17, Tinganes. The Kunningarstovan tourism authority and the city tourist office are open from Monday to Friday 8 am to 5 pm and Saturdays 10 am to 2 pm. (See also Tours, under Faroe Islands, Getting Around.)

Money Outside normal banking hours, the tourist office will exchange money. After hours, try the Hotel Hafnia which will charge a higher commission but is open evenings and Sundays.

Post & Telecommunications The central post office is on Vaglið behind the Ráðhús (city hall). It's open Monday to Friday from 9 am to 5 pm and on Saturdays from 10 am to noon. Fax and philatelic services are also available at the central post office. The telephone office is at Tinghúsvegur 76.

Laundry There's a laundrette opposite and just downhill from the police station. Alternatively, try Expert Vask at Undir Heygnum 24, one km south-west of the centre.

Bookshops The best place for foreign language publications is N Jacobsens Bókahandil.

Tinganes

Until the early 1900s, Tórshavn did not extend beyond Tinganes. The narrow Gongin was the main street. It's now lined with some lovely 19th century wooden houses.

   Munkastovan, probably dating from the 15th century, had a religious role. The 16th century **Leigubúðin** was the king's storehouse. When most of the old buildings on Tinganes burnt down in 1673 this and Munkastovan were spared. **Reynagarður**, once a parsonage, was constructed in 1630 and is a good example of typical Faroese architecture of the early 1600s. **Skansapakkhúsið**, at the far end of Tinganes, was constructed in 1750 and was an artillery cache. The stone **Myrkastovan** (Dark house), dating from 1693, was a guard house.

Museums

The Faroese Museum of Art **Listaskálin** (12 Dkr) north of Viðarlund park has works by Faroese artists. It's open daily from 3 to 5 pm between 15 May and 15 September.

   The historical museum **Forngripasavnið** contains religious artefacts, early art and practical household and farming implements from the Viking Age to the medieval period and modern times. Next door is the maritime museum **Bátasavnið** displaying Faroese boats and artefacts relating to local navigation and fishing. From 15 May to 15 September, these museums are free and open Monday to Friday from 10 am to noon and 2 to 4 pm, and 3 to 5 pm on weekends.

FAROE ISLANDS

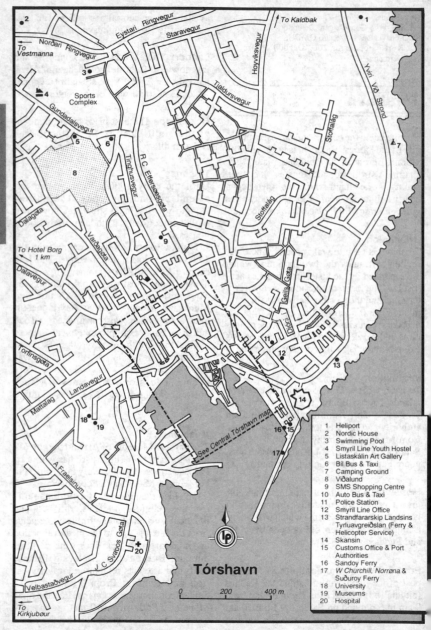

Tórshavn

1 Heliport
2 Nordic House
3 Swimming Pool
4 Smyril Line Youth Hostel
5 Listaskálin Art Gallery
6 Bil Bus & Taxi
7 Camping Ground
8 Viðalund
9 SMS Shopping Centre
10 Auto Bus & Taxi
11 Police Station
12 Smyril Line Office
13 Strandfararskip Landsins
   Tyrluavgreiðslan (Ferry &
   Helicopter Service)
14 Skansin
15 Customs Office & Port
   Authorities
16 Sandoy Ferry
17 W Churchill, Norrøna &
   Suðuroy Ferry
18 University
19 Museums
20 Hospital

Skansin

The fort Skansin, now in ruins at the eastern harbour, was ostensibly constructed to keep privateers and smugglers from upsetting the local monopoly trade.

Places to Stay

Camping The flood-prone camping ground is 1500 metres north along the coast from the centre. It costs 9 Dkr a tent and 18 Dkr a person which entitles you to use the facilities and a wet spot on the grass.

Hostels Smyril Line runs the youth hostel *Vallaraheimið* (☎ 19750) between 4 June and 31 August in Gundadalur. IYHF members/nonmembers pay 70/80 Dkr and breakfast costs 27 Dkr. From late June to mid-August, try *Undir Fjalli* (☎ 18900 or 15900) at Vesturgøta 15 south-west of Tórshavn. Singles/doubles cost 294/340 Dkr; extra beds are 102 Dkr. In the centre near Vaglið square, is *Tórshavn Sjómansheim* (☎ 13515) at Tórsgøta 4 where singles/doubles without bath cost 210/330 Dkr. Three meals are available for 132 Dkr.

Guesthouses Locals Ruth & Billy Olsen (☎ 10310) rent part of their home at Skrivaragøta 3 as dormitory-style accommodation for 70 Dkr a person. Private doubles cost 258 Dkr. From the northern end of the pedestrian mall, turn west and walk five blocks to Torfinsgøta and then turn right. Skrivaragøta is the fourth street.

The tourist office and Tora Tourist Traffic (☎ 15505), at Niels Finsensgøta 21, keep lists of families with rooms (singles/doubles average 215/390 Dkr) for tourists. They'll also help with finding accommodation elsewhere in the islands.

Tildhaldshúsið Skansin (☎ 12242) at Jekargøta 8 offers clean rooms, hot showers for 290/340 Dkr singles/doubles (breakfast included).

Hotels At the *Hotel Hafnia* (☎ 11270), a popular place situated near the harbour, singles/doubles with private bath begin at 684/858 Dkr. Extra beds are available for 174 Dkr.

Places to Eat

Self-Catering The best stocked supermarket is at the SMS Shopping Centre. You'll also find a small supermarket on Aarvegur opposite the Hotel Hafnia. In the centre, buy baked goods at *Frants Restorff* on Tórsgøta.

Snacks The nicest, but far from cheapest, place for a snack is the cosy *Konditoríið* on Niels Finsensgøta opposite the end of the pedestrian mall. Try also *Restaurant*, across the street from the ferry docks. A shop in the SMS Shopping Centre sells irresistible ice cream and cappuccino.

Highly recommended is *Pizzeria Fútastova* at Gongin 3 on Tinganes. For about 65 Dkr, you can feast on a small pizza and your choice from an endless salad bar.

Cafeterias *Tórs Cafeteria*, at Niels Finsensgøta 38 a couple of blocks up from the pedestrian mall, is convenient for typical cafeteria food. You can lunch for under 60 Dkr. A bit better is *Perlan* in the SMS Shopping Centre with a wide variety of salads, smørrebrød, desserts and hot snacks or a daily special, for fairly reasonable prices. The special is 36 Dkr. The *Sjómansheimið* cafeteria is open from 7 am to 9.30 pm with continental breakfasts, à la carte salads and smørrebrød as well as set specials.

Fine Dining At the *Hotel Hafnia* you'll find a huge buffet breakfast for 50 Dkr. Two-course lunches cost about 102 Dkr and Faroese specialities cost from 132 to 150 Dkr. Dinners normally include soup but salads cost extra.

Getting There & Away

For a concise schedule of intercity buses and inter-island ferries and helicopters, get a free copy of the booklet *Ferða Aetlan* from the tourist office or Strandfaraskip Landsins. Intercity buses depart from the eastern harbour and all (except the Kirkjubøur bus)

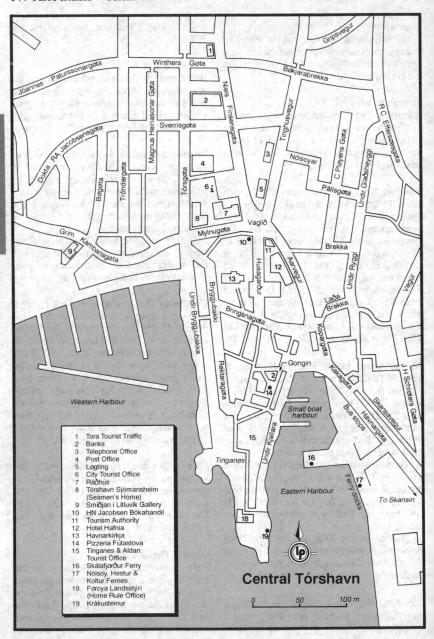

Central Tórshavn

0   50   100 m

1   Tora Tourist Traffic
2   Banks
3   Telephone Office
4   Post Office
5   Løgting
6   City Tourist Office
7   Ráðhús
8   Tórshavn Sjómansheim
    (Seamen's Home)
9   Smiðjan í Litluvík Gallery
10 HN Jacobsen Bókahandil
11 Tourism Authority
12 Hotel Hafnia
13 Havnarkirkja
14 Pizzeria Fútastova
15 Tinganes & Aldan
    Tourist Office
16 Skálafjørður Ferry
17 Nólsoy, Hestur &
    Koltur Ferries
18 Føroya Landsstýri
    (Home Rule Office)
19 Krákusteinur

stop at the Auto and Bíl taxi stands on their way out of town.

The Tórshavn heliport is just north of the camping ground along the coast road. For information and booking, contact Strand-faraskip Landsins Tyrluavgreiðslan International. Inter-island ferries leave from the eastern harbour.

Getting Around

To/From the Airport The airport for Tórshavn and the rest of the Faroes is on Vágar island. The airport bus (No 300) leaves from harbour bus stops about three hours before international flights depart. Book at the tourist office, through your hotel, or phone 12626.

Bus The red Bussleiðin city buses cover most of the city, running half hourly on weekdays and hourly in the evening, costing 7 Dkr a ride. Several kiosks sell passes.

Taxi Get taxis (☎ 11234 or 11444) from the Auto and Bíl stands and the Ráðhús.

Finland

Finland (Suomi) is usually grouped with the Scandinavian countries, an expedient of proximity that hides Finland's separateness. Finland has most in common today with Sweden, with which it shared almost 1000 years of history, but in recent times the Russian influence has been strongest in Finnish perceptions.

The Finns have one of the longest of traceable tenancies and stubbornly resisted servitude or eviction. But the flower of Finnish nationalism was late and delicate, based on improved relations with Russia.

Now Finland's ingenuity and greater understanding of Russia and the Baltic area will confirm its independence, but its misgrouping will be perpetuated here with apologies.

So the impression is of a country divided between traditions, and the truth of this is measured by the uniqueness and character of Karelia, the marchland extending from the Gulf of Finland to the central north and deep into Russia.

Karelian tradition and its rugged and beautiful landscapes are best studied in its museums and on its lakes, rapids and hiking trails. Only the magnificent castle at Savonlinna recalls the struggles between Russian and Swede that dominated for so long.

Helsinki is a place for seeing perhaps your first Russian Orthodox cathedral, and a night spent at Uusi-Valamo, near Heinävesi in North Karelia could be your first in a monastery.

North of Rovaniemi there are chances to see the midnight sun and the most northern of giant lakes, Inarijärvi. Experiencing either of these could introduce you to the Sami people, who also live in Russia, and their culture.

Should you brave the Finnish winter, brave the elements, go north during the eerie 'blue light' season and take a cruise on a Bothnian icebreaker.

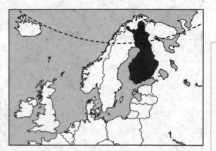

Facts about the Country

HISTORY

The ancestors of the Finns seem to have dominated half of northern Russia before arriving on the north of the Baltic coast well before the Christian era. They established themselves in the forests without disruption from the nomadic Sami people to the north.

By the end of the Viking Age, Swedish traders and perhaps chieftains had extended their interests to Ladoga and throughout the Baltic region. The growth of central power in Sweden and in Russian Novgorod anticipated Finland's fate as a marchland in play between the two countries.

In 1155 the Swedes made Finland a province but in 1240 Alexander Nevsky defeated the Swedes, beginning a strong Orthodox tradition in the east. The Treaty of Pähkinäsaari in 1323 delivered East Karelia to Novgorod.

In the 1520s the Reformation came to Swedish Finland which grew to include Lapland, North Karelia and the western shore of Ladoga. But Gustaf II Adolf began to Swedify his Finnish subjects, starting with the establishment of the first university in the capital Turku. His heavy-handedness began to split the country along religious lines and

FINLAND

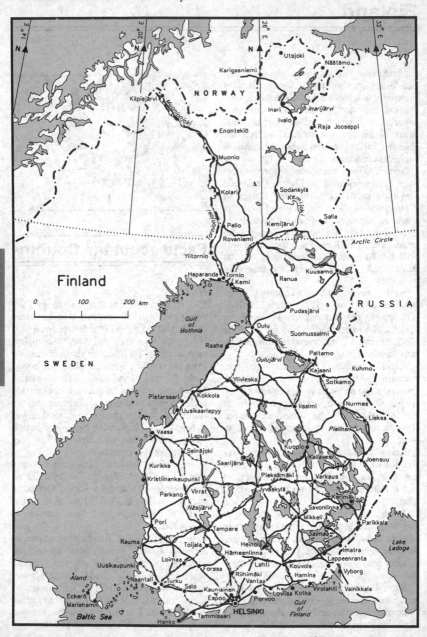

most followers of the Orthodox faith fled to Russia. Famine killed a third of all Finns and so brought a weaker Finland into the 18th century and an age of wars with Russia.

Russia took Ladoga and Vyborg (Finnish: Viipuri) and, in 1809, the whole country. But Finland gained greater autonomy as a Grand Duchy with its Swedish laws, Lutheran church and Finnish Senate. In 1812 the capital moved to Helsinki. Nationalism began to surge, although the first prominent Finns bore Swedish names. This suited the tsars until the 1880s, when a firmer policy appeared to dismantle and Russify the Finnish state.

From the end of WW I Finnish activists began to succeed in breaking Russian control and introducing reforms. Independence was declared in December 1917 under a bilateral coalition, but the divisions between socialists and conservatives, after a brief 'Red' coup in Helsinki, forced out the socialists and more moderate social democrats took their place. Complex relations with the new Soviet Union were further complicated by Finnish involvement in East Karelian bids for autonomy and British and German adventures in the Baltic area and the Soviet Red-White struggle.

The question of Åland's status soured relations with Sweden. Åland (Finnish: Ahvenanmaa) maintained its Swedish culture but submitted to Finnish sovereignty in 1921). Further anti-communist violence broke out early in the 1930s and Soviet relations remained uneasy after the non-aggression pact of 1932. Finland sought neutrality and formalised a commitment to Scandinavian solidarity, but it was probably concern about its security in the north-west that led to Soviet demands for Karelian territory and the Winter War in 1939.

Finnish defiance of the Soviet Union ended after months of fighting and it again lost part of Karelia and some nearby islands. Almost half a million people had to be resettled to the west. The Finnish predicament prompted concrete aid only from Germany, and Finland resumed hostilities late in 1941 (the Continuation War).

By September 1944, growing Soviet strength forced another armistice the terms of which meant Finns turning to fight entrenched German forces in Lapland until the general peace. This was the last of more than 40 wars with Russia. It cost Finland almost 100,000 people and heavy reparations.

Under President Paasikivi, Finland took a new line in its Soviet relations and signed a new treaty. Finland was to recognise Soviet security concerns and agree to Soviet aid in defending the frontier. This developed further during the 25 years of Urho Kekkonen's presidency and Finland was able to craft an independent view of East-West relations.

This meant opportunities to put Finland in the forefront of international dialogue and brought the security to develop its economy and welfare and its Scandinavian links through the Nordic Council and EFTA (European Free Trade Association). The several Helsinki conferences and accords have been markers in the development of international attitudes to security, disarmament and human rights.

GEOGRAPHY

Finland is Europe's sixth-biggest country, an uneven lowland apart from the northern tip of the Scandinavian spine. The post-glacial lakes of Saimaa are the dominant features, forests cover two-thirds of the country, and the Arctic zone covers one-third. Altogether there are 180,000 lakes and the winding ridges or eskers in between are therefore common.

Russia holds the Arctic coast to the north and the ecological damage caused by its northern mining towns has been among the strongest Finnish environmental concerns. Soil conservation and the quality of the extensive inland waters remain prime issues. The Turunmaa archipelago offshore from Turku almost merges with Åland and the Swedish coast.

GOVERNMENT

Finland is a presidential republic and a prime

minister is elected every four years by the assembly of about 200 members.

The president, chosen by separate delegates, has a six-year term and, in council with the prime minister and cabinet, forms the executive government. The president also appoints the chief judges, whose courts nominate people for the bench. The parliament is elected by proportional representation in 14 national districts. Finland's early governments under Russian auspices were innovative and the constitution has been little changed since independence. There are 12 provincial administrations, the *lääni*, and more than 450 *kunta* or municipalities.

The exception to this structure applies in Åland, which has a small local parliament and a high degree of autonomy. It also sends one member of parliament to Helsinki.

ECONOMY

In Finland 85% of all businesses are privately owned. Foreign trade is vital and the main trading partners have been EFTA and EC members (about two-thirds of all trade) and the former Soviet Union. Industry has fully developed only since WW II but delivered sustained growth of about 4% annually until about a decade ago.

Productivity in Finland is almost compatible per capita with that of its EFTA neighbours but in recent times consumer prices have risen at a rate of up to 10% a year. The Soviet economic collapse of the 1990s will influence any new eastern links as Finland moves towards the EC.

The metals and engineering sector, paper products and chemicals dominate foreign earnings and niches in such industries as shipbuilding have had to be developed: icebreakers and oil rigs are two examples. Crude oil accounts for a seventh of traded imports.

For the traveller the general cost structure is demanding on the pocket and the multistar comforts are downright expensive. A general value-added tax is set at 17%.

POPULATION & PEOPLE

There are about five million inhabitants of Finland, more than half of them collected in the south and south-west. Only in these areas is the population density greater than 30 people per sq km. Overall Finland is the third most sparsely populated country in Europe. There are more than 4000 Sami people, living mostly in the deep north, and a similar number of Romany people (Gypsies) in the south.

ARTS

The many libraries encapsulate well the focus of mainstream arts through their books and building design. The author of the Muminland stories, Tove Jansson, probably has the highest international profile among contemporary Finns although you cannot escape the design work of the late Alvar Aalto in public buildings, towns and furniture. One of the very greatest of modern composers, Jean Sibelius, was a Finn at the forefront of national aspirations and his keyboard works are at present interpreted by the piano master Erik Tawaststjerna.

Sibelius and the nationalistic painter Akseli Gallen-Kallela fell under the spell of Karelianism, a movement going back to the folk songs collected to form the national epic, the *Kalevala*, by Elias Lönnrot in the 1830s. That compilation has permeated the national consciousness and developed with the literary language during the 19th century as a bridge between liberal and Karelian folk tradition. But the greatest of Finnish writers, Aleksis Kivi, worked in a late Romantic framework.

CULTURE

The sketch of a log cabin with sauna by a forest lake may be an adequate symbol of Finnish culture if you can come to understand what it signifies: independence, endurance, open space and a capacity for reflection. Recourse to the music of Sibelius reveals a mysticism that cannot be explained or quantified, unless it speak through the *Kalevala* or stark simplicities of modern Finnish design. Perhaps the great Finnish distance runners sum up the society best by their very resilience.

More regional are the remains of the Sami reindeer-herding culture or the Karelian and Orthodox elements in the east.

RELIGION

About 90% of Finns are Evangelical Lutherans and only 50,000 or so are now Orthodox. Minority churches, including Roman Catholic, make up only a few per cent.

LANGUAGE

Introduction

Finnish is a Uralic language and belongs to to the Finno-Ugric group. Finnish is closely related to Estonian and Karelian and had common origins with Samoyed and languages spoken in the Volga basin. The most widely spoken of the Finno-Ugric languages is Hungarian, but similarities with Finnish are few.

Finnish is spoken by some five million people in Finland, where the country is known as *Suomi*, and the language as *suomi*. It is not a Scandinavian language, nor is it related to any other Indo-European languages. There are, however, many loan words from Baltic, Slavic and Germanic languages, and many words are derived from French and English.

Outside the big towns of Finland, few people speak fluent English, so it is advisable to learn a few phrases in Finnish to make your visit more rewarding. Finns appreciate any effort made by a non-native speaker and are eager to help further. Finnish is by no means an easy language to master but it is easy to read out loud, and mistakes made by visitors are usually disregarded. There is also a Swedish-speaking minority in south and west Finland, and all Finns do learn Swedish in school, so you may also need your Swedish vocabulary in Finland.

Pronunciation

Finnish has eight vowels, **a, e, i, o, u, y, ä** and **ö**. The alphabet also includes Swedish **å**, which is pronounced as the 'au' in 'caught'. **Å, ä** and **ö** are the final letters of the alphabet.

Vowels

y	is like the German 'ü'
ä	is pronounced as the 'a' in 'act'
ö	is like the 'e' in 'summer'

Consonants

Consonant sounds which differ from English are listed here.

z	which can be written and is pronounced as 'ts'
v & w	which Finns consider as more or less the same letter
h	is a weak sound, except at the end of a 'closed' syllable, when it is almost as strong as German 'ch' in 'ich'
j	like the 'y' in 'yellow'
r	which is rolled

Double consonants like **kk** in *viikko* or **mm** in *summa* are held longer. Note that **ng** and **nk** make two syllables, and are pronounced as **-ng-ng-** and **-ng-k-**. For example, *vangit*, 'prisons', is **vahng**-*ngit*. Note also that **np** is pronounced as **mp**, as in *olenpa*, **o**-*lehm-pah*.

Greetings & Civilities

Hello.	*Hei, Terve. (Moi)*
Goodbye.	*Näkemiin. (Moi.)*
Thank you.	*Kiitos. (Kiitti.)*
That's fine. You're welcome.	*Ole hyvä. (Eipä kestä.)*
Excuse me.	*Anteeksi.*
Sorry.	*Olen pahoillani. (Sori.)*
Do you speak English?	*Puhutko englantia?*
Does anyone speak English?	*Puhuuko kukaan englantia?*
I (don't) understand.	*Ei ymmärrän.*
Just a minute.	*Hetkinen.*
Please write that down.	*Olka hyvä ja kirjoittakaa se.*
How much is it ...?	*Paljonko se maksaa ...?*

Some Useful Signs

Camping Ground	*Leirint äalue*

FINLAND

Entrance	*Sis ään*
Exit	*Ulos*
Guesthouse	*Matkailijakoti*
Hotel	*Hotelli*
Information	*Opastus*
Open/Closed	*Avoinna/Suljettu*
Police	*Poliisi*
Police Station	*Poliisiasema*
Toilets	*WC*
Youth Hostel	*Retkeilymaja*

Getting Around

What time does ... leave/arrive?	*Mihin aikaan ... lähtee/saapuu?*
What time is the ...?	*Mihin aikaan on ...?*
next	*seuraava*
first	*ensimmäinen*
last	*viimeinen*
the boat	*laiva*
the bus (city)	*bussi*
the bus (intercity)	*bussi, linja-auto*
the train	*juna*
the tram	*raitiovaunu (raitsikka)*
the taxi	*taksi*
bus station	*linja-auto asema*
railway station	*rautatieasema*
departures	*lähtevät*
I would like ...	*Saanko ...*
a one-way ticket	*menolipun*
a return ticket	*menopaluulipun*
1st class	*ensimmäinen luokka*
2nd class	*toinen luokka*
Where is the bus/tram stop?	*Missä on bussi/raitsikka-pysäkki?*
I want to go to ...	*Haluan mennä ...*
Can you show me (on the map)?	*Voitko näyttää minulle (kartasta)?*
far/near	*kaukana/lähellä*
Go straight ahead.	*Kulje suoraan.*
Turn left ...	*Käänny vasempaan ...*
Turn right ...	*Käänny oikeaan ...*

Around Town

I'm looking for ...	*Minä etsin ...*
Where is ...	*Missä on ...*
a bank	*pankkia/pankki*
the city centre	*keskustaa*
the ... embassy	*...-n suurlähe-tystöä*
my hotel	*minun hotellia/ minun hotelli*
the market	*toria/tori*
the post office	*postia/posti*
a public toilet	*yleistä vessaa/ yleinen vessa*
the telephone centre	*puhelinta/puhelin*
the tourist informa-tion office	*matkailutoimistoa/ma tkailutoimisto*
beach	*uimaranta, ranta*
bridge	*silta*
castle	*linna*
cathedral	*tuomiokirkko, katedraali*
church	*kirkko*
hospital	*sairaala*
island	*saari*
lake	*järvi*
main square	*keskustori*
market	*tori, kauppatori, markkinat*
mosque	*moskeija*
old city	*vanhakaupunki*
palace	*palatsi*
ruins	*rauniot*
sea	*meri*
synagogue	*synagooga*
tower	*torni*

Accommodation

Where is a cheap hotel?	*Missä olisi halpa hotelli?*
What is the address?	*Mikä on osoite?*
Could you write the address, please?	*Voisitteko kirjoittaa osoitteen?*
Do you have any rooms available?	*Onko teillä vapaata huonetta?*
I would like ...	*Haluaisin ...*
a single room	*yhden hengen huoneen*
a double room	*kahden hengen huoneen*

FINLAND

a room with a bathroom	*huoneen kylpyhuoneella*	today	*tänään*
to share a dorm	*makuusalin sänkypaikan*	tomorrow	*huomenna*
		in the morning	*aamulla*
a bed	*sängyn*	in the afternoon	*iltapäivällä*
		in evening	*illalla*
How much is it per night/per person?	*Paljonko se on yöltä/hengeltä?*	Monday	*maanantai*
Can I see it?	*Voinko minä nähdä sen?*	Tuesday	*tiistai*
		Wednesday	*keskiviikko*
Where is the bathroom?	*Missä on kylpyhuone (vessa).*	Thursday	*torstai*
		Friday	*perjantai*
		Saturday	*lauantai*
Do you have a smoke sauna?	*Onko teillä savusaunaa?*	Sunday	*sunnuntai*
		January	*tammikuu*
		February	*helmikuu*

Food

breakfast	*aamiainen*	March	*maaliskuu*
lunch	*lounas*	April	*huhtikuu*
early/late dinner	*päivällinen/illalline*	May	*toukokuu*
		June	*kesäkuu*
		July	*heinäkuu*
Table for ..., please	*Pöytä ...-lle!, Saadaanko me pöytä ...-lle?*	August	*elokuu*
		September	*syyskuu*
		October	*lokakuu*
I would like the set lunch, please.	*Saanko päivän lounaan.*	November	*marraskuu*
		December	*joulukuu*
Service is included in the bill.	*Tarjoilu kuuluu hintaan.*		

Numbers

I am a vegetarian.	*Olen kasvissyöjä.*	1	*yksi (yks)*

At the Chemist

		2	*kaksi (kaks)*
		3	*kolme*
I need medication for ...	*Tarvitsen lääkitystä ...-a/ä varten*	4	*neljä*
		5	*viisi (viis)*
I have a prescription.	*Minulla on resepti.*	6	*kuusi (kuus)*
		7	*seitsemän (seittemän)*

At the Dentist

		8	*kahdeksan (kaheksan)*
I have a toothache.	*Minun hammasta särkee.*	9	*yhdeksän (yheksän)*
		10	*kymmenen*
I've lost a filling.	*Minulta on irronnut paikka.*	11	*yksitoista*
		12	*kaksitoista*
I've broken a tooth.	*Minulta on lohjennut hammas.*	13	*kolmetoista*
		14	*neljätoista*
My gums hurt.	*Ikeniä särkee.*	15	*viisitoista*
I don't want it extracted.	*En halua, että hammas poistetaan.*	16	*kuusitoista*
		17	*seitsemäntoista*
Please give me an anaesthetic.	*Voitteko puuduttaa.*	18	*kahdeksantoista*
		19	*yhdeksäntoista*
		20	*kaksikymmentä*

Time & Dates

		21	*kaksikymmentäyksi*
What time is it?	*Paljonko kello on?*	22	*kaksikymmentäkaksi*

30	*kolmekymmentä*
40	*neljäkymmentä*
50	*viisikymmentä*
60	*kuusikymmentä*
70	*seitsemänkymmentä*
80	*kahdeksänkymmentä*
90	*yhdeksänkymmentä*
100	*sata*
1000	*tuhat*
one million	*miljoona*

Health

I'm ...	*Olen ...*
diabetic/	*diabeetikko*
epilectic	*epileptikko*
asthmatic	*astmaatikko*

I'm allergic to ...	*Minä olen allerginen ...*
antibiotics	*antibiooteille*
penicillin	*penisilliinille*

antiseptic	*antiseptinen*
aspirin	*aspiriini*
some condoms	*kondomit/kondomej*
contraceptive	*ehkäisyväline*
diarrhoea	*ripuli*
medicine	*lääke*
nausea	*pahoinvointi*

Emergencies

Help!	*Apua!*
Call a doctor!	*Kutsukaa lääkäri!*
Call the police!	*Soittakaa poliisi!*
Go away!	*Mene pois! (Häivy!)*

Facts for the Visitor

VISAS & EMBASSIES

Citizens of the English-speaking countries require no visa for short stays (UK visitor's passes, national identity cards of a few European countries and the Nordic countries are accepted in place of a passport). Visas are generally required only for working or staying more than three months (see Documents following). These can be extended by application to local police. Visas for Russia take two weeks to process in Helsinki, so you may have to get one before leaving home (but see Tours to Russia following).

Finnish Embassies

Embassies include:

Australia & New Zealand
    10 Darwin Avenue, Yarralumla
    2600 ACT Australia
Canada
    Suite 850, 55 Metcalfe Street, Ottawa K1P 6L5
Denmark
    Hammerensgade 5, 1267 Copenhagen K
Germany
    Friesdorferstrasse 1, 5300 Bonn 2
Norway
    Drammensveien 40, 0255 Oslo 2
Poland
    ulica Chopina 4-8, 00559 Warsaw
Russia
    Kropotkinskij Pereulok 15-17,
    119034 Moscow G-36
UK
    38 Chesham Place, London SW1X 8HW
USA
    3216 New Mexico Avenue NW,
    Washington DC 20016

Foreign Embassies in Finland

The embassies and legations are in Helsinki, but Australia and New Zealand have none in Finland and citizens of these countries should contact the Australian ambassador in Stockholm (☎ 9800 1 0460 8-613 2900), or New Zealand consul-general (☎ 9800 1 0460 8-611 6824).

Canada
    Pohjoisesplanadi 25B (☎ 90-171 141)
Denmark
    Keskuskatu 1A (☎ 90-171 511)
Germany
    Frederikinkatu 61 (☎ 90-694 3355)
Norway
    Rehbinderintie 17 (☎ 90-171 234)
Poland
    Armas Lindgrenintie 21 (☎ 90-684 8077)
Russia
    Tehtaankatu 1B (☎ 90-661 876)
Sweden
    Pohjoisesplanadi 7B (☎ 90-651 255)
UK
    Itäinen Puistotie 17 (☎ 90-661 293)
USA
    Itäinen Puistotie 14A (☎ 90-171 931)

DOCUMENTS

A passport is generally all you require for a stay of up to three months. For a longer stay or to work you need a visa, available through national embassies and legations (workers need a full statement of job and conditions from the prospective employer). The immigration authority is the Interior Ministry's Centre for Alien Affairs, Haapaniemenkatu 5, 00530 Helsinki.

CUSTOMS

Currency can be brought in to Finland without declaration, or gift goods up to the value of 1500 mk (there are restrictions on edible fats and live plants). For alcohol the limit is two litres of beer, a litre of wine and a litre of spirits (special restrictions apply to travellers between aged between 18 and 20 years). Tobacco is restricted to 400 cigarettes or 500 grams (half this for Europeans). You can arrive with 50 litres of fuel in your tank without incurring tax.

MONEY

Visa and Eurocard-MasterCard are the main cards used in banks, but American Express, Diner's Club and Access are common in hotels and restaurants. American Express and Thomas Cook cheques are widely accepted. Banks are open from 9 or 9.30 am to 4 or 4.30 pm weekdays. Post office banks in big towns are open until 5 pm. Travellers' cheques cost about 5 mk each to exchange (in multiples) or singly, 25 mk, but beware of 40 mk charges (ask first).

Currency

The markka (= 100 penniä) is often called 'mark' and appears in much literature as FIM. The notes are 10, 50, 100, 500 and 1000 mk and coins one and five markka and 50 and 10 penniä (20 and five-penniä coins are now rare).

Exchange Rates

The markka is linked to the European currency unit. The following currencies convert at these approximate rates:

1 Dkr	=	0.70 Fmk
1 Ikr	=	0.07 Fmk
1 Nkr	=	0.70 Fmk
1 Skr	=	0.75 Fmk
A$1	=	3.34 Fmk
C$1	=	3.75 Fmk
DM1	=	3.17 Fmk
NZ$1	=	2.54 Fmk
UK£1	=	7.95 Fmk
US$1	=	4.67 Fmk

Costs

Camping or using the Finnish hostel association SRM (Suomen Retkeilymajajärestö) hostels allows a modest daily budget of 200 mk, but you would have to double this to stay in hotels. An ordinary SRM hostel bed costs from 45 to 60 mk, a cheap hotel costs 220/350 mk a single/double. A 400-gram loaf of bread costs about 9 mk, a Big Mac 21.90 mk, a 450 ml strong beer 20 to 25 mk (small bottles start at 6 mk), a cheap restaurant meal costs less than 50 mk. A litre of 99 octane super petrol costs 4.4 mk or more, a local telephone call 2 mk, 100 km by bus 49 mk, 100 km by train 45 mk. *Time* magazine costs 13 mk.

Ask at tourist offices about package and discount cards such as Helsinki card.

Tipping

Tipping will not be necessary unless you use porters and taxis.

Consumer Taxes

The general sales tax of 17% can be deducted if you post goods from the point of sale. At stores showing the 'Tax Free for Tourists' sign you can buy items priced over 200 mk at discounts of 12% to 16%. Show your tax-free cheque and sealed goods at the refund window at customs posts to claim the refund (not available on ferries to Sweden). A brochure (with a list of collection points) is available from Finland Tax-Free Shopping, Yrjönkatu 29D, 00100 Helsinki.

CLIMATE & WHEN TO GO

Winter north of the Arctic Circle is a frozen

FINLAND

experience of strange bluish light from November on, although February is the coldest month. In contrast, there is a July noon mean temperature of almost 20°C and the north gets a two-month 'day'.

At Inari in Lapland the July average temperature is almost 12°C (-13.5°C in January). Rainfall is less here, from 400 to 500 mm a year, and snowfalls grow from a mean of 10 cm in November to peak at 50 cm in March.

There are 18 hours of daylight per day in April, five hours in December. The midnight sun appears from about 20 May to 20 July, polar night reigns through December, New Year and Epiphany. The tourist season is from mid-June to the end of August, although in Lapland the mosquitoes are annoying in July – autumn *ruska* colours appear in September there. Helsinki has a average maximum of 20.5°C in July and snow starts to fall there in November, but March in Karelia or Lapland is better for skiing. See also the climate charts at the back of this book.

WHAT TO BRING

The winds from the east produce climatic extremes and taking an anorak (or waterproof and windproof jacket) is advisable even early in autumn. Waterproof boots (Wellingtons) and pants are best for spring hikers, considering the rain and lowland swamps. Self-catering gear, including utensils, a tea-towel and sheets are essential for hostelling. If you're staying in cabins and cottages bring linen and towels.

SUGGESTED ITINERARIES

Depending on the length of your stay you might like to see and do the following things:

Two days
    Inner Helsinki: national museum and main churches, plus a stroll down the Pohjoisesplanadi and a boat trip to Suomenlinna
One week
    Two days in Helsinki, two days in Savonlinna (castle and museums), by boat to Lappeenranta and then return by train

Two weeks
    Three or four days in Helsinki, a day each in Turku and Tampere, two days each in Savonlinna and Lappeenranta, Åland
One month
    One week Helsinki, 1½ weeks Karelia and the lakes, two days Tampere, two days Turku, three days Åland, four days Lapland (Inari)
Two months
    Two weeks Helsinki, three days each in Turku and Tampere, two weeks cruising in lakeland and North Karelia, one week Åland (cycling), two weeks Lapland

TOURIST OFFICES

The main tourist information centre is run by the Finnish Tourist Board (Matkailun edistämiskeskus or MEK) in Helsinki at Unionkatu 26, (Box 249, 00131 Helsinki). Their free literature covers most of the country.

Local Tourist Offices

The MEK head office is at Töölönkatu 11, Box 652 00101 Helsinki. MEK also has a northern regional office at Maakuntakatu 10, Box 8154, 96101 Rovaniemi. Other offices include:

Åland
    Ålands Turistinformation, Storagatan 11, 22100 Mariehamn
North Karelia
    Pohjois-Karjalan matkailutoimisto, Koskikatu 1, 80100 Joensuu
South-West Finland
    Varsinais-Suomen Matkailuyhdistys, Läntinen Rantakatu 13, 20100 Turku
Saimaa & South Karelia
    Saimaan Matkailu Ry, Puistokatu 1, 57100 Savonlinna

Tourist Offices Abroad

MEK's international offices include:

Canada
    Finnish Tourist Board, Box 246, Station Q, Toronto M4T 2M1
Denmark
    Finlands Turistbureau, Vester Farimagsgade 3, 1606 Copenhagen V
Norway
    Finlands Turistkontor, Lille Grensen 7, 0159 Oslo 1

Sweden
   Finska Turistbyrån, Kungsgatan 4A, 11143
   Stockholm
UK
   Finnish Tourist Board, 66-68 Haymarket,
   London SW1Y 4RF
USA
   Finnish Tourist Board, 655 Third Avenue, New
   York, NY 10017

USEFUL ORGANISATIONS

The national motoring organisation is Autoliitto, Kansakoulukatu 10, 00100 Helsinki. For youth there is Kompassi (see Helsinki), and a useful contact centre for environmental and alternative movements is the development centre and book café Ruohonjuuri, Mannerheimintie 13 in Helsinki (closed most Sundays).

There is an AIDS Information & Support Centre (☎ 90-665 081) at Linnankatu 2B in Helsinki. The organisation for gay and lesbian equality is SETA (Seksuaalinen tasavertaisus) at suite 5, Mäkelänkatu 36A (closed from Saturday to Monday, open to 9 pm Wednesdays, for telephone information call 90-769 642).

The national feminist organisation Unioni is based at Bulevardi 11A, Helsinki, where there is a book café (closed from Midsummer to the end of July). An extremely useful source of information is Santa Claus: you can write to him at Santa Claus' Village, Napapiiri, 96300 Rovaniemi.

BUSINESS HOURS & HOLIDAYS

Shops and post offices are generally open from 9 am to 5 pm weekdays, to 2 pm on Saturdays. But many supermarkets and the Helsinki department stores do open to 7 or 8 pm, although on holiday eves they shut at 6 pm. Town markets begin about 7 am weekdays and Saturdays and continue until at least about 2 pm. The public holidays are:

New Year's Day, 1 January
Epiphany, usually 6 January
Good Friday
May Day Eve & May Day, 30 April & 1 May
Ascension Day, May
Whit Sunday, late in May or early in June
Juhannus (Midsummer's Day) & Midsummer's Eve,
   third weekend in June
All Saints' Day, end of October or early in November
Independence Day, 6 December
Christmas Eve, 24 December
Christmas Day, 25 December
Boxing Day, 26 December

CULTURAL EVENTS

Finland Festivals coordinates annual feature events and produces several guides available from tourist offices. The foremost event is the Helsinki Festival late in August and early in September, involving all performing arts.

The Tampere Theatre Festival is an international professional gathering of more than 100 events during the third week of August. All types of music are catered for, but the greatest novelty is at the Savonlinna Opera Festival at Olavinlinna castle in July, the Naantali Music Festival at historic churches in June and Ruisrock, the longest-running of rock festivals, at Turku during the last weekend of June.

POST & TELECOMMUNICATIONS

Post offices are generally open from 9 am to 5 pm weekdays, but stamps can be bought at stations and newspaper shops. Postcards and letters weighing up to 50 grams cost 2.10 mk to Nordic countries, 2.90 mk to Europe, and 3.40 mk elsewhere (air-mail or lentoposti). Telegrams (☎ 021) cost 40 mk plus a charge per word varying with distance. Post faxes cost 18 mk and 6 mk per page. There is a poste restante at the main post offices in cities (open longer hours in summer).

Local calls are timed after you pay the base fee of 2 mk for five minutes (5-mk coins are accepted but you do not get change – this is the base cost for trunk calls and the '0' code numbers, such as the universal 041 taxi number). A few old phones accept only 1 mk. Credit-card phones charge a 5-mk minimum and allow calls costing up to 100 mk.

Telephone cards cost 10, 30, 50 and 100 mk. Internal trunk codes begin with 9 and are listed on page 20 in volume two of the Helsinki directory. For local enquiries dial 012, elsewhere dial 020. To neighbouring countries tariffs are 3.05 mk a minute, to

Europe 5.20 mk, to USA, Canada and Australia 7.55 mk, to New Zealand 12.20 mk (calls between 10 pm and 8 am are cheaper). The international prefix is 990, for direct-dial collect calls 9800 (these calls can be made free from a Tele office or TeleRing centre, where there are cards and booklets in English listing international codes). Finnish operators charge 30 mk to reverse charges on booked calls unless you are using a telephone card.

TIME
Finland is two hours ahead of GMT/UTC and summer time applies from April to the end of September. At noon in Finland it is 10 am in London, 5 am in New York, 2 am in San Francisco, 5 am in Toronto, 8 pm in Sydney, 10 pm in Auckland, 11 am in Stockholm, Copenhagen and Oslo and 1 pm in Moscow, St Petersburg and Tallinn.

ELECTRICITY
The electric current is 220 volts AC (some areas use 230 volts), 50 Hz, and plugs are of the standard European type with two round pins which require no switch.

LAUNDRY
There are few laundrettes but you can wash and dry a load for 50 mk. The traveller's best options are those SRM hostels with washing machines and the camping grounds.

WEIGHTS & MEASURES
Finland, like the rest of Europe, uses the metric system. Decimals are indicated by commas and thousands by points.

BOOKS & MAPS
Books and maps are relatively expensive. The best Helsinki bookshop is Akateeminen Kirjakauppa, Pohjoisesplanadi 39, especially for guidebooks and tourist maps. Suomalainen Kirjakauppa is in big towns; it's cheaper for most titles and English paperbacks are not hard to find. The following titles are recent offerings in translation:

A History of Finland, E Jutikkala & K Pirinen (hardback)
A Brief History of Finland, M Klinge (softback)
Finnish Museums, Suomen Museoliiton (softback)
Finland: Cultural Perspectives, V Kallio (hardback)
Sami: Europe's Forgotten People, N Valkeapää (hardback)
The Kalevala, translated by K Bosley (softback)
Helsinki: An Architectural Guide, A Ilonen (softback)

Also available in English is Lonely Planet's *Finland – a travel survival kit* by Marcus Lehtipuu & Virpi Mäelä.

Karttakeskus is the national map publisher and supplier (in Helsinki at Opastinsilta 12B in Pasila) and has all survey maps (ranging from 1:20,000 sheets to 1:100,000), sea and lake charts and hiking maps for the wilderness areas.

MEDIA
Radio Finland and national radio YLE-3 (and in Helsinki FM 103.7MHz) broadcast several BBC and Voice of America reports and local programmes. There are two national television networks and TV3 commercial stations in cities.

For good information seek the tourist papers *Discovering Helsinki* and *City in English* and the guide *Helsinki This Week*. The main newspaper *Helsingin Sanomat* has the biggest guides to entertainment, second-hand vehicles and travel. Dial Helsinki 040 for English news or 058 for daily events.

FILM & PHOTOGRAPHY
Standard 24-shot rolls of film need cost only about 22 mk and slide films cost about 30 mk (look for bargains). Consider the problems of taking shots on water or snow and the weird lighting conditions deep in the north whether in summer or winter.

The common-sense rule for security matters is not to photograph military personnel or installations which are not on display or parade. Do not photograph near the eastern border zone without checking with the Russian embassy.

HEALTH
The national pharmacies *(apteekki)* have

medicines and advice and some are open 24 hours a day in cities. Duty public hospitals, for emergencies and first aid, charge 67 mk for outpatients and 87 mk a day for ward beds (dial 008 for an emergency doctor, 000 for an ambulance). But surgery or private care would be expensive, so take the top scale of insurance cover. For telephone information dial 90-735 001, for Helsinki duty dentists it's 90-736 166.

The mosquito season is from June to August, particularly around the inland waters. For poisons information, call 90-4711.

WORK

You must arrange a job first and lodge the details when you fill in forms at a Finnish legation (see Finland, Documents). You must then wait up to three months. You should then be issued with work and residency visas, which you can apply to the police to extend. Students can apply for limited summer employment. Au pair arrangements are possible for up to 18 months.

ACTIVITIES
Boating

For boating you have the choice of sea and lake, but the prime sailing region, the Turku archipelago, is demanding to navigate. The south and south-west coast are best equipped for visiting craft and there are coastguard stations in Helsinki, Turku and Vaasa. The rescue channel is VHF 16.

Hire of small motorboats and sailing boats starts at about 1200 mk a week. To get information write to the navigation authority Merenkulkuhallitus, Vuorimiehenkatu 1, 00140 Helsinki. For charts choose those produced by Karttakeskus (see Books & Maps).

A principle of common access to nature applies but you can not light a fire except at marked site or with the landowner's permission, although you may camp in the open.

Canoeing

Canoeing is best on the lakes or in the Turunmaa archipelago early in spring; channels there are often marked, but only the experienced should try the sea. Packages are offered by tourist offices and the clubs of the Finnish Canoe Association (Radiokatu 20, 00240 Helsinki). Wilder rapids are available in Lapland and North Karelia. Canoe and kayak hire starts at around 100 mk a day and 500 mk a week.

Fishing

You may generally angle or fish with bait and fly in Finnish waters. You need an annual fishing licence (except in Åland or if you are under 18 years of age), which is available at post offices for 30 mk. Around the lake Inarijärvi and Enontekiö a regional system of 30-mk licences operates.

But most fishing spots are owned privately or by local or national authorities. So as well as the above licences you need a local permit for the day or week (available at varying rates from municipal or forestry authorities or from whoever owns the waters: tourist offices have information). The book *Welcome to Fish* is available from forestry authorities and the MEK booklet *Finland Fishing* from tourist offices. Important closed seasons include from September to November for salmon and trout varieties. There are also some summer restrictions. Check before you fish. It is customary to catch only the fish you need.

Hiking

The recommended time of year for hiking or trekking is from June to September, but April hikes are popular among the hardy and experienced. Mountain huts line the northern trails and can be used (and shared). Keep to marked trails, lodge plans with tourist offices or police, camp only at official sites and leave trail rubbish in proper bins. Light fires only at camp sites or with the landowner's permission.

Unprotected wildflowers, berries and mushrooms are usually free for picking (check on any local prohibitions) but do not experiment – know what you are doing.

Close-fitting waterproof boots and an anorak are essentials on the gear list. If you

FINLAND

are an inexperienced hiker, go into the developed hiking areas such as Ruunaa in Karelia or try a national park *(Kansallispuisto)*. Organised tours are available from MEK and routes such as Karhunkierros and the Lemmenjoki are very scenic. The huts in Lapland are free, but some are locked and you must get keys from tourist offices.

Sauna

The sauna symbolises the Finnish predilection for freedom and introspection. It is a cleansing physical and emotional experience that reveals much about people, hence an invitation to have a sauna is personal and most hospitable. The traditional type of sauna is in a wooden room with benches and a properly stoked wooden stove, but saunas at hotels, camping grounds and in homes tend to have more modern heating. Temperatures from 80°C to 100°C are common, but start off at 60°C. Lightly switching the body with birch twigs increases perspiration and then the cold swim or wash and scrub (fanatics roll in snow) completes the refreshment. Public saunas will cost about 50 mk, so go to a swimming pool that has one for around 12 mk.

Skiing

Nordic skiing is most popular on the flat landscapes and there are cross-country trails (some lit) of varying difficulty. Downhill skiers, jumpers and serious winter sportspeople will leave Helsinki for the complex at Lahti or go to a resort such as Kuopio or Koli in North Karelia. Expect to pay 70 mk a day to hire gear, but for downhill skiing you pay around 100 mk. Cheaper deals and weekly rates are available at some ski centres and SRM hostels.

The season runs from October (in the south, December) to mid-May and, although daylight is limited before Christmas, you can ski in nocturnal twilight in Lapland from late in October.

HIGHLIGHTS
Islands

The 6000 islands of **Åland** and the **Turunmaa archipelago** are regarded as one of the best sailing areas, an opportunity to experience a different environment. Handier to Helsinki are the fortress and museums of **Suomenlinna**, 20 minutes by ferry from the market square of Helsinki.

Museums & Galleries

In Helsinki begin with the big collections of the **National Museum**. Here you will find art as well as cultural collections, a pattern common in the regional museums. Better art venues are the refurbished **Ateneum** and the grottoes of the big **Retretti** complex at Punkaharju near Savonlinna. The open-air museums at **Seurasaari** near Helsinki and **Pielisen Museo** at Lieksa in North Karelia are two of the best in the country.

Castles

Olavinlinna at Savonlinna is the finest, mightiest and best preserved of northern medieval castles and is superbly set between lakes. Only a little less imposing are the castles of **Turku** and **Hämeenlinna**.

ACCOMMODATION

Check carefully when booking a place to stay from listings by locality – municipal names are common and your bed may be nowhere near the town.

If you want the best rates on hotels, come to town on Friday, this gives you two or three nights at holiday rates (check when booking). Summer rates are lower, but seasons vary by region at ski resorts where cheaper rates will apply in March and April). the most comprehensive annual hotel guide is *Suomen Hotelliopas* (92 mk).

Finncheques covering a night in a hotel bed cost 165 mk and are valid at about half of Finland's hotels from June to August (in some places you will pay an extra 75 mk). Hotel chains offer summer discounts and accept cards such as Scandinavian Bonus Pass. Holiday cabins can be booked through local tourist offices, generally for 1200 mk a week or more for four people. For listings on the mainland and booking information, write to Lomarengas, Malminkaari 23 C, 00700

Helsinki (for Åland bookings, see the Åland section).

The 160 SRM hostels and summer hotels are cheap for rooms or bed only (about half are open all year) and summer family deals cost 210 mk. Finnhostel cheques, available at SRM in Helsinki and in some hostels, costing 50 mk each are widely accepted (breakfast is extra). The national guide, including information on hotel packages, is on sale to youth-hostel card holders for 10 mk.

Camp sites cost from 30 to 80 mk, but if you have no International Camping Card (90 mk) buy a national card for 15 mk. MEK offers an annual budget accommodation guide free. For a B&B guide write to Lomarengas.

FOOD

Restaurant meals are expensive, and cafeteria specials costing around 40 mk often rely heavily on potatoes. Lunch is usually served between 11 am and 2 pm. The *grilli* is the usual venue for takeaways. Finnish cuisine is not easy to find: the *huffer* is rather like a smörgåsbord in its variety, but includes soups and fish and can be had for 60 mk in restaurants.

Helsinki is famous for Russian food, but high prices go with this reputation. Simpler experiments are the Karelian pasties and pastries, mostly costing under 15 mk.

Useful discount food chains are Siwa, Säästäri and Alepa. *Tarjous* means special price, but on food items can mean advancing age. When buying milk products, note that *rasvaton maito* is fat-free; *kevyt maito* is low-fat (1.9 grams per litre); and *kulutus maito* is conventional milk (3.9 grams of fats per litre).

DRINKS

Strong beers, wines and spirits are sold by the state network, aptly named Alko (open from 10 am to 5 pm, 6 pm Fridays and often until 2 pm Saturdays). Alcohol stronger than one-fifth by volume is not sold to those under 20 years of age. For beers and wines the age limit is 18. Group III ales (second rank in strength), however, can often be bought in supermarkets.

By law alcohol cannot strictly be consumed in the open air (or left in railway station lockers). Wines rarely cost less than 30 mk, though the popular and drinkable ones can be bought for less than 60 mk a bottle.

ENTERTAINMENT

Cinema tickets will cost from 25 to 40 mk (films are classified K for those up to 18 years old, S for general). English-language films have subtitles in Finnish. Discos charge from 20 mk at the door, nightclubs up to 60 mk (the usual age limit is 20 years, sometimes 24).

THINGS TO BUY

Duodji is authentic handicraft produced according to Sami traditions. A genuine item for sale, which can be expensive, should carry a round, coloured 'Duodji' token. The range of items in bone, hide, wood and metals includes the jewellery, clothing and characteristic knives of the various Sami communities.

Much of the work of the few master craftspeople can be regarded as original (in the traditional style) but, unlike other art purchases in Finland, duodji unfortunately attracts sales tax. Some, though, is sold under the tax-free for tourists system, so present your passport where appropriate (see the previous Consumer Taxes section).

Getting There & Away

AIR

Finnair and SAS dominate air traffic between Finland and Sweden. Together they have 14 flights per day between Helsinki and Stockholm (Finnish: Tukholma), 13 per week between Helsinki and Gothenburg, 17 per week between Tampere and Stockholm, nine per week between Turku and Stockholm and six per week between Helsinki and Malmö.

The small company Air Nordic flies four times per day between Vaasa (Finland) and Sundsvall (Sweden). There are seven or eight flights per day between Helsinki and Copenhagen (Finnish: Kööpenhamina) and three between Helsinki and Oslo.

Finnair also flies from Helsinki to St Petersburg (Finnish: Pietari) and Helsinki to Moscow daily, and Rovaniemi to Murmansk once a week. Finnair and Aeroflot fly from Helsinki to Tallinn, Aeroflot flies from Helsinki to Riga and Finnair and Lot fly from Helsinki to Warsaw (in summer Lot stops at Gdańsk). Services extend to most European cities including Istanbul, to London twice daily and to Berlin, Frankfurt, Hamburg, Munich and Stuttgart. Finnair and Delta fly daily from New York to Helsinki nonstop.

Discount flights are available to and from Finland for holders of YIEE (Youth International Educational Exchange) card or ISIC (International Student Identity Card) student cards from student travel agents. In Finland contact Kilroy Travels, Mannerheimintie 5C, 00100 Helsinki or in Turku, Tampere and Oulu.

LAND
To/From Sweden
Bus & Train Travelling to Sweden (from Finland) leave the Rovaniemi train from Oulu (Swedish: Uleåborg) at Kemi, 24 km from the border, and catch a connecting Tornio bus outside the station. Arrangements can vary and there is a one-hour time difference, so check connections at Kemi station before departure. Railcars run over the frontier river Tornionjoki between stations at Tornio (Swedish: Torneå) and Haparanda (Finnish: Haaparanta), however, on Saturdays you will need to take a cab or walk. Change money well in advance if you plan to cross the border at the weekend or if timetables mean tight connections.

From Haparanda you can take a train or bus west to Boden or Luleå (check timetables). From there you can travel by train to Stockholm or to Narvik in Norway.

If you are entering Finland from Sweden, take the connecting bus at Tornio station to Kemi. International rail passes and connecting rail tickets are valid on these buses. Expect to show your passport at the platform in Tornio.

Within Finland, trains run as far as Kolari from Oulu and Kemi on Tuesdays and Fridays or travel by bus from Rovaniemi. Norrbotten regional bus services Nos 052 (from Haparanda) and 003 (to Kiruna in Sweden) run to Pajala on the Swedish side of the border.

Rail journeys from Europe with ferry links are possible: holders of the Eurail pass can make free crossings from Stockholm to Turku with Silja Line and there are half-price crossings with the ScanRail and Nordturist passes.

Discounts are also available to holders of Inter-Rail pass from Travemünde to Helsinki, Stockholm to Turku and Stockholm to Helsinki. Eurolines' coaches via Copenhagen and Stockholm run to Turku and Helsinki.

Car The river Tornionjoki (Swedish: Torneälv) at Tornio is the frontier between Sweden and Finland. Cross over on the main bridge, where there is a border check. Take the green lane if you have nothing to declare.

To/From Norway
Bus Heading to Norway from Finland, buses run from Rovaniemi and Muonio to Skibotn (Norway) and return, and from Rovaniemi and Ivalo in Finland to Lakselv and Polmak in Norway twice daily.

Car At Nuorgam near Näätämo, the so-called Arctic Road crosses into Norway heading for Kirkenes. This border post is unstaffed from 10 pm to 7 am. Karigasniemi (on the road to Hammerfest and Lakselv), Kivilompolo and Utsjoki are also crossing points. On the road from Muonio (Finland) to Tromsö and Skibotn (Norway) you cross the Finnish border at Kilpisjärvi.

To/From Russia
Along the Russian frontier runs a border zone that is out of bounds to all visitors

except those holding visas and who are crossing the border; this zone is marked on some maps and extends in places four km into Finland. The same limit applies in waters of the Gulf of Finland.

On the heavily travelled Helsinki, Vyborg, St Petersburg corridor are one rail and two road crossings. The rail crossing is at Vainikkala (Russian side, Luzhayka). Highways cross at the Finnish border posts of Nuijamaa (Russian side, Brusnichnoe) and Vaalimaa (Russian side, Torfyanovka). From there to St Petersburg the road is said to be full of modern-day highwaymen so don't stop for anybody.

Further north, groups and individuals may be able to drive from Joensuu to the Finnish post of Tohmajärvi (Russian side, Vyartsilya) and 500 km on to Petrozavodsk; there's also a railway line on the Finnish side. From Ivalo (Finland), a road goes to Murmansk (Russia) via the Finnish border town of Raja-Jooseppi.

Train There is a Moscow sleeper running daily to and from Helsinki that carries cars twice a week. There are also daily St Petersburg services. You can buy Russian rail tickets from Helsinki (at the special ticket office in the central station) and cross the border at Vainikkala.

Car The crossings (on the roads to and from Vyborg and St Petersburg) are at Vaalimaa (open from 7 am to midnight) and Nuijamaa (departures between 8 am and 8 pm, arrivals between 8 am and 10 pm). You must return via the same crossing (unless you notify both border posts of your plans) and keep an itinerary card issued at the border post.

You need an international licence and certificate of registration, passport and visa and insurance. The state insurer Ingosstrakh (Salomonkatu 5C, 00100 Helsinki, open from 8 am to 3.30 pm weekdays) is the only body that will cover you in Russia and its associated republics, although you can make enquiries at travel agents. Intourist is in Helsinki at Mikonkatu 15 and can help with details of accommodation and petrol vouchers. Take basic auto spares with you.

Hitching It is best to avoid hitching at this frontier.

Tours Bus tours to St Petersburg are run by LS-Matkat Oy, Salomonkatu 5A, 00100 Helsinki. Regular express buses now run to St Petersburg from Helsinki (250 mk) and Turku. There is also a day express train from Helsinki to St Petersburg that arrives about 9 pm daily and departs again before noon the next day. The economy fare is 180 mk and you need a Russian visa.

From May to September you can book a two-day tour to Vyborg, the Karelian city to the south, that includes a trip on the Saimaa Canal and an Intourist tour of Vyborg.

This no-visa two-day tour requires 10-day advance bookings and full personal details in writing. The package costs 350 mk from Matka-Lappee Oy (☎ 953-534 22), Valtakatu 46, 53100 Lappeenranta. See also the following Sea section.

SEA

The Baltic ferries are some of the most impressive seagoing craft and have been compared to hotels and shopping plazas. You can pay a basic fee and find a seat or hire a cabin – taking a car is easy. Summer cruises in the 'Baltic ring' are starting up. On some routes services only run in summer or from March to December. Many ferries offer free deck passage or 50% discounts for holders of Eurail pass, Nordturist and ScanRail passes, and Inter-Rail pass. Some services offer pensioner reductions and discounts for ISIC and YIEE card holders. See also Estonia, Getting There & Away and the introductory Getting Around chapter.

Private boats entering Finnish waters are expected to report to customs posts immediately, using only harbours which have these posts. Otherwise notify the coastguard on VHF channels 10 or 16 and report to the appropriate harbour later (see Boating in the Activities section).

FINLAND

FINLAND

To/From Sweden
The Stockholm-Helsinki run is covered by Silja Line and Viking Line (Viking also sails via Mariehamn in Sweden to Turku in Finland and return). Birka Cruises and Ånedin-Line link Mariehamn and Stockholm; Eckerö Linjen sails return from Grisslehamn north of Stockholm to Eckerö in Åland most cheaply. Viking also sails from Kapellskär (via Mariehamn) to Naantali or direct from Stockholm.

Wasa Line and Jakob Lines sail between Vaasa (Finland) and Sundsvall (Sweden), Örnsköldsvik in Finland and Umeå in Sweden. Other services across the Gulf of Bothnia are from Umeå and Skellefteå in Sweden to Pietarsaari in Finland (Swedish: Jakobstad) and return, and from Skellefteå to Kokkola (Swedish: Karleby). Kristina also runs from Helsinki to Visby on the Swedish island of Gotland and Kalmar; Kristina and Polferries sail from Helsinki to Oxelösund in summer.

To/From Estonia
Kristina, Sally Lines, Saimaa Lines, Estonia New Line and Tallink sail from Helsinki to Tallinn and return.

To/From Latvia
Kristina operates a round trip connecting Helsinki, Riga (Finnish: Riika) and Visby on Gotland. Visas are needed for Latvia.

To/From Germany
Silja Line runs its Finnjet service from Travemünde to Helsinki (22 hours or more) and there is a bus link between Helsinki and Hamburg. Kristina Cruises has a service to Lübeck (Finnish: Lyypekki) which calls at Visby in Sweden.

To/From Poland
Polferries sails from Gdańsk to Helsinki at prices that vary according to season.

To/From Russia
In private craft you are obliged to report to the nearest customs post on either side, but do not enter border waters without a Russian visa. Sally Lines has a St Petersburg service and Kristina has summer cruises there (see Tours to Russia).

Kristina Cruises (☎ 90-629 968), Korkeavuorenkatu 45, 00130 Helsinki, offers two-day St Petersburg cruises (from 440 mk) and Sally Lines, K5, Terminal, Katajanokka (☎ 90-173 321, Box 127, 00161 Helsinki) offers similar packages without visas (book a fortnight in advance). Kristina also has a Kronstadt cruise package (from 390 mk) and a Vyborg day package (195 mk).

RIVER
To/From Norway & Sweden by Canoe
If you follow the frontier rivers Anarjokka or Tana you will come eventually to Norway. Such crossings require prior permission from the Finnish frontier guard or police. Write for information to the headquarters of the frontier guard: Rajavartiolaitoksen esikunta (☎ 90-161 6511), Box 3, 00131 Helsinki.

Getting Around

The comprehensive travel guide *Suomen Kulkuneuvot* (known as *Turisti*) costs 70 mk at kiosks and bus stations and gives full timetables and connections. It is issued three times a year.

AIR
Finnair, Finnaviation and Karair fly domestic services between big centres (extended in summer) and to Lapland, but not especially cheaply. From Helsinki to Rovaniemi costs 720 mk. But there are discounts such as advance return bookings (conditions apply and so-called Blue Flights are not included) and holiday tickets available from Finnair offices and travel agents. A holiday ticket for 15 days costs US$300 and an under-23 youth ticket costs US$250. Children aged under 12 pay half-price. Buses connect at most airports.

BUS

Buses are the principal carriers of domestic traffic and visitor travel to remote parts. A 500-km journey costs 204 mk. You can arrange discounts if you book (there are 30% savings with YIEE cards). There is little traffic during Juhannus or Midsummer and restricted services operate on other public holidays.

Oy Matkahuolto AB coordinates long-distance and express buses and maintains bus stations with cafeterias offering cheap food. National timetables are available from them and at tourist offices. Return tickets, family tickets and tickets for groups of three or more people can be booked at discount rates (for journeys over 80 km). It is always best to buy in advance to get the benefit of special offers, such as the cheap connections with Silja, Viking and Sally-line ferries when you buy the tickets together.

Reservations are recommended at holidays and weekends, too. Children under 12 years pay half-price, those under four pay nothing. Tourists aged over 65 can buy a senior discount card for 30 mk (bring a pass photo) that attracts 30% discounts. Holiday tickets valid for two weeks and 1000 km cost 280 mk (distributed like notes for 250, 100, 50, and 10 km so you must juggle them to suit journeys as there are no refunds).

Regional private operators and postbuses comprise the national network and charge at similar scales. No bus numbers are shown, so find the numbered berth for your destination at the bus station.

TRAIN

The many rail services do not reach all corners of Finland: the passenger services, mostly in 2nd class, are supplemented and sometimes replaced by buses (which sometimes will accept a rail pass). But they offer greatest economical comfort over the long-distance journeys and frequent intercity services. Rovaniemi is the main northern rail terminus (see Finland, Getting There & Away).

VR (Valtion Rautatiet) the Finnish national railway, has its own travel bureaus at main stations and can advise on all tickets. Special package tickets include 22-day, 15-day and eight-day Finnrail passes (2nd class costs 920, 730 and 470 mk, for 1st class add 50%) and Eurail, Inter-Rail, ScanRail and Nordturist passes apply. You can arrange personal or group tickets for specified periods and 10-trip discount tickets that save the cost of one journey.

There is a 30% discount for holders of Rail Europ S cards. Children under 17 pay half-fare, accompanied children under six pay nothing (and have no seat). You may break your journey once (regardless of changes) on a single ticket if you complete the journey in 15 days, but have the ticket stamped when you break off travelling. Return tickets are valid for a month. Seat bookings are essential on intercity expresses (1st/2nd class costs 25/60 mk). The normal reservation charge is 12/15 mk.

There are two and three-bed sleepers (costing from 120 to 180 mk extra, 60 to 90 mk extra and dearer on weekends) running on long routes. There are special family wagons and car-carriers to northern destinations.

TAXI

Taxi is an expensive travel option at 12 mk for flagfall (up to 25 mk at night and on Sundays) and about 100 mk for a trip from Helsinki to Vantaa airport. You can hail a cab on the street, but it's easier to pick one up at the airport or the station or dial 041 anywhere (5 mk).

CAR & MOTORBIKE

The highway and freeway network is good between centres, although in the forests you can find unsurfaced dirt and beaten tracks. There are many rest areas. Some northern roads are closed until mid-June. Studded or snow-mud tyres are needed in winter and early in spring. Drive only on public roads.

Road Rules

No international licence is needed to drive in Finland. The speed limits are 50 km/h in built-up areas (note the yellow signs with a

FINLAND

town silhouette) and from 80 to 100 km/h on highways (up to 120 km/h on motorways). Traffic keeps to the right and you must use headlights at dusk; snow, fog and rain; in towns and always on the open road. Wearing seatbelts is obligatory in all seats. The blood alcohol limit is 0.05%.

Foreign cars must display nationality and visitors must be fully insured (bring a Green Card if you have one). Accidents must be reported to the Motor Insurers' Bureau (☎ 90-192 51), Bulevardi 28, 00120 Helsinki. There are warnings about elk and deer on the northern roads (see Lapland).

Rental
The smallest car costs about 140 mk per day and 1.9 mk per km. Weekly packages start at about 1800 mk all up, 750 mk for a weekend. A modest middle-sized sedan can cost up to 220 mk per day and 2.5 mk per km.

Purchase
Small 10-year-old sedans and old vans can cost less than 10,000 mk, but anything costing less than 5000 mk is in the bomb class. New cars cost more than 60,000 mk. Second-hand 125-cc motorbikes cost less than 10,000 mk, older 500-cc models cost up to 15,000 mk.

BICYCLE
Daily hire at about 50 mk is common and there are weekly rates. SRM offers a cycling hostel package that takes in the flat south and lakes. New bicycles range from 1000 mk, but good second-hand models can cost as little as 500 kr.

HITCHING
Hitching works well, according to the practitioners, if you set up outside towns before motorway entrances. It might take three days to hitch from Helsinki to Oulu. The best season is from June to October.

BOAT
Lake and river ferries operate mainly during summer. The traffic is densest throughout the Saimaa lake lands and Karelia – a cruise leg is a pleasant and lazy travel variation.

LOCAL TRANSPORT
The only tram network is in Helsinki, but it is the best mode to use there. A fast metro is being developed from one line that serves the area north and east of the city. Otherwise, there are city bus services and networks in Helsinki, Turku and Tampere and local buses in other cities.

Helsinki

The capital did not come to Helsinki (Swedish: Helsingfors) until 1812. The first town was founded in the Vantaa area in 1550. It was later moved and the fortress on Suomenlinna was begun by the Swedes in 1748. It became the seat of the Russian Grand Duchy after falling to the tsar in 1808 when much of the town was wrecked. The monumental buildings of Senaatintori were designed by CL Engel, who recast the town as a city. Helsinki is best known today as the venue for important conventions and meetings on international security and human rights. For travellers it is a small and personal city, lively and not bustling. Its size makes it easy to walk around.

Orientation
Helsinki city occupies a peninsula and there are links by bridge and ferry with the nearby islands Suomenlinna, Korkeasaari, Seurasaari, Lauttasaari, Pihlajasaari, Laajasalo and Santahamina. There are three other city centres, Espoo and the enclosed Kauniainen to the east and Vantaa, with the international airport, to the north.

The city centre is around the main harbour Eteläsatama and market square Kauppatori and the ferry terminals lie either side. The main street axes are the twin shopping avenues Pohjoisesplanadi and Eteläesplanadi and Mannerheimintie.

Small boats can sail into the lake Töölönlahti around Katajanokka. Take a tram from the ferries or square north to the central railway station and square Rautatientori. North of the lake are the towers of the Olympic Stadium, marking the spread of parkland, and the church Kallion kirkko on the hill. A view from there, the stadium tower or from Linnanmäki might help you orient yourself.

Information

Apart from the tourist-office publications there is the excellent tourist paper *Exploring Helsinki* available free at the Jugendsali cultural centre, some cafés and tourist offices. *This Summer in Helsinki* is free and has good information on activities and rentals. Full maps and a street register of the Helsinki region are in volume two of the local telephone directory. To look at university notice boards enter the building at Fabianinkatu 33.

The youth information centre Kompassi, on the lower level of the Asematunneli subway from the main station, is open on Mondays from 9 to 11 am and 2 to 4 pm, Tuesday to Friday from noon to 7 pm (there are some useful travel books there). More information is available at Jugendsali (see Cultural Centres) and the International Youth Club, Humalistonkatu 4.

Tourist Offices The main tourist office of MEK, the Finnish tourist board, is at Unioninkatu 26 and has brochures and literature on most of the country. The City Tourist Office is nearby at Pohjoisesplanadi 19 and is open weekdays from 8.30 am to 4 pm, from mid-May to September 8.30 am to 6 pm and Saturdays from 8.30 am to 1 pm.

It is the best centre for current information, for getting the free guides *Helsinki This Week* and *Helsinki Guide*, and for buying a Helsinki card. This card gives free urban travel, entry to or discounts for many venues in Helsinki and the satellite cities (one day costs 75 mk, two days 105 mk, three days 125 mk; for children under 17 years it's 45, 55 and 65 mk). The card will be worthwhile if you take the free sightseeing tour and are keen to visit the main attractions.

A guide listing venues and bonus offers

for food and accommodation is supplied. Tourist information is also available at Finlandia talo in summer. For information about daily events dial 058.

The Helsinki Tourist Association has an information and guide-booking centre, at Lönnrotinkatu 7, open on summer weekdays from 9 am to 9 pm and at weekends.

There are tourist offices in Vantaa at Unikkotie 2 and Espoo at Itätuulenkuja 9, Tapiola.

Money Most city bank branches are open weekdays from 9.15 am to 4.15 pm. At the airport the counter is open daily from 6.30 am to 11 pm, although a machine operates 24 hours. You can exchange money on the ferries or at the Katajanokka terminal.

The main poste restante opposite the station in Asema-aukio can exchange money later (in summer until 9 pm weekdays, 6 pm Saturdays and from 11 am to 9 pm Sundays). There is also an exchange point on the second level of the big Stockmann department store, which is open Saturdays.

The American Express agency is at Pohjoisesplanadi 2.

Post & Telecommunications The main post office is at Mannerheimintie 11 and is open from 9 am to 5 pm weekdays. The Tele is in the same building and you can call to collect mail from the main post office (door F) until 9 pm weekdays and Sundays, 6 pm on Saturdays. There is a telegram counter. For Helsinki telephone numbers dial 012. The Helsinki directory consists of three volumes, including yellow pages. The telephone code for Helsinki is 90.

Foreign Embassies See Finland, Facts for the Visitor.

Cultural Centres Jugendsali, at Pohjoisesplanadi 19 next to the tourist office, has regular exhibitions, information and literature on cultural themes. The university book café at Mannerheimintie 5 is the centre of student arts and is open from 1 to 7 pm daily,

FINLAND

FINLAND

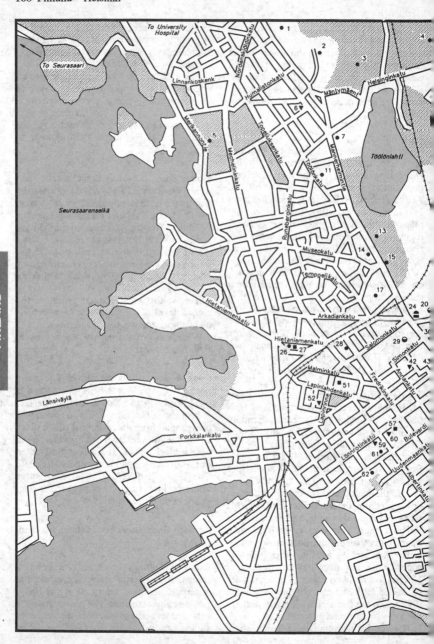

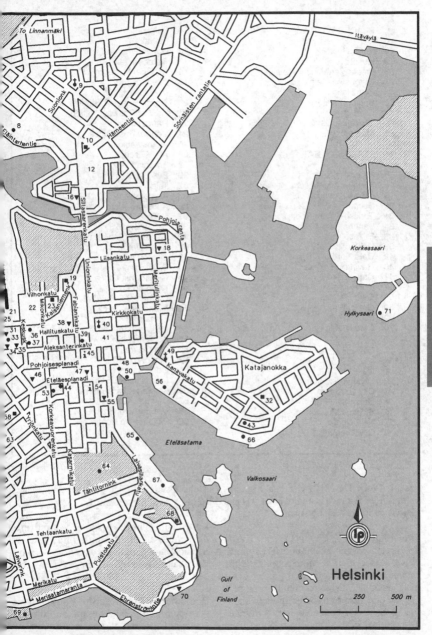

FINLAND

Helsinki

0   250   500 m

Gulf
of
Finland

■ PLACES TO STAY

10 Kallio Hostel
19 Hospiz
23 Irmala, Terminus & Pilvilinna
27 Domus Academica
43 Finn Hotel
51 Satakuntatalo
57 Lönnrot
58 Erottajanpuisto
63 Marttahotelli

▼ PLACES TO EAT

6   Piekka
16 Fanny & Alexander
18 Kolme kruunua
30 Socis
31 Turkish Kebab Room
34 Vanhan Kellari
35 El Taco
38 University Café
42 Café Nordia
46 Ravintola Fatima
47 Café Kappeli
52 Donnagreen
55 Café Caraveo
59 Green Way
60 Lönkan grilli
70 Café Ursula

OTHER

1   Ice Hall
2   Olympic Stadium
3   City Gardens
4   Limznmäkl Park
5   Sibelius Monument
7   New Opera
8   City Theatre

9   Kallion kirkko
11 Finnair
12 Hakaniementori
13 Finlandia talo
14 National Museum
15 City Museum
17 Parliament
20 Airport Buses & Sightseeing
21 Central Railway Station
22 Rautatientori
24 Central Post Office
25 Asema-aukio
26 Alibi Disco
28 Arkadia Disco
29 Bus Station
32 Tele
33 Kompassi
36 Ateneum
37 SAS
39 University
40 Lutheran Cathedral
41 Senaatintori
43 Viking Line
44 Silja Line
45 City Tourist Office
48 Kaupatori
49 Uspensky Cathedral
50 Island Boat Trips
53 Finnair
54 MEK Information
56 K5 Terminal
61 Old Opera
62 Sinebrychoff
64 Observatory
65 Makasiinilaituri Quay
66 Katajanokka Terminal
67 Olympia Terminal
68 Mannerheim Museum
69 Pihlajasaari Boats
71 Maritime Museum

except in July. The MUU Centre at Mannerheimintie 13 is aimed at audiovisual arts and there is an interesting book café.

Travel Agencies The budget agency Kilroy Travels is at Mannerheimintie 5. The Finnish Travel Association at Mikonkatu 25 is the central Finncheque agent and Finnair has a tours desk at Mannerheimintie 96. Ageba Oy, the organiser of package and city sightseeing tours, is at both main ferry terminals. The national B&B agency Lomarengas is at Malminkaari 23C. The Russian state agency Intourist is at Mikonkatu 15.

Laundry There is a laundrette (*itsepalvelupesula*) through the gate at Suonionkatu 1 (open weekdays from 8 am to 5 pm, Saturdays 8 am to 2 pm). Service washes cost 72 mk.

Bookshops The premier bookshop is Akateeminen Kirjakauppa at Pohjoisesplanadi 39 and it boasts stock in 40 languages. Next best (but often cheaper for guide books) is Suomalainen Kirjakauppa, Aleksanterinkatu 23, which has paperbacks and international papers and periodicals. A list of antiquarian dealers is in *Exploring Helsinki*. Kompassi in Asematunneli has rail and travel guides. In the city, try Valtikka at Eteläesplanadi 4 for maps.

Emergency The police have stations at Helsinki's main railway and bus stations (in emergencies dial 002). In Vantaa contact police at the airport (☎ 873 01), in Espoo (☎ 525 41). For duty doctors dial 008, for ambulances and fire brigade 000. English speakers should use the university's central hospital at Haartmaninkatu 4 or the first-aid centre at Töölönkatu 40. The 24-hour pharmacy is at Mannerheimintie 96.

Private doctors are listed in the yellow pages of the telephone directory. For emergency dentistry dial 736 166. For sea rescue dial 000 or 667 766. There is a police lost-property office at the police building, 7th floor, Päijänteentie 12.

Walking Tour
Ask for the *Helsinki on Foot* walking guide, which describes six self-guided routes, or in summer join a guided group for a Sunday walk. The commentary is in English on the tour that leaves at 1 pm from the main cathedral steps in Senaatintori (30 mk). There are also summer walks around Russian Helsinki on Tuesdays. For getting around faster, take the tourist tram (route 3T, normal fares). Do not forget to show your Helsinki card for free entry where this card's accepted. Many museums admit children free.

Art Galleries
The national art foundation of the **Ateneum**, Kaivokatu 2, is the principal gallery and covers Finnish and international art since the 19th century (10 mk, closed Mondays). The international art museum **Sinebrychoff**, at Bulevardi 40 (10 mk), has Continental works and Orthodox icons (nearby is the old and quaint **opera house**). The **city art museum**

at Tamminiementie 6 (10 mk) and the collection of the national painter at the **Gallen-Kallela museum** (see Espoo) are also worthy.

Mannerheim Museum
General Mannerheim was the most prominent of Finnish leaders and his home at Kalliolinnantie 14 is open Fridays, Saturdays and Sundays for tours (20 mk).

Around Töölönlahti
The monolithic **Parliament** dominates the Mannerheimintie entrance to the centre of Helsinki. Alvar Aalto's angular **Finlandia talo** is on the other side of the road, to the west of the railway, by the lake. The **City Museum** is in an adjacent old house (10 mk, closed Fridays).

The new **opera house** site is on the corner of Helsinginkatu, turn right there to reach the tiny and manicured **City Gardens**. The esoteric tubes of the **Sibelius monument** are the centrepiece of the park **Sibeliuksen puisto** off Mechelininkatu. The amusement park **Linnanmäki** on the hill north of the lake is open until 9 or 10 pm daily from late April to September (10 mk, day pass 70 mk).

Churches
Engel's sparse **Lutheran cathedral** marks the main square Senaatintori and the crypt has been opened for exhibitions.

The Orthodox **Uspensky cathedral** above the harbour at Kanavakatu 1 is the more magnificent inside and out (closed Mondays and Saturdays). The style of **Kallion kirkko** on the hill at the end of Siltasaarenkatu defines National Romanticism and **Temppeliaukion kirkko**, hewn into rock on Temppelikatu, symbolises the modern meanderings of Finnish religious architecture.

National Museum
The National Museum (Kansallismuseo), Mannerheimintie 34, has wide collections of Sami and Finno-Ugric ethnology as well as the Kalevala ceiling paintings of Gallen-

FINLAND

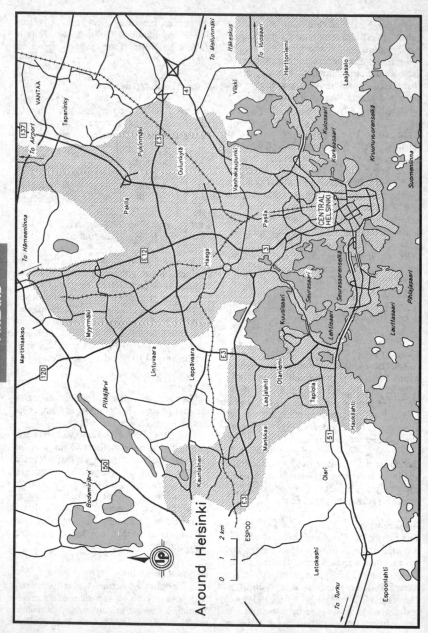

Around Helsinki

Kallela, royal portraiture, interiors and archaeology (10 mk).

Markets

The main produce and craft market is held daily in Kauppatori from 6.30 am to 2 pm (there are evening markets in summer). The flea market in Hietalahden tori (off Bulevardi) is popular locally and also is alive on summer evenings. There are also markets in Hakaniemen tori by Siltasaarenkatu (daily except Sundays).

Suomenlinna

Ferries and motorboats shuttle from Kauppatori and take only 20 minutes to dock at the island (from 16 to 20 mk return or use your Helsinki card). You can ramble in the ruins of the mighty fortress or look around the several museums.

The **Ehrensvärd Museum** (6 mk) is the best one and covers the history of the fortress and its many battles. There is also a separate **Military Museum** and the 1930s German-made U-boat *Vesikko* (5 mk).

Seurasaari

The open-air centre on the island Seurasaari is Helsinki's folk museum. It's open from May to August and a tour is included in the 10 mk entry fee. Seurasaari is also the venue for Helsinki's Midsummer bonfires. Take bus No 24 from the central railway station.

Korkeasaari

The island Korkeasaari has the **zoo** and is best reached by motorboat from Kauppatori (a return ticket costs 13 mk, plus 20 mk entry). Walk over the bridge to Hylkysaari and the maritime museum **Suomen merimuseo** (6 mk, closed weekdays from October to April).

Pihlajasaari

Pihlajasaari is a recreation, walking and bathing centre south of the city (take the motorboat from Laivurinkatu for 18 mk return).

Espoo

The most important sight at Espoo is the pastiche castle **Tarvaspää**, Gallen-Kallelantie 27, the studio and now museum of Akseli Gallen-Kallela (25 mk).

Vantaa

The technology and science centre **Heureka** at Tiedepuisto 1, Tikkurila was the first in Scandinavia. A visit is expensive (admission costs 75 mk) but practical and educational. Take the train (10 minutes from Helsinki's central station). There is an **aviation museum** at the airport (20 mk).

Activities

For local fishing permits go to the specialist store Schroder at Unioninkatu 25 near Pohjoisesplanadi. There are running and cycling paths and 200 km of cross-country ski trails (all facilities are shown on an outdoor and a tourist map). The popular site for sleds is Kaivopuisto. There are also three city-run skating areas. Enquire at the Sports & Outdoor Information Centre, at Kisahalli, Paavo Nurmen kuja 1B. If you go to the pool at Yrjönkatu 21 B, a swim and sauna will cost only 12 mk.

Organised Tours The Ageba coach tours range from 1½-hour tours (60 mk) to 2½-hour lunch tours (from 95 mk). Royal Line and Sun Lines operate city and island cruises for around 50 mk or combination bus and boat tours.

Festivals

The Helsinki Festival takes place over two weeks late in August and early in September, mostly involving scores of music events. The festival office is at Unioninkatu 28.

Places to Stay

The hotel-booking centre (☎ 171 133) in the central station is open in summer from 9 am to 7 pm weekdays and Saturdays and 10 am to 6 pm Sundays. In winter it is open from 9 am to 5 pm weekdays only. Hotel rooms in the city can be booked through the hotel booking centre from 320/550 mk for a

FINLAND

single/double. One-room apartments cost cost 1700 mk a week. The booking charge is 10 mk for hotel rooms and 5 mk for hostels.

Camping *Rastila Camping* (☎ 316 551), on Vuosaari near the bridge, is open from mid-May to mid-September. It charges a basic 20 mk per head or 40 mk per group (take bus No 96 from Itäkeskus).

Hostels *Lönnrot* (☎ 693 25 90), Lönnrotinkatu 16, has fine rooms with shared facilities (singles for 200 mk and doubles for less than 300 mk). The smaller, central *Erottajanpuisto* (☎ 642 169), at Uudenmaankatu 9, charges similar rates. *Eurohostel* (☎ 664 452), at Linnankatu 9, has singles/doubles for 160/230 mk.

Kallion retkeilymaja (☎ 7099 2590), Porthaninkatu 2, has dormitory beds from mid-May to August for 50 mk each. The linked hostels *Irmala*, *Terminus* and *Pilvilinna* (☎ 630 260), at Vilhonkatu 6, charge just over 200 mk for a single room.

The SRM hostel *Stadionin maja* (☎ 496 071) at the Olympic Stadium (enter from Pohjois Stadiontie) has beds in small rooms from 60 to 70 mk and dormitory beds for 55 mk a night. *Interpoint*, Merikasarminkatu 3, is open from July to mid-August and costs 40 mk a bed.

Vantaa The hostel *Vantaan retkeilyhotelli* (☎ 839 3310), at the Tikkurila sports complex, Valkoisenlähteentie 52, is handy to the airport and has doubles for 300 mk.

Espoo The sports institute *Otaniemen Urheilusäätiö* (☎ 460 544), Otaranta 6, has singles and doubles for under 200 mk.

Hotels There are several budget and mid-priced tourist hotels, the best are immediately west of the business district.

City Centre *Marttahotelli* (☎ 646 211), Uudenmaankatu 24, is open all year with singles at 300 mk during weekends (410 mk weekdays) and doubles from 500 mk. It is a pleasant walking distance from most venues.

From late May to August, *Satakuntatalo* (☎ 694 0311), Lapinrinne 1, has singles/doubles for 200/290 mk (discounts with Helsinki card). *Finn Hotel* (☎ 640 904), Kalevankatu 3, is central and reasonably priced charging from 270 to 310 mk a single.

Domus Academica (☎ 402 0206) is a hostel and summer hotel at Hietaniemenkatu 14 with singles from 185 mk and doubles from 245 mk. *Hospiz* (☎ 170 481), Vuorikatu 17, has a range of weekend and summer discounts, including singles for around 300 mk.

Espoo Hotelli *Säästöpankkiopisto* (☎ 887 61), on the beach at Rantamäki 3, Matinkylä, has summer prices from mid-June to mid-August: singles/doubles for around 200/300 mk (take buses No 131 or 132 from the Helsinki bus station).

Places to Eat
A good budget restaurant guide is available from tourist offices or you can look up the computer listings at the Olympic Stadium hostel.

Restaurants *Lönkan grilli*, Lönnrotinkatu 22, has an English menu and reasonably priced meals and specials, but usually closes at 8 pm. *Kolme kruunua*, in quieter Liisankatu near Pohjoissatama, has big cutlets for 80 mk and the cheapest dish costs around 40 mk.

Piekka, Mannerheimintie 68, is the pick of Finnish cuisine places but is mid-priced. A good vegetarian lunch café is *Donnagreen*, at Lapinrinne 2 (closed on weekends).

The *Turkish Kebab Room*, City-käytävä, is a cheap and central Middle Eastern lunch spot. For very reasonable Egyptian fare and dinner specials, try *Ravintola Fatima*, in the plaza off Eteläesplanadi. *Pizzapalati* is a good, central lunch bar and *Arun Thai* offers mid-priced dinners at Lönnrotinkatu 14.

Cafés The up-market crowds go to the swish music venue *Café Kappeli*, Eteläesplanadi 1, and *Socis*, opposite the railway station. *Café Caraveo*, at the harbour on the corner of

Pohjois Makasiinikatu, and *Café Nordia*, Yrjönkatu 28, are modest sandwich and confection houses. The *University Café*, Hallituskatu 13, is open during summer and has cheap cafeteria meals. *Café Ursula*, by the water at Kaivopuistonranta, is best in summer.

Pubs & Clubs *Vanha*, well situated with a balcony at Mannerheimintie 3, draws a young and animated drinking crowd. The bars, buffet, and dance floors of *Fanny & Alexander* near the bridge on Siltasaarenkatu make the door charge quite worthwhile.

Entertainment
Theatre tickets cost around 80 mk, usually more. The theatres are closed in July, when the outdoor summer theatres are popular. Expect to pay 30 mk or more at the cinema. Two discos are *Alibi*, next to Domus Academica, and *Arkadia*, at Fredrikinkatu 48.

Getting There & Away
You can get to Helsinki from anywhere in Europe by air and from almost anywhere in the Baltic area by sea. The ferries are of a high standard and offer many luxuries in entertainment and shopping.

Air Finnair flies to cities, main towns and Lapland, generally at least once a day but several times on such routes as Turku, Tampere, Kuopio and Oulu (see the Finland Getting There & Away section). The airline has an office at Aleksanterinkatu 17 and the main terminal is on Töölönkatu.

Bus Buy your long-distance and express bus tickets at the main bus station off Mannerheimintie (open from 7.30 am to 7 pm weekdays, 7.30 am to 3.30 pm Saturdays and noon to 5.30 pm Sundays).

Train An information booth is at the front hall of the main railway station, which is linked with the metro by Asematunneli. A VR travel agency is in the main ticket hall (open daily) and staff can answer all queries on national services. There is a Eurail counter, international ticket counter and a separate office for buying tickets to Russia.

Regular express trains run daily to Turku, Tampere, Lahti and Lappeenranta and there's a choice of day and overnight trains to Oulu, Rovaniemi and Joensuu. There are also daily trains to St Petersburg and Moscow. Luggage lockers cost 10 mk.

Car & Motorbike The centre of Helsinki is not impossible to drive in, but is a cul-de-sac with few arteries. The motorways are the E3, linking Porvoo and Espoo, to the north and running on to Turku. The E12 runs to Tampere and beyond, the E4 to Lahti.

Boat There are ferries to Stockholm (Sweden), Tallinn (Estonia), Gdańsk (Poland) and various destinations in Germany (see Finland, Getting There & Away). Ferry tickets can be bought at offices, terminals and the main railway station. To some destinations it is not necessary to book unless it is high season, perhaps from late June onwards. Silja is at Eteläesplanadi 14 and the Olympia terminal, Viking is at Mannerheimintie 14 and beside the Katajanokka terminal. Kristina at Korkeavuorenkatu 45 (departures from Makasiinilaituri), Sally Lines at Kluuvikatu 6 (departures from Matkustaja terminal), and Estonian New Line at Fabianinkatu 12 (departures from Olympia terminal).

Getting Around
Single journeys within Helsinki cost 8 mk for adults, 4 mk for children. Buy your tickets at stations or the R-kiosks, which are authorised sellers. Regional single tickets within the HKL transit network are 14 mk. Helsinki card gives you free travel anywhere within Helsinki, Vantaa and Espoo. HKL information and sales offices are open weekdays in Asematunneli, at Hakaniemi metro station and at Simonkatu 1. Tourist tickets are available at 48 mk for 24 hours and 144 mk for five days; 10-trip tickets cost 70 mk.

To/From the Airport Bus No 615 runs to

Rautatientori (14 mk). Bus No 519 links with the metro at Itäkeskus and bus No 521 at Herttoniemi. Buses also run to Asema-aukio, next to the main station, from 5 am to midnight (18 mk).

Bus City and local buses converge on Rautatientori, but Herttoniemi and Itäkeskus are also important hubs.

Train Regional trains run through Espoo and Kauniainen (towards Turku) and Vantaa (towards Tampere and Lahti). If your destination is north of the city, alight at Pasila junction, one stop short of the main station.

Tram This is the fastest and simplest mode for getting around Helsinki's central peninsula, although the city buses work a larger and tighter net. Walk on (centre doors only) and validate your ticket at the stamp port.

Underground The city metro station Rautatientori is linked with the central station by Asematunneli. Services run from about 6 am to 11.30 pm every day. The line extends to Kamppi in the western part of the city and north-east to Mellunmäki.

Taxi It is hard to go far by taxi for less than 70 mk at night and weekends. The general taxi telephone number is 041 or dial 651 766 or 651 866 in Helsinki.

Bicycle Cycling is practical outside the city centre, where there are tracks. You can rent bicycles for 40 mk a day (50 mk for a full 24 hours) or 180 mk a week at the Olympic stadium hostel. Catsport operates a rental centre on the lake behind Finlandia talo in summer.

Boat The main visitors' harbour (☎ 636 047) is on the island Valkosaari at the entrance to Eteläsatama (60 mk a night).

LAHTI

This small city 100 km north of Helsinki is the nearest winter and lake resort, easily reached on the E4 or by regular express trains. The tourist office is at Torikatu 3B, upstairs from the main square. There are several illuminated slalom slopes, ski jumps and tracks at the main sports centre near the centre of town off Hämeen Valtatie and at **Tiirsmaa** and **Messilä**.

Places to Stay The hostel *Lahden retkeilymaja* (☎ 918-826 324), at Kivikatu 1, two km south of the station, is open all year and charges 50 mk a bed or 130 mk a double. *Lahden Koti* (☎ 918-522 173), Karjalankatu 6, has group apartments for 250 mk a person per day.

Karelia

Karelia is a romantic region of lakes, rivers, locks and canals. Consider taking the ferries from inland port to port or try canoeing on lake and rapid. There is 50,000 km of shoreline!

Karelia has a culture which was once Orthodox and has close links over the Russian border. The museums, costumes, clothes and local foods are the traveller's proof of this. Runon ja Rajan tie (the Bard and Border Way), is a notable scenic road that hugs the border from Virolahti on the Gulf of Finland to Kuusamo in southern Lapland.

LAPPEENRANTA

Lappeenranta was a frontier garrison town until the building of the Saimaa canal made it an even more important port.

Information

The city tourist office and tourist service Lappeenrannan Matkailu Oy is in the bus station complex on the corner of Kauppakatu and Myllykatu.

Post & Telecommunications The main post office, at Pormestarinkatu 1, is open from 9 am to 5 pm weekdays. The Tele, in the adjacent building at Raatimiehenkatu 19,

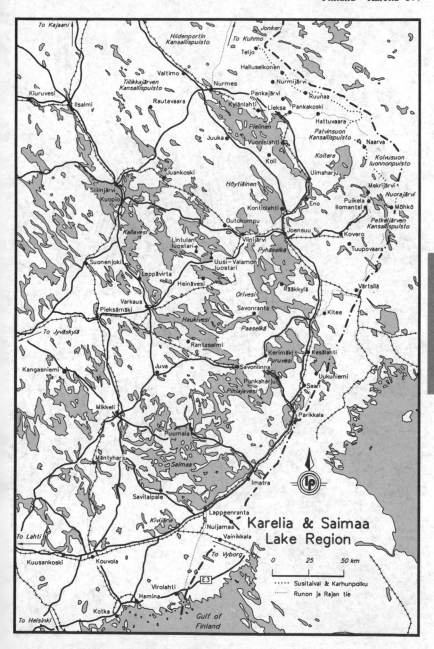

FINLAND

Karelia & Saimaa
Lake Region

0   25   50 km

········· Susitaival & Karhunpolku
········· Runon ja Rajan tie

FINLAND

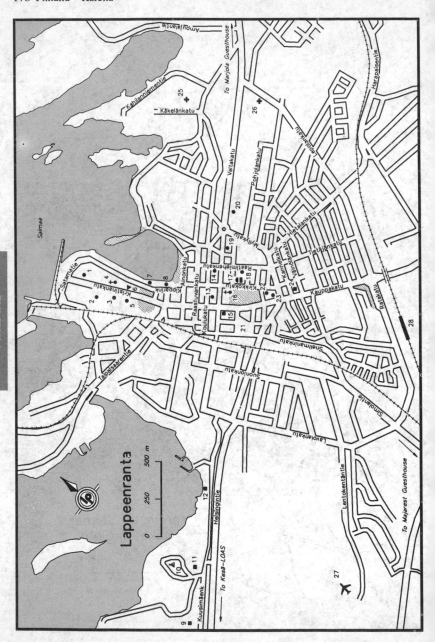

Lappeenranta

1 South Karelia Museum
2 Kristina Workshops
3 Art Museum
4 Orthodox Church
5 Cavalry Museum
6 Kahbila Majurska
7 Passenger Quay
8 *Prinsessa Armaada*
9 Retkeilyhotelli Karelia-Park
10 Huhtiniemi Camping
11 Finnhostel Lappeenranta
12 Hotel Carelia Congress
13 Café Galleria
14 Pifferia
15 Hotel Cumulus
16 Lappee Church
17 Post Office & Tele
18 Police
19 Library
20 Water Tower
21 Pink Burger
22 Bus Cafeteria
23 Bus Station & Tourist Office
24 Matkahovi Guesthouse
25 Hospital
26 Medical Centre
27 Airport
28 Railway Station

cultural reserve has been developed around fortress ruins and 15mk will admit you to all this. **Etelä Karjalan museo**, the South Karelia Museum, is linked with **Viipurin museo**, a celebration of Vyborg, where a large-scale model of the town is being built. There is a **cavalry museum** and uniformed riders still train (for summer tourists) between the fortress and the market square. There is also an **art museum**, the **Kristina studios** and art workshops and the **Orthodox church**.

Saimaa Cruise If you want to see lake Saimaa more closely, consider the Karelia Lines island cruise (from June to mid-August, daily except Mondays) for 55 mk. Ask at the tourist office about the one-hour bus tour of town for 15 mk.

Russia without a Visa From May to September you can book a two-day tour to **Vyborg**, the Karelian city to the south, that includes a trip on the **Saimaa Canal** and Intourist tour of Vyborg (see the Finland Getting There & Away section).

Places to Stay
Camping *Huhtiniemi Camping* (☎ 118 88) by the lake off Helsingintie is a big site charging 60 mk for vans.

Hostels *Finnhostel Lappeenranta* (☎ 155 55), Kuusimäenkatu 18, is open all year and singles/doubles cost 140/230mk a night (take bus No 26). *Huhtiniemi* (☎ 453 1888), on the same site, offers beds for 55 mk in summer. *Retkeilyhotelli Karelia-Park* (☎ 453 0405), the summer hotel in Korpraalinkuja beyond the camp site, charges from 65 to 110 mk from June to August. *Kesä-Loas*, (☎ 453 0900) Karankokatu 4, also has hostel beds in summer.

Guesthouses *Majarest* (☎ 691 110) at Mattilantie 1 and *Matkahovi* (☎ 184 35) at Kauppakatu 52 both offer singles with breakfast for 200 mk or less. Off-season *Marjola* (☎ 241 60), at Mikonsaarentie 15 in Hyötiö five km from town off the

is open until 6 pm weekdays. The telephone code is 953.

Emergency The emergency medical centre is Armilan sairaala on Lepolankatu and the central hospital is Etelä-Saimaan keskussairaala off Käkelänkatu. The ambulance emergency number is 000. You'll find the police (☎ 180 55, emergency 002) at Villimiehenkatu 2, where there is a lost property office.

Things to See & Do
The **Lappee wooden church** (Lappeen kirkko) on the corner of Valtakatu and Kirkkokatu is impressive and follows local fashion in having a separate **bell tower**. The water tower east of the town centre offers a lake view for 5 mk. There is a display of **old radios** and also a café.

Fortress Sector Above the main harbour a

FINLAND

Vehkataipale road past the bridge, costs 280 mk and is equipped for disabled people.

Hotels The *Hotel Carelia Congress* (☎ 522 10), at Marssitie 3, has weekend singles and doubles from 220 mk in summer. Weekend rates (from 250 mk) are also reasonable at the *Hotel Cumulus* (☎ 5781), Valtakatu 31, but prices rise by 150 mk or more during the week.

Places to Eat

The novelty restaurant is *Prinsessa Armaada*, a ship at the head of the harbour, offering some mid-priced lunches. *Pifferia*, Raatimiehenkatu 13, is more modest for meat and pizza, but the best lunch value is at *Café Galleria*, Koulukatu 15, if you are hungry. You can stick to your budget at the bus station cafeteria. *Kahvila Majurska* is a charming tea room opposite the cavalry museum.

Getting There & Away

There are Finnair flights to and from Lappeenranta. Take bus No 34 to the airport. Trains from Helsinki are frequent, as are the express buses. Kristina Cruises runs services to Savonlinna twice a week in midsummer (7½ hours, 130 mk). Karelia Lines is at the passenger quay off Satamatie.

KERIMÄKI

The small town of Kerimäki on lake Puruvesi 25 km east of Savonlinna is noted for its wooden parish **church**, which is claimed to be the world's biggest – it seats more than 3000 people. The church's size was not a mistake (local tradition says 'feet' on the plan was read as 'metres'), but was quite deliberately inflated from original plans when built by local people in 1848. The church's appearance and scale is impressive, the interior is imposing. You'll also find there's a **fishing museum** and a **Winter War museum**.

SAVONLINNA

Savonlinna grew up between lakes at the stronghold of Olavinlinna in some of the prettiest of waterscapes. As a summer spot or opera venue it is unbeatable.

Information

The tourist office and the tourist service, Savonlinnan Matkailupalevu, are at Puistokatu 1. The telephone code is 957.

Things to See & Do

The market at Kauppatori is open from dawn Monday to Saturday all year. Sweet pastries such as *omena-lörtsy*, an apple turnover, are not necessarily cheaper here than in the shops but it is more fun to select and buy them at the market.

There is a two-hour summer cruise (one-way 80 mk, return 110 mk) past the weird **Punkaharju esker** that carries the road and railway more than six km. You can get off at **Retretti**, the biggest arts centre in Finland, and take tours or buy a two-day pass for 70 mk. Several other 1½-hour cruises leave from Kauppatori and the going rate is from 30 to 40 mk per adult.

Olavinlinna The best preserved of medieval castles in the northern countries, Olavinlinna was used by both Swedish and Russian overlords but today is best known for the international opera festival in June. The performances are spectacular and you might pick up a casual ticket for around 100 mk, ask at the tourist office. There is also an **Orthodox museum**. You have to take the hourly guided tour for 14 mk, it is well worthwhile.

Savonlinnan Maakuntamuseo This museum in a main building by the lake near the castle and in the museum ships tied at Riihisaari. It has a Saimaa exhibition and features lake traffic, logging, hunting, fishing and nature. Admission costs 10 mk. There are exhibits about the threatened Saimaa ringed seals (of which less than 200 remain).

Places to Stay

You can camp at *Savonlinna Camping*

(☎ 537 353), at Vuohimäki seven km from town from 66 mk a site.

Malakias (☎ 232 83), a combined hostel and summer hotel over the footbridge from the market station, has four-bed rooms from 290 mk). Staying at the hostel costs 70 mk.

Next door, *Vuorilinna* (☎ 575 0495) is open from early June, and student flats with kitchen and balcony cost only 50 mk, but you need utensils. Hotel singles start at 220 mk. *Hospits* (☎ 224 43), an old building at Linnankatu 20 near the castle, has singles starting at 130 mk and hostel beds for 40 mk all year.

For grace and style, splurge on a stay at the summer hotel at *Rauhalinna* (☎ 523 119). It's a wooden villa 16 km from town or 40 minutes by boat. Doubles cost from 350 to 380 mk (open from June to August).

Places to Eat

The boat *Hopeasalmi* is moored at the market square and serves mid-priced pizza and salads. There is also an outdoor bar. The bar and restaurant *Captain Cook* nearby in Satamakatu is best for fish.

Paviljonki, the restaurant school on the left over the highway bridge at the east end, is 20% cheaper or cheaper than average for restaurant meals. A kebab and rice salad costs 30 mk at *Uskudar Kebab*, Pilikkakoskenkatu 3.

Getting There & Away

Finnair flies to and from Helsinki and regional centres. From Helsinki there are three express buses a day and trains via Parikkala. The main station is a long walk from the town centre, so get off at the Kauppatori platform instead. Kristina sails to and from Lappeenranta twice a week (7½ hours, 130 mk) in July. Roll Line makes a 12-hour trip to Kuopio every day except Mondays during June (220 mk).

KUOPIO

Kuopio, a provincial centre on the lake Kallavesi, is popular for its lakes in summer and snow in winter.

Information

The main tourist office and the tourist service *Kuopion Matkailupalvelu* (☎ 182 590) are at Haapaniemenkatu 17. The office is open from June to August from 8 am to 6 pm (closed Saturdays after 2 pm and Sundays). During the rest of the year it is open only to 4.30 pm weekdays. Other information booths are at the railway station and at the Roll Line building at the quay in mid-season. The telephone code for Kuopio is 971.

Things to See & Do

Walking is pleasant by the parks at **Piispanpuisto** and around the shore at the south end, where the wooden houses and the small Orthodox cathedral (the church's national seat) are clustered. There are indoor and outdoor markets in the main square and summer evening markets by the quay where you can try *kalakukko*, a local fish inside a rye loaf (eaten hot or cold).

Museums Natural history is the focus of **Kuopion Museo**, at Kauppakatu 23, open daily from May to August and closed Saturdays during other months. **Ortodoksinen kirkkomuseo**, at Karjalankatu 1, is the museum of the Orthodox archdiocese with monastic relics rescued from Russia. It is open from May to August and closed Mondays. **Korttelimuseo**, Kirkkokatu 22, and the attached quarter cover three centuries of local history and architecture (open from mid-May to mid-September). A museum at the old customs house **Tullihuone** off Satamakatu features engines from the old lake steamers. There are several two-hour lake cruises costing 40 mk.

Snow & Water Kuopio is popular for snow in winter. Under the spectacular lookout of **Puijo tower** is a **ski centre** with two slopes, a lift and ski jumps (take bus No 6). There are also 300 km of ski trails in the area and permanent snow from November. At the ski centre expect to pay 100 mk to hire downhill equipment for the day; the hostels hire gear more cheaply.

In summer Kuopio's lakes are popular, the

waters are demanding (350 local lakes and countless uninhabited islands) but you can hire all types of craft at Rauhalahti. The marina is at the north end of Satamakatu.

Places to Stay & Eat

The camping area *Rauhalahti* (☎ 312 244) charges from 30 to 55 mk for tenting. The hostels *Tekma* (☎ 222 925) at Taivaan-pankontie 14B and *Jynkkä* (☎ 312 361), seven km to the south, are the least expensive and cost from 50 to 60 mk.

Some hotels offer singles for 300 mk or less and doubles for about 350 mk from June to mid-August. These include *Savonia* (☎ 225 333) at Sammakkolammentie 2, *Hotelli Rauhalahti* (☎ 311 700), by the water off the highway at Katiskaniementie 8 five km to the south, (take bus Nos 20, 21 and 23) and *Sporthotel Puijo* (☎ 114 841) under the tower. Of the restaurants, *Zorba's* in Puijonkatu below Suokatu is fine value and *Rosso Ristorante* at Haapaniemenkatu 24 is the most popular budget option.

Getting There & Away

Finnair (which has an office at Asemakatu 22) flies to the airport, 20 km north of town, several times daily from Helsinki and you must catch a local bus into town. Kuopio is easy to reach by train or bus from Helsinki or Joensuu. The express bus station is north of the railway station and local buses converge on the market square.

Roll Line (☎ 126 744) has services to Savonlinna from early June until mid-August at 9 am daily except Mondays. The trips take nearly 12 hours and cost 220 mk (350 mk return).

JOENSUU

Joensuu is the centre for North Karelia and some keen fishing and still owes much to the timber industries.

Information

The fine wooden building at Koskikatu 1 is the North Karelian tourist office, which advises on all regional tourism. Local fishing permits (20 mk a day, 50 mk a week) and maps are available from the hunting and fishing authority there or at Koskikatu 1i (closed weekends) but check on what you want at the tourist office. The post office is at Rantakatu 6 and the Tele is at Kirkkokatu 22. The telephone code is 973.

Things to See & Do

Joensuu has sights of varied interest, though the quadrangular perspectives of the new town are not appealing. The main **park** and **market** are a relief: big and full of life from 7 am until mid-afternoon from Monday to Saturday. There is an outdoor stage for summer folk music and dance, some local crafts and small-tackle items. Sample Karelian sweet pastries and *Karjalan piirakka*, a rice-filled pasty.

At **Pohjois-Karjalan museo**, the regional museum on the island in Pielisjoki at the bridge, admission costs only 5 mk (closed Mondays). An extraordinary spectacle is the tropical butterfly and turtle garden **Perhos-puutarha** off Lukkotie north of town (open daily, 40 mk per adult). The university's **botanical gardens** at Heinäpurontie 70 have a tropical section (15 mk), and the world's smallest flowering plant.

The best example of the wooden architecture of the older town is the Orthodox **St Nicholas church** (open on summer weekdays) at the north end of Kirkkokatu.

Vintti is a textile workshop near the quay with an exhibition from June to August and some of the work is traditional.

Places to Stay & Eat

The camp site *Linnunlahden leirintäalue* (☎ 126 272) by the lake costs 35 mk per person or 75 mk per family, and there are cabins from 160 mk a night.

The summer hostel *Joensuun Elli* (☎ 259 27), Länsikatu 18, is big and charges from 60 mk for a bed. Singles/doubles cost 190/260 mk (take bus No 3 from the station, daily except Sundays). More modest is the scout-hall hostel *Partiotalo* (☎ 123 381), Vanamokatu 25, costing from 28 to 50 mk (open from June to August). Take bus No 2 to Kaislakatu. The regional sports institute

Itä-Suomen Liikuntaopisto (☎ 167 5076), on Papinkatu, offers singles/doubles for 170/240 mk.

Solid budget eating is available at the bus station *cafeteria*, but *Ravintola Kultapääsky* at Kirkkokatu 25 is a little more refined. *Punatulkku*, Kirkkokatu 21, has Karelian dishes and a good lunch smörgåsbord. *Café Helenna*, Siltakatu 16, has tempting cakes and confections.

Getting There & Away
Finnair, at Kirkkokatu 25, flies to and from Helsinki (45 minutes) a few times a day. You will need 17 mk for the 12 km trip on the airport bus.

Express and local buses come to the main bus station near the railway. The bus station ticket office has all timetables for northbound services.

Direct trains run from Helsinki, but from Savonlinna change at Parikkala, which sometimes means a wait of three hours. The Nurmes Marina ferry runs to Koli (from June to August, twice weekly) and has links to Lieksa and Nurmes. The quay and pleasure boats are at the south end of Rantakatu, past the bridge.

HEINÄVESI
The tiny town of Heinävesi on lake Kermajärvi is popular for lake trout and salmon fishing, get local permits at the tourist office at Kermanrannantie 10. The tall **wooden church** seats 2000 people. The hostel *Pohjataipaleen kartano* is by the river Koivuselkä, about seven km to the south of the station (served by trains from Joensuu and Pieksämäki) off the eastern road to Sävnelahti (turn left after Koivulahti).

UUSI-VALAMO
The monastery Uusi-Valamo, north of Heinävesi, is the centre of Finnish Orthodox culture and has traditions going back 800 years. The founders escaped from old Valamo and Soviet attentions in 1940; the new church was consecrated in 1977. The monks organise tours for 20 mk and courses on their faith, art and life style and you can attend some services. The monastery (☎ 972-619 11) is four km north of road 23 to Joensuu and is open to visitors from 10 am to 6 pm.

You can stay in a single room for 250 mk or in hostel accommodation for 100 or 125 mk (9 pm curfew) and there is a restaurant. Valamo can be reached by boat from Heinävesi or by bus from Joensuu (36 mk, daily except Sundays) or Kuopio. There is a bus direct from Helsinki (a six-hour ride, daily except Saturdays). Make telephone bookings between 8 am and 4 pm on weekdays. There are also boat trips to nearby **Lintula convent** (Lintulan luostari).

THE WOLF TRAIL & PATVINSUO
Susitaival, the path of the wolf, runs 90 km from the **Petkeljärvi national park** (Petkeljärven Kansallispuito) near Möhkö at the border about 20 km east of Ilomantsi (train or bus from Joensuu). There, *Möhkön Lomakylä* offers three-star camping and two-bed cabins for 130 mk a night (six-bed cabins cost 280 mk). The trail ends at the **Patvinsuo national park**.

Marked trails must be followed from March to early July. The birds, forests, and peatlands are protected, although in some parts berries and mushrooms may be picked. Chief among the fauna are moose, brown bear and wolf.

There are seven camp sites and more than 50 km of paths in the park. The hardy hiker will rest and then begin the **Karhunpolku** route farther north (see The Bear Trail). Foreigners may not enter the Russian border zone which, in places, extends four km inside Finnish territory.

LIEKSA
The small centre of Lieksa, lying about 100 km from Joensuu on lake Pielinen, will be important if you are hiking, paddling or sightseeing. It's best to visit from mid-May to September and has transport links, accommodation and services.

Information
Lieksan Matkailu Oy (☎ 205 00) is at

Pielisentie 7 and is open until 4 pm weekdays (from mid-May to mid-August until 6 pm and to 2 pm Saturdays, 3pm Sundays). It has information on bookings, paddling and national parks as well as local hiking maps. Banks are open until 4.15 pm daily and there are supermarkets. The local telephone code is 975.

Things to See & Do

The excellent **Pielisen Museo** is a complex of almost a hundred Karelian buildings and open-air exhibits with emphasis on the livelihood and life of the logging culture (open daily from mid-May to mid-August, 10 mk per adult) and an indoor museum of local war and folk history (open all year, but closed Mondays).

Fishing Fishing for trout, pike and perch is popular and you can buy a week's local permit (see Fishing, in the Finland Facts for the Visitor section) for state waters for 15 mk at the tourist office or upstairs at the forestry and police office facing the main square. Permits for the fishing centre at Ruunaa cost 33 mk for a season (permits are also available at Neitikoski).

Places to Stay

You can get a cabin at the river mouth at *Timitraniemen lomakeskus* (☎ 217 80), open from June to August. A two-bed cabin costs 150 mk, a four-bed one costs from 210 mk and there is space for tents and caravans for 60 mk a site. There's a hostel (☎ 421 10) at Vuonislahti.

Hotelli Puustelli (☎ 255 44), on Hovileirinkatu off Siltakatu, is the comfort hotel charging 300 mk a single in summer and 400 mk at other times. *Hotelli Kulma* (☎ 221 12), at Pielisentie 44 opposite the square, has a few simpler singles/doubles for 150/260 mk.

Getting There & Away

Lieksa is best reached by train from Helsinki or by train or bus from Joensuu (51 mk). The scenic mode of transport is by Nurmes Marina boat from Joensuu (via Koli, 130 mk). The Koli car ferry runs from mid-May to mid-August twice a day for 80 mk return. Cars cost 30 mk extra. Local buses operate from Mönninkatu, near the railway station.

RUUNAA

Ruunaa, 30 km north-east of Lieksa, is a recently developed area for easy hiking. The bus only goes as far as **Pankakoski**, so you might consider a 20-km hike from there as well. A wheelchair path goes a short distance to the rapids.

The trails vary in length from two km to more than 20 km and there are cabins and camp sites such as *Ruunaan Retkeilykeskus* (☎ 975-331 70) from June to September, 35 mk per head, 70 mk per family. The Neitakoski centre offers summer information and some comforts. There are six small rapids. Vehicles are restricted to marked roads.

THE BEAR TRAIL & JONGUNJOKI

The Bear Trail (Karhunpolku) is a hiking trail of medium difficulty leading just over 120 km from the southern shore of lake Suomunjärvi at the north end of Patvinsuo national park (there is an information centre directly across the lake).

This trail leads through the Ruunaa hiking area (see Lieksa) to the Teljo bridge over the river Jongunjoki on the Kuhmo road. There are 19 camp sites or cabins (some with sauna) as well as three main recreational complexes at Neitakoski or Nurmijärvi and Änäkäinen. Orange spots on trees are the waymarkers. Some of the route is through peatland and there are boggy areas. Remember to stay clear of the border zone.

Experienced paddlers can take the river route (70 km) back from Jonkeri to Nurmijärvi: there are 10 landing places, three wilderness huts and almost 40 rapids and falls. Several rapids, especially Hiidenportti, are classed as medium or difficult. High water is in spring; summer waters are rather more shallow. You will need spray covers. Do not shoot first – ask questions and check out the rapids beforehand.

The cabins cost 20 mk per person a night and must be reserved at the tourist office

(☎ 975-205 00) at Pielisentie 7, 81700 Lieksa.

Equipment can be hired locally at Pielisen Erämatkat (☎ 975-218 16) at Pielisentie 40 or in Pankakoski (☎ 331 66), and Erästely Räsänen Ky (☎ 975-561 50) near Nurmijärvi.

Maps & Information

Get the booklet *River Jongunjoki and The Bear's Path* from tourist offices at Joensuu, Lieksa, Nurmes or Kuhmo. There is a tourist map of the river (1:30,000) and two national survey maps. Karhunpolku is covered by a detailed strip map (1:30,000) available from tourist offices.

KOLI

Finns vote the views from the heights of Koli overlooking lake Pielinen as the best in the country. Nurmes Marina has boat services from Lieksa (less than two hours), Nurmes and Joensuu (seven hours) on various days from June to mid-August. A bus goes from the quay to the hilltop about 350 metres above the lake. There are two slalom centres, each with six slopes, and cross-country possibilities.

Places to Stay & Eat

At *Kolin Hüsi Camping* (☎ 973-672 108) there are four-bed cabins for 210 mk a night and camping for 55 mk a night per family.

The hostel *Kolin retkeilymaja* (☎ 973-673 131), at Niinilahdentie 47 near the lake, has beds from 55 to 65 mk. Both are, however, several km to the north and far from buses. *Kolin Loma-aitat* (☎ 973-672 257), Merilänrannantie 42, has cheaper cabins and some huts from 80 to 140 mk.

South-West Finland

TAMPERE

Tampere is Finland's second city and is set between lakes Näsijärvi and Pyhäjärvi. Manufacturing industry found it an ideal site and clustered its factories at the water's edge.

Now many factories have been reconstructed as cultural centres.

Orientation

The commercial centre is either side of the narrows of Tammerkoski and the industrial areas are on its banks; many of the buildings have been restored for community use. The sprawling parklands of Pyynikki face south on to the water and the tower of Näsinneula dominates Särkänniemi and the northern shore.

Information

The city tourist office is at Verkatehtaankatu 2 (closed weekends from September to May). The international youth centre Vuoltsu at Vuolteenkatu 13 provides free information, cheap snacks and free luggage storage. It is open from after Juhannus (Midsummer) to the end of August, from 2 to 10 pm daily. The local transport office is on Aleksis Kiven katu and open daily in summer.

Travel Agencies The Maija-Liisa Lahtinen Ky at Tuomiokirkonkatu 17 sells budget packages and air tickets. See also Tampere, Getting There & Away for more travel information.

Money

Banks are open weekdays from 9.30 am to 4.30 pm, but you can exchange money at some hotels and department stores and at the main post office.

Post & Telecommunications

The main post office is at Rautatienkatu 21, open in summer to 8 pm, on Saturdays from 10 am to 3 pm and Sundays from 2 to 8 pm. The Tele is in the same building, also open to 8 pm and to 2 pm Saturdays in summer. The telephone code is 931.

Emergency

The police building (☎ 195 111) is at Hatanpään valtatie 16 but closes at 3.15 pm most weekdays from June to August (there is a counter at the railway station). Emergen-

FINLAND

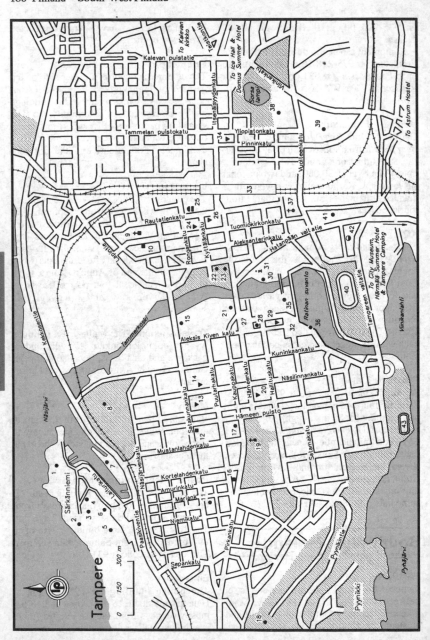

FINLAND

Tampere

Näsijärvi

Pyhäjärvi

Pyynikki

■ PLACES TO STAY		9	Cathedral
		11	Amurin Precinct
10	NNKY Hostel	15	Theatre 2000
12	Interpoint	17	City Library & Science Museum
16	Uimahallin Maja	18	Pyynikki Tower
		19	Aleksanterin Kirkko
▼ PLACES TO EAT		21	Tampere Theatre
		22	Finnair
13	Sokea Sika	23	Wasa Line & Sally Lines
14	Amerikan Eke	25	Post Office & Tele
20	Pizza Taxi	27	Keskustori
24	Foodwell	28	Transport Office
26	Kebab Suleima	30	Verkaranta Precinct
29	Cabaré Oscars	31	Tourist Office
34	Ravintola	32	Laukontori
		33	Railway Station
OTHER		35	Kehräsaari Precinct
		36	Laukontori Quay
1	Amusement Park	37	Orthodox Church
2	Sara Hildén Taidemuseo	38	Tampere-talo
3	Aquarium & Planetarium	39	University
4	Näsinneula Tower	40	Stadium
5	Zoo	41	Police
6	Dolphinarium	42	Bus Station
7	Mustalahti Quay	43	Speedway
8	Häme museo		

FINLAND

cies are dealt with by the central hospital (☎ 606 413) on Teiskontie and the duty doctor (☎ 008).

Things to See

Around the old industrial centre are the restored **Verkaranta** (handicraft) and **Kehräsaari** precincts, which combine textile and gift sales with displays. The **Tampere Theatre** and the **Theatre 2000** complex have also been reclaimed from mills and factories (the annual theatre festival is in late August). The big modern congress centre **Tampere-talo** is near the university.

Museums The city **library** and **Science Museum** give an example of modern architecture (inside is the **Muminlaakso** exhibition based on the children's books of Tove Jansson). The Häme **Regional Museum** is on Näslinna in parklands (10 mk, closed Mondays during the off season). The **City Museum** on the lake in Hatanpään

puistokuja and the **Amurin workers' precinct** (closed Mondays) on Makasiininkatu cover the town's history and working-class heritage.

Särkänniemi The parklands and amusements will fill in any family day (a general pass costs 70 mk for an adult and 45 mk for a child). There is a small **zoo**, **aquarium** (20 mk), **planetarium** and the **Dolphinarium** (30 mk). A trip up **Näsinneula tower** costs 12 mk. The art museum **Sara Hildén Taidemuseo** concentrates on modern and Finnish art and sculpture (10 mk).

Churches The **cathedral** built in National Romantic style features the weird interior frescoes of Hugo Simberg (open from 10 am to 6 pm daily). The small but ornate **Orthodox church** is open from May to August from 9.30 am to 3 pm weekdays.

Aleksanterin kirkko has interesting wooden interiors and the new **Kalevan kirkko** is an angular adventure in modern church architecture (take bus Nos 18, 19 and 20).

Views If you want to see both lakes, leave Näsinnuela. Go up to the older **Pyynikki tower** on the hill west of the centre where there is a café (take bus No 12 or 15).

Places to Stay
There is a hotel-booking centre (☎ 133 155) at Puutarhakatu 168.

Camping *Tampere Camping* (☎ 651 250) at Härmälä is five km south of the city centre (take bus No 1) and costs 60 mk a night.

Hostels The *NNKY hostel* (☎ 235 900) opposite the cathedral costs from 38 to 55 mk a bed during summer. *NMKY Interpoint* (☎ 125 046) at Hämeenpuisto 14 has a several beds from mid-July to mid-August. The hostel *Astrum* (☎ 235 317), Viinikankatu 22, has beds for 80 and 100 mk and rooms for 130 mk a person.

The tourist hotel *Uimahallin Maja* (☎ 229 460), Pirkankatu 10, charges from 70 to 85 mk a bed and offers discounts from late June to mid-August (closed during Juhannus). Its singles/doubles cost from 140/240 mk.

Summer Hotels *Domus* (☎ 550 000) at Pellervonkatu 9 offers singles from 150 to 200 mk from June to August. *Härmälän Kesähotelli*, (☎ 651 250), Nuolialantie 48, has singles/doubles for 130/195 mk.

Places to Eat
There is plenty of choice of places to eat and you can get a booklet listing city restaurants at the tourist office.

Foodwell, on Kyttälänkatu near the post office, is a reasonably priced lunch restaurant and bar. *Cabaré Oscars* at Aleksis Kiven katu 15 offers light lunches, a bar and steak menu. *Kebab Suleima*, on Rautatienkatu facing the railway station, is open late (after midnight at weekends) with inexpensive snacks. *Amerikan Eke*, Näsilinnankatu 17, offers sit-down hamburgers and meat dishes.

Pizza Taxi, at the avenue end of Hämeen-

katu, has moderately priced pizzas with salad. The university's student *Ravintola* on level one in the old building (enter from Yliopistonkatu) offers cafeteria meals from 20 mk.

Sokea Sika at Satakunnankatu 29 is a small, lively, smoky pub where you can drink for quite reasonable prices.

Getting There & Away
Air There are daily Finnair services from the Pirkkala airport (18 km to the south) to all parts of the country including Helsinki and direct flights from Stockholm. The Finnair office is at Kyttälänkatu 2.

Bus The main bus station is near the stadium. Express bus Nos 21 to 25 run from Helsinki and Nos 81 and 82 run from Turku; there are also frequent services to Hämeenlinna and Jyväskylä.

Train Express trains run hourly during the day between Tampere and Helsinki. Intercity trains continue to Oulu and there are trains to Pori, Vaasa and Joensuu. There's a VR agency at the railway station.

Boat Suomen Hopealinja (Silver Line) cruises from Hämeenlinna daily to Laukontori quay and from Mustalahti quay (near Kehräsaari) north to Ruovesi and Virrat (286 mk return). Silja Line is at Keskustori 1, Viking Line at Kuninkaankatu 17, Wasa/Jakob and Sally lines are on Koskikatu.

Getting Around
Bus The city transport and ticket office is at Aleksis Kiven katu 11. The bus service is good and a basic journey costs 7 mk, a day ticket is 25 mk and a 10-ride ticket, 55 mk.

Taxi You can get a taxi at the railway station or phone 970 41.

Bicycle You can use a bicycle for the day free of charge. Collect one (and a bike-path map) from the railway station luggage section, the tourist office, or the Domus and Uimahallin Maja hostels, leaving your full name and passport number. Second-hand bicycles sell for about 500 mk at Inter-Sport Järvinen on the corner of Hallituskatu and Aleksis Kiven katu.

HÄMEENLINNA

The big town Hämeenlinna and its medieval **castle** are at the southern tip of the lake network and 100 km north-west of Helsinki. The castle, off Tampereentie by the water, is open daily and costs 14 mk to visit. The home of composer Jean Sibelius, at Hallituskatu 11, is open daily (5 mk). The tourist office is upstairs at Palokunnankatu 11 (closed Sundays and weekends in the off season).

Getting There & Away Take a Tampere train from Helsinki or express bus No 21, 22, 24 or 25. To Tampere you can take a Silver Line eight-hour cruise to Tampere from June to mid-August for 170 mk one way. The main bus station is on Paasikiventie, over the bridge from the railway station.

TURKU

Turku, the oldest city in Finland and the former Swedish capital (Åbo), is now a big port and the third city of Finland.

Orientation

The ferry terminal is at the south-west end of Turku at the mouth of the river Aurajoki and has its own rail platform; it is best to take bus No 1 to the main square. The cathedral, university and old official sector are on the south-east bank of the Aurajoki and the main railway station is on the north-west side of the river, near the Naantali road.

Information

The main tourist office Kaupungin Matkailutoimisto, at Käsityöläiskatu 3, is open from 8 am to 4 pm weekdays, but the branch at Aurakatu 4 is open to 7.30 pm and in summer at weekends from 10 am to 5 pm.

The Tourist Association of South-west Finland, at Läntinen Rantakatu 13, is open from 8 am to 3.30 pm on weekdays and handles cottage bookings and tours. The

Inter-Rail Café, at Läntinen Rantakatu 47, has youth information and advice and is open on weekdays and Saturdays from 8 am to 10 pm from late June to mid-August. The café, which serves budget coffee and snacks, and a rest centre operate there during the day, but it is not a place to crash. You can store luggage free for a week or more. The Swedish consul (☎ 331 310) is at Kauppiaskatu 5.

Money

Banks are open from 9 or 9.30 am to 4.30 pm, but the exchange counter at the post office is open until 5 pm. You can also exchange money on the ferries.

Post & Telecommunications

The main post office is at Eerikinkatu 21, open from Monday to Friday 9 am to 5 pm (the poste restante is open from 8 am to 8 pm weekdays and 10 am to 4 pm weekends during summer). The Tele is nearby at Humalistonkatu 7. The telephone code is 921.

Emergency

To call police in Turku dial 002, but from surrounding areas dial 921-212 11. The central university hospital (☎ 692 211) is on Kiinamyllynkatu.

Things to See & Do

The cathedral, dating back to the 13th century, and its museum is open daily. The **Orthodox church,** facing Kauppatori, is open every day except Saturday to 3 pm. The two museum ships dominate the river banks. *Suomen Joutsen* (open daily from mid-May to mid-August) costs 10 mk to inspect and the wooden *Sigyn* 15 mk (open in summer except Mondays).

The **Sibelius Museum** at Piispankatu 17 collects musical instruments and exhibits memorabilia of the composer (15 mk, open daily except Mondays to 3 pm, and from 6 to 8 pm Wednesdays).

The **Samppalinna windmill** marks the park sector next to the **Wäinö Aaltonen Museum of sculpture.** The city **Art**

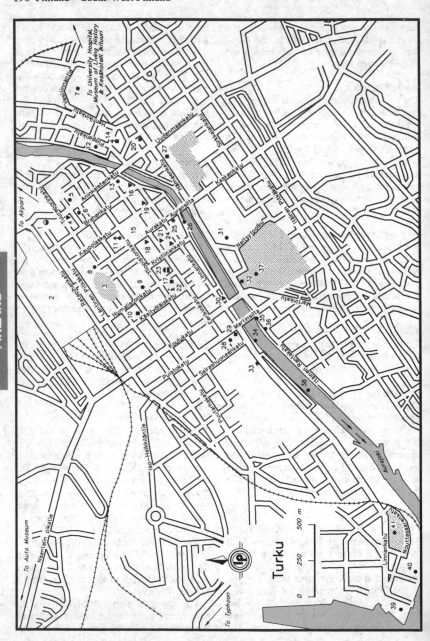

FINLAND

Turku

To University Hospital,
Museum of Living History
& Kesähotelli Ikituuri

To Airport

To Auto Museum

Naantalin pikatie

Iso-Heikkiläntie

To Typhoon

0   250   500 m

■ PLACES TO STAY

3	Matkakievari
9	Aura Hostel
10	Turisti Aula
27	Kåren Hostel
29	Kesähotelli Ikituuri

▼ PLACES TO EAT

4	Amir Kebab
5	Kasperi
16	Verso
17	Al Amir
18	Hesburger
19	Michelangelo Pizzeria
21	Myllärimatti
24	Ristorante Dennis
30	Le Pirate

OTHER

1	Bus Station
2	Central Railway Station
6	Naantali Buses
7	University
8	Art Museum
11	Orthodox Church
12	Sibelius Museum
13	Finnair
14	Cathedral
15	City Transpit (Kiosk & Buses)
20	Åobo Academy
22	Tourist Office
23	Post Office
25	Town Hall
26	Tourist Association & Waterbus
28	Police
31	Swimming Centre
32	Wäinoä Altonen Museum
33	Inter-Rail Centre
34	Archipelago Boats & Water Bus
35	Suomen Joutsen
36	Sigyn Museum
37	Windmill
38	Marina
39	Silja Line
40	Viking Line
41	Turku Castle

FINLAND

Museum is at the head of Aurakatu. The **Museum of Living History** (Kuralan kylämäki), on Kohmontie, is an experimental village open daily from mid-June to early September (take bus No 2). The big car collection at the **TS Auto & Communications Museum**, Pläkkikaupunginkatu 29, is open weekends from 10 am to 6 pm (20 mk). **Typhoon** is a big stadium and a main venue for the Ruisrock festival in the last weekend in June.

Walking Tours There are views of the river, parks and architecture on some beautiful walks. The best walk is along the river banks themselves between the little river ferry and Auransilta, and the park area above it.

A second walk follows the river banks for some time but diverts to the cathedral and old town. These walks are described in a pamphlet available from the tourist offices. Ageba runs a two-hour, 50-mk tour that leaves from the town hall on Aurakatu at 11.15 am daily in summer.

Turku Castle Part of the castle is a museum of old Turku and the remains of the medieval town. The castle is open daily to 6 pm from May to September, to 3 pm in the off season. Admission costs 15 mk (take bus No 1 from Kauppatori).

Market The market at Kauppatori is open from Monday to Saturday 7 am to 2 pm, although there are evening markets in the summer. The market hall at Eerikinkatu 16 is open until 5 pm weekdays and 2 pm Saturdays.

Places to Stay
Camping *Ruissalo Camping* (☎ 589 249), the big summer camping area on Ruissalo west of the city, costs 50 mk a site (take bus No 8).

Hotels & Hostels *Kesähotelli Ikituuri* (☎ 376 111) is a big student block, open to tourists from June to August but closed over Juhannus, and charges 200 mk a single.

Kaupungin retkeilymaja (☎ 316 578), the

city hostel at Linnankatu 39, costs from 50 to 60 mk per bed in shared rooms or dormitories.

Kåren (☎ 320 421), the summer hostel in student accommodation at Hämeenkatu 22, is older and simpler. The guest hostels *Aura* (☎ 311 973), at Humalistonkatu 13, and *Turisti Aula* (☎ 334 484), at Käsityöläiskatu 11, charge from 150 to 180 mk for singles and from 180 to 250 mk for doubles.

The *Hotel Seurahuone* (☎ 637 301), at Humalistonkatu 2, has both singles and doubles from 350 mk.

Places to Eat

There is plenty of choice in fine food and bars in the city. For novelty the boat restaurant *Le Pirate*, moored at Myllysilta, serves food on deck on summer evenings, although there are plenty of boat-restaurants.

Pizzeria Dennis is a reputable pizza and pasta restaurant at Linnankatu 17, though *Michelangelo Pizzeria* two blocks to the east might be a little cheaper. *Verso*, farther on in the courtyard by the river, is a vegetarian restaurant with hot dishes as well as salads (open to 5 pm).

Myllärimatti, on Eerikinkatu, has a variety of reasonably priced lunches and eating at *Hesburger* opposite is better than having takeaway food. *Al Amir Kebab* on Aninkaistenkatu, is a low-budget (sit-down) alternative.

Getting There & Away

Finnair is at Eerikinkatu 4. There are regular Finnair flights to all centres from the airport a few km north of the city. Counters at the Silja Line terminal open on summer mornings and evenings to greet ferry passengers.

Bus The express bus station is near the railway bridge at the north end of Aninkaistenkatu. International bus services such as Eurolines' from Copenhagen and Stockholm link up with the ferry services. Express bus No 1 runs to Helsinki and No 2 to Helsinki via Vantaa airport. There is a special express to Tampere or you can take

bus No 79, 81 or 82. Bus No 4 runs to and from the airport.

Train Express and local trains run frequently to and from Helsinki and Tampere and there are long-distance services to Lapland and towns such as Joensuu. Most trains continue to the ferry platforms.

Boat The Silja and Viking ferries come from Stockholm and nearby ports and Mariehamn (see To/From Sweden in the Finland Getting There & Away section). Silja and Viking lines have offices at the harbour and in the Hansa shopping centre off Aurakatu.

Getting Around

The city transit office has a kiosk on Kauppatori open in summer (from 8 am to 8 pm weekdays in May and August, from 9 am to 3.30 pm mid-June to July).

Bus The city and regional bus services (both gold and blue buses) are frequent and you pay 7 mk for a basic journey or 20 mk for a day tourist ticket. The bus stations are at Kauppatori and the ferry terminal.

Taxi Go to Kauppatori or dial 333 333 for a taxi.

Bicycle The cheapest bicycle hire is at the Inter-Rail Café for 10 mk per day, although you leave a deposit.

Boat Archipelago cruises and the steamer to Naantali depart from Martinsilta bridge and waterbuses leave from Auransilta.

NAANTALI

Naantali, a small port town 18 km from Turku, developed after the founding of a convent in the 1440s, although only the **church** (open daily in summer, on Sundays from noon to 3 pm in the off season) remains to dominate today.

Naantali is also the main venue of an international chamber music festival in the second week of June (for details and bookings write to Naantalin Matkailu Oy, Kaivotori 2, 21100 Naantali).

Walking is pleasant among historic houses. The gardens of the presidential palace **Kultaranta** on Luonnonmaa are open on Friday evenings in summer.

Several types of harbour for small boats are available and there is a summer tourist office at the square near the marina.

Getting There & Away Take express bus No 85 from Turku, which terminates at the harbour. For a day trip take the steamer from Turku at 12.15 pm daily in summer.

SEVEN CHURCHES ROAD

This is a popular road tour that takes in the historic churches at **Raisio**, **Masku**, **Nousiainen**, **Lemu**, **Askainen**, **Naantali** and **Merimasku**. The road from Merimaksu then passes south to the 14th-century vaulted and painted church at **Rymättylä**. Ask for a map at tourist offices.

Åland

Åland (Finnish: Ahvenanmaa) is a semi-autonomous, demilitarised and nuclear-free island zone with its own assembly, the Landsting, and its own language, Swedish. This situation goes back to a League of Nations decision in 1921, after a Swedish-Finnish dispute over sovereignty came to a head.

Local autonomy and limited legislative powers are guaranteed by the Finnish parliament; a separate delegate goes to the Nordic Council. Åland took its own flag in 1954 and has issued stamps since 1984. There is no separate customs authority. The telephone code is 928.

The islands are popular for boating and cycling, camping and cabin holidays. There are medieval parish churches, ruins and maritime villages. The islands are a popular place for celebrating over the Midsummer weekend. Nature is prized and a more restricted outdoor code operates in Åland.

Fishing waters are separately licensed and you should ask about appropriate fishing cards at tourist offices.

The centre for Åland is Mariehamn, a port with two harbours, in the south of the main island group. You can take your wheels almost anywhere in the islands using the bridges or the network of car and bicycle ferries.

Finnair flies to the airstrip two km northwest of Mariehamn. Eckerö, a port at the western edge of the islands, receives ferries from Sweden.

Information

The main tourist office is Ålands Turist-information (☎ 273 00), Storagatan 11, Mariehamn. Ålandsresor AB is at Storagatan 9. Write to Box 62, 22101 Mariehamn, to ask about cabins all over Åland. See also the following Åland Getting There & Away section.

The telephone code for the islands is 928.

Getting There & Away

Air Finnair is at Skarpansvägen 24 in Mariehamn and offers flights which leave three or four times daily from Helsinki and Turku and twice daily from Stockholm. AB Skärgårdsflyg has services from Naantali.

Boat Viking Line is at Storagatan 2, Silja Line at Torggatan 2, Eckerö Linjen at Storagatan 8 and Birka Line at Östra Esplanadgatan 7 in Mariehamn.

Viking and Silja lines have daily ferries to Mariehamn from Turku and Naantali as part of their links with Stockholm: you can stop off 'between' countries.

Birka Lines also sails from Stockholm, Eckerö Linjen sails from Grisslehamn (north of Stockholm) to Eckerö and Viking sails from Kapellskär (north of Stockholm). Packages offer hotel accommodation.

Getting Around

The speed limit on the roads in Åland is strictly 70 km/h. Within the eastern archipelago you can use free inter-island ferries, but to or from the central island group or to the

FINLAND

FINLAND

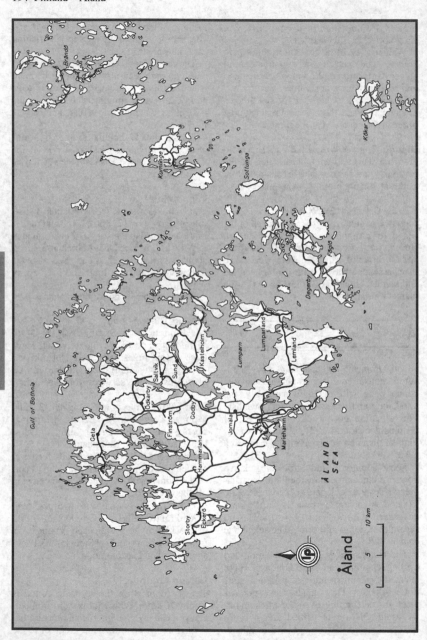

Åland

Finnish mainland you must pay 105 mk for cars and 42 mk per person. For details or timetables ask Ålands Turistinformation or Ålandstrafiken at Strandgatan 25, Mariehamn. The five main buses run from Mariehamn to Eckerö (cars free), Geta, Saltvik, Vårdö and Långnäs at fares up to 27 mk. Cycling is a great way to tour the strange landscape.

MARIEHAMN

Mariehamn's small port helped write some impressive chapters in maritime history. It retains its village flavour even with a rush of summer tourists.

Information

The banks are open from 10 am to 4.15 pm weekdays. Later exchange is possible at the main post office in Torggatan from 9 am to 5 pm weekdays (open late Thursdays in the off-season from September). There is a poste restante service. The Tele is behind the post office and at Nygatan 6.

You'll find the police on the corner of Styrmansgatan and Servicegatan. The hospital (☎ 5355) is on Norragatan. For sea rescue, phone 114 44 or 000.

Luggage storage is for 24 hours only in the lockers at the ferry terminal, but Ålandstrafiken will store backpacks for 5 mk a day or 10 mk for longer. Several supermarkets open until 8 or 9 pm in summer and at weekends. The cheapest ride from the ferry terminal is on the road train to the centre of the town (10 mk).

Consulates

The Swedish Consul is at Norragatan 44 and Russia, Germany, the UK and the Nordic countries all maintain consuls in the town.

Things to See & Do

The stalwarts of Åland are mariners and the **Maritime Museum** at Västra Hamnen, a sort of folk museum of fishing and maritime commerce, is devoted to them. Admission costs 13 mk. Nearby the ship *Pommern* is moored and you can clamber through it for 13 mk, it's open from May to October.

Trade and crafts are covered by the **Köpmannagården** in Parkgatan (free, open weekdays from 1 to 3 pm in summer). Of more general interest is the fine **Ålands Museum** and **Art Museum** at the east end of Storagatan (7 mk, closed Mondays from September to April).

The summer amusement park **Ålandsparken** is above the ferry terminal and open to 9 pm (entry costs 20 mk). Canoes can be hired at Ro-No on Havsgatan for 100 mk a day, and bicycles for 33 mk from there or at Eckerö Linjen. For local fishing licences ask at the tourist office.

Places to Stay & Eat

Gröna Udden (☎ 190 41) is the main camping ground and charges 10 mk a head per night.

The hotel boat *Alida* (☎ 137 55) is moored at the north end of Östra Hamnen and charges from 60 mk per bed in a two-bunk cabin. There are also reasonably priced fish dishes at the restaurant.

Gästhem Kronan (☎ 126 17), Neptunigatan 52, charges singles/doubles 180/265 mk and is open from mid-May to mid-August. Visitors' small-boat harbours are available on both sides of the town from 50 to 60 mk per night.

Café Iwa, Torggatan 12A, has sandwiches, cakes and Åland 'pancakes' (actually a sort of sweet quiche) for 15 mk.

SUND

In the municipality of Sund, about 20 km north-east of Mariehamn (take bus No 4), is the medieval ruin **Kastelholm**, now under restoration (12 mk). Nearby is **Jan Karlsgården**, a farm from last century open from May to September (free). Further east, the ruins of the Russian fortress at **Bomarsund** are always accessible. The jail museum of **Vita Björn** is open daily from May to September and is free.

ORRDALS KLINT

Hiking to the eminence Orrdals Klint above the shore north of Saltvik is popular and there is a bare but free hut for use (ask at the Mariehamn tourist office).

ECKERÖ

The westernmost municipality of Eckerö is linked by ferry to Sweden. The ferry terminal is at Storby and there is a bank, shops and tourist office at the harbour. The small-boat harbour is just to the north. Post offices are at Storby and Kyrkoby. Bus No 1 runs to Mariehamn. The medieval **Eckerö church** in the middle of the island has beautiful interior paintings.

KÖKAR

The island of Kökar is distant from the main Åland group and its sleepy villages are more quaint. The main sight is the old abbey of **Hamnö** where there is a museum of the island and its port. There are ferries four times a day from Långnäs, 28 km from Mariehamn on Lumparland. There are three visitors' harbours.

North-Central Finland

OULU

Oulu, a technologically oriented industrial centre of north Finland, was founded in 1605 and rebuilt after a fire in 1822.

Information

The tourist office is at Torikatu 10 (enter at the side), but is open only until 4 pm and is closed weekends, except in July when it's open weekdays and Saturdays to 6 pm and Sundays to 4 pm. VR has a travel bureau at the station (open weekdays to 5 pm). Supermarkets are open late on weekdays and to 6 pm on Saturdays and there is a full range of banks. July is the peak tourist season.

Post & Telecommunications The post office and Tele are together at Hallituskatu 36. The post office is open weekdays from 9 am to 5 pm and the Tele to 8 pm weekdays and 2 pm Saturdays. The telephone code is 981.

Emergency Emergency medical care is available at the university's medical centre off Kajaanintie east of the E4; the main hospital is to the north of this. The phone number for emergency care is 008. You'll find the police on Ratakatu behind the railway station, call 002.

Things to See & Do

Seeing over **Tietomaa**, a science and technology centre designed for visitors, could

■	PLACES TO STAY
20	Hotelli Turisti
21	Lanamäki
27	Välkkylä hostel

▼	PLACES TO EAT
13	Donér kebab
14	Musta Orkidea
15	Sultanhemmet
17	Café Marteija
18	Katri's Green Piece
24	Fantasia

	OTHER
1	Water Bus
2	Art Gallery
3	Tietomaa
4	Castle Ruin
5	Provincial Museum
6	Library
7	Theatre
8	Cathedral
9	Kauppatori
10	Tourist Office
11	Quay
12	Market Hall (Kauppahalli)
16	Finnair
19	Post Office & Tele
22	Railway Station
23	Police
25	Park
26	Bus Station
28	Swimming Centre
29	Indoor Rink
30	Sports Centre
31	Orthodox Church
32	Concert Hall

FINLAND

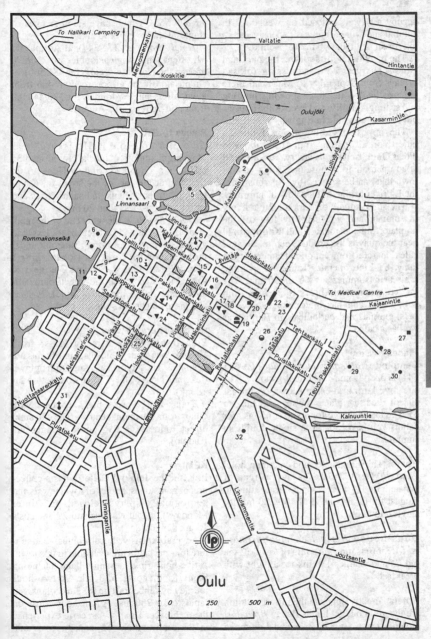

FINLAND

Oulu

0   250   500 m

occupy a day. It's closed on weekdays in autumn and winter, but it is expensive at 50 mk for an adult and 40 mk for a child.

The **provincial museum** in the parkland Ainola charges 5 mk admission (closed Fridays from September to May) and there are excellent collections showing hunting and sealing, folk-life and even dolls' houses, but there is no guide in English.

The imposing **cathedral** has Finland's oldest portrait (dating from 1611, about as old as Oulu itself) in its vestry. **Turkansaari** is an open-air folk museum 13 km east of town that can be reached by waterbus from the E4 river bridge or bus No 4 in summer.

The small square on Kirkkokatu is lively in summer and you can buy fish off the hotplate, but the market hall **Kauppahalli** near the quay is the produce centre. Several cafés operate from antique steamers at the quay. ST-Line operates four-hour evening cruises in summer for 60 or 80 mk. The modern **provincial library** is a refuge from spring rain and has international newspapers, journals and periodicals in English as well as a café.

Places to Stay

Camping *Nallikarin leirintäalue* (☎ 541 541) is open from May to mid-October. The site, five km north-east of town on the far side of Hietasaari, faces the sea (take bus No 5). The basic charge for a site is 65 mk, for cabins you pay 130/190 a single/double in summer.

Hostel The Finnhostel and summer hotel *Välkkylä* (☎ 377 707) is at the rear of Kajaanintie 36 and is open from June to August for 65 mk a bed or 170/220 mk for singles/doubles.

Guesthouse *Kempeleen moottorimaja* (☎ 515 566) is nine km south of town off the old E4 and charges 130 mk for a night with breakfast.

Hotels Directly opposite the railway station are the good budget hotels *Bed & Breakfast Hotelli Turisti* (☎ 377 233) and *Lanamäki*

(☎ 379 555), which have summer rates of singles/doubles 195/260 mk.

Hotel Apollo (☎ 374 344), at Asemakatu 31, offers some singles/doubles for 210/290 mk and the *Hotelli Vihiluoto* (☎ 481 500), at Oulunsalo off the airport road six km from town, offers singles/doubles for 320/440 mk from mid-June to mid-August.

Places to Eat

Café Marteija, on Hallituskatu near Mäkelininkatu, offers lunches for around 35 mk and a cheap second coffee. *Musta Orkidea*, at the end of the street on Kauppurienkatu, has salads and sandwiches and coffee will cost less than 20 mk.

Donér Kebab, at the other end of the mall, also offers grills and fast kebabs for less than 40 mk. *Fantasia* is a pizza restaurant under the arcade on the corner of Isokatu. *Katri's Green Piece* (closed Sundays), is next to Café Marteija and is all-vegetarian. *Sultanhemmet* on Asemakatu is Middle Eastern and more elegant in style.

Getting There & Away

Finnair has many direct flights: from Helsinki one-hour 'blue' discount flights are available. The airport is 15 km south of town (take bus No 9 or the Finnair connection for 18 mk).

Trains and express buses connect with Oulu from all main centres. The Helsinki direct train takes 9½ hours (longer via Kuopio).

KEMI

In Kemi the **Jalokivi Galleria** has a collection of gemstones, copies of royal jewels and geological displays (closed on winter Mondays). It is at Kauppakatu 29 and costs 15 mk per adult.

Several expensive but all-inclusive adventure tour packages are available in this town. A five-hour trip to a Sami village, including Sami food, costs 550 mk. A two-hour journey by rubber raft on the Kukkolankoski rapids costs 280 mk. A four-hour cruise on the icebreaker *Sampo* – an eerie experience in the semi-twilight of January, costs 600 mk. Ask at the tourist office (☎ 9698-199 469), Kauppakatu 22.

Getting There & Away
See the Finland Getting There & Away section for details on how to get to Sweden.

KUUSAMO
Kuusamo is a frontier town about 200 km north-east of Oulu and about the same distance east of Rovaniemi at the north end of the Bard and Border Way (see Karelia). The tourist centre Karhuntassu is at Torangintaival at the west end of the town and distributes an excellent free guide.

The **Ruka** skiing centre is about 25 km north of town. Lift cards for the 25 slopes cost around 100 mk a day, hire of basic gear is 80 mk. There is also a monster toboggan slope. There are many possibilities for hiking and fishing and many fast, rugged rapids on the river **Kitkajoki**.

Places to Stay
The local hostel *Kuusamon Kansanopisto* (☎ 989 221 32), at Kitkantie 35, is open only in summer and beds cost from 55 to 110 mk. *Hotel Martina* (☎ 989-852 2051), at Ouluntie 3, has singles for 280 mk. Good rooms are available at the guesthouse *Kuusamon Matkustajakoti* (☎ 989-852 2150), at Ouluntie 6, for 130 mk (100 mk for subsequent nights).

Getting There & Away
Finnair flies from Helsinki weekdays (3½ hours) and from all Karelian centres to the Kuusamo airport, which is four km to the north-east of the town centre.

Buses run daily from Kajaani, Oulu, Kemijärvi and Ivalo as well as Ruka and Ristikallio. In winter a special Helsinki train connects with bus No 189 at Taivalkoski.

KARHUNKIERROS
The circular Karhunkierros trail (with northern and southern branches which join at the rapids at Taivalköngäs) covers 75 km of rugged cliffs, gorges and suspension bridges from Rukatunturi, 25 km north of Kuusamo

(take the Ristikallio bus or bus No 189) to the Oulanka national park.

The hike to the information centre at Kiutaköngäs (open from June to August) can take several days but there are shelters and free overnight huts on the signposted and blazed trail, and there is a holiday centre at Juuma. The border zone is restricted and fires are permitted only at established sites on the trail.

For information and to check on trail huts and maps, go to Matkailukeskus Karhuntassu at Torangintaival 2 in Kuusamo.

KAJAANI
Kajaani, the home of Lönnrot, was a vital stronghold in the 18th century (until its castle was ruined by the Russians). The **castle ruins**, at the bridge over the river, are the main sight.

The beautiful wooden **church** on the corner of Pohjolankatu and Kirkkokatu is a rare example of neo-Gothic architecture. The **regional museum** on the corner of Asemakatu is open from noon daily except Mondays.

Places to Stay & Eat
The Finnhostel *Retkeilyhotelli Kajaani* (☎ 986-257 04) is at Oravantie 1 and is open from June to August; doubles cost 180 mk. *Matkustajakoti Nevalainen* (☎ 986-222 54), at Pohjolankatu 4 near the station, offers bed and breakfast for 160/215 mk for a single/double.

Getting There & Away
Kajaani can be reached by daily Finnair flights from Helsinki or from other centres. Trains connect with Kuopio and express bus No 171 runs from Joensuu and bus Nos 186 and 187 run from Oulu (No 187 continues to Kuhmo).

SUOMUSSALMI
The small town of Suomussalmi, off the E5 and 100 km north-east of Kajaani, was the scene of Winter War battles with the Russians. The road **Raatteen tie**, which runs 40 km to the border zone, was the battlefield and

FINLAND

the most eloquent of several monuments. At Raate there's a **guardhouse museum**.

Lapland

The Lapland region north of the Arctic Circle offers the spectacle of constant daylight (or, in winter, darkness) and the chance of seeing the Northern Lights (Aurora Borealis). The forests around Rovaniemi give way to tundra and marshes to the north. The lake Inarijärvi is popular winter and summer.

The annual average temperature in Rovaniemi is about 0°C, but in July it is almost 14°C; the December average minimum in Ivalo is almost -15°C. The *ruska* period from September produces exceptional autumn colours and in the far north *kaamos*, the season of eerie bluish light, begins late in October. There are many elks and reindeer but brown bears and the native lynx are now rarer, with only a few hundred of each.

The Sami People

There are fewer than 5000 Sami people and their living culture is best seen in the church village of Inari. Reindeer farming, fishing and forestry employ most people, although there is a tourist industry in handicrafts (see also Sweden, Facts about the Country).

Dangers & Annoyances

Floods (July is usually the wettest month) can affect hiking conditions in boggy lowlands and destroy trail bridges.

Mosquitoes are annoying in June and early in July. Wolves are not common but are likeliest in winter. Do not, as a matter of common sense, go walking alone in the wilderness. If you are hiking or skiing cross-country leave your plans with local police or the tourist office. Do not leave or burn rubbish – compress it and take it with you. Do not underestimate the risk of fire in this area during summer.

Driving hazards Beware of the elks, which can be found on or by roads (often in the morning and at dusk) and reindeer, which do not respond to motor horns. Badly injured animals should probably be destroyed and it is best to seek advice from police, or ask for help at a border post or at a nearby house.

Police must by law be notified about accidents involving elks. The same is true in the case of reindeer, which will have an owner who can claim from the state. Report the accident – only if you *don't* might there be legal trouble. To take meat is illegal (elk hunting is possible only if you have a permit).

It is recommended you carry studded or mud-snow tyres (coded MS) from November to March. Studded tyres can be hired at Isko stores from 650 mk for up to two weeks.

ROVANIEMI

Rovaniemi is the gateway for tourists entering Lapland and its skiing makes it a year-round destination.

Information

The city tourist office, at Aallonkatu 1, is open until 7 pm daily in summer (to 4 pm weekdays from September to May). Ask there about ski, snowmobile and bicycle tours. Lapland Travel Ltd, Maakuntakatu 10, 96100 Rovaniemi, organises many tours for winter and summer (closed weekends). The area telephone code is 960.

All national banks are represented and the town's branches are generally open from 9.30 am to 4.30 pm weekdays. They offer full exchange and credit-card services. The main post office is on Rovakatu and the Tele is at Ruokasenkatu 10.

The emergency medical centre (☎ 322 41) is at Sairaalakatu 1 and the central hospital is at Ounasrinteentie 22. You'll find the police station at Hallituskatu 1.

Things to See & Do

The **Ounasvaara** slalom centre is three km above the town. A lift ticket costs 75 mk for a day and gear hire, operating from mid-December to May, costs 70 mk. In summer you can bobsleigh for 10 mk.

The divisions of **Lapin maakuntamuseo**, at the side of the Lappia-talo at Hallituskatu 11 and at Poromiehentie 1A, include town history but the main exhibits deal with Sami culture and costumes (6 mk, open from May to August except Mondays). **Lapin metsämuseo**, Metsämuseontie 7, is a comprehensive open-air museum of forestry (take bus Nos 3 and 6 from Hallituskatu).

To see the **reindeer farm Napapiirin Porofarmi**, six km north-east of the town, you must book at the city tourist office (☎ 392 511). You can also book the river cruise there for 150 mk. Bus No 8 will take you to the **Arctic Circle marker**. The **Napapiiri Santa Claus complex** is near the airport.

Places to Stay

The camping at **Ounasvaara** (☎ 606 06), Taljatie, costs 55 mk a site. The hostel *Tervashonka* (☎ 344 644), Hallituskatu 16, is modest for 40 to 67 mk a bed. *Hotel Aakhenus* (☎ 220 51), Koskikatu 47, is a moderately priced summer option from 250/340 mk a single/double.

Places to Eat

Rinteenkulma, Koskikatu 25, is a good lunch cafeteria (open to 4 pm, closed Sundays). *Kisälli*, Korkalonkatu 35, is similar but open weekdays to 4 pm. At the *Union service station*, Lapinkävijäntie 37, is a roadhouse open to 9 pm daily. A cosy pub restaurant is *Roy Pub* at Maakuntakatu 24.

Getting There & Away

Air Finnair has several daily flights from Helsinki, Turku, Tampere and Oulu and there are connections to Ivalo, Sodankylä and Enontekiö (Ounas-Pallas national park). The bus connection from the airport costs 16 mk.

Bus Express bus No 190 to Rovaniemi runs from Oulu and Kemi (daily, except Sundays). Bus No 201 runs from Kajaani and No 202 takes you to Ranua on Fridays (also Saturdays from February to April and in summer). Eskelisen Lapin Linjat runs the express buses to Muonio, Ivalo and Kilpisjärvi and into Norway.

Train The train from Helsinki and Oulu usually terminates in Rovaniemi and you will probably take buses farther north or to Kemijärvi (there are only two train connections daily) – here your rail pass will not count. A VR travel office, at the railway station, sells tickets of all types.

RANUA

The Ranua wildlife park, 85 km south of Rovaniemi, regards itself as the northernmost of all such parks – certainly it offers your only chance to see a polar bear and probably the only chance to see a lynx in the wild in Finland. Express bus No 202 runs there daily except Sundays from Rovaniemi. The inevitable Santa village is attached.

SODANKYLÄ

Sodankylä, on the southern boundary of permanent winter snow, is best known for the Midnight Sun International Film Festival in mid-June. Each film costs 25 mk and casual tickets are available from Sodankylän Matkailu Oy (☎ 9693-134 74), Jäämerentie 9, 99600 Sodankylä. The summer hostel *Lapin opisto* (☎ 9693-21960), which is off the Savukoski road, fills up at this time. It costs 55 mk for a bed.

IVALO

Ivalo is the centre of the Inari lake district, where there is midnight sun from 23 May to 22 July and polar night from 3 December to 9 January. The tourist office is at the bus station in Piiskuntie, ask here about hiking trails and fishing permits for the area. There are banks in the town which are open until 4.15 pm weekdays.

Places to Stay

The *Hotelli Ivalo* (☎ 9697-219 11), Ivalontie 34, has singles/doubles for 300/360 mk from June to August, at other times it's dearer.

Getting There & Away

Air Finnair flies to Ivalo airport from several

FINLAND

centres daily. Some services involve changes at Oulu or Rovaniemi.

Bus Ivalo is best reached by express bus Nos 208 and 209 from Rovaniemi (or Norway) or bus No 189 from Kemijärvi.

SAARISELKÄ & URHO KEKKONEN NATIONAL PARK
Saariselkä is a ski resort 30 km south of Ivalo and hiking and cross-country trails lead into the Urho Kekkonen national park. This area is becoming a very popular up-market destination. For more details of trekking routes see Lonely Planet's *Finland – a travel survival kit* by Marcus Lehtipuu & Virpi Mäelä.

Just north of the Saariselkä region is Raja-Jooseppi, a border-crossing point to Russia, from where it's 250 km by road to Murmansk.

INARI
The lakeside settlement of Inari is a place to see living Sami culture. The express bus No 209 runs from Rovaniemi through Inari to Norway two or three times daily (except Sundays). Banks and the post office are open from 9.30 am to 4 pm daily.

Things to See & Do
Saamelaismuseo is a cultural centre on the shore of Inarijärvi run by the Sami community in summer (15 mk). It covers the craft, reindeer-farming and fishing traditions of this people. In summer, boat trips leave for ancient cult sites around the lake and you can see the prominent island of Ukko, god of the Inari fishermen. Visit the workshop

Samekki on Lehtolantie to look at or buy handicrafts. These are not inexpensive, but can be regarded as the products of genuine tradition.

There is a reindeer farm 15 km from the village on the Kittilä road, but there are 40,000 others in the area to catch sight of. Handicrafts are on display at the school in July and the tiny wilderness **church** is a five km hike to the north.

Places to Stay
The camping ground *Uruniemi* (☎ 9697-513 31), at Kirkonkylä, has sites for 40 mk in March and April and from June to late September. There are also cabins from 120 mk.

You'll find the hostel *Retkeilymaja Kukkula* (☎ 9697-512 144), on the Menesjärvi-Kittilä road, is open from March to September and charges from 55 mk a bed. The hotel *Inarin Kultahovi* (☎ 9697-512 21), off Kittiläntie by the river, has singles/doubles for 360/400 mk.

LEMMENJOKI
The mountain stream Lemmenjoki runs 50 km from the heart of the big **Lemmenjoki national park** through a deep valley into the lake above Inari. It is a natural hikers' challenge and extends for over 70 km, indicated by orange markers. There are closely spaced tent sites and you'll have a chance to do some gold-panning. Use the Inari 1:30,000 map sheet from Karttakeskus together with brochures from Inari tourist office, or the Lemmenjoki and Menesjärvi: 1:50,000 sheets.

Iceland

Nowhere are the forces of nature more evident than in Iceland (Ísland). You have glaciers, hot springs, geysers, active volcanoes, icecaps, tundra, snowcapped peaks, vast lava deserts, waterfalls, craters, and even Mt Snaefell, Jules Verne's gateway to the centre of the earth. On the high cliffs that characterise much of the coastline are some of the most densely populated sea-bird colonies in the world and the lakes and marshes teem with waterfowl. The island also provides a backdrop for the sagas, considered by literature enthusiasts to be the finest of all Western medieval works.

Facts about the Country

HISTORY

Although early Irish monks regarded Iceland as a hermitage until the early 9th century, the Age of Settlement is traditionally defined as the period between 870 and 930 AD when political strife on the Scandinavian mainland caused many people to flee westward.

The human history of Iceland was chronicled from the beginning. The *Íslendingabók* was written by a 12th century scholar Ari Þorgilsson (Ari the Learned) about 250 years after the fact. He also compiled the more detailed *Landnámabók*, a comprehensive account providing a chronicle of that era. The *Íslendingabók* credits the first permanent settlement to Norwegian Ingólfur Arnarson who set up in 874 at a place he called Reykjavík (Smoky Bay) because of the steam from thermal springs there.

Icelanders decided against a Scandinavian-style monarchy in favour of the world's first democratic parliamentary system. In 930, Þingvellir (Parliament plains) near Reykjavík was designated the site of the national assembly or parliament, the Alþing. Iceland was converted to Christianity around 1000.

In the early 13th century, the 200-year peace ended. Violent feuds and raids by private armies ravaged the countryside and the chaos eventually led to the cession of control to Norway in 1380. In 1397, the Kalmar Union (of Norway, Sweden and Denmark) brought Iceland under Danish rule. During the disputes between church and state, which resulted when the Reformation arrived in Iceland in 1550, Danes seized church property and imposed Lutheranism.

At the end of the 16th century, Iceland was devastated by natural disasters. Four consecutive severe winters led to crop failure; 9000 Icelanders starved to death while thousands were uprooted from their homes. In 1602, the Danish king imposed a trade monopoly whereby Swedish and Danish firms were given exclusive trading rights in Iceland. This resulted in large-scale extortion, importation of inferior goods and more suffering.

Over the next 200 years, natural disasters continued. In 1783, Lakagígar (Laki) erupted for 10 months and devastated much of south-east Iceland, spreading a poisonous haze that destroyed pastures and crops. Nearly 75% of Iceland's livestock and 20% of the human population perished in the resulting famine.

By the early 1800s, a growing sense of Icelandic nationalism was perceived in

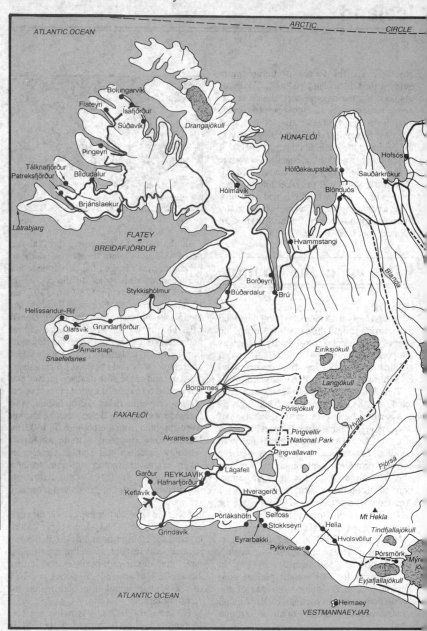

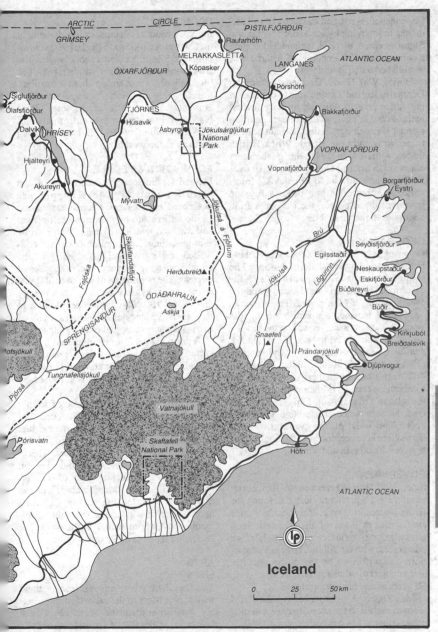

Iceland

0   25   50 km

ICELAND

Copenhagen. Free trade was restored in 1855 thanks to lobbying by Icelandic scholar Jón Sigurðsson and, by 1874, Iceland had drafted a constitution. The Republic of Iceland was established on 17 June 1944.

During WW II with Germany occupying Denmark, Iceland's vulnerability concerned the Allied powers. Without military forces, Iceland couldn't defend its strategic position against German aggression. Britain sent in forces to occupy the island. When British troops withdrew in 1941, the government allowed US troops to move in and take over Keflavík, now the site of Reykjavík's international airport. Despite protests by the government and people, the US occupation continues to the present day.

GEOGRAPHY

Covering an area of 103,000 sq km, Iceland is the second largest island in Europe. The south-east coast is 798 km from Scotland, the eastern end is 970 km from Norway, and the Westfjords lie 287 km east of Greenland.

Most of Iceland, a juvenile among the world's land masses, is characterised by desert plateaus (52%); lava fields (11%); *sandur* or sand deltas (4%); and icecaps (12%). Over 50% of the country lies above 400 metres and its highest point, Hvannadalshnúkur, rises 2119 metres from beneath the glacier Öraefajökull. Only 21% of the land, all near the coast, is arable and habitable. The bulk of the population and agriculture is concentrated in the south-west between Reykjavík and Vík.

GOVERNMENT

Since 1944, Iceland has been a democratic republic with a president elected to four-year terms by majority vote. Presidential duties are similar to those of the monarch in a constitutional monarchy and legislative powers rest with the Alþing. Executive functions are performed by the prime minister and a cabinet of ministers. Every citizen over 20 years of age has voting rights.

Ms Vigdís Finnbogadóttir, the first woman elected to the presidency of a democratic country, has held office since 1980.

ECONOMY

Iceland's economy is more or less dependent on fishing. A nationwide fleet of 900 vessels employs 5% of Iceland's workforce while fish processing occupies another 8%. The total annual catch averages about 1.6 million tonnes, 97% of which is exported. This amounts to over 70% of the total Gross National Product, representing around US$1000 million or the 15th largest fishing industry in the world.

POPULATION & PEOPLE

Iceland is the least Scandinavian of the Nordic countries. Most people are descended from the early Scandinavian and Celtic settlers and by nature are self-reliant and reserved which gregarious visitors may find unsettling. Immigration is strictly controlled and most foreigners living in the country are temporary workers or spouses of citizens. The population of just over 300,000 is increasing by only about 1.5% annually and nearly 150,000 of these people live in Reykjavík. Iceland has 100% literacy and its life expectancy is topped only by Japan's.

A person is very rarely addressed by title and/or surname in Iceland. Family names are illegal, unless they were adopted before the *Personal Names Act* which was passed by the Alþing in 1925.

Icelanders' names are constructed from a combination of their Christian name and their father's (or mother's) Christian name. Girls add the suffix *dóttir*, meaning daughter, to the patronymic and boys add *son*. Therefore, Jón, the son of Einar, would be Jón Einarsson. Guðrun, the daughter of Halldór, would be Guðrun Halldórsdóttir. Telephone directories are alphabetised by Christian name rather than patronymic so the aforementioned Guðrun would be listed before Jón rather than the other way around.

ARTS
Literature

The first literature to emerge from Iceland was poetry. Most of the early themes probably came from mainland Scandinavia even before the settlement of Iceland but weren't written down until the literary boom in the 12th century.

Icelandic poetry divides neatly into two categories: Eddic poetry, actually more like free-metre prose, and Skaldic poetry, written by court poets employing a unique and well-defined syntax and vocabulary. Eddic poetry dealt primarily with two themes, the heroic and the mythical. The heroic Eddas are based on Gothic legends and German folk tales while the mythical Eddas are derived primarily from stories of Norse gods and their antics. It's assumed Skaldic poetry was composed by Norwegian court poets to celebrate the heroic deeds of Scandinavian kings.

The most popular early works were the sagas. They were written in Old Norse which differed little from modern Icelandic. During the Saga Age (the late 12th and 13th centuries), epic tales of settlement, romance and dispute were recorded and sprinkled liberally with dramatic licence. For commoners, they provided entertainment and a sense of cultural heritage. One of the best known, *Egils saga*, is a biography of the skaldic poet, Egill Skallagrímsson. Authorship is attributed to Snorri Sturluson, Iceland's greatest historian. Other favourite works include *Grettis saga*, about a superhuman outlaw; *Laxdaela saga*, the tragic account of a northwest Iceland family; and *Njáls saga*, perhaps the most popular of all.

Icelanders have also contributed to the body of modern literature. In the late 1800s, Jón Sveinsson (Nonni), a priest from Akureyri, wrote a body of juvenile literature that was translated into 40 languages. Jóhann Sigurjónsson wrote *Eyvind of the Hills*, the biography of the 18th-century outlaw Fjalla-Eyvindar. The best known modern Icelandic writer is Nobel Prize winning Halldór Laxness, whose work deals with everyday life in Iceland, some autobiographical. *Independent People* describes the formerly harsh living conditions of Icelandic fishing and farming families. Other novels of his include *The Fish Can Sing* and *The Atom Station*.

Music

The pop music world was astounded in 1986 when the Icelandic band the Sugarcubes arrived on the scene. From the early '80s, there have been lots of spiky-topped teenagers with multicoloured hair wandering the streets of Reykjavík. Many were members of garage bands and put on fairly wild shows. Eventually, the Sugarcubes emerged. Their work may be sampled on the compilation *World Domination or Death*, but try to see some garage performances while you're there. You might catch the Sugarcubes' successors in action!

RELIGION

Although Iceland officially became a Christian nation in 999 or 1000 AD, many people continued to recognise the pantheon of Norse deities: Þór, the main god; Óðinn, the god of war and poetry; and Freyr, the god of fertility and sensuous pleasure. The Norse belief system was simple and not burdened with theology or dogma. No salvation was possible or necessary. A sort of immortality came only to those who died in battle. Such a warrior would be gathered up by the Valkyries, the warrior-maids, and carried into Valhalla where he could indulge in mead, feasting and women until the gods themselves fell in battle.

Currently, the Norse religion is gaining popularity as the officially recognised sect, *Ásatrú*. Led by a modern-day skald, sheep farmer Sveinbjörn Beinteinsson, it focuses on the natural forces and harmony represented by the ancient gods. Like the early religion, it has no sacred text, no rules and regulations and no philosophy about the progression of the human spirit. Ásatrú currently has several hundred followers.

LANGUAGE

Icelandic is a North Germanic language. By the 14th century Icelandic (Old Norse) and Norwegian, the original language of Iceland, had grown apart considerably. This was due to changes in Norwegian, whereas Icelandic remained largely unchanged.

Icelandic has changed remarkably little through the centuries. The treasures of the sagas and the poetic *Edda*, written about 700

ICELAND

years ago, can be enjoyed by a modern-day speaker of Icelandic. Icelanders are proud of their literary heritage. They are particularly conservative when it comes to the written word; borrowed vocabulary is ill tolerated and the policy of keeping the language pure is very strong. After all, Icelandic is spoken by a mere 250,000 people. Outside pressures on the language, in these times of easy travel and worldwide communications, are enormous.

The practice of creating neologisms (new words), instead of adopting foreign words is well established, in Iceland. Neologisms, such as *útvarp* 'radio', *sjónvarp* 'television', *tölva* 'computer', and *þota* 'jet', are just a few that have become part of the Icelandic vocabulary in the last 50 years.

Icelandic is a highly inflected language, which means that words change according to their form. Nouns are inflected in four cases: nominative, accusative, dative and genitive, and in singular and plural. Most pronouns and adjectives are also inflected. Prepositions and certain verbs determine cases. Nouns change their endings with each case. Plurals are formed with still different endings. There are three genders; masculine, feminine and neuter. Objects may be defined to be any of the three.

Icelandic has no indefinite article ('a/an' in English), only a definite article ('the' in English). The article changes according to gender: *hinn* (masculine), *hin* (feminine), and *hið* (neuter). It is normally attached to the end of a noun, when it drops the *h*: *maðurinn* (the man). The definite article also declines with the noun. Verbs are inflected in three persons, 1st, 2nd and 3rd, singular and plural.

Most Icelanders speak English, and often as many as three or four other languages, although, among themselves they only converse in Icelandic. Your efforts to speak Icelandic will most certainly be met with great enthusiasm.

Pronunciation

Stress is generally on the first syllable. Double consonants are pronounced as such.

Vowels

a   as the 'a' in 'father'

a   as in 'at'

e   as in 'fear'

e   as in 'get', 'bet'

i, y as the 'e' in 'pretty'

í, ý as the 'e' in 'see', 'evil'

o   as in 'pot'

u   there is no equivalent sound in English. It sounds a bit like the vowel sound in the French word *peur*. The 'u' in *Guð* 'god', is always pronounced as 'v'.

ú   as the 'o' in 'moon', 'woman'

ö   as in 'fern', 'turn', but without a trace of 'r'

Diphthongs

á   as in 'out'

ei, ey as in 'paid', 'day'

ó   as in 'note'

æ   as in 'eye', 'dive'

au   there is no equivalent sound in English

Semiconsonants

é   as in 'yet', 'yes'

Consonants

ð   as in 'lather'

f   as in English. When between vowels or at the end of a word it is pronounced as 'v'. When followed by **l** or **n** it is pronounced as 'b'.

g   as in 'good'. When between vowels or before **r** or **ð**, (*sagt* 'said'), it has a guttural sound as in 'loch'.

h   as in English, except when followed by 'v', when it is pronounced as 'k'

j   as in 'yes', 'yellow'

l   as in English, except when double 'l' occurs, when it is pronounced as 'dl' (*kalla* 'call')

n   as in English, except when double 'n' forms an end to a word, when it is pronounced as 'dn', 'einn' (one), but never when double 'n' forms part of the article 'hinn'.

p   as in English, except when before 's' or 't', when it is pronounced as 'f' (*skipta* 'exchange')

ICELAND

r	always trilled
þ	as in 'thin', 'three'

Greetings & Civilities

Hello.	*Halló.*
Goodbye.	*Bless.*
Yes.	*Já*
No.	*Nei*
Excuse me. (forgive me)	*Afsakið.*
Please.	*Gjörðu svo vel.*
Thank you.	*Takk fyrir.*
That's fine.	*Allt í lagi.*
You're welcome.	*Ekkert að þakka.*
How are you?	*Hvernig hefur þú það?*
Well, thanks.	*Gott, takk.*

Some Useful Phrases

Do you speak English?	*Talar þú ensku?*
Does anyone speak English?	*Talar einhver ensku?*
I speak a little Icelandic.	*Ég tala svolitla Íslenzku.*
I understand.	*Ég skil ekki.*
Just a minute.	*Bíddu aðeins.*

Useful Signs

Camping Ground	*Tjaldstæði*
Entrance	*Inngangur/Inn*
Exit	*Úthgangur/Út*
Free Admission	*Ókeypis*
Guesthouse	*Gistiheimili*
Hotel	*Hótel*
Hot/Cold	*Heitt/Kalt*
Information	*Upplýsingar*
Open/Closed	*Opið/Lokað*
Police	*Lögregla*
Police Station	*Lögreglustöð*
Prohibited	*Bannað*
Toilets	*Snyrting/Karlar*
Railway Station	*Lestarstöð*
Youth Hostel	*Farfuglaheimili*

Getting Around

What time does ... leave/arrive?	*Hvenær ... fer/kemur*
next	*næst*
first	*fyrst*
last	*síðast*
aeroplane	*flugvél*
the boat	*báturinn*
the bus	*vagninn (city bus)*
the train	*lestin*
the tram	*sporvagninn*
I would like ...	*Gæti ég fengid ...*
a one-way ticket	*miða, aðra leiðina*
a return ticket	*mið, báðar leiðir*
1st class	*fyrsta farrými*
2nd class	*annað farrými*
I want to go to ...	*Mig langar að fara til ...*
Where is the bus/tram stop?	*Hvar er biðstöðin?*
Can you show me (on the map)?	*Getur þú sýnt mér (á kortinu)?*
Go straight ahead.	*Farðu beint af augum.*
Turn left ...	*Beygðu til vinstri ...*
Turn right ...	*Beygðu til hægri ...*
far/near	*langt í burtu/nálægt*

Around Town

I'm looking for ...	*Ég er að leita að*
a bank	*banka*
the city centre	*miðbænum*
the ... embassy	*sendiráðinu*
my hotel	*hótelinu mi'nu*
the market	*markaðnum*
the police	*lögreglunni*
the post office	*pósthúsinu*
a public toilet	*almenningssalerni*
the telephone centre	*símstöðinni*
the tourist information office	*upplýsingaþjónustu fyrir ferðafólk*

Accommodation

Where is a cheap hotel?	*Hvar er ódýrt hótel?*
What is the address?	*Hvað er heimilisfangið?*

ICELAND

Could you write the address, please?	*Gætir þú skrifað niður heimilisfangid?*
Do you have any rooms available?	*Eru herbergi laus?*
I would like ...	*Gæti ég fengid ...*
a single room	*einstaklingsherbergi*
a double room	*tveggjamannaherbergi*
a room with a bathroom	*Herbergi með baði.*
to share a dorm	*að deila herbergi með öðrum*
a bed	*rúm*
How much is it per night/per person?	*Hvað kostar nóttin fyirir manninn?*
Can I see it?	*Má ég sjá það?*
Where is the bathroom?	*Hvar er baðherbergið?*

Food

breakfast	*morgunmatur*
lunch	*hádegismatur*
dinner	*kvöldmatur*
I would like the set lunch, please.	*Gæti ég fengið mat dagsins.*
Is service included in the bill?	*Er þjónusta innifalin?*
I am a vegetarian.	*Grænmetisæta.*

Time & Dates

What time is it?	*Hvað er klukkan?*
today	*í dag*
tomorrow	*á morgun*
in the morning	*að morgni*
in the afternoon	*eftir hádegi*
in the evening	*að kvöldi*
Monday	*mánudagur*
Tuesday	*þriðjudagur*
Wednesday	*miðvikudagur*
Thursday	*fimmtudagur*
Friday	*föstudagur*
Saturday	*laugardagur*
Sunday	*sunnudagur*
January	*janúar*
February	*febrúar*
March	*marz*
April	*apríl*
May	*maí*
June	*júní*
July	*júlí*
August	*ágúst*
September	*september*
October	*október*
November	*nóvember*
December	*desember*

Numbers

0	*núll*
1	*einn*
2	*tveir*
3	*þrír*
4	*fjórir*
5	*fimm*
6	*sex*
7	*sjö*
8	*átta*
9	*níü*
10	*tíu*
20	*tuttugu*
100	*eitt hundrað*
1000	*eitt þúsund*
one million	*ein milljón*

Health

I'm diabetic/epileptic/asthmatic	*Ég er sykursjúkur/ flogaveikur/ með asma*
I'm allergic to antibiotics/penicillin	*Ég er með ofnæmi fyrir fúkalyfjum/ pensilíni*
antiseptic	*sótthreinsandi*
condoms	*smokkar*
contraceptive	*getnaðarvörn*
diarrhoea	*niðurgang*
medicine	*lyf*
nausea	*ógleði*
tampons	*vatttappar/tampónar*

ICELAND

Emergencies

Help!	*Hjálp*
Call a doctor!	*Náið í lækni.*
Call the police!	*Náið í lögregluna!*
Go away!	*Farðu!*

Facts for the Visitor

VISAS & EMBASSIES

Scandinavians need only proof of citizenship if entering Iceland from another Nordic country. Citizens of the USA and Commonwealth countries need a valid passport to enter as tourists. Stays of up to three months during a nine-month period are normally granted with proof of sufficient funds for the declared length of stay. Officials are fairly liberal with this requirement but if they think you may run short of cash, they may ask for an onward ticket. Lengths of stay may be extended at police stations.

Icelandic Embassies

These include:

Australia
    Icelandic Consulate General, 44 St Georges Rd, Toorak Vic 3142 (☎ 03-827 7919)
Denmark
    Islands Ambassade, Dantesplads 3, DK-155 6 Copenhagen V (☎ 1-15 96 04)
Norway
    Islands Ambassade, Stortingsgaten 30, N-0161 Oslo 1 (☎ 22 41 34 35)
UK
    Embassy of Iceland, 1 Eaton Terrace, London SW1W 8EY (☎ 071-7305131)
USA
    Embassy of Iceland, 2022 Connecticut Ave NW, Washington, DC 20008 (☎ 202-2656653)
    Consulate of Iceland, 370 Lexington Ave at 41st, New York, NY 10017 (☎ 212-6864100)

Foreign Embassies in Iceland

All of the following addresses are in Reykjavík:

Canada
    Skúlagata 20 (☎ 91-25355)
Denmark
    Hverfisgata 29 (☎ 91-621230)
Norway
    Ánanaust, Grandagarður (☎ 91-28855)
UK
    Laufásvegur 49 (☎ 91-15883)
USA
    Laufásvegur 21 (☎ 91-29100)

CUSTOMS

Visitors may bring up to 10 kg of non-animal product food into Iceland. Those over 20 years of age may import duty-free a litre of spirits (less than 47% alcohol) and a litre of wine (less than 21%) or six litres of foreign beer (instead of wine or spirits). Those aged over 15 years may bring 200 cigarettes or 250 grams of other tobacco products.

For motor vehicles, you must present registration, proof of international insurance and a driving licence. A motor vehicle permit will be issued for the time of your stay but vehicles cannot be sold without payment of import duty. Those employed in Iceland must pay duty regardless of the length of stay.

MONEY

Foreign-denomination travellers' cheques, postal cheques, and banknotes may be exchanged for Icelandic currency at banks. A commission of 150 kr is charged for each transaction. Any leftover krónur may be exchanged for foreign currency before departure. Banks may require exchange receipts for the desired amount.

Major credit cards (Visa, MasterCard, Diners Club, American Express, Eurocard etc) will be accepted at most places. Icelanders use cards even for buying groceries and other small purchases. Credit cards may be used at banks to purchase cash. Eurocard (☎ 91-685499), Visa (☎ 91-671700), American Express (☎ 91-26611) and Diners Club (☎ 91-28388) all have service offices in Reykjavík.

Currency

The Icelandic unit of currency is the *króna* (kr) which is equal to 100 *aurar*. Notes come in 100, 500, 1000, and 5000 krónur denom-

ICELAND

inations. Coins come in one, five, 10, and 50-krónur, and 5, 10 and 50-aurar denominations.

Exchange Rates
The following currencies convert at these rates:

1 Dkr	=	10.40 Ikr
1 Fmk	=	14.62 Ikr
1 Nkr	=	10.19 Ikr
1 Skr	=	11.02 Ikr
A$1	=	37.95 Ikr
C$1	=	42.56 Ikr
DM1	=	36.03 Ikr
NZ$1	=	28.86 Ikr
UK£1	=	90.38 Ikr
US$1	=	53.05 Ikr

Departure Tax Iceland levies an airport departure tax of 950 kr, payable when airline tickets are issued.

Costs
The lowest average price of a single hotel room in Reykjavík is about 5700 kr. If you can forego some comforts and stay in youth hostels, eat at snack bars and travel with bus passes, you can keep expenses to around 1800 kr a day. Rock-bottom budget travel in Iceland is only possible with near total exposure to difficult weather conditions. If you must get by on less than 600 kr a day, you'll have to camp, self-cater and hitchhike, cycle or walk.

Those bringing a private vehicle, especially a camper van or caravan, can enjoy more comfort while keeping to a low budget. Petrol prices in Iceland tend to be high – 60 kr a litre – but the sting of fuel costs may be minimised by sharing expenses with travellers who lack vehicles.

In most cases, student-card holders are entitled to discounts on museum admissions and some transport fares. Students and Iceland bus-pass holders receive 10% discount on camping fees, ferry fares and sometimes even at hotels and restaurants. These discounts aren't advertised so it pays to ask.

Tipping
Tipping is not required in Iceland but finer restaurants automatically add service charges to the bill. If you feel compelled to tip for particularly good or friendly service, however, you won't be refused.

Consumer Taxes
Sales Tax A 15% sales tax is included in marked prices. Legislation passed in 1988, however, relieves foreigners of some of the sting if the items purchased amount to at least 3000 kr per sales ticket. The items must be bought in specially designated shops and exported within 30 days of purchase. Participating shops have a sign *'Iceland Tax-Free Shopping'*.

To collect the 13% to 15% refund, fill out a refund voucher at the time of purchase. Present all items purchased (except woollens which may be packed in your luggage) and your refund vouchers at the Keflavík international airport duty-free shop when departing Iceland. The refund will be made in Icelandic krónur. If you're leaving from another departure point, show your items and voucher to the customs official who will arrange for the refund (in your home currency) to be sent within 90 days.

CLIMATE & WHEN TO GO
The warm waters of the Gulf Stream and prevailing south-westerly winds from the tropical Atlantic combine to give the southern and western coasts mild winter temperatures. Unfortunately, this warmth combines with cold polar seas and mountainous coastlines to form condensation and, alas, rain. In January, Reykjavík enjoys an average of three entirely sunny days and in July, only one. Fierce, wind-driven rains alternate with partial clearing, drizzle, gales and fog to create a distinctively unpleasant climate. It's a matter of 'if you don't like the weather now, wait five minutes – it will probably get worse'.

Further north and east, especially around

Akureyri, Mývatn and Egilsstaðir, the situation improves. The interior deserts are also more prone to clear weather than coastal areas, but they may experience blizzards any time of year with icy winds whipping up dust and sand into gritty and opaque maelstroms. Similar conditions occur on the sandur of the northern and southern coasts. If you're trapped out of doors, they can be miserable.

Every year on 15 August, someone puts on the brakes and Icelandic tourism grinds to a halt: hotels close, youth hostels and camping grounds shut down and buses stop running. Late summer travellers may be disappointed to find that the most popular attractions are inaccessible by 15 September. By 30 September, the country has gone into hibernation.

WHAT TO BRING

The amount of stuff you'll have to carry will be dictated by your budget and intended activities. Shoestring travellers will need to load down with things that travellers on a higher budget won't need to worry about – a good case for bringing a vehicle where applicable. Items required by all but the most up-market travellers include a good synthetic-fibre sleeping bag, a Swiss army-style knife, a towel, a torch, a litre water bottle, lighters or waterproof matches, books for inclement weather, a copy of medical and optical prescriptions and camera supplies.

Warm, dry clothing is of utmost importance. Given the extreme weather possibilities, the layering method seems to work best. Between May and September, you'll need several pairs of thick wool or polypropylene socks, polypropylene or woollen underwear, windproof ski gloves, high protection sunglasses, a wool hat with ear protection, a T-shirt or two, a wool pullover, hiking shorts (canvas or polyester), wool shirt and wool trousers (jeans just won't dry!), a wind and waterproof jacket and trousers, hiking boots or strong hiking shoes with ankle support, and a swimsuit for hot springs and heated pools.

For camping and hiking, you'll need a tent that's easily assembled (because of the wind), sturdy, waterproof and free-standing. Get one with an outside annexe for dry storage of wet clothing, boots and cooking implements. You'll also need a camping stove and aluminium fuel bottle (MSR mountain stoves or alcohol stoves are preferable to butane stoves which are unstable and don't work well in wind), cooking implements (a nesting kit is best), waterproof ground cover or space blanket, gaiters, a compass and the relevant maps (which may be purchased in Iceland).

SUGGESTED ITINERARIES

Depending on the length of your stay you might wish to see and do the following things:

Two days
    The Golden Circle Tour: Gullfoss, Geysir and Þingvellir in south-central Iceland
One week
    Mývatn and Akureyri
Two weeks
    As above plus Fjallabak and Skaftafell
One month
    As above plus Vestmannaeyjar and the Landmannalaugar to Þórsmörk trek
Two months
    As above plus Westfjords, Jökulsárgljufúr, Askja, Lakagígar, Snaefellsnes, Vatnajökull and east Iceland

TOURIST OFFICES

The Icelandic tourist offices are very helpful and employees normally speak Scandinavian languages, English, German and French. Services are free but a charge may apply to telephone calls made on your behalf. National park brochures and commercial maps are sold at bookshop prices. In addition to providing information, the staff will book tours, sell bus passes and make advance hotel and transport reservations. There are information offices in Reykjavík, Vík, Kirkjubaejarklaustur, Höfn, Seyðisfjörður, Mývatn (Reykjahlíð), Húsavík, Akureyri, Sauðárkrókur, Ísafjörður, Stykkishólmur, and Akranes. The Reykjavík camping ground also provides information. For advance information, contact:

ICELAND

Iceland Tourist Board
Laugavegur 3, 101 Reykjavík, Iceland
Tourist Information Centre
Ingólfsstraeti 5, 101 Reykjavík, Iceland
Iceland Tourist Board 655 Third Avenue, New York,
NY 10017 USA
Isländisches Fremdenverkehrsamt
Brönnerstrasse 11, 6000 Frankfurt-Main,
Germany

BUSINESS HOURS & HOLIDAYS

Weekday shopping hours are from 9 am to 5 pm, although the odd shop may open at 8 am and close at 4 pm or later. On Saturdays, shops normally open at 9 or 10 am and close at noon or 1 pm. Petrol stations and kiosks are normally open on weekday evenings until 10 or 11 pm, Saturday afternoons and Sundays. Post offices will have varying opening hours, but most are open from 8.30 or 9 am to 4.30 or 5 pm on weekdays. Banking hours are between 9 am and 4 pm weekdays.

Icelandic Public Holidays

Icelanders observe the following holidays:

New Year's Day, 1 January
Maundy Thursday
Good Friday
Easter Day
Easter Monday
First Day of Summer, 21 April
Labour Day, 1 May
Ascension Day, 12 May
Whit Sunday, May
Whit Monday
Independence Day, 17 June
Shop & Office Workers' Holiday, first week in August
Leif Eiríksson Day, 9 October
Christmas Eve, 24 December (afternoon)
Christmas Day, 25 December
Boxing Day, 26 December
New Year's Eve, 31 December (afternoon)

CULTURAL EVENTS

The largest nationwide festival is Independence Day on 17 June, celebrating the day in 1944 on which Iceland gained independence from Denmark. According to tradition, the sun stays hidden, perhaps a psychological concession to what normally happens, anyway!

The first day of summer, or Sumar-dagurinn fyrsti, is celebrated in carnival style on the third Thursday in April with the biggest bash staged in Reykjavík. The first day of winter, Fyrsti vetrardagur, occurs on the third Saturday of October but it is, of course, not a cause that inspires much merriment.

Sjómannadagurinn, celebrated in the first week in June, is dedicated to seafarers and the Seamen's Union sponsors celebrations in every port city. In smaller coastal towns, this can be the greatest party of the year.

Midsummer is celebrated around 24 June in Iceland but with less fervour than it is on the Scandinavian mainland.

Another earth-shaking festival, Þjóðhátíð Vestmannaeyjar, takes place in early August in Vestmannaeyjar, commemorating the day in 1874 when foul weather prevented the islands from celebrating the establishment of Iceland's constitution. Elsewhere in Iceland Verslunarmannahelgi is held on the same weekend (or in some years on an adjacent weekend) with barbecues, horse competitions, campouts and family reunions.

In September, the *réttir* or roundup of the sheep from the highlands before the coming winter is also a festive occasion.

POST & TELECOMMUNICATIONS

The Icelandic postal system is both reliable and efficient and rates are comparable to those in other Western European countries. Poste restante is available in all cities and villages but Reykjavík is best set up to handle it. Mail should be addressed with your name to Poste Restante, Central Post Office, Reykjavík, Iceland.

Public telephone offices are affiliated with the postal system known as Póstur og Sími and both services normally occupy the same buildings. You'll wait about five minutes for an international call from any telephone office and reverse-charge calls may be made to many countries.

Direct dialling is available via satellite to Europe, North America and elsewhere. After dialling the international access code (90 from Iceland), dial the country code, area or city code and the telephone number.

Iceland's country code is 354. For operator assistance, dial 09. Directory assistance is (08).

Telefax services are available at communications offices in Reykjavík and most other places around the country. The telefax number in Reykjavík is 91-25901.

TIME

From 25 October to 24 March, Iceland is on the same time as London (GMT/UTC), five hours ahead of New York, eight hours ahead of Los Angeles and 11 hours behind Sydney, Australia. From 25 March to 24 October, it's one hour behind London, four hours ahead of New York, seven hours ahead of Los Angeles and 10 hours behind Sydney.

ELECTRICITY

The electric current is 220 volts, 50 Hz, and plugs have two round or two slanted prongs.

LAUNDRY

Laundrettes (Þrottahús) are thin on the ground. In Reykjavík, try Þvioð Sjálf at Barónsstígur 3. The camping grounds in both Reykjavík and Akureyri have machines for guests' use but plan on queuing. Large hotels also offer laundry services.

BOOKS & MAPS

A few of the sagas are available in translation. Since they are officially anonymous works, they're found in card catalogues and bookshops under the names of their translators, in most cases Magnús Magnússon, Hermann Pálsson or both. Available titles include *Hrafnkels Saga*, *Egills Saga*, *Laxdaela Saga*, *King Haralds Saga*, *Grettirs Saga* and *Njálls Saga*.

Halldór Laxness has written a great body of work, much of which has been translated into English. Some highly acclaimed novels include *The Atom Station*, *Salka-Valka*, *The Fish can Sing* and *Independent People*. The following publications may also be of interest:

Iceland Saga by Magnús Magnússon (paperback)
Letters from High Latitudes by Lord Dufferin (hardback)
Last Places – A Journey in the North by Lawrence Millman (hardback)
Iceland Road Guide by Einar Guðjohnsen and Pétur Kidson Karlsson (hardback)
Field Key to Flowering Plants of Iceland by Pat Wolseley (paperback)
Guide to the Geology of Iceland by Ari Trausti Guðmundsson and Halldór Kjartansson (paperback)
Iceland, Greenland & the Faroe Islands – a travel survival kit by Deanna Swaney (paperback)

Maps

The Landmaelingar Íslands (Iceland Geodetic Survey) offers three series of high-quality topographic sheets (1:25,000, 1:50,000 and 1:100,000) and a variety of thematic maps. Most travellers use the *Ferðakort 1:500,000* (touring map), the best general map of the country. It's cheapest if bought directly from Landmaelingar Íslands. Other useful maps are the 1:5000 map of Reykjavík, the 1:25,000 maps of Skaftafell and Þingvellir, the 1:50,000 maps of Hekla, Mývatn, and Vestmannaeyjar, and their 1:100,000 coverage of Hornstrandir and the trek from Þórsmörk to Landmannalaugar and Skógar.

For a catalogue, pricelist and order form, write to Landmaelingar Íslands (☎ 354-1-681611), Laugavegur 178, PO Box 5060, 125 Reykjavík, Iceland. Maps are available from their office or at the Mál og Menning bookshop at Laugavegur 18 in Reykjavík.

MEDIA

US military radio is at AM 1485. During June, July and August daily at 7.30 am, station 93.5 FM broadcasts English language news and a recorded version is available by phoning 91-693690. Two television stations operate during afternoon and evening hours. Many programmes deal with Icelandic themes but subtitled British and US programmes dominate prime time.

The only English language newspaper is the monthly *News From Iceland*, published for second and third generation Icelandic emigrants to Britain, the USA and Canada.

For subscription information, write to Höfdabakki 9, PO Box 8576, 128 Reykjavík, Iceland. The annual international rate is US$24.

German and English-language periodicals, including *Der Spiegel*, *Time* and *Newsweek* are available at Eymundsson's in Reykjavík and at Bókaverslunin Edda in Akureyri.

HEALTH

Travellers will have to concern themselves with very few health hazards. Tap water is safe to drink and surface water is potable except in urban areas. Glacial river water may appear murky but, if necessary, it's drinkable in small quantities. The murk is fine particles of silt glacier-scoured from the rock and drinking it can clog internal plumbing.

Because most unpopulated lands in Iceland serve as sheep pastures, giardia does exist in Iceland but isn't a major problem. It's still a good idea to purify drinking water.

Sunburn and windburn should be concerns on snow and ice. The sun will burn you even if you feel cold and the wind will cause dehydration and chafing of skin. Use a good sunblock and a moisture cream on exposed skin, even on cloudy days. A hat is recommended as is zinc oxide for your nose and lips. Reflection and glare from ice and snow can cause snow blindness so high-protection sunglasses are essential for glacier and ski trips.

WOMEN TRAVELLERS

Women travelling alone in Iceland will have fewer problems than they would travelling in their home country. Women hitchhikers, even those on their own, will not encounter any difficulties if they use common sense and aren't afraid of saying no to lifts.

DANGERS & ANNOYANCES

In Iceland, where petty larceny merits front-page headlines, police don't carry guns and parents park their children in prams on the street while they shop, there are few dangers or annoyances for travellers. Iceland even lets its prisoners go home on public holidays.

When visiting the many geothermal areas avoid lighter coloured soil around fumaroles and mudpots; snowfields which may overlie hidden fissures, loose sharp lava chunks; and slippery slopes of scoria (volcanic gravel).

FILM & PHOTOGRAPHY

The crystalline Arctic air combined with long, red rays cast by a low sun create excellent effects on film but because of glare from water, ice and snow, photographers should use a UV filter or a skylight filter and a lens shade. Film, photographic equipment and camera repairs are quite expensive. A 36-exposure roll of Kodachrome 64, for instance, will cost 1080 kr in Reykjavík so you may wish to bring a supply from home. Film is readily available in Reykjavík and Akureyri. Specialised processing for Kodachrome is not available.

WORK

High-paying jobs on fishing boats are hard to come by and normally go to friends and relatives of boat owners. Most foreigners will probably find themselves slopping fish guts eight hours a day for wages only slightly higher than could be earned at similar jobs at home – and well below an average Icelandic salary. Some companies, however, include food and/or accommodation in the deal. Intending workers will first need a job-offer while still outside Iceland. They must then apply for the necessary work permit. Icelandic embassies abroad keep lists of businesses hiring seasonal employees.

ACTIVITIES
Hiking

Most visitors to Iceland agree that the best way to see the country is on foot, whether on an afternoon hike or a two-week wilderness trek. The weather can prove a nuisance: rain is common and snow may fall all year round at higher altitudes. The best months for walking in the highlands are July and August. Earlier or later, some routes will be impassable without skis and complete winter gear. Lava fields can be very difficult to negotiate so strong boots will help. Be careful when walking with children, especially in fissured areas like Mývatn and Þingvellir where narrow cracks in the earth can be hundreds of metres deep.

Swimming

Thanks to an abundance of geothermal heat, every city and village has at least one public swimming hall *(sundlaug* or *sundhöll)*, with pools and jacuzzis. A session will normally cost about 120 kr; a shower is about 90 kr. Alternatively, visit one of Iceland's many natural hot springs.

Skiing

Skiers who enjoy out-of-the-way slopes will find some pleasant no-frills skiing available in Iceland. In the winter, nordic skiing is available throughout the country and in highland areas it continues until early July. The greatest drawbacks are the lack of winter transport in rural areas and almost constant bitter winds. Both Reykjavík and Akureyri have winter resorts for downhill skiing and a summer ski school operates at Kerlingarfjöll near Hofsjökull in central Iceland.

Horse Riding

The Icelandic horse *(equus scandinavicus)* has been prominent in the development of the country. It's small (about 133 cm high) and weighs between 390 and 400 kg, but is a sturdy animal perfectly suited to the rough Icelandic terrain. These horses are also used recreationally. They have a fifth gait called the *tölt*, so smooth that the rider notices scarcely any motion.

Farmhouse accommodation, tour agencies, and individual farmers rent horses and lead riding expeditions into the countryside. Icelandic horses are gentle and novice riders should have no problems. Horse tours normally cost about 6000 kr a day including tent or hut accommodation. Short-term rental costs about 800 kr an hour. In September, you can volunteer for the sheep round-up; the job normally provides room and board as well as an interesting experience. Arrange-

ments can be made through tourist offices or directly with individual farmers.

HIGHLIGHTS

Highlights for visitors are almost all natural. They include the geologically and biologically fascinating Mývatn and Krafla area; Landmannalaugar and the beautiful Fjallabak reserve; Skaftafell, Þingvellir and Jökulsárgljúfur national parks; the green glacial valley of Þórsmörk; the volcanically active islands Vestmannaeyjar; the immense Askja caldera; the wild coast of Hornstrandir; and the pleasant urban centre Akureyri.

ACCOMMODATION
Hotels

Major towns have at least one up-market hotel which will seem sterile and characterless, but has all the amenities: restaurants, pubs, baths, telephone and TV. For these creature comforts, you'll pay around 6000 kr to 10,000 kr for a double. If it's any consolation, a continental breakfast is normally included.

Edda Hotels

Most Edda hotels, operated by the Iceland Tourist Bureau, are school dormitories which are used as hotels during summer holidays. With adjoining restaurants and geothermally heated swimming pools, some offer sleeping-bag accommodation (just a soft and dry spot where you can roll out a sleeping bag) or dormitory facilities as well as conventional lodging. Single/double rooms cost about 2700/3600 kr. Sleeping-bag or dormitory accommodation, where available, will cost from 720 to 1000 kr.

Guesthouses

There are several types of guesthouses *(gistiheimilið)* some are private homes which let out rooms to bring in extra cash while others are quite elaborate. Some offer hostel-style sleeping-bag accommodation. In some cases, a continental breakfast is included. Sleeping-bag accommodation costs about 700 kr; double rooms range from

2700 kr to 4200 kr; and self-contained units, between 4200 kr and 5400 kr. Rooms are always cheaper if booked through an overseas travel agent. Most guesthouses are open only seasonally.

Farmhouse Accommodation

Farmhouse accommodation will allow you to become acquainted with everyday country life. Every farm is named and some are mentioned in the sagas and date back to Settlement times. A range of accommodation plans is available. Some offer meals and others just have cooking facilities. Most farms offer horse rentals and horse tours. Off-season (September to May) accommodation must be booked in advance. Prices are controlled by the government and are as follows:

bed & breakfast – 1560 kr a person
lunch – 720 kr
dinner – 960 kr
sleeping-bag accommodation (bed)
    – 780 kr a person
sleeping-bag accommodation (floor)
    – 510 kr a person
cottage (six-person weekly rate) – 24,000 kr
cottage (four-person weekly rate) – 20,400 kr
cottage (six-person daily rate) – 3720 kr
cottage (four-person daily rate) – 3120 kr
bed linen (daily, for one person) – 360 kr
child rate – half-price
horse rental – 780 kr an hour

Youth Hostels

In Iceland, hostels are called *farfuglaheimili*, which translates into something like 'little home for migrating birds'. All hostels offer hot water, cooking facilities, luggage storage and opportunities to meet other travellers. There are curfews, but with a few notable exceptions such as in Reykjavík, sleeping bags are welcome and guests will not have to provide or rent sleeping sheets. IYHF members pay 660 kr and others pay 780 kr.

Mountain Huts

Ferðafélag Íslands (Icelandic Touring Club) (☎ 91-19533 Reykjavík) and smaller local clubs maintain a system of mountain huts (*saeluhús*) in remote areas. A couple of these,

such as those at Landmannalaugar and Þórsmörk, are accessible by 4WD vehicle but most are in wilderness areas. Huts along the popular Landmannalaugar to Þorsmörk route must be reserved and paid for in advance through the club office. Some huts offer cooking facilities but accommodation is always dormitory-style and guests must carry food and sleeping bags.

The huts are open to anyone. In the more rudimentary ones, Touring Club members pay 300 kr while nonmembers pay about 465 kr. In the posher places, members pay up to 465 kr and nonmembers 700 kr. For further information, write to Ferðafélag Íslands, Öldugata 3, Reykjavík, Iceland.

Emergency Huts

The Icelandic Automobile Association and the government maintain orange emergency huts on high mountain passes, remote coastlines, and other places subject to life-threatening conditions. They're stocked with food, fuel and blankets and are open for emergency use only.

Camping

Camping provides the most effective relief from high accommodation prices. Bring only a stable, seam-sealed, well-constructed and durable tent. Most people probably can't imagine the forces meted out by North Atlantic storms.

Only a small amount of land in Iceland is privately owned. If you'd like to camp on a private farm, ask the owner's permission before setting up. Otherwise, apart from nature reserves, where camping is either forbidden or restricted to certain areas, you're free to camp anywhere you like. Take care to keep toilet activities away from streams and surface water and use biodegradable soaps for washing up. Natural fuel shortages and Icelandic regulations will preclude campfires so carry a stove and enough fuel for the duration of your trek.

Organised camping sites are called *tjaldstaeði*. Amenities and charges vary but normally, you'll pay around 180 kr a tent and another 180 kr for each person.

FOOD

Icelanders display little imagination when it comes to pepping up food and the only spices you're likely to encounter are paprika (on the chips) and a sprinkle or two of dried parsley. Although traditional delicacies may remind foreigners of the nightmare feast in *Indiana Jones and the Temple of Doom*, they aren't always as bad as they sound. The glaring exception is *hákarl*, putrefied shark meat that has been buried in sand and gravel for three to six months to assure sufficient decomposition. It reeks like a cross between week-old 'road kill' and ammonia – few foreigners can appreciate its appeal.

So what about *hrútspungur*, rams' testicles pickled in whey? Or *svið*, singed sheep's head (complete with eyes!) sawn in two, boiled and eaten either fresh or pickled; or *blóðmör*, sheep's blood pudding packed in suet and sewn up in the diaphragm; or stomach. In one variation, *lifrapylsa*, sheep's liver rather than blood is used.

Moving toward the less bizarre, Icelanders make a staple of *harðfiskur*, haddock which is cleaned and dried in the open air until it has become dehydrated and brittle. It is torn into strips and eaten with butter as a snack. Icelanders also eat broiled *lundi*, or puffin, which looks and tastes like calves' liver. Whale blubber, whale steaks and seal meat are also available but we recommend abstinence for environmental reasons.

The unique Icelandic treat is *skyr*. Few dislike this yoghurt-like concoction made of pasteurised skim milk, and a bacteria culture. Despite its rich and decadent flavour, it's actually low in fat but is often mixed with sugar, fruit and milk to give it a creamy, pudding-like texture.

Self-Catering

You can minimise food prices by self-catering. Every town and village has at least one *kaupfélagi* (cooperative), your key to inexpensive dining in Iceland. The most economical chain is Hagkaup. The cheapest groceries are tinned fish and coffee.

Icelandic greenhouse produce is very good but imported vegies are normally already past their peak when they hit the shelves. Street stands offer the best values on fresh produce.

Snack Bars & Restaurants

The least expensive prepared foods are available at petrol stations and snack kiosks. They normally serve chips, sausages, sandwiches, doughnuts, ice cream and coffee. For a light meal of chips and sausage with trimmings you'll pay around 200 kr. In larger towns, you'll find kiosks selling pizza, pastries and pre-packaged-pop-it-in-the-microwave items.

In Reykjavík and Akureyri, a couple of good-value restaurants offer all the bread, soup and salad you can eat for around 720 kr. (Iceland caught on to US-style salad bars when greens-starved foreigners resorted to nibbling on the grass.) Reykjavík has several intimate pub-style cafes where you can drink beer, eat a meal or chat over coffee for hours without attracting comment. These places serve some of the best meals available in Iceland for around 700 kr.

The word 'restaurant' in Iceland denotes an up-market establishment, often associated with expensive hotels. Restaurant meals normally consist of a meat dish, boiled potatoes bathing in an anonymous sauce, tinned vegetables, a brothy soup and possibly a cabbage-based salad. Lunches are often served cafeteria-style offering one 'daily special' and a limited selection of salads, fruit, breads and pastries on the side.

ENTERTAINMENT

A weekend evening in a Reykjavík disco is a never-to-be-forgotten experience!

THINGS TO BUY

Every visitor to Iceland seems to end up with a woolly pullover. Pullovers come in many designs but the traditional ones, which are more expensive than the delicate pastel fashion sweaters, are thicker and come in white and blue, violet or earth tones. For these you'll pay about 4500 kr. Reykjavík city tours stop at the Álafoss factory outlet, in the suburb Mossfellsveit, which is a bit cheaper than the tourist shops.

The Handknitting Association of Iceland has a shop at Skólavörðustígur 19 in Reykjavík with prices around 4000 kr for a traditional handknitted sweater. Rock-bottom prices are found in street stalls on Austurstraeti in Reykjavík. Quality isn't consistent, you'll find some garments for 3000 to 3300 kr. Seconds are available at Keflavík airport duty-free for less than 1200 kr.

Getting There & Away

AIR

There are no earth-shaking bargain fares available to or between points in the North Atlantic so the only way to keep transport costs down is to shop around for cheap air-fares. When purchasing a ticket keep in mind that Icelandair, Iceland's national carrier, is inflexible when it comes to ticket rescheduling.

Icelandair serves Reykjavík direct from Luxembourg, Glasgow, London, Paris, Frankfurt, Vienna, Copenhagen, Gothenburg, Stockholm, Oslo, Bergen and Vágar (Faroe Islands). In the high season, the Copenhagen flight operates daily. Once weekly, it connects with the flight from Reykjavík to the Faroe Islands.

Since Icelandair zealously promotes its European hub, Luxembourg, it runs free buses between that city and Frankfurt, Karlsruhe, Stuttgart, Dusseldorf and cities en route. It also offers discounted bus and train tickets to Amsterdam, Berlin, London, Paris, Madrid, Rome, Zurich etc. The cheapest return ticket to Reykjavík is from Luxembourg for US$431 and must be purchased 30 days in advance. You won't save anything taking the ferry one way from Denmark to Iceland and returning on the plane – the one-way air ticket costs US$517 so you'd do better buying the return ticket and throwing the other half away.

Other options from Europe include Lufthansa's direct service between Reykjavík and Frankfurt and Arnarflug's (Eagle Air's) services between Reykjavík and Hamburg, Zurich, Geneva, Milan, Munich, Basel and Brussels.

SEA
Ferry

A pleasant way to travel from the mainland is by ferry although it takes longer and isn't economically advantageous. It is, however, the only means of taking a vehicle. Smyril Line's *Norröna*, operates from mid-May to mid-September out of Hanstholm in north-western Denmark. Passengers travelling with Smyril from Hanstholm are provided with inexpensive transport from Copenhagen on the day of departure.

The *Norröna* sails from Hanstholm on Saturdays, arriving in Tórshavn in the Faroe Islands on Monday morning. All Iceland-bound passengers must disembark while the ship continues to Lerwick in the Shetland Islands, arriving Monday night. On Tuesday night the ferry is in Bergen, Norway, picking up more passengers. It arrives back in Tórshavn on Wednesdays, gathers up Iceland passengers, and sails overnight to Seyðisfjörður on the east coast. On the return journey, it sails back to Tórshavn, arriving Friday morning, then returning to Hanstholm.

Note that Iceland passengers cannot remain aboard while the ship sails to Shetland and Norway and must spend two nights in the Faroes en route. To stay longer in the Faroes, you'll have to break your journey there and pay for two sectors. The normal deck fare between Hanstholm and Seyðisfjörður (which includes a couchette or sleeper) is US$280 each way. Hanstholm to Tórshavn is US$188 and Tórshavn to Seyðisfjörður is US$164, adding up to US$352 for the broken trip. Discounts are available to holders of student cards.

To transport a vehicle up to five metres long will cost 75% of the deck-class passenger fare. Above deck class, there are three classes of cabins and a luxury suite. The ship also has a bar, cafeteria, restaurant, disco, casino and duty-free shops. For further information, schedules and fare lists contact: Smyril Line (☎ 97 96 22 44), Auktiongade 13, 7730 Hanstholm, Denmark.

Those coming from the UK can take Strandfaraskip Landsins' ferry, the *Smyril*, which sails weekly from Scrabster in Scotland to Tórshavn. From there, it's possible to connect with the *Norrøna* and continue to Iceland. For information contact: Strandfaraskip Landsins (☎ 298-14550 Tórshavn), Yvri við Strønd 6, Postbox 88, FR-110, Tórshavn, Faroe Islands.

Cargo Ship

The Icelandic cargo-shippers, Eimskip, whose vessels *Laxfoss* and *Brúarfoss* sail between Reykjavík, Immingham (UK), Antwerp, Rotterdam and Hamburg, have six cabins for passengers on each ship. Cabins accommodate two adults and two children and cost US$1200 between Hamburg and Reykjavík (a bit less from the other cities). For further information contact Eimskip (☎ 91-687100 Reykjavík), Posthússtraeti 2, IS-101, Reykjavík, Iceland.

Getting Around

AIR

Iceland's domestic airline, Flugleiðir, has daily flights in the summer between Reykjavík and Akureyri, Egilsstaðir, Grímsey, Höfn, Húsavík, Ísafjörður, Sauðárkrókur and Vestmannaeyjar. Smaller towns are served two to six times weekly. Some flights offer unadvertised discounted seats so enquire before paying full fare. Since inclement weather can lead to postponed or cancelled flights, flexible travel plans are essential. Don't book a flight from Vestmannaeyjar to Reykjavík, for instance, on the afternoon before you're scheduled to fly to Denmark. If the flight is cancelled, you may miss your connection.

Some gaps in Flugleiðir's schedule are filled by Arnarflug (Eagle Air) which links Reykjavík with Snaefellsnes and the Westfjords. Charter flights are available from Odin Air (☎ 91-610880 Reykjavík).

BUS

Although Iceland is small and has a well established public transport system, the interior is undeveloped and much of National Highway 1, the 'Ring Road', which was completed in 1971, remains unsurfaced. There are no railways and the highway system is Europe's least developed.

Bifreiðastöd Íslands Umferðarmiðstöðin (just BSÍ if you're in a hurry), a collective organisation of Iceland's long-distance bus lines, covers the country in feasible but often inconvenient connections. You can travel any one quarter of the Ring Road in a day but on minor routes you may wait several days for connections. Most buses stop running on 15 September and don't resume until June. Interior routes rarely open before July but in years of high snowfall, some don't open at all. Most are closed again by early to mid-September.

BSÍ (☎ 91-22300) offers two bus passes, the Hringmiði ('Ring Pass' or Full-Circle Pass) and the Tímamiði ('Time Pass' or Omnibuspass). The former allows one full circuit of the Ring Road in either direction, stopping anywhere you like. It costs 10,200 kr – not much less than the normal fare – but it entitles you to 10% discount at camping grounds and other accommodation, and on ferries and buses not covered by the pass. It also allows small discounts on some organised tours.

The Omnibuspass is good for one to four weeks and allows unrestricted travel on all but interior bus routes and a few other special routes. Some bus tours are included. On other tours, significant discounts are offered. The pass is also good for ferry and accommodation discounts.

With the one and two-week passes, you'd have to do a lot of travelling to get your money's worth but three and four-week passes are good value. One week costs 12,000 kr; two weeks cost 15,000 kr; three weeks, 19,200 and four weeks, 21,900 kr. Bus travellers may pick up a copy of the

Leiðabók (the timetable) free of charge at any tourist office.

TAXI

Taxis for up to five passengers and with an English or German-speaking driver may be hired for sightseeing at an average cost of 30 kr a km. Make arrangements through Reykjavík taxi services.

CAR & MOTORBIKE
Private Vehicles

It's easy to bring a vehicle on the ferry from mainland Europe. Drivers must carry the vehicle's registration, valid insurance and a driving licence. After the vehicle is inspected, a temporary import permit will be issued if the driver isn't employed in Iceland. Vehicles can't exceed 2.5 metres in width or 13 metres in length. Those which carry 15 or more passengers aren't permitted to tow trailers.

Most Icelandic roads and highways aren't suitable for high-speed travel. Due to excessive dust and flying rocks, some sort of headlight and radiator protection is advisable. Seat belt use in the front seat is compulsory.

Those travelling in the interior must have a 4WD vehicle and should keep in mind that there are no petrol stations or repair services anywhere on the F-numbered (interior) highway system. A suggested spares or repair kit includes extra oil, brake fluid, extra petrol, sealing compound for the radiator and petrol tank, a distributor cap, a rotor arm, a condenser, a fuel filter, a fan belt, at least two spare tyres and a puncture repair kit, spark plugs, insulated wire, fuses and headlights. You'll also need large-scale maps, a compass, extra rations, a shovel and some means of protecting your eyes and skin from wind-driven sand.

Tool kits should include a tow rope, a shovel, a crow bar, the relevant sockets and wrenches, a jack, a torch, batteries, flares, a fire extinguisher. Take emergency food rations too. And of course, you'll need the expertise to identify all this stuff and fix any mechanical problems.

While driving through the interior, it's best to travel with another vehicle. Even 4WD vehicles get bogged in sand drifts. The greatest threats are posed by unbridged rivers and drifting sand. Glacial rivers change course and fords change. Warm days may cause excessive glacial melting and placid rivers will turn into torrents without warning. Tyre marks leading into the water don't mean a river can be crossed.

Wade into the river before attempting to cross and check the depth and condition of the riverbed. Carry a pole to steady yourself in the current and face upstream while wading. Only cross where there are rocks or gravel, never sand. The narrowest fords are normally the deepest. Before entering the water, remove the fan belt, cover the distributor and ignition system with a woollen rag and switch off headlights. Don't stop in midstream unless you're sure you cannot continue and want to reverse out.

Car Rental

The Sultan of Brunei would think twice before renting a car in Iceland. The cheapest vehicles, compact eastern-European models, cost 1920 kr a day which seems reasonable until you add 19.20 kr per km, 25% sales tax, compulsory insurance and some very dear petrol to the price. Vehicles with 4WD will cost twice that. You must be at least 23 years old to rent a car from most of the following agencies:

ALP Bílaleigan (☎ 91-17570), Central Bus Terminal, Reykjavík

Arnarflug (☎ 91-29577), Síðumúli 12, Reykjavík

Ás Car Rental (☎ 91-29090), Skógarhlíð 12, Reykjavík

B & J (☎ 91-681390), Skeifan 17, Reykjavík

Bílaleiga RVS (☎ 91-19400), Sigtúni 5, Reykjavík

Geysir (☎ 91-688888), Suðurlandsbraut 16, Reykjavík

Icelandair (☎ 91-690200), Flugvallarvegur, Reykjavík

InterRent (☎ 91-86915), Skeifan 9, Reykjavík

InterRent (☎ 96-21715), Tryggvabraut 14, Akureyri

ALP Bílaleigan (☎ 91-43300), Hlaðbrekku 2, Kópavogur

BICYCLE

In Iceland, the wind, rough roads, gravel, river crossings, sandstorms, intimidating vehicles and horrid weather conspire against cyclists. Hard-core cyclists will find a challenge in Iceland but those after a pleasant experience should come prepared to pack up their bikes and travel by bus when the going gets miserable.

In areas better suited to cycling such as Mývatn or urban Reykjavík and Akureyri, bicycles can be hired for around 780 kr a day plus deposit. Bicycles may be carried on long-distance buses if there is space available (and there nearly always is).

HITCHING

Summer hitching in Iceland is possible but inconsistent. If there is traffic, you'll get a ride eventually but long waits are common in the Westfjords and Snaefellsnes. It's best not to hitch in groups of more than two people. Naturally, a lot of visible luggage will also put people off stopping.

BOAT

Major ferries operating in Iceland include the *Akraborg* which connects Reykjavík and Akranes; the *Herjólfur* between Þorlákshöfn and Vestmannaeyjar (a very rough trip); the *Baldur* between Stykkishólmur, Flatey and Brjánslaekur; the Hrísey ferry on Eyjafjörður; and the *Fagranes* between Ísafjörður, Jökulfjörður, Ísafjarðardjúp and Hornstrandir. The first three are car ferries and only the *Fagranes* does not operate year-round.

Ferry schedules are designed to coincide with buses. They are outlined in detail in the *Leiðabók* timetable. Holders of bus passes and student cards are sometimes entitled to a 10% discount on fares.

TOURS

Many of the nicest sights in Iceland are in remote locations where no public transport is available. If you don't have a hardy vehicle and don't want to walk, endure difficult hitching conditions or attempt cycling, tours will provide the only access. The least expensive and most loosely organised tours are offered by BSÍ, the consortium of long-distance bus companies, in association with small local operators. They run much like ordinary bus services but stop at points of interest for photos and walks. Sometimes a guide is included. It's also possible to leave the tour at any time and rejoin at a later, pre-specified date.

Several companies and groups operate hiking, trekking, horsepacking or photography tours. There are also up-market bus tours with accommodation in tents and mountain huts.

The following operators offer some of the more adventurous and interesting tours available:

Dick Phillips Tours (☎ 0498-81440 UK), Whitehall House, Nenthead, Alston, Cumbria, CA9 3PS, England
Ferðafélag Íslands (☎ 91-19533), Öldugata 3, 101 Reykjavík
Green Tours, Kultorvet 7, DK-1175, Copenhagen, Denmark
Guðmundur Jónasson Travel (☎ 91-83222), Borgartún 34, 105, Reykjavík
Icelandic Highland Travel (☎ 91-22225), Laekjargata 3, PO Box 1622, Reykjavík
Úlfar Jacobsen Travel (☎ 91-13499), Austurstraeti 3, PO Box 886, 101 Reykjavík
Útivistarferðir (☎ 91-14606), Grófinni 1, Reykjavík

Reykjavík

Iceland's capital Reykjavík, home to 150,000 of the country's 250,000 people, is unlike any other European city. Not only is it the world's northernmost capital, it's also one of the smallest capitals. Historically and architecturally, it's not very exciting but politically, socially, culturally, economically and psychologically, Reykjavík dominates Iceland: basically, everything that happens in the country happens in Reykjavík.

Reykjavík was the first place in Iceland to be intentionally settled. The original settler, Ingólfur Arnarson, tossed his high-seat pillars (a bit of pagan paraphernalia) overboard in 874 AD, and built his farm near

ICELAND

ICELAND

Greater Reykjavík

1	Sigurjón Ólafsson Museum
2	Cinema
3	Camping Ground & Youth Hostel
4	Laugardalur Swimming Pool
5	Höfdði House
6	Laugardalur Sports Centre
7	Pleasure Boat Port
8	Askur Restaurant
9	Hotel Esja & Pizza Hut
10	Kjarvalsstaðir
11	Kringlan Centre (Hard Rock Cafe & Hagkaup Supermarket)
12	Borgarleikhúsið (City Theatre)
13	Salmon Jumping (in season)
14	Árbaejarsafn (open air museum)
15	Nordic House
16	City Airport
17	Hótel Loftleiðir (bus to Keflavík & International Airport)
18	Hot Water Tanks & Restaurant
19	Kópavogskirkja (Church)
20	Cinema
21	Breiðholtskirkja (Church)

where they washed ashore, between the Tjörn (the Pond) and the sea, where Áðalstraeti now intersects with Suðurgata. He called the place Reykjavík (Smoky Bay) because of the steam rising from nearby geothermal features. Ingólfur claimed the entire south-west corner of the island then set about planting his hayfields at Austurvöllur, the present town square.

Orientation

The heart of Reykjavík is still between the Tjörn and the harbour and many old buildings remain. Nearly everything in the city is within walking distance of the old settlement. Most meeting and lounging activity takes place in Laekjartorg and the adjacent pedestrian shopping street, Austurstraeti. The shopping district extends east along Laugavegur from Laekjargata to Hlemmur bus terminus.

Information

The tourist office is at Ingólfsstraeti 5 near Laugavegur. It's open from 1 June to 15 September from 8.30 am to 7 pm weekdays,

8.30 am to 4 pm Saturdays, and 10 am to 3 pm Sundays. There's a second tourist office at the BSÍ long-distance bus terminal. Pick up a copy of *What's on in Reykjavík*, published monthly during summer.

Money

After-hours banking is available at Keflavík international airport daily between 6.30 am and 6.30 pm and at the Hotel Loftleiðir (Reykjavík city airport) daily from 8.15 am to 7 pm (except Sundays in winter). During non-banking hours, hotels exchange foreign currency but at a higher commission.

Post & Telecommunications

Poste restante and the long-distance telephone office are at the main post office on the corner of Posthússtraeti and the Austurstraeti pedestrian mall. There's a sub-station in the BSÍ terminal. The telephone exchange is open weekdays from 9 am and 7 pm and on Sundays 11 am to 6 pm.

Bookshops

The widest variety of English language books is at Sigfús Eymundsson's on Austurstraeti and Mál og Menning (which also sells topographic maps) at Laugavegur 18. There's a second-hand bookshop on Tryggvagata, one block west of Posthússtraeti.

Emergency Services

The following phone numbers may be useful: police (☎ 91-11166), ambulance & fire brigade (☎ 91-11100) and emergency medical service (☎ 91-696600, after hours 91-21230).

Left-Luggage

Luggage storage at the BSÍ terminal is open weekdays from 7.30 am to 9.30 pm, Saturdays 7.30 am to 2.30 pm, and Sundays 5 to 7 pm.

Old Town

Old Town includes the area bordered by the Tjörn, Laekjargata, the harbour and the suburb of Seltjarnarnes, including the east

ICELAND

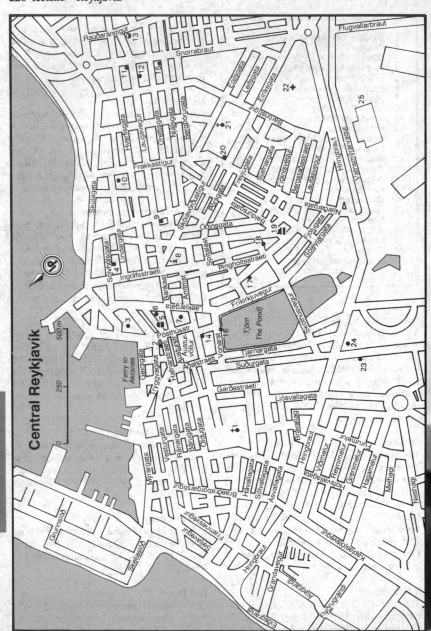

ICELAND

Central Reykjavík

1	Landakotskirkja
2	Gaukur á Stöng
3	Kolaportið Flea Market
4	National Library & National Theatre
5	Central Post Office
6	Café Torg
7	Kaffi Straeto, Icelandair Office, Tunglið Disco & Café Opera
8	Tourist Office
9	One Woman Vegetarian Restaurant
10	Cinema
11	Natural History Museum
12	Cinema
13	Hvammur Bus Terminal
14	The Alþing
15	Cinema
16	Reykjavík Theatre Company
17	Listasafn Íslands (National Museum of Art)
18	Volcano Show
19	Central Youth Hostel
20	Einar Jónsson Museum
21	Hallgrímskirkja
22	National Hospital
23	University
24	National Museum
25	BSÍ Bus Terminal

bank of the Tjörn and both sides of Laekjargata. Laekjartorg is the socialising centre of town.

The houses on the south side of **Hafnarstraeti** were used by Danish traders during the trade monopoly between 1602 and 1855. Today, tourist shops sell woollens, pottery and souvenirs.

Old Reykjavík grew up around the **Tjorn**, the pleasant lake in the centre of town. The park on the Tjörn has jogging and bike trails, a fountain and colourful flower gardens. The **National Gallery**, behind the church Fríkirkjan near the Tjörn, is worth visiting for exhibitions by Icelandic artists. It's open daily except Mondays, from 11 am to 5 pm. Admission is free.

Stjórnarráðið, the white building opposite Laekjartorg, contains executive offices. It's one of the city's oldest buildings, originally an 18th century jail. On nearby **Árnarhóll** (Eagle Hill) is a statue of the first settler, Ingólfur Arnarson.

The grey basalt building south of Austurvöllur (Ingólfur's hayfields and the old town square) built in 1881, houses the **Alþing**. The present building is too small for the growing government and a new building will be constructed nearby.

Fógetinn, at Aðalstraeti 10, is housed in Fógeti (Sheriff) Skúli Magnússon's weaving shed, the oldest building in Reykjavík, which was constructed around 1752. Although the shed burnt down in 1764, it was immediately replaced on the same foundation. It's now a popular restaurant.

Hallgrímskirkja

The immense church at the top of Skólavöðustigur, Reykjavík's most imposing structure, was unashamedly designed to resemble a mountain of basaltic lava. The bland interior is offset by the superb view from its 75-metre tower. The lift costs 100 kr an adult. In the summer, it's open daily except Mondays from 10 am to noon and 2 to 6 pm.

Kjarvalsstaðir

Jóhannes Kjarval, born in 1885, was Iceland's most popular artist. The surrealistic style that characterises his work was derived from the ethereal nature of the Icelandic landscape; when seen from a distance of 10 metres or so, its magic appears. The Kjarval museum is in Miklatún park on Flókagata. It's open from 11 am to 6 pm daily. Admission is free.

Árbaejarsafn

Also known as the Open Air Museum, Árbaersafn is a 12.5-hectare historic farm set up as a museum in 1957. It also includes a collection of old homes and buildings moved from various places to illustrate life in early Iceland. In the summer, it's open daily except Mondays from 10 am to 6 pm. Take bus No 10 or 100 from the city centre.

Volcano Show

To appreciate Vestmannaeyjar or Mývatn, first see the Volcano Show. Filmed by locals Vilhjálmur and Ósvaldur Knudsen, it offers

ICELAND

insight into the volcanic spectre under which Icelanders live. The 2½-hour show is at 10 am, and 3 and 8 pm daily in the summer. Shows are normally in English but French or German presentations may be arranged in advance. The theatre is at Hellusund 6a near the Central Youth Hostel. Admission is 600 kr.

National Museum

The National Museum on Hringbraut is obligatory for those interested in Norse culture and Icelandic history. Most interesting are the Settlement Era religious and folk relics and tools; nautical and agricultural artefacts, fishing boats, and some ingenious early farm implements. It's open daily except Mondays from 11 am to 4 pm between 15 May and 15 September and for limited hours the rest of the year. Admission is free.

Places to Stay

In the summer, finding a place to stay can be difficult. Bring a tent or book accommodation in advance if you'd rather not risk being left out in the cold.

Camping The Reykjavík camping ground, with cooking and laundry facilities, is in Laugardalur, 15 minutes on bus No 5 from Laekjartorg and a 420-kr taxi ride from the BSÍ terminal. At the height of summer, you'll be lucky to find space for a tent on this immense piece of real estate. It's open from 1 June to 15 September and costs 150 kr a person plus 150 kr a tent. At 7 am daily a shuttle bus runs to the BSÍ terminal.

Hostels In the summer, it's wise to book hostels a month in advance. Otherwise, try in the evening and hope for a cancellation. The crowded *Central Youth Hostel* (☎ 91-24950) is at Laufásvegur 41, seven minutes on foot from Laekjartorg and five minutes from the BSÍ terminal. The *Laugardalur Youth Hostel* (☎ 91-38110), at Sundlaugavegur 34 beside the camping ground, is less claustrophobic. It closes down on 15 September.

Guesthouses The cheapest guesthouse is the *Salvation Army* (☎ 91-613203) at Kirkjustraeti 2 near Austurvöllur in the centre. It offers singles/doubles for 1560/2280 kr.

It's followed by a number of others which charge from 2700 to 3600 kr a night for comfortable but not elegant doubles. They include the central *Borgarstjarnan* (☎ 91-621804) at Ránargata 10 near the harbour, the *Guesthouse #1* (☎ 91-623477) at Miklabraut 1 near Miklatún park, the *Svanurinn Guesthouse* (☎ 91-25318) at Lokastígur 24, the *Matteu Guesthouse* (☎ 91-33207) at Bugðulaekur 13 in Laugardalur, *Guðmundur Jónasson* at Borgartún 34, *Snorra* at Snorrabraut 61 and a number of others. For a complete list of guesthouses and homes which let out rooms, contact the tourist office.

Hotels *Hotel Óðinsvé* (☎ 91-25640), at Þórsgata 1, charges 3900/5340 kr for singles/doubles. At *Hotel Holt* (☎ 91-25700), at Bergstaðastraeti 37, rooms start at 6900/7920 kr. Other up-market hotels include the *Geysir* (☎ 91-26477) at Skipholt 27, the *Borg* (☎ 91-11440) at Pósthússtraeti 11, the *Lind* (☎ 91-623350) at Rauðarárstígur 18, and the *City Hotel* (☎ 91-18650) at Ránargata 4a. Doubles range from 6000 to 7800 kr.

The most up-market hotel is the international-class *Saga* (☎ 91-29900) at Hagatorg 1 with a view over the city. Double rooms start at 8700 kr.

Places to Eat

Some up-market restaurants offer a *Sumarréttir*, a scaled-down menu for budget-conscious tourists (from 600 to 720 kr for lunch and 900 to 1200 kr for dinner). However, many less pretentious places serve better food for similar prices.

Self-Catering The least expensive supermarket chain is *Hagkaup* with stores in the Kringlan Centre and on Laugavegur near Snorrabraut. The former has a salad bar for

90/150 kr for small/large serves but it's open only during shopping hours.

Restaurants At *Svarta Pannan*, at Hafnarstraeti 17, expect to pay from 360 to 480 kr for fried chicken, fish and chips, burgers etc. Great deli snacks and sandwiches are available at *Hlölla Deli* at Austurstraeti 1. For a change, try the pitta bread sandwiches at *Pítan*, Skipholt 50. Reasonable pizzas are served at *Puzzahúsið* at Grensásvegur 10 and at *Jón Bakan*, Nýlbýlavegur 14. The well-known US chain *Pizza Hut* at the Hotel Esja offers a self-serve salad bar, pizzas, pasta, beer and wine. You only need spend 1200 kr for a meal including beer.

For smorgasbord, try *Eldvagninn* at Laugavegur 75. *Potturinn og Pannan*, at Brautarholt 22, has soup and salad specials at lunch time. In the evening they serve fish, lamb, and beef dishes for around 1500 kr.

Near the camping ground at Suðurlandsbraut 4 is *Askur*, specialising in fish and lamb dishes. In addition to the daily soup and salad bar, they have a Sunday buffet.

For budget travellers, nothing beats small pub-style cafes for good food and lively, friendly atmosphere. The most popular is *Gaukur á Stöng*, at Tryggvagata 22, which is especially lively at the weekends. By day, *Café Hressó* on Austurstraeti and Laekjartorg is a good choice. At the corner of Laekjargata and Laekjartorg is the *Kaffi Straeto* which specialises in stuffed pancake dishes for around 600 kr.

Café Torg overlooking Laekjartorg is one of the friendliest places in town to drink morning coffee or eat a light meal. At the Kringlan Centre is the famous but overpriced *Hard Rock Cafe*.

The *El Sombrero* at Laugavegur 73 is a mid-range Spanish restaurant. The most genuine Italian fare is at *Ítalia*, Laugavegur 11, with lunch specials for less than 960 kr. An odd combination, the *Taj Mahal Tandoori & Sushi Bar* at Laugavegur 34a serves Indian curries, tandoori and sushi with 600-kr lunch specials. *Sjanghae* at Laugavegur 28 serves Mandarin Chinese dishes, including 600-kr lunch specials.

An excellent vegetarian restaurant is the *One Woman Vegetarian Restaurant* at Laugavegur and Klapparstígur. It has both macrobiotic and standard vegetarian fare.

Entertainment

Reykjavík has five cinemas and there's another in nearby Kópavogur. Daily newspapers list shows and show times. There are several theatre groups, an opera, a symphony orchestra and a dance company. Information on current events will be available in the daily papers or at the box offices. In the summer, the Viking-theme tourist show *Light Nights* plays Thursday to Sunday at 9 pm in the summer at Tjarnargata 10e.

Discos are the height of Icelandic teen life but they aren't for the destitute; cover charges range from 780 to 900 kr and there are queues on weekend evenings. The once wild *Hollywood*, at Ármúli 5 in Laugardalur, has toned down for yuppie tastes but is still one of the 'four-in-one' discos (a consortium offering admission to four discos for a single cover charge). Others are *Hotel Ísland*, also on Ármúli, and *Hotel Borg* at Pósthússtraeti 11. The fourth is the immense *Broadway*, at Álfabakki 8 near Kópavogur, take bus No 11.

The most frantic is *Tunglið* at Laekjargata 2. Other popular spots include *Abracadabra* at Laugavegur 116, *Casablanca* at Skúlagata 30, *Utopia* at Suðurlandsbraut 26 and *Cuba* at Borgartún 32.

Getting There & Away

Air Reykjavík city airport serves all domestic flights, Odin Air flights to and from Kulusuk in Greenland and flights to the Faroe Islands. All other flights leave from Keflavík international airport.

Bus Long-distance buses use the BSÍ terminal (☎ 91-22300) at Vatnsmýrarvegur 10. In the summer, there's a daily service between Reykjavík and Akureyri, Skaftafell, Höfn, Akranes, Snaefellsnes, Þorlákshöfn and Reykjanes as well as a twice-weekly service to the Westfjords. Travellers between Reykjavík and eastern Iceland must stay

ICELAND

over in either Höfn or Akureyri before making connections.

Ferry The car-ferry *Akraborg* (☎ 91-16420) does four trips daily between Reykjavík and Akranes for 465 kr a person or 825 kr for a car and driver.

Getting Around
To/From the Airport The Flybus to Keflavík international airport leaves the Hotel Loftleiðir two hours prior to international departures. Buses from Keflavík airport into town leave about 45 minutes after arrival of an international flight. The fare in either direction is 350 kr.

Bus Reykjavík's city bus system is excellent, running from 6 am to 1 am. Buses pick up and drop passengers only at designated stops which are marked with the letters *SVR*. The two central terminals are at Hlemmur near Laugavegur and Rauðarárstígur and on Laekjargata near Laekjartorg. The fare is 50 kr and exact change is required. Discount tickets (45 kr) are available at the terminals and the camping ground.

Taxi Reykjavík is small but taxis will come in handy if you have a lot of luggage or hope to catch an early airport bus. They aren't inordinately expensive and, since there's no tipping, they work out cheaper than in the USA or most of Europe. There are five taxi stations: Hreyfill (☎ 91-685522), Baejarleiðir (☎ 91-33500), BSR (☎ 91-11720), BSH (☎ 91-51666) and Borgarbíll (☎ 91-22440).

BLUE LAGOON
The Blue Lagoon (Bláa Lónið) is actually a pale blue 20°C pool of effluent from the Svartsengi power plant. Although it's affectionately known as the 'chemical waste dump' by visitors, its deposits of silica mud combined with an organic soup of dead algae have been known to relieve psoriasis. A swim can be an ethereal experience with clouds of vapour rising and parting at times to reveal the stacks of the power plant and moss-covered lava in the background. Bring enough shampoo for several rinses or your hair will be left a brick-like mass after swimming. The bath house is open from 10 am to 10 pm daily in the summer. In the winter, it's open Monday to Friday from 2 to 9 pm and weekends 10 am to 9 pm. Admission is 300 kr a person.

Getting There & Away
From BSÍ in Reykjavík, take one of three daily Grindavík buses. The one-way fare is 300 kr.

The South

THE GOLDEN TRIANGLE
The term 'Golden Triangle' refers to Gullfoss, Geysir and Þingvellir, the 'Big Three' destinations for Icelandair's stopover visitors.

If Iceland has a star attraction, it's **Gullfoss**. The river Hvitá drops 32 metres in two falls. Ten km down the road is Geysir, after which all the world's spouting hot springs are named. The **Great Geysir** died earlier this century, plugged by tourists tossing in debris to encourage it to perform. Fortunately, it has a faithful stand-in, **Strokkur** (Butter churn), which spouts approximately every three minutes.

Þingvellir has been the most significant historical site in Iceland since the Alþing was established in 930. It was selected for its topography, acoustics and proximity to population. It was set apart as Iceland's first national park *(Þjóðarðurinn)* in 1928 for its history and wealth of natural attractions.

Most historical buildings are concentrated in a small area of the park and the remainder is left to nature. A maze of hiking trails crisscrosses the plain and leads through the woods to points of interest or simply through scenic areas. Of particular interest are **Almannagjá**, a large tectonic rift; **Lögberg** (Law rock) which served as the podium for the Alþing from 930 to 1271; **Þingvallavatn,**

Iceland's largest lake; and the clear blue wishing spring, **Peningagjá**.

Places to Stay & Eat

Þingvellir has several camping grounds, the main one at Leirur, and the *Hotel Valhöll* (☎ 98-34700), across the Öxará river from the church. It has three dining rooms and fairly elegant accommodation for 5000 kr a double. Nearby at Leirur is the main camping ground and a petrol station selling basic snacks. Geysir has an up-market summer hotel, the *Hotel Geysir* (☎ 98-68915) with a beautiful dining room.

Getting There & Away

The popular Golden Circle day tours leave Reykjavík at 8 am daily in the summer. The standard route includes a long stop at Eden shop in Hveragerði, the Kerið crater, the southern bishopric at Skálholt followed by lunch then Gullfoss, Geysir and a snack then Þingvellir. The cost is 3100 kr without lunch. Book through Reykjavík hotels, youth hostels or tourist offices.

There is a daily bus service from Reykjavík to Gullfoss and Geysir. Public buses travel between Þingvellir and Reykjavík once or twice daily from 1 June to 15 September.

VESTMANNAEYJAR

The 16 islands of Vestmannaeyjar were formed by submarine volcanoes between 10,000 and 5000 years ago and, in 1963, the world witnessed on film the birth of its newest island, Surtsey. Only the island of Heimaey (the Home Island) with 5000 residents supports a permanent population. Characterised by brightly coloured roofs, Heimaey village spreads across about a third of the island. Its spectacular setting is defined by the *klettur* escarpments which rise abruptly behind the well-sheltered harbour, the steaming red peak of Eldfell and the green hill Helgafell.

Things to See & Do

The **Vestmannaeyjar Natural History Museum** has an aquarium of bizarre Icelandic fish and a wonderful collection of polished agate and jasper slices which form natural landscape paintings. Admission is 150 kr and it's open daily from 11 am to 5 pm between 1 May and 1 September. There's also a **folk museum** upstairs in the library.

Páll Helgason Travel Service and Hjálmar Guðnason and Ólafur Gränz (☎ 98-11195) offer two-hour boat trips from Heimaey. The latter takes the more novel approach with a trumpet-tooting captain and old sailors' rituals.

Hiking opportunities abound; for information, visit the tourist office at Westmann Islands Travel, Kirkjuvegur 65.

Places to Stay

The camping ground is in Herjólfsdalur near the village. Alternatively, try *Vestmannaeyjar Youth Hostel* (☎ 98-12915) at Faxastígur 38, open from 1 June to 15 September. It fills up quickly when the ferry arrives. *Heimir Guesthouse* (☎ 98-11515), Heiðarvegur 1, offers doubles for 3500 kr and cheap sleeping-bag accommodation.

Hotel Gestfjafinn (☎ 98-12577), at Herjólfsgata 4, costs 4700 kr for a double. Next down the line is the *Skútinn* (☎ 98-11420), at Strembugata 10, which charges 3200 kr. The expensive *Hotel Þórshamar* (☎ 98-12900) has a guesthouse *Sunnuhöll* with sleeping-bag accommodation.

Places to Eat

For Vestmannaeyjar delicacies, try the *Muninn* at the Hotel Þórshamar or the *Skútinn* at Kirkjuvegur 21. *Bjössabar* on Bárustígur serves burgers, pizzas, sandwiches, and (as the sign proclaims) 'Texas Fried Chicken'. The *Skansinn* pub and restaurant, at the Hotel Gestfjafinn, is open weekdays until 1 am and on Fridays and Saturdays until 3 am.

Getting There & Away

The *Herjólfur* ferry trip from Þorlákshöfn to Heimaey is dreaded as a nauseating corkscrew ride through rough seas. This ferry sails from Vestmannaeyjar to the mainland at 7.30 am on weekdays and returns at 12.30 pm. On Saturdays it leaves at 10 am and

ICELAND

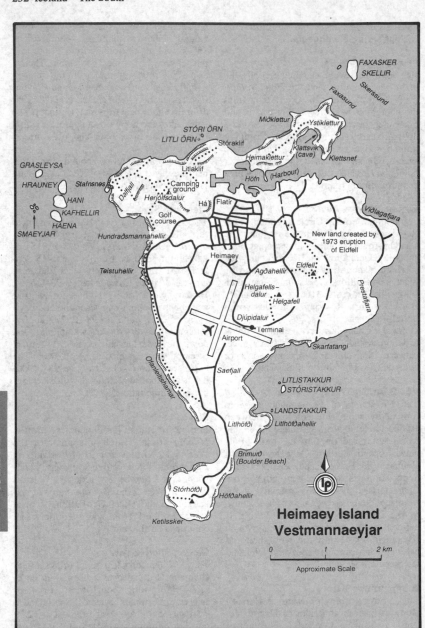

**Heimaey Island
Vestmannaeyjar**

returns at 2 pm, and on Sundays it leaves at 2 pm and returns at 6 pm. The fare is 1035 kr. BSÍ runs buses between Reykjavík and Þorlákshöfn to connect with the ferry.

There are flights at least once daily between Reykjavík city airport and Vestmannaeyjar but inclement weather can interrupt schedules.

ÞÓRSMÖRK

The valley of Þórsmörk (the Woods of Þór) is one of the most beautiful in Iceland, a forested glacial valley full of flowers, braided rivers and clear-running steams surrounded by snowy peaks and glaciers. There's great hiking but it can get crowded on weekends. Þórsmörk is the terminus for two of Iceland's most popular hikes, Landmannalaugar to Þórsmörk (see under Fjallabak Reserve) and Þórsmörk to Skógar.

Places to Stay

All grassy lawns and valleys around Þórsmörk are open to camping but if the area gets much more littered and trodden, expect establishment of a formal camping area. There's also a brutally packed mountain hut;

book in advance through the Ferðafélag Íslands (☎ 91-19533) in Reykjavík. Guests must supply their own food and sleeping bags. Hot showers cost 180 kr.

The hut at Húsadalur costs 640 kr a person and reservations are necessary; book through BSÍ in Reykjavík. Cooking facilities are available.

Getting There & Away

In the summer, a bus leaves the BSÍ terminal in Reykjavík daily at 8.30 am, arriving at Húsadalur (over the hill from Þórsmörk) at around noon. It departs Húsadalur for Reykjavík at 3.30 pm. On Friday nights, there's a special weekenders' bus departing Reykjavík at 8 pm. The return fare is 3120 kr.

To reach the cosy farmhouse youth hostel at nearby Fljótsdalur, get off the Þórsmörk bus at the intersection of routes 261 and 250 and walk the nine km from there. Traffic is sparse so hitching can be slow. On the return trip, you'll have to hitch all the way back to the Ring Road because the bus takes another route back.

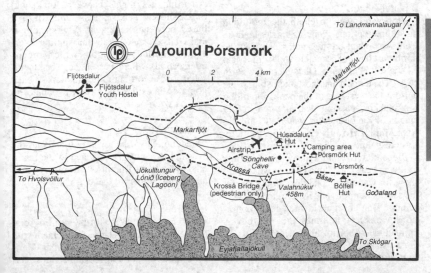

ICELAND

The North

SNAEFELLSNES

French science-fiction author Jules Verne wrote that the 100-km-long peninsula called Snaefellsnes was 'very like a thigh-bone in shape'. Those with less sophisticated imaginations will probably look at the map and see something else. One of Iceland's most renowned landmarks, the 1446-metre volcano Snaefell is capped by the glacier Snaefellsjökull. Its crater led Verne's characters to the underworld in *A Journey to the Centre of the Earth*.

Most of Snaefellsnes' population lives in the north coast villages of Stykkishólmur, Grundarfjörður, Ólafsvík, and Hellissandur-Rif. The bird life is rich, people are laid-back, the scenery is good, and the weather...well that just has to be experienced.

Stykkishólmur

Snaefellsnes' largest village, Stykkishólmur, is known as the start of the popular boat trip through the 'innumerable islands of Breiðafjörður'.

Snaefellsjökull

Visitors who want to climb the mountain have three options. Walking tracks lead up from Arnarstapi on the south coast past the north-east flank of Stapafell, and from Route 54 about 1.5 km east of Ólafsvík on the north coast. The longest and most interesting route is from the west end of the peninsula along Móðulaekur, passing near the red scoria craters of Rauðhólar, the waterfall Klukkufoss, and through the scenic valley Eysteinsdalur.

Prepare for harsh weather on all three routes and and carry food and a stove to melt snow for water. Ice conditions may warrant the use of crampons and ice axes to reach the summit. Don't hesitate to turn back if conditions worsen – at times the weather is unimaginably horrid. From either Ólafsvík or Arnarstapi, in good weather, allow at least four hours for the climb. The western approach will take much longer and you'll have to stay overnight on the icecap.

With 4WD vehicles, you can drive in some four km on the Móðulaekur route and nearly three quarters of the way to the summit on the other routes, snow conditions permitting.

Places to Stay & Eat

Stykkishólmur has a youth hostel, camping ground and up-market hotel, the *Hotel Stykkishólmur* (☎ 93-81330) with doubles for 6720 kr.

The *Egillshusið Guesthouse* (☎ 93-81450), where doubles with/without linen cost 3240/2100 kr, is more pleasant. Sleeping-bag accommodation costs 600 kr. The snack bar and cafeteria are recommended.

In Olafsvík, the *Hotel Nes* offers comfortable doubles for 3480 kr and sleeping-bag space for 720 kr. The camping ground lies one km east of town. For meals, try *Hafnarkaffi* at the harbour; soup and salad cost 300 kr. The grill near the hotel has burgers, sausages, chips and lunch specials and there's a bakery in the same building.

Getting There & Away

Arnarflug has flights between Reykjavík, Stykkishólmur and Hellissandur-Rif. All buses between Reykjavík, Stykkishólmur and Ólafsvík meet at an unassuming intersection called Vegamót (which means intersection) where passengers sort themselves out according to destination. What's going on is explained only in Icelandic, so stay on your toes.

THE WESTFJORDS

Extending claw-like toward Greenland, the Westfjords peninsula, attached to the mainland by a narrow isthmus, is the most rugged and remote corner of Iceland.

Ísafjörður

Ísafjörður, the Westfjords' commercial centre, is the region's largest settlement with about 3500 people. The **Westfjords Maritime Museum**, one of Iceland's finest, has

Snæfellsnes West End

historical displays and lovely old photographs of the early settlement.

Places to Stay & Eat The *Hotel Ísafjörður* (☎ 94-4111) is a typically sterile Icelandic hotel with doubles for 6600 kr including a buffet breakfast. An affiliated *Summer Hotel* (☎ 94-4485) operates at the school west of town; doubles without bath cost 4800 kr. Dormitory accommodation is 620 kr. The free camping ground is in Tungudalur several km from town but there's also camping behind the Summer Hotel.

Hotel Ísafjörður's dining room is expensive but the breakfast buffet is good at 420 kr. *Frábaer* on the main street serves good quick meals and the *Seamen's Cafeteria* out on the spit does simple inexpensive set meals.

Hornstrandir
The wildest corner of the Westfjords, the uninhabited Hornstrandir peninsula, offers excellent hiking and camping. It's accessible on the *Fagranes* ferry from Ísafjörður.

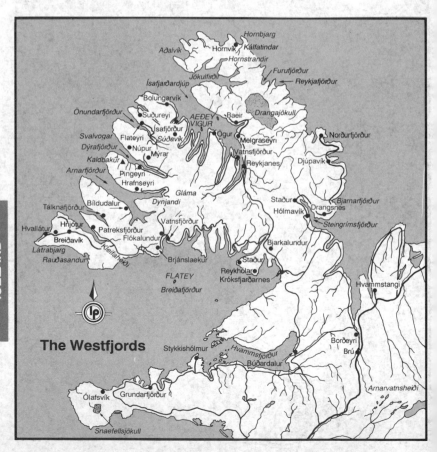

There's no accommodation or food available on Hornstrandir.

Látrabjarg

The cliffs of Látrabjarg wrap around the westernmost end of the Westfjords and are home to one of Iceland's greatest concentrations of bird life. The 12-km-long cliffs range from 40 to 511 metres high. Puffins and seals are normally the main attractions.

There's a *youth hostel* at Breiðavík 12 km away. From Ísafjörður, the only reliable transport to Látrabjarg is the two-day BSÍ tour. It's a long and trying affair and allows only an hour on the cliffs.

Getting There & Away

Air Flugleiðir has daily flights between Akureyri and Ísafjörður. Between Reykjavík and Ísafjörður, there are both morning and evening flights daily.

Bus Westfjords' bus schedules are complicated; they're geared to coincide with bus tours wherever possible as well as ferry sailings between Brjánslaekur and Stykkishólmur.

There are two highway trips a week each way between Reykjavík and Ísafjörður. Sometimes the southbound bus takes the Ísafjarðardjúp route to Bjarkalundur rather than going down the west coast to Flókalundur. When it goes to Flókalundur, it sometimes connects with a bus to Brjánslaekur ferry terminal; or to Breiðavík and Látrabjarg. When it goes to Bjarkalundur, it sometimes connects with the bus between Reykjavík and the Strandir coast to Norðurfjörður. BSÍ tours in the Westfjords use some combination of these buses.

Ferry The car ferry *Baldur* operates between Stykkishólmur (Snaefellsnes) and Brjánslaekur (Westfjords) at least once daily between 1 May and 30 September. The ferry connects with Reykjavík buses in Stykkishólmur and with Westfjords buses at the other end of the journey.

AKUREYRI

Akureyri (Meadow Sandspit) is the best of urban Iceland and sunny days are common in this small and tidy town beneath perpetually snow-capped peaks. Along the streets, in flower boxes and in private gardens grow Iceland's most colourful blooms and the summer air is filled with the fresh scent of sticky birch.

Things to See & Do

The geologic theme that pervades modern church architecture in Iceland has not been lost on Akureyri **church**. Less blatantly 'basalt' than Reykjavík's Hallgrímskirkja, Akureyrarkirkja is basalt, nonetheless. Inside there's an angel sculpture by renowned Danish sculptor Bertel Thorvaldsen. It's open daily from 9.30 to 11 am and 2 to 3.30 pm.

Most of Akureyri's **museums** are the homes of locals 'done good'. Icelanders' proudly commemorate their artists, poets and authors but without a particular admiration for their work, non-Icelanders will find this of limited interest. The best of these is **Nonnahús**, at Aðalstraeti 45b, the childhood home of children's writer Reverend Jón Sveinsson (nicknamed 'Nonni') who lived from 1857 to 1944. This cosy old home, built in 1850, is a good example of an early village dwelling.

The **Akureyri Folk Museum**, at Aðalstraeti 58, houses interesting artwork and historical household items. Admission is 150 kr. It's open daily from 1.30 to 5 pm between 1 June and 15 September.

The **Lystigarður Akureyrar**, the botanical gardens, were opened in 1912. They include every species native to Iceland and high-latitude and altitude plants from around the world. They're open from 1 June to 30 September from 8 am to 10 pm weekdays, 9 am to 10 pm on weekends

A good day's walk from Akureyri is up the **Glerá valley** and to the summit of 1144-metre **Mt Sulur**. With more time, you can continue up to Baugasel mountain hut and turn the walk into a two-day trip.

ICELAND

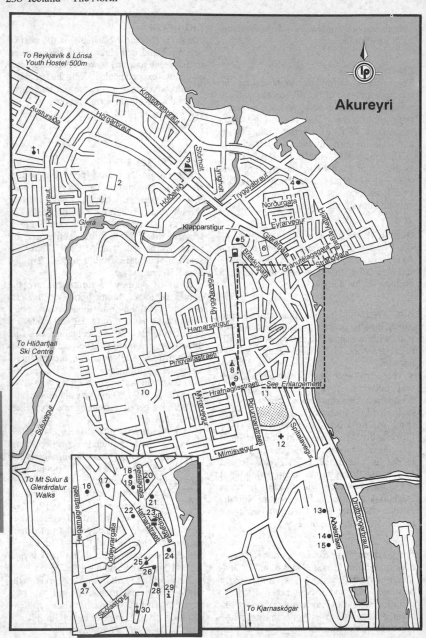

Akureyri

1 Glerá Church
2 Sports Stadium
3 Youth Hostel
4 Hagkaup Supermarket
5 View Disc & Helgi the Lean Statue
6 Sports Stadium
7 Police
8 Camping Ground
9 KEA Supermarket
10 Sports Stadium
11 Botanic Gardens
12 Hospital
13 Friðbjarnarhús
14 Nonnahús
15 Akureyri Folk Museum
16 Davíðshús
17 Library & Archives
18 Cinema
19 Bank & Foreign Exchange
20 Bank & Foreign Exchange
21 Uppinn Pizzeria & Bar
22 Bank & Foreign Exchange
23 Post & Telephone Office
24 Bautinn Restaurant
25 Akureyri Church
26 Natural History Museum
27 Swimming Pool
28 Matthías Jochumsson Memorial Museum (Sigurhaeðir)
29 Tourist Information Office & Bus Terminal
30 Catholic Church

Places to Stay

The nice central camping ground costs 260 kr a person, including use of the washing machine. There's free coffee in the office every morning.

The *Akureyri Youth Hostel* (☎ 96-23657), at Stórholt 1, is a 15-minute walk from the city centre. It's open year-round and advance bookings are essential. The *Lónsá Youth Hostel* (☎ 96-25037) is three km from the centre near the river Lónsá. A city bus stops within 300 metres; if you arrive after 5 pm, phone and they'll fetch you. It's open from 1 June to 1 October.

All the middle-range accommodation in Akureyri is guesthouse-style. Consistently recommended is the *Salka Guesthouse* (☎ 96-22697) in the centre of town at Skipagata 1. It's small and friendly, offering singles/doubles for 1650/2280 kr and sleeping-bag accommodation for 720 kr with cooking facilities. Nicer is *Ás Guesthouse* (☎ 96-26110) at Skipagata 4. It offers bed and breakfast. Singles/doubles cost 2280/3210 kr.

Other guesthouses have singles/doubles for 1650/2280 kr. They include the *Brauðstofan* (☎ 96-23648) at Skólastígur 5, the *Dalakofinn* (☎ 96-23035) at 20 Lyngholt and houses at Þórunnarstraeti 93 (☎ 96-21345), and the one at 13 Gilsbakkavegur (☎ 96-26861). All but the last offer sleeping-bag accommodation for 720 kr.

The plushest hotel is the *Kea* (☎ 96-22200) which advertises a mini-bar in every room; doubles start at 7680 kr. The *Akureyri* (☎ 96-22525), at Hafnarstraeti 98, charges 4140/3000 kr for doubles with/without bath. The *Edda Hotel* (☎ 96-24055) at Hrafnagils-straeti 98 is similarly priced.

Places to Eat

The supermarket at the camping ground is open evenings and weekends. Near the river at Tryggvabraut 22 is *Einars Bakery* which sells fresh bread and cakes. Along the pedestrian shopping mall are quite a few small kiosks selling sausages and chips, burgers and sandwiches. On Ráðhústorg is *Uppinn Pizzeria*, a pizza restaurant and bar. *Elefant Disco* on the shopping street also has a pizzeria.

If you have only one splurge in Iceland, save it for the *Bautinn*. For 615 kr, you'll get all-you-can-eat soup and salad and if you buy a complete meal (main dish, potato dish and vegetable dish) for around 900 kr, the soup and salad are included.

Getting There & Away

Air In summer, Flugleiðir (☎ 96-22000) has up to seven flights daily between Akureyri and Reykjavík. For information and ticketing, contact Akureyri Travel Bureau (☎ 96-25000) on Ráðhústorg. A popular trip is to the island of Grímsey which straddles the Arctic Circle.

Bus Between Akureyri and Reykjavík, there

ICELAND

are buses departing at least once daily year round. Buses travelling over the Kjölar Route to Reykjavík, through the interior, leave on Wednesdays and Saturdays at 8 am in July and August.

Buses to Mývatn and Egilsstaðir run daily from 19 June to 31 August. Buses to Dalvík, the Hrísey ferry and Ólafsfjörður leave at least once daily Monday to Friday.

Getting Around

The tourist information office at the bus terminal rents bicycles for around 900 kr a day.

MÝVATN

In the Mývatn area, travellers can settle in and spend a week camping, sightseeing and relaxing. The Mývatn basin sits on the spreading zone of the Mid-Atlantic Ridge and although most of the interesting sights are volcanic or geothermal features, the centrepiece of the reserve is the blue lake itself and its numerous waterfowl. Mývatn's main population and service centre, **Reykjahlíð**, was one of the area's Settlement Age farms.

Around the Lake

From the petrol station in Reykjahlíð you can hire a one-speed bicycle for the 37-km trip around the lake (525/825 kr for six to 12 hours). There are a number of walks and side trips away from the main roads. The most interesting begins at **Stóragjá**, a hot spring near the village. After a few minutes, the walk reaches a dead end at a pipeline. From there, turn left and walk several hundred metres until the track turns southward. It crosses an overgrown lava field before reaching **Grjótagjá**, another hot spring. It then continues to **Hverfjall**, the prominent tephra crater south of Reykjahlíð, and **Dimmuborgir**, a maze of oddly shaped lava pillars and crags created 2000 years ago.

Other sites of interest around the lake include the forested lava headland of **Höfði**; the *klasar* pinnacle formations at **Kálfa-strönd**; the swarms of **pseudocraters** at **Skútustaðir** where ponds, bogs and marshlands provide havens for nesting birds; the climb up 529-metre **Vindbelgjarfjall**; and

the high-density waterfowl nesting zone along the north-western shore (off-road entry is restricted between 15 May and 20 July).

Námafjall

Produced by a fissure eruption, the pastel coloured Námafjall ridge lies south of the Ring Road, six km east of Reykjahlíð. It sits squarely on the spreading zone of the Mid-Atlantic Rift and contains numerous steaming vents. A short trail leads from the highway.

Krafla

The impressive and colourful crater at **Leirhnjúkur** is Krafla's primary attraction. From the rim above Leirhnjúkur, you can look out across **Kröfluöskjunni** lava flows created by the original Mývatnseldar eruptions and from the 1975 eruptions, all overlain in places by still steaming 1984 lava. Nearby **Viti**, a 320-metre-wide explosion crater whose name means hell, contains a hot lake but now appears to be inactive.

Tours BSÍ tours operate only in the summer. The two-hour tour around the lake departs from either Skútustaðir or Reykjahlíð and costs 1020 kr. The Grand Mývatn tour leaves Hotel Reynihlíð three times weekly at 8.30 am. The morning segment is a four-hour version of the round-the-lake tour, visiting Krafla in the afternoon. Segments cost 1320 kr each. These tours also operate from Akureyri.

Places to Stay & Eat

Reykjahlíð The main camping ground, 150 metres uphill from the church, fills to overflowing. Sites cost 150 kr a person and 135 kr a tent. *Eldá* (☎ 96-44220) guesthouse charges 320 kr a person for camping and 840 kr for sleeping-bag accommodation. *Hotel Reykjahlíð* (☎ 96-44442) is a small 12-room hotel on the lakeshore charging 3960 kr a double. The largest hotel is the *Reynihlíð* (☎ 96-44170) which charges 5100/6720 kr for singles/doubles, including a continental

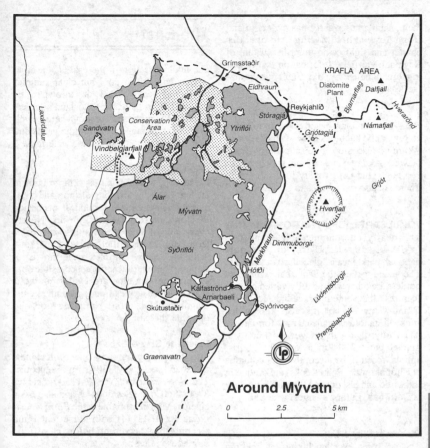

Around Mývatn

0   2.5   5 km

breakfast. The TV lounge and pub serve as a community centre.

The Hotel Reykjahlíð has a low-key dining room but the Hotel Reynihlíð is larger and more popular. The staff aren't impressed with travellers who order coffee and chips (around 300 kr) and occupy seats which could be used by big spenders. The cheapest snack bar food is at the Reykjahlíð petrol station. Be sure to sample the local bread, a gooey cake-like concoction called *hverabrauð* (hot spring bread). Buy it at the supermarket rather than expensive tourist shops.

Skútustaðir Skútustaðir at the southern end of the lake has a general store, cafeteria and a snack bar at the petrol station. Sleeping-bag accommodation is available at the school and costs 520 kr a person and private doubles cost 670 kr a person. The camp site beside the pool costs 290 kr a person. The *Skútustaðir Farm Guesthouse* (☎ 96-44212) has private rooms, cooking facilities and sleeping-bag accommodation.

Getting There & Away
Air Flights to Mývatn from Reykjavík go via the Húsavík or Akureyri airports. From

there, shuttle buses carry passengers to and from Reykjahlíð. Mýflug Air operates charter and sightseeing tours in and out of Reykjahlíð airfield. Information and ticketing are handled by the Eldá guesthouse (☎ 96-44220).

Bus The main long-distance bus terminal is at Reykjahlíð but buses between the lake and Akureyri also stop at Skútustaðir. Buses between Akureyri and Mývatn take less than 1½ hours and depart daily in the summer. There are also daily buses to Egilsstaðir.

JÖKULSÁRGLJÚFUR NATIONAL PARK

The nearly unpronounceable name (try 'YEW-kl-sour-GLYU-fr') of this new national park means glacial river canyon. The name belies the fact that within its borders are other wonderfully varied natural features. It's sometimes called 'Iceland's Grand Canyon', but it's also known for sticky birch forests, unusual rock formations and **Ásbyrgi**, a canyon gouged out by a glacial burst 200 km away. The swirls, spirals, rosettes, honeycombs, and columns at **Hljóðaklettar** (Echo Rocks) are unique in the world and just outside the park boundary is **Dettifoss**, Europe's largest waterfall.

Places to Stay & Eat

The park offers excellent hiking and trekking opportunities but unfortunately, camping inside park boundaries is limited to expensive official camping sites at Ásbyrgi and Vesturdalur. Meals are available only at the snack bar, supermarket and petrol station at the Ásbyrgi farmstead on Route 85.

Getting There & Away

Day tours to major sights of Jökulsárgljúfur operate from Húsavík twice weekly and from Mývatn six times weekly (3180 kr). Apart from the bus from Húsavík to Vopnafjörður, which passes Ásbyrgi, tours provide the only public transport to the park.

The East

The main attraction in the east is sunshine; visitors can expect cool but clear summer weather with the odd rainy day thrown in just to keep things interesting. Iceland's largest forest and longest lake are found here as well as a wealth of rugged and remote peaks and headlands, and some very nice waterfalls.

EGILSSTAÐIR

Egilsstaðir, which began as a large farm in the late 1800s, is now the transport and commercial hub of eastern Iceland. It sits beside the long narrow lake **Lögurinn**. Nearly everything of interest to visitors – the cafeteria, bank, tourist office and supermarket – is in the tourist complex near the petrol station. The main attractions, accessible only by private vehicle, are **Hallormsstaður woods** with a nice camping ground; and the magnificent waterfall **Hengifoss** on the opposite shore of the lake.

Places to Stay & Eat

The camping ground is one of Iceland's nicest and costs only 330 kr for two people. The *Hotel Valaskjálf* (☎ 97-11500) charges 3780/4860 kr singles/doubles and also has a cinema. More reasonable is the *Farm Guesthouse* (☎ 97-11114) with horse rental and sleeping-bag accommodation at official farmhouse prices.

Apart from the bland dining room in the Hotel Valaskjálf, there's only the tourist complex cafeteria. In season, a farm market north-east of the bank sells produce, smoked salmon and snacks.

Getting There & Away

Air Flugleiðir has several flights daily between Reykjavík and Egilsstaðir.

Bus Egilsstaðir is a hub city and one of the four 'corner stones' of the Ring Road so you'll have to stay the night here if you're travelling between southern and northern Iceland. The terminal is at Hotel Valaskjálf.

On Mondays, Tuesdays, Thursdays and Fridays the Egilsstaðir to Seyðisfjörður bus leaves Seyðisfjörður at 10 am and Egilsstaðir at 11.15 am. On Wednesdays, it does three runs in either direction for passengers travelling on the *Norrøna* to or from mainland Europe and the Faroes. They depart from Egilsstaðir at noon, 4.15 and 8.40 pm, and from Seyðisfjörður at 10.45 am, 2.45 and 7.40 pm.

BORGARFJÖRÐUR EYSTRI
Beneath a stunning backdrop of rugged rhyolite peaks on one side and the spectacular **Dyrfjöll** mountains on the other, this town enjoys the nicest setting in eastern Iceland. It's popular with rock hounds after jasper, zeolite, obsidian, basalt and agate.

Places to Stay
Sleeping-bag accommodation is found at *Fjarðarborg* (☎ 97-29920) for 525 kr and at *Stapi* (☎ 97-29983), 500 metres south of town, for 780 kr. *Greiðasalan Borg* (☎ 97-29943), a B&B, is on the main street and the free camp site beside the church has sinks and flush toilets.

Getting There & Away
There are three buses weekly to and from Egilsstaðir.

SEYÐISFJÖRÐUR
Seyðisfjörður, the terminal for ferries from the European mainland, is a pleasant introduction to Iceland for many travellers. It's an architecturally interesting town surrounded on three sides by mountains and on the other by a deep, 16-km-long fjord. The tourist information desk in the Smyril Line office will book your onward accommodation. The bank is 300 metres from the dock and becomes quite a mob scene with everyone clamouring to change money after the ferry docks.

A great introduction to walking in Iceland is the popular trip up the valley **Vestdalur** and around Mt Bjólfur to the Seyðisfjörður-Egilsstaðir road.

Places to Stay
Seyðisfjörður has a recently renovated *youth hostel* (☎ 97-21410) and there's farmhouse accommodation with sleeping-bag space at nearby *Þórsmörk* (☎ 97-21324). The pleasant and well-located *Hotel Snaefell* (☎ 97-21460) costs 3660/4860 kr for singles/doubles. The camping ground is beside the Shell petrol station in the town centre. Alternatively, excellent camp sites may be found below the first Vestdalur waterfall about 40 minutes walk from town.

Places to Eat
The only fully fledged restaurant is at the *Hotel Snaefell* but prepare for a financial blow-out. Alternatively, there's a reasonably priced coffee shop beside the bridge which serves home-baked goods, quiche and specials. It's open weekdays and Saturdays from 2 pm, and on Fridays between 9 am and noon.

Getting There & Away
For bus information, see under Egilsstaðir. Details of the ferry service from mainland Europe is described in the Getting There & Away section of this chapter.

SKAFTAFELL NATIONAL PARK
Skaftafell national park, beneath a breathtaking backdrop of peaks and glaciers, is ideal for daywalks and longer wilderness hiking trips. Don't approach or climb on the glaciers without proper equipment and training.

One of the most popular walks is the effortless one-hour return walk to the glacier **Skaftafellsjökull**. The track begins at the service centre and leads to the glacier face where you can experience first-hand evidence of glacial activity: bumps, groans and flowing water as well as the brilliant blue hues of the ice itself.

If Skaftafell has an identifying feature, it's **Svartifoss**, a waterfall flanked by unusual overhanging basalt columns. A well-worn trail leads from the camping ground. If you have a fine day, the entire loop walk around **Skaftafellsheiði** is highly recommended. The longer day walk from the camping

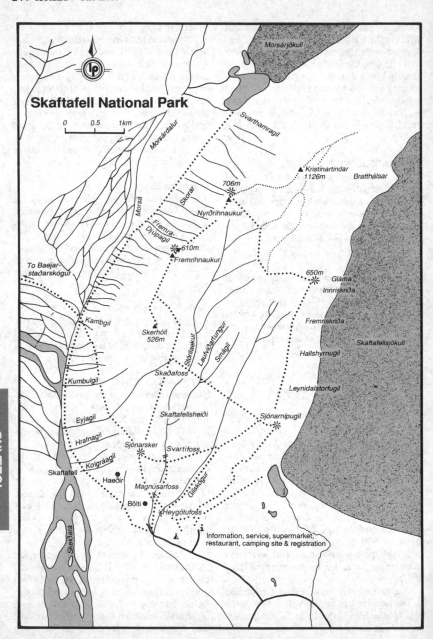

Skaftafell National Park

0   0.5   1km

Morsárjökull

Svarthamragil

Morsárdalur

Skorar

706m

Kristinartindar
1126m

Bratthálsar

Nyrðrihnaukur

Fremra-
Djúpagil

610m

Fremrihnaukur

Morsá

To Baejar-
staðarskógur

650m

Gláma
Innriskriða

Kambgil

Fremriskriða

Skerhóll
526m

Skaftafellsjökull

Stórilaekur

Laufskálatungur

Smágil

Hallshyrnugil

Kumbulgil

Skaðafoss

Leynidalstorfugil

Eyjagil

Skaftafellsheiði

Sjónarnípugil

Hrafnagil

Sjónarsker

Svartifoss

Kolgráagil

Skaftafell

Haeðir

Magnúsarfoss

Gljáskógur

Bölti

Heygótufoss

Skeiðará

Information, service, supermarket,
restaurant, camping site & registration

ICELAND

ground to the glacial lagoon in **Morsárdalur** is tiring but enjoyable; plan on about seven hours for the return trip.

Places to Stay & Eat
The camping ground, an immense, grassy field, is broken only by the odd windbreak hedge or barbecue spit. Showers cost 100 kr for five minutes but queues can be long, especially on weekends. The service area has an information office, coffee shop, cafeteria, supermarket and toilet block. Prices at the coffee shop/cafeteria are surprisingly reasonable but budget travellers will have to avoid the alcohol.

Another nice option is the farm *Bölti* (☎ 97-81626) on Skaftafellsheiði above the western end of the camping ground. They offer private double rooms and a five-bed dorm with sleeping-bag accommodation.

Getting There & Away
From Reykjavík, take the bus to Höfn (from 1 June to 31 August) or Fjallabak (from 15 July to 31 August). The latter follows the incredibly scenic inland route through Landmannalaugar and Eldgjá rather than the relatively drab coastal Ring Road. From Skaftafell to Reykjavík, the Fjallabak bus departs at 8 am. The the bus from Höfn to Reykjavík departs Höfn at 9 am and passes Skaftafell at noon daily.

VATNAJÖKULL
Vatnajökull, in places one km thick, is Iceland's greatest icecap. It rests atop 8400 sq km of otherwise rugged territory with scores of smaller valley glaciers flowing down in crevasse-ridden rivers of sculpturing ice.

Jökulsárlón
This 100-metre-deep lagoon near the Ring Road is more or less an obligatory stop between Skaftafell and Höfn. It is full of icebergs calved from the glacier Breiðamerkurjökull, one of the valley glaciers descending from the Vatnajökull icecap.

Glacier Tour
The easiest way to visit the icecap is to join the BSÍ glacier tour which departs from the hotel in Höfn daily at 9 am from 20 June to 31 August. It stops at Jökulsárlón and costs 840/1560 kr with/without the Omnibuspass. The tour can be booked through your place of accommodation in Höfn (there's a camping ground, hotel and youth hostel). Sleeping-bag accommodation at the ski hut costs 600 kr.

The tour allows about two hours on the glacier. You can walk around on the ice or hire snow machines for an extortionate 1980 kr. A trip in the *thiokols* (glacier buggies) costs 2460 kr a person. Walkers are cautioned not to wander beyond the red poles planted about a km from the hut. There are lots of extremely dangerous snow-bridged crevasses. If you see a narrow depression in the snow, steer clear and don't continue further.

The Interior

The vast and barren interior of Iceland comprises one of Europe's greatest wilderness areas. Gazing across the expanses, you could imagine yourself in Tibet, Mongolia or, as many have noted, on the moon. The Apollo astronauts held training exercises there in preparation for their lunar landing. The uninhabited centre is remote wilderness. There are no services, no accommodation, no bridges and no guarantees should something go awry. Unless you're on a guided tour, careful preparations are essential.

ROUTES OF CENTRAL ICELAND
Historically, the interior routes were used as summer short cuts between the northern and southern coasts. The harsh mountains, valleys and broad expanses were considered the haunt of *utilegumenn*, outlaws fleeing justice. For commoners, the vast deserts were considered places of fear and tragedy.

ICELAND

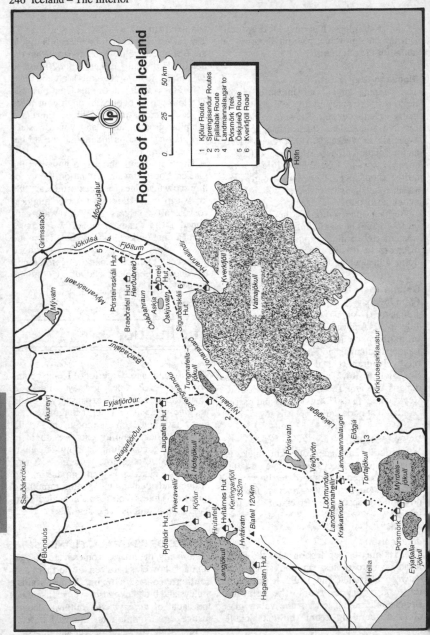

Routes of Central Iceland

1 Kjölur Route
2 Sprengisandur Routes
3 Fjallabak Route
4 Landmannalaugar to
  Þórsmörk Trek
5 Öskjuleið Route
6 Kverkfjöll Road

0   25   50 km

Kjölur Route

The Kjölur (Keel) Route was named in reference to its topographic shape. Although it was greener, more interesting and geographically more inviting than its counterpart, the Sprengisandur, it was historically the less popular, probably due to legends of superhuman outlaws inhabiting its remote ranges.

Its main attraction for modern visitors is **Hveravellir**, a geothermal area of fumaroles and multicoloured hot pools at the northern end of the pass. This route is better suited to walking or cycling than other interior routes thanks to its smoother nature and lack of sand and lava flows.

BSÍ tours leave from Akureyri on Wednesdays and Saturdays at 8.30 am during July and August and arrive in Reykjavík 15 hours later. The normal fare is 6480 kr but Omnibuspass holders pay 4260 kr. If you have the Hringmiði (Full-Circle Pass), you can opt to replace the Akureyri to Reykjavík section of the Ring Road with the Kjölur Route for the Omnibuspass fare.

Sprengisandur Route

The Sprengisandur Route (F28) may be the least interesting of the interior routes but it offers great views of Vatnajökull, Tungnafellsjökull and Hofsjökull glaciers as well as Askja and Herðubreið from the western perspective. Travellers may want to break the journey at **Nýidalur** which has a camp site and two Ferðafélag Íslands' huts accommodating 160 people. They're open from 1 July to 31 August. From the huts, you can take a leisurely hike up the lush valley or do a day hike to colourful pass **Vonarskarð**, a broad 1000-metre saddle between Tungnafellsjökull, the green Ógöngur hills, and the Vatnajökull icecap.

There are a couple of variations on the Sprengisandur tour. From south to north, BSÍ tours travel from Reykjavík to Akureyri on Mondays and Thursdays. On Wednesdays and Saturdays, they go to Mývatn, a slightly shorter trip. From north to south, they operate on Thursdays and Saturdays only from Mývatn. The fare is 6600 kr from Akureyri and 5940 kr from Mývatn.

Herðubreið & Askja

Herðubreið and Askja are the most visited wonders of the Icelandic desert.

Herðubreið The oddly-shaped mountain Herðubreið (1682 metres high) has been described as looking like a birthday cake, a cooking pot and a lampshade but the tourist industry calls it 'Queen of the Icelandic Desert'. The track that circumnavigates it makes a nice day hike from **Herðubreiðarlindir**, a grassy oasis created by springs flowing from beneath the lava. There's a tourist office, a camp site and Ferðafélag Íslands' Þórsteinsskáli hut (open from June to August) with gas and coal stoves. It's an ideal stop before continuing to Askja or returning to Mývatn.

Askja Bitterly cold and windy, Askja is an immense 50-sq km collapsed caldera that sets one thinking about the power of nature. Part of the collapsed magma chamber contains the sapphire blue (when it's liquid) lake **Öskjuvatn**, Iceland's deepest at 217 metres. At its north-eastern corner is **Víti**, a vent which exploded and formed a tephra crater and a hot lake. Nearby Dreki Hut at **Drekagil** (Dragon Ravine) accommodates 20 people but the cold is brutal, so be prepared with warm and hefty sleeping bags.

Getting There & Away

The BSÍ tour from Mývatn leaves three times weekly in July and August *if* the road is passable. It's a gruelling 15-hour return trip and many participants opt to stay at Herðubreiðarlindir or Drekagil and rejoin the tour later. The fare is 4680 kr.

FJALLABAK RESERVE

Fjallabak reserve is a landscape of rainbow-coloured rhyolite peaks, rambling lava flows, blue lakes and soothing hot springs that can hold you captive for several days. There are numerous worthwhile day hikes around Landmannalaugar. The star attractions are **Laugahraun** lava flow; the hot vents at colourful **Brennisteinsalda** (Burning Stones Crest); and the blue lake

ICELAND

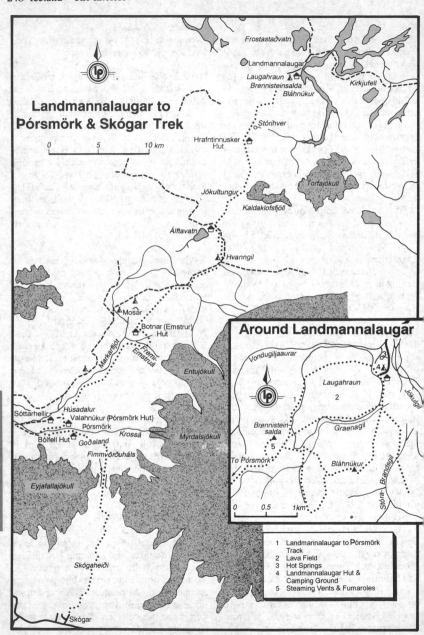

Landmannalaugar to Þórsmörk & Skógar Trek

Frostastaðvatn

Landmannalaugar

Laugahraun
Brennisteinsalda
Bláhnúkur

Kirkjufell

Stórihver

Hrafntinnusker
Hut

0   5   10 km

Torfajökull

Jökultungur

Kaldaklofsfjöll

Álftavatn

Hvanngil

Mosar

Botnar (Emstrur)
Hut

Markarfljót

Fram-
Emstruá

Entujökull

Sóttarhellir

Húsadalur
Valahnúkur (Þórsmörk Hut)
Þórsmörk

Bólfell Hut   Goðaland

Krossá

Myrdalsjökull

Fimmvörðuháls

Eyjafjallajökull

Skógaheiði

Skógar

Around Landmannalaugar

Vondugiljaaurar

Laugahraun

1

2

Brennisteins-
alda

Graenagil

5

To Þórsmörk

Bláhnúkur

Jökulgil

Stóra-
Brandsgil

4

0   0.5   1km

1	Landmannalaugar to Þórsmörk Track
2	Lava Field
3	Hot Springs
4	Landmannalaugar Hut & Camping Ground
5	Steaming Vents & Fumaroles

ICELAND

Frostastaðavatn, just over the rhyolite ridge north of Landmannalaugar. **Bláhnúkur** (Blue Peak), a 943-metre peak immediately south of the Laugahraun, offers a good scree scramble with a view.

Landmannalaugar to Þórsmörk Trek

The four-day trek from Landmannalaugar to Þórsmörk (or vice versa) is the premier walk in Iceland and can be completed by anyone in reasonable physical condition. Most people walk the track from north to south because of the net altitude loss and the shower at the Þórsmörk hut. Some continue to Skógar making a six-day trip. Due to its popularity, those staying in the three huts along the track must pay hut fees and pick up keys from hut wardens in Landmannalaugar or Þórsmörk, or from Ferðafélag Íslands in Reykjavík. Wardens can also answer specific questions and provide information on trail conditions.

Places to Stay

The Ferðafélag Íslands' hut at Landmannalaugar accommodates 115 people on a first-come-first-served basis. In July and August, it's normally booked out by tour groups and club members. You'll probably have to resort to the soggy and gravel-covered camping area which shares facilities with the hut.

Getting There & Away

The only public transport over the Fjallabak Route is the BSÍ tour which operates (river conditions permitting) each way between Reykjavík and Skaftafell daily from 15 July to 31 August.

It stops at Landmannalaugar at 12.30 and departs at 2.30 pm. It also stops at **Eldgjá** (Fire Gorge) allowing an hour for a walk to the spectacular **Ófaerufoss**, a two-level waterfall spanned by a natural stone bridge. The total fare is 3600 kr.

ICELAND

Norway

Norway (Norge) is a ruggedly beautiful country of high mountains, deep fjords, and icy blue glaciers. It stretches 2000 km from beach towns in the south to treeless Arctic tundra in the north. Norway offers incredible wilderness hiking, year-round skiing, and some of the most scenic ferry, bus and train rides imaginable. Summer days are delightfully long, and in the northernmost part of the country the sun doesn't set for weeks on end.

In addition to the lure of the spectacular western fjords, Norway has pleasantly low-key cities, unspoiled fishing villages and rich historic sites that include Viking ships and medieval stave churches.

Norway retains something of a frontier character, with even its biggest cities surrounded by forested green belts. Wilderness camping is one of the best ways to see the country up close and a good way to beat some of Norway's high costs.

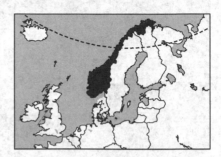

Facts about the Country

HISTORY

The first settlers to Norway arrived more than 10,000 years ago with the end of the Ice Age. As the glaciers retreated north, these early hunters and gatherers followed, pursuing migrating reindeer herds.

Norway's greatest impact on history was during the Viking Age, a period usually dated from the plundering of England's Lindisfarne monastery by Nordic pirates in 793 AD. Over the next century, the Vikings made raids throughout Europe and established settlements in the Shetland, Orkney and Hebrides islands, the Dublin area and Normandy, the latter named for the 'North men'. Harald I (Harald Finehair) unified Norway around 900 and St Olaf converted its people to Christianity a century later.

With their sleek seaworthy ships, the Vikings became the first to cross the Atlantic Ocean beginning with Erik the Red's visit to Iceland and Greenland. Shortly after, in the year 1001 according to the sagas, Leif Eriksson, the son of Erik the Red, explored the coast of North America which he called Vinland the Good.

The Viking Age ended in 1066 with the defeat of the Norwegian king Harald Hardrada at the Battle of Stamford Bridge in England.

In the 1200s Oslo emerged as a centre of power and a period of prosperity and growth followed until the mid-1300s when the bubonic plague swept the country, wiping out nearly two-thirds of the population. In 1380 Norway was absorbed into a union with Denmark which lasted over 400 years.

Denmark's ill-fated alliance with France in the Napoleonic Wars resulted in its ceding of Norway to Sweden in January 1814 under the Treaty of Kiel. Tired of forced unions, on 17 May 1814 a defiant Norway adopted its own constitution, though its struggle for independence was quickly quelled by a Swedish invasion. In the end Norwegians were allowed to keep their new constitution but were forced to accept the Swedish king.

In 1884 a parliamentary government was introduced in Norway and a growing nationalist movement eventually led to this

NORWAY

country's peaceful secession from Sweden in 1905. By referendum Norwegians voted in favour of a monarchy over a republic. Having no royalty of their own, Norway's parliament selected Prince Carl of Denmark to be king. Upon acceptance, he took the title Håkon VII and named his infant son Olav, both names from Norway's Viking past.

Norway stayed neutral during WW I. Although it restated its neutrality at the start of WW II, it was attacked by the Nazis on 9 April 1940 and after a two-month struggle fell to the Germans. King Håkon set up a government in exile in England and placed most of Norway's huge merchant fleet under the command of the Allies. Though Norway remained occupied until the end of the war, it had an active Resistance movement.

In one of the most renowned sabotage efforts of WW II, Norwegian Resistance fighters parachuted into the German heavy-water plant at Rjukan, in southern Norway, and blew the plant, along with Germany's efforts to develop an atomic bomb, sky-high. Upon retreating at the end of the war, the Nazis torched and levelled nearly every town and village in northern Norway.

The royal family returned to Norway in June 1945, exactly five years after going into exile. King Håkon died in 1957 and was succeeded by his son, Olav V, a popular king who reigned until his death (when he was aged 86) in January 1991. Crown Prince Harald, Olav's son, was crowned king of Norway (Harald V) in a grand ceremony in Trondheim on 23 June 1991.

Norway joined the European Free Trade Association (EFTA) in 1960 but has been reluctant to forge closer bonds with other European nations, in part due to concerns about losing its national identity and its ability to preserve small-scale farming and fishing. Norway is once again debating whether it should seek membership into the European Community (EC), a procedure that requires a national referendum. The last such referendum, which took place in 1972, resulted in a heated national debate, a serious rift in the government and a 52% vote against EC membership.

GEOGRAPHY

Norway, occupying the western part of the Scandinavian peninsula, has a land area of 324,220 sq km and shares borders with Sweden, Finland and Russia. The country is long and narrow, with a coastline deeply cut by fjords – long, narrow inlets of the sea between high, steep cliffs. Mountains, some capped with Europe's largest glaciers, cover more than half of the land mass. Only 3% of Norway is arable.

'The Land of the Midnight Sun' is more than just a promotional slogan, as over 500 km of Norway lies north of the Arctic Circle, the point at which there is at least one full day when the sun never sets and one day when it never rises.

GOVERNMENT

Though officially a monarchy, Norway is a constitutional democracy with a parliamentary form of government, similar to the UK's. General elections are held every four years for the 165 seats in parliament (Storting). Gro Harlem Brundtland has been Norway's prime minister since 1986. The first woman to hold this office, she is a member of the labour party, the largest of the six major parties represented in parliament.

Norway's politics has few extremes. The major conservative party is quite moderate by European standards, the two communist parties have only minuscule membership, and there is no right-wing neofascist movement. The labour party is social-democratic in orientation, promoting extensive social programmes supported by high taxation.

ECONOMY

North Sea oil fields, discovered on the Norwegian continental shelf in the 1960s, have brought prosperity to Norway which has one of the world's highest per capita incomes.

Fishing, shipbuilding and shipping are mainstays of the economy and abundant hydroelectric power provides the basis for a number of industries including aluminium, steel and paper production. Norway has a comprehensive cradle-to-grave social welfare system. All citizens are entitled to free university education, free hospital treatment and a guaranteed pension.

POPULATION & PEOPLE

Norway has 4,274,000 people and the lowest population density in Europe. The largest cities are Oslo with 462,000 residents, Bergen with 215,000, Trondheim with 137,000 and Stavanger with 97,000.

Norwegians are of Germanic (Nordic, Alpine and Baltic) origin. In addition, there are about 30,000 Sami people, a Lapp ethnic minority, many of whom still live a traditional nomadic life herding reindeer in the far north.

ARTS

Norway's best known artists include Edvard Munch, composer Edvard Grieg, playwright Henrik Ibsen and sculptor Gustav Vigeland.

Norway's unique stave churches, some of the oldest wooden buildings on earth, have one foot in the Viking Age and the other in the 11th century early Christian era. The churches, named for the vertical boards of the walls, are distinguished by dragon-headed gables that resemble the ornately carved prows of Viking ships and by their unique pagoda-like shape.

CULTURE

Norwegians tend to be independent and outdoor-oriented people. On summer weekends hiking is popular, in winter it's skiing. Other favourite pastimes include fishing, boating and white-water rafting. 'No trespassing' signs are virtually unknown and public access to wilderness areas is guaranteed.

Norway holds onto many of its cultural traditions. The wearing of elaborate regional folk costumes is still commonplace at weddings and other festive events. Traditional folk dancing and singing is enjoying a resurgence in popularity and visitors can enjoy these activities at festivals around the country.

Storytelling is another centuries-old tradition. Trolls are an essential element in Norwegian folklore, borne from a custom of fireside storytelling that helped pass the dark winter months. Trolls are especially associated with mountainous areas. While some trolls could be befriended, others were pesky creatures who lived in the ground under houses and barns, and were a convenient source of blame for all of life's woes. Trolls live on in Norway's place names, as mascots, as carved figurines and in scores of folk tales.

Norwegians tend to be straightforward and easygoing, and nothing out of the ordinary is expected of visitors. One simple rule of etiquette: as a guest in a Norwegian home, you shouldn't touch your drink before your host makes the toast 'skål', which you should answer in return.

RELIGION

More than 90% of all Norwegians belong to the Church of Norway, an Evangelical Lutheran denomination.

LANGUAGE

Norway has two official written languages. They are quite alike, and every Norwegian learns both at school. Bokmål, literally 'Book-language', referred to in this language section as BM (or indicated within brackets), is the urban-Norwegian variety of Danish, the language of the former rulers. BM, also called Dano-Norwegian, has high prestige in some circles. It is written by more than 80% of the population, but not widely spoken (it wasn't really designed for speaking). Nonetheless, many business people, officials, and others, do speak it.

The other written language is Nynorsk, or 'New Norwegian' – as opposed to Old Norwegian, the language in Norway before 1500 AD, before Danish rule. Nynorsk, referred to here as NN, is a kind of common denominator of everyday speech in all its dialects. It is therefore very appropriate for the traveller who wants to communicate with Norwegians all over the country. NN is disliked by some members of society, especially class-conscious people, and you may even come across people who claim that NN doesn't really exist!

In speech the distinction between BM and

NN is no problem, since Norwegians understand either. Both are used in the media, although BM is predominant in the daily papers. A striking feature of both written languages is that many words have two or more officially authorised forms of spelling.

English is widely understood and spoken in Norway, especially in the urban areas and tourist destinations. In the rural (and therefore mostly NN) areas you may come across people who will speak little English. If you show an effort to speak their tongue, it will help a great deal to establish contact.

Pronunciation

Length, as a distinctive feature, of vowels is very important in the pronunciation of Norwegian. Every vowel has a (very) long and a (very) short counterpart, when appearing in a stressed syllable. Generally, it is short when followed by one consonant, and long when followed by two or more consonants.

Vowels

a	as in 'cut'
a long	as in 'father'
å	as in British English 'pot'
å long	as in British English 'lord'
æ	has the same pronunciation as the first four varieties of e
e	before r, as in British 'bat'
e	before r, as in British 'bad'
e	as in 'bet'
e long	as in posh British 'day'; close to German *sehen*
e	as the 'u' in 'lettuce', always unstressed
i	like 'beat', but very short, as the French *si, il*
i long	as in 'seethe'
o	as in British 'pot'
o long	like the American 'zoo', but more like the German *u* in *Suchen*
o	as the 'u' in put
o long	as in 'lord'
ø	as in German *zwölf*, or French *boeuf*
ø long	as in British 'fern'
u	as in French *sud*
u long	like British 'soon', but more like German *süss*
u	as in 'put'
y	between French *sud* and *si*
y	between 'seethe' and German *süss*

Diphthongs

ai	similar to 'dive'
ei	similar to Australian English 'day'
au	similar to Australian English 'shown'
øy	as the French *eui* in *fauteuil*

Consonants & Semivowels

d	at the end of a word, or between two vowels, it is often silent
g	as the 'g' in 'get', but before the letters or combinations ei, i, j, øy, and y it is, in most cases pronounced like the 'y' in 'yard'. The combination gn is pronounced as the 'ng' of 'sing', followed by an 'n'.
h	like the 'h' in 'her', but before v and j it is silent
j	always like the 'y' in 'yard'
k	a hard sound as in 'kin', but before the letters or combinations ei, i, j, øy, and y, it is, in most words, pronounced as the 'ch' in 'chin'. In many areas though, these combinations are pronounced like the 'h' in 'huge', or like the German *ch* in the word *ich*.
l	pronounced thinly, as in 'list', except after the phonetic 'ah', 'aa', 'o' and 'or' sounds, when it becomes the 'l' sound of 'all'
ng	in most areas, like the 'ng' sound in 'sing'
r	trilled, as in Spanish. In south-west Norway, however, the r is pronounced gutturally, as in French. The combinations rd, rl, rn, rt sound a bit like American 'weird', 'earl', 'earn' and 'start', but with a much weaker 'r'. The resulting consonants are made with the tip of the tongue curled behind the teeth, and the preceding vowel is lengthened. These consonants occur even when the r is the last letter of one word and the d, l, n, or t is the first letter of the

next word. In some words, however, where the **d** in the combination **rd** is silent, the preceding vowel is often lengthened but the **r** trilled: for example, the word gard, meaning farm, is pronounced gaarr, not gahrd. The combination **rs** is pronounced 'sh' as in 'fish'.

s   always voiceless, like the 's' in 'us'. The combination **sk** followed by **ei, i, j, øy** and **y** is pronounced as 'sh': so the Norwegian word ski sounds like the English 'she'.

t   like the English 't', except in two cases where it is silent: in the Norwegian word det (meaning 'it, that'), roughly pronounced like British English 'dare'; and in the definite singular ending -et of Norwegian neutral nouns

v   is nearly always pronounced like the English 'w' but without rounding the lips – rather like a German speaker would pronounce a 'w'

Greetings & Civilities

Hello./Goodbye.	Goddag./Morna.
Yes./No.	Ja./Nei.
Please.	Ver(Vær) så snill.
Thank you.	Takk.
That's fine. You're welcome.	Inga årsak. (NN)
	Ingen årsak. (BM)
Excuse me. (Sorry.)	Unnskyld.
Do you speak English?	Snakkar du engelsk? (NN)
	Snakker du engelsk? (BM)
Does anyone speak English?	Er det nokon som snakkar engelsk her? (NN)
	Er det noen som snakker engelsk her? (BM)
I (don't) understand.	Eg forstår (ikke). (NN)
	Jeg forstår (ikke). (BM)
Just a minute.	Vent litt.

Useful Signs

Camping Ground	Kamping/Leirplass
Entrance	Inngang
Exit	Utgang
Guesthouse	Gjestgiveri/Pensionat
Hotel	Hotell
Information	Opplysningar (NN)
	Opplysninger (BM)
Open/Closed	Open/Stengd (NN)
	Åpen/Stengt (BM)
Police	Politi
Police Station	Politistasjon/Lensmannskontor
Prohibited	Forbode (NN)
	Forbudt (BM)
Toilets	Toalettar (NN)
	Toaletter (BM)
Railway Station	Jernbanestasjon
Youth Hostel	Vandrerhjem

Getting Around

What time does ... leave/arrive?	Kva tid går/kjem ...? (NN)
	Når går/kommer ...? (BM)
What time is the ... bus?	Kva tid kjem ... bussen? (NN)
	Når kommer ... bussen? (BM)
next	neste
first	første
last	siste
the boat	båten
the bus (city bus)	bussen (bybussen)
the bus (intercity)	bussen (linjebussen)
the train	toget
the tram	trikken
I would like ...	Eg (Jeg) vil gjerne ha ...
a one-way ticket	enkeltbillett
a return ticket	tur-retur
1st class	første klasse
2nd class	andre klasse (NN)
	annen klasse (BM)
Where is ...?	Kor er ...? (NN)
	Hvor er árr ...? (BM)

I want to go to ...	Eg (Jeg) skal til ...
Can you show me (on the map)?	Kan du vise meg (på kartet)?
Go straight ahead.	Det er rett fram.
Turn right.	Ta til høgre. (NN)
	Ta til høyre. (BM)
Turn left.	Ta til venstre.
far/near	langt/nær

Around Town

I'm looking for ...	Eg (Jeg) leiter etter ...
a bank	banken
the city centre	sentrum
the ... embassy	den ... ambassade
my hotel	hotellet mitt
the museum	museet
the police	politiet
the post office	postkontoret
a public toilet	eit offentleg toalett (NN)
	et offentlig toalett (BM)
the telephone centre	televerket
the tourist information office	turistinformasjon

beach	strand
castle	slott
cathedral	domkirke, katedral
church	kyrkje (NN)
	kirke (BM)
main square	(stor)torget
market	torget
monastery	kloster
monument	historisk bygning
mosque	moské
the old city	gamlebyen
palace	slott
ruins	ruinar (NN)
	ruiner (BM)

Accommodation

Where is a cheap hotel?	Kvar er eit billig hotell? (NN)
	Hvor er et billig hotell? (BM)
What is the address?	Kva (Hva) er adressa?

| Could you write the address, please? | Kan du vere (være) så snill å skrive opp adressa? |

At the Hotel

| Do you have any rooms available? | Har du ledige rom? |

I would like ...	Eg (Jeg) vil gjerne ...
a single room	ha eit enkeltrom
a double room	ha eit dobbeltrom
a room with a bath-room	ha eit rom med bad
to share a dorm	ligge på sovesalen

How much is it per night/per person?	Kor mykje er det pr. dag/pr. person? (NN)
	Vor mye er det pr. dag/ pr. person? (BM)
Can I see it?	Kan eg få sjå det? (NN)
	Kan jeg få se det? (BM)
Where is the bath-room?	Kor (Hvor) er badet?

Food

breakfast	frukost (NN)
	frokost (BM)
lunch	lunsj
dinner	middag

I would like today's special, please.	Eg (Jeg) vil gjerne ha dagens rett, takk.
Is service included in the bill?	Er bevertninga medrekna? (NN)
	Er bevertninga iberegnet? (BM)
I am a vegetarian.	Eg er vegetarianar. (NN)
	Jeg er vegetarianer. (BM)

Time & Dates

| What time is it? | Kva (Hva) er klokka? |

NORWAY

today	*i dag*	60	*seksti*
tomorrow	*i morgon* (NN)	70	*sytti* (NN) *sytti* (BM)
	i morgen (BM)	80	*åtti*
in the morning	*om formiddagen*	90	*nitti*
in the afternoon	*om ettermiddagen*	100	*hundre*
in the evening	*om kvelden*	1000	*tusen*
		one million	*ein million* (NN)
Monday	*måndag* (NN)		*en million* (BM)
	mandag (BM)		

Monday	*måndag* (NN)
	mandag (BM)
Tuesday	*tysdag* (NN)
	tirsdag (BM)
Wednesday	*onsdag*
Thursday	*torsdag*
Friday	*fredag*
Saturday	*laurdag* (NN)
	lørdag (BM)
Sunday	*søndag* (NN)

January	*januar*
February	*februar*
March	*mars*
April	*april*
May	*mai*
June	*juni*
July	*juli*
August	*august*
September	*september*
October	*oktober*
November	*november*
December	*desember*

Numbers

0	*null*
1	*ein* (NN) *en* (BM)
2	*to*
3	*tre*
4	*fire*
5	*fem*
6	*seks*
7	*sju* (NN) *syv* (BM)
8	*åtte*
9	*ni*
10	*ti*
11	*elleve*
12	*tolv*
13	*tretten*
20	*tjue* (NN) *tyve* (BM)
30	*tretti*
40	*førti*
50	*femti*

Health

I'm diabetic/epileptic/asthmatic	*Eg (Jeg) har sukkersjuke/fallesjuke/astma*
I'm allergic to antibiotics/penicillin	*Eg (Jeg) er allergisk mot antibiotika/ penicillin*
antiseptic	*antiseptisk middel*
aspirin	*dispril*
contraceptive	*prevensjonsmiddel*
diarrhoea	*magesjau*
medicine	*medisin*
nausea	*kvalme*

Emergencies

Help!	*Hjelp!*
Call a doctor!	*Ring ein lege!*
Call the police!	*Ring politiet!*
Go away!	*Forsvinn!*

Facts for the Visitor

VISAS & EMBASSIES

Citizens of the USA, Canada, UK, Australia and New Zealand need a valid passport to visit Norway, but do not need a visa for stays of less than three months.

Norwegian Embassies & Consulates

The following are useful addresses:

Australia
    Royal Norwegian Embassy, 17 Hunter St, Yarralumla, Canberra, ACT (☎ 06-2733 444)
Canada
    Royal Bank Center, 90 Sparks St, Suite 532 CDN, Ottawa, Ontario K1P 5B4 (☎ 613-238-6570)

New Zealand
  Royal Norwegian Consulate General, PO Box 2825, Wellington (☎ 4-712 503)
UK
  Royal Norwegian Embassy, 25 Belgrave Square, London SW1X 8QD (☎ 071-235-7151)
USA
  Royal Norwegian Embassy, 2720 34th St, Washington DC 20008 (☎ 202-333-6000)

Foreign Embassies in Norway

These overseas embassies are in Oslo:

Canada
  Oscars gate 20, Oslo (☎ 22 46 69 55)
Denmark
  Olav Kyrres gate 7, Oslo (☎ 22 44 18 46)
Finland
  Drammensveien 40, Oslo (☎ 22 43 04 00)
Russia
  Drammensveien 74, Oslo (☎ 22 55 32 78)
Sweden
  Inkognitogata 26, Oslo (☎ 22 44 38 15)
UK
  Thomas Heftyes gate 8, Oslo (☎ 22 55 24 00)
USA
  Drammensveien 18, Oslo (☎ 22 44 85 50)

There are no Australian or New Zealand embassies – contact the British embassy instead.

DOCUMENTS

In addition to your passport, take your home driving licence. It will be valid in Norway. Also take a youth hostel association card to get lower hostel rates. A student identity card will get you some discounts at museums and occasionally on buses and ferries.

CUSTOMS

Alcohol is expensive in Norway, so you might want to bring in your duty-free allotment: one litre of spirits and one litre of wine (or two litres of wine), plus two litres of beer. You're also allowed to bring in 200 cigarettes duty free. There are no restrictions on the amount of currency you can bring into Norway, but if you're carrying the equivalent of more than 25,000 kr in cash you must declare it upon entry.

MONEY

Post offices and banks exchange major foreign currencies and accept all travellers' cheques. Travellers' cheques command a better exchange rate than cash by about 1%.

Post offices charge a service fee of 10 kr a travellers' cheque or 15 kr for any size cash transaction. A few banks, including Kreditkassen, match those rates, but most banks charge 20 kr per travellers' cheque. Because of these per-cheque fees, you'll save money by bringing travellers' cheques in higher denominations.

Visa, Eurocard, MasterCard, American Express and Diners Club cards are widely accepted throughout Norway and generally you'll be better off using a credit card as you avoid the transaction fees. However, credit cards cannot be used to buy train tickets or most domestic ferry tickets other than those for the coastal steamer.

Currency

The Norwegian krone is most often written NOK in international money markets, Nkr in northern Europe and kr within Norway.

One Norwegian krone equals 100 øre. There are one, five, and 10-kroner coins, as well as 10 and 50 øre coins, while bills come in 50, 100, 500 and 1000-kroner denominations.

Exchange Rates

The following currencies convert at these approximate rates:

1 Dkr	=	1.00 Nkr
1 Fmk	=	1.45 Nkr
1 Ikr	=	0.01 Nkr
1 Skr	=	1.10 Nkr
A$1	=	4.29 Nkr
C$1	=	4.81 Nkr
DM1	=	4.07 Nkr
NZ$1	=	3.26 Nkr
UK£1	=	10.22 Nkr
US$1	=	6.00 Nkr

Costs

Norway can be very expensive, but if you

tighten your belt there are ways to take some of the sting out of this.

If you use only camping grounds and prepare your own meals you might squeak by for 140 kr a day. If you stay at hostels, breakfast at a bakery, lunch at an inexpensive restaurant and pick up cheap eats at a grocery store for dinner, you can get by for 225 kr a day. If you stay at 'cheap' hotels which include a buffet breakfast, have one meal at a moderately priced restaurant and eat a snack for the other meal, expect to spend 375 kr a day if you're doubling up, 475 kr if you're travelling alone. This is still pretty bare-bones – entertainment, alcohol, even a couple of Cokes are going to cost extra.

To this you need to add transport costs. If you've got a rail pass and stick mainly to train routes these costs will be low. Trying to cover the whole country can be quite expensive – not because the per-km rate is particularly high, but because the distances are great.

Happily, admission to museums is sometimes free. It often costs from 10 to 15 kr and rarely more than 25 kr – flashing a student card will frequently get you a discount.

Tipping

Service charges and tips are included in restaurant bills and taxi fares with no additional tip expected.

Consumer Taxes

The 20% value-added tax (VAT), which is written 'mva' but pronounced 'moms', is already included in the price you pay for goods and services, including hotel rooms. One exception is car rentals, where you may be quoted rates with or without the tax.

If you buy goods totalling 300 kr or more from a store with a 'Tax Free for Tourists' sign you're entitled to a refund of the value-added tax (VAT), minus a service charge, which comes to between 10% and 15% of the purchase price. Ask the store for a 'tax-free cheque', which you present along with

your purchases at your departure point from Norway to get the refund.

CLIMATE & WHEN TO GO

Due to the warming effects of the Gulf Stream, which flows north along the Norwegian coastline, Norway's coastal areas have a surprisingly temperate climate. In Bergen the average monthly temperature in winter never drops below 0°C and in Vardo in the far north the average December temperature is only -4°C. The mountainous inland areas see a more extreme range of temperatures with colder winter weather.

Norway is at its best and brightest from May to September. Late spring is a particularly pleasant time – fruit trees are in bloom, daylight hours are long, and most youth hostels and sights are open but uncrowded.

Unless you're heavily into winter skiing or searching for the Aurora Borealis of the polar nights, Norway's cold dark winters are not the prime time to visit.

Midnight-sun days, when the sun never drops below the horizon, extend from 14 May to 30 July at Nordkapp and from 23 May to 17 July in the Lofoten islands. Even southern Norway has daylight from 4 am to 11 pm in midsummer.

WHAT TO BRING

Norwegians are quite casual – even executives carry daypacks as often as briefcases – and most travellers are unlikely to need dressy clothing. As the weather can change quickly it's best to have layers of clothing that can be put on and taken off.

Even in summer you're unlikely to regret having a jacket, or at least an anorak (windbreaker), for windy fjord cruises and the high country. Good walking shoes are important. You should bring hiking boots if you plan to do some wilderness hiking, a warm sleeping bag and appropriate gear if you're camping. Consider bringing snacks such as trail mix, peanut butter and instant coffee to save a few bucks. Youth hostellers and those renting cabins will save money by bringing their own sheets as hiring linen sets adds from 30 to 40 kr to the bill.

SUGGESTED ITINERARIES
Depending on the length of your stay you might like to see and do the following:

Two days
    Bergen, rail to Flåm, and a combination boat/bus trip back to Bergen allowing you to see some of the fjords
One week
    Two days in Oslo, two days in Bergen and a three-day jaunt through the western fjords
Two weeks
    As above, plus continue north through Åndalsnes, Trondheim and the Lofoten islands
One month
    As above, plus a coastal steamer cruise breaking at Tromsø and Nordkapp
Two months
    Explore the country thoroughly – spend some time skiing and hiking in the Jotunheimen and Hardanger areas

TOURIST OFFICES
Local Tourist Offices
There are tourist offices in almost every town of any size in Norway, usually near the railway station, dock or town centre. In smaller towns they may be open only during peak summer months, while in cities they're open all year round. Many offices will mail out brochures on request. These are some of the larger regional offices:

Bergen Tourist Board
    Slottsgate 1, 5003 Bergen (☎ 05 31 38 60)
Finnmark Tourist Board
    Postboks 1223, 9501 Alta (☎ 08 43 54 44)
Lofoten Tourist Board
    Postboks 210, 8301 Svolvær (☎ 08 87 10 53)
Oslo Promotion
    Grev Wedels plass 2, 0151 Oslo 1
    (☎ 22 33 43 86)
Sogn og Fjordane Tourist Board
    Postboks 299, 5801 Sogndal (☎ 05 67 23 00)
Stavanger Tourist Association
    Postboks 11, 4001 Stavanger (☎ 04 53 51 00)
Troms Reiser
    Postboks 1077, 9001 Tromsø (☎ 08 31 00 00)
Trondheim Travel Association
    Postboks 2102, 7001 Trondheim (☎ 07 51 14 66)

Representatives Abroad
Representatives abroad include:

Australia
    Royal Norwegian Embassy, 17 Hunter St, Yarralumla ACT 2600 (☎ 06-2733 444)
Denmark
    Norges Turistkontor, Trondhjems Plads 4, 2100 Copenhagen (☎ 31-38 41 18)
New Zealand
    Royal Norwegian Consulate General, PO Box 2825, Wellington (☎ 4-712 503)
Sweden
    Norska Turistbyrån, World Trade Center 5 tr, Mässansgata 18, 412 51 Gothenburg (☎ 031-83 69 70)
UK
    Norwegian Tourist Board, Charles House, 5 Lower Regent St, London SW1Y 4LR (☎ 071-839 6255)
USA & Canada
    Norwegian Tourist Board, 655 Third Ave, New York, NY 10017 (☎ 212-949-2333)

USEFUL ORGANISATIONS
For information on hostels, contact Norske Vandrerhjem (☎ 22 42 14 10), Dronningens gate 26, 0154 Oslo 1.

Disabled travellers can get information on available services from the Norwegian Association of the Disabled (☎ 22 17 02 55), Postboks 9217 Vaterland, 0134 Oslo 1.

If you're of Norwegian descent and want to trace your roots, contact the Norwegian Emigration Centre (☎ 04 52 07 08), Bergjelandsgata 30, 4012 Stavanger.

For gay issues, there's Det Norske Forbundet av 1948 (☎ 22 36 19 48), St Olavs plass 2, 0165 Oslo 1. For general information about the gay scene, call Homofile og Lesbiskes Opplysningstelefor, or HOLT (☎ 22 11 33 60), after 8 pm on weekdays.

The Norges Automobilforbund (NAF), the national automobile club, is affiliated with a number of international clubs, including the AA in Britain and the AAA in the USA. NAF's main office (☎ 22 34 14 00) is at Storgata 2, 0155 Oslo 1. However NAF has very little to offer in English and the only road map they provide free is one listing member camping grounds, so you're best off asking your home association for materials before your trip.

BUSINESS HOURS & HOLIDAYS

Business hours are generally from 9 am to 4 pm Monday to Friday, though stores often stay open to 6 or 7 pm on Thursdays and to 2 pm on Saturdays. Be aware that many museums have short hours (from 11 am to 3 pm is quite common) which can make things tight for sightseeing. On Sundays most stores are closed, including bakeries, grocers and many restaurants.

Public holidays are:

New Year's Day, 1 January
Maundy Thursday, the Thursday before Easter
Good Friday, the Friday before Easter
Easter Monday, the day after Easter
May Day, 1 May
Constitution Day, 17 May
Ascension Day, the 40th day after Easter
Whit Monday, the seventh Monday after Easter
Christmas Day, 25 December
Boxing Day, 26 December

CULTURAL EVENTS

Constitution Day, 17 May, is Norway's biggest holiday, with marching bands and thousands of traditionally costumed schoolchildren parading beneath the Royal Palace in Oslo. Midsummer's Eve, which is celebrated by bonfires on the beach, is generally observed on 23 June, Saint Hans day.

The Sami people (Lapps) hold their most colourful celebrations at Easter in Karasjok and Kautokeino with reindeer races, *joik* (traditional chanting) concerts and other festivities. The 1994 Winter Olympics will be hosted by the mountain resort town of Lillehammer, 180 km north of Oslo, from 12 to 27 February 1994.

POST & TELECOMMUNICATIONS

Norway has an efficient postal service. Postcards and letters weighing up to 20 grams cost 3.30 kr to mail to Nordic countries, 4.20 kr to the rest of Europe, and 5.20 kr elsewhere. Mail can be received c/o poste restante at any post office in Norway.

Most pay phones accept one, five and 10-kr coins and will return unused coins but won't give change, so it's best to use coins in small denominations. Domestic calls cost a minimum of 2 kr. You get three times as much calling time per krone after 5 pm and on weekends for local calls, twice as much time for regional calls.

Phone cards, which are valid for 22 units of calls (44 kr worth), cost 35 kr and can be purchased at Narvesan kiosks. The cards can only be used in special green phones which are readily found at railway stations but are less common elsewhere.

The country code for calling Norway from abroad is 47. To make international calls from Norway dial 095 and then the country code for the country you're calling.

Changing Phone Numbers

All Norway telephone numbers are scheduled to change in 1993. The changes will take place in steps throughout the year, with the first series occurring in Oslo in late January. The Oslo phone numbers given in this book are the new numbers. As phone numbers in other locales are changing after publication, this book lists the old phone numbers in all but the Oslo area. This means, for example, that after 9 September 1993 (the day the Bergen phone numbers change) the Bergen numbers listed in this book will no longer ring through.

If you dial an old phone number after the change, a recording will give you the new phone number; however it's expected to be in Norwegian only, so it'd be quite helpful to learn the numbers zero to nine in Norwegian.

Tourist offices should have updated listings of the new numbers for accommodation and other visitor services as the changes occur. You can also get numbers by calling the directory service at 0180 as operators speak English, but the cost is a steep 8 kr for 30 seconds.

You can tell if you have an old or new number, as the new phone numbers will all have eight digits and no number will begin with zero.

TIME

Time in Norway is one hour ahead of GMT/UTC, the same as Sweden, Denmark and most of Western Europe. When it's noon in Norway, it's 11 am in London, 1 pm in Finland, 6 am in New York and Toronto, 3 am in San Francisco, 9 pm in Sydney and 11 pm in Auckland.

Norway observes daylight-saving or summer time, when clocks are set ahead one hour in late March and back an hour at the end of September. Timetables and business hours are posted according to the 24-hour clock.

ELECTRICITY
The electric current is 220 volts, from 50 to 60 Hz, and plugs have two round pins.

LAUNDRY
Coin laundries *(mynt-vaskeri)* are expensive and surprisingly rare, though washers and dryers can often be found at hostels and camping grounds. It's a good idea to bring a little laundry soap and plan on doing some hand washing.

WEIGHTS & MEASURES
Decimals are indicated by commas and thousands by points. Norway uses the metric system, with unit measurements written in grams and kg. At delis, 100 grams is often written with the price followed by pr/hg. Fruit and other single items are commonly sold by the piece *(stykke)*, which is abbreviated 'stk'.

BOOKS & MAPS
A good multi-purpose map is the fold-out *Campsites in Norway* road map, which is updated annually and distributed free from Norwegian tourist offices abroad. Request a copy before you go, as it's rather difficult to find in Norway.

For drivers, the best road maps are the Cappelens series, available in Norwegian bookstores. Local tourist offices often have simple town maps.

Mountain Hiking in Norway by Erling Welle-Strand has information on wilderness trails, hiking itineraries, sketch maps and details about trail huts. *Motoring in Norway*

also by Welle-Strand is a concise book describing scenic motor routes.

Norwegian in Ten Minutes a Day is an easy approach to learning the basics of the language, though Berlitz's pocket-size *Norwegian-English Dictionary* is more useful when you're travelling around.

The Vinland Sagas: The Norse Discovery of America (Magnusson/Palsson) is a translation of two medieval sagas that tell of the discovery of America 500 years before Columbus arrived there. *A Brief History of Norway* by John Midgaard covers Norwegian history from prehistoric to modern times.

The Viking World by James Graham-Campbell is a softcover book with handsome photos that traces the history of the Vikings by detailing excavated Viking sites and artefacts.

Norwegians Sigrid Undset and Knud Hamsun have both won the Nobel Prize for Literature. Undset is best known internationally for *Kristin Lavransdatter*, a trilogy that portrays the struggles and earthy life style of a 13th-century Norwegian family. Hamsun won the Nobel Prize for his 1917 novel *The Growth of the Soil*; other works of his such as *Hunger* and *Mysteries* delve into the more troubled aspects of the human character.

There are numerous books on Norse mythology, Vikings, trolls and Thor Heyerdahl's explorations – or to get a different view of Norwegian society pick up one of Henrik Ibsen's classics, such as *A Doll's House*.

Bookstores in Norwegian cities typically have good English-language sections including books on Norway. Sons of Norway's Heritage Books (1455 West Lake St, Minneapolis, MN 55408 USA) has a mail-order catalogue with a few hundred English-language books about Norwegian history, culture, travel and language, as well as maps.

MEDIA
Norway's three largest newspapers are *Verdens Gang*, *Aftenposten* and *Dagbladet*, all available in Norwegian only. The *Inter-*

NORWAY

national Herald-Tribune and British newspapers can be found at major transport terminals and large city kiosks.

Most TV broadcasts are in Norwegian, though US and British programmes are presented in English with Norwegian subtitles. Hotels with cable TV often have CNN and English-language sports channels.

FILM & PHOTOGRAPHY

Though both print and slide film are readily available in major cities, prices are high. A 24-exposure roll of Kodacolor Gold 100 will cost about 50 kr to buy, 120 kr to develop and print. A 36-exposure roll of Kodachrome 64 with processing costs about 140 kr.

HEALTH

Norway is a very healthy place and no special precautions are necessary when visiting. More health information is in the introductory Facts for the Visitor section of this book.

WOMEN TRAVELLERS

Norway is a very safe country and travelling presents no unusual hassles for women. If you're interested in Norwegian feminist issues, contact Kvinnefronten (Women's Front) (☎ 22 37 60 54), Helgesens gate 12, 0553 Oslo.

WORK

The unemployment rate is high in Norway and work is difficult to get. Foreigners who intend to work must apply for a resident-and-work permit through the Norwegian embassy or consulate in their home country before entering Norway. However a ban on most work permits is currently in effect, with exceptions being granted only in cases where highly skilled workers are in demand in a special occupation and that demand cannot be met by Norwegians.

The Atlantis-Norwegian Foundation for Youth Exchange (☎ 22 67 00 43), Rolf Hofmosgate 18, 0655 Oslo 6, has a 'working guest' cultural exchange programme which places people aged from 18 to 30 with Norwegian families. Guests pay their own way to and from Norway plus a registration fee of 830 kr, and then work about 30 hours a week as an au pair or farmhand in exchange for room, board and about 500 kr pocket money a week. Note that arranging a stay can take up to three months.

ACTIVITIES

Much of Norway is wilderness. Åndalsnes and the Lofoten islands are centres for mountain climbing, Nigardsbreen near Sogndal has guided glacier hikes and birdwatchers can see flocks of puffins and kittiwakes in the Lofoten islands of Røst and Værøy.

Hiking

Norway has some of Europe's top hiking, though much of it is seasonal; in the high snow country, hiking is often limited to the period from June to September. The most popular areas are the Jotunheimen and Rondane mountains and the Hardanger plateau. The Norwegian Mountain Touring Association, or DNT, maintains a network of mountain huts a day's hike apart throughout much of Norway's wilderness area. Contact their head office Den Norske Turistforening (☎ 22 83 25 50), Postboks 1963 Vika, 0125 Oslo 1 for information on trails, maps and lodging.

Skiing

'Ski' is a Norwegian word and Norwegians make a credible claim to have invented the sport. It's no exaggeration to say it's the national pastime in winter and no matter where you are in the country you're seldom far from a ski run.

Norway has thousands of km of maintained cross-country ski trails and scores of resorts with downhill runs. The Holmenkollen area on the outskirts of Oslo, Geilo on the Oslo-Bergen railway line, and Lillehammer and the surrounding Gudbrandsdalen region are just a few of the more popular spots. If you're a summer skier, head for the glaciers near Finse, Stryn or the Jotunheimen mountains. DNT is a good source for information on skiing throughout Norway.

Fishing

Norway's salmon runs are legendary, Finnmark in June and July is tops. The 174-page book *Angling in Norway*, available from tourist offices for 120 kr, has details on the best salmon and trout-fishing areas, fees and regulations.

HIGHLIGHTS
Train Rides

The 470-km trip on the **Oslo-Bergen railway** is Norway's finest: a scenic journey through lush green fields, a snow-capped mountain range and the windswept **Hardanger plateau**. A side trip that's a must is on the branch line which hairpins its way down the **Flåm valley**, stopping at a thundering waterfall midroute. Another special train trip is on the **Rauma line** from Dombås to Åndalnes passing **waterfalls** galore.

Museums & Churches

Oslo's **Bygdøy** peninsula holds a fascinating collection of **explorers' ships**: the polar *Fram*, the *Kon-Tiki* raft, and three ships used by the Vikings a millennium ago. Be sure to visit one of the 30 remaining wooden **stave churches** that were built in Norway during medieval times. Ironically, a fair number of the original 800 stave churches stood until the 19th century, when they were torn down by congregations set on building more modern edifices in brick and stone. A few of those spared this fate can now be found in open-air folk museums with other historic timber buildings. Bygdøy has Norway's largest folk museum, while the one in Lillehammer is the most evocatively presented.

Top Fjord Sights

Nothing typifies Norway more than its multitude of glacier-carved fjords and ferrying along these inland waterways is Norway's top sightseeing activity. The **Geirangerfjord** has the most spectacular waterfalls, the **Nærøyfjord** provides the most stunning scenery in the Bergen region and the less-famed **Fjærlandsfjord** has a wonderful pastoral character with small farms hugging the shore.

While the fjords are quite scenic from the water, often the most majestic angle is looking down on them from the surrounding mountainsides. Many fjord-side villages have hiking trails that lead up to lookouts offering some of Norway's finest views. In addition, the road from Gudvangen to Voss, and the Trollstigen and Eagle roads between Åndalsnes and Geiranger, have high vantages with breathtaking fjord scenery.

ACCOMMODATION

Next to camping and hostels, the cheapest places to sleep in Norway are in private rooms booked through tourist offices, usually costing from 150 kr. Many towns have pensions and guesthouses in the 200 to 350 kr range.

Some hotels substantially cut their rates on weekends and in the summer season, which are slow periods for business travel. The Rainbow Hotels chain offers the best deals nearly halving its rates to around 375/500 kr for singles/doubles. The missionary-run NorStar/Havly chain is almost as cheap and the rooms are also quite pleasant. These hotels are alcohol-free, but in all other ways are standard hotels open to everyone.

When weighing accommodation values, one important consideration in this land of sky-high food prices is that hotels usually include an all-you-can-eat buffet breakfast, while most pensions do not.

Camping & Cabins

Norway has nearly 1000 camping grounds. Tent space generally costs from 40 to 70 kr and many camping grounds also rent simple cabins. The cabins often have cooking facilities though linen and blankets are rarely provided, so you'll need your own sleeping bag. In addition Norway has an 'everyman's right' rule dating back 1000 years. This allows you to pitch a tent anywhere in the wilderness (*utmark*) for two nights, as long as you camp at least 150 metres from the nearest house or cottage and leave no trace of your stay.

Den Norske Hytteformidling (☎ 22 35 67 10), Postboks 3207 Sagene, 0405 Oslo 4, has information on cabins where you self-cater.

Hostels

There are 90 vandrerhjem (youth and family hostels) in Norway. Some are quite comfortable lodge-style facilities open all year round, while others operate out of school dorms in summer only. Most have two to six beds to a room and cost from 55 to 160 kr a person, with breakfast generally included at the higher priced hostels. Many hostels also have single, double and family rooms at higher prices. During the summer it's best to call ahead and make reservations, particularly for popular destinations.

Almost all Norwegian youth hostels have kitchens that guests may use to cook their own meals, including all hostels listed in the Norway chapter of this book unless otherwise noted.

Prices given throughout the Norway chapter are for hostel members; if you're not a member you'll have to pay 25 kr more for each night's stay.

You can pick up a free brochure listing youth hostels from tourist offices or get the 70-page detailed Vandrerhjem i Norge in Norwegian, which is available free from many travel agents. Note that the word lukket next to a hostel listing simply means 'closed' and not 'lock-out' and refers to the hours (usually from 11 am to 4 pm) when the reception office is closed and the phone is not answered.

FOOD

Food prices can give you a shock. To keep within a budget, expect to frequent grocery stores and bakeries. Some grocery stores have reasonably priced delis where you can pick up salads sold by weight or half a baked chicken for about 30 kr. Grocery stores also charge about half of what a bakery charges for a loaf of bread.

Common throughout Norway is the konditori, which is a bakery with a few tables where you can sit and eat pastry and inexpensive sandwiches. Other relatively cheap eats are found at gatekjøkken, a term used for food wagons and streetside kiosks, which generally have hot dogs for around 20 kr and hamburgers for 30 to 40 kr. Only marginally more expensive, but with more nutritionally balanced food, are kafeterias which have simple meals for around 50 kr. Meals at moderately priced restaurants often cost from 90 to 120 kr, though many places feature a daily special (dagens rett) for about 65 kr.

Norwegian specialities include the ubiquitous smørbrød or open-faced sandwich as well as grilled or smoked salmon (laks), boiled shrimp (reker), cod (torsk) and other seafood. Expect to see sweet brown goat cheese called geitost, flatbrød and pickled herring with the breads and cereals included in the breakfast buffet. Lutefisk, dried cod made near-gelatinous by soaking in lye, is popular at Christmas time but it's definitely an acquired taste.

DRINKS

The legal drinking age is 18 years for beer and wine, 20 for spirits. On Sundays and public holidays, restaurants and cafés are permitted to serve only beer and wine.

Beer (of any strength) can be purchased in supermarkets, but wine and spirits can only be purchased at government liquor stores called vinmonopolet. These shops are open to about 4.30 pm on weekdays (6 pm on Thursdays) and to 1 pm on Saturdays. Wine is the most reasonably priced alcoholic beverage, costing from 55 kr a bottle.

In addition to the government monopoly on alcohol sales, some local communities in rural areas have stricter restrictions on alcohol sales and a few have virtual prohibition.

ENTERTAINMENT

While Norway is not known for its riveting entertainment scene, you can usually find reasonable nightlife in the bigger cities. Entertainment tends to be pricey. A movie ticket or the cover charge for a disco averages 50 kr, while a glass of beer (øl) will set you back a good 30 kr.

THINGS TO BUY

Norway has high-quality products at high prices. Specialties include wool sweaters and other hand-knitted clothing, pewterware, silver jewellery, Sami sheath knives, reindeer leather products and troll figurines.

Getting There & Away

AIR

SAS, British Airways, KLM, Air France, Lufthansa, Sabena, Swissair, Alitalia, Iberia, Finnair and Icelandair link Oslo with other major European cities. Bergen and Stavanger also have direct international flights.

LAND

To/From Sweden

Bus Nor-Way Bussekspress runs numerous express buses daily between Gothenburg and Oslo (five hours, 230 kr). There's a Friday and Sunday bus between Stockholm and Oslo (nine hours, 340 kr) and, from mid-June to mid-August, a Sunday bus from Stockholm to Trondheim (14 hours, 470 kr).

Train There are daily trains from Stockholm to Oslo (522 kr), Trondheim (603 kr) and via Kiruna (Sweden) to Narvik (631 kr). Trains also run daily to Oslo from Helsingborg (569 kr) via Gothenburg.

Car The main highways between Sweden and Norway are the E6 from Gothenburg to Oslo, the E18 from Stockholm to Oslo, the E14 from Sundsvall to Trondheim and the E12 from Umeå to Mo i Rana. Numerous secondary roads also cross the border.

To/From Denmark

Trains run daily from Copenhagen to Oslo (614 kr) via Helsingborg in Sweden (where you cross on the rail ferry to Helsingør in Denmark).

To/From Finland

The E8 highway runs from Tornio (Finland) to Tromsø and there are secondary highways connecting Finland with the Sami towns of Karasjok and Kautokeino. All three have bus services.

To/From Russia

Russia has a short Arctic border with Norway, see the Kirkenes section for more specific details.

SEA

To/From Sweden

Scandinavian Seaways runs daily overnight ferries between Oslo and Helsingborg, with fares varying according to the season and day of the week, but usually beginning around 500 kr. Scandi Line runs five ferries daily between Strømstad (Sweden) and Sandefjord (Norway) that take 2½ hours and cost 100 kr for a passenger, 130 kr for a car.

To/From Denmark

Color Line runs an average of four ferries daily between Hirtshals (Denmark) and Kristiansand, the shortest connection (four hours) between Norway and Denmark Fares vary from 148 kr in winter to 308 kr on summer weekends for a passenger, from 210 to 420 kr for a car. There's also a 7.30 pm ferry crossing from Oslo to Hirtshals daily in summer, weekdays in winter, which costs from 150 to 310 kr for passengers, 280 to 420 kr for cars.

Scandinavian Seaways runs daily overnight ferries from Oslo to Copenhagen, with the cheapest cabin fare costing from 395 kr (Sunday to Wednesday in the off season) to 685 kr (on summer weekends). Car fares range from 200 to 300 kr.

The Stena Line operates ferries from Oslo to Frederikshavn daily in summer, slightly less frequently the rest of the year. Boats leave Oslo at 7.30 pm, take 10 hours and cost from 190 to 410 kr for a passenger, 290 to 500 kr for a car. Stena also operates a daily ferry from Moss to Frederikshavn that leaves Moss at 12.45 am, takes 7½ hours and costs from 140 to 360 kr for a passenger, 290 to 410 kr for a car.

The Larvik Line makes at least one daily crossing from Larvik to Frederikshavn, with fares ranging from 210 to 340 kr for passengers, 260 to 470 kr for cars.

To/From Iceland & the Faroe Islands
The Smyril Line runs weekly in summer between Seyðisfjörður (Iceland) and Bergen, via the Faroe and Shetland islands. One-way fares from Bergen begin at 460/610 kr to Lerwick in the Shetland Islands, 830/1100 kr to Tórshavn in the Faroe Islands and 1340/1780 kr to Iceland. These fares are for a couchette, with the lower fares for the first three sailings in June and the last three sailings in August, and the higher fares for midsummer travel. The boat leaves Bergen at 3 pm on Tuesdays.

To/From the UK
Color Line sails from Bergen to Newcastle, via Stavanger, twice weekly in winter and thrice weekly from late May to mid-September. Fares for a reclining chair range from 195 kr in midwinter to 895 kr on weekend sailings in summer. The fare to transport a car is 450 kr.

Getting Around

Public transport in Norway is quite efficient, with trains, buses and ferries often timed to coordinate with one another. The handy *NSB Togruter*, available free at any railway station, has rail schedules and information on linking buses. Boat and bus departures vary with the season and the day (services on Saturdays are particularly sketchy), so pick up the latest timetables *(ruteplan)* from regional tourist offices.

AIR
Norway has nearly 50 airports with scheduled commercial flights, from Kirkenes in the north to Kristiansand in the south. Because of the great distances, air travel in Norway may be worth considering even by budget travellers.

Norway's domestic airlines are SAS, Braathens SAFE and Widerøe/NorskAIR.

Typical fares from Oslo are 995 kr to Trondheim and 1855 kr to Tromsø, but a variety of discounts can make air travel competitive. Minipris return tickets cost only about 15% more than full-fare one-way tickets. There's a family rate allowing spouses a 50% discount and anyone aged under 25 years can fly standby for half-fare.

Braathens SAFE's Visit Norway Pass, valid all year round, divides Norway into northern and southern sectors at Trondheim. Flights between any two points in one sector cost $US66. Tickets or a Miscellaneous Charges Order (a voucher which is used like cash with any IATA airline) must be purchased prior to arrival in Norway.

Widerøe/NorskAIR has a summer ticket (valid from 1 July to 15 August) allowing flights for 410 kr within any one of four sectors that are divided at Trondheim, Bodø and Tromsø.

In addition to these domestic discount fares, SAS offers its international passengers $80 advance-purchase tickets that allow travel on direct flights between any two Scandinavian cities they serve, which include a number of Norwegian cities (see the Introductory Getting Around chapter).

BUS
Norway has an extensive bus network and long-distance buses are quite comfortable. Tickets are sold on the buses, with fares based on distance, averaging 95 kr per 100 km. Some bus companies have student and family discounts of 25% to 50%, always ask.

Nor-Way Bussekspress operates the largest network of express buses in Norway, with routes connecting every main city and extending north as far as Kirkenes.

TRAIN
Norway has a good, though somewhat limited, national rail system. All railway lines are operated by the Norwegian State Railways (Norges Statsbaner or NSB). From Oslo lines go to Stavanger, Bergen, Åndalsnes, Trondheim and Bodø, and some continue to Stockholm and Gothenburg in Sweden.

Second-class travel, particularly on long-distance trains, is very comfortable, with reclining seats, footrests, reading lights and the like – 1st-class travel simply isn't worth the extra money.

The introductory Getting Around chapter has details of rail passes. If you're not travelling with a rail pass, there's a minipris ticket available for travel on long-distance trains. You must buy the ticket at least one day in advance and minipris doesn't apply to many of the trains that leave on Fridays, Sundays and holidays. Regular/minipris fares from Oslo are 450/360 kr to Bergen, 440/300 kr to Åndalsnes and 510/360 kr to Trondheim. For the maximum minipris fare of 490 kr, you can even go all the way from Stavanger to Bodø, the greatest rail distance in the country. There's a 50% discount on train travel for people aged 67 and older (and their spouses) and for children under 16.

To be assured of a seat you can always make reservations for an additional 20 kr, and on many long-distance trains, including all those between Oslo and Bergen, reservations are mandatory. If you're on a train that doesn't require reservations and you don't have one, skip empty seats that have a yellow slip of paper attached to them, as they indicate the seat is reserved for some portion of the journey.

Second-class sleepers offer a good way to get a cheap sleep, for 100 kr a bed in a three-berth cabin. Two-berth cabins cost 180 kr a person in old carriages and 200 kr in new carriages which are far more comfortable and well worth the 20 kr difference.

Railway stations almost invariably have luggage lockers for 10 to 20 kr and many also have a baggage storage room.

TAXI

Taxis are available in most towns but are expensive, averaging 17 kr at flagfall and 10 kr per km.

CAR & MOTORBIKE

In Norway, you drive on the right side of the road. All vehicles, including motorcycles and mopeds, must have dipped headlights on at all times. The use of seat belts is obligatory for all passengers. On motorways and other main roads the maximum speed is generally 90 km/h, while speed limits on through roads in built-up areas are generally 50 km/h unless otherwise posted.

Drink driving laws are strict in Norway: the maximum permissible blood alcohol concentration is 0.05% and violators are subject to severe fines. Driving with a blood alcohol level of 0.08% or greater warrants a 21-day prison sentence.

You are required to carry a red warning triangle in your car to use in the event of a breakdown. Third party auto insurance is compulsory and carrying a Green Card is recommended.

If you plan to drive through mountainous areas in winter or spring, check first to make sure the passes are open, as many are closed until May or June. However main highways, such as route 11 from Oslo to Bergen and the entire E6 from Oslo to Kirkenes are kept open all year round. Drivers who expect to drive in snow-covered areas should have studded tyres or carry chains, which can be hired or purchased in Norway.

If you plan to travel along Norway's west coast, keep in mind that it is not only mountainous but deeply cut by fjords. While it's a spectacular route, travelling along the coast requires numerous ferry crossings, which can be time consuming and rather costly. For a complete list of ferry schedules, fares and reservation phone numbers, consider investing in the latest copy of *Rutebok for Norge*, a phone-book-size transport guide (159 kr) available in bookstores and at larger Narvesan kiosks.

Fuel costs average 7.1 kr for a litre of unleaded petrol, 7.9 kr for super petrol and 3.5 kr for diesel.

Motorbikes are not allowed to be parked on the pavement and must follow the same parking regulations as cars.

Caravanning

The speed limit for caravans (cars pulling

NORWAY

trailers) is usually 10 to 20 km/h less than for cars. There are a few mountain roads where caravans are forbidden and numerous other roads that are advisable for experienced drivers only, as backing up may be necessary to allow approaching traffic to pass. For a map outlining these roads, and caravan rules, write to Vegdirektoratet, Postboks 6390 Etterstad, 0604 Oslo 6.

Rental

Renting a car is very expensive, as the walk-in rate for a compact car with unlimited km costs about 850 kr a day. Generally you'll get much better deals by booking with an international agency before you arrive in Norway.

One good deal readily available in Norway is the weekend rate offered by many companies, including Avis and Hertz, which allows you to pick up a car after noon on Friday and keep it until 10 am on Monday, for around 1100 kr, including VAT and unlimited km.

BICYCLE

Given its great distances, hilly terrain and narrow roads, Norway is not ideally suited for extensive touring by bicycle. There are a number of places good for cycling on a regional basis, however, and bikes can be rented at some tourist offices and hostels.

For information on long-distance cycling routes, contact Syklistenes Landsforening (☎ 22 71 92 93), Maridalsveien 60, 0458 Oslo 4.

HITCHING

Hitching is not very common in Norway and you'll probably get mixed results if you try it. One good approach is to ask for rides from truck drivers at ferry terminals and petrol stations.

BOAT

An extensive network of ferries and express boats links Norway's offshore islands, coastal towns and fjord districts. See specific destinations for details.

Coastal Steamer

For more than a century Norway's coastal steamer, *Hurtigruten*, has been the lifeline linking the tiny fishing villages scattered along the north coast. One boat heads north from Bergen every night of the year, pulling into 35 ports on its six-day journey to Kirkenes, where it then turns around and heads back south. If the weather's agreeable, the fjord and mountain scenery along the way is nothing short of spectacular.

The ships are accommodating to deck-class travellers, offering free sleeping lounges, 5-kr lockers, a shower room, a 24-hour cafeteria and a cheap coin laundry. Deck passengers can also rent cabins for 60 to 300 kr, if space is available.

Sample deck fares from Bergen are 1010 kr to Trondheim, 1721 kr to Stamsund, 2072 kr to Tromsø, 2612 kr to Honningsvåg and 3214 kr to Kirkenes. One stopover is allowed.

There are some great off-season deals. From 1 September to 30 April, all passengers are entitled to a 60% discount off the basic fare for voyages beginning any day other than Friday or Sunday. If you're aged between 16 and 26 and are travelling between the previously mentioned dates you can get a coastal pass for 1750 kr that allows unlimited travel for 21 days; this gives you plenty of time to make the return trip from Bergen to Kirkenes and still do quite a bit of exploring along the way.

TOURS

Norway's most popular tour is the *Hurtigruten* coastal steamer cruise from Bergen to Kirkenes. The one-way six-day journey, including meals and cabin, can be done for as little as US$500 in winter and US$695 in summer. At peak times the boats are booked out far in advance. Reservations are made through the Bergen Line (☎ 800-666-2374 in the USA, 800-343-7226 in

NORWAY

Canada) and NSR Travel (☎ 071-930-6666 in the UK).

Oslo

Founded by Harald Hardrada in 1050, Oslo is the oldest of the Scandinavian capitals. After being levelled by fire in 1624, the city was rebuilt in brick and stone by King Christian IV who renamed it Christiania, a name which stuck until 1925 when Oslo took back its original name.

Despite being Norway's largest city, Oslo has barely 500,000 residents and for a European capital it is remarkably low-key, casual and manageable. The city centre is a pleasant jumble of old and new architecture.

Oslo sits at the head of the Oslofjord, an inlet of the Skagerrak. Its northern border is the Nordmarka, a forested green belt crossed by hiking and skiing trails. The city has good museums, plenty of parks and an abundance of statues. The Nobel Peace Prize is awarded in Oslo each year in December.

Orientation
Oslo's central railway station (Oslo Sentralstasjon or Oslo S) is at the east side of the city centre. From there Karl Johans gate, the main street, leads through the heart of the city to the Royal Palace.

Oslo is easy to get around. Most central city sights, including the harbourfront and Akershus Fortress, are within a 15-minute walk of Karl Johans gate, as are the majority of Oslo's hotels and pensions. Many of the sights outside Oslo centre, including Vigeland Park and the Munch Museum, are a short bus ride away, and even Bygdøy peninsula is a mere 10-minute ferry ride across the harbour. The trails and lakes of the Nordmarka wilderness are also easily reached by public transport.

Information
Tourist Offices The main tourist office (☎ 22 83 00 50) is west of the Rådhus (city hall), near the harbour. It's open from 9 am to 6 pm weekdays and to 4 pm on Saturdays from early May to late September, and from 9 am to 5 pm Monday to Friday the rest of the year. Pick up an Oslo map and the *Oslo Guide* there or at the Oslo S tourist-information window, which is open from 8 am to 11 pm daily. Only the main tourist office has brochures for the rest of Norway.

Use It, the youth information office at Trafikanten, outside Oslo S, is open mid-June to mid-August from 7 am to 5 pm weekdays, 9 am to 2 pm Saturdays. They can give you the lowdown on what's happening around Oslo and provide advice on anything from accommodation to hitching.

Oslo Card If you plan on doing a lot of sightseeing consider using the Oslo card which provides free entry to most museums and attractions, and travel on all Oslo public transport. It costs 95/140/170 kr for one/two/three days (half-price for children aged from four to 15 years) and is sold at the tourist office, post offices and hotels. If you're a student or a senior citizen you'll get half-price entry into many sights anyway and may do better with one of the public transport passes.

Money Fornebu airport and Oslo S both have post office and bank windows that exchange money. The post offices charge lower fees but are open shorter hours. The post office at Oslo S is open weekdays from 7 am to 6 pm and Saturdays from 9 am to 2 pm, while the bank at Oslo S is open from 7 am to 11 pm daily from mid-May to 1 September and to 7.30 pm the rest of the year. American Express, at Karl Johans gate 33 opposite the Grand Hotel, changes major currencies and all types of travellers' cheques without transaction fees. It's open from 9 am to 6 pm on weekdays, from 10 am to 3 pm on Saturdays.

Post & Telecommunications The main post office, at Dronningens gate 15, is open from 8 am to 8 pm weekdays, 9 am to 3 pm Saturdays. To receive mail, have it sent to Poste restante, Oslo Sentrum Postkontor, Dronningens gate 15, 0101 Oslo 1.

Oslo

NORWAY

■ PLACES TO STAY

6	Hotell Munch
8	Anker Hotell
25	Grand Hotel
27	Norrøna Hotell
29	KFUM Inter-Rail Point
42	Cecil Hotel
46	Vika Atrium Hotel
65	Hotell Astoria
66	Fønix Hotel
69	City Hotel
70	Sjømannshjemmet

▼ PLACES TO EAT

1	Molina Pub & Spiseri
2	Happy In
3	Café Nordraak
10	Tempus Grocery Store
12	University Cafeteria
14	Helios Health Food
17	Vegeta Vertshus
21	Baker Hansen
23	Oluf Lorentzen Grocery Store
25	Grand Hotel
28	Bakery
31	Djengis Khan
35	Stortorvets Gjæstgiveri
40	Samson's
41	Peppe's Pizza
47	Smør-Petersen
48	La Piazza
52	Bakery
53	Rimi Grocery Store
64	Nador Restaurant
71	Kafé Celsius

OTHER

4	Royal Palace
5	Historic Museum
7	Library
9	Medical Clinic
11	National Gallery
13	T-bane Subway
15	Norli Bookshop
16	Tanum Libris Bookshop
18	DNT
19	Saga Cinema
20	National Theatre
22	Vinmonopolet
24	American Express
26	Heimen Husflid
30	Husfliden
32	Skiforeningen
33	Oslo City Shopping Centre
34	NAF (Norges Automobilforbund)
36	Bank
37	Kilroy Travels
38	Stortinget T-bane Station
39	Stortinget
43	Rådhus
44	Tourist Office
45	Den Rustne Eike
49	Aker Brygge
50	Bygdøy Boats
51	Sightseeing Boats
54	Telegraph Office
55	Smuget
56	Oslo Domkirke
57	Pharmacy
58	T-Bane Subway
59	Bus Station
60	Jerbanetorget
61	Trafikanten
62	Oslo S (Railway Station)
63	Norsk Vandrerhjem
67	Post Museum
68	Main Post Office
72	National Museum of Contemporary Art
73	Fortress Entrance
74	Christiania Museum
75	Norway's Resistance Museum
76	Akershus Castle

You can send telegrams, telex and fax and make long-distance calls from 8.30 am to 9 pm weekdays, 10 am to 5 pm weekends, at the telegraph office at Kongens gate 21 (entrance on Prinsens gate).

Note that all Oslo-area phone numbers were scheduled to change on 28 January 1993. If you have a number that starts with 02 or is only six digits, it's an old number; in many cases if you add 22 at the start of the old six-digit number or replace 02 with 22, the call will go through. All Oslo numbers used in this book are the new numbers.

Foreign Embassies For details see Norway, Facts for the Visitor.

Travel Agencies Kilroy Travels (☎ 22 45 32 00), Nedre Slottsgate 23, specialises in student and budget travel. They also sell international student cards, travel books, maps and backpacks.

Laundry Coin-operated laundrettes include Myntvask, Ullevålsveien 15, open from 8 am to 9 pm daily; and Majorstua Myntvaskeri, Vibes gate 15, open to 8 pm weekdays, 3 pm on Saturdays.

Bookshops Tanum Libris, Karl Johans gate 43, has a comprehensive selection of English-language books, maps and travel guides. If you don't find what you want, walk around the corner of Universitetsgata to Norli, another huge bookshop.

Emergency Dial 002 for police and 003 for an ambulance. Jernbanetorvets Apotek, opposite Oslo S, is a 24-hour pharmacy that can provide medical and dental referrals. Oslo Kommunale Legevakt (☎ 22 11 70 70), Storgata 40, is a medical clinic with 24-hour emergency services; it costs 80 kr for office visits before 4 pm, 140 kr after.

Things to See

Oslo's highlights include the Bygdøy peninsula with its folk museum and Viking ships, Vigeland Park filled with the sculptures of Gustav Vigeland, and Akershus Fortress with its castle and views of Oslo harbour.

Walking Tour Many of Oslo's city sights can be combined in a half-day walking tour. Starting at Oslo S, head north-west down Karl Johans gate, Oslo's main pedestrian street, which is lined with shops and pavement cafés and is a popular haunt for street musicians. After walking a couple of blocks you'll reach **Oslo Domkirke**, the city cathedral, built in 1697. It's open from 10 am to 3 pm weekdays all year round, as well as to 1 pm on Saturdays in summer. Admission is free.

Midway along Karl Johans gate is **Stortinget**, the yellow-brick parliament building. There are free midday tours during the summer recess. Just as architecturally striking is the stately **Grand Hotel** across the street, built in the 1870s, a decade after Stortinget.

Eidsvollsplass, a city square filled with fountains and statues, stretches between Stortinget and the **National Theatre**. The theatre, which has a lavish Rococo hall, was built a century ago to stage Henrik Ibsen's plays.

Across Karl Johans gate is the University of Oslo's law and medical campus and one block to the north is the university's Historic Museum and the National Gallery. Karl Johans gate ends at the Royal Palace, which is surrounded by a large public park.

Heading down from the National Theatre, Roald Amundsens gate leads to the Rådhus and the bustling harbourfront. For a hilltop view of it all, walk down Rådhusgata and turn right on Akersgata to Akershus Fortress, where you could easily spend a couple of hours exploring the castle and museums inside.

The Rådhus Oslo's twin-towered red brick city hall, opposite the harbour, is surrounded by prosaic statues of labourers at work. Of more interest are the wooden reliefs depicting scenes from Norse mythology that line the outside entranceway and the huge splashy murals that decorate the inside halls and chambers.

You can get a good look at the main hall from the front corridor or, for 15 kr (students 5 kr), walk through it all. It's open from 9 am to 3.30 pm Monday to Saturday (to 7 pm on Thursdays), noon to 3 pm Sundays.

National Gallery The National Gallery (Nasjonalgalleriet) has the nation's largest collection of Norwegian art, including some of Munch's best known works, and a respectable collection of other European art including works by Gauguin, Monet and Picasso. The museum, at Universitetsgata 13, is open from 10 am to 4 pm Mondays, Wednesdays, Fridays and Saturdays; 10 am to 8 pm Thursdays and 11 am to 3 pm Sundays. Admission is free.

Historic Museum The Historic Museum

NORWAY

(Historisk Museum) of the University of Oslo, Frederiks gate 2, is three museums under a single roof. Most interesting is the ground floor **antiquities collection** displaying medieval and Viking Age finds and the richly painted ceiling of a 13th century stave church. The **numismatic collection** on the 2nd floor has antique coins, while the top floor holds the **Ethnographical Museum** with displays on Oceania, Asia and Africa. Opening hours are from 11 am (noon in winter) to 3 pm daily except Mondays and admission is free.

Royal Palace The Royal Palace, on a hill at the end of Karl Johans gate, is the official residence of the king of Norway. The palace building itself is not open to visitors but the rest of the grounds are a public park. If you happen to be around at 1.30 pm you can catch the changing of the guard, but it's not worth rushing across town to see.

Akershus Fortress Strategically located on the east side of the harbour, this medieval fortress and castle was built by King Håkon V around 1300. The park-like grounds offer excellent views of the city and Oslofjord, and are the venue for a host of concerts, dances and theatrical productions during the summer.

Entry into the fortress (free) is either through a gate at the end of Akersgata or over a drawbridge spanning Kongens gate that's reached from the south end of Kirkegata. The fortress grounds are open to 9 pm in summer, 7 pm in winter; after 6 pm use the Kirkegata entrance.

In the 17th century, Christian IV renovated **Akershus Castle** into a Renaissance palace, though the front is still decidedly medieval. In its dungeons you'll find dark little cubbyholes where outcast nobles were kept under lock and key, while the upper floors have banquet halls and staterooms.

The chapel is still used for royal events and the crypts of King Håkon VII and Olav V lay beneath it. Tours led by university students wearing period dress provide a good anecdotal history (in English at 11 am, 1 and 3 pm) and are included in the 10-kr admission fee, or you can wander through on your own. The castle is open from 1 May to mid-September from 10 am to 4 pm Monday to Saturday, 12.30 to 4 pm Sunday. In late April and from mid-September to the end of October, it's open on Sunday afternoons only.

During WW II the Nazis used Akershus as a prison and execution grounds, today it's the site of **Norway's Resistance Museum**, which gives a vivid account of German occupation and the Norwegian struggle against it. It's open from 10 am to 4 pm daily (Sundays from 11 am) in summer and from 10 am to 3 pm weekdays in winter. Admission is 15 kr.

Of interest mainly to history buffs, the **Christiania Museum** at the northern edge of the fortress features a model of the old city and a 20-minute video display of its history. It's open daily from 10 am to 4 pm from 1 June to 15 September. Admission costs 20 kr (students 10 kr).

National Museum of Contemporary Art This museum, at Bankplassen 4, in an Art-Nouveau building formerly housing the Central Bank of Norway, features Scandinavian modern art. Opening hours are from 11 am to 7 pm Tuesday to Friday, to 4 pm weekends. Admission is free.

Munch Museum Dedicated to the life work of Norway's most famous painter, Edvard Munch (1863-1944), this museum, at Tøyengata 53, contains more than 5000 drawings and paintings which Munch bequeathed to the city of Oslo. Despite the artist's tendency towards tormented visions, the museum is thought provoking rather than disturbing – *The Scream, The Sick Child* and *The Maiden & Death* are exhibited here but so are other works with lighter themes such as *The Sun* and *Spring Ploughing*.

The museum is open from 10 am (noon on Sundays) to 6 pm daily in summer, with shorter winter hours. Admission is 40 kr (students 15 kr). Take T-bane line 3, 4, 5 or 6 to Tøyen and follow the signs, it's a five-minute walk.

Botanical Garden & Museums Next door to the Munch Museum is the university's **Zoological Museum** with well-presented displays of stuffed birds and animals and its **Mineralogical-Paleontological Museum** with rocks, gemstones and a few dinosaur bones. The museums are inside a fragrant botanical garden. All are free.

Vigeland Park Frognerparken or Vigeland Park (Vigelandsparken) is a wonderful city park with expansive green spaces, duck ponds and rows of shade trees – a fine place for leisurely strolls and picnics on the lawn. Its central walkway is lined with life-sized statues by Gustav Vigeland. In nearly 200 works in granite and bronze, Vigeland presents the human form in a range of emotions from screaming pot-bellied babies and entwined lovers to tranquil elderly couples.

The most impressive piece is the monolith of writhing bodies, said to be the world's largest granite sculpture. The circle of steps beneath the monolith are lined with voluptuous stone bodies and provide a popular spot for sitting and contemplating it all. The park is free and always open, making this a good place to come in the evening when the museums have closed. Take bus No 72 (or tram No 2) from the National Theatre.

Vigeland Museum For a more in-depth look at the development of Gustav Vigeland's work, visit Vigeland Museum at Nobels gate 32, across from Vigeland Park. The museum was built by the city as a home and workshop for Vigeland in exchange for the bulk of his life's work and contains his early statuary, huge plaster moulds, woodblock prints and sketches.

It's open from 10 am to 6 pm (from noon to 7 pm Sundays) in summer, from noon to 4 pm in winter. It's closed on Mondays. Admission is 20 kr (10 kr students) in summer, free in winter.

Holmenkollen The Holmenkollen **ski jump**, perched on a hillside above Oslo, draws the world's top jumpers in a ski festival each March and doubles as a concert site in summer. From the top of the ski jump there's a bird's-eye view of the steep ramp as well as a panoramic view of Oslo city and fjord – an elevator goes part of the way up and then you climb 114 steps on your own.

The 35-kr admission fee includes a ski museum below the jump. Its collection of skis and sleds dating back as far as 600 AD includes some found in bogs and glaciers. There's a cafeteria with reasonable prices beside the museum.

From Stortinget, take T-bane line 15 for the 20-minute ride to Holmenkollen station, from where it's a 10-minute walk up to the jump. It's open from 10 am to 3 pm weekdays and 11 am to 4 pm weekends from October to April, and daily from 10 am to 5 pm in the shoulder seasons, 10 am to 7 pm in June, 9 am to 10 pm in July and 10 am to 10 pm in August. If you intend to also visit Tryvannstårnet be sure to get the combination ticket which includes that sight for just 5 kr more.

Tryvannstårnet North of the ski jump, the Tryvannstårnet **observation tower** offers superb views of the Nordmarka wilderness as well as snow-capped Mt Gausta to the west, the Oslofjord to the south and the forests of Sweden to the east. For 25 kr, an elevator zips you up to the top. The opening hours are the same as at Holmenkollen.

To get to Tryvannstårnet from Holmenkollen, get back on the T-bane for a scenic ride past sod-roofed cottages to **Frognerseteren**, where the tram literally ends in the woods. A signposted trail above the stop leads to the tower, a 20-minute walk.

Bygdøy Bygdøy peninsula holds some of Oslo's top attractions: an open-air folk museum, excavated Viking ships, Thor Heyerdahl's raft *Kon-Tiki* and the *Fram* polar exploration ship. You can rush around all the sights in half a day, though allotting a few hours extra will be more enjoyable.

Though only minutes from central Oslo, Bygdøy (pronounced 'big duh') has a rural character and a couple of good **beaches**. The royal family maintains its summer residence on the peninsula, as do many of Oslo's more well-to-do people.

Ferries operate from mid-April to late September, making the 10-minute run to Bygdøy (15 kr) every 30 minutes, starting at 7.45 am (8.45 am on weekends). The last crossing returns from Bygdøy at 5.30 pm in April and September, 8.30 pm in summer (9.30 pm from 15 June to 15 August). The ferries leave from Rådhusbrygge 3 (opposite the Rådhus) and stop first at Dronningen, from where it's a 10-minute walk up to the folk museum. The ferry continues to Bygdøynes, where the *Kon-Tiki, Fram* and maritime museums are clustered. You can also take bus No 30 from Jernbanetorget to the folk museum. From the folk museum it's a five-minute walk to the Viking ships and 15 minutes farther to Bygdøynes. The route is well signposted and makes a pleasant walk.

Bygdøy Kolonial, a small grocery store a few minutes beyond the Viking ship museum, sells pastry and fruit. There are restaurants at the folk and maritime museums.

Norwegian Folk Museum

More than 170 buildings, mostly from the 17th and 18th centuries, have been gathered from around the country and are clustered according to region in Norway's largest open-air museum. Dirt paths wind past rough-timbered farmhouses whose sod roofs sprout wildflowers, storehouses on stilts *(stabbur)*, old barns and mills.

A highlight is the restored **stave church**, built around 1200 in Gol and brought to Bygdøy in 1885. There are also two separate **museums** just inside the main entrance, one with excellent displays of **Sami culture, folk costumes** and **jewellery**, the other featuring **Norwegian furnishings**.

In the summer, Sunday is the big day for special events, which usually include afternoon folk dances in the courtyard. The museum is open daily from 10 am to 6 pm from 15 June to 15 September, from 11 am to 4 pm mid-May to mid-June and from noon to 4 pm (closed Mondays in winter) the rest

of the year. Admission is 35 kr (students 25 kr) in summer, and 20 kr in winter when the viewing of the building interiors is more restricted.

Viking Ship Museum

This captivating museum houses three Viking ships which were excavated from the Oslofjord region. The ships had been drawn ashore and used as tombs for nobility, who were buried with all they would need in the hereafter: jewels, furniture, food and a servant or two. Built of oak in the 9th century, the ships were buried in blue clay which preserved them amazingly well.

The impressive **Oseberg ship**, which has elaborate dragon and serpent carvings, is 21½ metres long and took 30 people to row. It was excavated with a burial chamber containing the largest collection of Viking Age artefacts yet found in Scandinavia. The other main ship *Gokstad* is the finest example of a longship. The museum is open daily, from 10 am to 6 pm May to August, from 11 am to at least 3 pm the rest of the year. Admission is 15 kr (students 7 kr).

Kon-Tiki Museum

This museum displays the *Kon-Tiki* balsa raft which Norwegian explorer Thor Heyerdahl sailed from Peru to Polynesia in 1947 to prove that Polynesia's first settlers could have come from South America.

Also on display is the papyrus reed boat *Ra II* in which he crossed the Atlantic in 1970. The museum is open from 10 am to 6 pm daily from mid-May to August, 10.30 am to 4 or 5 pm the rest of the year. Admission is 15 kr (students 8 kr).

Polarship Fram

The *Fram* Museum, opposite the *Kon-Tiki* Museum, holds Fridtjof Nansen's 39-metre rigged schooner *Fram* launched in 1892 and used for polar expeditions, including the 1911 discovery of the South Pole by Roald Amundsen. You can clamber around inside the boat, go down to the hold where the sled dogs were kept and check out fascinating photo displays of the *Fram* in the polar ice. Opening hours are

NORWAY

from 10 am to 5.45 pm daily from mid-May to August, with shorter off-season hours. Admission is 15 kr (students 8 kr).

Norwegian Maritime Museum Least interesting of Bygdøy's museums, the Norwegian Maritime Museum (Norsk Sjøfartsmuseum) has small fishing boats, displays of dried cod and an abundance of model ships. The balcony on the top floor of the larger wing has a good view of the Oslofjord islands. It's open daily from 10 am to 7 pm from mid-May to September, with shorter off-season hours. Admission costs 15 kr (students 8 kr).

Islands & Beaches Ferries to half a dozen islands in the Oslofjord leave all year round from Vippetangen, south-east of Akershus Fortress. **Hovedøya**, the closest island, has a rocky coastline though its south-west side is a popular sunbathing area. There are walking paths around the perimeter and the **ruins of a 12th century monastery** up near the restaurant.

Farther south, the undeveloped island of **Langøyene** offers far better swimming and free tenting. It has both sandy and rocky beaches, including one on the south-east side designated for nude bathing.

Boats to Hovedøya leave about every 45 minutes between 6.30 am and 11.15 pm in summer, to 6.45 pm the rest of the year, while boats to the other islands are somewhat less frequent. The boat to Langøyene runs only from early June to mid-August, with the first service leaving at 10.15 am and the last returning at 7.30 pm.

The Bygdøy peninsula also has two popular beaches, Huk and Paradisbukta. To get to these beaches take bus No 30 from Jernbanetorget (or the National Theatre) to its last stop. **Huk,** which is right at the bus stop, is separated into two beaches by a small cove, with the beach on the north-west side a nude bathing area. While there are some sandy patches, most of Huk is comprised of grassy lawns and large smooth rocks ideal for sunbathing. If the crowds are too large, a 10-minute walk through the woods north from the bus stop leads to the more secluded

Paradisbukta. For freshwater swimming, try the east side of the lake **Sognsvann** at the end of T-bane line 13.

Other Sights Oslo's oldest building is **Gamle Aker Kirke**, a medieval stone church built in 1080 and still used for services. It's open from noon to 2 pm Monday to Saturday, admission is free. Take bus No 37 from Jerbanetorget, get off at Akersbakken and walk up past the cemetery.

The **Post Museum** is worth a walk through if you're at the main post office – the entrance is at the opposite end of the block. Exhibits include a reindeer sledge once used for mail delivery and Norway's best stamp collection. It's open from 10 am to 3 pm weekdays, with free admission and souvenir postcards.

Oslo also has a number of other fairly esoteric museums, including ones dedicated to skating, transport, children's art, customs and tolls, architecture, the armed forces, theatre and the like. For more details see the *Oslo Guide*.

Activities
Hiking A network of trails leads off into the Nordmarka from Frognerseteren, at the end of T-bane line 15. One good hearty walk is from Frognerseteren over to lake Sognsvann, where you can take T-bane line 13 back to the city.

Cycling Den Rustne Eike (**☎** 22 83 72 31), near the harbour by the tourist office, rents six-speed bicycles for 60 kr for six hours, 95 kr for 24 hours, and mountain bikes for 100/145 kr. They have maps and information on bike paths, including the route to Bygdøy and paths in the Nordmarka, and organise cycling tours. Hours are 10 am to 6.30 pm daily May to October, to 3.30 pm weekdays only in winter.

One popular outing is to take the weekend bike train (*sykkeltoget*) to Stryken, 40 km north of Oslo, and cycle back through the Nordmarka. The train leaves Oslo S at 9.30 am on Saturdays and Sundays from May to October and you can carry your bike along for free. If you want to try something shorter, you could take the local train to Kjelsås and follow the bike route along the river Akerselva back down to the city.

Skiing Oslo's ski season is roughly from December to March. There are numerous ski trails in the Nordmarka area north of Oslo, many of them floodlit. Easy-access tracks begin right at the end of T-bane lines 13 and 15. Tomm Murstad Skiservice (☎ 22 14 41 24) at the Voksenkollen station, one T-bane stop before Frognerseteren, has skis for hire. The Ski Society (Skiforeningen) (☎ 22 92 32 00), can provide more information; they have a convenient winter office on the 2nd floor at Storgata 20.

Organised Tours Oslo is so easy to get around that there's little need for organised tours. However if time is tight, Båtservice Sightseeing (☎ 22 20 07 15) does a tidy full-day tour of the Bygdøy sites, Vigeland Park and Holmenkollen ski jump plus a cruise of the Oslofjord for a reasonable 250 kr, or a three-hour version minus the cruise for 150 kr.

Places to Stay
You'll find some of the best accommodation deals at the tourist information window at Oslo S, open from 8 am to 11 pm daily. The staff will book rooms in private homes (for two nights' minimum stay) for 150/250 kr singles/doubles.

They also book unfilled hotel rooms at cut rates, though it's strictly a supply and demand situation. When the hotels are busy discounts are slim – at most other times rates are generally about half-price for luxury hotels and one-third off for moderately priced hotels. There's a 20 kr booking fee per person.

Use It, in the Trafikanten building, can give you the latest information on hostels and student accommodation, including subletting if you're staying a fortnight or more. It can sometimes get special rates at a few hotels, including City Hotel. Use It's services are free, but it's only open in summer.

Camping Oslo has two large camping sites with full facilities. Both charge 70 kr to pitch a tent. *Ekeberg Camping* (☎ 22 19 85 68), at Ekebergveien 65 on a knoll above the city, is open from 1 June to 31 August. Take bus No 24 from Jernbanetorget to the Ekeberg stop, a 10-minute ride.

The lakeside *Bogstad Camp & Turistsenter* (☎ 22 50 76 80), at Ankerveien 117 up in Holmenkollen, is open all year round. Take bus No 41 from Jernbanetorget to the Bogstad Camping stop, a 30-minute ride.

Free summer camping is allowed on the Oslofjord island of Langøyene. Other possibilities for camping rough are to take T-bane line 15 to Frognerseteren at the edge of the Nordmarka or take line 13 to Sognsvann. Camping is not permitted at the lake itself, so you'll need to walk a km or two beyond it.

Hostels *Haraldsheim Youth Hostel* (☎ 22 15 50 43), Haraldsheimveien 4, has 270 beds, mostly in rooms with two to four people. Prices are 136 or 156 kr in a dorm, 220 or 310 kr for a single room and 380 or 450 kr for a double room. The higher rates are for rooms with private showers and toilets. Prices include breakfast and there are kitchen and laundry facilities. The hostel is four km from the city centre; take tram No 1 or 7 to the end of the line (Sinsen), from where it's a five-minute walk. Haraldsheim is open all year round except from 23 December to 1 January.

Pan Youth Hostel (☎ 22 23 76 40), Sognsveien 218, is open from mid-June to 20 August only. There are 119 beds, mostly two to a room, which cost 148 kr a person, breakfast included, or for 248 kr you can have a room to yourself. There's a guest kitchen and free parking. Pan is a 20-minute, six-km ride from the city centre; take T-bane line 13 from Stortinget to Kringsjå, one short stop before the line terminates at Sognsvann, a bathing lake and popular recreational area.

KFUM Inter-Rail Point (☎ 22 42 10 66), a YMCA hostel at Møllergata 1(the entrance is on Grubbegata), has Oslo's cheapest beds at 70 kr and a great central location, a 10-

minute walk from Oslo S. It's only open from early July to mid-August and often fills early. Reception is open from 8 to 11 am and 5 pm to midnight. Guests can store packs there during the day.

Pensions *Ellingsen's Pensjonat* (☎ 22 60 03 59) at Holtegata 25, in a neighbourhood of older homes five blocks north of the Royal Palace, is the best low-end accommodation value. There are 20 small but adequate rooms, each with a desk, chair and sink. There are toilets and showers in the corridor, and singles/doubles cost 160/260 kr. During the summer it's best to call ahead for reservations. To get there take bus No 1 (towards Majorstuen) from Jernbanetorget and get off at Uranienborgveien.

Somewhat overpriced but closer to the centre is *Cochs Pensjonat* (☎ 22 60 48 36) at Parkveien 25, just north of the Royal Palace. The 65 rooms are a bit spartan, though not uncomfortable, and cost 280/360 kr for singles/doubles with shared bath, 360/470 kr for rooms with a private bath and cooking facilities.

Bella Vista (☎ 22 65 45 88), Arrundveien 11B, is a 16-bed pension six km north of the city centre by bus No 31or 41. Rooms with shared baths cost 200/300 kr. Guests have kitchen privileges.

Hotels Most Oslo hotels are expensive though there are a few deals, particularly in summer, that moderate the cost. Almost all these hotels include a free buffet breakfast, the only one listed here that doesn't is Sjømannshjemmet.

Sjømannshjemmet or the Seamen's Hostel (☎ 22 41 20 05), at Tollbugata 4 near the harbour, sees more land travellers than sailors these days. The facilities are bareboned and the furniture's a little past it, but the location's fine, the beds are comfortable enough and the price is right with singles/doubles costing 210/280 kr. The entrance is on Fred Olsens gate.

City Hotel (☎ 22 41 36 10), Skippergata 19, is an older hotel with 60 rooms. It's lightly faded but has character, including a front parlour with Victorian furniture. Rates are 365/535 kr in rooms with shared showers and toilets, 455/635 kr with private baths. If you're sensitive to traffic noise, be sure to ask for a courtyard room.

Anker Hotell (☎ 22 11 40 05), Storgata 55, has standard rooms with private baths for 530/650 kr weekdays and 375/560 kr weekends. In summer a student dormitory wing also becomes available for 375/560 kr. It's a 15-minute walk from the railway station on the scruffier east side of town; there's free parking.

Fønix Hotel (☎ 22 42 59 57), at Dronningens gate 19 just a couple of blocks from Oslo S, has small adequate rooms with shared bath from 300/450 kr.

Norrøna Hotell (☎ 22 42 64 00), Grensen 19, is a pleasant mission-room hotel with comfortable rooms on a par with those in many of Oslo's best hotels. All rooms have private baths, TV, telephones and hair dryers. Some rooms are wheelchair-accessible. Rates are 395/550 kr on weekends and holidays from autumn to spring, 550/650 kr from late June to mid-August, 685/795 kr at other times.

The following Rainbow-chain hotels have weekend (including Sundays) and summer (from around 20 June to 10 August) rates that are roughly half their standard rates. All are central 1st-class hotels with private baths, TVs, minibars and the like.

The newly renovated *Hotell Astoria* (☎ 22 42 00 10), at Dronningens gate 21, costs 355/480 kr on weekends and in summer. *Hotell Munch* (☎ 22 42 42 75), at Munchs gate 5 and the oldest and least appealing, costs 355/480 kr on weekends and in summer. *Vika Atrium Hotel* (☎ 22 83 33 00) at Munkedamsveien 45, a modern highrise a couple of blocks from Aker Brygge, charges 450/550 kr on weekends and in summer.

The recently constructed *Cecil Hotel* (☎ 22 42 70 00), on the corner of Stortingsgata and Rosenkrantz gate, has a great location a stone's throw from parliament. Rooms are modern and quiet, and there's an excellent breakfast buffet and free coffee and fruit during the day. Rates are 400/580 kr on weekends, 500/650 kr in summer; there's also a cheaper 'combi' double, but it's claustrophobically small and the second bed is an uncomfortable fold-out couch.

For period character it's hard to beat the *Grand Hotel* (☎ 22 42 93 90), at Karl Johans gate 31. Rooms are large with all the expected amenities, though they're understated rather than poshly elegant. The standard rates of 1450/1600 kr for singles/doubles drop to 675/990 kr on weekends and to 675/830 kr from mid-June to mid-August.

Places to Eat

Eating is an expensive proposition in Oslo. One way to save money is to buy snacks from bakeries, many of which have reasonably priced sandwiches as well as breads and pastries. *Baker Hansen* and *Samson's* are two good chains with numerous shops around Oslo.

Many of the more inexpensive eateries are closed on Sundays. Notable exceptions are at Aker Brygge, where most food stalls and even the bakery is open, and fast-food chains such as *Peppe's Pizza, McDonald's* and *Burger King*.

Food Markets The *Rimi* grocery store, at Rosenkrantz gate 20, and the *Tempus* grocery store, at Youngs gate 11, both have good prices. A little more expensive is *Oluf Lorentzen*, at Karl Johans gate 33, which in addition to selling groceries has a simple salad bar, and offers baked chicken and other takeaway deli dishes at reasonable prices. It's open to 7 pm weekdays, 5 pm Saturdays. Fruit stalls set up daily except Sundays in front of Oslo S and at the harbour. *Helios*, Universitetsgata 22, sells health foods and produce.

Oslo S & Around Oslo S has a *Caroline Café* with fairly good cafeteria fare at average prices, a hot-dog stand and a sandwich shop. There's a small grocery store near the main entrance that's open to 11.30 daily.

Oslo City, a shopping complex opposite the north side of Oslo S, has several fast-food restaurants including *Chopsticks* with Chinese food, *Tysk City Grill* with gyros, a hamburger joint, a pizzeria and a couple of bakeries. Oslo City is open to 8 pm weekdays, 6 pm Saturdays, closed on Sundays.

Aker Brygge Aker Brygge, the shopping complex along the west side of the harbour, has a good collection of inexpensive eateries at ground level. *Chopsticks* has Chinese dishes for under 50 kr. Just opposite is *Bakeriteater*, with good bread, pastries and hearty baguette sandwiches. The Tex-Mex-style *Cactus*, two doors down, has specials from 11 am to 3 pm weekdays when a taco with salad is 50 kr, about half the dinner price. Nearby *Deniz Kebap* serves up a large kebab on pitta bread for 35 kr.

At the rear of Aker Brygge is a *Rema 1000* grocery store, with *Smør-Petersen*, a popular deli, just inside the entrance. The deli sells excellent Norwegian salmon dishes, including a delicious baked salmon in a pastry crust, creative salads and other deli foods. You can order takeaway or eat inside at one of the café tables. It's a terrific bargain, with food on a par with that served in top-end restaurants but at prices cheaper than in many cafeterias.

Just south of the Rema grocery store is *La Piazza*, an Italian restaurant with excellent pizza and pasta dishes from around 75 kr.

At the harbourside stalls across from Aker Brygge look for signs saying *'ferske reker'* where freshly boiled unshelled shrimps sell for around 30 kr a half-litre. You can pick up a loaf of bread, grab a harbourside bench and peel your way through one of Oslo's cheapest treats.

Other Oslo Restaurants *Vegeta Vertshus*, at Munkedamsveien 3B near the National Theatre, has an excellent vegetarian buffet that includes wholegrain pizza, casseroles and salads. It costs 61 kr for all you can stack on a small plate, 69 kr for a bigger dinner plate. Hours are from 10 am (11 am Sundays) to 10 pm daily.

Legenden Musikk Pub at Sankt Olavs plass 1 has pepperoni or vegetarian pizzas large enough to feed a couple of people for 90 kr, plus some of the cheapest beer (24 kr a half-litre) in town. It's open from 10 am to 1 am. More expensive is *Peppe's Pizza*, part of a nationwide chain with good pizza. The branch at Stortingsgata 4 is open daily to midnight.

Café Nordraak, Sankt Olavs gate 32, is a popular hang-out for Norwegian students from the art academy and has inexpensive food. It's also a good alternative place to have a few beers. It's open from around 11 am daily to 3 am Wednesday to Saturday, to midnight other days.

Another place popular with local artists is *Kafé Celsius*, at Radhusgata 19, a low-key café with a pleasant courtyard beer garden, classical music in the background and good sandwiches, Greek salads and pastas at the usual café prices. It's open from 11 am (12.30 pm on Sundays) to about 2 am.

The university has a cheap *cafeteria* in the rear of the stately columned building at Karl Johans gate 47.

The *Stortorvets Gjæstgiveri* at Grensen 1 has a weekday meat-and-vegetable special for 55 kr and soup, sandwiches and other light meals served cafeteria-style.

Molina Pub & Spiseri, Sankt Olavs Plass 2, is a popular gathering place for gay men and women. Though it's predominately a café, there's also a pool table and an adjacent gay resource centre.

Onkel Oswald is a trendy café two blocks north of the Royal Palace at Hegdehaugsveien 34. While it's best known for its drinks menu which features over 50 regional beers, it also serves reasonably good food including salad, pasta and chicken dishes for around 75 kr. It's open from 9 am to 2 am weekdays, from 10 am Saturdays and noon on Sundays.

Nador Restaurant, Dronningens gate 22, has Moroccan dishes from about 90 kr and a three-course daily dinner special for about 100 kr.

If you have a big appetite, try *Djengis Khan*, in the alley at Torggata 11, where 100 kr buys an all-you-can-eat Mongolian barbecue of grilled meats, vegetables and your choice from a simple salad bar. Other dinners, such as sweet and sour pork, begin around 70 kr. It's open from noon to 11 pm daily.

The *Grand Café* at the Grand Hotel on Karl Johans gate has been serving Oslo's cognoscenti for more than a century and, as a reminder, a full-wall mural depicts the restaurant in the 1890s bustling with the likes of Munch and Ibsen. Some of the more affordable dishes include the light meals from the *småretter* menu which average 75 kr and the weekday special (from 3 to 6 pm) that commonly features poached salmon and costs about 100 kr.

More elegant is the genteel *Palmen*, a glass-domed café inside the lobby of the Grand Hotel, which features light meals such as lamb stew, lasagne or quiche and salad for around 85 kr. Palmen is open weekdays from 11.30 am to 8 pm, Saturdays to 6 pm.

Entertainment

The tourist office's monthly *What's on in Oslo* brochure lists current concerts, theatre and special events. The six-screen *Saga cinema* on Roald Amundsens gate shows first-run Western movies in their original language with Norwegian subtitles.

For the gay scene, the most happening place is *Den Sorte Enke* (The Black Widow), Møllegata 23, a popular pub open from 6 pm to 4 am, with a disco from Wednesday to Sunday.

Stortorvets Gjæstgiveri, Grensen 1, has live jazz from 8 pm to midnight on Fridays (30 kr cover charge) and from 1 to 5 pm Saturdays. *Smuget*, Kirkegata 34, is one of Oslo's hot spots with live rock, jazz or blues nightly and a disco from 8 pm to 4 am. There's usually a cover charge of 30 to 50 kr.

Or take advantage of summer's long daylight hours and spend evenings outdoors – go down to the harbour and enjoy the live jazz wafting off the floating restaurants, have a beer at one of the outdoor cafés at Vigeland Park, or take a ferry out to the islands in the Oslofjord.

Things to Buy

Husfliden, at Møllergata 4 not far from Oslo

Domkirke, has a wide selection of Norwegian handicrafts. Another spot with quality items is Heimen Husflid, at Rosenkrantz gate 8, which sells traditional Norwegian clothing and crafts, ranging from carved wooden trolls to reindeer-wool sweaters and colourful folk costumes. Items are expensive, but it makes for good window shopping.

Getting There & Away
Air Oslo's main airport, Fornebu, is nine km from the city centre. Gardermoen airport, 50 km outside Oslo, is mostly used for charter flights.

The SAS ticket office (☎ 22 17 00 20) is in the Oslo City shopping centre. SAS also handles ticketing for Widerøe airlines. Braathens SAFE (☎ 67 12 20 70) is at Håkon VII's gate 2.

Bus Long-distance buses arrive and depart from Galleri Oslo, east of Oslo S. The train and bus stations are linked via an overhead walkway.

Train All trains arrive and depart from Oslo S in the city centre. The station is quite modern and conveniently laid out (though the 5-kr restrooms are a fleecing). The reservation windows for domestic trains are open Monday to Saturday from 6 am to 11 pm, Sundays to 11.45 pm, and for international trains from 6.30 am to 11 pm daily. There's also a helpful information desk with staff who can answer questions on travel schedules throughout Norway.

The station has backpack-sized lockers for 20 kr and an Inter-Rail Centre, which is open from 7 am to 11 pm daily from mid-June to September, where travellers with rail passes can shower (20 kr) and wait around in between catching trains.

Car The main highways into the city are the E6 from the north and south, the E18 from the east and west. You'll have to pass through one of 18 toll stations and pay 10 kr each time you enter Oslo. Be aware that if you use one of the lanes for vehicles with passes and get stopped there's a 250-kr fine. Motorbikes

aren't subject to the tolls and there are no fees to leave Oslo.

Hitching Leaving Oslo it's generally best to take a train to the outskirts of the city in whatever direction you're heading and start hitching from there. The ride board at Use It is worth checking, though there are usually far more people seeking rides than offering them.

Boat Boats to and from Copenhagen and Frederikshavn (Denmark) use the docks off Skippergata, near Vippetangen. Bus No 29 brings you to within a few minutes' walk of the terminal.

Boats from Hirtshals (Denmark) and Kiel (Germany) dock at Hjortneskai, just west of the central harbour, from where there are connecting buses to Oslo S.

The summer boat to Arendal, Risør and Kragerø docks at Rådhusbrygge, opposite the Rådhus. For information contact Båtservice (☎ 22 20 07 15).

Getting Around
Oslo has an efficient public transport system with an extensive network of buses, trams, subways and ferries. A single one-way ticket on any of these services costs 15 kr and includes a free transfer within an hour. A day ticket *(dagskort)* good for unlimited 24-hour travel (30 kr) and one-week cards (130 kr) are sold at Trafikanten, Narvesen kiosks and staffed subway stations. In addition, all city transport is free if you have an Oslo card. Note that while it may seem easy to board the underground and trams without a ticket, if confronted by an inspector you'll receive an automatic 350-kr fine.

Trafikanten, below the tower at the front entrance of Oslo S, has free schedules and a public transport map, *Sporveiskart Oslo.* The office is open from 7 am to 8 pm weekdays, 8 am to 6 pm on weekends.

To/From the Airport SAS airport buses, Flybussen, run between Fornebu airport and Oslo S every 15 minutes (30 kr). The less frequent public bus No 31 runs from in front of the airport to Oslo S. Taxis from Fornebu to the city centre cost about 100 kr.

Bus & Tram Bus and tram (trolley) lines crisscross the city and extend into the suburbs. There's no central station but most converge at Jernbanetorget in front of Oslo S. Most westbound buses, including those to Bygdøy and Vigeland Park, also stop at the south side of the National Theatre.

Underground T-bane, which in the city centre is an underground system, is faster and goes farther outside the city centre than most bus lines. All eight lines converge at Stortinget station, from where four run west and the other four go east.

Taxi Taxis charge 17 kr (21.30 kr after 7 pm and on weekends) at flagfall and about 10 kr per km. There are taxi stands at the railway station, shopping centres and city squares. Taxis with lit signs can be flagged down, or call 22 38 80 90. Oslo taxis accept major credit cards.

Car Oslo has its fair share of one-way streets, which can complicate city driving a bit, but otherwise traffic is not terribly hard to deal with. Still, the best way to explore central sights is to walk or take local transport, though a car can be quite convenient for exploring outlying areas such as Holmen-kollen.

Metered street parking, identified by a solid blue sign with a white letter 'P', can be found throughout the city. Hours written under the sign indicate the period in which the meters are in effect, which is usually from 8 am to 5 pm, with Saturday hours written in brackets. Unless otherwise posted, parking is free outside of that time and on Sundays. Parking at most meters costs from 5 to 20 kr an hour – busy spots, such as those around post offices, have the highest rates. There are also numerous parking houses in the city, including large ones at major shopping centres such as Oslo City and Aker Brygge. The free tourist office maps show the locations. If you buy an Oslo card, you'll get a pass that allows you to park free at municipal car parks.

Boat Ferries to Bygdøy leave from Rådhusbrygge, while ferries to the islands in the Oslofjord leave from Vippetangen.

ØSTFOLD

The Østfold region, on the east side of Oslofjord, is a mixture of farmland and small industrial towns based on the timber trade.

Trains leave every couple of hours from Oslo to the border town of Halden, with six trains a day continuing on to Sweden. Halden has an imposing 17th century fortified hilltop castle which was the site of many battles between Norway and Sweden. There's a camping ground on the castle grounds and a youth hostel in town.

From Moss, 55 km south of Oslo, there's a overnight boat to Frederikshavn, Denmark. Moss itself is lined with factories and saw-mills and is not a place that invites you to linger.

The most interesting Østfold excursion from Oslo is to Fredrikstad, which takes 1½ hours and costs 105 kr each way by train.

Fredrikstad

The city of Fredrikstad has an old enclosed fortress town complete with moats, gates and a drawbridge, built in 1567 as protection against a belligerent Sweden. You can walk around the perimeter of the fortress walls that were once ringed by 200 cannons and through narrow cobbled streets lined with still-lived-in historic buildings, mostly dating from the 1600s. The fort's long arsenal and infantry barracks are also still in use. The central square has a bank, a sand-wich café and a statue of King Frederik II who founded the town.

From Fredrikstad station it's a five-minute walk down to the waterfront, where a ferry (two minutes, 4 kr) shuttles across the river Glomma to the fortress' main gate.

After exploring the fortress you can cross the moat and walk 15 minutes down Kongens gate to the intact Kongens fort which sits on a bluff above a city park. It all

Around Oslo

makes for pleasant strolling and there are no admission fees. There's a camping ground near Kongens fort.

Southern Norway

Sørlandet, the curving south coast, is magnetic for Norwegians when the weather turns warm. The coast is largely rocky with a heavy scattering of low stone islands, and Sørlandet's numerous coves and bays are ideal for the many Norwegian holidaymakers who have their own boats. The attraction is generally not as great for foreign travellers, the majority of whom have just arrived from places with warmer water and better beaches.

The Sørland train line, which runs 586 km from Stavanger to Oslo via Kristiansand, stays inland most of the way, though buses which connect with the train go to several south coast towns. The E18, the main highway and bus route, runs inland from Stavanger to Mandal, while eastward from there it passes through a number of coastal towns.

STAVANGER

Stavanger, Norway's fourth largest city, was a bustling fishing centre at the turn of the century and in its heyday had more than 50 sardine canneries. By the 1960s the depletion of fish stocks had brought an end to the industry, but the discovery of North Sea oil spared Stavanger from hard times. The city now holds the title of 'Oil Capital of Norway' – perhaps no greater tourist attraction than pickled herring, but it has brought prosperity and a cosmopolitan community that includes more than 3000 British and US oil people.

Most visitors to Stavanger arrive on the ferry from England and make a beeline for Bergen or Oslo. If your time is limited, doing that is not a bad idea. Otherwise, it's worth spending a day in Stavanger – it has an historic harbour area, a medieval cathedral and a few local museums.

Orientation & Information
The adjacent bus and railway stations are a 10-minute walk from the harbour. The main tourist office is in Kulturhus and it's open all year round from 9 am to 5 pm Monday to Friday, to 2 pm on Saturdays. In summer there's also a tourist booth at the inner harbour which is open daily from 9 am to 8 pm. Most of Stavanger's sights are within easy walking distance of the harbour.

The modern Kulturhus, a town centre of sorts, also holds the public library, a cinema, an art gallery, a café and a restaurant. On sunny days the pedestrian streets behind the Kulturhus are alive with street musicians, pavement vendors and students hanging around. There's a small fish market at the inner harbour and a colourful produce and flower market across the way at Torget. You can pick up a free Stavanger card wherever you're staying for 50% off museum fares as well as some discounts on sightseeing tours, boats and buses.

The Norwegian Emigration Centre, which helps foreigners of Norwegian descent trace their roots, is at Bergjelandsgata 30 and is open from 10 am to 2 pm Monday to Friday.

Things to See & Do
For a little Old World charm stroll through **Gamle Stavanger** on the west side of the harbour where cobblestone walkways lead through rows of early 18th century whitewashed wooden houses. With more than 150 houses, it's said to be Northern Europe's best preserved wooden-house settlement.

Stavanger Domkirke, on the south end of Kirkegata, is an impressive medieval stone cathedral dating back to the 12th century. It's open free to the public daily from 9 am to 6 pm (Sundays from 1 pm) from 15 May to 15 September, from 9 am to 2 pm Monday to Saturday the rest of the year. On Thursdays at 11.15 am there's an organ recital; it's an atmospheric time to visit.

You can get a good free view of the city and the harbour oil rigs from the top of **Valbergtårnet**, a tower at the end of Valberggata.

The **Stavanger Museum** at Muségata 16

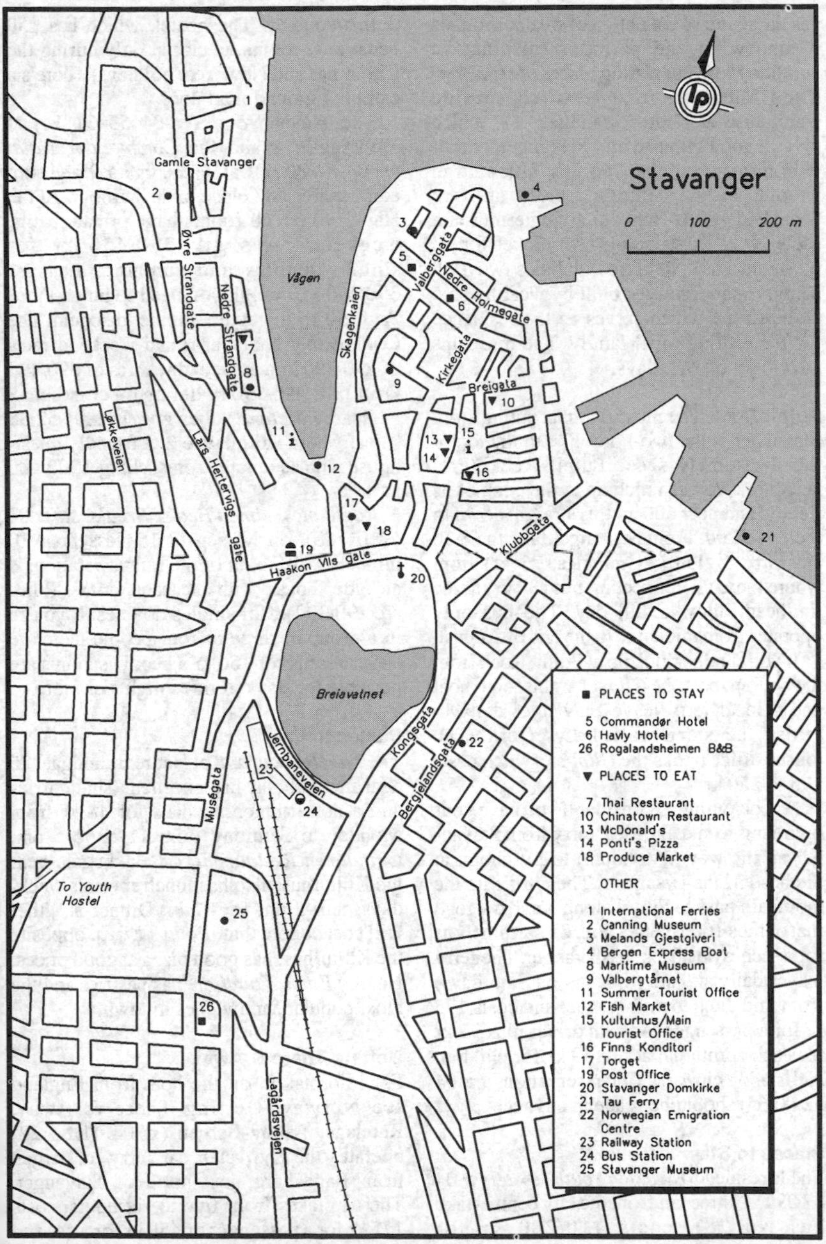

Stavanger
0
100
200 m
Gamle Stavanger
Øvre Strandgate
Nedre Strandgate
Vågen
Skagenkaien
Valberggata
Nedre Holmegate
Kirkegata
Breigata
Løkkeveien
Lars Hertervigs gate
Klubbgata
Haakon VIIs gate
Breiavatnet
Kongsgata
Bergjelandsgata
Jernbaneveien
Musegata
To Youth Hostel
Lagårdsveien
PLACES TO STAY
5 Commandør Hotel
6 Havly Hotel
26 Rogalandsheimen B&B
PLACES TO EAT
7 Thai Restaurant
10 Chinatown Restaurant
13 McDonald's
14 Ponti's Pizza
18 Produce Market
OTHER
1 International Ferries
2 Canning Museum
3 Melands Gjestgiveri
4 Bergen Express Boat
8 Maritime Museum
9 Valbergtårnet
11 Summer Tourist Office
12 Fish Market
15 Kulturhus/Main Tourist Office
16 Finns Konditori
17 Torget
19 Post Office
20 Stavanger Domkirke
21 Tau Ferry
22 Norwegian Emigration Centre
23 Railway Station
24 Bus Station
25 Stavanger Museum

has the standard collection of stuffed animals in one wing and period furnishings in another. More interesting places are the **Maritime Museum**, in a restored seaside warehouse at Nedre Strandgate 17, which gives a good glimpse into Stavanger's maritime history, and the **Canning Museum** in an old sardine canning factory at Øvre Strandgate 88A. Entry to a single museum costs 20 kr or a combination ticket for all museums costs 30 kr and includes two 19th century manor houses built by wealthy ship owners, one which serves as the residence for the visiting royal family. The museums are closed on Mondays.

Pulpit Rock The most popular outing from Stavanger is the two-hour hike to the top of the awesomely sheer Pulpit Rock (Prekestolen). You can inch up to the edge of its flat top and peer 600 metres straight down to the Lysefjord. From Stavanger take the 8.30 am ferry to Tau (40 minutes, 23 kr) from where there's a connecting bus (30 kr) to the trailhead, allow a full day. The bus only operates from mid-June to the end of August.

If you'd rather look up at Pulpit Rock from the bottom, both the *Clipper* sightseeing boat and a local ferry leave Stavanger daily to cruise the steep-walled Lysefjord. The tourist office books the *Clipper*, which costs 175 to 250 kr.

A good outing to consider if you have your own car is to take the local ferry from Stavanger all the way (3½ hours) to Lysebotn, at the head of the Lysefjord. Then drive up the mountain pass to Sirdal along a narrow road that climbs 1000 metres with 27 hairpin turns for a scenic ride back to Stavanger. The ferry leaves daily at 9 am (8.45 am on Saturdays) from mid-June to mid-August and costs 175 kr for a passenger car with driver plus 77 kr for each additional adult, 39 kr for children and senior citizens. Car reservations (☎ 04 52 00 65) should be made in advance.

Places to Stay
The lakeside *Mosvangen Youth Hostel* (☎ 04 87 09 77), three km from the city centre (take bus No 78), costs 110/280 kr for

dorms/doubles. The hostel, which has 150 beds in 57 rooms, is closed only during the Christmas and New Year holidays. There's a camping ground next door.

The *Havly Hotel* (☎ 04 53 31 14) at Valberggata 1 and the *Commandør Hotel* (☎ 04 52 80 00) at Valberggata 9 are both comfortable and close to the harbour. At the Havly, where all rooms have private baths, weekend rates are 350/450 kr for singles/doubles and summer rates are 350/460 kr, though you need to buy a Fjord Pass (50 kr) to get the summer discount. The Commandør has year-round weekend rates of 290/390 kr and weekday rates of 390/490 kr in July, 490/590 kr during other months.

Nearby *Melands Gjestgiveri* (☎ 04 52 38 21) at Nedre Holmegate 2, a friendly guesthouse with adequate rooms, charges 300/400 kr.

Rogalandsheimen Bed & Breakfast (☎ 04 52 01 88), on Muségata 18, less than 10 minutes walk south of the railway station, is an older house with pleasant rooms. Rates are 290/390 kr for singles/doubles. If you're in a group of three or four people there are larger rooms for 150 kr a bed. Discounts are possible for stays of three nights or more.

Places to Eat
The *Thai Restaurant*, at Nedre Strandgate 25 near the harbour, has excellent Thai curries and a dozen lunch specials for 48 kr from Monday to Saturday from 11.30 to 5 pm. *Chinatown Restaurant*, on Bakkegata near the Kulturhus, also has lunch specials weekdays until 5 pm for 52 kr. Dinner at either will cost double that. *Ponti's Pizza*, opposite the Kulturhus, has good pizza at good prices. Nearby *Finns Konditori* has pastries and the most popular sandwiches in town.

Getting There & Away
For information on the boat from England see Norway, Getting There & Away. Rutelaget Askøy-Bergen (☎ 04 41 81 22) operates the *Kystveien* car ferry to Bergen from Randaberg, just north of Stavanger. The trip takes from five to six hours, costs 175 kr for a passenger or 450 kr for a car and

driver. Heading north it's an overnight ferry, leaving Randaberg at 11.50 pm daily except Saturdays. There's also a 12.50 pm sailing on Saturdays and Sundays from late June to mid-August and daily during much of July. From Bergen, the ferry leaves at 5.30 pm daily except Saturdays most of the year, with additional weekend sailings in summer and a different and more frequent schedule in July.

There's an express passenger catamaran (☎ 04 52 20 90) to Bergen that leaves directly from Stavanger and is two hours faster, but the boats have all the character of a 747 aeroplane – you can even rent headsets! The fare is 450 kr, with 25% off for spouses and youth hostel members. There are three sailings each way on weekdays, two on weekends.

Stavanger's only train line runs to Oslo (eight hours, 540 kr), via Kristiansand and Bø, a couple of times a day. Departures from Stavanger are at 7.25 am and 1.40 pm daily and weekdays at 10 pm; all require reservations. There's also a daily express bus to Oslo (10 hours, 435 kr) that leaves Stavanger at 8.45 am.

The main south coast highway, the E18, terminates in Stavanger, where it turns into Motorveien. Turn south on Madlaveien to get to the city centre. To drive to Randaberg take Randabergveien (route 14) west from Stavanger centre.

Getting Around

The city centre is a combination of narrow streets and pedestrian walkways that are best explored on foot. There are car parks next to the post office and at the south side of the railway station.

KRISTIANSAND

Kristiansand, the closest port to Denmark, offers the first glimpse of Norway for many travellers. The capital of Sørlandet, Kristiansand has a grid pattern of wide streets laid out by King Christian IV, who founded the city in 1641. It's a busy seaside holiday resort for Norwegians but of less interest to foreign visitors who generally pile off the ferries and onto the next train.

Orientation & Information

The train, bus and ferry terminals are together on the west side of the city centre. There's parking in this area and along most of the city's wide streets. Meters take 1 kr for 15 minutes. Markens gate, a pedestrian street a block inland, is the central shopping and restaurant area. The tourist office is at Dronningens gate 2, six blocks down Vestre Strand gate from the railway station. Change money at the post office, on the corner of Markens and Rådhus gate, or in the bank at the ferry terminal.

Things to See & Do

For a quick look around, walk south-east along Vestre Strand gate to its end and then along Strandepromenaden and the yacht harbour to **Christiansholm Fortress** (circa 1674) where there's a coastal view from the cannon-ringed wall. From there walk inland along the tree-lined Festningsgata and turn left onto Gyldenløves gate, passing the **town square** and **cathedral** on the way back to the transport terminals.

Ravnedalen, a park with lakes and trails, is just north of the city centre and there's the **Vest-Agder folk museum**, the 11th century church **Oddernes kirke** and a **zoo** not far outside town. In summer the MS *Maarten* cruises to the offshore islands. Tour time ranges from one to three hours, with the price from 40 to 90 kr; you can book through the tourist office.

Places to Stay

Roligheden Camping, at a popular beach three km east of town, can be reached by bus No 1. *Kristiansand Youth Hostel* (☎ 04 29 53 69), at Badminton Senteret, Kongsgård allé 33C, two km from the city centre, is open from 1 June to late August and costs 120 kr with breakfast.

The best hotel value is the central *Hotel Bondeheimen* (☎ 04 22 44 40), Kirkegata 15, which has weekend and summer rates of

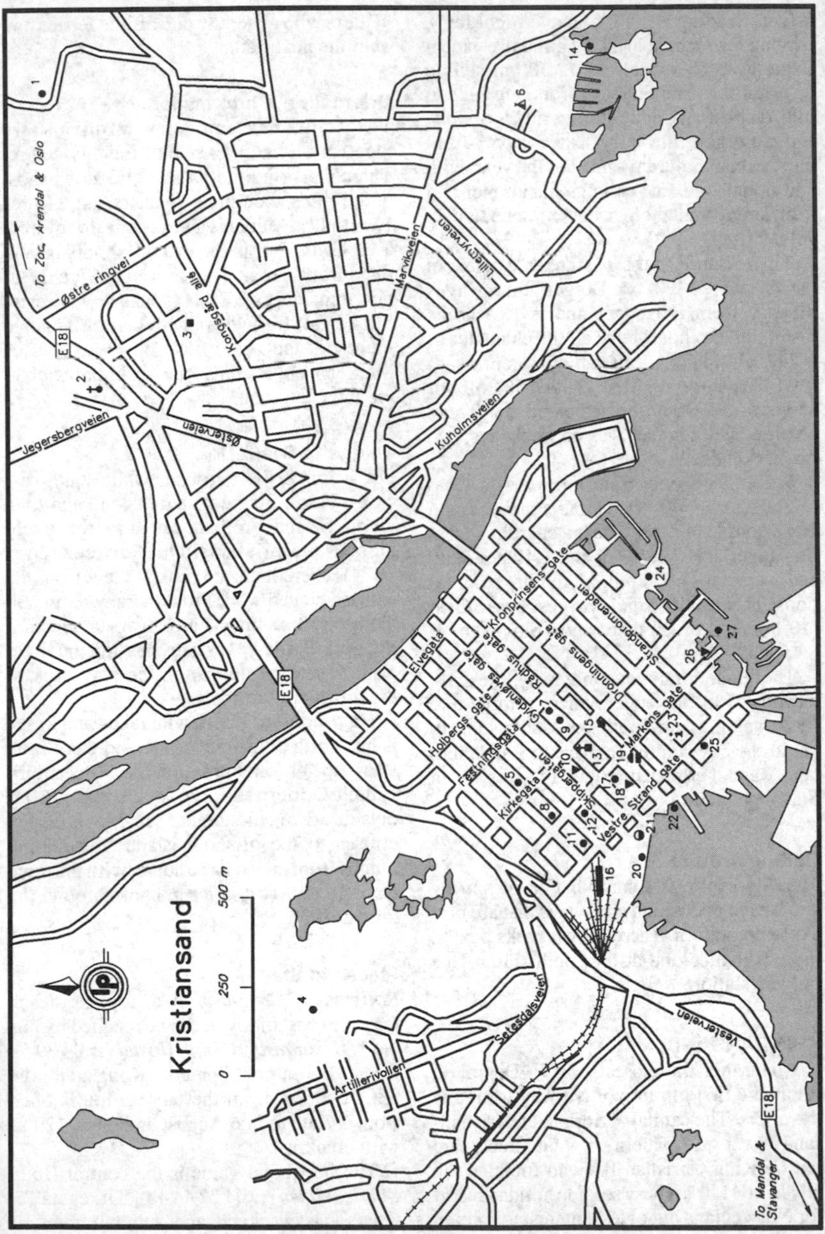

Kristiansand

500 m

250

0

NORWAY

To Zoo, Arendal & Oslo

Østre ringvei

E18

Jegersbergveien

Setesdalsveien

Kongsgård Allé

Marviksveien

Lillemarkveien

Kuholmsveien

E18

Artillerivollen

Selesdalsveien

Vesterveien

To Mandal & Stavanger

E18

Elvegata

Kronprinsens gate

Dronningens gate

Kirkegata

Festningsgata

Holbergs gate

Rådhus gate

Skippergata

Tollbodgata

Gyldenløves gate

Vestre Strand gate

Kirkegata

Markens gate

Strand gate

PLACES TO STAY

3 Kristiansand Youth Hostel
6 Roligheden Camping
15 Hotel Bondeheimen

PLACES TO EAT

10 Peppe's Pizza
18 Bakery
26 Sjøhuset

OTHER

1 Vest-Agder Folk Museum
2 Oddernes Kirke
   (11th Century Church)
4 Ravnedalen
5 Artisjokken Health Food Store
7 Rimi Grocery Store
8 Bella Italia
9 Town Square
11 Domus Grocery Store & Cafeteria
12 China Palace
13 Cathedral
14 Beach
16 Railway Station
17 Libris Bookstore
19 Post Office
20 Ferry Terminal
21 Bus Station
22 MS *Maarten* Excursion Boat
23 Tourist Office
24 Christiansholm Fortress
25 Fønix Movie Theatre
27 Yacht Harbour

singles/doubles 280/480 kr, 360/540 kr at other times.

Places to Eat

Bella Italia, Markens gate 42, has pizza for 39 kr until 4 pm and the nearby *China Palace* has lunch specials for 50 kr to 5 pm. *Domus* grocery store, opposite the railway station, is open weekdays to 10 pm, Saturday to 6 pm, and has a cheap cafeteria.

There's a good bakery on Rådhus gate near the post office. If you're looking for somewhere more up-market, you could join the crowd at the popular harbourside

Sjøhuset at Østre Strandgate 12A – prices are high, but the food's good and there's a very good fish soup.

Getting There & Away

Express buses head north at 8.45 am daily to Voss (10 hours, 413 kr) and Bergen (11 hours, 469 kr) via Odda. There are numerous daily trains and express buses to Oslo and Stavanger. Regional buses depart a few times daily for towns along the southern coast. It takes 1¾ hours to Arendal (69 kr), 3¼ hours to Risør (114 kr) – catch the early bus and you can break your journey at both places and still reach Oslo the same day. Fares are half-price for students and spouses. The E18 runs along the north side of the city centre and is reached via Vestre Strand gate.

In July there's a morning ferry from Kristiansand to Arendal via Lillesand and Grimstad, and a connecting ferry to Oslo via Risør and Kragerø. For information on ferries to Denmark see Norway, Getting There & Away.

ARENDAL

Arendal is the administrative centre of Aust-Agdar county. The most interesting part is the old harbourside area of Tyholmen (just south of the bus station) with its restored 19th century wooden buildings and town hall.

The tourist office is on the east side of Tyholmen, across from the DNT mountaineering office. DNT has information on the trails and wilderness cabins in the hills north of Arendal.

Places to Stay & Eat

The *Ting Hai Hotel* (☎ 04 12 22 01), at Torvgate 5 two blocks north of the bus station, costs 420/570 kr for singles/doubles and has a Chinese restaurant. The waterfront fish market sells good inexpensive fish cakes and the *Rimi* grocery store opposite the bus station has a cafeteria.

Getting There & Away

Arendal is connected with the main railway

NORWAY

line by a trunk line that runs from Nelaug, and is a stop for express buses between Kristiansand and Oslo.

RISØR

Risør, with its cluster of historic white houses built up around a busy little fishing harbour, is one of the most picturesque villages on the south coast. It's a haunt for artists, and many well-to-do yachties make it their summer hang-out.

Next to wandering around the harbour, one of the most popular things to do is visit the offshore islands, which can be reached by taking inexpensive water taxis. The most frequented island, **Stangholmen**, has a restaurant in an old lighthouse, and is reached by the water taxi (10 kr) that docks by the police station. The harbourfront tourist office is open to 8 pm daily in midsummer.

Places to Stay & Eat

Most visitors to Risør stay on their boats and rooms at the *Risør Hotel* (☎ 04 15 07 00),the only in-town hotel, start at 450/650 kr for singles/doubles. From 1 July to mid-August there's a *youth hostel* (☎ 04 15 09 93), at Sirisvei 13 one km from the harbour, with beds for 110 kr. If you want a double room (220 kr) it's easy to arrange as all 30 rooms have two beds. You could consider camping – roughing it on one of the offshore islands.

The pavement *Solsiden Café* at the harbour has surprisingly reasonable prices. You can pick up fruit at the harbourside market and there's a bakery one block up Kragsgate west of the harbour.

Getting There & Away

Buses to and from Risør connect with the train at Gjerstad, three times a day. There are also daily Arendal and Oslo-bound buses. The midsummer ferry from Oslo costs 260 kr, with a 25% discount for students.

OTHER SOUTH COAST TOWNS

Mandal, 45 km west of Kristiansand, is the southernmost town in Norway, with nice sandy beaches, numerous skerries (small, rocky islands) and two youth hostels. The nearby **Lindesnes** lighthouse marks Norway's southernmost point.

Between Kristiansand and Arendal you'll pass **Lillesand**, with its unspoiled village centre of old whitewashed houses befitting the 'white town' image that so many other south coast towns claim, and **Grimstad**, where the house that Henrik Ibsen lived in has been incorporated into a museum.

TELEMARK

Most of the Telemark region is sparsely populated and rural, with steep mountains, deep valleys, high plateaus and a myriad of lakes. Unfortunately, travel around Telemark is geared primarily to the automobile. Train lines run only through the south-eastern part of Telemark and buses are infrequent.

Telemark's most visited attraction is the impressive **Heddal stave church** (circa 1242) the largest stave church in Norway. It's on highway E76 five km west of **Notodden**, the closest rail stop.

Telemark's two largest cities, **Porsgrunn** and **Skien**, are among the most industrialised in Norway. If you get stranded in Skien, one of the best hotel deals is the *Høyers Hotell* (☎ 03 52 05 40), at Kongensgate 6 near the canal in the city centre, which costs 420/520 kr for singles/doubles in summer and on weekends all year round.

From late May to early September sightseeing boats leave Skien for an unhurried, if not rather sluggish, 10-hour trip through the Telemark canal system (105 km of waterways with 18 locks) that ends at **Dalen**. The cost is 200 kr one way. Dalen has a summer *camping ground* (☎ 03 67 71 91) with cabins.

The long, narrow industrial town of **Rjukan** is squeezed into the deep Vestfjord valley at the base of the 1883-metre Mt Gausta. A trail to the mountain top starts at lake Hedder, 16 km from town.

The **Industrial Workers Museum** has an exhibit of the Norwegian Resistance's daring sabotage of the heavy-water plant which was built by the Nazis in Rjukan during WW II.

The easiest way to get to Rjukan is via the 10 am train from Oslo to Kongsberg where a bus connects daily except Sundays, arriving in Rjukan at 2 pm. Rjukan's *youth hostel* (☎ 03 69 05 27), Birkelandsgate 2, charges 80/200 kr for dorms/doubles.

From Rjukan it's a nine-hour walk north to the Kalhovde mountain hut and a network of trails that stretches north and west across the expansive moors of **Hardangervidda**, a popular wilderness hiking area that boasts Norway's largest wild reindeer herd.

At **Bø**, Telemark's westernmost rail station, the train connects with buses that lead west to Dalen, Amot and on to Odda in Hardanger.

Kragerø, a popular seaside resort with narrow streets and whitewashed houses, has long been a retreat for Norwegian artists. The simplest approach is by rail from Oslo or from Kristiansand to Neslandsvatn, where three daily trains running in each direction meet a connecting bus to Kragerø.

There's also a summer ferry from Oslo. Kragerø's summer *youth hostel* (☎ 03 98 18 66), two km from the harbour, has dorms/doubles for 150/300 kr including breakfast.

KONGSBERG

The settlement of Kongsberg was founded in 1624 following the discovery of one of the world's purest deposits of silver in the nearby valley Numedal. Kongsberg became the largest town in Norway as a result of the ensuing silver rush.

In the early 19th century, the silver works closed and a Royal mint helped the town continue to florish. The **national mint** is still located in town, but the last mine closed in 1957.

Nowadays in summer there are daily tours of the old **silver mines** at **Saggrenda**, eight km from Kongsberg, which include a train ride through cool subterranean shafts (40 kr) – bring a sweater! The noon bus (15 kr) from Kongsberg (daily except Sundays) will get

you to Saggrenda in time for the 12.30 pm tour.

There are two worthwhile museums to visit in Kongsberg. The **Norwegian Mining Museum** (25 kr), at Hyttegata 3 just over the bridge, has exhibits of mining, minting and skiing in an 1844 smelting building.

The **Lågdal folk museum** (10 kr), which has 20 historic buildings and an indoor museum with recreated 1800s workshops, is 10 minutes south of the railway station: go down Storgata, turn left on Bekkedokk, take the walkway parallel to the tracks and follow the signs.

The tourist office is opposite the railway station. After hours, you can pick up a free town map at the nearby Gyldenløve Hotel.

Places to Stay & Eat

Lågdalsmuseets Camping (☎ 03 73 22 28), in the folk museum grounds, has cabins for 200 kr or you can pitch your tent beside one of the sod-roofed farmhouses for 50 kr.

Kongsberg Youth Hostel (☎ 03 73 20 24) is two km from the railway station: walk down Storgata, cross the bridge, turn right at the post office and take the pedestrian walkway over the E76. Dorms cost 145 kr, doubles 430 kr including breakfast.

Of Kongberg's two hotels the *Gyldenløve Hotel* (☎ 03 73 17 44) offers the best summer rate at 410/580 kr for singles/doubles with a Fjord Pass (which you can buy at the hotel for 50 kr).

The country-clubbish *Gamle Kongsberg Kro*, on the south side of the river, has a stewed beef meal *(dagens gryte)* until 11 pm daily for 50 kr. There's a cafeteria at *Arena grocery store*, just west of the railway station, and a bakery at Storgata 28.

Getting There & Away

Kongsberg is a 1½-hour 105-kr train ride from Oslo. Express buses connect Kongsberg with Rjukan (2¼ hour,s 104 kr), Notodden (45 minutes, 35 kr) and Oslo (1¾ hours, 83 kr). Kongsberg's railway and bus stations are side by side.

Kongsberg

0   250   500 m

To Geilo

To Oslo (E76)

Drammensveien

Lågen

E76

To Saggrenda &
Notodden (E76)

1 Arena Grocery Store
2 Bus Station
3 Railway Station
4 Tourist Office
5 Taxi Stand
6 Gyldenløve Hotel
7 Bank
8 Bakery
9 Grand Hotel
10 Lågdal Folk Museum
   & Camping
11 Kongsberg Youth Hostel
12 Gamle Kongsberg Kro
13 National Mint
14 Norwegian Mining Musuem
15 Post Office
16 Kongsberg Church

NORWAY

Central Norway

The central part of Norway, stretching west from Oslo to the historic city of Bergen and north to the mountaineering town of Åndalsnes, takes in Norway's highest mountains, largest glacier and most spectacular fjords. Not surprisingly, this region is the top destination for travellers to Norway.

FROM OSLO TO BERGEN

The Oslo-Bergen railway line is Norway's most scenic a seven-hour journey past forests, small farms, alpine villages and the starkly beautiful plateau Hardangervidda.

Midway between Oslo and Bergen is **Geilo**, a ski centre where you can practically get off the train and onto a lift. Geilo has a *youth hostel* (☎ 06 78 53 00) near the railway station and there is good summer hiking in the mountains above town.

From Geilo the train climbs 600 metres through a tundra-like landscape of high lakes and snow-capped mountains to the tiny village of **Finse**, near the glacier Hardangerjøkulen. Finse has year-round skiing and is in the midst of a network of summer hiking trails. One of Norway's most frequently trodden trails winds from the Finse railway station down to the fjord town of Aurland, a four to five-day trek. There's breathtaking mountain scenery along the way as well as a series of DNT mountain huts a day's walk apart – the nearest is the Finsehytte, 200 metres from the Finse station. There's also a bike route from Finse to Flåm on the century-old railroad construction road.

Myrdal, the next stop, is the connecting point for the spectacularly steep Flåm railway which twists its way 20 splendid km down to **Flåm** village on the Aurlandsfjord, an arm of the Sognefjord.

Many people go down to Flåm, have lunch and take the train back up to Myrdal where they catch the next Oslo-Bergen train. A better option is to take the two-hour ferry from Flåm up the waterfall-laden Nærøyfjord to Gudvangen where there's a

connecting bus that climbs up the steep valley on the dramatically scenic ride to Voss. From Voss, trains to Bergen run nearly hourly. To include a cruise of the Nærøyfjord in a day trip from Oslo to Bergen, you'll need to take the 7.30 am train from Oslo which connects with the 2.30 pm ferry from Flåm. For details on Flåm see the Sognefjord section.

Voss

Voss is another winter-sports centre with attractive surroundings, though the town itself is not particularly special. Buses stop at the railway station. The tourist office is a 10-minute walk away, to the right (south) of the prominent 13th century stone church.

Places to Stay & Eat There's a lakeside camping ground a few minutes' walk from the tourist office and several moderately priced pensions around town. The modern *Voss Youth Hostel* (☎ 05 51 20 17) has a nice lakeside location, a km west of the railway station, but it's a rather impersonal place and prices are high at 136 kr for a dorm bed, 236/360 kr for singles/doubles. There's no guest kitchen, though an ordinary breakfast is included in the price. Bicycles, canoes and rowing boats can be hired at 20 kr an hour, 75 kr a day, and there's a free sauna.

There's a grocery store and bakery on the north side of the church, or you can pick up fruit and snacks at the petrol station opposite the railway station.

BERGEN

Bergen was the capital of Norway during the 12th and 13th centuries and in the early 1600s had the distinction of being Scandinavia's largest city – with a population of 15,000.

Set on a peninsula surrounded by seven mountains, Bergen's history is closely tied to the sea. It became one of the central ports of the Hanseatic League of merchants which dominated trade in northern Europe during the late Middle Ages. The Hanseatic influence is still visible in the sharply gabled

Bergen

0   150   300 m

■ PLACES TO STAY

11	Kloster Pension
12	Augusta Conditori
18	Kalmar Inn
42	Håkon Hotell
43	Myklebust Pensjonat
44	Bergen Gjestehus
48	Olsnes Guesthouse
57	InterMission

▼ PLACES TO EAT

15	Bryggenstuen & Bryggeloftet
20	Peppe's Pizza
23	Burger King
25	Bakery
26	Kebab Expressen
28	Café Opera
33	Kaffistova BUL
36	Banco Rotto
40	Dickens
41	Michelangelo
45	Kinsarvik Frukt
46	Bakery
52	Spisestedet Kornelia
59	Mira Indian Café

OTHER

1	Aquarium
2	International Ferries
3	Håkonshallen
4	Rosenkrantz Tower
5	Stavanger Express Boat
6	Post Office

7	Vinmonopolet
8	Mariakirken
9	Bryggens Museum
10	Schøtstuene
13	Theta Museum
14	Sjøboden
16	Fjord Express Boats
17	Stavanger Ferry
19	Hanseatic Museum
21	Funicular
22	Torget
24	Terra Nova
27	Cinema
29	Maxime
30	Bank
31	Tourist Office
32	Galleriet
34	Laundrette
35	Kunsthåndverk
37	Sykkel Buttiken
38	Post Office
39	Telegraph Office
47	Domkirke
49	Leprosy Museum
50	Municipal Art Museum
51	University Museums
53	Rasmus Meyer's Collections
54	Library
55	Railway Station
56	Old Town Gate
58	Bus Station
60	Grieghallen
61	University Student Centre
62	Coastal Steamer Quay
63	Medical Clinic

terrace houses that line Bergen's picturesque harbour front.

Even though it's Norway's second largest city, Bergen (population 215,000) has a pleasant, slow pace. A university town and the cultural centre of western Norway, it has theatres, museums, a noted philharmonic orchestra and plenty of statues and parks.

Odds are that you'll see rain, as it falls 275 days a year. Still, the weather is not as dismal as it sounds – the rain keeps the city green and flowery, and the low skyline of red-tiled roofs manages to look cheery even on damp drizzly days.

Bergen is the main jumping-off point for journeys into the western fjords: numerous buses, trains, passenger ferries and express boats set off daily.

Orientation
Bergen is a fairly compact city and easy to get around, albeit hilly. The bus and railway stations are a block apart on Strømgaten on the east side of the city, and the tourist office and city centre are a 10-minute walk down Kaigaten. Much of the city is built up around the waterfront and many of the sights, restaurants and hotels are within a few blocks of Vågen, the inner harbour.

NORWAY

Information

Tourist Office The tourist office, on Torgalmenning pedestrian square, has brochures on destinations throughout Norway. Be sure to pick up the detailed *Bergen Guide*. Hours are from 8.30 am to 9 pm daily (10 am to 7 pm Sunday) from May to September, 10 am to 4 pm Monday to Saturday the rest of the year.

Money Change money at post offices or at the bank opposite the tourist office. After hours the tourist office changes money, though the rate's not as good.

Post & Telecommunications The main post office, on Småstrandgate, is open from 8 am to 5 pm weekdays, 9 am to 2 pm Saturdays. The telegraph office is on its south side and open from 8 am to 8 pm weekdays, 9 am to 2 pm Saturdays.

Library The public library, between the bus and railway stations, has a good selection of foreign newspapers. It's open on weekdays to 8 pm, Saturdays to 2 pm, with shorter midsummer hours.

Travel Agency Terra Nova, the Norske Vandrerhjem travel agency at Strandgaten 4, specialises in budget travel and books tours, including a five-day bicycle trip between Voss and Geilo.

Laundry Bergen's only coin laundrette, Jarlens Vaskoteque, 17 Lille Øvregate, charges about 50 kr a load, though for 10 kr more you can drop your clothes off with the manager and pick them up a couple of hours later. It's open from 10 am to 8 pm Monday to Friday, 9 am to 3 pm on Saturdays.

Emergency Dial 002 for police and 003 for an ambulance. The medical clinic (☎ 05 32 11 20) at Lars Hillesgate 30 is open 24 hours a day for emergencies. There's a pharmacy at the bus station open to midnight daily.

Things to See

The waterfront **fish market** at Torget is a bustling place in the morning and a good starting point for an exploration of historic Bryggen on the north side of the harbour.

Bergen also has lots of quaint cobbled streets lined with older homes. One of the best areas for strolling around is up above Bryggen and the funicular station.

Bryggen Bryggen, the site of the old medieval quarter, is a compact area that's easily explored on foot. The streetfront with Bryggen's long timber buildings has museums, restaurants and shops, while the alleys that run along their less-restored sides offer a closer look at the stacked-stone foundations and rough-plank construction of centuries past.

Hanseatic Museum This museum, in a well-preserved timber building dating from the 16th century, offers a glimpse of the austere working and living conditions of merchants in the Hanseatic period which reached its height during the 15th century. The museum is open daily from 9 am to 5 pm in summer, and from 11 am to 2 pm daily in May and September and on Sundays, Mondays, Wednesdays and Fridays in the off season. Admission costs 15 kr.

Bryggens Museum When this modern museum was being constructed, 800-year-old building foundations from Bergen's earliest settlement were unearthed and incorporated into the museum's exhibits, along with excavated medieval tools, pottery, skeletons and the like. It's open daily from 10 am to 5 pm May to August, from 11 am to 3 pm (from noon on weekends) September to April. Admission costs 10 kr.

Schøtstuene Schøtstuene, at Øvregaten 50, houses the assembly halls where the fraternity of Hanseatic merchants met for their business meetings and beer guzzling. It's open from 10 am to 4 pm daily in summer, and from 11 am to 2 pm daily in May and September and on Sundays, Mondays, Wednesdays and Fridays in the off season. Admission costs 15 kr.

Theta Museum This museum is at the back of the building marked Sjøboden: go through the alley and up the stairs to the 3rd floor. This clandestine one-room Resistance headquarters uncovered by the Nazis in 1942 is now Norway's tiniest museum. It's open Tuesdays, Saturdays and Sundays from 2 to 4 pm from mid-May to mid-September. Admission costs 10 kr.

Mariakirken Situated opposite the Bryggens Museum, this Romanesque stone church with twin towers dates from the 1100s and is Bergen's oldest building. The interior has frescoes, some dating back to the 15th century, and a splendid Baroque pulpit donated by Hanseatic merchants in 1676. It's open from 11 am to 4 pm weekdays from mid-May to mid-September and from noon to 1.30 pm Tuesday to Friday the rest of the year. Admission costs 10 kr.

Rosenkrantz Tower Alongside the harbour is the Rosenkrantz tower, built in the 1560s by Bergen's governor as a residence and defence post. The tower incorporates parts of an earlier building that dates back to 1260. You can climb up spiral staircases past halls and sentry posts to the lookout on top. The tower is open from 10 am to 4 pm daily mid-May to mid-September, but only from noon to 3 pm on Sundays in the off season. Admission costs 10 kr.

Håkonshallen This large ceremonial hall built by King Håkon Håkonsson in 1261 for the wedding of his son is next door to the Rosenkrantz tower. The roof was blown off in 1944 when a German ammunition boat exploded in the harbour and the building has been extensively restored. It's open from 10 am to 4 pm daily mid-May to mid-September, from noon to 3 pm (3 to 6 pm on Thursdays) the rest of the year. Entry costs 10 kr.

Other City Sights The university, at the end of Christies Gate, has a **Natural History Museum** full of stuffed creatures and mineral displays, a **Maritime Museum** with models of Viking ships and, of greater interest, an **Historical Museum** with Viking weaponry, medieval altar fronts, folk art and period furnishings. The Natural History Museum is closed on Thursdays, the Historical Museum on Fridays and the Maritime Museum on Saturdays, but they are otherwise open from 11 am to 2 pm. Admission is 10 kr at the Maritime Museum, free at the other two.

The **Municipal Art Museum** and the **Rasmus Meyer's Collections**, on Rasmus Meyers Allé opposite the lake fountain, exhibit a superb collection of Norwegian art from the 18th and 19th centuries, including works by Munch and JC Dahl; and contemporary works by Picasso, Klee and others. These collections are open daily from 11 am to 4 pm (Sundays from noon to 3 pm) from 15 May to 15 September; there's a combined entrance fee of 15 kr, students free. In the off season hours are shorter, but admission is free.

Bergen's **aquarium** has a big outdoor tank with seals and penguins as well as indoor fish tanks. It's out near the northern tip of the peninsula, reached by bus No 4 or a 15-minute walk from the city centre. The aquarium is open daily from 9 am to 8 pm May to September, 10 am to 6 pm October to April, and costs 30 kr. The public park just beyond the aquarium is a pleasant place for strolling and has shaded lawns, sunbathing areas and an outdoor heated swimming pool.

Bergen Environs A modest open-air museum, **Gamle Bergen**, with about 35 buildings from the 18th and 19th centuries, is north of the city centre and reached by bus No 1 or 9. Open all year, guided tours begin on the hour from noon to 5 pm in summer and cost 25 kr.

The well-preserved **Fantoft stave church**, built in Sognefjord in the 12th century, was moved to the southern outskirts of Bergen in 1884. From Bergen take bus No 18 or 19, get off at Fantoft and walk uphill for 10 minutes. The church is open from 10.30 am to 5.30 pm daily from mid-May to mid-September, admission costs 10 kr.

If you want to continue on to the former lakeside home and workshop of composer Edvard Grieg, get back on the bus until the Hopsbroen stop and follow the signs to **Troldhaugen,** a 20-minute walk. If you're not a big Grieg fan, however, you might not find this low-key museum worth the effort. It's open from 10.30 am to 5.30 pm daily in summer, admission is 15 kr.

The **cable car** (40 kr) up 607-metre Mt Ulriken provides a hilltop view of the Bergen area. Take bus No 2 or 4 to Haukeland hospital.

Activities

Funicular & Hiking For an unbeatable view of the city, take the steeply rising funicular to the top of 320-metre Mt Fløien. If you also want to do some hiking, there are well-marked trails leading into the forest from the hilltop station. Trail 3 makes a 1.3-km loop around a lake and trails 1 and 2 each make five-km loops through hilly woodlands. For a delightful 40-minute walk back to the city, take trail 4 and connect with trail 6. The funicular runs to 11 pm daily and costs 13 kr one way.

Norway in a Nutshell The railway sells a packaged ticket combining a morning train from Bergen to Flåm, a ferry up the Nærøyfjord to Gudvangen, a bus to Voss and a train back to Bergen in time for dinner. It makes for a very scenic day trip at 370 kr.

Places to Stay

Bergen has its fair share of 1st-class hotels, though few are outstanding, prices are invariably high, and seasonal and weekend discounts are miserly when compared to those in Oslo and Trondheim. Overall the city's best values are found in pensions.

Camping The closest camping ground is *Bergenshallen Camping* in Landås, 10 minutes from the city centre by bus No 3.

Hostels The most central cheap place to crash is at *InterMission* (☎ 05 31 32 75), Kalfarveien 8, where the Christian Student

Fellowship provides mattresses on the floor of a 1780s house for 90 kr. The staff is friendly, guests have kitchen privileges and laundry facilities are available. It's a five-minute walk from the railway station and is open from mid-June to mid-August from 5 pm. Arrive early to get a bed.

Bergen Inter-Rail Point (☎ 05 31 81 25), at Kalfarveien 77 about 10 minutes beyond InterMission, also has mattresses on the floor for the same price. It's open from 1 July to mid-August.

The 200-bed *Montana Youth Hostel* (☎ 05 29 29 00), at Johan Blytts vei 30, five km from the city centre by bus No 4, is open from mid-May to the end of September. Dorm beds cost 136 kr, breakfast included.

Private Rooms The tourist office books rooms in private homes. Singles/doubles cost from 145/235 kr, plus a 15/20 kr booking fee.

Pensions *Olsnes Guesthouse* (☎ 05 31 20 44), Skivebakken 24, is in a quiet neighbourhood of older homes, a five-minute walk from the railway station (turn uphill opposite the Leprosy Museum). There are nine adequate rooms, guests have use of a kitchen and there's a good mix of Norwegian and foreign travellers. Rooms cost 135/245 kr with shared bath, 170/295 kr with private bath, with rates negotiable for longer stays.

The 30-bed *Kloster Pension* (☎ 05 90 21 58), Klosteret 12, is a popular lodge-style guesthouse which has clean, simple rooms from 250/380 for singles/doubles including a continental breakfast.

The *Myklebust Pensjonat* (☎ 05 90 16 70), Rosenbergsgaten 19, has six delightfully comfortable rooms with natural wood floors and tasteful decor. Rates start at 350/380 kr, with breakfast an optional 45 kr a person.

Hotels *Håkon Hotell* (☎ 05 23 20 28), Håkonsgaten 27, has rooms that are simple and clean, with rates from 295/435 kr for singles/doubles with shared bath. As military personnel get a hefty discount, Håkon Hotell sometimes fills with sailors.

The *Kalmar Inn* (☎ 05 23 18 60), Jon Smørs gate 11, has 40 rooms occupying four floors above the Rema 1000 grocery store on a busy central intersection. Though the size and decor of the rooms vary, overall they're quite adequate for the price, which begins at 250/375 kr singles/doubles with shared bath and kitchen privileges. Breakfast is an additional 30 kr a person. It's a good bet if other places are full, as the Kalmar has just purchased 50 more rooms in the same neighbourhood.

Bergen Gjestehus (☎ 05 31 96 66), Vestre Torvgate 20A, is a 24-room hotel with commodious rooms, simple but not cheerless, most with kitchenettes and all with TV, phone and private baths. Rates are 500/600 kr in the summer, about 100 kr cheaper in winter.

Places to Eat

The bus station is a mecca of cheap eats with food stalls serving inexpensive sandwiches and Chinese food, a good fruit stand, a grocery store, and Sol Brod bakery with huge cinnamon rolls for 6 kr.

Mira Indian Café, opposite the bus station on V Strømkaien, has vegetarian dishes for 45 kr and meat dishes with rice and nan for 75 kr. It's open from 3 to 11 pm daily.

Café Opera, at Engen 24 and open to 1 am daily, has excellent food at reasonable prices. Home-made soups with fresh herbs are 34 kr and a chalkboard lists dinners like lamb or trout for 55 kr. *Kebab Expressen*, Engen 33, has good inexpensive felafels and kebabs.

Spisestedet Kornelia, a pleasant vegetarian restaurant at Fosswinckelsgate 18, has salads, omelettes and pastas for 50 to 80 kr. It's open from noon to 7.30 pm weekdays.

Dickens, Bergen's most popular café, has a sunny dining room overlooking Ole Bulls plass. Salads, pizzas and pasta dishes cost around 65 kr, fish and meat dishes are roughly double that. However, there's a special daily menu that features a good-value light meal for about 50 kr and a hearty meal

for 80 kr. The kitchen is open from 11.30 am to 11 pm, from 1 pm on Sundays.

The best pizza in town is from *Michelangelo*, Neumannsgate 25, which has both indoor and outdoor dining. If you're in Bryggen, the old standby *Peppe's Pizza*, Finnegården 2A, is not a bad second choice.

Kaffistova BUL, opposite the fish market, has inexpensive cafeteria food, such as lasagne with salad for 50 kr. There's a harbour view from the 2nd-floor dining room and it's open weekdays and Sundays to 6 pm, Saturdays to 3.30 pm. The more up-market *Augusta Conditori* at the Augustin Hotel has soups, pastas and good pastries at reasonable prices at lunch time.

Banco Rotto, Vågsalmenningen 16, has Bergen's most unusual café setting, with tables spread across the spacious lobby of a former 19th century bank. They have sandwiches for about 25 kr, salads for 50 kr and hot dishes around 75 kr, but the real attraction here is the tantalising cakes. It's open Monday to Wednesday from 11.30 am to 5.30 pm, Thursday to Saturday to about midnight, Sunday from 1 to 6 pm.

Bryggestuen & Bryggeloftet, a two-storey restaurant in the midst of the historic district at Bryggen 6, has a pleasant atmosphere with traditional Norwegian food. At all times except midsummer they feature a generous daily special for about 60 kr, but otherwise most dishes begin around 100 kr. It's open from 10 am to 11.30 pm, Sundays from 1 pm.

The *fish market* at Torget is the place to buy fruit and seafood, including tasty open-faced salmon rolls for 10 kr – or pick up a bag of boiled shrimp or crab legs for around 35 kr and munch away down at the harbour. The fish market is open Monday to Saturday from about 8 am to 3 pm.

Grocery stores abound in Bergen. The cheapest prices are at the *Mekka* chain, which is also open later than other stores (weekdays to 8 pm, Saturdays to 6 pm); there's a Mekka at the bus station, another near Banco Rotto.

Kinsarvik Frukt on Olav Kyrres Gate is a small grocery store with a health-food section. *Lie Nielsen* bakeries, found around town, have good reasonably priced sandwiches and breads. Bergen brews its own beer under the Hansa label.

Entertainment

Café Opera, Engen 24, is a popular student hang-out with live music in the upstairs lounge, usually there's no cover charge. *Maxime* and *Polar Bear Bar*, at Ole Bulls plass, are side-by-side hot spots with a disco and live bands. They sometimes offer cheap food to draw customers.

Sjøboden, a lively pub in the heart of Bryggen, has a decidedly nautical ambience, a piano player nightly, and Hansa beer on tap.

Bergen Kino on Neumannsgate has 13 cinema screens and first-run Western movies. The Bergen International Festival, held for 12 days at the end of May, is the big cultural event of the year with quality dance, music and folklore events taking place throughout the city.

Things to Buy

The Galleriet shopping centre, between the tourist office and post office, has a couple of camera shops and a good bookshop, Malvær Libris. The new bus station contains the other major shopping centre. Kunsthåndverk, Lille Øvregate 17, is an artists co-op with good pottery and crafts.

Getting There & Away

Air Bergen airport is in Flesland, 19 km south-east of Bergen's city centre. The SAS Flybussen runs to the Bergen bus station for 36 kr.

Bus Daily express buses run to Odda in Hardanger (3¾ hours, 172 kr) and to the western fjord region. From Bergen it costs 307 kr (6¾ hours) to Stryn, 433 kr (10½ hours) to Ålesund and 673 kr (15 hours) to Trondheim. Inter-Rail pass holders get a 50% discount on the northbound buses.

Train Trains to Oslo (seven hours, 450 kr) depart several times a day; seat reservations are required. In addition, local trains run regularly between Bergen and Voss (95 kr).

The railway station has a bank, café and lockers for 20 kr.

Car The main highway into Bergen is the E16. There's a 5-kr toll for vehicles entering the city on weekdays from 6 am to 10 pm.

Boat There's a daily Sognefjord express boat to Balestrand, Flåm and Gudvangen, a northbound express boat to Måløy and both an express boat and ferry to Stavanger. All express boats leave from the south side of Vågen.

The coastal steamer, *Hurtigruten*, leaves from the quay south of the university at 10 pm daily. Details are in Norway, Getting Around.

Boats to Newcastle and Iceland dock down past Rosenkrantz tower; information is in the Norway, Getting There & Away section.

Getting Around

The bus fare within the city boundaries is 11 kr per ride, or 60 kr for a two-day tourist pass. A free bus runs between the post office and the bus station. There's a taxi stand (☎ 05 99 09 90) south of the tourist office on Ole Buls plass.

If you have a car, you're best off parking it and exploring the city centre on foot. Except in spots where there are parking meters, street parking is reserved for residents with special zone-parking stickers. Thus if you see a big 'P' for parking but the sign has the word *'sone'* on it, it's a reserved area. Most metered parking is limited to 30 minutes or one hour, though there's two-hour metered parking on the west side of the Grieghallen concert hall and off Christies Gate on the north side of Lille Lungegårdsvann. Still, your best bet is to park in one of the indoor car parks; the largest and the only one open 24 hours a day is Bygarasjen at the bus station, which charges 35 kr to park from 7 am to 5 pm, 15 kr from 5 pm to 7 am.

Sykkel Butikken, Østre Skostredet 5, rents three-gear bicycles for 30 kr a day. It's open from 9 am daily except Sundays.

Western Fjords

0   25   50 km

SOGNEFJORD

The Sognefjord is Norway's longest (200 km) and deepest (1300 metres) fjord – a wide slash across the map of western Norway. In some places sheer lofty walls rise more than 1000 metres straight up from the water, while in others there is a far gentler shoreline with farms, orchards and small towns sloping up the mountainsides.

The Sognefjord's broad main waterway is impressive, but it's by cruising into the fjord's narrower arms that you get closest to the steep rock faces and cascading waterfalls. The loveliest branch is the deeply cut Nærøyfjord, Norway's narrowest fjord.

Getting There & Away

Fylkesbaatane operates a year-round express boat that runs daily between Bergen and Årdalstangen, at the head of the Sognefjord, stopping at a dozen small towns along the way. From 1 June to 15 September, Fylkesbaatane runs a second express boat that links Bergen with Flåm. The boat leaves Bergen at 8 am daily and arrives in Flåm at 1.20 pm; stops en route include Balestrand, Vangsnes and Aurland.

The return boat leaves Flåm at 2.35 pm, arriving in Bergen at 8.30 pm. From Bergen it costs 345 kr to Balestrand, 415 kr to Flåm. There are discounts for students, families and most rail pass holders.

There are numerous local ferries linking the fjord towns and an extensive (if not always frequent) network of buses, all detailed in the 150-page *Sogn og Fjordane* timetable available free at larger tourist offices and some bus and railway stations.

Flåm

Flåm, a tiny village at the head of the Aurlandsfjord, is a transit point for travellers taking the Gudvangen ferry or the Sognefjord express boat. It's also the only place on the Sognefjord with rail connections. Despite its heavy day-traffic few people stay overnight and it's a pleasantly quiet place to be in the evening when the last train pulls away. The tourist office booth at the railway station rents bikes, has information on hiking and sells ferry tickets. The docks are just beyond the railway station.

Places to Stay & Eat *Flåm Camping Ground & Youth Hostel* (☎ 05 63 21 21), with dorm beds for 75 kr and doubles for 210 kr, is a few minutes' walk from the station; go up the track and over the bridge. It's open from 1 May to 15 October. *Heimly Pensjonat* (☎ 05 63 23 00) has a great fjord view and straightforward rooms for 390/590 kr for singles/doubles, breakfast included.

The *Heimly Cafeteria* has reasonably priced sandwiches and a fine fjord-side location, or try the cafeteria in the *Fretheim Hotel*, which is not as expensive as it looks.

Getting There & Away The Flåm railway runs between Myrdal and Flåm (48 kr) six to eight times a day in sync with the Oslo-Bergen services. At Flåm, a bus to Aurland meets the train and there are various boats heading out to towns around the fjord. The most scenic boat ride from Flåm is the ferry up the Nærøyfjord to Gudvangen, which departs at either 1.50 or 2.30 pm daily and costs 85 kr. At Gudvangen a connecting bus will take you on to Voss.

In addition to the Sognefjord express boat between Flåm and Bergen, a local express boat runs all year round between Flåm and Balestrand (1¾ hours, 120 kr), departing from Flåm at 8.15 pm daily except Saturdays, and from late June to mid-August at 6 pm daily. In summer on Saturdays only there's also an 11.30 am sailing from Flåm to Balestrand that continues on to Fjærland. These boats all stop in Aurland and Vangsnes en route to Balestrand.

Vangsnes

Vangsnes, across the fjord from Balestrand, is a little farming community crowned with a huge hilltop statue of saga hero Fridtjof. Though it has both ferry and express boat connections there's not much to the village. There is a small grocery store near the dock and the cosy *Vangsnes Youth Hostel* (☎ 05 69 66 22), a few minutes' away, charges only 80 kr for a bed, 160 kr for a double room.

Solvang Camping, above the dock, has cabins and motel rooms for 130 to 225 kr. Buses go to nearby Vik, a factory town that has a stave church about a km from its centre.

Balestrand

Balestrand has a backdrop of snowy mountains and a genteel British hill-country feeling. Considering that it's the main resort destination on the Sognefjord, the village is remarkably low-key and there are some pleasant, inexpensive places to stay.

The village road that runs south along the fjord has little traffic and is great for strolling along. It's lined with apple orchards, ornate older homes and gardens, a 19th century English church and Viking burial mounds. One mound is topped by a statue of the legendary King Bele, erected by Germany's Kaiser Wilhelm II who spent vacations here regularly until WW I.

For a longer hike take the small ferry *Bianca* (10 kr) across the Esefjord to the Dragsvik side, where an abandoned country road is the first leg of an eight-km walk back to Balestrand. The tourist office at the dock has a free trail map and rents bikes for 100 kr a day.

Places to Stay & Eat At *Sjøtun Camping*, a 15-minute walk south along the fjord, you can pitch a tent amidst apple trees or rent a rustic four-bunk cabin for 130 kr.

Balestrand Youth Hostel (☎ 05 69 13 03), in the lodge-style Kringsjå Hotel, has beds for 85 kr and double rooms for 220 kr. The Victorian *Bøyum Pensjonat* (☎ 05 69 11 14) has singles/doubles for 175/260 kr. Both places are minutes from the dock and open from mid-June to late August.

Midtnes Pensjonat (☎ 05 69 11 33), next to the English church, is popular with returning British holiday-makers, and costs from 320/420 kr with breakfast.

There are two fast-food cafés near the post office, opposite the dock, and the hostel restaurant has a complete daily meal for 70 kr.

Getting There & Away In addition to the Sognefjord express boat, local boats run daily to Flåm, Hella and Fjærland. Buses run from Balestrand to Sogndal (63 kr) and Bergen (186 kr). Taking the bus to Bergen is cheaper and more scenic than going by the express boat, as the bus passes by Vik's Hopperstad stave church and climbs through the impressive and usually snow-packed Vika mountains on the way to Voss.

Fjærland

Fjærland is a small farming village which is at the head of the scenic Fjærlandsfjord and near two arms of the massive glacier Jostedalsbreen, an inviting combination for daytrippers.

From Balestrand you can take a morning ferry to Fjærland and a connecting bus to the glacier. En route the bus stops at the sleek new glacier museum (55 kr!).

Another option is the private taxi run by George Mundal (☎ 05 69 31 78), who provides an unhurried tour to the glacier and charges only 75 kr a person (minimum of two people), the same as the bus.

Both bus and taxi go within a few hundred metres of the two glacier arms: the Supphellebreen, where you can walk up to the edge and touch the ice; and the creaking blue-iced Bøyabreen, where it's not uncommon to witness small breaks dropping into the meltwater beneath the glacier.

If you get stuck in Fjærland after the last boat, your accommodation options are the turn-of-the-century *Hotel Mundal* (☎ 05 69 31 01), where rooms cost 695/730 kr for singles/doubles, and a less appealing guesthouse with rates that are nearly as steep. There's a fast-food stand at the dock.

Getting There & Away Ferries run five times daily each way between Fjærland and Balestrand (35 kr), stopping in Hella en route. The last ferry from Fjærland to Balestrand leaves at 5.35 pm (6.40 pm daily except Saturdays from late June to mid-August), though there's an 8.45 pm ferry as far as Hella daily except on Saturdays.

In summer a daily bus (114 kr) departing at 10.30 am runs from Fjærland to Stryn connecting onwards to Hellesylt and Geiranger.

Sogndal

Sogndal is a modern regional centre of little note and even its tourist office focuses on day trips outside the town. Of top interest is the glacier Nigardsbreen 70 km to the north, followed by Norway's oldest **stave church** (circa 1130) in Urnes across the Lustrafjord and the **Sogn Folk Museum** near Kaupanger.

Places to Stay & Eat The tourist office at the bus station books rooms in private homes at 130/200 kr for singles/doubles. There's a summer *youth hostel* (☎ 05 67 20 33) in a school dorm 15 minutes east of the bus station. The hostel charges 80 kr for a dorm room, 150/200 kr for singles/doubles, and is closed from 10 am to 4.30 pm.

Otherwise the cheapest places are the central *Loftesnes Pensjonat* (☎ 05 67 15 77) at Fjørevegen 17 costing 300/400 kr, and the *Lægreid Hotel* (☎ 05 67 11 33) at the bus station, with large, comfortable rooms for 420/590 kr including breakfast. For cheap eats try the cafeterias in the adjacent *Domus* and *K-Sentret* supermarkets on Gravensteinsgata, open to 4.30 pm weekdays, to 2 pm Saturday.

Getting There & Away Buses run from Sogndal to Kaupanger (18 kr) and Hella (41 kr): points for the nearest boat connections. Daily buses go north-east to Lom (135 kr) and on to Otta (177 kr), a hiking centre between the Jotunheimen and Rondane mountains on the Dovre railway line. Sogndal has Sognefjord's only airport.

Nigardsbreen

Nigardsbreen, the most attractive arm of the Jostedalsbreen glacier, is a popular summer destination. Various guided hikes go daily across the glacier's rippled blue ice from June to early September. These hikes range from easy 1½-hour family walks (50 kr) to physically demanding day-long treks (290 kr) that cross deep crevices and require hiking boots and warm clothes. Detailed programmes are available from Jostedalen Braførarlag (☎ 05 68 32 73) 5828 Gjerde or at nearby tourist offices.

From Sogndal, take the Otta-bound bus at 8.50 am and get off in Gaupne where a 10.45 am bus leaves weekdays (9.55 am on Saturdays) for Nigardsbreen, an hour away. A 5 pm bus from Nigardsbreen connects back to Sogndal. If you're doing a longer hike it's best to stay in rural Gjerde, five km from Nigardsbreen, where there are a couple of pensions and camping grounds.

NORDFJORD

For most travellers the 100-km-long Nordfjord is but a stepping stone between the Sognefjord and the Geirangerfjord. The latter two fjords are linked by a road that winds around the head of the Nordfjord past the villages of Utvik, Innvik, Olden and Loen to the larger town of Stryn.

If you want to break your journey there are fjord-side lodging and camping sites en route and a *youth hostel* at Stryn (☎ 05 77 11 06) open from 15 May to 15 September (80 kr).

The chief Nordfjord attraction is **Briksdal glacier**, one of Jostedal's icy arms. Though a barrage of tourist buses make the drive up Olden valley to Briksdal there's only one public bus. It leaves Stryn (10 am, 44 kr) and Olden (10.20 am, 27 kr) daily from mid-June to mid-August, arriving at Briksdal at 11 am.

From there it's a three-km hike to the glacier. Briksdal has a lodge *Briksdalsbre Fjellstove* (☎ 05 77 38 11), which charges 240 kr a person with food and souvenirs, a camping ground and pony cart rides to the glacier for those who don't want to walk. The return bus leaves Briksdal at 2.15 pm.

Getting There & Away

On weekdays a bus heads south from Stryn to Fjærland at 8.45 am and from late June to late August there's also a daily afternoon bus at 3 pm. The bus takes 2¼ hours and costs 114 kr.

Afternoon buses run in both directions between Stryn and Hellesylt (one hour, 52 kr), connecting with the Geiranger ferry.

Måløy, a fishing town at the mouth of the Nordfjord, can be reached by daily buses from Stryn (two hours, 100 kr), the express boat from Bergen (4¼ hours, 410 kr) and the coastal steamer.

JOTUNHEIMEN NATIONAL PARK

The road between Sogndal and Lom passes through Jotunheimen national park, Norway's most popular wilderness destination. Hiking trails lead to the park's 60 glaciers, up to the top of Norway's loftiest peaks (2469-metre Mt Galdhøpiggen and 2452-metre Glittertinden) and along ravine-like valleys with deep lakes and plunging waterfalls. There are DNT huts and private lodges along many of the routes.

From Turtagrø, a rock-climbing centre midway between Sogndal and Lom, there's a three-hour hike to Fannaråkhytte, Jotunheimen's highest (2069 metres) DNT hut, with great panoramic views from the top. Krossbu is in the midst of a network of trails, including a short one to the Smørstabbreen glacier.

The 75-bed *Krossbu Turiststasjon* (☎ 06 21 29 22) has singles/doubles for 175/350 kr. The town of Bøverdalen, 18 km south of Lom, has the 220-bed *Elveseter Hotel* (☎ 06 21 20 00) with singles/doubles for 240/310 kr and a *youth hostel* (☎ 06 21 20 64) which is open from late May to the end of September and has dorm beds for 65 kr.

ÅNDALSNES

Åndalsnes, at the edge of the Romdalsfjord, is the northern gateway to the western fjords. Most visitors arrive on the train from Dombås, travelling along a gorgeous route that descends through a deep valley with dramatic waterfalls. Just before reaching Åndalsnes the train passes Trollveggen, whose jagged and often cloud-shrouded summit is considered the ultimate challenge among Norwegian mountain climbers. The road (route 9) between Dombås and Åndalsnes runs parallel to the railway line and is equally spectacular.

The town of Åndalsnes is rather nondescript, but the scenery is top notch. Camping grounds are plentiful and it has one of the finest youth hostels in Norway.

The mountains and valleys surrounding Åndalsnes offer excellent hiking and climbing. One trail, which goes up to the top of Mt Nesaksla, starts right in town 50 metres south of the Esso petrol station, and makes a fine half-day outing. While the path is quite steep, at the top you'll be rewarded with a terrific view of the surrounding fjords and mountains.

In summer the ascent can be quite hot in the midday sun, so get an early start and be sure to take water. For information on other trails and rock climbing, enquire at the helpful tourist office, which is five minutes from the railway station, just over the bridge. The tourist office, youth hostel and Åndalsnes Camping rent bicycles for 20/60 kr per hour/day.

Serious mountain climbers will want to contact the Aak Fjellsportsenter (☎ 07 22 64 44), 6300 Åndalsnes, which is four km from Åndalsnes centre on the way to Dombås. The centre sells topographic maps; offers mountaineering courses; rents out skis, canoes and mountain climbing equipment and also has a few rooms which rent for 300 kr.

Places to Stay & Eat

Åndalsnes Camping (☎ 07 22 16 29), three km from the centre on the south-east side of the river Rauma, has cabins from 80 kr and rents canoes (30 kr an hour), motorbikes (200 kr a day) and cars (550 kr a day).

The best place to stay in Åndalsnes is at the sod-roofed *Setnes Youth Hostel* (☎ 07 22 16 29), two km from the railway station on route 9. It's refreshingly personal, rooms are clean and pleasant, and scores of travellers return there. Dorm beds cost 90 kr, while singles/doubles cost 160/250 kr. Don't miss the famous pancakes-to-fried-fish breakfast (40 kr), complete with home-made currant jam and candles on the tables. Laundry facilities are available. The hostel shuts down for the first two weeks in May and advance reservations are necessary in winter. Reception is closed from 10 am to 4 pm. The bus to Ålesund goes by the hostel and will drop you off for 10 kr.

If the hostel is full, the nearby *Romsdal Guesthouse* (☎ 07 22 13 83) has straightforward rooms for 250/350 kr singles/doubles and pleasantly rustic two-bedroom cabins with complete kitchens for 300 kr.

The railway station sells fruit and sandwiches and there's a grocery store near the tourist office. The *Grand Hotel* dining room, which is open from 4 to 10 pm (2 to 6 pm on Sundays), has a full-meal daily special for around 75 kr and many of the similarly priced dishes on its *småretter* (light dishes) menu are good-sized portions.

Getting There & Away
The train from Dombås runs three times daily (1½ hours, 117 kr), in sync with the Oslo-Trondheim train services. Buses to Ålesund, an attractive central coast town, and Molde, noted for its summer jazz festival, meet the trains. Buses to Geiranger (three hours, 85 kr) via the Trollstigen highway operate from 15 June to 31 August, leaving Åndalsnes at 6.45 am and 5.05 pm. If you have your own car, the mountain pass is cleared and open by 1 June every year, and in early season it's an awesome drive through deep walls of snow.

FROM ÅNDALSNES TO GEIRANGER
The **Trollstigen** (Troll's Path) winding south from Åndalsnes is a thriller of a road with hairpin bends, a 1:12 gradient and, to add a daredevil element, it's practically one lane all the way. The bus makes photo stops at the thundering 180-metre waterfall **Stigfossen** on its way up to the mountain pass. At the top it usually stops long enough for you to walk to a lookout with a dizzying view back down the valley.

There are **waterfalls** galore smoking down the mountains as you descend to **Valldal**. You could break your journey in Valldal – there are camping grounds, cabins and a youth hostel – though most travellers continue on, taking the short ferry ride across to **Eidsdal**. There a waiting bus continues along the Ørneveien (Eagle's Highway),

ending with a magnificent bird's-eye view of the Geirangerfjord before descending into Geiranger village.

GEIRANGERFJORD
The 16-km Geirangerfjord is narrow and winding with towering rock faces, a scattering of abandoned farms clinging to the cliffsides, and breathtakingly high waterfalls with names like Seven Sisters, Suitor and Bridal Veil.

The villages of Geiranger and Hellesylt, at either end of the fjord, are connected by ferry. The cruise down the Geirangerfjord is Norway's most stunning and shouldn't be missed.

Geiranger
Geiranger, snuggling at the head of the Geirangerfjord, is surrounded by high mountains with cascading waterfalls. Though the village has only 300 residents, it's one of Norway's most visited spots. Nevertheless, it's reasonably serene in the evening when the cruise ships and tour buses have gone.

There's great hiking all around Geiranger to abandoned farmsteads, waterfalls and some beautiful vista points. One special walk is to **Storseter waterfall**, a 45-minute hike that actually takes you between the rock face and the cascading falls. The tourist office, at the pier near the post office, has a hike album detailing trails.

Places to Stay & Eat Hotels in Geiranger can be quickly booked out by package tourists, but cabins and camping spots are plentiful. A dozen camping grounds skirt the fjord and hillsides, including *Geiranger Camping*, right in town at the head of the fjord.

The *Grande Fjord Hotell* (☎ 07 16 30 67), on the fjord two km north-east of the village, has cabins for 200 kr, tent space and moderately priced motel rooms. You can find *husrom* signs around the village advertising rooms for rent, generally costing 150/250 kr for singles/doubles. One such place, *Oddebjørg Hjelle*, just uphill from the Hotel Geiranger, has cosy rooms and fjord views.

If you don't find anything on your own the tourist office also books rooms in private homes for a 20 kr fee.

The best place to eat is at *Naustkroa Bistro* at the pier, with good inexpensive food and hearty servings. Buy groceries at the store next to Meroks Hotel or at the Shell station near the dock.

Getting There & Away In summer there are daily buses to Åndalsnes leaving Geiranger at 1 and 6.10 pm, as well as buses to Ålesund and Molde. The Geiranger-Hellesylt ferry (70 minutes, 26 kr for a passenger, and 103 kr for a car) cruises the fjord five to nine times a day from 1 May to mid-September.

Hellesylt

Though this end of the fjord is not as spectacular as at Geiranger, Hellesylt does have an enthusiastic tourist office that rents rowing boats and fishing rods, and a fine summer *youth hostel* (☎ 07 16 51 28) perched just above town with dorms (75 kr) and a row of cabins (180 kr) with fjord views. Buses heading south to Stryn (one hour, 52 kr) leave from the pier where the ferry pulls in.

LILLEHAMMER

Lillehammer, host of the 1994 Winter Olympics, is 180 km north of Oslo. This small town (population 23,000) is abuzz with activity in preparation for the Olympic Games, which will be held from 12 to 27 February 1994. Hotels, sports facilities and a new railway/bus station are all going up and new ski jumps are being built on the hillsides above town.

While the main ceremonies and many of the 120 sporting events will take place in Lillehammer, other events such as alpine skiing and bobsleigh competitions will be held in the mountains north of Lillehammer and the skating competitions will be based in the city of Hamar, to the south.

Orientation & Information

Central Lillehammer is small and easy to explore. The tourist office, bus station and railway station are at a single site and Storgata, the main pedestrian walkway, is two short blocks to the east. For the lowdown on the Olympics, visit the Lillehammer Olympic Information Centre (☎ 06 27 19 00), at Elvegata 19, which has displays and runs a short film on the Olympic sites. The centre is open daily: from 10 am to 6 pm (from noon on Sundays) June to August and from 11 am to 5 pm September to May. To purchase tickets or make other arrangements for the Olympics, contact the Olympic committee in your home country.

Things to See & Do

After winter sports, Lillehammer's main attraction is the exceptional **Maihaugen folk museum**, a collection of historic farm buildings and a stave church in a traditional village setting. There are workshop demonstrations by people wearing period costumes and guided tours in English. The museum is open from 10 am to 4 pm in May and September and from 9 am to 6 pm June to August. Admission costs 40 kr for adults, 15 kr for children. Maihaugen is a 20-minute walk from the railway station; go up Jernbanegata, right on Anders Sandvigs and left up Maihaugvegen.

Lillehammer is at the northern end of **Mjøsa**, Norway's largest lake. The lake is long, almost fjord-like in places and dotted with farms, stretches of forests and small towns. The train to Oslo runs alongside much of lake Mjøsa and from mid-June to mid-August the *Skibladner*, the world's oldest operating **paddle steamer**, cruises from one end to the other. On Tuesdays, Thursdays and Saturdays the boat sails at 11 am from Hamar to Lillehammer (3¾ hours, 120 kr) and leaves Lillehammer at 3 pm for the return trip to Hamar.

Places to Stay & Eat

Lillehammer Youth Hostel (☎ 06 25 09 87), at Smestad Sommerhotell two km north of the railway station, is open from mid-June to mid-August. It costs 95 kr for a dorm bed and 260/310 kr for singles/doubles. The cheapest hotel, *Dølaheimen Hotell*, opposite the

NORWAY

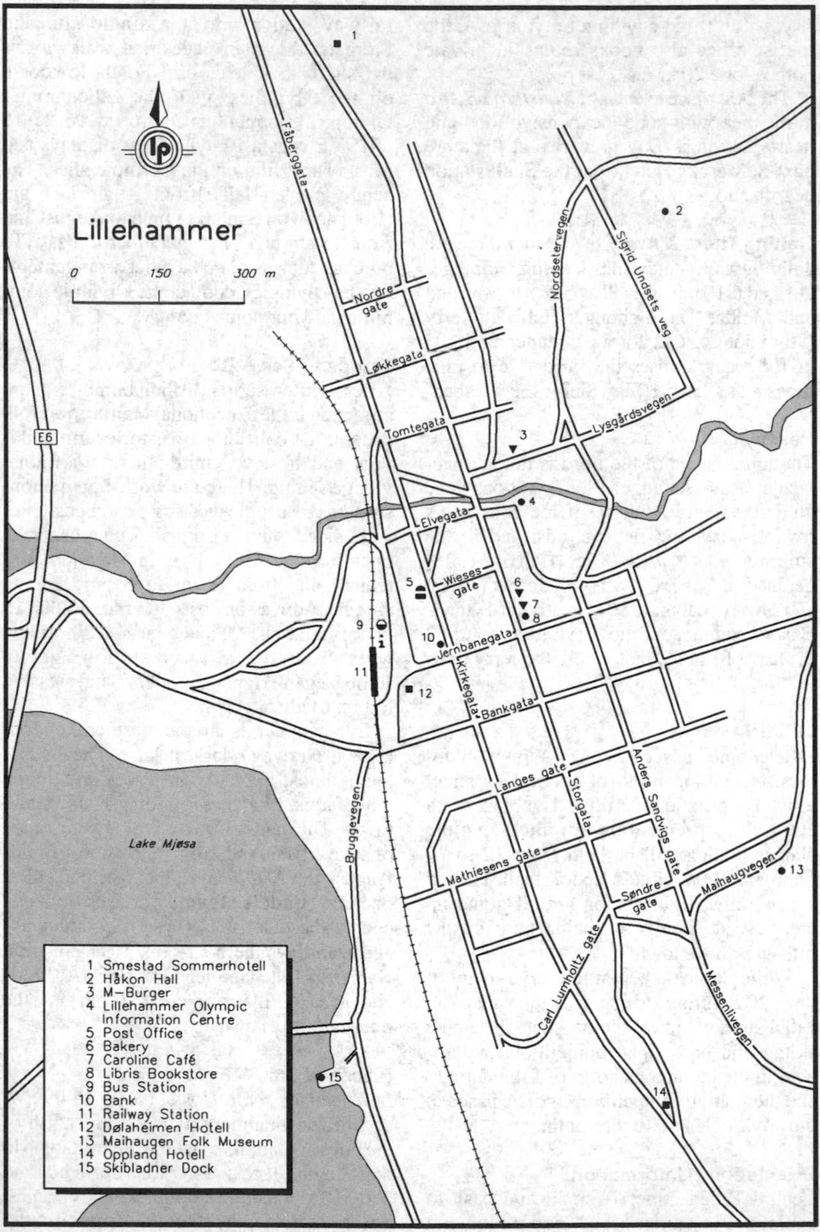

Lillehammer

0   150   300 m

1 Smestad Sommerhotell
2 Håkon Hall
3 M–Burger
4 Lillehammer Olympic
   Information Centre
5 Post Office
6 Bakery
7 Caroline Café
8 Libris Bookstore
9 Bus Station
10 Bank
11 Railway Station
12 Dølaheimen Hotell
13 Maihaugen Folk Museum
14 Oppland Hotell
15 Skibladner Dock

Fåberggata

Nordre gate

Løkkegata

Tomtegata

Lysgårdsvegen

Nordsetervegen

Sigrid Undsets veg

Elvegata

Wieses- gate

Jernbanegata

Kirkegata

Bankgata

Langes gate

Storgata

Anders Sandvigs gate

Maihaugvegen

Mathiesens gate

Søndre gate

Carl Lumholtz gate

Messenliesgen

Brugevegen

Lake Mjøsa

E6

NORWAY

railway station, charges 400/525 kr without breakfast for rooms in the older wing.

The *Oppland Hotell* (☎ 06 25 85 00) on Hamarveien 2, a km south of the centre, has rooms from 425/600 kr.

For the best food value in town head to the Lillehammer Olympic Information Centre where a rooftop café, *Det Olympiske Spiskammer*, features traditional Norwegian cuisine. You can sample such tasty regional dishes as marinated reindeer, smoked salmon with honey-mustard sauce and delicate cakes. It's gourmet-quality food at cafeteria prices and a pleasant setting to boot. The café is open the same hours as the centre.

Otherwise, Storgata is lined with shops and restaurants and you can take your pick. The *Caroline Café*, Storgata 63, has standard fare at low prices and there's a good bakery next door. *M-Burger*, a pavement stand, up Lysgårdsvegen from Storgata, has the best burgers in town.

Getting There & Away

Lillehammer is on the Dovre railway line between Oslo (2½ hours, 195 kr) and Trondheim (five hours, 360 kr). There are four daily trains from Trondheim and at least six daily trains from Oslo.

Northern Norway

The counties of Sør and Nord Trøndelag, Nordland, Troms and Finnmark comprise a vast and varied area stretching over 1500 km, mostly north of the Arctic Circle. The terrain ranges from majestic coastal mountains that rise above tiny fishing villages and scattered farms to the barren treeless Arctic plateau in the far north.

Trains run as far north as Bodø and from there it's all buses and boats. Because distances are long, bus travel costs can pile up, though Inter-Rail and Nordturist pass holders get a 50% discount on the express bus from Bodø to Kirkenes. A fine option to land travel is the *Hurtigruten* coastal steamer which pulls into every sizeable port between Bergen and Kirkenes, passing some of Europe's best coastal scenery along the way.

RØROS

Røros is an old copper mining town with a well-preserved historic district that's on UNESCO's World Heritage list. The first mine opened in 1644 and the last one closed in 1986. The main attractions are **turf-roofed miners' cottages** and other centuries-old timber buildings, a prominent **1784 church** with a Baroque interior, slag heaps and the **old smelting works**, which is now a **mining museum**. The museum (30 kr) features intricate scale models of life in the mines and is open all year round, from 11 am to 3.30 pm on weekdays, to 2 pm on weekends, with longer hours in summer. The town makes for delightful strolling and everything's an easy walk from the railway station.

You can also visit the defunct **Olav copper mine**, 12 km north-east of town, which is open for tours (35 kr) on Saturdays at 3 pm all year round and daily from 1 June to late September. The midsummer schedule is the heaviest, with six tours a day, including a 6 pm tour which is accompanied by a musical performance inside the mine chamber. Book the tours at the Røros tourist office, a two-minute walk north-east of the railway station.

Places to Stay & Eat

Idrettsheimen Youth Hostel (☎ 07 41 10 89), open from mid-May to the end of August, is one km from the railway station at Øra 25 and has camping, dorm beds (125 kr) and cabins (250 kr). To get there, walk east from the railway station and cross the tracks opposite Bergstadens Turisthotel; the rest of the way is clearly signposted. The hostel is in a rather lacklustre location on the edge of a sports field.

Better value is *Ertzscheidergården* (☎ 07 41 11 94), at Spell Olaveien 6, a family-run guesthouse which has 15 comfortable and squeaky clean rooms and is but a stone's throw from both the church and mining museum. Rooms with shared kitchen and bathroom are 220/320 kr for singles/doubles. Rooms with private bathrooms cost 100 kr more.

There's a health-food store called *Soloppgangen Helse & Miljø* at Kjerkgata 6, a *Domus supermarket* with a cafeteria and a couple of bakeries within a block of the tourist office. For something more substantial, *Vertshuset Røros*, Kjerkgata 34, in an old inn below the church, has a great atmosphere, reasonable prices and good hearty Norwegian food, including reindeer for 70 kr at lunch, 120 kr at dinner. The *pizzeria* in the historic stone-walled cellar below is another good option.

Getting There & Away

Røros is 46 km west of the Swedish border, via route 31. Røros is also on the eastern railway line between Oslo (5¾ hours, 390 kr) and Trondheim (2½ hours, 175 kr). With Røros having the distinction of being the town with the highest altitude in Norway, it's not surprising that there's splendid mountain scenery in the area. The ride between Røros and Trondheim, both on the railway line and the parallel route 30, passes snow-capped mountains, rushing streams, scattered farmhouses and tiny villages tucked into hillside valleys.

TRONDHEIM

Trondheim, Norway's third largest city, is a lively university town with a rich medieval history. Norway's first capital, it was founded at the estuary of the winding Nidelva river in 997 AD by the Viking king Olaf Tryggvason. After a fire razed most of the city in 1681, Trondheim was redesigned by General Caspar de Cicignon with wide streets and a Renaissance flair. The steeple of the medieval Nidaros cathedral is still the highest point in town.

Orientation & Information

The central part of town is on a triangular, island-like piece of jutting land that's easy to explore on foot. The railway station and coastal steamer quays are across the canal, a few minutes north of the centre. Torvet, the central square, has a summer produce market, a head-on view of the cathedral, a statue of King Olaf and a 12th century stone church, though all unfortunately are overwhelmed by asphalt paving and drab commercial buildings.

The tourist office at Torvet is open to 8 pm weekdays and 6 pm weekends in summer, to 4 pm weekdays and 1 pm Saturday in winter. At ESP, Jomfrugaten 6, you can do laundry for 56 kr until 4.30 pm weekdays, 2 pm Saturdays.

Nidaros Cathedral

The grand Nidaros Domkirke is the city's most dominant landmark and Scandinavia's largest medieval building. The first church on this site was built in 1070 over the grave of St Olaf, the Viking king who replaced the worship of the Nordic gods with Christianity. The oldest wing of the current building dates back to the 12th century.

Perhaps the most spectacular part of the cathedral is the ornately embellished exterior west wall which is lined with the statues of Norwegian kings and bishops and a collection of biblical characters.

The interior of the cathedral is open daily. Weekday hours are from 9.30 am to 5.30 pm from mid-June to mid-August, noon to 2.30 pm October to April, and 9 am to 2.30 pm the rest of the year. It always closes at 2 pm on Saturdays and is open from 1 to 4 pm (to 3 pm October to April) on Sundays. Admission is 10 kr, which includes entrance to the adjacent 12th century **Archbishop's Palace**, the oldest secular building in Norway.

The cathedral, which is the site of Norwegian coronations, also displays the crown jewels in summer from 9.30 am to 12.30 pm weekdays and 1 to 4 pm on Sundays, the rest of the year from noon to 2 pm on Fridays only. From mid-June to mid-August visitors can climb the cathedral tower (3 kr) for a rooftop view of the city.

If old swords, armour and cannons sound interesting, visit the **Rustkammeret military museum** (5 kr) out the back.

Museums

The **Museum of Applied Art**, Munkegata 5, has a fine collection of contemporary arts and crafts ranging from Japanese pottery by Shoji Hamada and Bernard Leach to tapestries by Hannah Ryggen, Scandinavia's best known tapestry artist. It's open from 9 am to 5 pm weekdays and from noon on Sundays 20 June to 20 August, with slightly earlier closings the rest of the year. Admission is 20 kr for adults, 30 kr for a family.

There's an **art gallery** (20 kr) at Bispegata 7 with a hallway of Munch lithographs. Trondheim also has a small **maritime museum** and the **University Museum of Natural History & Archaeology**.

The **Ringve Museum**, four km north-east of the city centre, is a fascinating music history museum. Music students from the university give guided tours, demonstrating the antique musical instruments on display. Tours in English are at 11 am, 12.30 and 2.30 pm daily from mid-May to the end of August (plus 4.30 pm in midsummer), at noon and 2 pm daily in September and at 1.30 pm on Sundays only the rest of the year. Admission costs 40 kr (25 kr for students and pensioners).

Old Trondheim

The excavated **ruins of early medieval churches** can be viewed free in the basement of the Sparebanken, Søndre gate 4, and in the public library nearby. Also not to be missed are the old **waterfront warehouses** resembling Bergen's Bryggen which are best viewed from Gamle Bybro (the Old Town Bridge). There's a good city view from the top of the 17th century **Kristiansten Fort**, a 10-minute uphill walk from Gamle Bybro. It's open daily in summer to 3 pm, admission 3 kr. A good strolling area is the cobblestoned west end of Dronningens gate which is lined with wooden buildings from the mid-1800s.

Trøndelag Folk Museum

At Sverresborg, this open-air folk museum has good hilltop views of the city and fjord and 60 period buildings including **Sami turf huts** and a **stave church** that is one of Norway's smallest. It's open from 20 May to 1 September (11 am to 6 pm) and admission costs 30 kr. Take bus No 8 or 9 to Wullumsgården, a 10-minute ride.

Activities

A popular place to sunbathe and picnic is **Munkholmen** island, the site of an 11th century Benedictine monastery later converted into a prison fort. From 30 May to 30 August, boats (23 kr) leave on the hour from 10 am to 6 pm from Ravnkloa, next to the indoor fish market.

The west side of Trondheim is bordered by a green area, the **Bymarka**, that's crossed with good skiing and wilderness trails. To get there, take the tram (12 kr) from St Olavs gate to Lian, which has good city views, a bathing lake and hiking paths.

Places to Stay

The nearest camping ground is *Sandmoen Camping*, 10 km south of the city on the E6. In midsummer, university students operate an informal crash pad at *Studentersamfundet* (☎ 07 89 95 38), a five-minute walk south of the cathedral. It's open from mid-July to late August, mattresses on the floor cost 60 kr and the centre's café has inexpensive food and Trondheim's cheapest beer. While it's geared to students and Inter-Railers, it's open to all.

The *Rosenborg Youth Hostel* (☎ 07 53 04 90), two km east of the railway station at Weidemannsvei 41, is neither conveniently located nor special, though it is open all year round except from 22 December to 5 January. Dorm beds cost 130 kr, a rather ordinary breakfast is included, and reception is closed from 11 am to 4 pm.

Singsaker Sommerhotell (☎ 07 52 00 92), Rogerts gate 1, is a student dorm that rents rooms in summer at 250/400 kr for singles/doubles. There's a sauna, a fitness room, billiards and parking. The more central *Pensjonat Jarlen* (☎ 97 51 32 18) has simple rooms with kitchenettes and private baths for 250/400 kr singles/doubles and group rooms at 150 kr a person.

Two Rainbow hotels – the *Trondheim*

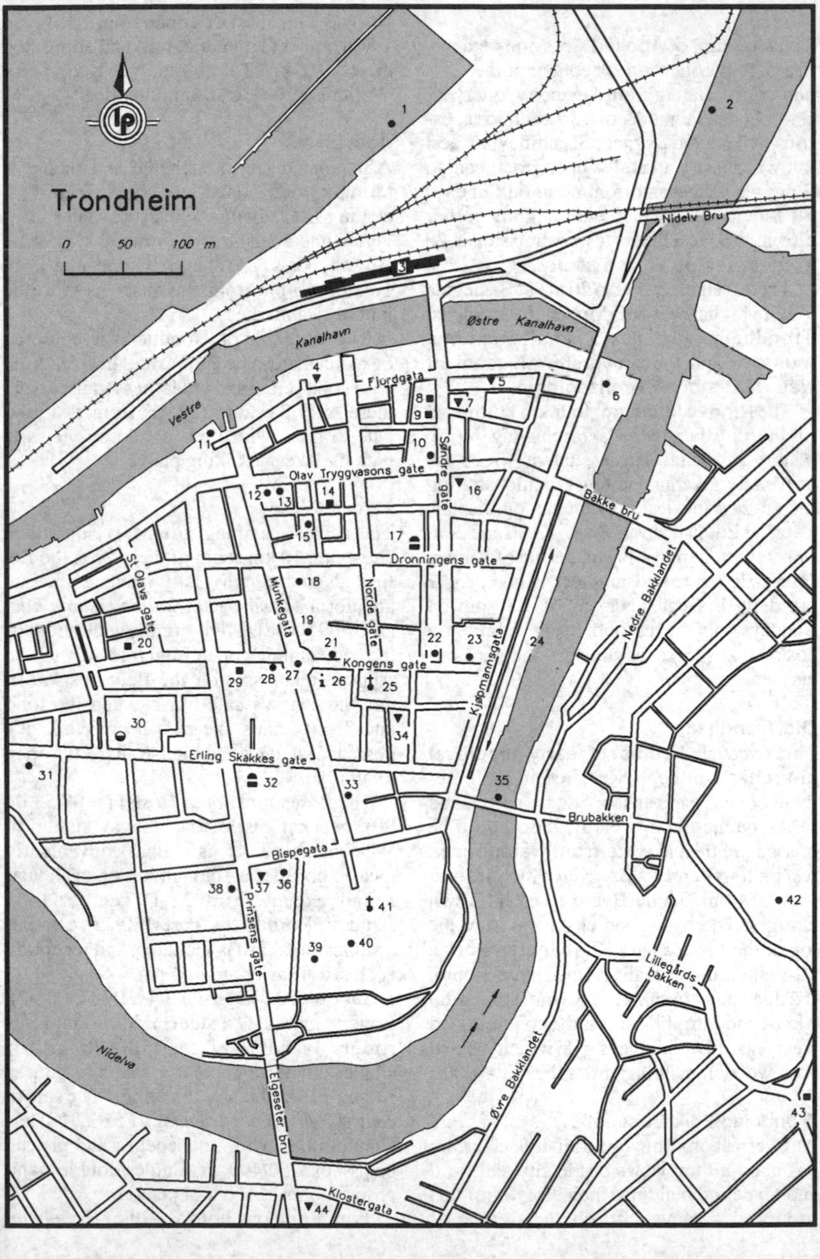

Trondheim
0
50
100 m
Nidelv Bru
Østre Kanalhavn
Kanalhavn
Vestre
Fjordgata
Olav Tryggvasons gate
Søndre gate
Bakke bru
Dronningens gate
St Olavs gate
Munkegata
Nordre gate
Kongens gate
Kjøpmannsgata
Nedre Bakklandet
Erling Skakkes gate
Brubakken
Bispegata
Prinsens gate
Lillegårds bakken
Nidelva
Elgeseter bru
Øvre Bakklandet
Klostergata
1
2
3
4
5
6
7
8
9
10
11
12
13
14
15
16
17
18
19
20
21
22
23
24
25
26
27
28
29
30
31
32
33
34
35
36
37
38
39
40
41
42
43
44

■ PLACES TO STAY

8	Chesterfield Hotel
9	Gildevangen Hotell
14	Norrøna Hotell
20	Pensjonat Jarlen
29	Trondheim Hotell
43	Singsaker Sommerhotell

▼ PLACES TO EAT

4	Hardangerfrukt
5	Grønn Pepper
7	Det Lille Franske
16	Burger King
21	Bakery
34	Zia Teresa
37	Café ni Muser
44	Studentersamfundet

OTHER

1	Coastal Steamer Quay (Southbound)
2	Coastal Steamer Quay (Northbound)
3	Railway Station
6	Maritime Museum
11	Ravnkloa Fish Market
10	Libris Bookshop
12	Kreditkassen Bank
13	SAS Ticket Office
15	ESP Laundrette
17	Post Office
18	Stiftsgården (Royal Residence)
19	Kreditkassen Bank
21	Bookshop
22	Sparebanken (Church Ruins)
23	Library (Church Ruins)
24	Old Waterfront Warehouses
25	Vår Frue Kirke
26	Tourist Office
27	Torvet
28	Rema 1000
30	Bus Station
31	University Museum of Natural History & Archaeology
32	Post Office
33	Museum of Applied Art
35	Gamle Bybro
36	Art Gallery
38	Cinema
39	Rustkammeret
40	Archbishop's Palace
41	Nidaros Domkirke
42	Kristiansten Fort

Hotell (☎ 07 52 70 30) at Kongens gate 15 and the charming turn-of-the-century *Gildevangen Hotell* (☎ 07 52 83 40) at Søndre gate 22 – have summer walk-in rates of 375/450 kr and somewhat higher reservable weekend and summer rates.

The new *Chesterfield Hotel* (☎ 07 50 37 50) on Søndre gate 26, just a few minutes south of the railway station, has big modern rooms with private baths and cable TV. A few rooms have cooking facilities at no extra cost. If you want to bask in the midnight sun, ask for one of the corner rooms on the 7th floor which have huge skylights and broad city views. Rates are 495/595 kr for singles/doubles on weekdays and 395/495 kr on weekends, except in summer when they become 450/550 kr daily.

The *Norrøna Hotell* (☎ 07 52 65 70), Thomas Angells gate 20, also has modern rooms with private baths and good-value weekend rates of 350/450 kr.

If you have your own transport, a good option is the *Trondheim Leilighetshotell* (☎ 07 52 39 69), a renovated apartment building at Gardemoens gate 1A, three km north-east of the city centre. Each flat has a kitchen, bath, TV and washing machine. The smallest flats (40 sq metres in area) cost 300/400 kr for singles/doubles, plus 150 kr for each additional person. The largest costs 900 kr and can accommodate seven people. Breakfast is included and there's free parking.

Places to Eat

Travellers stumbling off the night train can head to *Det Lille Franske*, Søndre gate 25, which opens at 8 am on weekdays and has coffee, fine pastries and a pavement table. Another *Det Lille* bakery opposite the tourist office has huge pizza slices for 21 kr at lunch time.

Gjest Baardsen in the library is a good

NORWAY

place to meet international students. This café serves standard pastries, coffees and sandwiches as well as good shrimp salads. *Café ni Muser*, in an older house on the corner of Bispegata and Prinsens gate, is a pleasantly casual spot with inexpensive light meals and sandwiches. It's busiest on sunny afternoons when the outdoor terrace becomes a little beer garden. Hours are from 11.30 am (from 6 pm on Mondays) to at least midnight daily.

Zia Teresa, a cosy Italian bistro on Vår Frue Strete, offers an excellent lunch special which includes the pasta of the day, French bread and a salad bar for 55 kr from noon to 3 pm weekdays. At other times, pizza and pasta dishes start around 60 kr. It's open to 11 pm daily.

The *Grønn Pepper*, Fjordgata 7, is a Mexican restaurant with moderate prices, open for dinner only. On Mondays they have an all-you-can-eat taco bar from 4 to 11 pm for 69 kr.

For a traditional Norwegian experience, try the centuries-old *Tavern* in Sverresborg, by the folk museum, which serves a good, filling meal of Norwegian food for about 80 kr.

There's a health food store, *Hardanger-frukt*, at Fjordgata 64, while for more standard fare *Rema 1000* at Torvet has good prices on groceries and bakery items – or munch out on fish cakes (55 kr a kg) from the Ravnkloa fish market.

Entertainment

Studentersamfundet, on the left just over the bridge Elgeseter bru, is a student centre with a disco, pub, cinema, lounges and some good alternative music, though most of the activities gear down in the summer. During the school year, Friday's the main party night.

The *Sola Bar* at the Trondheim Hotell offers a rare chance to try the Viking drink *mjød* (mead), a honey-based liquor that tastes a bit like sweet white wine and is made on site.

Getting There & Away

Northbound buses, trains and the coastal steamer all stop in Trondheim. Train fares are 510 kr to Oslo, 600 kr to Bodø. If you're moving quickly with a rail pass consider taking the overnight train from Oslo, tossing your gear into a locker at the station and spending the day exploring Trondheim before continuing on an overnight train to Bodø – which, incidentally, goes through Hell just before midnight. There are trains from Trondheim to Storlien in Sweden (2¾ hours, 110 kr) at 7.38 am and 5.30 pm daily and also on weekdays at 10.15 am, all with a connecting service to Stockholm.

From early July to late August, the Trondheim railway station has an Inter-Rail Centre open from around 7 am to 11 pm where backpackers can hang around between catching trains, take a shower (20 kr) or prepare a meal.

Getting Around

The central transit point for city buses is the intersection of Munkegata and Dronningens gate. The bus fare is 12 kr and you must have exact change.

The E6, the main north-south motorway, passes right through the heart of the city. Trondheim has a toll system (10 kr) for vehicles entering the city weekdays from 6 am to 5 pm. As the city doesn't have a lot of pedestrian-only streets, it's easy to drive between sights. There's metered parking along many streets in the centre – look for zones marked *P Mot avgift* or *P Avgift*. Standard meters cost 8 kr for one hour up to 33 kr for a three-hour maximum, however, green meters cost only 3 kr an hour for up to four hours. Avoid red meters which cost 5 kr for 15 minutes and have a 30-minute maximum. If you prefer to explore Trondheim on foot, you could park by the railway station, where there are no time limits. The tourist office rents bicycles for 50 kr a day from early May to late September.

BODØ

Besides being the terminus for the northern railway line, Bodø is Nordland's biggest town, a coastal steamer stop and a jumping-off point for the Lofoten islands. Though it has a lovely mountain backdrop, Bodø was rebuilt in the characterless box-style of the 1950s after having been levelled in WW II air raids. There's not much to see in the centre other than a small **museum of Nordland history** (10 kr) and a modern **cathedral** with limited viewing hours, both four blocks up Torvgata from Sjøgata. Get midnight-sun views on Mt Rønvik, a 30-minute walk from the youth hostel up Rønvikveien to Fjellveien.

The tourist office at Sjøgata 21 and a Kreditkassen bank are five minutes west of the railway station. The bus station is at the end of Sjøgata, a few minutes farther along.

Places to Stay & Eat

The nearest camping ground is *Bodøsjøen Camping* (☎ 08 12 29 02), three km from town via bus No 12. *Flatvold Youth Hostel* (☎ 08 12 56 66) is a 15-minute walk from the railway station, left on Sjøgata and left on Rønvikveien to Nordstrandveien 1. The 163-bed hostel, which is open from late June to mid-August only, has dorm beds for 90 kr, single rooms for 130 kr, and doubles for 220 kr, all in small rooms with private baths. Reception is closed from noon to 5 pm.

The tourist office books private rooms at 100 kr a person. Most hotels in Bodø offer competitive summer rates: cheapest is the *Norrøna Hotel* (☎ 08 12 55 50) at Storgata 4 which is central and charges 250/350 kr for singles/doubles. If you prefer to be near the railway station, the 13-room *Bodø Gjestegård* (☎ 08 12 04 02), at Storgata 90, is open all year round and costs 270/380 kr, breakfast included.

Koch at the corner of Torvgata and Storgata has a supermarket and cafeteria and there are other eateries nearby on Storgata. *The Beef* at the Central Hotel, Professor Schyttes gate 6, has good fish and reindeer dishes which include a choice from the salad bar and cost from 80 to 120 kr.

Getting There & Away

Trondheim trains arrive in Bodø at 10 am and 7.15 pm. If you're on your way north get off one stop before Bodø at Fauske, where the two daily express buses to Narvik (250 kr) and Alta (682 kr) leave 15 minutes after the train pulls in. The southbound train leaves Bodø at 10.30 am and 8.35 pm. Information on the Lofoten boats is in the Lofoten islands section.

AROUND BODØ

The 19th century trading station **Kjerringøy**, on a sleepy island 40 km north of Bodø, has been preserved as an open-air museum. Guided tours cost 20 kr. On weekdays in summer a bus leaves Bodø at 1.10 pm and returns at 6.30 pm. Or you could stay nearby at the former rectory which is now a guesthouse called *Kjerringøy Prestegård* (☎ 08 18 34 60), with hostel-style beds for 90 kr.

There are also buses from Bodø to **Saltstraumen**, the world's largest maelstrom, 33 km south of Bodø, where at high tide an immense volume of water swirls and churns its way through a three-km strait that links two fjords. Though much touted as a sight, it's really not terribly impressive to look at.

NARVIK

Narvik was established a century ago as an ice-free port for iron-ore mines in Swedish Lapland. The city is bisected by a monstrous transshipment facility where the ore is off-loaded from rail cars onto ships bound for Germany and Japan.

Narvik is basically a transit point for travellers too, though if you've got time on your hands there's a **war museum** (20 kr) on the town square that commemorates the fierce battles fought here in WW II. Behind the town a cable car runs 650 metres up **Fagernesfjellet** (30 kr each way) for views of the midnight sun.

The post office is at Kongens gate 14. The tourist office and bus station are at Kongens gate 66 and the railway station is a five-minute walk to the west. The Lofoten express boat and the youth hostel are on Havnegata, two km south down Kongens gate.

Narvik

1 Narvik Camping
2 Railway Station
3 Tourist Office
4 Bus Station
5 Midnight Sun Viewpoint
6 Domus Supermarket
7 Rosa
8 Sentrumsgården
9 SAS Office
10 Kreditkassen Bank
11 War Museum
12 Breidablikk Gjestgiveri
13 Cable Car Station
14 Ore Transshipment Facility
15 Bank
16 Post Office
17 Nordkalotten Youth Hostel
18 Lofoten Express Boat

Rombaksfjord

Rombaksveien

E6

Hamsunsvei

Reinsveien

Narvik Havn

Ofotfjord

Havnegata

Flyplassveien

0   250   500 m

NORWAY

Places to Stay & Eat

Narvik Camping, two km north-east of town on the E6, has tent space for 60 kr. *Nord-kalotten Youth Hostel* (☎ 08 24 25 98), Havnegata 3, costs 125 kr with breakfast and is a surprisingly good place to eat dinner. They also have singles/doubles for 215/315 kr. More central is the *Breidablikk Gjest-giveri* (☎ 08 24 14 18) at Tore Hunds gate 41. This is a good-value pension with singles/doubles for 200/250 kr with a hillside fjord view.

Rosa, at Brugata 3 just over the bridge from the town square, is the best place to eat. It has pizza, a daily special for 75 kr and a piano bar. *Domus* supermarket, opposite Rosa, has a cheap cafeteria. *Myklevold Bakeri*, on the 2nd floor of Sentrumsgården at Kongens gate 51, has good cinnamon rolls for 5 kr and there's a coffee shop next door.

Getting There & Away

Some of the express buses between Bødo and the far north make an overnight break in Narvik. A couple of trains run daily to Kiruna in Sweden with connections to Stockholm. There's an express boat between Narvik and Svolvær.

LOFOTEN ISLANDS

The spectacular Lofoten islands are peaks of glacier-carved mountains that shoot straight up out of the sea. From a distance they appear as an unbroken line, known as the Lofoten Wall, and are separated from the mainland by the Vestfjord.

The Lofoten islands are Norway's prime winter-fishing grounds. The warming effects of the Gulf Stream draw spawning Arctic cod from the Barents Sea south to the Lofoten waters each winter, followed by migrating north coast farmers who for centuries have drawn most of their income from the seasonal fishing. Though fish stocks have dwindled greatly in recent years, fishing continues to be the Lofoten islands' largest industry and the cod is still hung outside on wooden racks to dry through early summer.

Fishermen's winter shanties (*rorbu*) and dorm-style seahouses (*sjøhus*) double as summertime tourist lodges, providing some of Norway's most atmospheric accommodation.

The main islands of Austvågøy, Vestvågøy, Flakstad and Moskenes are all ruggedly beautiful. Artists are attracted by Austvågøy's light and there are art galleries in Svolvær, Kabelvåg and the busy fishing village of Henningsvær.

Vestvågøy has Lofoten's richest farmland and Norway's largest Viking hall (83 metres long), which is being excavated in Borg near the island centre. Flakstad and Moskenes islands have sheltered bays, sheep pastures, and sheer coastal mountains that loom above extremely picturesque fishing villages.

The four main islands are all linked by bridge or tunnel, with buses running the entire Lofoten road (E10) from Fiskebøl in the north to Å at road's end in the south-west. Bus fares are half-price for Inter-Rail pass holders.

Svolvær

By Lofoten standards the main port town of Svolvær on the island of Austvågøy is busy and modern. The post office and banks are on the square facing the harbour, as is the helpful regional tourist office which has information on nearby hiking and mountain climbing.

Daredevils like to scale **The Goat**, an odd two-pronged peak visible from the harbour, and then jump from one horn to the other – the graveyard at the bottom awaits those who miss!

Excursion boats from Svolvær run daily to the **Trollfjord**, which is just two km long but spectacularly steep and narrow. The northbound coastal steamer also makes a jaunt into the Trollfjord, the huge ship practically kissing the rock walls at the innermost point where it makes a 180° turn.

Places to Stay & Eat The *youth hostel* is in the Polar Hotel (☎ 08 87 07 77), one km from the dock. A bed costs 145 kr. A better choice is *Svolvær Sjøhus* (☎ 08 87 03 36), a rustic dockside seahouse with rooms from 200 kr;

turn right on the first road past the library, five minutes east of the harbour. *Sentrum Kafeteria* on the town square has sandwiches and hamburgers. There's a cheap cafeteria in the *Rimi* grocery store two blocks up and the nearby *Hotel Havly* has a good café.

Getting There & Away Flights from Bodø to Svolvær (or Leknes) cost 580 kr one way, 700 kr return. Buses to Leknes leave Svolvær (two hours, 72 kr) at 6.50 and 10.20 am daily except Sundays, 4.20 pm daily, and 10 pm daily except Saturdays. A car ferry runs between Svolvær and the mainland town of Skutvik (two hours, 46 kr for a passenger, 155 kr for a car) several times a day. The coastal steamer leaves Bodø at 3 pm daily, arriving in Svolvær (236 kr) at 9 pm. Express boats leave Narvik for Svolvær (3½ hours, 239 kr) at 3.15 pm weekdays, noon on Sundays. There are no express boats on Sat-urdays in either direction and no Monday sailing from Svolvær to Narvik.

Kabelvåg

The road into the quiet hamlet of Kabelvåg passes a **wooden church** which is one of Norway's largest. Built a century ago to min-ister to the influx of seasonal fisherfolk, the 1200 seats far surpass the village's current population.

Kabelvåg's small square has a market, café and post office. Behind the old prison a trail leads uphill to the **statue of King Øystein** who in 1120 ordered the first rorbu to be built to house fishermen who had been sleeping in their overturned rowing boats – it was more than a touch of kindness, as the tax on the exported dried fish was the main source of the king's revenue.

Excavations of those original **rorbu** are now taking place just beyond the **Lofoten Museum**, a regional history museum (20 kr).

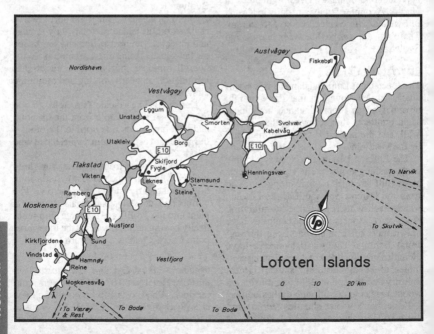

Lofoten Islands

0   10   20 km

Nearby there's an **aquarium** (40 kr) with an outdoor tank containing harbour seals. From Svolvær you can walk the five km to Kabelvåg or catch one of the hourly buses.

Leknes

Other than to change buses or catch a flight, there's little reason to visit Leknes,the island of Vestvågøy's sterile municipal centre. There's a tourist office and a moderately priced restaurant at the bus station and a mediocre bakery across the street. The town hall, next to the station, has a post office and taxi stand.

Stamsund

The traditional fishing village of Stamsund makes a fine destination largely due to its dockside *youth hostel*, a magnet for travellers who sometimes stay for weeks on end. Manager Roar Justad lends rowing boats for free (catch and cook your own dinner!), rents bicycles and mopeds, and knows all the hiking trails.

A bakery with good pastry and breads, a grocery store, post office and bus stop are five minutes uphill from the hostel. The nearby petrol station sells snacks until 10 pm.

Places to Stay The coastal village of Steine, three km west of Stamsund, has a camping ground (☎ 08 88 92 83) with cabins from 250 kr. At the previously mentioned youth hostel, *Justad Rorbuer* (☎ 08 88 93 34), bunks in the old seahouse cost 70 kr, double rooms 180 kr and new four-person cabins are available from 330 kr. It's open from mid-December to the end of October and laundry facilities are available. If the hostel's full *Ytterviks Rorbuer & Sjøhus* (☎ 08 88 94 21) has four-bed rorbu from 425 kr, rooms from 200 kr.

Getting There & Away The coastal steamer stops en route (7.30 pm northbound, 9 pm southbound) between Bodø (220 kr) and Svolvær (78kr). Buses run every hour or two from Leknes to Stamsund (20 minutes, 23 kr). The last one leaves at 10 pm (except Saturdays) in summer, 8.20 pm daily the rest of the year.

Reine

The village of Reine, on the island of Moskenes, is on a calm bay backed by lofty mountains and an almost fairy-tale setting.

Ferries run from Reine to **Vindstad** through the scenic Reinefjord every day but Sunday. From Vindstad you can make a one-hour hike over a ridge to the abandoned beachside settlement of **Bunes** on the other side of the island. If you take the morning ferry from Reine you can catch the afternoon ferry back. All buses from Leknes to Å stop in Reine. The main bus stop is between the library and post office.

Places to Stay & Eat The rustic *Gammelbua* at the road's end has superb food. A big pot of fish soup with bread makes a delicious meal for 70 kr, or try the Lofoten speciality *torsketunger* (cod tongues!). There's a small market opposite Gammelbua. *Reine Rorbuer* (☎ 08 89 22 22) at Gammelbua has seaside rorbu from 600 kr in summer, 200 kr in the off season. There are *'sjøhus'* signs along the road for cheaper private rooms.

Å

Å is a special place – a preserved fishing village with a shoreline of red rorbu, cod drying on racks everywhere and picture-postcard scenes at almost every turn. Many of Å's 19th century buildings have been set aside as the **Norwegian Fishing Village Museum** (guided tours in summer, 35 kr) complete with old boats and boathouses, a period bakery, storehouses and so on.

The camping ground at the end of the village has a hillside view of Værøy island which lies on the other side of the maelstrom Moskenesstraumen, a mighty whirlpool which has inspired tales by Jules Verne and Edgar Allen Poe.

Places to Stay & Eat *Moskenesstraumen Camping* (☎ 08 89 11 48) has tent space for 50 kr, simple cabins for 280 kr. *Å Youth Hostel* (☎ 08 89 11 21), open from 1 May to

30 September, offers accommodation in some of the museum's historic buildings for 95 kr. Best is Sjøhus Salteriet, a restored 1920s waterfront warehouse with comfortable rooms, mostly doubles, and the sound of lapping waves. Å-Hamna Rorbuer (☎ 08 89 11 00), also at the museum, has pleasant single and double rooms in a restored 1860s home from 75 kr a person.

Food choices are limited – the best bet is to use the kitchen where you're staying. Some of the rorbu sell fresh fish and you can pick up supplies at the small grocery store behind the hostel office. The museum has a café in the white Victorian house on the hill and the camping ground has a food kiosk that's open late.

Getting There & Away There's a daily bus at 7.45 pm from Leknes to Å (two hours, 69 kr), a daily bus from Å to Leknes at 4.15 pm and an earlier weekday bus in each direction. From the second week of June until late August, Ofotens og Vesteraalens Dampskibsselskab runs car ferries from Bodø to Moskenes, five km north of Å, at 6.30 am daily, and at 11 am and 9 pm daily except Saturdays. The schedule is much less frequent for the rest of the year. The trip takes four hours; the fare is 86 kr for a passenger and 335 kr for a car under five metres long. Make car reservations by calling 08 00 31 15 for the 6.30 am sailing and 09 01 59 53 for the others. The car ferries continue on, connecting Moskenes with Værøy and Røst.

Værøy & Røst

Lofoten's southern islands of Værøy and Røst have some of the finest bird-watching in Norway, with huge colonies of colourful puffins, razorbills, guillemots, kittiwakes and terns. There's also a good chance you'll spot the rare sea eagle.

Craggy Værøy has only 900 people, but hundreds of thousands of sea birds. Hiking trails take in some of the more spectacular sea bird rookeries. The main trail goes along the north coast, beginning a few hundred metres past the airport and continuing all the way to the deserted fishing village of Mostad. This 10-km hike makes for a full day outing, but is not terribly strenuous. Other birding outings, including boat tours, can be arranged through the youth hostel.

Røst, south of Værøy, enjoys one of the mildest climates in Norway, thanks to its location in the midst of the Gulf Stream. Access to the best bird-watching requires a boat, as the largest rookeries are on offshore islands. The Røst youth hostel arranges an all-day boat trip (110 kr) which cruises by the major sea-bird colonies and then drops you off for a few hours on an island where a trail up a mountain provides a good view of Røst. On the return, it's common to spot seals basking in the sun. Røst itself is flat and other than the boat trip there's not much to do, so when planning your trip check the ferry timetable carefully – three days between boats can be a bit long.

Places to Stay The Røst Youth Hostel (☎ 08 89 61 09) charges 75 kr, is open from 1 May to 30 August and has a café on site. Breakfast is quite good, but costs a steep 55 kr. There's a sauna available and the warden has a rowing boat which you can use for 10 kr. The Værøy Youth Hostel (☎ 08 89 53 52) provides accommodation in an old seaside sjøhus and rorbu, is open from 15 May to 15 September and also charges 75 kr a bed.

Getting There & Away There are scheduled flights to Røst from Bodø and Leknes, but only private charter flights to Værøy. In summer, ferries (which originate in Bodø) leave Moskenes for Værøy on Mondays and Saturdays at 10.45 am and on Sunday, Wednesday and Thursday evenings, with the latter three ferries continuing south to Røst. The ferry from Bodø to Værøy takes six hours and costs 81 kr, while the 2½-hour trip from Moskenes to Værøy costs 36 kr. The trip from Moskenes to Røst takes four hours and costs 64 kr.

A second boat departs from Moskenes daily in the afternoon in July and early August, stopping at Værøy en route to Røst.

TROMSØ

Tromsø (population 50,000) boasts itself to be the world's northernmost university town. It's also the capital of Troms county. In contrast to some of the more sober communities dotting the north Norway coast, Tromsø is a spirited town with street music, cultural happenings and more pubs per capita than any other place in Norway – it even has its own brewery. Snow-capped mountains provide a scenic backdrop for the city and good skiing in winter. Many polar expeditions have departed from Tromsø, earning the city the nickname 'Gateway to the Arctic'. A statue of explorer Roald Amundsen, who headed some of the expeditions, stands in a little clearing down by harbour.

Orientation & Information

Tromsø's city centre and airport are on the island of Tromsøya, which is linked by a bridge to the mainland where the city's eastern outskirts spill over. The tourist office, at Storgata 61, is open from 8.30 am to 7 pm weekdays and from 10 am to 5 pm weekends from 1 June to mid-August, from 8.30 am to 4 pm weekdays for the rest of the year.

Things to See & Do

The city centre has some older buildings, including the cathedral **Tromsø Domkirke**, one of Norway's largest wooden churches, and a **Catholic church**, both built in 1861. However Tromsø's most striking church is the **Arctic Cathedral** (open in summer from 10 am to 5 pm, 5 kr) on the mainland just over the bridge. It's a modernistic building that resembles Australia's Sydney Opera House.

The modern **Tromsø Museum**, at the southern end of Tromsøya, is north Norway's largest museum, with well-presented displays on geology, Sami culture and regional history. It's open daily all year round and from 9 am to 9 pm in summer. Admission costs 10 kr. There's a small **aquarium** nearby. Take bus No 27 from Bananas, opposite the Domkirke.

The harbourside **Polar Museum** has some frontier exhibits that are interesting and others, such as the display on clubbing and gutting baby seals, that are offensive. It's open from 11 am to 6 pm daily from 15 May to 31 August, to 3 pm daily the rest of the year. Admission costs 20 kr.

The nearby **Tromsø City Museum** contains the furnishings of a wealthy 19th century merchant who traded Norwegian fish for Russian goods. While not a must, a walk through will give you a feeling for the era when Tromsø was known as 'the Paris of the North'. It's open from 11 am to 3 pm weekdays all year round as well as on weekends from 15 May to 15 September. Admission costs 10 kr.

You can get a fine city view by taking the **cable car** 420 metres up Mt Storsteinen. It runs from 10 am to 5 pm daily May to September, and from 9 pm to 12.30 am on clear nights June to August when the midnight sun is in view. The ride costs 45 kr. Take bus No 28 from the Domus grocery store.

Places to Stay

The closest tent space and cabins are at *Tromsdalen Camping* (☎ 08 33 80 37) on the mainland, two km east of the Arctic Cathedral; take bus No 36.

Tromsø Youth Hostel (☎ 08 38 53 19) is in Elverhøy at Gitta Jønsonsvei 4, two km west of the city centre via bus No 24. It's open from 20 June to 19 August and costs 85 kr for dorms, 185/220 kr for singles/doubles. Reception is closed from 11 am to 5 pm.

The tourist office books rooms in private homes from 150/200 kr plus a 25 kr booking fee. The *Park Pensjonat* (☎ 08 38 22 08), Skolegata 24, has comfortable rooms at 260/330 kr for singles/doubles. While closer to the waterfront, the *Skipperhuset Pensjonat* (☎ 08 38 16 60), Storgata 112, costs 310/380 kr for singles/doubles and has a dreary boarding-house feel.

The *Polar Hotel* (☎ 08 38 64 80), at Grønnegate 45, has a summer and weekend rate of 420/520 kr and a cheery breakfast room with a city view. Rates are 630/770 kr at other times.

The *Saga Hotel* (☎ 08 38 11 80), Richard

Tromsø

0   150   300 km

■ PLACES TO STAY	6 Cinema
	7 Post Office
4 Skipperhuset Pensjonat	8 Bakery
15 Park Pensjonat	9 Domus
20 Polar Hotel	10 Stortorget
22 Saga Hotel	11 Catholic Church
	12 Bookshop
▼ PLACES TO EAT	13 Prelaten
	16 Bank
1 Studenthuset	17 Tromsø Domkirke
13 Prelaten	18 Bakery
14 Quick Lunch'en	19 Tourist Office
	21 Post Office
OTHER	23 Bus Station
	24 Coastal Steamer Quay
2 Library	25 Mack Beer Hall
3 Tromsø City Museum	26 Hospital
5 Polar Museum	

Withs plass 2, is a centrally located, alcohol-free hotel with 52 rooms (some reserved for nonsmokers), each with private bath and TV. It has weekend and summer (1 July to 1 September) rates of 450/600 kr, a steep discount off the normal rate of 815/940 kr.

Places to Eat

Buy fresh boiled shrimp from fishing boats at Stortorget harbour and a loaf of bread at the nearby bakery and you've got yourself a meal – there are even dockside picnic tables. The harbourside *Domus* grocery store has a cheap 2nd-floor cafeteria and a water view.

The student-run *Studenthuset*, at Skippergata 44, has good inexpensive pizza and is a popular hang-out with darts, music, and Mack on tap. It's open from 3 pm (from 1 pm on Saturdays) to 1.30 am daily. *Prelaten*, an underground pub at Sjøgata 12, has omelettes, baked potatoes and salads at reasonable prices and often features live folk and alternative music.

Quick Lunch'en, a hole-in-the-wall behind the expensive Pomar Russian Restaurant at Storgata 73, has fishburgers, pitta sandwiches and burritos from 30 to 40 kr.

Getting There & Away

Tromsø is the main airport hub for the northern region, with direct flights to Oslo, Bergen, Trondheim, Honningsvåg and Kirkenes, among others. There are a few daily express buses to Narvik (five hours, 244 kr) and an afternoon bus to Alta (seven hours, 314 kr). Both services pass through beautiful scenery as they leave Tromsø.

The coastal steamer arrives at 2.15 pm and departs at 5 pm northbound and arrives at 11.45 pm and departs at 1.30 am southbound. The fare is 680 kr to Bodø, 433 kr to Alta.

Finnmark Fylkesrederi og Ruteselskap (☎ 08 41 16 55) operates an express boat from early June to mid-August which leaves Tromsø at 4pm Sunday to Thursday and arrives in Honningsvåg at 10 pm, stopping in Hammerfest en route. The one-way fare from Tromsø to Honningsvåg is 600 kr, however, there are family, student and return-ticket discounts available.

Getting Around

The bus from the airport to the city centre costs 20 kr, while a taxi will cost about 75 kr. Thoroughly exploring Tromsø can take time, as the city is split up and many of the sights are outside the centre. Most rides on city buses cost 13 kr, or you can buy a one-day pass at the tourist office for 40 kr.

If you have your own car, you'll find it's quite convenient for getting around. Tromsø has numerous parking areas spread around the city and a huge underground car park between Grønnegata and Vestregata due east of the harbour.

FINNMARK

Finnmark's curving north coast is cut by fjords and dotted with fishing villages. The interior is populated by nomadic Sami people who for centuries have herded their reindeer across the vast mountain plateau Finnmarksvidda, a stark wilderness with only two major settlements, Karasjok and Kautokeino.

Virtually every town in Finnmark was razed to the ground at the end of WW II by retreating Nazis whose scorched earth policy was meant to delay the advancing Soviet troops. The rebuilt towns are all alike with buildings in standard box-style.

ALTA

Alta is a sprawling town with fishing and quarrying (including slate) industries. The two main centres, Sentrum and Bossekop, are two km apart. Alta's main sight is the **rock carvings** at Hjemmeluft on the E6, a couple km south of Bossekop. A boardwalk leads past some of Hjemmeluft's 3000 carvings of hunting scenes, fertility symbols and reindeer that date back as far as 4000 BC. The admission fee of 25 kr includes the new **Alta Museum**. Alta is also renowned for its salmon run; several local companies provide fishing tours.

Places to Stay & Eat

Skogly Camping is off the E6 near the rock carvings. The *Alta Youth Hostel* (☎ 08 43 44 09), Midtbakken 52, a short walk from the

Sentrum bus station, costs 95 kr. It's open from 20 June to 20 August and the reception is closed from 11 am to 5 pm. The Alta tourist office in Bossekop books rooms in private homes. *Alta Motell* and *Alta Gjestestue* in Bossekop and *Café Eden* at the SAS Alta Hotell in Sentrum have moderately priced food.

Getting There & Away

Some of the express buses between Bodø and the far north stop in Alta at night and depart in the morning, requiring an overnight stay. In summer, buses for Nordkapp, Kirkenes, and Karasjok leave Alta at 7.35 am daily except Sundays and 3.35 pm daily.

The northbound coastal steamer stops at Alta at 3.30 am daily.

HAMMERFEST

Hammerfest has a population of 7000, an economy based on fishing and a claim to being the 'northernmost town in the world' – a matter of semantics as Honningsvåg 'village' is farther north!

Most visitors arrive on the coastal steamer and have an hour to look around. The tourist office is straight up from the dock, opposite the town hall where the Royal & Ancient Polar Bear Society has Arctic hunting displays.

A better way to spend your time is to climb the 86-metre Salen Hill for lovely views of the town, coast and mountains. The 10-minute trail begins on stairs behind the small park directly up from town hall. Or walk up Kirkegata to the contemporary church where there's a fair chance you'll find reindeer grazing in the graveyard.

Places to Stay & Eat

NAF Camping Storvannet (☎ 08 41 10 10), two km east of the town centre, is open from 1 June to 15 September and has cabins for 190 kr. The cheapest hotel rooms are at the *Håja Hotell* (☎ 08 41 18 22), Storgata 9, where singles/doubles with shared bath cost 375/540 kr. There's a *Domus* supermarket on Strandgata a few minutes east of the town hall and a café a little beyond that.

Getting There & Away

The coastal steamer stops daily at 7 am northbound and 11.45 am southbound. The Express 2000 bus leaves for Oslo via Sweden at noon on Mondays, Wednesdays and Saturdays. Finnmark Fylkesrederi og Ruteselskap (☎ 08 41 16 55) runs an express boat to Honningsvåg (two hours, 226 kr) from early June to mid-August, leaving Hammerfest at 7 pm on Fridays and Saturdays and at 8 pm Sunday to Thursday.

You can also get an excursion ticket for 550 kr that includes the express boat, a bus to Nordkapp to see the midnight sun and an early morning return to Hammerfest.

HONNINGSVÅG

Honningsvåg, the only sizeable settlement on the island of **Magerøy** has a little museum and a church built in 1884, but the centre of attention is **Nordkapp**, 34 km away.

Places to Stay & Eat

Nordkapp Camping & Youth Hostel (☎ 08 47 51 13) is in a scenic fjordside locale eight km north of Honningsvåg on the road to Nordkapp (by bus it costs 13 kr). Dorms cost 100 kr, cabins start at 250 kr. Honningsvåg's in-town hotels are expensive. The cheapest is the *Hotel Havly* (☎ 08 47 29 66) at 495/730 kr. Two km north of Honningsvåg, *Valanbo Gjestehus* (☎ 08 47 31 88), Kjelviks gate 2, has singles/doubles for 360/600 kr.

There's a grocery store on Storgata up from the coastal steamer quay and the reasonably priced *Café Corner* is behind the tourist office, midway between the bus station and quay.

Getting There & Away

From late June to late August the Nordkapp Express bus leaves Alta at 7.35 am Monday to Saturday and 3.35 pm daily, stopping briefly in Honningsvåg (five hours, 202 kr) before continuing on to Nordkapp.

The road approach from E6 is via Olderfjord, from where you take route 69 north-west to Kåfjord. Car ferries (☎ 08 41 16 55) cross from Kåfjord to Honningsvåg every couple of hours (45 minutes, 24 kr for a passenger, and 75 kr for a car).

The coastal steamer stops at Honningsvåg at 1.30 pm northbound and 6.45 am southbound. The northbound stop is four hours, long enough for passengers to make the trip up to Nordkapp. There's also an express boat from Hammerfest.

NORDKAPP

Nordkapp (North Cape), a high rugged coastal plateau at 71°10'21", is Europe's northernmost point. The sun never drops below the horizon between 14 May and 30 July. North Cape, which was an ancient power centre for the Sami people, was named by Richard Chancellor, the English explorer who drifted this way in 1553 on a search for the Northeast Passage. Following a much-publicised visit by King Oscar II in 1873, Nordkapp became a pilgrimage spot of sorts. Nowadays there's a 90 kr entrance fee and a touristy complex with exhibits, eateries, souvenir shops and a post office. The 180° theatre runs a good short movie but beyond that you're best off walking out along the cliffs. If the weather is fair you can perch yourself on the edge of the continent and watch the mist roll in.

Getting There & Away

In summer, buses run four times a day from Honningsvåg to Nordkapp (one hour, 38 kr), the first at 11.50 am and the last at 10.30 pm. The road, which winds across a rocky barren plateau and past herds of grazing reindeer, is open from May to October, the exact dates depend on the snow.

VARDØ

Vardø, Norway's easternmost village, is on an island linked to the mainland by a 2.9-km tunnel under the Barents Sea. It's a coastal steamer stop, but is otherwise out of the way for all but the most die-hard travellers. The only sight of interest is the small 1737 star-shaped **fort** with cannons and sod-roof buildings, a five-minute walk directly up from the coastal steamer quay.

Places to Stay & Eat

The seven-room *Gjestgården B&B* (☎ 08 58 75 29), Strandgata 72, has singles/doubles for 235/350 kr. *Nordpol Kro*, just up from the harbour, offers bacon and eggs, pizza and live music.

KIRKENES

Kirkenes, a mining town beneath a smoke-belching factory, was Norway's most bombed village during WW II. The biggest attractions are a statue dedicated to the Soviet soldiers who liberated the town and an anti-climactic ride to the Russian border-crossing point of Storskog. While tourists from the coastal steamer are still bused to the border to point cameras towards the former 'forbidden territory', this outing has lost most of its intrigue with the normalisation of relationships between East and West.

Travel between Norway and Russia is now slowly opening up to tourism. The region's main transport company, Finnmark Fylkesrederi og Ruteselskap (FFR) runs a high-speed catamaran between Kirkenes and Murmansk daily except Sundays from mid-June to mid-August.

The boat, which leaves Kirkenes early in the morning and returns at midnight, is geared for day passengers who are provided with a special 24-hour visa upon arrival in Murmansk. Bookings to FFR (☎ 08 41 16 55) must be made at least seven days in advance. The cost of 1135 kr includes a sightseeing tour and dinner in Murmansk. For travellers who are continuing on to Russia, the one-way fare is 505 kr.

A new bus service is starting up between Kirkenes and Murmansk and negotiations are underway to begin air travel between the two cities. For the latest information, contact the Kirkenes Tourist Office (☎ 08 59 25 01), Postboks 8, 9901 Kirkenes. Independent travellers who want to enter Russia on their own must still obtain a regular visa in advance at a Russian embassy.

Places to Stay & Eat

The nearest camping ground and cabins are at *Kirkenes Camping* (☎ 08 59 80 28), 6½

km west of town on the E6. It's open from 1
June to 30 September. *Fredrikke Gjestehus*
(☎ 08 59 13 83) on Doktor Wessels gate 3
near the bus station has singles/doubles for
425/525 kr including breakfast. The *Rica
Arctic Hotel* (☎ 08 59 29 29), Kongensgata
1, charges 550/800 kr, with a 15% discount
on weekends. There are two grocery stores
in the town square, a *Go Biten* café on Doktor
Wessels gate and a bakery a block away.

Getting There & Away
The airport is a 20-minute drive from town.
There's an SAS airport bus (40 kr) but it
doesn't meet all flights. A bus leaves
Kirkenes daily at 9 am, arriving in Karasjok
at 2.30 pm (307 kr) and Alta at 8 pm (540
kr). Kirkenes is at the end of the line for the
coastal steamer, which departs southbound
at 1.45 pm on Tuesdays, Thursdays and
Sundays and at 11.30 am other days, after a
two-hour layover in port.

KARASJOK
Karasjok is the most accessible Sami town
and the site of the newly established **Sami
Parliament**. It has Finnmark's oldest

church (circa 1807) the only building left
standing in Karasjok after WW II.

The tourist office in the **Samiland
Centre**, at the junction of highways E6 and
92, can book reindeer and dog-sled rides and
arrange gold panning, canoeing and river-
boat trips. There's an interesting **Sami
museum** (15 kr); from the tourist office
walk up the E6 and turn right on Museums-
gata.

Places to Stay & Eat
Karasjok Camping (☎ 08 46 61 35), a well-
equipped camping ground on the outskirts of
town on the road to Alta, has cabins as well
as tent and caravan space. *Anne's Overnatt-
ing* (☎ 08 46 64 32), Tanaveien 40, charges
295/375 kr for singles/doubles, though if you
have your own sleeping bag it's about 100 kr
cheaper. *Lailas Kafé*, over the bridge on
Markangeaidnu 1, has moderately priced
meals.

Getting There & Away
Buses leave Karasjok at 7 am and 3 pm daily
for Alta (five hours, 237 kr) via Olderfjord
(2½ hours, 136 kr) and at 2.30 pm for
Kirkenes.

Sweden

Sweden (Sverige) is much recognised but not very well known. Its destiny has been shaped by its being, in particular respects, both big and small. On the fringe of Europe, it is at once a Western country and a culture with an independent outlook, but these paradoxes make it a more fascinating place to visit.

It would be difficult to imagine more starkly beautiful landscapes than those in the north of Sweden. The forests and giant lakes lend themselves to outdoor activities. The coastal archipelagos *(skärgård)* around Stockholm and Bohuslän are a unique environment, popular for summer getaways. The many boat and canal trips available are a treat and it is often said that Stockholm is best seen from the water. The more adventurous will want to paddle their own canoe.

Walking is a national pastime and there are plenty of marked and attractive paths minutes from the cities. More rugged are the slopes of Sarek national park in Lapland: a national jewel, but no playground for the inexperienced.

Also take advantage of the Swedes' preoccupation with their cultural heritage. The *Wasa* ship museum in Stockholm exemplifies the national investment in preservation and reconstruction. Skansen in Stockholm is the prototype and should not be missed.

At a local level, seek out the villages and town quarters maintained by heritage groups. Each region has collected its art and reminders of the past in a representative museum.

In this country unravaged by war, monuments of prehistory abound. There are about 3000 rune stones, carved and decorated inscriptions that are the main records of paganism and the coming of Christ, and the unique picture-stones of Gotland.

In Sweden, one of the most expensive countries for visitors, the simple and relatively cheap joys of its fresh air, the landscape and culture are among the least

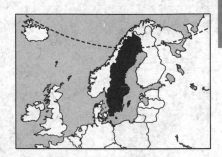

extravagant and most rewarding of pleasures.

Facts about the Country

HISTORY

Proper written records survive only from late in the Middle Ages. But the number and variety of fortifications, assembly places, votive sites and graves is impressive. Of these the densest concentrations are around the Mälaren valley, in Uppland (the ancient region centred on Uppsala) and on the Baltic islands Gotland and Öland.

Humankind and metallurgy made late appearances and only in the Bronze Age, after the arrival of Indo-Europeans, are we aware of rich trade. But the early cultural life is still eloquently expressed by the *hällristningar*, rock paintings that survive in many parts of Sweden and depict ritual or mythological events through familiar symbols of the warrior, the boat, the sun and the beasts of the hunt. Stone Age dolmens and chambered tombs gave way to cairns and small mounds. Stone settings in the shape of ships were in use by the Iron Age as graves or cenotaphs for this warrior society that kept chieftains (and slaves until the great manumission of 1335). In the Mälaren valley, the

SWEDEN

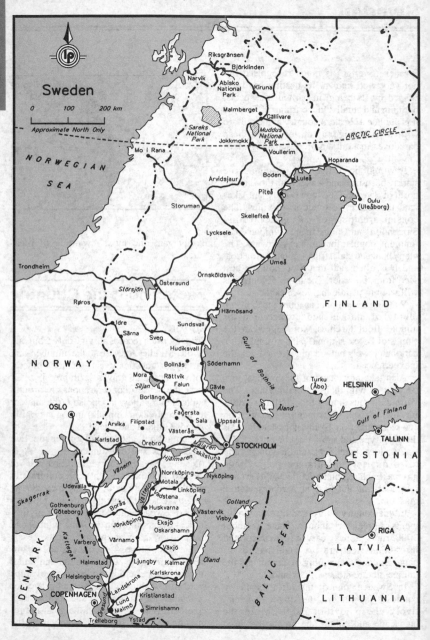

Sweden

0   100   200 km

Approximate North Only

first known trading posts were established and monuments with runic inscriptions appeared.

In the 9th century the missionary St Ansgar visited Birka near modern Stockholm when what we call the Viking Age was just getting under way: Gotland and the Svear already had links throughout the Baltic area and Swedish adventurers meddled in Russia. Roman, Byzantine and Arab coins appeared in huge numbers. The wealth and power of the Svear overwhelmed the Gauts or *götar* to the south before the 11th century and only then was a Christian, Olof Skötkonung, made king just as a Swedish state began to take shape. In 1164 an archbishopric was established in Uppsala.

King Magnus Ladulås instigated a national law code in 1350. Sweden avoided feudalism, but a privileged aristocracy owed allegiance to the king and the wealth of the church grew. St Birgitta, the fascinating spiritualist and reformer of Rome, began an order at Vadstena.

The south belonged to Denmark and was strongly influenced by it. A third influence, that of the Hanse and the city of Lübeck, established walled trading towns such as Visby and a strong German presence in early Stockholm. But Denmark interceded and with Norway joined Sweden in the Union of Kalmar in 1397. Danish monarchs held the Swedish throne for a while, tolerating an assembly of four estates which was the forerunner of the modern *Riksdag*.

The regent Sten Sture loosened the Danish hold with the sword at Stockholm in 1471. The execution of his son and namesake there in 1520 by the Danish king Christian II caused further rebellion that began in Dalarna under the leadership of the young nobleman Gustaf Vasa. In 1523 he was crowned as Gustaf I and set about introducing the Reformation and a powerful, centralised nation-state. In mainly Catholic Småland Nils Dacke defied Gustaf, but his death in 1543 left a strong throne firmly in control of a Lutheran Sweden.

A period of expansion began under Gustaf II Adolf, who interfered in the Thirty Years' War to champion the Protestant German princes and remove the imperial threat to his ambitions in the Baltic. He fell at Lützen in 1632, yet Sweden was to gain territory on the Baltic coast and in Sweden. Sweden then controlled much of Finland and the Baltic countries.

The so-called age of great power passed. The megalomania of the young Karl XII was crushed by Peter the Great at Poltava. Karl's adventures cost Sweden its Baltic territories and the crown much prestige. Greater parliamentary power marked the next 50 years.

Gustaf III led an absolutist coup that interrupted this development. He brought French culture to his court, and introduced a Swedish academy of culture. His foreign policy was less auspicious and he was murdered, quite properly at the opera while in fancy dress, by a conspiracy of aristocrats in 1792. Absolutism was ended by aristocratic revolt in 1809 and Finland was lost to Russia.

The same year Sweden produced a constitution that divided legislative powers between king and Riksdag. The king's advisory council also was responsible to the Riksdag, which controlled taxation. The post of ombudsman appeared as a check on the powers of the bureaucracy. Sweden also made a deal with Denmark which swapped Swedish Pomerania for Norway. Napoleon's marshal Bernadotte was chosen to fill a gap in the succession and, as Karl Johan, became regent. This began the rise of liberalism and Sweden's policy of neutrality. The military enforcement of the 1814 union with Norway was Sweden's last involvement in war.

Industry arrived late but was based on efficient steelmaking and the safety match, a Swedish invention. Iron mining, important for at least 300 years, and then steel manufacture, began to expand and produce a middle class. But the 1827 statute which scattered the agricultural villages of much of the Swedish countryside had more immediate and far-reaching effects – the old social fabric disappeared. Potatoes had become the staple crop, producing among other things *brännvin*, sometimes called schnapps or Swedish vodka.

In 1866 a very limited franchise was introduced for a new and bicameral Riksdag. Many farmers preferred to migrate and endure the hardships in the USA, but when US corn began to penetrate the Swedish market tariffs became the great issue. This led to tensions with free-trading Norway and ultimately to the end of the union in 1905.

By 1900 almost one in four Swedes lived in the cities and industry (based on timber, precision machinery and hardware) was on the upswing. In this environment the working class was radicalised.

Conscription was first introduced as a measure against Russian power in 1901 and men aged over 24 years received the vote in 1907. Moves to cut wages caused a great strike by 300,000 people two years later, a setback for the labour movement. Temperance movements profoundly influenced the workers and the labour movement and alcohol restrictions became policy.

Sweden declared itself neutral at the outbreak of WW I and was governed bilaterally until 1917. But food shortages caused unrest and consensus was no longer possible: for the first time a social democratic government, a coalition, took control. Reforms followed quickly and suffrage for all adults aged over 23 years was introduced, as well as the eight-hour working day.

The social democrats dominated politics after 1932 and the liberal tendencies of the 1920s *statsminister* Hjalmar Branting joined with economic intervention (under Per Albin Hansson) and measures to introduce a welfare state.

These trends were scarcely interrupted in Sweden's studied and ambiguous approach to WW II. The social democrats sponsored models for industrial bargaining and full employment which attracted imitators and allowed the economy to blossom in harmony under Tage Erlander. The economic pressures of the 1970s began to cloud Sweden's social goals and it was under Olof Palme that support for social democracy first wavered. Palme's murky assassination in 1986 and subsequent government scandals shook national confidence and in 1991 a right-of-centre coalition under the moderates won power.

GEOGRAPHY

Sweden covers an area of 450,000 sq km and its maximum north-south extent is over 1500 km. This size allows for a little diversity, but the dominant characteristics of the landscape go back to the time of the glaciations. The flatness and openness of Skåne is like Denmark but the forests, mainly conifer but sprinkled with birch and hardwoods, thicken farther north into Småland.

The rocky south-west coast is most notable for its fjords and skerries, although the Göta älv scarcely compares with the barrage of rocky archipelago that shields Stockholm. (Fjords, shaped mainly by glaciers, are much shallower at the mouth than at the centre.) There are approximately 100,000 lakes. The islands of Öland and Gotland consist of flat limestone and sand.

The lake Mälaren is the heart of Sweden, although of the south and central lakes Vänern is by far the biggest. In Norrland (a practical term for the northern 60% of the country) there is a nearly uniform expanse of forest, river and rapid. Only in Lapland and Norrbotten do the trees seem to thin out and the low mountains of the far north-west assert themselves. The Norwegian spine provides a natural frontier in the west.

It is no surprise that Sweden led Europe in setting up national parks and that the biggest and best of these are in Lapland. Rules that govern the parks vary locally, but the principle is that responsible and careful people may have access to open areas (see Sweden, Activities). Beaches are also protected and there are secondary areas maintained at local level throughout Sweden. The level of ecological consciousness is high and reflected in concerns for native animals, clean water and renewable resources.

GOVERNMENT

Sweden has maintained its monarch under the constitution as head of state but the statsminister is chosen by the Speaker of the Riksdag. Since 1971 there has been only one chamber in the Riksdag. From it come the cabinet ministers, who then lose their parliamentary vote. After several constitutional reforms in the 1970s, cabinet was confirmed as the ultimate decision-making power. The Riksdag with about 350 members is elected every third September, but representatives of union, business and cooperative movements also sit and serve on its commissions.

There are 24 *län*, or administrative counties in Sweden, not to be confused with the ancient provinces. Their councils are convened by cabinet appointees, can levy taxes and are responsible for the administration of regional services such as health. At municipal level, 284 *kommuner* provide housing, roads and water.

ECONOMY

Sweden is most closely associated today with high technology and precision hardware such as ball-bearings. This is partly a result of Sweden's brand of neutrality, which requires self-sufficiency in advanced communications, vehicles, and military technology. International deals by big companies have reduced the importance of Swedish-built automobiles and made technological leaders such as Asea (now ABB) multinational concerns.

Sweden has a very big public sector and the share of workers employed in administration and services is 37%, compared to about 23% in mining and manufacturing. Perhaps the main economic drawback is the country's dependence on raw imported crude oil. The pillar of economic policy has been full employment – unemployment was relatively low until 1991.

Timber and ore are vital to industry. About half the country is forested and half of this is in the hands of government or forestry companies. The iron mines of Kiruna and Gällivare in the Arctic north are of greatest importance. Only 10% of Sweden is farmland and most of this is in the south.

POPULATION & PEOPLE

There are 8.5 million people, which makes Sweden the most populous country in the north, but there is no comparison with similar-sized countries on the Continent; the density is just over 20 people per sq km.

There are two native minorities included in these figures: the 15,000 Sami or Lapps (less than a third of them live in the northern countries and Russia) and about 30,000 Finns who live in the north-east. The Sami people can be considered the 'original' inhabitants of the north and developed a system of belief based on hunting magic and sacred places. They are believed to have wandered into the area from the north-west of Russia and Finland long before the birth of Christ. Today they keep reindeer or are engaged in tourism and forestry.

The birth and mortality rates in Sweden are low, but there has been a net immigration of more than 600,000 since WW II, mostly from other countries in the Nordic group, which has a single labour market. Other immigration has been closely restricted.

Stockholm and its surrounding area contain more than one million people, Gothenburg is home to more than 700,000 and Malmö has up to 500,000. Several other Swedish cities have 100,000 or more residents. Apart from a sprinkling of towns up the Bothnian coast there is only sparse settlement in Norrland.

ARTS

The best known members of Sweden's artistic community have been writers: chiefly the influential dramatist and author August Strindberg and the widely translated children's writer Astrid Lindgren. But to the Swedish soul the Gustavian balladry of Carl Michael Bellman is perhaps dearest. Vilhelm Moberg, a representative of 20th-century proletarian literature, won international acclaim with *The Immigrants* and *The Emigrants*. The most important figure from Swedish culture, however, has been the scientist Carl von Linné, who classified plant species under Latin names in the 18th century and made pioneering field studies. Still better known is Alfred Nobel, first patron of the Nobel Institute and the international prizes.

CULTURE

The modern impression of Sweden is of a progressive state with advanced technology and social policy and the great cultural and economic wealth neutrality can bring. Future events can be expected to modify this image, because Sweden is shifting and the greatest challenges to its courage and ingenuity lie ahead. Its deserved reputation as a social innovator has led to a misunderstanding in the West of the reasons for Sweden's successes.

Western reformers have pointed to systems and offered models based on Swedish practices, largely ignoring the reality that the nation is a product of its unique experience and has come a very different path from the English-speaking countries. Swedes and the powerful industrial democracies, or at least English speakers, tend to see the the world in quite different terms.

The strong rural traditions have not been forgotten. In the past 30 years the so-called 'green wave' has taken many Swedish families out of town, partly through nostalgia and partly because of their concern for quality of life. The summer cottage by the lake has become a cliché, but many families do own such retreats (there are 600,000 second homes). The traditional Midsummer festival, which celebrates the mercies of a rugged climate, incorporates popular tunes, parish ('national') costumes, flowers and various styles of maypole. Folk culture is a consistent refrain in Swedish life and is closely associated, for instance, with Dalarna.

The main 'customs' you will observe as a traveller are few. When in state agencies such as the post office or Systembolaget, take a number and wait until it comes up on a digital display (perhaps with a window number). This may happen in big tourist offices as well. In private homes and such places as indoor sports centres remove your shoes and any outer winter clothing inside the door. You should formally respond after eating a home-cooked meal; Swedes are in the habit of saying simply, 'Thank you for the meal'.

As for greetings, *hej!* is the most common, the response often *hej, hej!* and *hej då!* is the usual (clipped) farewell.

RELIGION

Sweden has a Lutheran state church, which all citizens in principle join (in fact about 95% of citizens are members). The state however guarantees religious freedom. All but objectors of conscience pay a flat-rate church tax. Members also have rights of baptism and marriage in the home parish. The church synod is elected through delegates by members 18 years or over. Women may be ordained.

LANGUAGE

Swedish is a Germanic language, belonging to the Nordic branch, and is spoken throughout Sweden and in parts of Finland and Estonia. Swedes, Danes and Norwegians can, however, make themselves mutually understood since their languages are similar, while most Swedes speak English as a second language.

Since they share common roots the Old Norse language with sprinklings of Anglo-Saxon, you will find many similarities between English and Swedish. However, the pronunciations alter, and there are sounds in Swedish which are not found in English. There are, for instance, three more letters in the Swedish alphabet: **å**, **ä** and **ö**.

Swedish grammar follows the Nordic Germanic languages. Verbs are the same regardless of person or number: 'I am, you are', etc are, in Swedish, *Jag är, du är* and so on. Definite articles in Swedish ('the' in English) are determined by the ending of a noun: -en and -et for singular nouns and -na and -n for plural. To determine if it is -en or -et as an ending can be difficult and has to be learnt word by word.

One suggestion is to try to learn the common phrases for politeness, as your attempts will be greatly appreciated by the Swedes, who are not used to foreigners speaking Swedish.

Sami dialects (there are three main groups) are Uralic (hence not Indo-European) and ancestrally related to Finnish. English is the popular second language and spoken throughout the tourist industry.

Pronunciation

Sweden is a large country but with a relatively small population. Since people in the past lived scattered and isolated, there is a great variety of dialects. There are sounds in Swedish which do not exist in English, so we have tried to give as close approximations as possible.

Vowels

The vowels are pronounced as short sounds if there is a double consonant afterwards, otherwise they are long sounds. Sometimes the o in Swedish sounds like the **å**, and e as the **ä**. There are, however, not as many exceptions to the rules as there are in English.

Vowel	Long	Short
a	as the 'a' in 'father'	as in 'cut' or the French *ami*
o	as in 'zoo'	as in 'pot'
u	sounds like 'ooo'	when you don't like something as in 'pull'
i	as in 'see'	as in 'in'
e	as in 'fear'	as in 'bet'
å	as in 'poor'	almost like the 'o' in 'pot'
ä	as in 'act'	as in the French *et*
ö	similar to 'fern'	or the German *schön* as in the French *deux*
y	as in the German *über*	as in the French *tu*

Consonants

The consonants are pronounced almost the same as in English. The following letter combinations and sounds are specific to Swedish:

c	as the 's' in 'sit'
ck	like a double 'k' which gives the vowel before a short sound
tj, rs	a 'sh' sound, as in 'ship'
sj, ch	a 'kh' sound, as in the Scottish *loch*, or German *ich*

g, lj a 'y' sound, as in 'onion'. Sometimes the g is pronounced as the 'g' in 'get'.

Greetings & Civilities

Hello./Goodbye.	*Hej./Hej då/ Adjö.*
Yes./No.	*Ja./Nej.*
May I? Do you mind?	*Får jag? Gör det något?*
Please.	*Snälla, vänligen.*
Thank you.	*Tack.*
That's fine. You're welcome.	*Det är bra. Varsàgod.*
Excuse me.	*Ursäkta mig.*
Sorry. (excuse me, forgive me)	*Förlåt*

Some Useful Phrases

Do you speak English?	*Talar du engelska?*
Does anyone speak English?	*Talar någon engelska?*
I (don't) understand.	*Jag förstår (inte).*
Just a minute.	*Dröj en minut.*
How much is it?	*Hur mycket kostar den?*
Can you write down the price?	*Kan du skriva ner priset?*

Useful Signs

Camping Ground	*Campingplats*
Entrance	*Ingång*
Exit	*Utgång*
Full/No Vacancies	*Fullt/Inga Lediga Rum*
Guesthouse	*Gästhus*
Hotel	*Hotell*
Hot/Cold	*Varm/Kall*
Motel	*Motell*
Open/Closed	*Öppen/Sängd*
Police	*Polis*
Police Station	*Polisstation*
Prohibited	*Förbjudet*
Rooms Available	*Lediga Rum*
Toilets	*Toalett*
Railway Station	*Tågstation*
Youth Hostel	*Vandrarhem*

Getting Around

What time does the ... leave/ arrive?	*När avgår/kommer ... ?*

SWEDEN

(aero)plane	*flygplanet*
boat	*båten*
bus (city)	*stadsbussen*
bus (intercity)	*landsortsbussen*
train	*tåget*
tram	*spårvagnen*

I would like ...	*Jag skulle vilja ha ...*
a one-way ticket	*en enkelbiljett*
a return ticket	*en returbiljett*
1st class	*första klass*
2nd class	*andra klass*

Where is the bus/tram stop?	*Var är buss/ spårvagnshåll platsen?*
I want to go to ...	*Jag vill gå till ...*
Can you show me (on the map)?	*Kan du visa mig (på kartan)?*

Go straight ahead.	*Gå rakt fram.*
Turn left ...	*Sväng till vänster ...*
Turn right ...	*Sväng till höger ...*
far	*långt*
near	*nära*

Around Town

I'm looking for ...	*Jag letar efter ...*
the art gallery	*kontsgalleriet*
a bank	*en bank*
the church	*kyrkan*
the city centre	*stadscentrum*
the ... embassy	*... ambassaden*
my hotel	*mitt hotell*
the market	*marknaden*
the museum	*museet*
the police	*polisen*
the post office	*postkontoret*
a public toilet	*en offentlig toalett*
the tourist information office	*turistinformation*

ancient	*forntida, forntids-*
beach	*strand*
bridge	*bro*
building	*byggnad*
castle	*slott*
cathedral	*domkyrka*
church	*kyrka*

hospital	*sjukhus, lasarett*
island	*ö*
lake	*sjö*
main square	*stortorget*
market	*torg (handel)*
old city	*gamla stan*
palace	*palats*
ruins	*ruiner*
sea	*hav*
square	*torg*

Accommodation

Where is a cheap hotel?	*Var är billiga hotell?*
What is the address?	*Vilken adress?*
Could you write the address, please?	*Kan du vänligen skriva adressen?*
Do you have any rooms available?	*Finns det några lediga rum?*

I would like ...	*Jag skulle vilja ha ...*
a single room	*ett enkelrum*
a double room	*ett dubbelrum*
a room with a bathroom	*ett rum med badrum*
to share a dorm	*dela sovsal*
a bed	*säng*

How much is it per night/per person?	*Hur mycket kostar det per natt/per person?*
Can I see it?	*Får jag se det?*
Where is the bathroom?	*Var är badrummet?*
sauna	*bastu*

Food

breakfast	*frukost*
lunch	*lunch*
dinner	*middag*

I would like the set lunch, please.	*Jag skulle vilja ha lunchmenyn, tack.*
I am a vegetarian.	*Jag är vegetarian.*

Time & Dates

In Sweden, you tell the time using the 24-hour system.

What time is it?	*Vad är klockan?*
in the morning	*på morgonen*
in the afternoon	*på eftermiddagen*
in the evening	*på kvällen*
today	*idag*
tomorrow	*imorgon*

Monday	*måndag*
Tuesday	*tisdag*
Wednesday	*onsdag*
Thursday	*torsdag*
Friday	*fredag*
Saturday	*lördag*
Sunday	*söndag*

January	*januari*
February	*februari*
March	*mars*
April	*april*
May	*maj*
June	*juni*
July	*juli*
August	*augusti*
September	*september*
October	*oktober*
November	*november*
December	*december*

Numbers

0	*noll*
1	*ett*
2	*två*
3	*tre*
4	*fyra*
5	*fem*
6	*sex*
7	*sju*
8	*åtta*
9	*nio*
10	*tio*
11	*elva*
12	*tolv*
13	*tretton*
14	*fjorton*
15	*femton*
16	*sexton*
17	*sjutton*
18	*arton*
19	*nitton*
20	*tjugo*
30	*trettio*
40	*fyrtio*
50	*femtio*
60	*sextio*
70	*sjuttio*
80	*åttio*
90	*nittio*
100	*ett hundra*
1000	*ett tusen*
one million	*en miljon*

Health

I'm ...	*Jag är ...*
diabetic	*diabetiker*
epileptic	*epileptiker*
asthmatic	*astmatiker*

I'm allergic to antibiotics/penicillin	*Jag är allergisk mot antibiotika/penicillin*

antiseptic	*antiseptisk*
condoms	*kondomer*
contraceptive	*preventivmedel*
diarrhoea	*diarré*
medicine	*medicin*
nausea	*illamående*
tampons	*tamponger*

Emergencies

Help!	*Hjälp!*
Call a doctor!	*Ring efter en doktor!*
Call the police!	*Ring polisen!*
Go away!	*Försvinn!*

Facts for the Visitor

VISAS & EMBASSIES

Temporary residency visas *(uppehållstillstånd)* are generally required only for stays of more than three months in Sweden and are issued free for specified periods. But citizens of many African, Asian and Eastern European countries require special tourist visas for entry, which are valid for 90 days. Work permits *(arbetstillstånd)* are necessary (see the following Work section). You cannot collect a visa inside Sweden and cannot normally extend your stay. You will probably wait two months before receiving your visa.

Guest students need special student residency permits and are allowed to take only summer jobs between mid-May and mid-September. These permits are not normally available to those wishing to attend folk high schools or local adult education centres.

Swedish Embassies

These legations handle visa applications in the English-speaking countries:

Australia
    5 Turrana St, Yarralumla ACT 2600
Canada
    Consulate-General, 377 Dalhousie St,
    Ottawa K1N 9N8
Denmark
    Sankt Annæ Plads 15A, 1250 Copenhagen K
Finland
    Pohjoisesplanadi 7B, 00170 Helsinki
Germany
    Consulates-General, Kurfürstendamm 151,
    W 1000 Berlin 31
    Alsterufer 15, W 2000 Hamburg 36
New Zealand
    8th floor, Greenock House, 39 The Terrace,
    Wellington 1
Norway
    Nobelsgate 16, 0244 Oslo 2
UK
    11 Montague Place, London W1
USA
    Consulates-General, 1 Dag Hammarskjöld
    Plaza, New York, NY 10017
    10880 Wilshire Blvd, Los Angeles CA 90024

Foreign Embassies in Sweden

These embassies and legations are in Stockholm, although some neighbouring countries have consulates in Gothenburg, Malmö and Helsingborg (see the Information sections under those cities):

Australia
    Block 5, Sergels torg 12 (☎ 08-613 2900)

Canada
    7th floor, Tegelbacken 4 (☎ 08-237 920)
Denmark
    Gustav Adolfs torg 14 (☎ 08-2318 60)
Finland
    Jakobsgatan 6 (☎ 08-676 67 00)
Germany
    Skarpögatan 9 (☎ 08-670 15 11)
New Zealand
    Consulate-General, Arsenalsgatan 8C
    (☎ 08-611 6824)
Norway
    Strandvägen 113 (☎ 08 66 7 0620)
Poland
    Consulate-General, Prästgårdsgatan 5,
    Sundbyberg (☎ 08-764 4800)
UK
    Skarpögatan 6-8 (☎ 08-667 0140)
USA
    Secretariat, Strandvägen 101 (☎ 08-783 5300)

DOCUMENTS

Statens invandrarverk, the immigration authority, handles all applications for visas and work permits lodged at overseas diplomatic posts. This means that a minimum of six weeks (allow eight) is needed to process applications, which are examined by the police. You may have to post away your passport to have it stamped inside. Work permits can be renewed by Statens invandrarverk (☎ 011-15 60 00), Vikboplan 5, Box 6113, 600 06 Norrköping.

Citizens of the Nordic group of countries do not need passports to travel direct to Sweden or permits to work. UK citizens need only a British Visitor's Passport. Citizens of Belgium, France, the Netherlands, Italy, Liechtenstein, Luxemburg, Switzerland, Germany and Austria need only their national identity cards for visits of up to three months. Identification must be carried.

CUSTOMS

You will usually choose the red or green gates in customs depending on whether you have anything to declare. If you bring duty-free goods from elsewhere you must display them. To bring in a car you should obtain a special red or green symbol indicating your declaration. These come with the special brochures for motorists issued at highway customs posts, some of which also have the red and green gates.

Souvenirs from overseas being taken through Sweden (up to a value of 600 kr for Europeans and 2700 kr for other visitors) are not liable for duty and tax. Goods apart from alcohol and tobacco and duty-free purchases up to a value of 1000 kr are exempt, although there is no partial exemption for items over that amount.

Untinned meats, dairy produce and eggs should not be imported without permission from Livsmedelsverket, the food authority, although food from other Nordic countries is normally conceded. You can bring personal prescribed drugs and medicines in three months' supply. Leave your flick knife behind.

If you are aged 20 years or over you may import duty-free one litre of spirits, one litre of wine or an apéritif less than 22% alcohol (or two litres if you have no spirits) and two litres of strong beer. If you are aged 15 or over you may bring in 400 cigarettes or 500 grams of tobacco (half of these amounts if you are a European resident). You may bring up to five further litres of wine and of spirits and unlimited tobacco if you pay duty.

There are exceptions for regular boats or ferries from Denmark and Norway to most places except Gothenburg, and on the hovercraft from Copenhagen to Malmö. You will then be restricted to 40 cigarettes or 100 grams of tobacco and duty will be payable on all alcohol. There is more detail, including prohibitions on firearms and animals, in the official leaflet *Red or Green in the Customs?*.

MONEY

Unrestricted amounts of money can be taken in or out of Sweden, but no more than 6000 kr in Swedish currency is allowed. The currencies most often exchanged are those from the Nordic countries; your dollars, Deutschmarks and pounds sterling. For travellers' cheques Thomas Cook and American Express are fine. Eurocheques are not as common in Sweden as they are on the Continent. They must be written in kronor and

you should bring your Eurocard as guarantee when cashing them.

Visa and MasterCard-Eurocard, in that order, are the preferred cards. But cash withdrawals against them depend on finding the bank that has an affiliation with the bank issuing your card. It is best to check at home before leaving as this is also the best way to have money sent to you through the home bank. Postal orders for up to 10,000 kr can be claimed at the post office banking counters.

You can sometimes use any of the main credit cards in specially marked electronic tellers. Banks, however, advise that there are risks involved in using these machines when travelling overseas and don't recommend your using them: errors may lead to the machine's swallowing the card. There are minimum charges for automatic withdrawals too, for Visa they are 35 kr or 3%. American Express, Diner's Club and Access are the more common minor cards.

The cheapest and often easiest place to exchange money is the Forex bank, in the big ports. Forex charges much less than the savings banks and offers competitive exchange rates on main currencies. If you keep your receipts, you can change back to the original currency for no cost. You can find offices open until 9 pm. Otherwise you will pay 35 kr or more per exchange at the banks (generally open from 9.30 am).

Late in the day, you can usually exchange at post offices at rates comparable to the banks', and this can be handy if banks close about 3 pm (which is usual, except on Thursdays or at city branches where closing time is 5 or 5.30 pm). Some small branches close for lunch.

On the ferries and at many terminals you can exchange at set times, but check charges and rates. Currencies of neighbouring countries (but not roubles) are accepted on board.

Currency

The Swedish krona is usually called 'crown' by Swedes speaking English. There are only four coins: 50 öre and the one, five and 10-kronor pieces. Prices are often shown to within five öre but the sum is rounded off. The common notes are 20, 50, 100, 500 and 1000-kronor (the 10-kronor note is being phased out and travellers would rarely use the 10,000-kronor note). The 50-öre, one and five-kronor coins are accepted by telephones (but you get no change from five kronor) and five-kronor coins by luggage lockers.

Exchange Rates

The following currencies convert at these approximate rates:

1 Dkr	=	0.95 Skr
1 Fmk	=	4.90 Skr
1 Ikr	=	0.10 Skr
1 Nkr	=	0.90 Skr
A$1	=	3.97 Skr
C$1	=	4.45 Skr
DM1	=	3.77 Skr
NZ$1	=	3.02 Skr
UK£1	=	9.45 Skr
US$1	=	5.55 Skr

Costs

For the budget traveller the high cost structure in Sweden will be brought home by the price of food and accommodation. The basics such as milk and bread, however, are kept reasonable as a matter of policy. Most STF hostels charge 90 or 83 kr a night to card-holding members. If you are a non-member there is an extra charge of 35 kr. Few hotels will charge less than 400 kr for a single, even in holiday season, but it can be hard to find any asking less than 500 kr from Sundays to Thursdays. Cheap restaurants are those asking less than 50 kr for a main course.

A 450-gram loaf of bread can be discounted to under 10 kr, but 14 kr is the usual price. The standard strong beer, varying between 370 ml and 450 ml, will usually cost about 30 kr in restaurants, though you can find it cheaper. Big Macs will cost 25.50 kr, making them one of the cheaper burgers.

The grades of petrol are 98 octane super, 96 octane standard or regular, and 95 octane unleaded. The base prices are high at 6.69,

6.53 and 6.30 kr per litre respectively, the result of the need to import. Diesel costs 4.75 kr per litre. You can sometimes save 10 öre per litre by looking around; expect the ruling prices to be about 20 öre per litre higher in the far north. Unleaded varieties are slightly cheaper and some auto pumps use 50 and 100-kronor notes *(sedlar)*.

You can make a 100-km train trip for 120 kr 2nd-class and 100 km by express bus will cost about 90 kr, but it gets cheaper the farther you travel. Local phone calls are 2 kr and *Time* magazine costs 19 kr.

Tipping

Tipping is not necessary in restaurants, where there is provision for service in the bill, but adding an extra few kronor is still quite common. In taxis round up the meter tariff if you can manage it, particularly if there is luggage. Cloakrooms can cost you 10 kr anyway, and you will need the wherewithal for drinking.

Bargaining

This is not customary: a price is generally a price. If you want bargains (by European or US standards there are few) look for the signs *rea* (sale) and *lågpris, extrapris* or *rabatt* (discounts).

Consumer Taxes

The main extra cost for the traveller is *mervärdeskatt* or *moms*, the value-added tax on goods and services, paid at point of sale but refundable to travellers on exportable items. (This can vary but imagine you are paying almost 20% of the advertised price in tax.)

The dreaded moms adds up to as much as 22% on the base prices of most of your goods and services, including all tickets, although tax on hotel and restaurant services is lower. Most, but not all advertised prices in restaurants include the value-added tax. Foreigners buying souvenirs and gifts can avoid it or be reimbursed if the goods leave the country within seven days.

By showing your passport in business premises with the blue-and-yellow 'Tax-free for tourists' sign, you can get a certificate for the tax paid (at a small charge and valid for a month unless you specify longer) and take the item to the refund desk (if there is one) when you leave the country. The goods will be sealed at the shop, or you can sometimes arrange to have them posted home.

If the shop is not in the tax-free system, you will have to note the address and post back a copy of the purchase receipt and a customs import certificate when you reach home or the next country and receive the refund by mail. But make sure this is agreed by the trader: they are under no obligation to make refunds in this way. You should check that your port of departure has a cash desk. To make that easier, get the *Shopping in Sweden* tax-free guide at shops and tourist offices or write to Sweden Tax-free Shopping, Information Department, Box 128, 23122 Trelleborg, for a copy.

CLIMATE & WHEN TO GO

If you want the sunshine, visit between late May and late July, bearing in mind that August can be wet. Monthly average temperatures in Stockholm and Malmö are highest in July at about 17°C. Then the average in the northern mountains is about 11°C and there is usually plenty of sun in August. Humidity is generally low.

Light refraction in the northern latitudes increases the length of the day in the far north by 15 minutes before dawn and after sunset. Malmö in the south gets 17½ hours of light in midsummer, Sundsvall has constant light during the second half of June, and Kiruna has 45 days of continuous light. Stockholm has an average of about nine hours of sunshine daily from May to July, but Luleå leads the country in July with more than 10 hours. At 69° north, there is an average 'day' of only four twilight hours in December. There can be occasional minus temperatures and snow falls in the mountains and the north even in summer: the range of temperatures north of the Gulf of Bothnia is almost 30°C.

Annual rainfall is greatest around Gothenburg at well over 700 mm, although this city's annual average temperature is among

the warmest at just under 8°C. About a third of the precipitation in Lapland is snow, which lies on the ground for anything between 150 and 200 days a year.

WHAT TO BRING

Raincoat and jumper (sweater) are necessary luggage at all times of year, because rainy changes can spoil summer weather quite quickly, especially when they come with a Baltic wind. From at least November to March only scarf and mittens and anorak or overcoat will suffice. In the more temperate months, aim to use layers of thinner clothing that will dry more quickly.

Budget travellers will need an internationally valid youth hostel or camping card. Self-catering on the road demands a lunch box or two, a breadknife, plastic bottle and a camper's can opener or multiple tool.

SUGGESTED ITINERARIES

Depending on the length of your stay you might like to see and do the following:

Two days
> Stockholm only: Gamla Stan, *Wasa* Museum, Skansen, Nationalmuseet, a boat cruise in Saltsjon, Drottningholm

One week
> Stockholm as above (two days), Visby (one day), Uppsala (one day), Gävle (one day), Falun and the copper mine (two days)

Two weeks
> Stockholm (three days), Uppsala (one day), Gävle (one day), Falun (one day), Siljan (one day), Örebro (one day), Vadstena (one day), Gothenburg (two days), Malmö (one day), Lund (one day)

One month
> Stockholm (five days), Uppsala (two days), Gävle (two days), Falun (one day), Siljan (three days), Östersund (two days)
> Return to Stockholm then visit Visby and Gotland (two days), Kalmar (one day), Öland (three days), Malmö (one day), Lund (one day), Gothenburg (two days), Jönköping (one day), Vadstena (one day)

Two months
> Explore the country thoroughly, you could include an extended visit to Abisko national park

TOURIST OFFICES

Sweden has about 350 local tourist information offices. Most are open long hours in summer and short hours (or not at all) in winter: others exhibit nomadic tendencies. Even in June it can be hard to find information at weekends; the office might be open a few hours on Saturday. In small destinations these offices are open only from June to August. If you'll be relying on their information get the free booklet *Discover Sweden: Regional tourist organisations and tourist information offices*.

Svenska Turistföreningen or STF, a national club, provides services to its members and general information and books. It also coordinates the *vandrarhem* (hostels) and mountain huts. Paying annual membership (adults 205 kr, juniors 65 kr, families 65 kr a member) attracts the same discounts as a youth hostel card and discounts on books. There are also outdoor activities members can book for. The services, discounts and opportunities might make a year's membership worthwhile. Write to: Svenska Turistföreningen, Box 25, 10120 Stockholm. Their offices are at Drottninggatan 31, Stockholm; Östra Larmgatan 15-21, Gothenburg; and Skeppsbron 1, Malmö.

The Swedish Institute offers books and fact sheets about Sweden at Sverigehuset, upstairs from the Stockholm Information Service. The Statoil petrol company offers motorists tourist information at many of its service stations, so ask if you need help. For information about guides from the Internordic Guide Club, write to Sveriges Turistråd or Sveguide, Skottsätter, 61800 Kolmården.

Local Tourist Offices

These are the main tourist information offices and a selection of regional offices:

Stockholm
    Upptäck Sverige (Discover Sweden) shop, Stureplan 8,
    The Swedish Institute, Box 7434, 10391
    Stockholm Information Service, Box 7542, 10393 Stockholm

Gothenburg
    Göteborgs Turistråd, Kungsportsplatsen 2, 41110 Gothenburg
Malmö
    Destination Malmö, Skeppsbron 2, 21122 Malmö
Dalarna
    Dala Turism AB, Tullkammaregatan 1, 79131 Falun
    Siljan Turism AB, Box 21, 79500 Rättvik
Gävle & district
    Gästrike/Hälsinge Turistråd, Box 552, 80107 Gävle
Gotland
    Gotlands Turistförening, Box 2081, 62102 Visby
Norrbotten
    Norrbottens Turistråd/Nordkalottresor AB, Sandviksgatan 53, 95132 Luleå
Östersund and district
    Jämtland/Härjedalens Turistinformation
    Östersunds Turist & Kongressbyrå, Rådhusgatan 44, 83182 Östersund
Skåne
    Skånes Turistråd, Skiffervägen 38, 22378 Lund
Uppland
    Uppsala Turist och Kongress, Fyris torg 8, Box 1833, 75148 Uppsala

Tourist Offices Abroad

These offices can assist with tourist promotional material and enquiries:

Australia
    SAS, 5th floor, 8-12 Bridge St, Sydney NSW 2000
Canada
    SAS, suite 205, 6205 Airport Rd, Mississanga, Ontario L4V 1E1
Denmark
    Sveriges Turistbureau, Vester Farimagsgade 1, 1606 Copenhagen V
Finland
    Ruotsin Matkailutoimisto, Yrjönkatu 11, 00120 Helsinki 12
    SAS, 4th floor, Keskuskatu 7, 00100 Helsinki
Germany
    Schwedisches Touristik-Amt, Burchardstrasse 22, 2000 Hamburg 1
New Zealand
    SAS, 4th floor, Emcom House, 75 Queen St, Auckland 1
Norway
    Sveriges Turistbyrå, Fridtjof Nansens Plass 8, 0160 Oslo 1

UK

Swedish Tourist Board, 5th floor,
29-31 Oxford St, London W1R 1RE
SAS, SAS House, 52-53 Conduit St,
London W1R 0AY

USA

Swedish Tourist Board, 18th floor,
655 Third Ave, New York, NY 10017
Scandinavian Tourist Board, 8929 Wilshire Blvd,
Beverly Hills, CA 90211
SAS Scandinavian Airlines, suite 3015, 1270
Avenue of the Americas, New York, NY 10020

USEFUL ORGANISATIONS

The Swedish Institute (see Information) is
the distributor of cultural information. The
National Academic Mobility Information
Centre, at the same address, answers overseas queries about educational exchanges.
STF (most of whose literature unfortunately
is not available in English) is the national
tourist club and hostel organisation and operates budget tours and packages.

SFS-Resor, the national student travel
agency, can help with bookings and information on discounts (write to Box 7144, 10387
Stockholm).

Sveriges Riksidrottsförbund, 12387
Farsta, is the umbrella for sporting unions
around Sweden and can put you in touch
with them.

De Handikappades Riksförbund, Stora
Nygatan 4, Box 2053, 10312 Stockholm, is
the coordinator of strategies and information
for handicapped people and issues books in
English.

There should be no problem with local
attitudes towards women, but in emergencies
you can turn to the local kvinnojouren (see
Women Travellers following). The national
umbrella organisation is Riksorganisation
för Kvinnojourer i Sverige (☎ 08-652 0720),
Hantverkaregatan 7, Box 22114, 10422
Stockholm. The organisation concerned for
equality for lesbians and gay men is Riks-
förbundet för Sexuellt Likaberättigande
(☎ 08-736 0212), based at Stockholms Gay-
hus, Sveavägen 57, Stockholm.

BUSINESS HOURS & HOLIDAYS

Businesses and government offices are open

from 8.30 or 9 am to 5 pm, although they can
close after 3 pm in summer. Banks usually
open at 9.30 am and close at 3 pm, but some
open from 9 am to 5 or 5.30 pm in cities.

Normal shopping hours are from 9.30 am
to 6 pm weekdays and 9.30 am to 2 or 3 pm
on Saturdays, but department stores are open
longer and sometimes on Sundays. Some
supermarkets will be open until 7 or 9 pm in
big towns. Lunch often begins at 11 am and
is over by 2 pm in restaurants.

There is a concentration of public holidays
in spring and early in summer, and Midsummer in particular brings life almost to a halt
for three days. Transport and other services
are reduced, even on Midsummer's Eve, so
read your timetables carefully. Some food
stores are open and many tourist offices, but
not all the attractions. Some hotels are closed
from Christmas to New Year. Public holidays, which often close the attractions (and
even some businesses early the day before
and all day after) are:

New Year's Day, 1January
Epiphany, 6 January
Good Friday
Easter Monday
Labour Day, 1 May
Ascension Day, (May)
Whit Monday, (late May or early June)
Midsummer's Day, (Saturday, late June)
All Saints' Day, (Saturday, late October or early
    November)
Christmas Day, 25 December
Boxing Day, 26 December

CULTURAL EVENTS

In Sweden New Year's Eve is not a big event
in itself, but is a busy time for eating and
entertainment: in some places there are fireworks. Valborgsmässoafton (30 April) is
strongly connected with students who are
easy to spot in Uppsala and Lund. Bonfires
and fireworks are lit and some museums may
close early.

May Day (1 May) is observed by marches
and events of the labour movements which
stop the traffic in the name of the red rose.
Flag Day, the national day, is 6 June.

Midsummer is the festival of the year.

Maypole dancing is a traditional activity on Midsummer's Eve and everyone who can, goes to the country, perhaps to the old family home or summer cabin. For the folk touch, Dalarna is one place to celebrate, but music, dancing, drinking and eating are normal no matter where you are, so enjoy it: not much will be open.

The crayfish season begins on the second Wednesday in August, ushered in by feasting on the first catch (or frozen batch from abroad). In the north, where crayfish are still fewer, they substitute the sour Baltic herring and hold a similar festival on the Thursday of the following week.

In just 60 years the Lucia festival on 13 December has become most popular. Oddly, it seems to merge the folk tradition of the longest night and the story of St Lucia of Syracuse. A choir in white, led by Lucia, who wears a crown of candles, leads the singing and *glögg*, a hot alcoholic fruit punch, is drunk. Christmas Eve is the main day of celebration during this season: the night of the *smörgåsbord* and the arrival of *jultomten*, the Christmas gnome with the sack of gifts.

POST & TELECOMMUNICATIONS

City post offices are open from 8.30 am to 6 or 6.30 pm weekdays and sometimes until 1 pm Saturdays. Stamps can be bought at branches of Pressbyrån. Letters to other parts of Sweden and the Nordic countries will cost 2.80 or 5.50 kr. Basic letters or postcards sent by air mail to Europe are 4.50 kr. Normal surface post overseas costs 5.50 kr. Not all classes of mail may be available from Sweden to your home country, so ask at the post office.

A package weighing 2 kg costs 150 kr by air mail outside Europe, but there may be a limit of 500 grams or 1 kg on parcels to your country. If this or the quoted rate worry you, ask about the 40% savings of *ekonomibrev* (surface post that can take a month or more). You may have to be stubborn at some windows if you know a certain price-weight combination is possible. There are fewer restrictions on printed matter, which is also a lot less trouble to post. Air mail will take a

week to reach most parts of North America, perhaps a little longer to Australia and New Zealand. Specify the mode or else air mail may be assumed.

Local telephone calls cost a minimum of 2 kr, but you will have to feed in coins for long conversations and distances and to talk over 100 km will cost 1.57 kr per minute. One economical way to phone anywhere is with the throwaway plastic telephone cards (costing 45 and 80 kr at Televerket's Telebutik, Pressbyrån and some kiosks), which can be used at special phones in many (not all) cities and big towns. Credit-card phones are in some hotels and public buildings. Most calls from hotel rooms will attract extra charges before being added to the bill. Area codes for cities are given in the Post & Telecommunications section of particular cities.

Overseas telephone calls can be awkward to make and expensive. Avoid dialling direct from the Telebutik, which is terribly expensive and attracts tax (see Consumer Taxes). But collect calls must be made from the Telebutik which is in cities and big towns. There you order the call, take it in a cubicle and pay no charge. You can not order overseas collect (reverse-charge) calls (☎ 0018) from public phones. For direct dialling ask for the *009* international dialling booklet, which includes base charges. Direct dialling is cheaper at the Tele Center at Stockholm's central station or you can dial your home operator for a collect call with a 020-79 number:

USA: AT&T 020-79 56 11, MCI 020-79 59 22,
    Sprint 020-79 9011
Canada: 020-799 015;
UK: 020-79 51 44
Australia: 020-79 90 61
NZ: 020-79 90 64

From mid-June to mid-August you can make half-price direct calls from any specially labelled pay phone (Turist Telefon), which are in cities.

For directory information in Sweden dial 079 75 from orange phones (this is impossible from green phones), dial 0013 from all phones for Nordic countries, dial 0019 for other countries. Instructions and call details in English are on page 19 of the country telephone books. The country telephone code for Sweden is 46.

Calls to Norway, Denmark and Finland cost 6.05 kr per minute (with tax), to Germany and Poland 11.10 kr, to the UK 11.10 kr, to North America 18.75 kr and to Australia and New Zealand 37.50 kr. The charge for operator-connected calls is 25 or 30 kr. The international code is 009.

Overseas telegrams cost 75 kr and from 3 to 6 kr a word. Lettergrams cost only 60 kr for 50 words or less. To send them dial 0021 or submit them at a Telebutik. For faxes the Telebutik rates are cheapest at just over 30 kr a page.

In the phone books, private numbers are on the grey-edged white pages, companies and organisations on the plain white pages, businesses (listed by category) on the yellow pages, community services on the green pages and regional services on the blue pages. In regional phone books, numbers are listed by area under the separate telephone codes. The free general emergency number is 90 000.

Note that telephone numbers throughout Sweden were being systematically changed during 1992 and 1993. Where possible we have published the new, changed numbers (which in a few cases will not be in use until late 1993). Expect some confusion about numbers even in all but the most recent travel booklets and brochures. If you have difficulties, contact the national directory-assistance service in Sweden (☎ 079 75) or, from overseas, your country's international service for current numbers.

TIME

Sweden is one hour ahead of GMT/UTC, but summer time (from the end of March to the end of September) is another hour ahead. Otherwise, at noon in Sweden, it is 11 am in London, 6 pm in New York and Toronto, 3 pm in San Francisco, 9 pm in Sydney, 11 pm in Auckland, noon in Oslo, Copenhagen and Berlin and 1 pm in Helsinki.

ELECTRICITY

The electric current in Sweden is 220 volts AC, 50 Hz, plugs have two round pins and often clip in. Some hotels do have 110 volt-sockets or suitable adapters.

LAUNDRY

For cultural reasons doing laundry is difficult for travellers: most Swedes have no use for the laundrette. A 'quick wash', where you leave clothes for laundering, is not available everywhere and can actually take a week or more. Many hostels and camping grounds have laundry facilities (look for small symbols in listings) and some hotels can offer a wash service. Swedish-made washing machines and automatic dryers are thorough but slow, so select short cycles if you can. It is best to have portable tube soap or soap powder in your luggage for doing your washing in basins. Y-3, a local powder sold in boxes with separate packets, costs about 21 kr at supermarkets.

WEIGHTS & MEASURES

The metric system applies in Sweden, but note the *mil*, which is simply 10 km but often used in conversation or for long distances. There's also a fondness for using the decilitre (0.1 litres) and centilitre (0.01 litres) on packaging. Decimals are indicated by commas and thousands by points.

BOOKS & MAPS

There is a good range of general books at the Sweden Bookshop (see Information in the Stockholm section). Some useful titles are:

Nature in Sweden P Hanneberg/Swedish Institute
    (softback)
Swedish Forest National Board of Forestry
    (paperback); write to Skogsstyrelsen,
    55183 Jönköping
Management and Society in Sweden
    P Lawrence & T Spybey (hardback)
A Concise History of Sweden A Åberg
    (paperback)

SWEDEN

Swedish Politics During the 20th Century
    S Hadenius (paperback)
Gustavus Adolphus: A History of Sweden 1611-1632
    Vol I-II, M Roberts (hardback)
Nordic Folk Art M Nodermann (hardback)
Manor Houses and Royal Castles in Sweden
    B Söderberg (hardback)
Traditional Festivities in Sweden
    I Liman, Swedish Institute (paperback)
A Small Treasury of Swedish Food
    Federation of Swedish Farmers (softback);
    write to LRF Konsument, 10533 Stockholm
Skåne I Matanle (hardback)
Gamla Stan B & G Glase (softback)
Museer i Sverige/Museums of Sweden (softback)

For maps start at Kartbutiken, Kungsgatan 74, 11122 Stockholm. The recommended maps are Lantmäteriverket's survey series coded in green (1:50,000), blue (1:100,000) and red (1:250,000). These are also available at big bookshops along with commercial tourist and motoring maps at scales smaller than 1:200,000.

A cheap way to get specific information is from the fact sheets and articles (on many topics) from the Swedish Institute (see Tourist Offices), which cost 1 kr a sheet.

MEDIA

Radio Sweden, the overseas network, broadcasts a few programmes in English (1179 kHz nationally or FM 89.6 in Stockholm), though you can tune to the BBC's European frequencies. Radio Stockholm (FM 103.3 mHz) relays BBC news at 7 pm weekdays.

Of the four main television channels, TV1 and TV2 are the national outlets and TV3 the main internal broadcaster of films and entertainment. Subtitled English films and series are common. Two Danish networks can be received in the south and the popularity of cable and satellite brings the English programmes within reach.

You will not lack news in English. Pressbyrån in cities will display international news magazines and you can usually find a copy of *The International Herald-Tribune*, *The Times*, *The Guardian* or *Wall Street Journal* at the main railway stations.

FILM & PHOTOGRAPHY

The only problem with buying film in Sweden is the cost. For your snaps sort through the bargain bins for 24-shot rolls under 30 kr at photo stores, but for 36-shot slide films you will commonly pay 70 kr (often much more). Processing is also expensive. So look for specials and take advantage of free developing where you can.

Note that you might well be photographing on water or in snow, but do not disregard the question of twilight photography in winter and on summer nights: some of the colours in the north are quite superb and you might hunt out the weird lights of the Aurora Borealis north of the Arctic Circle. When photographing the midnight sun with an automatic camera, try shading the light-meter for longer exposure. When using manual settings start with medium or wide apertures at $\frac{1}{30}$ second. Consider using a filter or put the sun nearer the margin than the centre of your shot.

Do not risk photographing the military if they are not on parade or displayed in a museum. Photography is forbidden in certain militarily restricted areas in the north of Gotland around Fårö and off the north Bothnian coast.

HEALTH

No vaccinations are required of visitors. The national pharmacist, Apoteket, provides prescription and non-prescription medicines (the usual maximum charge is less than 100 kr) and advice on how to deal with everyday ailments and conditions. The *nattapotek* are open 24 hours. For emergencies and casualty services local medical centres (*vårdcentral* or *lasarett*) are the best places to go (you must show your passport). This is the public health system and duty doctors (*distrikts-läkare* or *jourhavande läkare*) are standing by. Ordinary outpatient visits cost 60 kr. There are centres in all districts and main towns. They are listed in the green pages of local telephone books (don't forget they are indexed by area). The general emergency telephone number, including the ambulance, is 90 000.

The early summer crowds will face mosquitoes. These annoying creatures are not especially dangerous, but are perhaps worst in the northern lowlands near water or marsh and some forests. Take a trusted repellent because a few proven local preparations are being banned from sale in Sweden. For guidance go to Apoteket.

Winter travellers should note that there are long cold stretches. If you are out of doors in the far north or during winter, exposure is a threat best avoided by common-sense use of clothing and shelter. Complicated health treatment in Sweden can cost foreigners a great deal and travel insurers recommend top levels of coverage. Private doctors (*läkare*) are also listed in telephone books, but check that they are affiliated with the national health scheme in Sweden (UK citizens enjoy reciprocity). Dentists (*tändläkare*) can be expensive: travellers will pay at least 60% of costs up to 2500 kr.

WOMEN TRAVELLERS

Equality of the sexes is emphasised in Sweden and there should be no question of discrimination. Kvinnojouren is the national organisation that deals with violence against women; its local centres are listed in the green pages of telephone directories. Pregnant women with health emergencies should contact the nearest *mödravårdcentral* in the blue pages of the local telephone directory under the municipality.

Ask for a women-only compartment, if you do not want male company in a 2nd-class rail sleeping section. A few Stockholm taxi concerns offer women's cut rates at night.

DANGERS & ANNOYANCES

Sweden is one of the safest countries imaginable and crimes perpetrated against travellers are fairly rare. In the cities the otherwise welcome prominence of bicycles could concern the pedestrian – recognise that there are separate bicycle paths next to thoroughfares in most places and stay off them and keep alert when walking or catching

buses. Note also that the mosquitoes can be a nuisance (see Sweden, Health).

WORK

If you can get one, a job requires a permit. For this you need an application form from a Swedish diplomatic post and you must apply for a temporary residency visa at the same time. The basis for application is a letter from the potential employer confirming a job offer and some idea of proposed accommodation.

Students enrolled in Sweden can take summer jobs and get leads from student services, but these jobs are not offered to travelling students. To ask about prospects in particular fields, write to Arbetsmarknadsdepartmentet, 10333 Stockholm, which can give advice or addresses for regional employment organisations that keep lists of vacancies (see Sweden, Visas & Embassies and Documents).

ACTIVITIES

The outdoor pastimes are precious to Swedes, who are active on bicycles, forest jogging tracks, the rivers and lakes, the mountain trails and the snow and ice. Only about 5% of the forest area is virgin and about 200 animal species are threatened, but it is estimated there are about 15 wolves, 600 bears, 200 lynx and 100 wolverines in the wild.

General right of access, *allemansrätten*, applies to private uncultivated land outside dwelling areas. According to it you can camp away from dwellings for one night in small tents. You may take mushrooms and berries and unprotected flowers (there are some local restrictions, so it is best to check at tourist offices). You may not take living wood, bark, leaves, bushes or nuts.

Fires may be set where safe (not on bare rocks) with fallen wood. Local fire restrictions may be in force, so check at tourist offices or police stations. To make sure the fire's out you must drown it and dig in the fireplace afterwards.

There is also the right of access to beaches and swimming places off private blocks of

SWEDEN

land. Do not leave litter unless it is inside a bin. Cars may not be driven across open land or on private roads. Close all gates and climb no fences. Do not disturb reindeer.

Skating

There is skating in winter wherever the ice is thick enough. Stockholm's lake and canal system is exploited by the local children and enthusiasts seeking the longest possible 'run'. Safety and local knowledge are paramount, so follow or join the locals. In Stockholm you can hire cheap skates and follow bus groups, but if conditions are not good, go and watch a wild crowd of ice-hockey spectators.

Cycling

The cycling season is from May to September in the south and July and August in the north. It can seem especially attractive around the flat country of the lakes and Skåne or the concentrated worlds of Öland and Gotland. In towns simple bicycles can often be hired through tourist offices for about 50 kr a day or 200 kr a week and, given the network of tracks through and around most cities, doing this is quite practical. To buy second-hand cycles, try bicycle workshops, especially near universities. Excellent maps of cycle paths are available at tourist offices. To cover long distances you can book your bicycle on the train (75 kr).

There are over 20 off-road and signposted national routes (all with prepared information) and, if you want an epic challenge, follow the green signs along Sverigeleden, the national circuit, linking up over 6000 km of tracks. Plans (for the routes that are usually near to hostels) are sold as packages by STF and include hostel accommodation. Write to STF or Cykelfrämjandet, Box 6027, 10231 Stockholm (see also the Sweden Getting Around section).

Skiing

World Cup downhill skiing has come to Mora on the lake Siljan, but to Swedes it is better known for nordic or cross-country skiing. Vasaloppet is a long-distance event

that attracts thousands to the town. Snow permitting, you can watch or compete on the first Sunday in March. The resorts around Siljan have some of best skiing, or go deep into Dalarna from Idre. Gällivare in Lapland might sound more romantic, but the ski centres of Västmanland, north of Mälaren, are handy and Stockholm has several ski centres.

Do not leave marked cross-country routes without a good map, local advice, and proper equipment including plastic sheet and ropes. Wind-chill temperatures of -30°C are possible, so you should know the daily forecasts. Police and tourist offices have information on local warnings. In the mountains there is the risk of avalanche (lavin) and susceptible areas are marked by yellow multilingual signs and buried-skier symbols. Risk is generally significant on ice faces or slopes with a gradient of more than 25°. Avoid slopes off marked runs and all but the gentlest of slopes holding new snow. Conditions can also be risky three days after heavy snow, in high winds or rising temperatures. Avalanche transmitters are expensive.

Hiking

Hiking is popular anywhere, but the mountain challenge of the northern national parks is most compelling. But these parks are rarely snow-free and the jewel, Sarek, is only for experienced hikers (see National Parks in the Norrland section). For information on organised group walks, write to or visit STF or, better still, pay a year's membership. For guides, contact Sveguide (see Sweden, Tourist Offices). Good waterproof jackets, pants and boots (Wellingtons) are important equipment.

Easy walking trails are common. There are about 7000 km of signed trails in Norrland. These are rated as suitable for summer (the season is from late June to September) and winter (from February to May). Summer trails are marked with raised or painted stones, all-seasons routes with crosses.

The STF mountain huts (about 90 of them are maintained by Naturvårdsverket) are placed at intervals averaging about 20 km.

You may stay the night (or camp nearby and pay 15 kr to use the facilities). The eight STF mountain stations have shops, showers and restaurants. Nights cost 90 kr at huts and more than 100 kr at stations for members of STF (add 30 kr if you are not a member).

A special card is available to those aged under 26, it allows hut accommodation for 10 nights (340 kr). Visit STF or buy a card at a mountain station, where up-to-date maps are also available. Conditions are self-service, similar to in STF hostels, and you must bring sheets. The *STF Fjällhandbok* (79 kr) is written in Swedish but maps show all huts and facilities.

Canoeing

There are 80 approved canoeing centres and excellent areas on the lakes, such as in Dalsland, or the exciting northern river rapids or mountain lakes. You can hire canoes from 300 to 700 kr a week. The national body, Svenska kanotförbundet, produces the annual guide *Kanotvåg* and maps of 800 routes all over the country. Write to Skeppsbron 11, 61135 Nyköping. According to the right of common access there is the right to boat, paddle or moor temporarily. The brochure *Important Information for You Who Paddle* is recommended and available from Naturvårdsverket, Box 1302, 17125 Solna.

Fishing

There are national fishing ordinances, but local restrictions on inland waters may also apply, especially concerning salmon, salmon trout and eel, so check with tourist offices or the county authority before dropping a line. You generally need the owner's permission (in the case of government authorities this is covered by local permits), but open areas include parts of lakes Vänern, Vättern, Mälaren, Hjälmaren and Storsjön and most of the coastline (except for fishing the Baltic salmon off Norrland and in some protected areas).

Three authorities maintaining fishing waters should be noted: Kronofiske, with its centres of farmed stocks and developed facilities; Domänfiske, which administers 1500 charted lakes and rivers; and Vattenfall, which has salmon farms in south and central Norrland. Kronofiske cards cost from 100 kr a day, but Domänfiske cards are cheap for 190 kr a year and will cover a family. Day cards are 40 kr, weekly cards 115 kr. These are available at tourist offices and sports and camping stores. For brochures write to Domänfiske, 79181 Falun.

Boating & Sailing

The lake and canal routes offer pleasant sailing in spring and summer (the canals are mostly open for limited seasons) but the lock fees can be high. Some simpler harbours are free, but one with good facilities can cost 75 kr a night.

The dotted skärgård (archipelago) areas, particularly around Stockholm, are a different if demanding setting for sailing or motor boats. A useful guide is STF's annual *Båtturist* book (65 kr), with details of 460 guest harbours and facilities, prices and services and radio details. To operate a VHF radio you need a permit from Televerket (write to Televerket Tillståndsexpedition, 12386 Farsta, or get a form from radio shops).

The 90 000 emergency telephone number covers the sea rescue network, the normal boat safety channel is 27.095 mHz. For a customs brochure write to Generaltullstyrelsen, Box 2267, 10316 Stockholm; for information on sea rescue write to Sjösäkerhetsrådet, af Pontinsväg 6, 11521 Stockholm. For charts go to Kartcentrum, Vasagatan 16, Stockholm, or ask at tourist offices. For a different kind of excitement, STF organises raft and rapids packages.

Exploring on Inlandsbanan

The train from Mora to Gällivare through the interior covers more than 1000 km of valley and forest, a quaint summer adventure through villages (you can get on or off at Östersund and other stations for regional buses and buy tickets on board).

HIGHLIGHTS

National Parks

There are about 20 national parks in all kinds of landscape, but the best places to admire the mountains are the giant **Sarek** and **Stora Sjöfallet** parks and the tiny **Abisko** in Lapland. **Muddus national park** is old forest which you traverse between Gällivare and Jokkmokk. Different again is the forest at **Tiveden** at the north end of Vättern. There are also different types of protected nature reserves administered at local level.

Islands

The Baltic islands **Gotland** and **Öland** are of different character to the mainland and this is reflected in the rare rock forms *raukar* and the flora. The islands are also summer centres and cabin holidays are popular. Visby on Gotland is six hours from Stockholm by train and ferry and Öland is reached by bridge from Kalmar.

Historic Towns

Hailing from a mute antiquity is **Birka**, the Viking town on an island near Stockholm, and the rebuilt **Eketorp** fortified village on Öland. **Visby** is the only walled medieval town remaining. A survival of similar but livelier character is **Gamla Stan** in Stockholm as well as parts of **Lund**. Do not miss the old centre of **Malmö**, however, or a later wooden town such as **Eksjö** near Jönköping.

Museums

Regional museums and museum villages are very popular in Sweden and are better presented than most in Europe. **Skansen** combines folk-life, wildlife and livestock in a way followed elsewhere and runs special events. The new *Wasa* **museum** is one of the latest and best, **Musikmuseet** in Stockholm is a small museum that is equally well presented, while **Östindiska huset** in Gothenburg and **Malmöhus** castle combine human and natural history on a large scale. The regional *länsmuseer* are generally free although they may be open only from noon to 4 pm (often 8 pm on Wednesday). *Museer*

i Sverige is a national guide in Swedish and English (80 kr).

Castles

Castles exist in good order and bad, and include laid-out palaces with gardens such as **Drottningholm** near Stockholm, lakeside residences such as **Skokloster slott** by Mälaren and **Vadstena slott**, formidable fortresses such as **Kalmar** and **Örebro** castles and impressive ruins such as those at **Borgholm** on Öland. **Uppsala slott** and **Malmöhus** are also museums.

Churches

Entry to churches is free, except for the burial church **Riddarholmskyrkan** in Stockholm. There are all styles of cathedrals; the *domkyrkor* of **Lund** (Romanesque), **Uppsala** (Gothic) and **Kalmar** (Baroque) are fine examples.

Early stone churches abound on the Baltic islands and the wooden **Särna gammalkyrka** in upper Dalarna is also worthy.

ACCOMMODATION

There will be a style of accommodation to suit your budget, but many travellers of all ages will opt for hostel savings, as many Swedes do. Tourist offices can often supply B&B or farm accommodation guides, sometimes listing places with double rooms for less than 200 kr. Swedes often register the date you arrive and will leave on, so consecutive dates usually mean one night only. Facilities for the handicapped are generally good and camping grounds usually provide at least modified toilets. Ask at tourist offices for the annual *Holiday Guide for the Disabled*.

Camping

Some camping grounds are open in winter and offer comforts, but the best time for camping is from May to August (although there are sometimes off-season discounts). Prices vary with facilities: from 30 to 100 kr a site plus electricity. The better equipped places have all kitchen and laundry facilities.

Caravans can be rented for 2000 kr a week or more from several operators.

Don't forget that you can camp a night in the open under common access rights (see the introduction to Sweden, Activities). Primus and Sievert are the common gas products available at service stations.

Hostels

About 280 vandrarhem (hostels) are affiliated with STF, which produces a detailed guide for 69 kr (worth getting for its detailed information and transport details, easily decipher without a phrasebook). STF members (membership costs 205 kr a year for adults, 65 kr for those aged 20 years and under) or holders of international youth hostel cards can stay for the budget rates of 60, 76, 83 or 190 kr. Others will pay a premium of 35 kr, but guest cards can be bought at most hostels.

About half of all hostels are open all year (many close only at Christmas), others are in schools and open for six weeks in summer (or only by pre-booking). Expect these to close during the day, and you often must arrive by 6 pm. Rooms usually hold from two to six beds, though some hostels have family rooms for about 60 kr extra. Breakfast usually costs about 40 kr.

The principle is that you clean up yourself, but some hostels push optional 'cleaning fees' of up to 35 kr. If you do not clean up, they will.

Many hostels have kitchens, but you often need utensils and usually a tea towel. Washing machines and dryers are often available but are worked hard. Bring sheets (not sleeping bags). Mountain huts and stations are also affiliated with STF (see Hiking in the introductory Sweden Activities section).

Cabins

Rented cabins are popular for groups and families seeking fresh air, forests, lakes and relief from heavy costs. Weekly rates vary widely, however, from as little as 400 kr (for two beds, cold water and little else) to more than 3000 kr. Conditions vary locally, and the discounts at 'summer' resorts apply off-season. Booking in some cases needs to be done six months in advance and cancellations are costly; some owners will not accept foreigners. Mostly you must bring sheets and tea towels, sometimes cooking utensils.

Regional rental agencies and some tourist offices produce guides and price lists; you can sometimes snap up a good place to stay from vacant stock at little notice.

Hotels

These are expensive, usually costing more than 500 kr a single. If you want discount rates, it is best to confine hotel stays to weekends (usually Friday and Saturday nights, sometimes Sundays, so check if you are booking ahead). Prices are also cheaper from June to mid-August (the periods vary), when traffic and competition is greatest. Price ranges can be confusing, so if you want the cheapest room available, ask. We attempt here to mention a base price and some discounts. A comprehensive guide to all hotels and packages is available at big tourist offices.

Sometimes prices are expressed as 'per person in a two-bed room', so be careful. Portable beds are often available for children in double rooms for a small fee. There are discount cards, some Scandinavia wide, run by the big chains and which may fit in with your plans.

If you are driving, package rates are available for 200 hotels. These work out to less than 200 kr per person a night. The pass and guide costs about 60 kr from Biltur Logi, 79303 Tallberg, or is available at city tourist offices and some bookshops. The Pro Skandinavia vouchers available in the UK (from Haman Skandinavia UK, Box 244 Wembley, Middlesex HAO 2UU) are valid for one-night singles (including breakfast) at 400 hotels in Scandinavia and confer discounts with some ferry companies and car-rental agencies. They cost £22 each.

FOOD

The prices of restaurant dinners with a drink easily climb above 150 kr. At the budget end solid, meat-based, cafeteria-style meals, usually with a big helping of potatoes (boiled, mashed or chipped) can come in at 50 kr. The *husmanskost* specials are often meatballs; they usually include potato and are high in cholesterol, but if this suits you will pay as little as 35 kr. The *sallad* is often simply coleslaw and rolls at the buffet. Prices generally, but not always, include charges.

Lunch can be most reasonable: look for *dagens rätt* (today's special) which will generally include bread, salad and coffee or a drink. It might pay to eat lightly at dinner. Lunch usually starts at 11 am and sometimes is over after 2 pm. Chinese restaurants are less likely to be a cheap option in Sweden, but Middle Eastern fare down to takeaway kebabs and many pizzas are budget alternatives. *Fullständiga rättigheter* means fully licensed.

The cafeteria tray at cheaper lunch houses, department stores and railway stations is a viable option, but don't forget to stack the actual tray in the rack afterwards. Be careful buying food in railway cafeterias, however, because many of these places are by no means cheap.

Pure vegetarian restaurants exist but there are not many and they are usually closed at weekends. Salads and pizzas cater for the 'green toothed' in many places, sometimes costing less than 50 kr.

In cafés, getting a coffee of any size for less than 10 kr is rare, although quite often the practice of *påtår* gives you a free or 5-kr refill.

Self-Catering

Shopping is easy enough in supermarkets and worth it if you are hostelling. In supermarkets note the item price and comparative price per kg, which are shown by law. Plastic carry-bags will usually cost about 1 kr at the checkout.

Bread and milk prices are kept low at around 13 kr per 450-gram loaf and 7 kr per litre. To some people, the selection of fresh vegetables and fruit will seem limited. At produce markets prices are not always displayed, but the selection is better. Low-fat milk is *lättmjölk* and *filmjölk* is the processed sour milk that Swedes like with breakfast cereals. *Mellanmjölk* is all-purpose with reduced fats.

DRINKS

Strong beer, wines and spirits are sold by the state monopoly Systembolaget at outlets in the cities and towns, which are open weekdays from 9 am to 5 or 6 pm (you must be aged over 20 and have identification). You must normally decide what you want from price lists and displays and then take a number and wait: Friday-afternoon queues can be long.

Alcohol prices are kept high as a matter of policy, but drinkable wines can be bought for less than 50 kr a bottle. Strong beer, or *klass III*, is also sold at these outlets in 375-ml bottles for about 15 to 25 kr each. Only the lighter beers, known as *folköl* and *klass II*, are sold in supermarkets and some unlicensed restaurants.

ENTERTAINMENT

Discos and nightclubs admit no-one aged under 20, although the maximum age limit for men is usually 23 and sometimes 25. Drinking at these places is the most expensive of options, but the strength of the brews might restrict your outlay. Cloakroom charges average 10 kr. Pubs and restaurants can charge 30 kr or less for the standard *storstark*, 450 ml of klass III, although the cheaper 375-ml bottle is common in pubs.

Theatre tickets cost around 200 kr or more if there is no subsidy, and for the cinema it's anything from 35 kr (rare) to 60 kr (common in cities). Going to the cinema is a good option as many subtitled features in English are shown.

THINGS TO BUY

Souvenirs, handicrafts or quality Swedish products in glass, wood or pewter are relatively expensive. Typically Swedish is the Dalarna painted wooden horse and, if you want a good hand-made one, go to the workshops in Dalarna (see Mora).

On Sami handicrafts, which are quite

expensive, look for the *'Duodji'* label (a round coloured token of authenticity) on knives, textiles and trinkets, although the fakes are dear enough. Handicrafts carrying the round token *'Svensk slöjd'* are endorsed by the national handicrafts organisation Svenska hemslöjdsföreningarnas riksförbund, whose symbol is found on affiliated handicraft shops.

Getting There & Away

Eurail, Inter-Rail, ScanRail and Nordturist passes attract extra discounts on some international ferries (or even free passages, such as from Stockholm to Helsinki on Silja Line). The ISIC brings discounts on some airfares, ferries, tours tickets and international rail tickets to those under 26 years (at student travel agents such as STA or SFS-Resor in Stockholm, see details under Useful Organisations in Sweden, Facts for the Visitor).

AIR
SAS is an international and domestic airline and flies frequently from European hubs and intercontinental cities to Arlanda airport north of Stockholm and to Copenhagen. SAS hovercraft run from Malmö to Copenhagen airport (Swedish: Köpenhamn) to link up with international flights. Apex fares for about half-price are available on some bookings a fortnight ahead and stays including a weekend.

There are daily SAS nonstop services from Stockholm to New York, London and Amsterdam (also KLM services) and to Berlin, Düsseldorf, Hamburg and Frankfurt (also Lufthansa services). Lufthansa also flies from Stockholm to Munich and from Stockholm to Hanover daily. British Airways as well as small concerns such as Transwede fly to Stockholm from London. Passengers from Montreal or Toronto must change in New York.

From Australia SAS and Thai International fly to Stockholm via Bangkok or Singapore (although you change in Copenhagen) or you can connect with flights to Stockholm in London, Amsterdam or Frankfurt. SAS and All Nippon Airways fly from Stockholm to Tokyo twice weekly. SAS has Monday and Thursday flights to Hong Kong from Copenhagen.

Airport buses link the main cities: from Arlanda to Stockholm (five routes) costing 50 kr, from Landvetter to Gothenburg for 50 kr and from Sturup to Malmö for 45 kr. The Flygbuss taxi from Arlanda costs 185 kr to Stockholm (the taxi is provided between your room and the nearest Flygbuss terminal, where you board the bus). Book at the Flygbuss desk at Arlanda or Cityterminalen (☎ 08-670 10 10) in Stockholm. At Arlanda S-E Banken is open for changing money from 6.30 am to 10 pm daily in the departure hall and from 7 am to 10.30 pm at the luggage claim.

To/From Denmark
SAS flies frequently from Stockholm and Gothenburg to Copenhagen every day, although the Malmö-Copenhagen hovercraft link might be more useful. (See also Malmö, Getting There & Away.) SalAir flies from Linköping to Copenhagen a few times daily (except Saturdays, when there is only one early flight).

To/From Finland
SAS has a score of daily flights to Helsinki (Swedish: Helsingfors) and services Turku and Tampere most days from Stockholm (for Finnair services see Finland, Getting There & Away). SAS also flies from Gothenburg to Helsinki every day except Saturday.

To/From Norway
There are many daily SAS flights from Stockholm and Gothenburg to Oslo as well as a direct Air France flight from Gothenburg to Stavanger every day except Saturday.

To/From Germany
SAS flies from Stockholm to Hamburg two or three times daily and from Stockholm and Gothenburg to Frankfurt just as often. The

Berlin-Stockholm service is daily (except Saturdays), although you have a choice of daily Lufthansa (or DLT) flights there or to Hamburg, Frankfurt and Munich. SalAir has several flights a week from Malmö to Hamburg.

To/From Russia
SAS and Aeroflot fly from Stockholm to Moscow daily and Aeroflot flies direct to St Petersburg on Sundays.

LAND
Coach companies link up with ferries to provide services to Sweden, such as Eurolines' services from London via Amsterdam to Stockholm, Gothenburg and Malmö. Swebus runs the Continentbus services throughout Europe to Swedish cities (for timetables write to Swebus Continent AB, Gullbergs Strandgata 34, 41104 Gothenburg).

Car & Motorbike
You do not need to display a Green Card for insurance purposes, but you should be fully insured before entering Sweden and have a recognised full driver's or motorcyclist's licence (no international licence is needed, except as a condition of some rental agencies). Cars can be loaded on most ferries and caravans on many.

To/From Denmark
Bus Express bus No 998 from Halmstad and Helsingborg crosses by ferry to Copenhagen and Kastrup airport. Bus No 999 runs Lund-Malmö-Copenhagen. At weekends bus No 860 runs a Stockholm-Helsingborg-Malmö-Copenhagen service.

To/From Finland
Bus Services from Luleå to Haparanda, Övertorneå and Pajala on the Swedish side are operated by Länstrafik i Norrbotten bus Nos 052, 053, and 601) and some long-distance buses run from Stockholm or Sundsvall. On the Finnish side the Matka-huolto express buses run to Tornio, Pello and Kolari (see Lapland, Getting There & Away in the Finland chapter).

Train The Luleå-Boden-Tornio link can be frustrating, sometimes serviced by the buses of Norrbottens länstrafik, sometimes by railcar (rail passes will cover any bus journeys). There are no non-bank exchange shops and no Saturday link between Haparanda and Tornio (so you have a long walk or a 70-kr taxi ride to Tornio bus station). Do not forget the time in Finland is one hour ahead of that in Sweden (see Finland, Getting There & Away). If you want to get to Helsinki with a rail pass, check which ferry company accepts it (or gives discounts).

Car & Motorbike You can easily put your car or motorbike (even cars with a caravan) on the main ferries from Stockholm to Helsinki and Turku. The northern road crossings and customs posts are always open.

To/From Norway
Bus Bus No 820 runs from Gothenburg to Oslo and at weekends bus No 879 runs from Stockholm to Oslo via Karlstad. Bus Nos 802 and 870 (at weekends) cross the border near Sälen and terminate at the village of Trysil. In Norrbotten bus No 001 runs a Kiruna-Riksgränsen service but stops at the border.

Train The main railway links are those from Stockholm to Oslo via Hallsberg, from Gothenburg (Malmö) to Oslo, from Sundsvall (Gävle) to Trondheim and from Luleå to Narvik. Winter-sport traffic can be heavy at the top end of Malmbanan and may make seat bookings prudent.

SEA
To/From Denmark
The ferry links to Copenhagen and Helsingør in most cases have connections with other forms of transport and can carry all vehicles. The exception is the hydrofoils of Flygbåtarna, a 45-minute Malmö-Copenhagen shuttle, although the Malmö-Dragør

(Swedish: Dragör) service of SFL is little slower and cheaper.

From Malmö the Flygbåtarna (Danish: Flyvebådene) hydrofoils commute to Copenhagen at least hourly from 5 am to 1 am, although summer departures from Copenhagen run as late as 4 am. City Jet Line, Pilen, Shopping Linje, and the restaurant boats of Copenhagen Line also depart daily (except Sundays) from Skeppsbron. The SAS hovercraft for Kastrup airport near Copenhagen leave from Skeppsbron 10, beyond the hydrofoil terminal. SFL runs services to Dragør from the Limhamn ferry terminal (take bus Nos 12A and 19A).

From Helsingborg, SFL car ferries shuttle at least twice an hour and the railway ferries dock near the main station. Sundsbussarna depart for Helsingør every 15 or 20 minutes from Hamntorget. The ScandLines shuttle-bus takes 20 minutes and Sundskatten 15 minutes.

Stena Line cruises from Gothenburg to Frederikshavn daily and takes just over three hours. Small concerns run services from Halmstad and Varberg to Grenå, car and restaurant ferries from Landskrona to Copenhagen and from Helsingborg to Tuborg near Copenhagen.

Going to Bornholm, Bornholmstrafikken and Bornholms Express sail daily from Östersjöterminalen Ystad to Rønne (three hours). The number of services increases from June to August and Cars and caravans are carried.

To/From Finland

Viking Line cruises direct from Stockholm to Helsinki overnight (14 hours), but offers alternative services between Stockholm, Mariehamn, and Turku (around 11 hours), and between Kapellskär, Mariehamn, and Naantali (eight hours). All services carry vehicles and operate all year. Silja operates from Stockholm to Helsinki (up to 16 hours) and from Stockholm to Turku (13½ hours). These big carriers offer bus links to cities in both countries.

Ånedin-linjen sails from Skeppsbron in the centre of Stockholm to Mariehamn five times a week from April to December (no vehicles). Birka's Mariehamn service carries vehicles and runs all year except early in January. Eckerö linjen sails from Grisslehamn near Stockholm to Eckerö (Åland) from late March until December. Jakob Lines sails from Umeå to Pietarsaari in Finland (Swedish: Jakobstad) and from Skellefteå to Jakobstad or Kokkola (Swedish: Karleby) in Finland between mid-May and mid-December (vehicles are carried).

Wasa Line sails to Vaasa from Sundsvall and Umeå and from Skellefteå to Jakobstad or Kokkola between May and the end of August.

Kristina Cruises sails from June to August, from Norrköping to Helsinki and return on cruises and includes Riga on its Visby-Helsinki route. Polish Baltic Shipping Company sails a round trip (up to 19 hours) from Oxelösund near Nyköping to Helsinki once a week all year.

To/From Norway

From Helsingborg, Scandinavian Seaways cruises to Oslo from Sundsterminalen every evening.

To/From Germany

TT-Line sails from Trelleborg to Travemünde daily and the journey takes seven hours, but the TS-Line Trelleborg-Sassnitz service takes less than four hours and is cheaper. TR-Line is a Trelleborg-Rostock service and Scarlett Line links Ystad with Mukran near Sassnitz. Stena Line cruises from Gothenburg to Kiel each evening, taking 14 hours. Vehicles are carried on these ferries.

From Malmö, Nordö-Link goes to Travemünde from Stockholmskajen but Euroway's parallel service continues to Lübeck. Baltic Express has services from Nynäshamn to Kiel (25 hours).

To/From the Netherlands

Scandinavian Seaways sails from Gothenburg to Amsterdam twice weekly and carries vehicles.

To/From Poland

Polish Baltic Shipping Company cruises twice daily from Ystad to Swinoujście (daily, nine hours) and from Ystad and Oxelösund to Gdańsk (one round trip a week, about 18 hours). From Karlskrona, Polen Ferries cruises overnight to Gdynia.

To/From the Baltic States & Russia

Estline sails overnight between Stockholm and Tallinn in Estonia (cheaper Sundays to Thursdays). Baltic Express has St Petersburg cruises from Stockholm and Nynäshamn and Riga (Latvia) cruises from Stockholm. Sally Lines' summer cruises stop at Visby, Helsinki, St Petersburg and Tallinn.

To/From the UK

Scandinavian Seaways sails Gothenburg-Harwich and Gothenburg-Newcastle. The trip takes 24 hours or more.

LEAVING SWEDEN

To collect tax refunds on gifts and souvenirs when leaving Sweden you must go to the tax-free collection counters at airport halls and ferry terminals with documents and the items. At Arlanda airport, counters are in halls A and B and there is a check desk in the departure hall. Many points have no desk or customs stamp, so check your departure point beforehand (see Consumer Taxes in the Facts for the Visitor section of this chapter).

Getting Around

Bus and train are the likeliest tourist modes of transport: they carry passengers to every corner of Sweden for at least part of the year. Discount schemes combining bus and train fares can cut a great deal from your costs, so you should ask about possible discounts before paying full price, at least on bus, rail or ferries, where free or half-price passages are offered for some cards and routes.

ISIC discounts are few and varied and visiting students generally will pay full fares unless they explore other deals. Pensioners are luckier and should conduct thorough interviews at tourist offices or ticket windows before paying up (Rail Europ S cards commonly discounts by 30% or 50%). Some good deals are listed (following) by section.

Disabled people will find special services and adapted facilities of a generally high standard (particularly in new railway wagons, which use lifts with 225 kg capacity). Taxi drivers are briefed to deal with collapsible wheelchairs and almost everywhere guide dogs can be taken with few restrictions. For details the Sveriges Turistråd book *Holiday Guide for the Disabled* is recommended (see Accommodation in the Sweden Facts for the Visitor section).

AIR

SAS internal daily flights serve Malmö, as far north as Luleå and Kiruna, and there are flights from Stockholm to Gothenburg every hour. SAS also flies to Copenhagen from Jönköping, Kalmar, Norrköping, Västerås and Växjö. Linjeflyg is a sister internal network, covering smaller destinations. Conditional discounts with Linjeflyg allow spouses or children to travel accompanied for no more than 350 kr return. Passengers under 26 years of age can pick up casual vacancies for single journeys at discount rates. There are also return and scheduled discount flights cutting prices by up to 65% if you book. Sometimes children can fly for half-fare.

Seats on the last SAS Stockholm-Gothenburg plane each night can be snapped up casually for 200 kr.

Tickets can be bought at Upptäck Sverige at Stureplan in Stockholm or travel agents. For local airport taxis and buses see To/From the Airport in the particular Getting Around sections.

BUS

Länstrafik (county regional service) is the basis of Swedish local transport and the services are designed for those needs. So services may seem to wander or will vary in frequency and route number according to the hour or time of year. Read days and times carefully from the timetable and check again when you board, especially on public holidays and during the Midsummer weekend.

A cross on the timetable usually means the bus will stop only on request, and a vertical line shows no stop on that journey. Nattrafik (night buses) and lågtrafik (off-peak) is common part or all of the night in the cities. Timetables are available at the railway and bus stations. SJ also uses buses to connect some towns with rail services.

Local and regional traffic tends to use systems of validated *kuponger* (coupons) in zones (often as magnetic cards) and any discount cards can be cómpared for value on the basis of the standard kupong price. For longer services and tour buses, there are the big Swebus in Gothenburg (with express and weekend services throughout the country) and Svenska Buss, which runs weekend buses in the southern half of the country only. Linjebuss (from Sundsvall) and the postbuses of Postens Diligenstrafik operate to and around Norrland. Timetables for these buses are available at bus stations and tourist offices. Svenska Buss (☎ 08-14 37 20) and Snabbuss (☎ 0922-129 55) are two services which require advance seat reservations.

Pensioners qualify for 30% discounts on SJ express buses, and holders of the European Youth Card can travel on Swebus weekend services for half-fare.

TRAIN

The Swedish national railways SJ (Statens järnvägar) runs intercity and express services (often you must reserve seats for a fee of 20 kr, but ask first).There are also regional trains and the futuristic X2000 fast trains, which are in daily Stockholm-Gothenburg service at speeds up to 200 km/h, cutting the travelling time to three hours or less (1st-class premium is 265 kr, 2nd-class 137 kr). A 1st-class intercity ticket or rail pass gets you a free cup of coffee.

There are normally restaurant cars on long routes; 2nd-class couchettes and 1st-class sleeper compartments are available on the main north-south long routes (to Narvik and

Luleå). Some trains have car transporters during the summer peak which cost 25 kr for each 10 km. Ordinary bicycles cost 75 kr.

Sleeper charges vary from 80 to 900 kr for individual compartments with shower and toilet. All options are marked on national timetables, issued as books (5 kr) three times a year. Play wagons with facilities for children are running on several intercity services.

When buying tickets ask for 1st class if you want it, it's not always available on short services. You can buy tickets at all stations and some travel agencies, but phone bookings are possible. At most stations you can use a touch-sensitive map and get price information and times in English for all trips. To buy on board will cost 25 kr extra.

The international passes Inter-Rail, Eurail pass, Nordturist, Scanrail and Rail Europ S are accepted on SJ services. Inter-Rail senior passes cost 1850 kr for 15 days and 2650 kr for a month, Nordturist costs 1680 kr travelling 2nd class for 21 days (under 26 year olds pay 30% less). They are available at the SJ ticket office at Stockholm Central or the many agencies at main stations.

Normal fares are reasonable at a ceiling of around 1200/750 kr for 1st/2nd class, Stockholm-Malmö costs about 500 kr (2nd class) but discounts are not hard to find. There is travel for half a 2nd-class fare (for a minimum of 84 kr) on *röda avgångar* or off-peak single services marked in red on the timetables, but to use them you must buy the Reslustkort at a station. The card, valid for a year, costs 250 kr and offers half-price 2nd class travel for six weeks from late June and 25% discounts in 2nd class on Tuesdays, Wednesdays, Thursdays and Saturdays. Two children under 12 years old can travel free with an adult and those aged from 12 to 16 years pay half-fares.

Holders of Rail Europ S cards pay 50% of all fares and pensioners travel for a 30% discount.

If changing to or from regional trains or buses (not Inlandsbanan), you can book connections with SJ services and claim any discounts on the joint price. Otherwise the only discounts on these networks are local or for multiple or day tickets, which may include bus connections. Do not expect international rail passes to be valid on these, although Pågatågen and Bohus Trafik are two exceptions.

To travel Inlandsbanan 1000 km from Mora to Gällivare costs 300 kr a single, but a special card allows two weeks' unlimited travel on the route for 700 kr (including regional bus connections and discounts from Gällivare to Narvik) and a day-section card costs 110 kr. Service on this line is slow (14 hours direct from Östersund to Gällivare) but so is that on the 'main' line from south to north, where only SJ night trains operate (the best place to change between Sundsvall and Boden/Luleå is at Ånge). The trains on the Malmbanan line from Narvik to Luleå are not famous for punctuality, by contrast with most SJ services, (regional trains are better but are not shown on the SJ national timetable).

In summer narrow-gauge passenger cars operate on little-used lines such as the Smålspåret Västervik-Växjö service (about 160 kr for a full trip).

Station luggage lockers cost between 10 and 25 kr for 24 hours, depending on their vintage (machines or ticket counters should provide change). Check that the station building (or left-luggage room, if there are no lockers) will be open when you want to collect: some places close just after the last arrival or departure and weekend hours, outside the cities and in winter, may be short.

TAXI

The flagfall for taxis can be 10 or 20 kr in cities, but rates are higher in smaller towns so that journeys of five km can cost up to 100 kr. To book in advance may cost 40 kr. Women can ride at discount rates at night with some Stockholm lines.

CAR & MOTORBIKE

The good road network and the excellent E-class motorways are far from crowded except at the height of summer in the south. You need only a recognised full licence to

drive in Sweden, an international licence is unnecessary (unless you want to rent a car).

If your vehicle breaks down, telephone the local number (listed in the directory) of the Larmtjänst 24-hour towing service. According to law, in case of an accident exchange names and details with other drivers or the property owners involved although injuries and serious accidents should be reported to police (on no account move any car before the police arrive). Insurance Green Cards are not necessary but will give peace of mind.

In the far north reindeer and elk are road hazards around dawn and dusk. They wander near roads and car horns will rarely shift them, although signs warn of the worst areas. Reindeer should be considered as property and elk to be protected animals. If there's an accident ask for help at the nearest house (a badly injured animal may need to be destroyed by someone with the proper permit). Report incidents to police, because you have no charge to fear other than that associated with a failure to do so. Sandboxes on many roads may be a help in mud or snow. The national motoring association is Motormännens Riksförbund (☎ 08-67 05 80), Sturegatan 32, 10240 Stockholm.

Road Rules

In Sweden you drive on the right and give way to the right. Headlights should be dipped but must be on at all times when travelling on the roads. Seat belts must be worn in all seats, children under seven years old should be in appropriate harnesses or in child seats, if fitted.

You cannot afford to drink and drive as the blood-alcohol limit is stringent at 0.02%. The normal maximum speed in the open is 110 km/h, but this falls to 90 km/h in summer in most areas (except the northern half of Norrland). Speeds in built-up areas are 50 or 70 km/h, depending on the red-and-yellow speed signs. The general speed limit for cars towing caravans is 70 km/h (40 km/h if the caravans don't have brakes).

Most road signs match international standards. Give way to pedestrians on zebra crossings and cyclists crossing at cycle tracks (marked by broken lines either side). On motorways broken lines define wide paved edges, and the vehicle being overtaken is expected to ease into this area to allow faster traffic to pass comfortably.

Petrol is cheaper at 24-hour automatic pumps operated with notes (*sedel*) of 50 or 100 kr. Otherwise most service stations are staffed self-service outlets.

Rental

Car rental with the international chains is expensive (climbing to 1000 kr a day for medium-sized sedans for short rental periods) although railway and airline packages can bring some savings. Weekend and summer packages are also offered at discount rates which can be better but are not always available at airport branches. Generally rental is cheaper per day over a week or more.

Basic small cars cost from 150 to 200 kr per day (plus 1.65 kr per km), although the Happy Rental national chain (☎ 0 59 59 12) at the Globen stadium charges as little as 99 kr a day and offers low rates per km for the smallest model car and some small operators offer similar rates. SJ offers a rental package service from about 50 stations at rates from 600 kr for a weekend.

To rent a car it is commonly required that you be at least 19 years of age (or older to rent a big model) and you often need to show an international licence.

Two rules of thumb are: plan to rent for as long as you can (for more than one month the daily rates sink by up to 60%) and avoid renting at the airports. The airport stations are excluded by companies from special and weekend packages.

MC-huset (☎ 040-21 04 35), at Jägershillsgatan 6, 201 21 Malmö will rent motorbikes for up to a week from 1395 to 2495 kr (with 3500 kr deposit) plus 65 öre per km. Honda MC-center (☎ 08-23 51 98), Vanadisvägen 6, 11346 Stockholm, rents 250-cc models for 1430 kr a week or 4570 kr a month on a 1000 kr deposit.

Purchase

The used-car columns of *Dagens Nyheter* on Thursdays are best for car hunting, although anything under 10,000 kr will be at least 10 years old and well-used. If you think you have been ripped off, ask Konsumentverket (☎ 08-759 83 00), Sorterargatan 26, Box 503, 162 15 Vällingby about your rights.

BICYCLE

The motorways are not open to cyclists, but the long, specially designed and scenic cycle routes (on which mopeds are also allowed) are better. They link up with main roads at the edge of towns and the cycle-track networks in the cities (for which tourist offices can usually provide maps). The network takes you on generally good surfaces from town to town and you can escape to the minor roads to take in sights. The booklet *Discover Sweden by Bike* gives an overview and brochures are available for most routes from Cykelsällskapet, Box 6006, 16406 Kista (see Cycling, in the Activities section of Sweden, Facts for the Visitor). You must turn on lamps after dusk and extra reflectors are advisable (though not mandatory for travellers).

Bicycles can be carried as registered luggage on SJ trains for 75 kr (book three days ahead in summer), or for 200 kr if there is some urgency. Bicycles are allowed on the SL trains of Stockholm, Pågatågen in Skåne and the local railways of Gothenburg, but not during rush time. Dismantled bicycles, however, can be taken with other luggage into your compartment. On ferries sometimes there's a fee for bicycles which can be be taken as luggage or on deck for short crossings. Taxis can usually oblige with carrying bikes and länstrafik can generally stow a few at a time on the bus, but town or city buses generally cannot accept them.

A variant is the *dressin* or pedal-powered rail trolley, which can be hired for use on one of several old, closed railway lines (ask at tourist offices). They are mostly used for short jaunts, but in Dalarna and Värmland you can take on routes of 50 to 90 km. Sometimes a dressin leg is included in bicycle-tour packages.

Hire generally costs about 50 kr a day for ungeared bicycles or from 200 to 250 kr a week. If you want to buy second-hand try the bicycle workshops in university towns first. Solid models can be found for less than 1000 kr.

HITCHING

Hitching is not so popular in Sweden, where the consensus is that you have less luck getting lifts (winter weather can make it impossible). Perhaps the truck drivers are likeliest to oblige, but they tend to stay on motorways, which are off-limits to hitch-hikers. The best pick-up areas are outside main towns before the motorways begin.

BOAT

Mariners should get the annual guide *Båtturist* for 65 kr from STF, which lists all visitors' harbours and prices. Overnight fees for the harbours are commonly about 80 kr, though facilities vary.

Lake & Canal Ferries

The canals provide cross-country routes linking the main lakes and there are several services into Uppland from Mälaren (see Stockholm). The longest cruise is on the Göta canal from near Stockholm across to Gothenburg (running from May to mid-September, which takes four days and includes the lakes in between at fares of more than 4500 kr a bed (and more for single cabins). Rederiaktiebolaget Göta Kanal (☎ 08-80 63 15) operates over the whole distance, but day trips or sections are also available.

Archipelago Ferry

From Stockholm and Gothenburg, most of these ferry services run only in summer. You can cruise from Stockholm to Oskarshamn down the island-dotted east coast with KustLinjen (☎ 08-24 94 70).

TOURS

The packages offered by big concerns such as SAS, SJ, the ferry companies, STF and the affiliated local tourist offices are many and various, designed to suit general or special interests and usually include accommodation or transport.

Books are usually available in English if you write (see Tourist Offices in the Sweden Facts for the Visitor section). The Upptäck Sverige shop in Stockholm specialises in tours and bookings and has the best range of literature.

Other useful concerns are Swebus (see Buses in the Sweden Getting Around section) and the guide organisations Sveriges Guideförbund (☎ 011-39 24 20), Skottsätter, 61800 Kolmården and the Scandinavian Guide Service (☎ 042-14 84 65).

Stockholm

The name Stockholm goes back at least to the 1250s and the regent Birger Jarl is remembered for fortifying the old town in this period. Stockholm was and is ideally suited to trade and maritime connections, protected from the open seas (but hardly from the Baltic winds) by the archipelago or *skärgården*. The town spread out on similar island formations, pushed up and filled out over centuries, and spilled out to accommodate the million or so people who live in Greater Stockholm now. The city is indeed best when seen from the water (thus the silly 'Venice of the north' tag) but you'll enjoy seeing the parklands of Djurgården or the alleys of Gamla Stan on foot.

Orientation

The modern centre of the city is Norrmalm, focused on the ugly Sergels torg. This is the business and shopping hub and is linked by a network of subways to the central station and the gardens of Kungsträdgården, popular and packed in summer. The subways link with the metro (T-banan) stations.

The triangular island Stadsholmen and its appendages is the old centre Gamla Stan, separated from Norrmalm by the narrow channels of Norrström around the royal palace but connected by several bridges. To the west of this is the lake Mälaren.

On the south side the main bridge Centralbron and the Slussen interchange connect the southern part of the city Södermalm and its spine Götgatan. From its top end the giant golf ball of the stadium Globen is the southern landmark, although you will cross water again at Skanstull before reaching it.

To the east of Gamla Stan is the small island Skeppsholmen, and further down Strandvägen and past the berths you cross to Djurgården, topped by Skansen, where the tower Kaknästornet dominates from the north (see Views).

Information

There is a telephone information service (☎ 22 18 40) in English giving all events. The best overall guide is the monthly *Stockholm This Week*, available free at tourist offices, which includes events and a shopping, restaurant and accommodation guide. For a little more background buy *Discover Stockholm* for 35 kr.

For help with archipelago visits and accommodation, *Skärgårdsguiden* lists boat services, camp sites, hotels and hostels and the 1:250,000 activities map *Utflyktskarta Stockholms län* is a pocket reference (10 kr) for attractions around Greater Stockholm. The black pocket softcover guide *Hur, Var?* has a full route guide to Stockholm transport and services and is available from the Pressbyrån or tobacconists for 70 kr.

The Friday supplement *Gajden* in *Svenska Dagbladet* covers all events and has a detailed museum guide with all opening times. The Saturday *Dagens Nyheter* guide *På Stan* or the *Puls* guide in Friday's *Expressen* covers all arts, music and entertainment. The monthly free paper *Nöjesguide* concentrates on contemporary music, theatre, film and pubs.

For information about culture and the arts go to the ground-floor information counter (☎ 700 01 42) in Kulturhuset on Sergels torg. For student activities go to the University of Stockholm's union, Nobelhusen, Frescativägen 14, open to 4.30 pm on weekdays (metro: Universitetet).

Tourist Offices The main tourist office is the Stockholm Information Service (☎ 789 20 00, weekends ☎ 789 24 18) on the ground floor of Sverigehuset in Kungsträdgården on Hamngatan. Literature here deals with outdoor activities as well as sights and tours for which you can can book. It is open daily all year from 9 am to 5 pm (to 2 pm at weekends) and in summer from 8.30 am to 6 pm weekdays (to 5 pm at weekends). Upstairs you'll find the Sweden Bookshop and information in English about Swedish life provided by the Swedish Institute. You can park nearby on Regeringsgatan or take the metro to Kungsträdgården.

Other tourist offices are Hotellcentralen at tunnel level in the central station, where you also book accommodation and some sightseeing tours (closed weekends from September to May); at Kaknästornet (open daily until 10.30 pm from mid-April to mid-September) and through the courtyard at Stadshuset (open daily from May to November).

For tour information and brochures about all of Sweden, go to the Upptäck Sverige 'Discover Sweden' shop (☎ 611 74 30) at Stureplan 8, open on weekdays from 10 am to 6 pm, Saturdays 11 am to 3 pm. You can book air tickets and tour packages and browse through information about favourite activities there.

Outside Stockholm, offices are at Järnvägsgatan 2, Nynäshamn (open all year); the old central station at Södertälje (open from June to mid-August) or the nearby Nämndhus at Järnagatan 12; the ferry station at Grisslehamn (open in summer) and at Söderhamnsplan on Vaxholm (open all year). Small offices are open on the archipelago from June to August on Dalarö, Utö and Värmdö and at Älmsta.

Stockholm Card This will cover all needs of transport and sightseeing for an adult and two children aged under 18. Cards cost 135/270/405 kr for one/two/three days. For getting around you can have free travel on buses, metro and local trains (not airport buses), trips on the lift Katarinahissen and

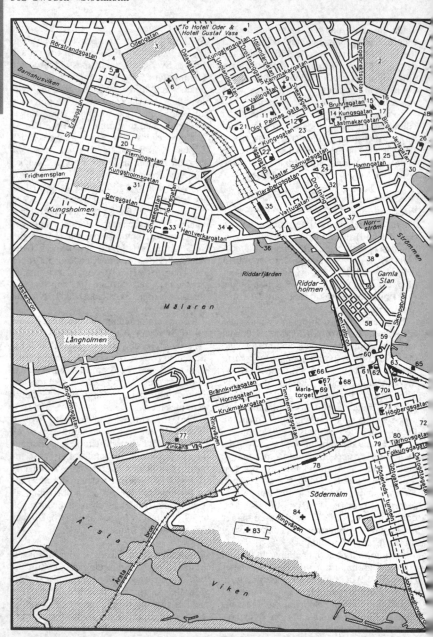

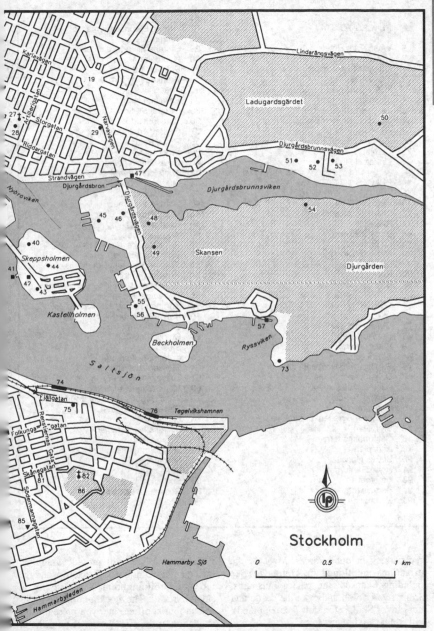

Stockholm

0   0.5   1 km

■ PLACES TO STAY

5	Wasa Park Hotell
7	Hotell Bema
11	Queen's Hotel
22	Freys Hotel
26	Hotell Örnskjöld
41	af Chapman Hostel
42	Skeppsholmen Hostel
47	Djurgårdsbrunnsviken
57	Ryssviken Marina
65	Gustaf af Klint
72	Columbus Hotell
77	Zinken Hostel

▼ PLACES TO EAT

10	Café Da Vinci
12	Svensk matkultur
14	Aktuell
66	Black & Brown
69	La Fontana
70	Old Beefeater Inn
71	Lilla Budapest
80	Kelly's
85	Blecktornskällaren

OTHER

1	Observatorielunden
2	Humlegården
3	Vasaparken
4	St Eriksplan
6	Sabbatsberg Hospital
8	Dansmuseet
9	Adolf Fredriks kyrka
13	Central Telebutik
15	Silja Line
16	'Discover Sweden' Shop
17	Stureplan
18	Östermalms torg
19	Karlaplan
20	St Erik Hospital
21	Norra Bantorget
23	Hötorget
24	Sergels torg
25	Norrmalms torg
27	Hedvig Eleonora kyrka
28	Armémuseum
29	Statens historiska museum
30	Nybroplan
31	Police Centre
32	Brunkebergs torg
33	Post Office
34	Serafim Hospital
35	Central Station
36	Stadshusbron
37	Gustav Adolfs torg
38	Royal Palace
39	Stortorget
40	Östasiatiska museet
43	Arkitekturmuseet
44	Moderna museet
45	Vasamuseet
46	Nordiska museet
48	Vattenmuseet
49	Biology Museum
50	Kaknäs tower
51	Sjöhistoriska museet
52	Tekniska museet
53	Folkens Museum Etnografiska
54	Rosendals slott
55	Gröna Lund Tivoli
56	Djurgårdsstaden
58	Kornhamnstorg
59	Karl Johans torg
60	Birka Line
61	Stadsmuseet
62	Slussen
63	Katarinahissen Lift
64	Slussen Bus Station
67	Leksaksmuseet
68	Maria Magdalena kyrka
73	Prins Eugens Waldemarsudde
74	Stadsgårdsterminal
75	Fjällgatan
76	Viking Line Terminal
78	Södra Station
79	Medborgarplatsen
81	Nytorget
82	Sofia kyrka
83	Söder Hospital
84	Rosenlund Hospital
86	Vita Berget

free parking in public areas. Most of the attractions mentioned in Things to See including Skansen, the palace museums, Gröna Lund Tivoli and even the castle and museum at Skokloster slott (see Uppland), will admit card holders free.

The tourist bus will provide unlimited travel; sightseeing boats, a free trip; and the ferry to Drottningholm, a return trip at single-fare rate. The Stockholm card is available at tourist offices and you present it for validation at the first venue. If you like to move around and see museums, it will be worthwhile (if only for convenience) but plan your sightseeing, add an estimate of travel costs and decide.

Money City bank branches are open from 9 or 9.30 am to 5 or 5.30 pm (others may close at 3 pm). The cheapest exchange is at the Forex bank at ground level in the central station, open from 8 am to 9 pm daily, from 7 am in summer. It costs 10 kr per cheque. At the post centre in the station you will pay 35 kr. A Forex counter is open at City-terminalen from 9 am to 7 pm weekdays, and at Värta Hamnen.

You can also exchange money at the central post office on Vasagatan or Valuta-specialisten at Kungsgatan 30 on Saturdays, or at Upptäck Sverige at Stureplan. At Arlanda airport you can change money daily from 6.30 am to 10.30 pm. American Express is at Birger Jarlsgatan 1.

Post & Telecommunications The central post office and poste restante is at Vasagatan 28, open weekdays from 8 am to 6.30 pm. The postal centre at the central station is open most holidays and until 10 pm weekdays and 7 pm at weekends. The central Telebutik is at Kungsgatan 36 and the central station Telecenter is open daily from 8 am to 9 pm (better and cheaper for overseas calls). The telephone code for Stockholm is 08.

Foreign Embassies See Sweden, Facts for the Visitor.

Cultural Centres The main information centres are Kulturhuset and the Swedish Institute at Sverigehuset above the tourist office. Look also at the hall in the National-museum (see the following Museums section). Also at Kulturhuset is a reading room with periodicals and newspapers from all over the world which you can read free.

Travel Agencies The STF central office and travel bureau is at Drottninggatan 31 (closed weekends and from 1 pm the day before public holidays) there you can join, buy books and reserve tour packages. For student discount bookings go to SFS-Resor at Kungsgatan 4.

Laundry Laundry options are limited and it is best to find a hotel or hostel with facilities or a fast washing service. The washing services are not fast, taking a week or longer (for around 40 kr per kg). You might get your laundry done in two days (sometimes 'faster') at Farsta Snabbtvätt (☎ 94 97 60) at Farstagränd 1, Farsta. City Tvätt Staffan at Sveavägen 106 has a one-week service (around 40 kr per kg).

Bookshops For maps and guidebooks go to Nya Akademibokhandeln on the corner of Mäster Samuelsgatan and Regeringsgatan. It's three minutes' walk from Sverigehuset.

There are many English paperbacks and a useful information counter. The Sweden Bookshop (see the previous Stockholm Tourist Offices section for the address) has the broadest selection of thematic books. For newspapers and paperbacks in English try the Pressbyrån at the central station. Bok och Bild at the front of Kulturhuset has books of artistic and cultural interest.

Emergency The central 24-hour pharmacy is at Klarabergsgatan 64. The clinic City Akuten (☎ 11 71 02) at Holländargatan 2 receives casualties from around the city. At night, in emergencies, contact the duty doctor (☎ 644 92 00). In the suburbs seek the nearest municipal medical centres listed in the green pages of the telephone directory or try Information Stockholm (☎ 785 81 90) during business hours (except Friday afternoons).

Hospitals near the city are Sabbatsberg and Sankt Erik (north-west of the central station), Söder and Rosenlund (on Ring-vägen in Södermalm) and Roslagstull (on Valhallavägen, directly north of the city).

Dentists are on duty at Sankt Eriks, Flemminggatan 22, from 8 am to 7 pm daily (for acute cases up to 9 pm). Overnight contact the duty dentist (☎ 644 92 00) for advice. The free general emergency number is 90 000.

The police are near to the central station behind Cityterminalen, Bryggargatan 19 and Tulegatan 4. Police headquarters (☎ 769 30 00) is at Agnegatan 33. The police lost-property office (☎ 769 30 00) is at Bergsgatan 39. The central station's lost property is on the lower level. For motor vehicle breakdowns and towing contact Larmtjänst (☎ 020-91 00 40).

Things to See

Many of Stockholm's sights are closed on Mondays, so plan on mainly being in the open air then. Children under 16 are generally admitted for half-price to sights and museums and small children can usually enter free if accompanied by a paying adult.

Walking Tour The best walking tour is the one you can do yourself with the recommended books (see Stockholm Information). Sverigehuset is a good starting point for either of the proposed walks. To Gamla Stan, walk south through **Kungsträdgården** and turn west at the opera house to **Gustav Adolfs torg** and cross the bridges to the palace area and **Slottsbacken**. Move past **Storkyrkan** to **Stortorget**, get onto Västerlånggatan and follow it to **Järntorget**. Then follow Österlånggatan back to the palace area and go underground to the **Medeltidsmuseum** (Medieval Museum) (see Museums).

The Djurgården walk will be a longer strand-and-park stroll of several km and is at least a morning's adventure. Pass **Nybroplan**, by the graceful buildings and boats along Strandvägen to **Djurgårdsbron**, where you cross and pass **Nordiska museet** to the west. With **Skansen** to the east, continue through the park to the period houses of **Djurgårdsstaden**. After that you have the choice of going south to **Waldemarsudde**, the garden and mill, or to the north (a park walk) to **Rosendals slott**. If you have run out of time or breath take a bus back from Skansen (bus No 44 or 47).

Gamla Stan The island where Stockholm began has attracted habitation since the early hunting and fishing economies (even though it was much smaller then). The city emerged in the 13th century and took on the newer pursuits of trade and the accents of its German guests from the Hanse. It grew with Sweden's power until the 17th century, when the castle of Tre Kronor, symbol of that power, was burned to the ground. The present **palace** dates from the mid-18th century.

It was in this period that the town quarters were named from classical traditions and mythology rather than from the Norse. Most streets are medieval enough, still winding along their 14th century lines and linked by a fantasy of lanes, arches and stairways. This environment lends itself to restaurants (often in medieval cellars and elegantly priced), ice-cream cafés and all manner of galleries and gift shops. The cartouches and their dates over the doors map the architectural tradition for the strolling traveller: to bring a car to Gamla Stan is impractical, so use the Gamla Stan metro station. The colourful Esselte *Gamla Stan Map & Guide* (36 kr) will also help.

On the adjacent Riddarholmen is **Riddarholmskyrkan**, no longer a church but the royal necropolis and displayed armorial glory of the knights of the Serafim order. See the **sarcophagus** of Gustaf II Adolf, Sweden's mightiest monarch, and the massed wall-plates displaying the arms of the members of the order. There are so many exhibits that they must be rotated in twos and threes for display. Entry is 10 kr. The church is open daily to 3 pm from May to August, on Wednesdays and weekends in September.

The old hub is **Stortorget**, scene of the brutal murders of the Sture vice-regal faction by the treacherous Danish king Christian II in 1520; it moved the Vasas and their supporters to throw off the foreign yoke forever. There is the old **stock exchange** building in the shadow of the coronation cathedral **Storkyrkan**, where Sankt Göran has toyed with the dragon for 500 years. One strong reminder of the medieval German influence is the German church **Tyska kyrkan**, but the ornate **Riddarhuset** in Dutch Baroque style at Riddarhustorget 10 is perhaps the most attractive of the buildings. Inside, the collection of more than 2000 arms is a who's who of Swedish history (20 kr, open weekdays from 11.30 am to 12.30 pm only).

Royal Palace The **apartments** behind the Renaissance exteriors are open daily (except Mondays) until 3 pm. Admission costs 25 kr. The **royal armoury** combines coaches and costumes to survey the story of the royal livery (40 kr, enter from Slottsbacken). The **regalia** on show is a sample collection, open daily until 4 pm (25 kr, enter from Slottsbacken).

Skansen This was perhaps the world's first open-air museum, certainly it pioneered the type and its influence on other Scandinavian museums is visible and profound. Entry is free but it is worth buying the guide in English (35 kr) to understand the themes displayed. Village conditions are reproduced and the birds wander with little concern around the crowds. The point to Skansen is that it gathers its exhibits from all over Sweden, so if you see only one open-air museum, let this be it.

The folk culture of the past is the strongest theme, but the attached **zoo** is no small affair and you can see the brown bears, wolves and lynx in their enclosures. The **aquarium** is also a must. Folk-dancing is demonstrated during summer and a more modern touch is the small **forestry pavilion**. The hilltop location is part of the attraction, but the lazy can take the railway (20 kr) to the top and make their own way down. Take bus No 47 from the central station or the summer ferry services from Nybroplan or Slussen, because the parking is limited during the week and prohibited at weekends, when Djurgårdsvägen is closed to traffic.

Djurgården This is the real garden of Stockholm, the sanest of places, although its topsy-turvy history as both zoo and a hunting park reflects the swinging tastes of the absolutist monarchs. The abiding impression is of a rambling range with postcard settings, such as the manor house **Rosendals slott** (30 kr, open from June to August except Mondays) or **Prins Eugens Waldemarsudde**, where the gallery has a focus on Scandinavian painting (30 kr, closed Mondays). But do not neglect the period houses of Djurgårdstaden on the western side and you can fill in half a day just wandering about for free.

Museums There are more than enough museums covering all manner of specialities and not all are noted here. Make intelligent use of a Stockholm card and note free admission at some venues one day a week. Several are also open late on Wednesdays.

Musikmuseet, Sibyllegatan 2, is the best presented of the small collections and you can handle some instruments from all periods – they're the ones specially marked in green. Admission costs 20 kr (closed on Mondays). On Sunday afternoons, wander around the corner to the yard of the royal stables **Kungliga hovstallet** on Väpnargatan (open from 1 to 3 pm, except in July and August).

The famous museum **Vasamuseet**, on the west shore of Djurgården, allows you simultaneously to look into the lives of 17th century sailors and to appreciate a brilliant achievement in marine archaeology. The flagship *Wasa* went almost straight to the bottom when launched and the literature or tour guides will explain the extraordinary 300-year story of its death and resurrection without a shot fired (30 kr, open daily, bus Nos 44 and 47). In front of the *Wasa* at Djurgårdsbron is the folk collection of **Nordiska museet**, depicting home life since the Middle Ages (30 kr, closed Mondays from September to May).

Aquaria Vattenmuseum, on Djurgårdsvägen near Gröna Lund, is an all-senses experience in aqua-ecology (40 kr, closed from October to April and some Mondays).

The **Biology Museum** on Djurgården near Nordiska museet explains the animals of the north and their place in the wild (6 kr, open daily). More comprehensive is the

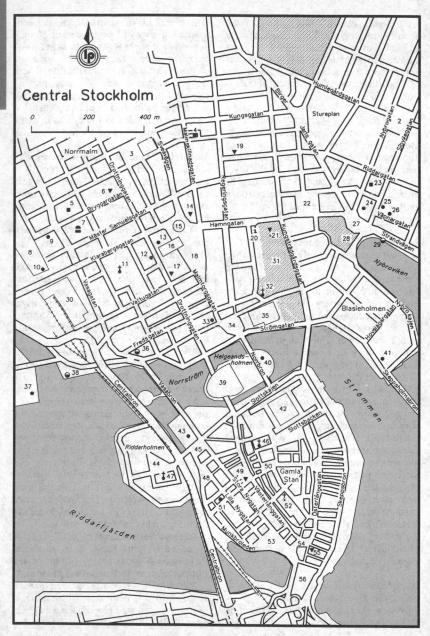

Central Stockholm

0   200   400 m

Norrmalm

Stureplan

Kungsgatan

Riddargatan

Vapnargatan

Strandvägen

Nybroviken

Nybrokajen

Blasieholmen

Hamngatan

Helgeands-
holmen

Norrström

Strömmen

Slottskajen

Slottsbacken

Riddarholmen

Gamla
Stan

Riddarfjärden

Munkbroleden

■ PLACES TO STAY

5 Freys Hotel
23 Hotell Örnskjöld

▼ PLACES TO EAT

6 Café London
14 Sergels Pärla
17 City Hallen
19 Gröna Linjen
21 Monarch
49 Spegeln
55 Bacchi Wapen

OTHER

1 Engelbrektsplan
2 Östermalms torg
3 Hötorget
4 Oxtorget
7 Central Post Office
8 Cityterminalen
9 Police
10 SAS Office
11 Klara kyrka
12 STF Office
13 SL Information
15 Sergels torg
16 Kulturhuset
18 Brunkebergs torg
20 Sverigehuset

22 Norrmalmstorg
24 Theatre
25 Musikmuseet
26 Kungliga hovstallet
27 Nybroplan
28 Wallenbergs torg
29 Nybrohamnen
30 Central Station
31 Kungsträdgården
32 Jakobs kyrka
33 Medelhavsmuseet
34 Gustav Adolfs torg
35 Opera
36 Tegelbacken bus stop
37 Stadshuset
38 Klara Mälarstrand boats
39 Parliament
40 Medeltidsmuseum
41 Nationalmuseum
42 Royal Palace
43 Riddarhuset
44 Birger Jarls torg
45 Riddarhustorget
46 Storkyrkan
47 Riddarholmskyrkan
48 Munkbron
50 Stortorget
51 Post Museum
52 Tyska kyrkan
53 Kornhamnstorg
54 Järntorget
56 Karl Johans torg

Natural History Museum at Frescativägen 40. Entry costs 20 kr and the museum is closed on Mondays (metro: Universitetet).

The main national historical collection, however, is at **Statens historiska museum** at Närvavägen 13. It covers archaeology and culture, particularly from the Viking Age, and also features coins. Entry is 30 kr and the museum is closed on Mondays (metro: Karlaplan).

The medieval museum, **Medeltids-museet**, at Strömparterren beside the palace, takes you below ground to examine the remains of medieval Stockholm in the proper place (20 kr, closed Mondays and open Wednesdays to 8 pm). Guided tours in English are at 1 pm.

More classical in taste are the Mediterranean collections (including items from

Egypt) in the Mediterranean Museum, **Medelhavsmuseet**, at Fredsgatan 2 near Kungsträdgården (30 kr, closed Mondays).

The **Post Museum** at Lilla Nygatan 6 in Gamla Stan is one of Europe's best collections and is free. The City Museum **Stadsmuseet** at the Slussen interchange covers Stockholm's past since the Reformation (15 kr, open daily).

The technical museum **Tekniska museet**, at Musievägen 7, (25 kr, open daily, take bus No 69 from Sergels torg) covers industrial and technical development and the **Telemuseum** is adjacent. General maritime history, so important to Stockholm, is on display nearby at the maritime museum **Sjöhistoriska museet**, Djurgårdsbrunns-vägen 24 (20 kr, open daily). The wine and liquor museum **Vin-och sprithistoriska**

museet, at Dalagatan 100, sounds eccentric but might make sense of the weird story of brännvin as a folk intoxicant and the birth of a conservative Swedish alcohol policy (20 kr, closed Mondays, metro: Odenplan or take bus No 58). The little-known martial past of Sweden is revealed at the army museum, **Armémuseum** at Riddargatan 13. The cost is 15 kr (Sundays free) and the museum is closed on Mondays. Films in English on military history are often shown. The architecture museum **Arkitekturmuseet** has shifting exhibits as well as the Swedish and international context (20 kr, Thursdays free, closed Mondays).

The ethnographic museum **Folkens Museum Etnografiska**, Djurgårdsbrunnsvägen 34, is strong on collections from Third World cultures and holds thematic exhibitions. The cost is 20 kr and the museum is closed on Mondays (take bus No 69).

The Oriental museum **Östasiatiska museet** on Skeppsholmen displays past and present with ceramics and crafts of beauty from the East. The cost is 30 kr (students 15 kr, Wednesdays free) and the museum is closed on Mondays.

The dance museum **Dansmuseet**, Barnhusgatan 12, claims to be unique and covers all aspects of staging and costume.

The toy museum **Leksaksmuseum**, at Mariatorget 1C, is an oversized fantasy nursery full of whatever you probably wanted as a child. Admission costs 25 kr (children 10 kr) and the museum is closed on Mondays.

Churches In the centre of the city south of Klarabergsgatan, is **Klara kyrka** with free organ and choral concerts a speciality at almost any time of year. The 'soul' of Stockholm, the balladeer Carl Michael Bellman, rests in the churchyard. The Renaissance portals of **Jakobs kyrka** at the south end of Kungsträdgården are fine examples of the type.

At the north end of town are the impressive **Gustav Vasa kyrka** on Karlbergsvägen near Odenplan, and **Adolf Fredriks kyrka** on Sveavägen in 18th century Rococo style

has vault paintings depicting the suffering of Christ. There is a monument to the brilliant Enlightenment thinker René Descartes, who succumbed, according to legend, to Queen Christina's punishing pre-dawn mathematics tutorials. **Hedvig Eleonora kyrka** near Östermalms torg and **Sofia kyrka** and the period village surrounding the hill **Vita Berget** in Södermalm are slices of the 18th century.

Art Museums There are regular exhibitions of the visual arts at **Kulturhuset** and many small galleries. Of the popular attractions **Millesgården**, at Carl Milles väg 2, Lidingö, the outdoor sculpture collection by Carl Milles, is the most singular (30 kr, open daily, summer Wednesdays to 9 pm). Take the metro to Ropsten and bus Nos 201 to 206.

Nationalmuseum on Blasieholmskajen has the main national collection of painting and sculpture but hosts other exhibitions on a variety of themes including design, so it is worth checking even if mainstream art is not your province (40 kr, free on Fridays, closed Mondays). There is also an excellent museum shop.

For a contemporary selection there is the modern art museum **Moderna museet** and the adjacent museum of photography **Fotografiska museet**on Skeppsholmen. The cost is 40 kr (free on Thursdays) and the museums are closed on Mondays (take bus No 65 from the central station). **Liljevalchs konsthall**, Djurgårdsvägen 60, offers a different perspective on modern art and crafts. Entry costs 30 kr and the museum is closed on Mondays (take bus Nos 44 and 47).

Views Mandatory views of Stockholm are from the **Stadshuset** tower for a look over Gamla Stan, or the sweep afforded by the platform of the lift **Katarinahissen** or to the east from **Fjällgatan**, where the street has been restored with wooden houses in the style of 200 years ago.

The panorama from Scandinavia's biggest tower, **Kaknästornet** off Djurgårdsbrunnsvägen east of the city, is exceptional on a clear day, bringing Stockholm's layout and the archipelago to the east into clarity. Take the lift up for 18 kr (take bus No 68 from the central station or Sergels torg and bus No 69 from the metro at Karlaplan). The view atop Skansen is not bad either and the gallery level of Kulturhuset is good for regarding the concrete handiwork around Sergels torg.

Markets The central outdoor produce market is at **Hötorget** off Vasagatan, open from dawn on weekdays and Saturdays. On Sundays craft stalls appear. The indoor **Saluhallen** at Östermalms torg has the cheeses and delicacies. The traders' blankets in the pedestrian mall of Drottninggatan are frequently unlicensed.

Gröna Lund Tivoli The amusement park on the shore of Djurgården (to the south-west of Skansen) is open from late April to mid-September (to 10 pm during the height of summer). Admission costs 25 kr before 6 pm, 35 kr at night (small children are free). Fun coupons are 7.50 kr each or 97 kr for 15, but if you just enjoy rides buy the daily pass bracelet for 140 kr (children 70 kr). Take bus No 44 or 47 from the central station or Sergels torg.

Activities
Sightseeing A simple trip to take in the inner city is with the Turistlinje buses, linking city attractions (see Stockholm, Getting Around). Stockholms Sightseeing, at Skeppsbron 22, runs an interesting cruise from May to September around the central bridges and canals from Strömkajen (near the Grand Hotel) or at Klara Mälarstrand, opposite Stadshuset (two hours, 95 kr). Morning and afternoon city coach tours last 2½ hours and cost 200 kr.

The Djurgårdslinjen No 7 tram from Norrmalmstorg costs 12 kr. Evening prawn and jazz cruises will satisfy a different aesthetic. If you cannot resist, book at a tourist office.

Mälar Ferries There are day trips to **Sigtuna** and **Skokloster slott** with Strömma kanalbolaget (☎ 24 11 00), whose boats depart

from Klara Mälarstrand and Nybrokajen daily (except Mondays, Fridays and Midsummer from early in June to mid-August, 120 kr return). Waxholmsbolaget (☎ 14 08 30) makes the trip daily in summer for 95 kr return. You can also sail to Birka (see Around Stockholm).

Winter Warm-Ups The bus tour (about 1½ hours, 100 kr) in winter starts from Sverigehuset at 11 am daily but is not available between Christmas and New Year. You must book a seat at the Stimulating Stockholm counter at Stockholm Information Service. Cheaper and perhaps more fun is the skating rink in Kungsträdgården open daily from November until mid-March; you can hire skates for only 10 kr for the day and enjoy the music. Also wintry is nordic skiing from Stora Skuggan near the university at Norra Djurgården (metro: Universitetet or take bus No 40). You can reserve equipment at the tourist office.

From November to April you can join the mad long-distance skaters on the Mälar ice. On Friday evenings or Saturdays contact Friluftsfrämjandet (☎ 711 22 08) for information about Sunday skating groups and local conditions and arrangements. The runs are gruelling and potentially dangerous hence the need for a little experience, local knowledge and being part of a group. Rug up.

For maps and details on ski trails and slopes around Stockholm, get the *Vintertips* booklet from tourist offices or contact STF (see Information).

Festivals
Stockholm Water Festival This festival runs for 10 days in mid-August and involves all manner of concerts, exhibitions and cultural events as well as boat sports, regattas and exhibition skiing, a triathlon and a special religious service on the lakeshore. A special city tour is organised by Stadsmuseet.

Places to Stay
Camping Close to the city, *Östermalms*

Camping (☎ 10 29 03), on Fiskartorpsvägen, is open in summer for caravans only.

Bredäng Camping (☎ 97 70 71), on Stora Sällskapets väg in Bredäng 10 km south of Stockholm, is open all year with sites for 80 kr a night (metro: Bredäng).

Hostels The private *Columbus Hotell* (see Hotels, City Fringe) has excellent hostel-class singles/doubles for 250 kr, but in a three or six-bed room you can get beds for 105 kr. The boat *Gustaf af Klint* (see Hotels, City Fringe) has beds for 120 kr in four-bed cabins and you can arrange to arrive any time (but it's closed at Christmas and New Year).

The popular STF boat hostel *af Chapman* (☎ 679 50 15), now moored at Skeppsholmen, has done plenty of travelling of its own but now is a big hostel rolling gently in sight of the centre of the city (take bus No 65 from the central station). Beside the boat hostel on dry land is the even bigger hostel *Skeppsholmen* (☎ 679 50 17), in Hantverkshuset, where there are rooms and dormitories. Across the water in Södermalm is *Zinken* (☎ 668 57 86) at Zinkens Väg 20 (metro: Zinkendamm) and *Långholmen* (see Hotels, City Fringe).

Hotels The hotel booking office is Hotellcentralen (☎ 24 08 80), at the lower level of the central station and open weekdays from 9 am to 5 pm, or ask at any of the tourist offices. Kaknästornet (☎ 667 80 30) is open until 10.30 pm from mid-April to mid-September. You can book hotels for a fee of 25 kr the same day (for hostels it's 12 kr) or free if booking in advance. There are also private singles or doubles for a minimum of two nights. The push-button video screen and map in the hall may be of some use after hours but, with few exceptions, lists expensive hotels.

If you are not in the city at weekends or from late June to mid-August you will pay high rates at most hotels. One way around this is the Stockholm holiday and weekend hotel packages (from 350 kr a night, including Stockholm card, with two children free) offered by tourist offices. For information

write to Destination Stockholm, Stora Hoparegränd 5, 11130 Stockholm.

City Near the station off Vasagatan (enter from Bryggaregatan) is *Freys Hotel* (☎ 20 13 00), which has singles/doubles for 540/690 kr on Fridays, Saturdays, holidays and during July. The small *Hotell Örnskjöld* (☎ 667 02 85) at Nybrogatan 6 is handy to the ferry harbour and discounts singles to 375 kr late in June and in July (metro: Östermalmstorg).

In the middle of the city is the pleasant *Queen's Hotel* (☎ 24 94 60) above the shopping street at Drottninggatan 71A – a mild splurge on weekends and in summer with singles/doubles from 335/435 kr and baths 100 kr extra. At other times you will pay up to 600 kr a single. Another place for a splurge is *Hotel Oden* (☎ 34 93 40) on Karlsbergsvägen (metro: Odenplan). At weekends and in summer there are singles/doubles for 520/610 kr, at other times singles start at 770 kr. The hotel has full services, cable TV, sauna and car park and you could hold a small day conference in any room.

Hotell Gustav Vasa (☎ 34 38 01) is a little uptown at Västmannagatan 61 and has reasonably priced singles/doubles for 310/430 kr that are even cheaper in July and early August. *Hotell Bema* (☎ 23 26 75), at Upplandsgatan 13, discounts single/double rates to 450/520 kr during the same period.

City Fringe *Wasa Park Hotell* (☎ 34 02 85), at Sankt Eriksplan 1, is handy just north-west of the business district (metro: Sankt Eriksplan) and has singles for 325 kr in summer and for 360 kr the rest of the year.

The big student hotel *Frescati* (☎ 15 94 34), in the university belt north of the city at Professorsslingan 13, has singles/doubles for 250/350 kr from June to August (metro: Universitetet and bus No 40, or Roslagsbanan: Freskati).

The hotel and hostel *Columbus Hotell* (☎ 644 17 17) is a popular restored housing block in Södermalm. You'll find it at Tjärhovsgatan 13. Bathless singles/doubles there cost from 250 to 390/490 kr. At the old jail Gamla Kronohäktet at Långholmsbron is the hotel and STF hostel *Långholmen* (☎ 668 05 00). In the restored building are singles/doubles for 430/630 kr on Friday and Saturday nights and in July. The personal hotel and restaurant boat *Gustaf af Klint* (☎ 640 40 77), on Stadsgårdskajen near Slussplan, has single/double cabins for 380/480 kr (and there is occasional live rock).

Further from the city at Solna is *Solna Hotel Pensionat* (☎ 82 60 65) at Råsundavägen 163 (metro: Sundbybergs C and bus No 515). Singles/doubles cost 320/420 kr but in July you pay 100 kr less.

The small *Hotell Sabima* (☎ 704 02 20), at Västerled 14 in Bromma, has singles for 350 kr but in July and early August there are showerless singles/doubles for 200/350 kr (metro: Abrahamsberg or Alvik, then take bus No 114).

Marinas For private boats there are three harbours within the near city area. *Rålambshov* (☎ 618 42 50) at Västerbron is open from May to September and charges 75 kr a night for a berth (depth up to 12 metres). *Djurgårdsbrunnsviken* (☎ 661 11 00) at Hundudden inside the canal entrance charges 60 kr (open from June to August, depth up to eight metres). At *Ryssviken* (☎ 662 11 27) in Djurgården near Waldemarsudde the charge is 65 kr (open from May to October).

Places to Eat

City Restaurants *Spegeln* on Västerlånggatan near Kåkbrinken is a pleasant restaurant with a variety of meats, pastas and salads if you want a mid-priced meal in old-town style. The brasserie and bar *Monarch* in Kungsträdgården on Hamngatan is a city alternative offering other entertainments and a garden but is hard to get into on Saturday evenings when the music starts.

Svensk matkultur, at Holländargatan 2 opposite Hötorget, has a range of dishes but boasts a full Swedish menu, some of which is mid-priced.

The corner restaurant *Aktuell*, at Oxtorget

near Kungsgatan, is one of the cheaper restaurants for drinking but is small and closed on Sundays. *City Hallen*, on Drottninggatan on the corner of Vattugatan, is one of the budget options around the city centre and *Sergels Pärla*, on the lower level of Sergels torg, is informal and mid-priced for pizzas, salads and daily lunches (no alcohol).

To the north of city, *Pancho's* at 60 Odengatan near Odenplan is open to 1 am and has a happy hour at 3 pm daily. *Bofri* on the corner of Sveavägen and Surbrunnsgatan is a small, smoke-free pub eatery with some character, vegetarian dishes and big steaks for about 90 kr.

Vegetarians (or anyone) can eat heartily from the buffet in graceful surroundings at Gröna Linjen, upstairs at Mäster Samuels gatan 10.

Södermalm Eating dinner can be cheaper in Södermalm. *Lilla Budapest*, on the corner of Götgatan and Svartensgatan, has Eastern European cuisine at middling prices. The small but lively *Blecktornskällaren*, on the corner of Ringvägen and Södermannagatan, has a more straightforward variety of food priced in the low to middle range.

Cafés The *Café Panorama* at the top level of Kulturhuset is very reasonable for sandwiches, coffee and cake if you like the view. The little *Café Da Vinci*, on Drottninggatan in front of Centralbadet, is a pleasant breakfast or lunch place handy to the shopping area but a little quieter and not at all expensive. The budget *Café London*, situated on Bryggargatan just off Drottninggatan, has some of the cheapest lunches in the inner city.

Pubs & Clubs Stockholm is not renowned for late nightlife, but certain clubs on Kungsgatan and a little out of the city centre carry the demand. The bar *Monarch* (see City Restaurants) packs fairly full with a younger crowd for late evening music and bar service. A little less expensive is *La Fontana* at Mariatorget, a popular club among people in their early 20s.

SWEDEN

Bacchi Wapen is a late-opening piano bar, club and disco on Järntorgsgatan in Gamla Stan (open to 3 am from Wednesday to Saturday). The panelled pubs *Black & Brown*, on the corner of Hornsgatan and Blecktornsgränd, and *Old Beefeater Inn*, on the corner of Götgatan and Urvädersgränd, are probably the most congenial drinking places in Stockholm. An often crowded restaurant and pub is *Kelly's* on Folkungagatan near Götgatan.

Getting There & Away

Air Arlanda airport is just over half an hour from the city centre by Flygbuss (see Stockholm, Getting Around for details).

The air services to Copenhagen, Oslo, Helsinki, Tampere and Turku are run by SAS (☎ 020-91 01 50) and Finnair (☎ 679 93 30). British Airways (☎ 679 78 00), KLM (☎ 676 08 80) and Lufthansa (☎ 611 22 88) also have regular European services. Finnair, British Airways and Lufthansa are at Norrmalmstorg 1.

Internal flights are dominated by SAS (☎ 751 59 50) and Linjeflyg (☎ 797 50 80), with offices at Cityterminalen. They fly to about 40 destinations, principally Gothenburg, Borlänge, Luleå, Malmö, Umeå, Visby, Ängelholm (near Helsingborg) and Östersund. SalAir has services to Linköping and Mora from Arlanda (see also Sweden, Getting Around).

Bus Regional buses arrive at and depart from Cityterminalen at Klarabergsviadukten opposite the central station. All cities and main towns are serviced from Stockholm and full timetable information is available here. SJ buses also run to Arlanda, Uppsala, Västerås, Norrtälje, Södertälje and Nyköping. Express bus Nos 835 and 837 run to Norrköping and Kalmar. For services to Arlanda airport see the Stockholm Getting Around section.

Train SJ's direct national services run to Narvik (Norway), Trondheim (Norway), Sundsvall, Mora, Uppsala, Hallsberg via Örebro, Oslo via Karlstad, Gothenburg,

Copenhagen via Helsingborg and Malmö. All services depart from the central station (Stockholm C). The X2000 fast train operates on the Gothenburg run and is being extended (running from Stockholm Syd at Flemingsberg). The SL-pendeln commuter service runs to Uppsala, Södertälje, Gnesta, Nykvarn and Nynäshamn via Västerhaninge (departing from Stockholm C).

Car & Motorbike The E20 and E4 motorways run together from the centre of Stockholm to Södertälje and then branch: the E20 heads south to Nyköping and Norrköping and the E4 heads west to Eskilstuna and Örebro. To the north the E20 continues to Norrtälje and the E4 to Uppsala and Gävle. The E18 runs north-west to Västerås.

For rentals, Budget (☎ 33 43 83) is at Sveavägen 153, Happy Rental (☎ 59 59 12) is at Globen, Hertz (☎ 24 07 20) is at Vasagatan 26, InterRent (☎ 21 06 50) is at Tegelbacken 6.

Boat The Turku and Helsinki ferries of Viking Line (☎ 714 56 00) depart from the terminal at Tegelvikshamn (bus No 53 from Slussen). Viking Line has an office in the central station off Centralplan.

Silja Line (☎ 22 21 40) at Stureplan has similar services from Värta Hamnen (Silja buses to and from the Ropsten metro station). Birka Line and Ålandlinjen's Åland ferries depart from Stadsgårdsterminalen (metro: Slussen). Eckerö linjen (☎ 0175-309 20) sails to Åland from Grisslehamn on Väddö about 100 km north of Stockholm. Sally Lines (☎ 14 11 15) is at Vasagatan 15.

Getting Around

The SL (Storstockholms Lokaltrafik) information centre (☎ 23 60 00) for all timetables and enquiries is at Sergels torg (open daily from 7 am to 9 pm or to midnight in summer). A Stockholm card for one to three days (see Stockholm, Information) covers travel on SL trains and buses in greater Stockholm. The best collected 'how to' guide to destinations and transport lines is the pocketbook *Hur, Var?* (see also Stockholm, Information).

Rail passes are not valid on the SL trains. You buy 6 kr coupons and use a minimum of two coupons per trip (in one zone), three for two zones (maximum four zones, 30 kr). The ticket will last one hour and must be stamped at the start of the journey. Coupon sheets can be bought cheaply (60 kr for 15) or there are tourist day or three-day cards for the whole of the SL system (55 and 105 kr) or day cards for the city only (30 kr). Monthly cards cost 325 kr. Children aged from six to 17 years travel for half-price, younger children travel free. Children aged from seven to 11 years may travel accompanied by a paying adult free at Christmas, New Year and on certain holidays.

Lockers at the lower level of the central station cost 15 or 25 kr for 24 hours, the toilets 5 kr and a shower 20 kr. The lost property office (☎ 736 07 80) is at the Rådmansgatn metro station.

To/From the Airport Flygbuss services to/from Arlanda airport (30 minutes) leave every 10 or 15 minutes and go to/from Cityterminalen opposite the central station or via other routes to Bromma and Solna, Kista and Nacka terminal (50 kr). The Flygbuss desk is in the international arrivals terminal at the airport.

Bus The inner-city buses radiate from Sergels torg, Odenplan, Fridhemsplan west of the city, and Slussen. Night services are separately numbered except for bus No 47 from Sergels torg to Djurgården. Bus No 68 runs to Kaknästornet only in summer. The Nattbus services are numbered in the 90s.

From Brommaplan bus Nos 301 to 323 service Lövö, Ekerö and the Mälar islands west of Stockholm city and bus No 311 connects with a ferry to Adelsö. The Lidingö buses run from Ropsten and there is a separate gold summer timetable.

For orientation and sightseeing purposes you can use the Turistlinje, which passes the central station, Sergels torg, Slussen, Sverigehuset, Kaknästornet and Djurgården.

A 24-hour ticket is 40 kr and you can make trips and stops according to whim. The buses run on the circuit from 9 am to 5 pm in summer (to 4 pm in autumn and spring).

Train Four SL services besides the metro run to Nockeby (metro link: Alvik), to Lidingö (metro link: Ropsten), to Kårsta, Österskär and Näsbypark (metro: Stockholm Östra) and to Saltsjöbaden (metro: Slussen), Märsta and Kungsängen.

Underground The most useful mode of transport in Stockholm is the T-bana, which converges on T-Centralen, a tunnel walk from the lower level of the central station. There are three main through lines with branches. Off-peak services vary but no trip to or from the city centre will take longer than 40 minutes. The metro has the most comprehensive connections, including those with the SL-pendeln regional trains.

The pedestrian tunnels and their horrible wall-art are an easy link from Sergels torg across to Kungsträdgården and the shopping streets around Hamngatan.

Tram The Lidingö tram No 21 runs from Ropsten to Gåshaga and connects with the metro.

Taxi The taxis gather at Centralplan in front of the central station or you can order one by phoning 15 00 00 or 670 00 00. They charge 25 kr at pick-up and you will pay 50 kr just to cross the water, going through Gamla Stan. Taxikurir (☎ 30 00 00) offers a fare ceiling of 75 kr in the city.

Car & Motorbike If you are driving, note that Djurgårdsvägen is closed near Skansen at night, on weekends and some holidays. Parking houses are marked on all city maps and evening rates can be as low as 10 kr. Blue-ticket street parking in marked areas uptown costs 7 kr per hour on weekdays between 8 am and 6 pm and is free at weekends and on holidays. In these areas you get tickets from the machine indicated by the blue sign on the post.

Bicycle Maps of cycle tracks around Stockholm (92 kr) are available from the tourist offices. Nynäsleden to Nynäshamn joins Sommarleden near Västerhaninge and swings west to Södertälje. Roslagsleden leads to Norrtälje (linking with Blåleden to Vaxholm). Upplandsleden leads to Märsta north of Stockholm and you can ride to Sigtuna and then take the track to Uppsala. Sörmlandsleden leads south-west from Södertälje.

Bicycles can be carried on the SL-pendeln, except at weekdays between 6 and 9 am and 3 and 6 pm or from the central station. You can ride where the paths are divided in white for cyclists and pedestrians.

Boat You can use the services of Waxholmsbolaget's archipelago boats for 16 days with the Båtluffarkort (235 kr). The ferries wind through the archipelago to Arholma, Ljusterö, Ingmarsö, Möja, Sandhamn, Nämdö, Ornö, Utö and Nynäshamn (from Strömkajen near the Nationalmuseum and Nybrokajen on the other side at Nybroviken).

Gripsholms Rederi AB (☎ 0159-102 07) sails from the quay at Stadshusbron to Mariefred twice daily for 100 kr return (see also Mälar ferries in the Activities section). The steamers depart for Vaxholm (from Nybroplan), Sandhamn (from Strömkajen) and Mariefred (from Stadshusbron). For all details on water traffic there is a daily information service (☎ 14 08 30).

Katarinahissen The lift from street level near Slussen takes you up to the crest of Södermalm, rather a climb any other way. The lift, which provides quite a view, costs 3 kr a trip.

Around Stockholm

DROTTNINGHOLM
West of the city, the royal residence and parks of Drottningholm on Lövön are among the best loved walking places and tourist attractions of Stockholm. The main **palace** of Renaissance inspiration was built about the same time as Versailles late in the 17th century. The highlights of the chambers inside are the **Karl X Gustaf Gallery** in Baroque style, the painted ceilings of the **State Hall** and the dazzling colours of the **Stone Hall**. The palace is open daily from May to September (25 kr). The court theatre **Slottsteater** has a museum but you can see opera and concerts in summer in the original surroundings for prices ranging from 50 to 400 kr, phone 660 82 25 or ask at post offices.

The **Baroque gardens** spread geometrically in the contemporary manner. To the left at the far end is the pavilion of **Kina slott**. Take the metro to Brommaplan and change to bus Nos 301 to 323 or take the boat from Stadshuset (60 kr return). For 200 kr you can take the cruise and a guided tour with Stockholms Sightseeing (see Activities). Put aside most of a day.

VAXHOLM
The 16th century **castle** Vaxholm, north-east of Stockholm, is a popular cruise destination and there are summer picnic boat tours featuring Baltic herring (175 kr), book at the tourist office. The castle is now a **fortress museum**, rather like the collections of summer houses that were fashionable last century. Take bus No 670 from the metro station Tekniska Högskolan or the boats from Strömkajen.

BIRKA
Summer cruises to the **Viking Age trading town** Birka, on Björkö in Mälaren, have increased in popularity as archaeologists unearth more of the town and its cemetery, harbour and fortress. You can cruise with Waxholmsbolaget or Stockholms Sightseeing from Rastaholm in summer (from 100 kr return).

MARIEFRED & GRIPSHOLM SLOTT
Visiting the quaint 18th century village Mariefred and the 16th century castle Gripsholm slott (25 kr) will make one of the best days out if you are tiring of Stockholm.

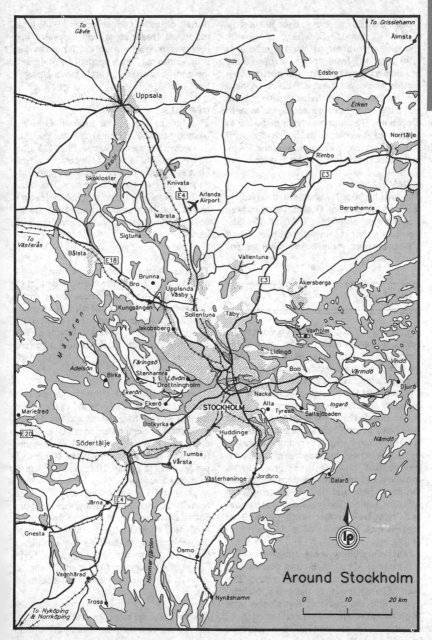

Around Stockholm

0   10   20 km

Take the E20 motorway about 50 km west of the city through Södertälje or use the summer motorboats of Waxholmsbolaget (190 kr return). Inside the castle (open daily in summer) is the **old national portrait collection** and **royal theatre**. You can book a tour for 180 kr that includes a museum train and a trip on the steamer *Mariefred* back to Stockholm. The tour runs from mid-May to September at weekends and holidays, as well as from Tuesday to Friday in summer. Book at the Stockholm Information Service.

NYNÄSHAMN

The boat harbour Nyäshamn is dwarfed by the ferry terminal of Gotlands City, where ferries depart nightly for Gotland. The SL-pendeln runs from Stockholm C to Västerhaninge, where you change for Nynäshamn.

Uppland

Uppland was the cradle of Sweden, and its centre Uppsala was the earliest focus of the emerging nation. An archbishop first sat there in 1164, but it seems to have long been a cult centre. But this was 'old' **Gamla Uppsala** just to the north, a **burial site** that probably attracted ancient assemblies and a votive cult. Perhaps it was the greatest such holy place in pre-Christian Scandinavia, but it was profane by the 12th century, upstaged by the beginnings of the **stone church** now on the site. But the three great **burial mounds** and an **Iron Age cemetery** attest the pagan past, and finds of contemporary weapons, armour and grave goods at **Vendel** and **Valsgärde** further north (as well as legends such as accounted in *Beowulf*) hint at its glory.

The surrounding areas are dotted with hundreds of Viking Age **rune stones** and **forts** dating from an even earlier time. The lake Mälaren is just to the south. Nearby you'll find the castle of **Skokloster** and **Sigtuna**, a small town itself steeped in history. There are more than a score of parish churches with remains of fine **late-medieval frescoes** around Uppsala. The best preserved are probably at **Tensta kyrka**, near Vattholma 25 km north of Uppsala, and the churches at Vendel and Gamla Uppsala have others.

UPPSALA

The landmarks of the modern Uppsala (sometimes spelt Upsala) are old enough. The cathedral was consecrated in 1435 after 150 years of building and the castle was first built in the 1540s, although today's appearance belongs to the 18th century. The focus is the sprawling university, Scandinavia's oldest, and its hospital: some of the town's hotels close for part of July, coinciding with university holidays.

Orientation

The main railway and bus stations are 15 minutes' stroll from the business district of Uppsala and the river Fyrisån, where you'll find yourself in the old cathedral and university quarter; the prominent castle to the south of the street grid is at least as far again. The shopping mall of Kungsängsgatan is centred on Stora Torget.

Information

A tourist office of Uppsala Turist och Kongress AB is handy at the castle (open from mid-April to mid-June and late August to the end of September; Monday to Saturday 11 am to 3 pm, Sundays 11 am to 4 pm; from mid-June to late in August 10 am to 6 pm Monday to Friday, 10 am to 5 pm Saturdays and Sundays).

The central office at Fyris torg 8 is open from 10 am to 6 pm weekdays (and to 2 pm Saturdays from late August to late June). Students in search of information can go to the student union next to the restaurant Ubbo, on the corner of Åsgränd and Övre Slottsgatan. Luggage storage at the station costs 25 kr per item for 24 hours (lockers 15 kr).

Money There are branches of all main banks, but you can also exchange money at the main post office until 5 pm weekdays or on Saturday mornings. Forex is at Fyris torg (open from 9 am to 6 pm, to 3 pm on Saturdays).

Post & Telecommunications The Uppsala telephone code is 018. The Telebutik is at Bangårdsgatan 7 and the main post office is at Vaksalagatan 10.

Travel Agencies SJ sells all tickets and packages (including tickets abroad until 7 pm on weekdays) at the railway station every day from dawn until 10 pm (Saturdays to 8 pm only). The student travel agency opposite the main university building on Övre Slottsgatan sells some reasonably priced air tickets.

Books & Maps The excellent Bokhandel Lundeqvistska on the corner of Östra Ågatan and Drottninggatan has paperbacks and books about Sweden in English, guidebooks, maps, as well as helpful staff and computerised search resources.

Emergency The police are at Salagatan 18. There is a 24-hour pharmacy at Svartbäcksgatan 8, but for emergency treatment go to the university medical centre (☎ 16 60 00); enter from Sjukhusvägen. There is a dentist at Vretgränd 18.

Dangers & Annoyances Half the city seems to be out on a bicycle at any time and the white lines on the cycle/walking paths can mean little. Keep a lookout and do not risk being bowled over.

Things to See
The French Gothic **cathedral**, dominates the city as some of the dead who rest there dominated their country: St Erik, Gustaf Vasa, Johan III, Carl von Linné. The **archiepiscopal museum** is in the north tower (closed weekdays from September to May). The nearby **Trefaldighets kyrka** is of rather lesser stature.

The museums at the **Gustavianum** (20 kr) cover Egyptology, anatomy and Swedish archaeology, but only the last two are open all year (at weekends, but daily in summer). The **Uppland Museum**, in the old mill at Sankt Eriks gränd 6, comprises the county collections from the Middle Ages and later as well as natural history exhibits (free entry, closed Sundays from October to April).

Carolina Rediviva, the university library, has a display hall with maps and historical and scientific literature, the pride of which is the surviving half of the 6th century bible **Codex Argentus**, written on purple vellum in the extinct Gothic language (entry costs 5 kr on Sundays and in summer).

The **Linnéum** and **botanic gardens** and greenhouse are below the castle hill and are not to be confused with the **Linné Museum** and **garden** at Svartbäcksgatan 27, open from May to September. The museum, which holds memorabilia of the great scientist's (Carl von Linné's) work in Uppsala, closes on Mondays. The garden, with more than 1000 herbs, has been shaped according to its 18th century plan.

The regional **art museum**, next to the tourist office at Fyris torg 6, is best for works on local themes and is free (closed Mondays). Take sandwiches and sit by the main **university** building (which is imposing enough to demand a glance inside) and take in the ambience of a historic university (first opened in 1477). On the lawn in front are nine typical Uppland **rune stones** which you will not have to detour to see. On 30 April the students gather dressed in white for procession and song to celebrate Walpurgis.

Walking Tour The best walk would begin at the cathedral and follow the river to the Uppland Museum, then go farther to the bridge on Skolgatan; the Linné gardens are on the other side. Follow Skolgatan back across the river to Övre Slottsgatan and begin a sweep through the university quarter to the botanic gardens and the castle.

Markets The indoor produce market, Saluhallen, is at Sankt Eriks torg between the cathedral and the river (open on weekdays and Saturdays), and an open six-day market is at Vaksala torg, behind the railway station.

SWEDEN

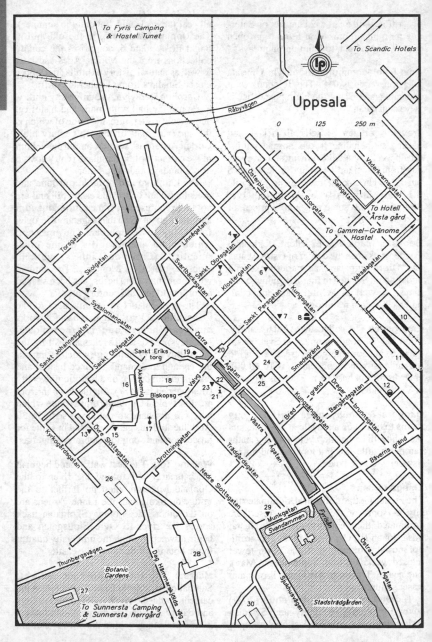

To Fyris Camping
& Hostel Tunet

To Scandic Hotels

Råbyvägen

Uppsala

0   125   250 m

Österplan

To Hotell
Årsta gård

To Gammel–Gränome
Hostel

Uppsala Slott The castle (with tourist office inside wing A) is open daily from mid-April to September (except 30 April and Mid-summer's Eve) and entry is 40 kr. The features are the genuinely death-stained dungeons, the state hall and the so-called **Vasa vignettes**: dioramas showing the colour and treachery of the castle's past. The bell tower **Gunillaklockan** and cannon look out over the old town from the courtyard. Allow two hours so you can take everything in.

Activities
You can ride the steam train *Lennakatten* on the narrow-gauge museum railway into the countryside (on Sundays from mid-June to

early in September for 55 kr return). The two tours depart from the museum station behind the main station.

You can also take river-and-lake cruises to Sigtuna (about five hours) and connect with the service to Stockholm (about eight hours; see Uppsala, Getting There & Away).

Places to Stay
Camping *Fyris Camping*, by the river at Fyrisfädern north of the city, is small and has basic facilities but offers sites for 110 kr in summer. There are four-bed cabins with cooking facilities for 260 kr (from June to August) or 200 kr at other times of year (take bus No 10, 14, 24, 25 or 26). Reception is at the office of the indoor sports complex.

Sunnersta Camping (☎ 27 60 84), off Dag Hammarskjölds väg on the lake Ekoln seven km to the south of the city centre, is open from May to the end of August and has camping charges between 60 and 80 kr. There are also two-bed cabins for 90 kr.

Hostels *KFUM Hostel Tunet*, Torbjörnstorg 2, is open from late June to mid-August and beds are cheap at 70 kr.

Sunnersta herrgård (☎ 32 42 20), a hostel in the manor house at Sunnerstavägen 24, is open all year and charges 83 kr, but it is hard to get beds. Take bus No 14, 20 or 40 six km to the south.

Twenty-five km to the north-east at Stavby on road 288, the STF hostel *Gammel-Gränome* (☎ 0174-131 08) is a pleasant rural hostel established on a preserved farm dating from the 1600s. The charge is 83 kr a bed. Bus Nos 811 and 886 run to Uppsala.

Private Rooms Various rooms around the city can be booked at the tourist office from 145 kr a night, although you pay a 40 kr booking fee.

Hotels The *Scandic Hotel*, at Gamla Uppsalagatan 50, is a big hotel-motel north of the city and the most reasonable of the summer alternatives for 550 kr a double from late June until the first week of August. More modest is *Hotell Årsta gård*, Jordgubbsgatan

14, where singles cost 420 kr or 225 kr at weekends.

Places to Eat
In the centre of town *Restaurang Näktergalen* at Stora Torget has solid meals starting at 50 kr and there is a bar; *Saffet's* downstairs offers variety in takeaway food. *William's*, Övre Slottsgatan 7, is a British-style pub.

Brunnen, on Dragarbrunnsgatan near Sankt Persgatan, has solid mid-priced dishes and *Bar Celona* on Sysslomangatan near Skolgatan has similar fare: at both places you can eat heartily for 50 kr.

Vågen at Fyris torg has everything from fish of the day to kebabs and is open long after midnight. *Guldtuppen* is a mid-priced steak restaurant, on Kungsgatan, and the pizza-grill *Ram-Boo*, on Sankt Olofsgatan, can provide takeaways and kebabs. The pizzas and salads are good at *Carolines*, behind the main university building on Övre Slottsgatan and the tone is more elevated.

Vegetarian fare is available at the *Govindas* Vedic centre, at the corner of Kungsgatan and Sankt Olofsgatan, open daily from 11.30 am to 6 pm.

Cafés *Konditori Fågelsången*, at Munkgatan 3, looks on to the duck pond – a pleasant view to go with coffee and cake or ice cream.

Getting There & Away
Air Uppsala is not far from Arlanda airport and regional buses and the airport Flygbuss (bus Nos 801 and 802) depart at least twice an hour from the Uplandia Hotel and the bus station (55 kr).

Bus There is the choice of the town-to-town Upplandstrafik (silver buses, where you can alight only at intermediate stops) and the green-and-white local buses. Timetables are available at the main bus station off Kungsgatan.

Train The SJ Uppsalapendeln makes shuttle runs from Stockholm. If you are commuting to the capital, ask about the discount 10-trip

coupons (buses make one-hour trips late at night and leave Stockholm as late as 2.15 am åt weekends). Normal SJ services heading north also stop there. SL coupons take you only as far as Märsta.

Car & Motorbike The E4 runs south to Stockholm (80 km) and north to Gävle (100 km). Road 55 connects with the E18 near Enköping.

Boat Boat trips allow you to link Skokloster castle (one way/return 70/105 kr), Sigtuna (five hours, 75/141 kr) and Stockholm (eight hours, 175 kr) – a pleasant way to see some of Sweden's most sensual country. The service, from the south bridge Islandsbron beside Östra Ågatan, runs from late June to mid-September, except Mondays and Fridays (change at Sigtuna for Stockholm). It is the most relaxed way to introduce yourself to the landscape after the pace of Stockholm. Tickets can be bought on board or booked with Strömma-kanalbolaget (☎ 018-12 12 30).

Getting Around
Bus The route numbers of local buses vary according to the day and time. Some routes have off-peak *(lågtrafik)* or nocturnal *(nattrafik)* services. Timetables and route maps are at the bus station or some city stops.

Taxi There are plenty of taxis at the railway station, but you can dial 13 90 90 or 14 90 90 to order one.

Bicycle The bicycle paths lead into and around the town and riding is only uncomfortable on some cobbled inner streets. You can hire a bicycle at Cykelstället, Svartbäcksgatan 20, for 50 kr a day and 180 kr a week or buy a simple reconditioned second-hand model from Cykelreparatur, Övre Slottsgatan 9, from 600 to 700 kr.

GAMLA UPPSALA
Uppsala began at the three great **grave mounds** at Gamla Uppsala, three km north of the modern city. The mounds, said to be

the howes of legendary pre-Viking kings, mark a cemetery of about 200 small mounds. It has also been suggested that it was a great heathen temple site. But Christianity came in the 12th century and with it the bishops: from 1164 the archbishop had his seat in a cathedral on the site of the present **church**, which, by the 15th century, was enlarged and painted with **frescoes**. Parts of the frescoes and some late-medieval items survive. Pope John Paul II celebrated mass there in 1989.

Next to the flat-topped mound **Tingshögen** is the inn **Odinsborg**, known for its horns of mead, although daintier refreshments are offered on site in summer. The museum village **Disagården** to the north of the mounds is open daily from June to August (tours are free, except at Midsummer). The old **railway station** is also a museum piece: take bus No 14, 20 or 24 from Uppsala.

VALSGÄRDE
The **Iron Age graves**, four km north of Gamla Uppsala at Valsgärde, yielded the trappings of a warrior society. The **cemetery**, a mound and several stone-settings lie east of road 290, a pleasant bicycle ride from Uppsala (there is no bus).

VENDEL
The village of Vendel, almost 40 km north of Uppsala, gave its name to the period just before the Viking Age. In the **cemetery** used during the 6th, 7th and 8th centuries fine ornamented helmets and weapons and gravegoods buried in boats were found; copies are now in the small **Vendel Museum** on the site (closed Mondays).

The 14th-century **Vendel kyrka** has remains of late-medieval frescoes. Turn north-east off the E4 after Björklinge or take bus No 814 from Uppsala.**Ottarshögen**, to the west between the village and the E4, is a big mound associated with a legendary king.

SIGTUNA
The kernel of Sigtuna is on the west shore of an arm of Mälaren, across the bridge if you approach from the E4. An early trading

centre was developed here; the church and the remains of the period are the ruins of the churches of St Per, St Olof and St Lars and the abbey **Mariakyrkan** with restored interior paintings. The ruins are strung over half a km of Stora Gatan (probably Sweden's oldest main street) and Olofsgatan.

The **town museum** at Lilla torget preserves the town's more recent past and copies of medieval finds (10 kr, open daily). The quaint 18th century **town hall** (the smallest in the country) is at Stora torget and is the best of many buildings from that period. In the setting of trees and rose gardens, you can have the most pleasant of town walks.

Information
Sigtuna Turistbyrå is at Stora Gatan 33 and is open daily in summer.

Places to Stay
The STF hostel *Gula skolan*, on Stora Gatan by the bus station, charges 76 kr a night and is open from early June until mid-August.

Getting There & Away
You can connect with trains from Stockholm or Uppsala (take bus No 570 or 575 from Märsta station). Strömma-kanalbolaget boats from Stockholm (eight hours) and Uppsala arrive at the quay south of the town centre.

SKOKLOSTER SLOTT
The angular and singular palace Skokloster slott, on Skohalvön, combines the delights of a Mälar manor and Baroque museum and there are often concerts inside during summer. The superb and whimsical palace interiors are the highlights of a visit. The palace is open from May to August and there are hourly tours each afternoon. The abbey dating from the 13th century stands nearby. The **Motor Museum** near the palace (open all year, entry 30 kr) actually contains all types of machinery, including aircraft.

Getting There & Away
You can take bus No 894 from Uppsala or the special museum bus on summer Satur-

days (ask at the tourist office). The palace is best reached by car from Sigtuna (take road 263 from Haga). The occasional No 557 bus runs from Kungsängen railway station.

WIKS SLOTT

The tiny castle Wiks slott, south-west of Uppsala by the inlet Lårstaviken, dates from the 1400s but has been much remodelled, especially the spired roof. A café is open in summer so you can enjoy the lake view there. Take bus No 847 from Uppsala, or take road 55 south-west and turn left about three km past the church at Ramsta.

Central Sweden

The region of the central lakes takes in the provinces Västmanland, Närke, Värmland and Dalsland, areas not as flat as the south but transitional geographically and economically. The emphasis is on mining and timber. Rich folk culture has always belonged to Dalarna (Dalecarlia), making it popular with tourists all year around when considering winter sports. But it was a mining centre early in the 17th century and so old clashed with new for 200 years before giving way.

VÄSTERÅS

Both an old and a modern city, Västerås is a centre of ABB (formerly Asea) industrial technology. It is only 80 minutes by rail from Stockholm.

Information

The tourist office is at Stora Torget 5 (closed Sundays, and closed Saturdays from November to February).

Money The main banks are open in the city until 5.30 pm weekdays or you can change money at the central post office.

Post & Telecommunications The main post office is at Sturegatan 18 and the Telebutik is nearby at Gallerian 7. The telephone code is 021.

Emergency The duty pharmacy is at Stora Gatan 34 (you may have to press an emergency button) and the medical centre is on Kopparbergsvägen. You'll find the police at Västgötegatan 7.

Things to See

Västerås slott, the castle housing the **Västmanlands Länsmuseum** (Västmanland Museum), has a strong historical collection but diverts into peculiarities such as the carved **calendar sticks** used in the 16th century and Swedish china. The neighbouring turbine house **Turbinhuset** has part of the collection. The museum is free (open daily in summer, otherwise closed on Mondays).

The art museum **Konstmuseum**, at Fiskartorget, concentrates on Swedish painting of this century (free, closed Mondays). The **cathedral** and its **museum** reflect 700 years of episcopal activity.

The **Vallby museum**, off Vallbyleden near the E18 north-west of the city, is an open-air collection assembled from the region to recreate village life. There's the usual array of cottage manufactures. The area is open daily until 10 pm from June to August. Take bus Nos 12 or 92 from Munkgatan.

The ancient cult site **Anundshög**, six km north-east of the city along Tortunavägen, has a full complement of prehistoric curiosities such as mounds, stone ship-settings and a big rune stone. But the row of stones beside the modern road may be the ancient road **Eriksgata**. It is possible, then, that the people of the region came here to receive their would-be kings in high ceremony.

Places to Stay

Camping The best camp sites are on Mälaren's shores. *Johannisbergs camping* (☎ 14 02 79), six km south of the city, is open from May to September. *Sundängens camping* (☎ 0171-410 43) is about 20 km east of the city on the road at Ängsösund.

Hostel The STF hostel is *Lövudden* (☎ 18 52 30), five km south-west of the city off

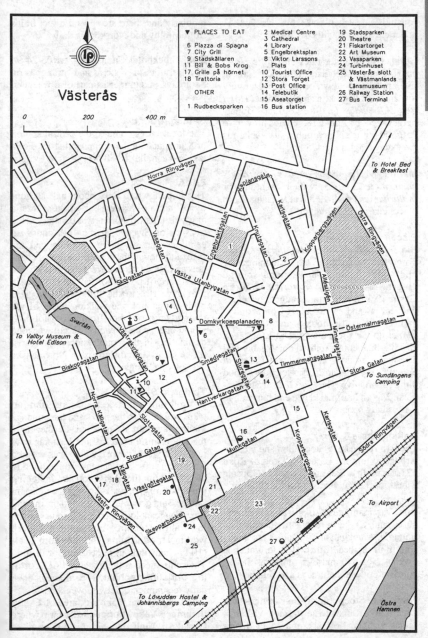

Västerås

0   200   400 m

▼ PLACES TO EAT

6 Piazza di Spagna
7 City Grill
9 Stadskällaren
11 Bill & Bobs Krog
17 Grille på hörnet
18 Trattoria

OTHER

1 Rudbecksparken

2 Medical Centre
3 Cathedral
4 Library
5 Engelbrektsplan
8 Viktor Larssons
   Plats
10 Tourist Office
12 Stora Torget
13 Post Office
14 Telebutik
15 Aseatorget
16 Bus station

19 Stadsparken
20 Theatre
21 Fiskartorget
22 Art Museum
23 Vasaparken
24 Turbinhuset
25 Västerås slott
   & Västmanlands
   Länsmuseum
26 Railway Station
27 Bus Terminal

Johannisbergsvägen (take bus No 25). A better class of bed will cost 250 kr.

Hotels The summer rates at *Traffic Hotel* (☎ 30 04 00), at Hallsta Gårdsgata 1 about five km from the town centre, are relatively low from 380/540 kr a single/double. *Hotel Bed & Breakfast* (☎ 14 39 80), at Kopparbergsvägen by the E18, comes down to 350/500 kr a single/double at weekends (weekday singles are 475 kr).

Marinas Visiting boats can use *Lögarängshamnen* (☎ 13 00 25) at the river mouth or *Mälarparken* (☎ 18 10 85) at Viksäng. Both places charge 75 kr a night.

Places to Eat
Bill & Bobs Krog and *Stadskällaren* at Stora Torget are the pick of the restaurants, for mid-priced outdoor lunches and splurge dinners respectively. *Trattoria*, at Stora Gatan 45, is for the more budget-conscious with pizzas and salads (closed on Monday and Tuesday afternoons) and *Grille på hörnet* up the street near Västra Ringvägen also has budget fare (closed on Monday and Tuesday afternoons and Sundays). *Piazza di Spagna*, at Vasagatan 26, is pricier but a good dinner alternative. The *City Grill*, at Smedjegatan 2, is an informal kebab and burger bar. It is usually open.

Getting There & Away
The E18 runs east to Stockholm and west to Arboga to join the E3 before Örebro. Road 67 leads north to Sala and Gävle and Uppsala is best reached by road 55 from Enköping.

Bus Västmanlands Lokaltrafik regional buses and SJ buses come to the railway station or Munkgatan. Timetables are available from the head office at Retortgatan 7. Swebus Nos 870 and 871 run from Stockholm on Fridays, Saturdays and Sundays.

Train The Stockholm-Oslo services via Örebro and Karlstad run through Västerås. Trains to Sala, Borlänge and Mora depart regularly and there are several direct trains from Mjölby and Norrköping daily.

Boat Stockholm Sightseeing (☎ 08-24 94 70) has tours to Västerås and Strängnäs on Saturdays in summer as part of a weekend package.

Getting Around
The local buses come to the central station or Munkgatan in the shopping district. For a taxi you can dial 18 50 00.

SALA
The small town of Sala, about half an hour by rail north of Västerås, is worth at least a day's visit. Its silver mine was considered the treasury of Sweden in the 16th and 17th centuries and its importance changed the face of the town: the peaceful series of channels and pondages that weave around it were the source of power for the mines. This in turn gave rise to the little white wooden bridges that link the walking paths of the town. Only 100 km from Stockholm, it would make a restful and different weekend destination in the countryside. The tourist office **Sala Gruvturism** is in Norrmanska Gården on Gillegatan.

Things to See & Do
A stroll along the sleepy **Gröna gången** takes you through the parks and the pondage **Mellandammen** at Sofielund. Further on is the **silver mine area** (off the Västerås road just south of the town), which was worked from the 1400s. You can take tours down to 60 metres in the shafts (60 kr, including museum entry) or walk through the museum village **Sala gruvbyn**, devoted to the mining life. You can look at the displays in the information centre, including a superb working **model mine**, the **museum** itself (10 kr) and films in the **Hjulhuset** theatre. The centrepiece is the minehead of **Drottning Christinas schakt**. The village is open daily in summer, otherwise weekends.

In town by the main park area of **Ekeby dammar** is **Väsby kungsgård**, a farm where Gustaf II Adolf and his mistress used to rendezvous. Excitement for the traveller is limited to the beautiful preserved interiors and the comprehensive **weapons** collection of the sort wielded by the mighty Swedish armies of the 17th century. The vaulted cellars and wine benches have been restored. There is a small **textile museum** attached (10 kr inclusive, open weekday afternoons and daily from May to August.

The rebuilt 17th century **Kristina kyrka** on Gruvgatan is impressive enough today, but once had a spire 83 metres high! Older is **Sala sockenkyrka** off Hyttvägen, with the remains of frescoes by the esteemed Albertus Pictor from the 15th century.

Places to Stay

The pleasant STF hostel *Sofielund* (☎ 0224-136 59, winter 101 64) and *Sofielunds Famijliecamping* (☎ 0224-101 64) are by the pondage at the south end of Gröna gången (or take the round-about bus No 61 from the railway station). The camping ground is open from mid-May to September and charges from 50 kr.

Hotell Svea (☎ 0224-105 10), Väsbygatan 19, discounts singles/doubles to 375/500 kr in the middle of summer.

Getting There & Away

The train from Västerås is convenient but the network of regional buses will take you from Uppsala or Gävle. Västmanlands Lokaltrafik's bus Nos 69 or 569 runs a few times daily from Västerås. There is also a Flygbuss Arlanda service.

ÖREBRO

The wealth of Örebro was built on a prosperous textile industry. Its dubious legacy is the first of the 'mushroom' water towers, which now earns small change as a lookout.

Information

The main tourist office is at the library on Näbbtorgsgatan (open weekdays and on Saturday mornings in summer). There's an office in the castle during summer. You can also get useful information at the museum shop at Wadköping.

Money Main banks are open until at least 3 pm, or you can exchange at the central post office.

Post & Telecommunications The post office is at Storgatan 3 and the Telebutik is at Våghustorget 1. The telephone code is 019.

Things to See

The once powerful **Örebro slott**, on the water at the centre of town, is taken up today by restaurants and administrators, but it has been consequently much restored and is perhaps the most photogenic castle in Sweden.

An exhibition on its history is open daily (except on Sundays) from May to August. Tours run daily until mid-August (12 kr). On the river at Skytteparken is the museum village **Wadköping**, which has craft workshops and period buildings. The fine **Örebro länsmuseum** in the castle park is free and open daily.

Places to Stay

The STF hostel is *Adolfsberg* (☎ 24 09 21) on Sanatorievägen in the woods three km from town and a short walk from Mosåsvägen (take bus No 11 or 31 from Järntorget).

Ansgar Hotell (☎ 10 04 20), at Järnvägsgatan 10, has singles/doubles discounted to 290/340 kr in summer.

The *Good Morning Hotel* (☎ 17 07 07), on Stenbackevägen at the Gustavsvik centre, has singles/doubles for 495/590 kr discounted to 345/420 kr at weekends and in summer (take bus No 117).

Getting There & Away

The regional bus station is at Klostergatan 37. Swebus No 844 runs to Norrköping and Karlstad. The main railway station is a little apart from the town centre and SJ services from Stockholm run to both Oslo and Gothenburg.

Getting Around

The local bus office at Klostergatan 37 has all timetables. City buses converge on

Järntorget. At the tourist office you can buy a day card for all buses for 25 kr (single trips cost 12 kr).

KARLSTAD

The port Karlstad is on Vänern, Sweden's biggest lake. A tourist office is at the library at Västra Torggatan 26 (closed on Sundays). The main post office is at Järnvägsgatan 2 and the Telebutik, at Drottninggatan 30.

Things to See & Do

The leisure park **Mariebergsskogen** by the water on Långövägen combines amusements with an open-air museum and animal park. **Skogens mini-zoo** is open daily, but the amusements are open only from May to the end of August. The 18th century stone bridge **Östra Bron** is the longest such bridge in Sweden and is the best place to admire the river. The steamer *Polstjärnan* offers daily lake tours each morning from Inre Hamn (90 kr).

Places to Stay

The STF hostel *Ulleberg* (☎ 054-56 68 40) is off the E18, three km from the town (take bus Nos 16 or 31), but closes on some holidays. The *Grand Hotel* (☎ 054-11 52 40) at Västra Torggatan 8 has singles/doubles for 400/500 kr all year. The *Carlton Hotel*, at Järnvägsgatan 8, has excellent singles from 350 kr.

Getting There & Away

Trains from Stockholm to Oslo pass through Karlstad and also run to Gothenburg. Express bus No 844 runs to Örebro and Jönköping and bus No 803 runs to Gothenburg. You'll find the Swebus terminal at Drottninggatan 43.

DALARNA

The Dalarna area provides the richest tract of folk culture for the traveller in Sweden. Dalarna is known for its art, music and dancing. Add the prospects for winter sports at Falun, around Siljan and at Säarna, Idre and Grövelsöjon (where STF has a mountain station, 40 km north-west of Idre on the

Norwegian border) and you have worthwhile destinations all year. Actually, the list of ski resorts is much longer, and the summer activities are too numerous to list, so investigate at the local tourist offices.

SJ trains terminate at Mora and you will rely on the Dalatrafik buses (72 kr takes you to Särna, although bus No170 continues up to Grövelsjön) and the novelty of Inlandsbanan, which extends to Östersund and, eventually, to Gällivare in Lapland. Local trains run from the junction at Borlänge to Malung. You can hike the course of Vasaloppet (see Mora) from Sälen with support from the bus (No 95). Otherwise, your personal demands or the restrictions of timetabled services may make you decide to hire a car at Mora.

FALUN

Falun, the traditional centre of Dalarna, is synonymous with mining and with Stora, perhaps the world's oldest public company. The tourist office at Stora Torget is open weekends and to 1 pm on Saturdays. The post office is at Slaggatan 19 and the Telebutik, on Falugatan in the Falanhuset.

Things to See & Do

The copper mine **Falu koppargruva** was the world's most important by the 17th century and generated many of Sweden's international aspirations during that period. The mines also provided, as a by-product, the red coatings which became the characteristic house paint of that past age in Sweden. (The minerals and vitriol in this paint protect wood – the paint is still popular today.)

In the **Stora museum** are many exhibits showing the miners' wretched life and work and the folk tale of Fett-Matts, the shocking story of a lad plucked, in a perfect state of preservation, from rubble two generations after the mine took his life. The museum (open daily) is above the town at the top end of Gruvgatan in front of the present open-cut mine. Admission costs 5 kr, but to enter the bowels of the mine for a once-only experience will cost 50 kr.

A gentler experience is available at

Dalarnas Museum by the bridge on Stigare-gatan (admission free, open daily). The feature of this fine museum is the stories and sounds of the famous minstrels of Dalarna's folk life and the culture that spawned it. Homes of the period are grouped around **Bergshauptmansgatan**, making the stroll back to town pleasant. The Baroque interiors of **Kristine kyrka** at Stora Torget show the riches that came into the town.

Places to Stay & Eat
The big *STF hostel* (☎ 023-105 60) is at Hälsinggårdsvägen 7, three km east of the town and a 10-minute walk from the bus stop (take bus No 701 from Vasagatan, under the bridge north-east of the station).

Hotel Bergmästaren (☎ 023-636 00), at Bergskolegränd 7, has singles for 615 kr (reduced to 450 kr in July).

McEwan's Inn, at Holmgatan 15, is a lively bar serving good mid-priced meals, but is closed on Sundays. The little restaurant and café *Kopparhatten* at the Dalarna museum serves some traditional folk-cuisine delights at friendly prices and is open daily.

Getting There & Away
Buses arrive at the terminal outside the station at Promenaden 3 (take bus No 53 from Borlänge, No 70 from Mora and Rättvik). Coming by train from Stockholm you must change at Borlänge for Falun (the station there can close by 8 pm) and the line to Mora.

SILJAN
The big lake Siljan is one of the country's popular destinations for summer campers and winter skiers. An activities map is available at local tourist offices (25 kr) and a hiking map detailing 300 km of trails costs 50 kr. The discount card Siljanspasset (which has bonuses) also costs 50 kr.

RÄTTVIK
Rättvik, a popular skiing centre, offers other diversions. There is a big information office, at Torget across the lawn from the railway station. You can exchange money there if need be, although there are banks and a post office in town. The pseudo-rune stone beside the church on the lake commemorates the rising (of Gustaf Vasa's band against the Danes in the 1520s) which created modern Sweden.

The ski slopes are right above the lake and town. There are four lifts (one for beginners) and six runs up to one km long from **Tolvås-tugan**. There is artificial snow and a lift card costs 80 kr for a morning or afternoon. The main nordic run is from **Jarlstugan** near Genvägen.

In summer there are cruises on the steamer *Gustaf Wasa* or rides in the long rowing boats (*kyrkobåtar*) of ancient pedigree (rowed to the church in ceremony at Whitsun and the international dance festival late in July). Book at the tourist office. You can hire bicycles at the equipment shop Cykel & Motor at Torget for 70 kr a day.

Places to Stay
Siljansbadets Camping (☎ 0248-116 91), on the lake shore near the railway station, has four-bed cabins all year from 345 kr (270 kr in spring and autumn). The *STF hostel* (☎ 0248-105 66), on Centralgatan towards the hills from the station, is one of the newest and best equipped in the country.

MORA
The legend is that Gustaf Vasa took off in high dudgeon to take on the Danes alone in 1521. The good yeomen of Dalarna, after due consideration, chose to brave the winter and follow. Vasaloppet, the ski race which ends at the entrance to the town and involves 90 km of gruelling nordic skiing, is entered by thousands of people each March. The tourist office is by the lake on Ångbåtskajen not far from the church and its prominent bell tower.

Things to See & Do
If, for you, art seems more congenial or better than the skiing, visit the **Zornmuseet** celebrating the works and private collections of Mora painter Anders Zorn. Aside from the characteristic portraits and nudes are collec-

tions of art including the odd traditional *dalmålningar* paintings. Admission costs 15 kr (open daily all year).

The most reputable of the painted Dalecarlian wooden horses *(dalahästar)* are produced by the well-known makers Nils Olsson Hemslöjd at Nusnäs, 10 km south of Mora, open daily (except Sundays from September to May). The Zorn family farm **Zorngården** (20 kr, open daily) and **Zorns Gammelgård** (10 kr, open daily in summer), a collection of local building traditions, are noteworthy.

Places to Stay & Eat

Hotell Moraparken (☎ 0250-178 00) at Parkgatan 1 has doubles from 480 kr (in summer and at weekends). *Restaurang Lilla Björn* at Kyrkogatan 5 is the most pleasant and reasonably priced of the restaurants.

Getting There & Away

Linjeflyg and SalAir fly direct to the airfield (south-west of town on the Malung road) from Stockholm. The buses to and from Rättvik and Falun (No 70) run to the bus station at Moragatan 23. The railway station is about one km around the lake from town and there are direct trains from Stockholm and Borlänge. Bus No 170 continues to Särna. For car rental, try Happy Rental (☎ 0250-109 84) or Hertz (☎ 0250-117 60).

SÄRNA

The little town of Särna is the start of some of the most beautiful highland wilderness for hikers. The wooden 17th century **Särna gammelkyrka** is matched by contemporary buildings.The forestry museum **Lomkällan** (open in July and August) is three km north of the town on road 70. The tourist office at Särnavägen 6 is not open all year so ring 0253-102 05 for information.

Places to Stay

The friendly STF hostel *Turistgården* (☎ 0253-104 37), at Sjukstugvägen 4 near the main bus stop, is open all year round. The hostel *Björkhagen* (☎ 0253-103 08) nearby is also open all year. *Knappgården* (☎ 0253-

180 60) at Särnaheden has doubles for 330 kr and beds for 125 kr in multi-bed rooms.

Getting There & Away

Dalatrafik bus No 170 runs from Falun and Mora.

MICKELTEMPLET

For one of the best views in Sweden, drive up or climb the peak Mickeltemplet two km above Särna village. There, from an altitude of 625 metres, you can see much of upper Dalarna and the peaks around Städjan. There is a lift and two simple runs (up to 350 metres) and 30 km of nordic trails. For lessons or ski hire book at Halvarssons Alpin (☎ 0253-106 00).

FULUFJÄLLET

The mountain Fulufjället, west of Särna, feeds **Njupekärs** Sweden's tallest waterfall at 100 metres. Road 1056 from Särna leads towards the Norwegian border through rugged and beautiful country. The road leading south from the junction at Mörkret, 30 km from Särna, turns into a mountain trail (you can park near Stormorsvallen) and leads about two km to the falls at the beginning of the ancient forests of the **nature reserve**. Maps are available at the tourist office at Särna.

IDRE

Idre, the ski centre, gives a view of the singular peak **Städjan** (not a volcano) from the Nipfjället road. Bus No 70 runs from Mora, although there are occasional direct services from Stockholm.

Most sports gear, including canoes, can be hired at the resort **Idre Fjäll**, but the attraction is the countryside and the skiing. There are 30 downhill runs (lift cards cost 115 kr a day), a bank, post office and a small supermarket.

You can also try driving dog sleds (book first on 0253-412 32) and snow scooters (90 minutes instruction from 300 kr). For other bookings and details dial 0253-400 00.

Places to Stay
There is a hostel *Larsgården* (☎ 0253-202 28) at Byvägen 35. *Lövåsgården fjällhotel* (☎ 0253-290 29) has single/double flats from 195/320 kr. The price drops to 140/190 kr from mid-June to September.

Norrland

The northern half of Sweden, Norrland, has always been considered separately from the rest of the country, associated with forest and dale and the pioneers' struggle with them. The development of the Swedish working class here was decisive.

The timber remains but most mining moved north to Kiruna and Malmberget. The wilderness attracts walkers and skiers for much of the year.

Inlandsbanan, the train service from Mora to Gällivare via Östersund, Storuman and Arvidsjaur, will cost 300 kr to travel the whole distance in one go, but a tourist ticket for 710 kr allows you to jump on and off the train at will for a fortnight.

Getting north from Sundsvall by train is a night exercise only; you can change trains in some comfort at Ånge.

GÄVLE
Gävle is probably the most pleasant of the northern cities to walk in, mainly because of its architecture (note the contrast between the wooden residences of Villastaden and Gamla Gefle).

Information
The tourist office is through the courtyard of the Berggrenska gården quarter by the river off Kyrkogatan.

Money All main banks have branches in the city and several are open to 5 pm on Thursdays. You can also exchange money at the central post office.

Post & Telecommunications The central post office is at Drottninggatan 16 off Stortorget. The Telebutik is at Drottninggatan 29. The telephone code is 026.

Emergency The duty pharmacy at Nygatan 31 is not open at night; go to the medical centre off Västra vägen. The police are at Centralgatan 1.

Things to See
The **castle** on the south bank of Gävleån is now far from its state of former splendour and is closed to the public, but you can get an idea of the town's past at the regional **Gästriklandsmuseum** on Södra Strandgatan. This museum has remains of the **Björkebåten** wooden boat from the 5th century and emphasises all aspects of the city's maritime past. Admission is free, it's closed on Monday.

The **Silvanum** forestry museum (free, closed Mondays), by the river, features aspects of forestry and conservation and there is a practical demonstration at the small wood **Boulognerskogen** over the footbridge and **Valls Hage** further west. The oldest of the churches in Gävle is the **Heliga Trefaldighets kyrka** at the west end of Drottninggatan, which has an 11th century **rune stone** inside.

Railway buffs or big children will not resist the preserved **steam locomotives** of **Järnvägsmuseet**, on Rälsgatan off Österbågen, (closed most Mondays and public holidays). Admission costs 20 kr.

The leisure park **Furuvik** about 12 km south-east of Gävle aims to provide a little of everything; you can behave like a monkey on the loops and mini-train rides and then see the real thing at the **Gibbon House**. The park is open daily from mid-May to mid-August to 5 or 6 pm. Admission is 85 kr (children 55 kr) in summer and a day token for all rides costs 75 kr.

Summer boat tours to the island **Limön** can be booked at the tourist office. Limön, part of an archipelago, has a **nature trail** and there is a mass grave and **memorial** to the sailors of a ship that was lost early last century.

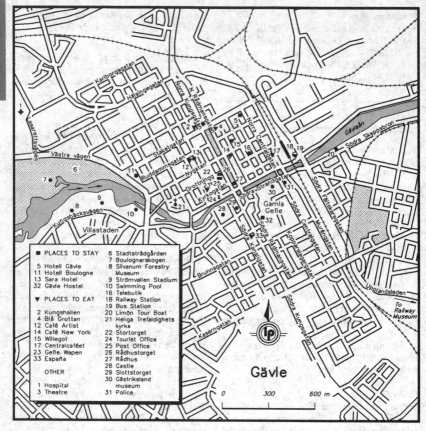

PLACES TO STAY

- 5 Hotell Gävle
- 11 Hotell Boulogne
- 13 Sara Hotel
- 32 Gävle Hostel

▼ PLACES TO EAT

- 2 Kungshallen
- 4 Blå Grottan
- 12 Café Artist
- 14 Café New York
- 15 Willegot
- 17 Centralcaféet
- 23 Gefle Wapen
- 33 España

OTHER

- 1 Hospital
- 3 Theatre
- 6 Stadsträdgården
- 7 Boulognerskogen
- 8 Silvanum Forestry Museum
- 9 Strömvallen Stadium
- 10 Swimming Pool
- 16 Telebutik
- 18 Railway Station
- 19 Bus Station
- 20 Limön Tour Boat
- 21 Heliga Trefaldighets kyrka
- 22 Stortorget
- 24 Tourist Office
- 25 Post Office
- 26 Rådhustorget
- 27 Rådhus
- 28 Castle
- 29 Slottstorget
- 30 Gästrikland museum
- 31 Police

Gävle

0   300   600 m

Places to Stay

Eleven km south of the city, *Furuviks Camping* (☎ 980 28) on road 76, is open from mid-May to September.

The STF *Gävle hostel* (☎ 62 17 45), at Södra Rådmansgatan 1, is excellent and is open all year. The hostel *Engeltofta* (☎ 961 60) is at Bönavägen 118 about six km northeast of the city.

Hotell Gävle (☎ 11 54 70), at Staketgatan 44, has singles/doubles for 350/525 kr at weekends and from mid-April to mid-August.

Hotell Boulogne (☎ 12 63 52) at Bygg-mästargatan 1 has some budget beds and singles/doubles cost from 300/410 kr in summer and at weekends.

At Hemlingby Friluftsgård's, *Hemlingby stugan* (☎ 11 70 15), on Hemlingbyvägen four km from the city (take bus No 3), singles/doubles cost 230/340 kr.

Places to Eat

Gefle Wapen, at Norra Slottsgatan 3, is a little over mid-priced for lunch but is a pleasant steak restaurant with a rock pub downstairs.

Café Artist, at Norra Slottsgatan 9, is elegant but subdued. *Café New York*, at

Nygatan 24, and *Kungshallen,* at Norra Kungsgatan 17, are the budget options at any time. *Centralcaféet* opposite the railway station is cheap for solid meals. Its clientele is animated.

España, at Södra Kungsgatan 18A, is mid-priced and provides some vegetarian pizzas. There is a disco as well as lunch specials at *Blå Grottan,* at Norra Rådmansgatan 20, and the pub-restaurant *Willegot,* on Norra Köpmangatan, offer happy-hour specials of dinner and ale.

Getting There & Away
Direct trains run from Stockholm via Uppsala and continue on to Östersund or Sundsvall and Luleå. Express bus No 800 runs to Falun and on to Gothenburg via Karlstad. Regional buses run to Uppsala and Falun from Hamntorget and SJ services are supplemented by regional trains.

Getting Around
Most local buses come to Nygatan near Stora torget or Rådhustorget. For a taxi dial 12 90 00 (flagfall is only 10 kr).

SUNDSVALL
The town of Sundsvall developed around the timber industry, but was built in stone. Determined rebuilding after a fire more than 100 years ago has left a legacy of **stone façades** up and down Storgatan and at Stora Torget, monuments to the wealth of the forest industry.

The tourist office at Stora Torget is open daily from June to August. The post office is at Köpmangatan 19 and the Telebutik, at Kyrkogatan 11.

Things to See
The big **Kulturmagasinet** has been redesigned from the original stone buildings on Packhusgatan. Its museums record the industrial strife that happened in the forests during the last century and was so formative in modern Swedish working-class attitudes. The museums are free and open daily.

The beautiful frescoes of the medieval church **Alnö gamla kyrka** north of the

bridge on Alnö are open daily from 9 am to 7 pm from mid-June to mid-August. In fine condition today, they were painted in the 1500s.

Getting There & Away
Sundsvall is on the E4 and the Stockholm-to-Haparanda railway line, and there are also train services to Östersund, where you change for Trondheim. Getting north by train is a struggle as the trains only operate at night. You can change at Ånge (the most comfortable option) or Bräcke. For ferries to Finland see the Sweden Getting There & Away section.

STORSJÖN
The lake Storsjön attracts people for summer and winter sports and its share of campers. This area used to be Norwegian and many of the locals maintain an independent spirit. The island **Frösö** is reached by road or footbridge from the middle of Östersund.

The features are the animals at **Frösöns djurpark** (open from mid-May to August, 65 kr), the old **Frösöns kyrka** and its characteristic separate **bell tower**, and the fishing (get local permits from Domänverket at Storgatan 16). For skiers there are slalom and nordic runs on the island at Ostberget (lift cards cost 200 kr a day). Lake cruises on an old steamship from Östersund cost from 40 to 75 kr (for up to five hours). Most importantly, there is a monster in the lake.

ÖSTERSUND
In the town of Östersund **Jämtlands läns museum**, with its fine prehistoric and music collection, is free and open daily. The curiosity is the **Överhögdal tapestry**, a Viking Age relic that appears to depict churches from a time 200 years before Christianity properly arrived. The museum village **Jamtli fornby** is open from Midsummer to mid-August (50 kr).

Information
The regional tourist office on the small square on Kyrkgatan deals with all of the Storsjön area. The budget card Storsjökortet,

valid for nine days, gives discounts or free entry to activities in the area (95 kr). The post office is at Storgatan 38 and handles currency exchanges until 5 pm. The Telebutik is at Kyrkgatan 62. The telephone code is 063.

Places to Stay & Eat

The *Vandrarhemmet Jamtli* (☎ 10 59 84), at Museiplan, has reasonably priced beds in multi-bed rooms and the STF hostel *Alléhemmet* (☎ 10 23 43) is at Tingsgatan 12 (open from mid-June to early August).

The small *City Hotellet* (☎ 10 84 15), at Artillerigatan 4, has singles/doubles starting at 350/450 kr. Private rooms and cabins can be booked at the tourist office (for a fee of 40 kr) at rates from about 125 kr a night.

The *Brassière Le Coq* on Residensgränd might be good value, but *Volos* at Prästgatan 38 is open daily. *Lilla Cafét* at No 44 is good for sandwiches and there is a budget-conscious countercultural crowd at *Café Tingshuset* on the corner of Rådhusgatan and Samuel Permans Gata.

Getting There & Away

Linjeflyg flies from Stockholm to the airport on Frösö. Express buses also run from Sundsvall. The railway station is a short walk from the town centre, but the main regional bus station is at Gustaf III Torg. Trains run direct from Stockholm through Gävle or from Sundsvall, some to Trondheim. (If you're travelling on the train from Sundsvall you'll have to change.) Regional trains shuttle from Sundsvall.

Getting Around

Local buses run to the railway station and past the main bus station: bus Nos 3 and 4 go to Frösön. Cycling on Frösön is popular and a free map of paths is available at the tourist office.

LULEÅ

The tourist office in Luleå is at Rådstugatan 9 and other offices operate at Trekanten and Lule Gammelstad in summer. The post office is at Storgatan 59, the Telebutik is at Kungsgatan 29.

Things to See

The shipping of iron ore established Luleå economically and an evening walk around the harbour offers some atmosphere. More potent reminders of the past are at **Lule Gammelstad**, the biggest of the restored 'church villages' that housed the pioneers on their weekend pilgrimages (happening in this case since at least the 1400s). There are more than 400 buildings. Take bus No 8 (No 32 alternates there at weekends). Guided tours can be booked at the tourist office in summer.

The rail museum **Karlsvikshyttan** at Karlsvik is claimed as unique in its focus on hopper wagons for iron ore. The regional **Norbottens Museum** is in Hermelinsparken (open daily).

Places to Stay

A summer option is the cabins at Klubbviken (☎ 0920-585 91) on an island 20 km from the town centre; you take the boat from the small boat harbour No 1 at Södra hamn. The two-bed cabins cost 150 kr a night, four-bed 450 kr from mid-June to mid-August. Camp sites are also available.

Örnvik (☎ 0920-523 25) is a holiday village with a hotel charging 315/500 kr a single/double in summer. There are cabins and a small STF hostel with extra rooms from 165 kr. Örnvik is eight km from town (take bus No 6 to Norra Gäddvik and follow the walking track). The tourist office can arrange private rooms costing from 150 kr.

Getting There & Away

There are daily flights from Stockholm and Kiruna to the local airport, seven km south of the town (the airport bus costs 40 kr). Luleå is the start of Malmbanan, the 500 km iron-ore route to Narvik in Norway (coming from the south, you change trains at Boda).

Getting Around

The regional bus station is near the railway on Prästgatan, although most local buses run nearby, along Storgatan. Some buses stop in the evenings, but if you are stuck, the yellow

Sexan taxis (☎ 666 66) will take you anywhere nearby for up to 100 kr.

ARVIDSJAUR

Welcome to Lapland. The small settlement of Arvidsjaur on Inlandsbanan was an early Sami market. The museum village **Sita Sameland** is run by the Sami community. There are almost 100 buildings as well as forestry and reindeer breeding. Tours cost 20 kr. The tourist office (☎ 0960-175 00) on Garvaregatan will help you book accommodation.

Road 95 leads to Arvidsjaur from Skellefteå (bus No 351) and road 94 from Luleå (bus No 354). Road 88 leads north to Jokkmokk and Gällivare and Linjeflyg has flights from Stockholm.

VUOLLERIM

Road 97 runs from Boden to Jokkmokk, following the beautiful wooded valley of the Lule älv. Vuollerim, a village about two-thirds of the way to Jokkmokk, sells petrol and groceries and has a post office. Of deeper interest is the **Stone Age museum** – reconstructive archaeology that tries to make sense of how harsh life must have been. You can use some of countless objects collected by the research group Arkeologi Vuollerim.

JOKKMOKK

The village of Jokkmokk, reached by Inlandsbanan, is just north of the Arctic Circle and started as a Sami market and mission. The Sami winter fair still takes place early in February, when you can shop seriously for handicrafts *(sámi duodji)*.

Information

The tourist office (☎ 0971-121 40) at Stortorget is open daily from 8 am to 4 pm (to 8 pm in June, July and August). It also has information you need for braving the snows or mountainous interior, although you should see the mountain information room at the museum. Fill out your travel plan on a special postcard and submit it before you leave.

The police are on the corner of Storgatan

and Klockarvägen. The medical centre (☎ 0971-11350, after hours 11356) is at Lappstavägen 9. Banks are open to 3 pm weekdays (to 4 pm on Fridays).

Things to See & Do

On Kyrkogatan, **Ájtte** is a Sami and mountain museum with **handicrafts** on sale, although they are not cheap. The information on the national parks is excellent and includes slides (20 kr, open daily in summer, closed Mondays from October to April).

The beautiful **wooden church** on Storgatan should be seen; the 'old' church in Hantverkargatan has been rebuilt, as the original was burned in the 18th century. The wooden museum buildings off Lappstavägen behind the medical and dental centre are small but complete and recall the age of the Sami missions. Track bikes and snow mobiles can be hired at Rosengrens El, Ulleniusgatan 12 (closed weekends).

Fishing The Kronogård areas are ideal for fishing, but you will need a local Domän fishing card (85 kr a day, 325 kr a week) from the tourist office in Luleå or Fritidsmagasinet in Jokkmokk (ask at the tourist office). The information centre is 10 km off road 88, about 50 km due south of Jokkmokk. The tourist office has a small brochure with a map and can explain restrictions.

Solar Photography If you are visiting the area just to photograph the midnight sun, don't point and shoot. Firstly, remember the sun is always dangerous to look at. Secondly, try a few settings in combination or else you may be disappointed. Success is possible through narrow to medium apertures at exposures of about $\frac{1}{30}$ of a second and some people use red or orange filters. On automatic cameras it might help to trip the light meter into a slightly longer exposure. Experiment and avoid disappointment.

Places to Stay & Eat

For accommodation ring ahead and book a private room from 120 kr a night. *Hotell Gastis* (☎ 0971-100 12) has mid-priced rooms and the *STF hostel* (☎ 0971-119 77) is open during June, July and August. At *Jokkmokks Turistcenter* (☎ 0971-123 70), three km south-east of town, four-bed cabins are 230 kr. The liveliest restaurant is *Restaurang Milano* in Berggatan.

Getting There & Away

Bus No 251 runs from Luleå to Jokkmokk and Gällivare. Bus No 102 runs from Gällivare (66 kr, a good cheap tour through Muddus national park) and bus No 253 from Luleå is also useful. The ride to Murjek (42 kr), from where you can pick up the Malmbana train, is also beautiful. Buses stop at the old railway station.

GÄLLIVARE & MALMBERGET

The twin towns of Gällivare and Malmberget are important for mining and winter sports, exploiting the bald hill Dundret. The tourist office (☎ 0970-166 60) is at Storgatan 16 and is most helpful in organising accommodation and tours to national parks. The Telebutik is in the Domus at Västra Kyrkallén 7. The police (☎ 0970-110 60) are at Prästgatan 1. The hospital is at Källgatan 14.

Things to See & Do

In Malmberget the museum village **Kåkstan** and **mining museum** are open from mid-June to early August. Gold-panning and tours of the **Aitik copper mine** can be arranged at the tourist office.

The top of the hill **Dundret** is a nature reserve and the view is reputed to encompass a twelfth of Sweden; the ski lifts are all on the town side. Gear hire starts at 130 kr a day (620 kr a week) for downhill. There are six lifts, 13 runs of varying difficulty and four nordic courses. Nordic gear is a little cheaper, from 80 kr.

Places to Stay

Hotell Polar (☎ 0970-111 90), at Per Högströmsgatan 9, has rooms from 290/450 kr a single/double. The *STF hostel* (☎ 0970-147 81) is at Barnhemsvägen 2A and is open all year. *Lapphärbärget*, over the footbridges by the river, has beds for 100 kr.

Getting There & Away

Linjeflyg flies direct to the airport (10 km from town) from Luleå, Gothenburg and Stockholm. Länstrafik i Nörrbotten buses run to the regional bus station on Lasarettsgatan.

KIRUNA

The midnight sun lasts from the end of May to mid-July in Kiruna and there is darkness throughout December and New Year. The tourist office (☎ 0980-188 80), next to the library at Hjalmar Lundbohmsvägen 42, will not book accommodation by phone. But you can organise tours of the **LKAB iron mine**, the world's biggest underground dig in summer (daily, 65 kr) or the space base **Esrange** (95 kr). The post office is at Föreningsgatan 1 and a Telebutik is at Geologgatan 2.

Places to Stay

Hotels are expensive. The *STF hostel* (☎ 0980-171 95 or 0980-127 84) at Skyttegatan 16A opens only from mid-June to the end of July. Try *Yellow House* (☎ 0980-114 51), at Renstigen 1, where rooms cost 150/270 kr for a single/double or try Vildmarkshörnan (☎ 0980-19234).

Getting There & Away

There are daily nonstop SAS flights from Luleå and Stockholm to the airfield about 10 km from the town. The ticket office is at Hannugatan 1. Bus No 101 runs from Gällivare, No 001 to Riksgränsen at the Norwegian border. These stop by the tourist office. Kiruna is on Malmbanan and there are trains from Narvik and Luleå.

NATIONAL PARKS

The parks are scarcely mapped and only a couple of rude roads lead into the glacier area. But STF runs summer boats on Torneträsk and from Saltoluokta. The vegetation thins out to bald hills and rugged peaks that provide exceptional views. Waterproof boots are essential at any time of the year: the thaw is in May and June, and the best hiking is available from midsummer to September, but be careful when wading across streams nonetheless. It can still be cold, especially in the valleys, despite the midnight sun. Winter escapades are too risky for the uninitiated because of the risk of an avalanche (see Activities, Skiing in the Sweden Facts for the Visitor section). The rescue telephone number is 90 000.

Good information is available at the tourist offices and the mountain centre at the museum in Jokkmokk. Let the tourist office or police know your plans and stick to them. Get someone to help fill in a *färdmeddelande* postcard with your plans. The range of 1:100,000 Fjällkartor maps costs 70 kr or more each. Tours are organised by STF, which maintains huts and several big mountain stations with excellent facilities and services. Various types of phones are installed in or near mountain huts and hikers are urged to use them to check weather or conditions: the huts are listed in the *STF Fjällhandbok*. For weather reports dial 0971-100 54 (Jokkmokk, from January to the start of May), 0970-158 08 (Gällivare, from mid-February) or 0980-113 50 (Kiruna, from mid-February).

Using buses is a good way to begin your adventures in this region. You can send on extra luggage with bus drivers to an agreed destination for 40 kr.

Sarek

The magical landscape of Sarek national park covers an area of 2000 sq km. It comprises 100 glaciers and countless peaks, only a handful of which are over 2000 metres high. This is most beautiful yet demanding country, only for the tough and experienced (who will need to do their homework thoroughly). Perhaps the best views are over the lake and delta of **Laiture** on the Rapa älv, not far from the eastern boundary of the park. The most experienced hikers (and only they should go without a group tour) will take a week or more to get in and out. There are no huts and few bridges. General access rights

(see Activities in the Sweden Facts for the Visitor section) apply, and fires may only be set where and when safe. No vehicles!

A common way in is from the south from STF's Kvikkjokk Fjällstation (☎ 0971-210 22), more than 100 km up a rough but beautiful lakeside road north-west of Jokkmokk (take bus No 253 from Luleå, Boden or Jokkmokk a few times daily). From Gällivare take bus No 103 to the STF cabin at Ritsem.

Please read the Sarek STF sheet in English or Naturvårdsverket's brochure *Sarek – Myth and Reality*, available at tourist offices in the region.

Stora Sjöfallet

The highlight of the Stora Sjöfallet national park is the mountain lake **Langas** and the **waterfall**, which wanders back down the valley and widens into Stora Lulevatten. The falls are near the south-east edge of the park at the end of a mountain road. Sarek shares the southern boundary.

Abisko

The tiny Abisko national park is on the long lake Torneträsk, well served by the mountain highway from Kiruna to Narvik. It is the soft option of the northern parks, less rugged and more accessible following the Kamajåkka valley. Trains stop at Abisko Östra, Abisko Turist (the STF station (☎ 0980-400 00), closed in the afternoons, when you buy tickets on board) and Björkliden (two hours from Kiruna) at the western edge of the park or take bus No 001 from Kiruna. Björkliden is a complete tourist village.

Apart from the north gate to Kungsleden and the nearby Sami camp there are three paths and a cabin and camp site at Abiskojaure.

KUNGSLEDEN

You could need a month to cover Kungsleden, a 500-km well-marked hiking trail, properly (bring rubber boots, map and compass). August and September are recommended months for hiking because in June and July there is still some boggy ground which attracts the mosquitoes.

The Kungsleden trail leads south from Abisko, skirts Sarek and offers a diversion to the summit of **Kebnekaise**, Sweden's highest peak, where STF has a mountain station (☎ 0980-550 42). The trail finishes at Hemavan north-west of Tärnaby on the E12 near the Norwegian border. It is easier to take on sections or just take day walks with leaders from the mountain stations.

Huts are spread at 10 to 20 km intervals between Abisko and Kvikkjokk, but then there are none until Ammarnäs (pay at the nearest STF station if there is no warden). You need a sleeping bag only as there are blankets and gas inside. The mountain station Saltoluokta (☎ 0973-410 10) offers succour and comfortable facilities, sports gear for hire and buses out (connecting with the lake boat in summer). STF produces an information sheet in English and packages information on the trail in three stages.

Götaland

The rolling country of Götaland in south central Sweden is crossed by the **Göta canal**, which links with Roxen north of Linköping and flows eventually into the great lake **Vättern** at Motala. The forested province of Småland deserves a section to itself, but the traveller will probably be drawn to the glassworks country and the southern half of Vättern. Using buses in Östergötland can be cheaper with the tourist tickets you can buy at ÖstgötaTrafiken bus stations, tourist offices or post offices (60 kr for a day, 120 kr for three days). A länskort (300 kr) covers all travel in July and August.

NORRKÖPING

The principal attraction of the area around Norrköping is the animal park at Kolmården, 30 km north of Norrköping, but there is plenty to see in the city as well.

Information

The summer tourist card Kolmården-Norrköpingskortet (185 kr) is valid for three days and includes free bus travel with Östgöta-Trafiken and entry at Kolmården and other attractions. There are also restaurant discounts and bonuses. Children's cards are 65 kr. The tourist office Destination Norrköping is at Drottninggatan 11 and open daily. The office sells the one and three-day tourist cards.

Money All main banks have branches in the city and you can exchange money at the central post office until 5 pm on weekdays.

Post & Telecommunications The central post office is at Drottninggatan 20 and the Telebutik at Drottninggatan 28. The local telephone code is 011.

Emergency The duty pharmacy is at Hantverkaregatan 24 and the hospital is on Södra Promenaden (enter from Gymstikgatan). You'll find the police at Stockholmsgatan 4.

Things to See

Admission to the art museum **Norrköpings konstmuseum**, at Kristinaplatsen, is free (closed Mondays in summer). The most important works are from early this century. The city museum **Stadsmuseum** (free and open daily) at Västgötegatan 19 is concerned with the town's industrial past. More general is Sweden's only museum of work, **Arbetets Museum**, nearby (open daily). For a view of the city and out on to Bråviken climb the **Rådhuset** tower (10 kr, open in summer except Sundays). **Sankt Olai kyrka** in the park at the centre of town is one of the few noteworthy Baroque specimens in Sweden.

Good examples of the characteristic northern Bronze Age **rock carvings** are near the city at Himmelstalund, painted red on a smooth outcrop overlooking the playing fields west of the E4 (take bus No 115 from Repslagaregatan).

Activities

The tiny vintage tram No 1 runs three times

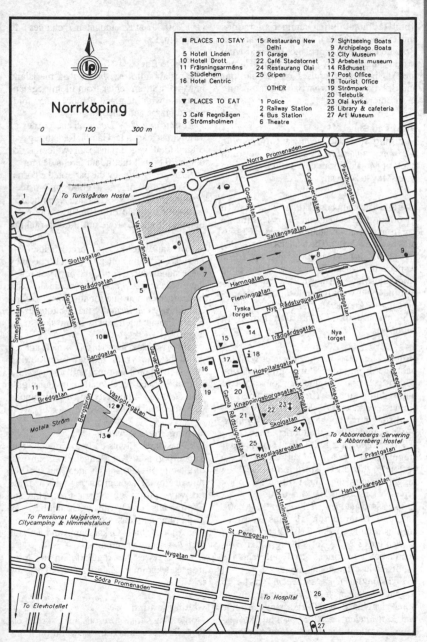

Norrköping

0   150   300 m

PLACES TO STAY
5 Hotell Linden
10 Hotell Drott
11 Frälsningsarméns Studiehem
16 Hotel Centric

PLACES TO EAT
3 Café Regnbågen
8 Strömsholmen
15 Restaurang New Delhi
21 Garage
22 Café Stadstornet
24 Restaurang Olai
25 Gripen

OTHER
1 Police
2 Railway Station
4 Bus Station
6 Theatre
7 Sightseeing Boats
9 Archipelago Boats
12 City Museum
13 Arbebets museum
14 Rådhuset
17 Post Office
18 Tourist Office
19 Strömpark
20 Telebutik
23 Olai kyrka
26 Library & cafeteria
27 Art Museum

from **Rådhuset** during summer afternoons and evenings (25 kr). Boats cruise around Bråviken and the archipelago from mid-May to mid-August (55 kr, 1½ hours from Hamnbron). Sightseeing cruises on the harbour and Bråviken depart from Saltängsbron daily in summer (55 kr).

Places to Stay
Camping Sites near the city at *Citycamping & Himmelstalund* (☎ 17 11 90) on the south bank of Motala Ström cost 110 kr. It's open from May to August.

Hostels The main hostel *Turistgården* (☎ 10 11 60), at Ingelstadsgatan 31, is less than a km from the railway station (closed at Christmas and New Year). The hostel *Abborreberg* (☎ 11 93 44) is camping-class in some respects but is beautifully situated. It's open from mid-May to August. Take bus No 111 to Lindö and walk through to the Abborreberg park. Another hostel (☎ 39 11 22) is seven km from Kolmården (open in summer).

Hotels The hotels become cheaper with the package Kolmården-Norrköpingspaketet, which fixes prices in double rooms for two nights during summer (from 585 kr a person, singles 200 kr extra). Prices for each hotel are listed in the booklet *DIN Norrköpings-guide* available from the tourist office.

Hotel Centric (☎ 12 90 30) at Gamla Rådstugugatan 18 is a good city hotel at the bottom of this price-list. If you are seeking bigger savings, the tourist office can book private rooms from 110 kr a night.

The associated *Hotell Drott* (☎ 18 00 60), at Tunnbindaregatan 19, has summer singles/doubles from 320/420 kr. *Hotell Linden* (☎ 12 25 33), at Vattengränden 7, is dearer but holds prices steady all year. It's small and has shared amenities.

Frälsningsarméns Studiehem (☎ 12 15 33), at Bredgatan 46, is a summer student hotel charging 240/340 kr a single/double and *Elevhotellet* (☎ 22 27 50), at Ektorpsgatan 2, is similarly priced. *Hotel Kneippen*

(☎ 13 30 60), at Kneippgatan 7, charges 340 kr for singles.

Places to Eat
The restaurant *Strömsholmen* on the island in Motala Ström (enter from Fleminggatan) is stylish with meat and fish but offers mid-priced pizzas and salads.

Restaurang New Delhi on the corner of Trädgårdsgatan and Gamla Rådstugugatan offers food vegetarians will welcome for under 70 kr, but the Indian fare is dearer.

Restaurang Olai by the park on the corner of Skolgatan offers a good mid-priced dinner. The lunch specials at *Gripen* nearby on Drottninggatan offer the best low-price options. It and *Garage* are the top-ranking nightspots.

For sandwiches and breakfasts *Café Regnbågen* at the railway station is cheap by these standards, so don't wait until you reach the city centre. *Café Stadstornet* in the park is in the open and fine for sit-down burgers. The *library cafeteria* at Stadsbiblioteket off Södra Promenaden makes a fair shoestring lunch.

Abborrebergs Servering is a pleasant tea room by the youth hostel overlooking Bråviken (open in summer until about 9 pm). The mid-priced lunch restaurant and nightclub *Garage* is in the city on Drottninggatan opposite Stadstornet.

Getting There & Away
SAS has direct flights daily to Copenhagen. The airport is at Kungsängen, four km east of the city on Arkösundsvägen (bus No 115 runs nearby). The main bus station is near the railway station on Norra Promenaden. Express bus No 830 runs to Gothenburg via Jönköping and bus Nos 835 and 837 run from Stockholm to Oskarshamn and Kalmar (and to Öland in summer).

Rail services run regularly on the lines from Stockholm to Malmö and from Mjölby to Västerås.

Getting Around
Norrköping's transport runs on 13-kr tickets that allow one hour's travel, valid on trams

and city buses. The welcome trams cover the city and are the quickest for short or long hops, especially to and from the central station up along Drottninggatan.

KOLMÅRDEN

The Kolmården zoo is billed as the biggest in Europe and has about 1000 animals from all climates and continents. The complex is divided into a main **zoo** and **tropical house** (40 kr), a **safari park** (70 kr) and **dolphinarium** (70 kr). A general ticket will cost 190 kr in summer (children under 14 years pay 30% of this, those under five pay nothing). The cable car is the best way to view the animals reposing in the open areas.

The zoo is open all year from 10 am to 5 pm (to 6 pm in summer) and you'll need all day to take it in fully. Kolmården is on the north shore of Bråviken, turn east off the E4 near Strömfors (take bus No 432 from Norrköping).

LINKÖPING

The city of Linköping is one of Sweden's oldest and the attractions are its churches and museums.

Information

The tourist office is at Ågatan 39 (closed Saturday afternoon and Sundays).

Money The main banks have city branches open to 5 pm or you can change money at the central post office.

Post & Telecommunications The central post office is at Kungsgatan 20 and the Telebutik is at Ågatan 29. The telephone code is 013.

Emergency The duty pharmacy is at Stora Torget 5. The duty hospital is on Westmansgatan at Valla, south-west of the city. The police are at Kungsgatan 23.

Things to See

Gamla Linköping on Malmslättsvägen near the Valla roundabout west of the city is one of the biggest of the Swedish living-museum villages. Some of items you can see include a **post office, pottery** and a small **chocolate factory**. Most buildings are open at weekends and on Wednesdays. The information office is open daily in summer and on weekdays during the rest of the year. At other times you can wander among the 19th century buildings at will. There is no general admission charge. Take bus Nos 204 to 207.

Exhibits in the **Flygvapenmuseum** illustrate air-force history from all periods and include familiar biplanes in unfamiliar Swedish livery and the admired Swedish technology of the jet age. There are about 50 aircraft in all. The museum is on Carl Cederströms gata, Malmslätt (10 kr, take bus No 551 from the main bus terminal).

Östergötlands länsmuseum at Raoul Wallenbergs plats has a big collection by a variety of European painters. This collection includes Cranach's view of Eden, *Original Sin*, and Swedish art reaching back to the Middle Ages. The **prehistoric collection** is well organised and there is a Linköping collection. Shifting exhibitions are in the display hall. Entry is free but special exhibitions cost 20 kr, including a cup of coffee at the café, and the museum is closed Mondays. The regional **handicrafts collection** is at the rear of the old library at Ågatan 65 (open Mondays and Tuesdays).

The episcopal and monastic influences have been strong. The **cathedral** in Romanesque and Gothic styles on Sankt Persgatan is one of Sweden's oldest and biggest, although **Sankt Lars kyrka** on Storgatan is also superb and has an 11th century **gravestone** carved with runes. The Baroque veneer comes from this century. The old Cistercian convent **Vreta kloster** at the intersection 11 km north-east of the city near Berg has been restored in its Romanesque features (bus No 521or 620 from Linköping).

Activities

Boat cruises on Kinda kanal and Roxen run from mid-May to August from Tullbron on Järnvägsgatan across the lake or down the canal to Rimforsa. The canal trip, on MF *Kind*, takes more than six hours in all and

SWEDEN

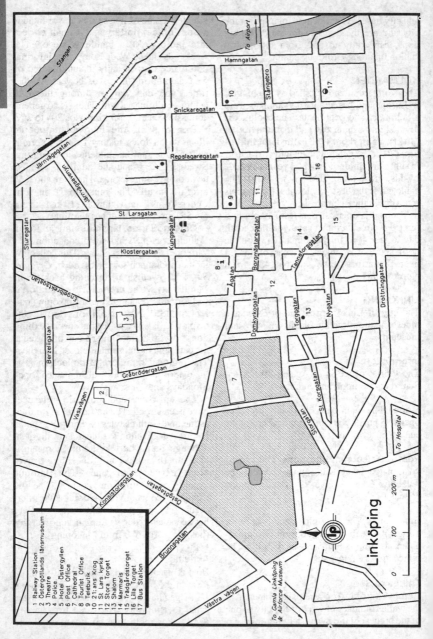

Linköping

1 Railway Station
2 Östergötlands länsmuseum
3 Theatre
4 Police
5 Hotel Östergyllen
6 Post Office
7 Cathedral
8 Tourist Office
9 Telebutik
10 21:ans Krog
11 S:t Lars kyrka
12 Stora Torget
13 Shalom
14 Marmaris
15 Trädgårdstorget
16 Lilla Torget
17 Bus Station

costs from 235 kr (return trip by bus or train included). Book at the tourist office or Rederi AB Kind (☎ 0141-148 25).

Places to Stay

The *STF hostels* are at Björnkärrsgatan 14 off Malmslättsvägen (☎ 17 64 58), open from early in June to mid-May (take bus Nos 204, 205, 206 and 219); and at Klostergatan 524 (☎ 14 90 90), open all year. Another hostel (☎ 666 56) is at Ljungsbro and is open from mid-May to mid-August (take bus Nos 521 or 522).

The tourist office (☎ 20 68 35) books rooms costing from 150 to 185 kr a night. *Hotell Östergyllen* (☎ 10 20 75) at Hamngatan 2B has singles/doubles from 230/300 kr.

Filbyter Motell (☎ 27 00 27) on Norrköpingsvägen at Tallboda cuts prices to 290/365 kr for singles/doubles at weekends and the nearby *Blåklinten* (☎ 12 41 81) charges only 150 kr for simple rooms or 500 kr for a week; neither place includes breakfast. Take bus No 211 to either.

Places to Eat

The *21:ans Krog* on the corner of Ågatan and Snickaregatan caters generally but offers vegetarian fare including pies. *Shalom* in Torggatan and *Marmaris* on Tanneforsgatan offer the pick of the budget pizzas, kebabs and salads. *Wärdhuset* on Gästgivaregatan at Gamla Linköping has style but serves a budget lunch downstairs. While at the village you can lift the calorie count with some of the cakes at the small garden café *Grands Veranda* off Kryddbodtorget.

Things to Buy

The regional handicrafts league runs the shop Östgöta hemslöjd at Storgatan 41, where approved handmade items are for sale.

Getting There & Away

SalAir flies to Malmö and Arlanda and direct to Copenhagen daily. Express bus No 830 runs to Gothenburg and Norrköping. Regular trains run from Stockholm to Malmö through Linköping and local trains

run to Västervik, Hultsfred and Oskarshamn in Småland.

Getting Around

The bus station is at Nygatan 8. Bus No 202 runs from the railway station through the centre of the city. Bus Nos 209 and 210 run past the airport.

VADSTENA

The town of Vadstena on Vättern lake is a legacy of both church and state power. The dominant figure was St Birgitta, who established her order here in the 1370s. The **abbey** and the **castle** compete for the visitor's interest. The atmosphere in the old town and by the lake make it perhaps the most pleasant spot in Sweden. Visit in June or July if you want to see the main sights.

Information

The main tourist office is at Rådhustorget and another office operates inside the castle at weekends (both open from May to September). A coupon giving free admission to the castle and convent and the street train is available for 55 kr.

Things to See

The Renaissance castle **Vadstena slott** looks straight on to the harbour and lake beyond. It is a mighty family project of the early Vasa kings, at first a spare fortress that grew to become an imposing lakeside residence. In the upper apartments are some items of period furniture and paintings including a Van Dyck. The castle and chapel are open daily from June to August, at weekends in September. Admission costs 25 kr.

The 15th century **klosterkyrkan** combines Gothic and Renaissance features. Inside are the accumulated **relics of St Birgitta** and late-medieval art and some of the painted vaulting has been restored. Among the works is the saint depicted during revelation. The **monastery** is to one side and the old convent is now the manor house **Bjälboättens palats** (15 kr, open weekends in June and August, daily in July). The tower

Rödtornet on Sånggatan is the remains of the town church of the period.

The **Rådhus** and the **Vadstenaortens museum** at the square also remain from the 16th century.

Activities

A short museum **steam railway** runs 10 km from Fågelsta from the **station museum** on Järnvägsgatan near the castle (30 kr return) on various Tuesdays, Thursdays and weekends from the end of May to August. The town's street train rattles around the sights in half an hour for 25 kr (June and July only).

The tour boats of Wetterns Båttrafik cruise the lake and stretches of the Göta canal in summer (on Wednesdays in July) to Motala for 40 kr a section. Book at the tourist office.

Places to Stay

A good camping site is *Vätterviksbadet* (☎ 0143-127 30) on the lake two km north of the town (90 kr), open from May to mid-September. The STF hostel (☎ 0143-103 20 or 104 04) is at Skänningegatan 20 near the fire station. The small *Pensionat Solgården* (☎ 0143-143 50), situated at Strågatan 3, has singles/doubles from 290/450 kr and three-bed rooms from 550 kr (with breakfast). You can also stay, expensively, at the *Klosterhotell* (☎ 0143-114 20) in the abbey grounds.

Places to Eat

Rådhuskällaren under the old town hall is a pleasant stone-and-timbered atmosphere and has mid-priced courses. *Hamnserveringen* in the park in front of the castle is an open-air café outside the castle.

Things to Buy

The crafting of bobbin lace is an old industry in Vadstena and several boutiques in the old town ply their wares. There's a range of items at Föreningen Svenska Spetsar at Rådhustorget or Elsa Petersons Spetsaffär at Storgatan 23. Small brochures about Vadstena lace are available there.

Getting There & Away

Bus is the best mode of travel to and from Vadstena (take bus No 610 or 620 from Motala or Linköping). Bicycle is an option as the scenic flatlands around Vättern lend themselves to the pedal. Cycling maps are available at the tourist office.

ALVASTRA KLOSTER

The once powerful 12th century Cistercian monastery Alvastra kloster is largely a garden ruin but the walls of the abbey and some buildings still stand. The monastery is at the south end of the hill **Omberg** off road 50 about 25 km south-west of Vadstena (take bus No 610 from Vadstena). It is a favourite site on a summer evening for plays and music.

RÖKSTENEN

A whole series of ancient legends is alluded to here on Rökstenen, Sweden's biggest and most famous **rune stone**, at the church at **Rök** just off the E4 on the road to Heda and Alvastra (take bus No 665 and get off at Hejla). In ancient and intricate verse, the sections we may understand refer to the Ostrogothic hero-king Theodoric, who conquered depleted Rome in the 6th century, but the stone is dated to 9th century. There is a small tourist centre on the site.

JÖNKÖPING & HUSKVARNA

The towns Jönköping and Huskvarna are as good as linked at the south tip of the lake Vättern. The two places are known to many: Jönköping for safety matches and Huskvarna for precision machines, especially sewing-machines, and for motorcycles.

Information

The main tourist office is in the Djurläkartorget complex above the railway station (open daily in summer, on weekdays from September to May).

Money All main banks are represented and open to 3 pm, or you can exchange money at the central post office to 5 pm and on Saturday mornings.

Post & Telecommunications The central

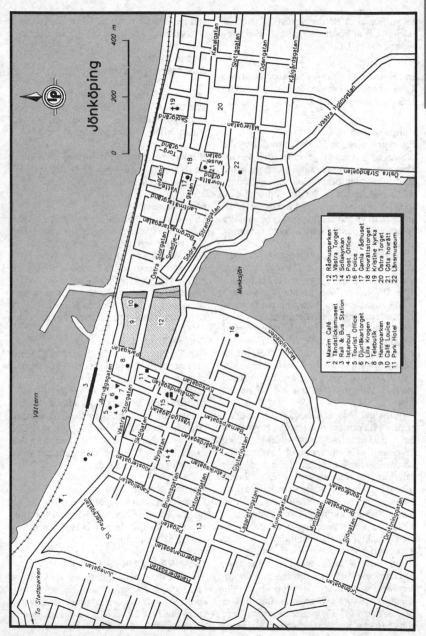

Jönköping

1 Maxim Café	12 Rådhusparken
2 Tändsticksmuseet	13 Västra Torget
3 Rail & Bus Station	14 Sofiakyrkan
4 Istanbul	15 Post Office
5 Tourist Office	16 Police
6 Djurkartorget	17 Gamla rådhuset
7 Lilla Kronen	18 Hovrättstorget
8 Telebutik	19 Kristine kyrka
9 Hamnparken	20 Östra Torget
10 Café Louice	21 Göta hovrätt
11 Park Hotel	22 Länsmuseum

post office is at Barnarpsgatan 17 and the Telebutik is at Västra Storgatan 4. The telephone code is 036.

Emergency The duty pharmacy is at the Ryhov medical centre on Ryhovsgatan. The police are at Vallgatan 3.

Things to See
The match museum **Tändsticksmuseet,** the centre of a tourist precinct off Västra Storgatan west of the railway station, is the most interesting destination. A good guide (in English) explains the development of a Swedish innovation much taken for granted. Entry is 15 kr and the museum is open daily in summer, closed Mondays from September to early in June.

Nearby is the **Radio Museum** with a collection of all manner of TV, phonographs, and memorabilia – a playground for technical buffs (10 kr, closed Mondays).

Above the town to the west is the expanse of **Stadsparken** and its curiosities, which include the 1400 ornithological stuffings of **Fågelmuseet** (10 kr, open daily from May to September), and the little Baroque **Bäckaby kyrka.** The **bell tower** dominates a fine lookout over the towns and Vättern towards Visingsö (take bus No 1C up the hill).

In the old town square of Hovrättstorget are the 17th century buildings of **Hovrätten** and red **Gamla rådhuset,** which is being developed as a **museum of justice.** The **Länsmuseum** collections (free and open daily) at Dag Hammarskjölds plats include art and local history, and no-one should miss the haunting fantasy works of the tragic John Bauer. **Kristine kyrka** on Östra Storgatan is the centre of a restored part of the old town.

In Huskvarna the handicrafts village **Smedbyn,** over the bridge off Jönköpings-vägen south of the town centre, is the most popular local sight and you can buy wares. A **weapons museum** (10 kr) is also in the village. **Dr Skora's Waxworks Cabinet,** at Grännavägen 24, is a bizarre offering where you can leer at Swedes famous (or infamous)

and an eclectic range of other international celebrities (50 kr, open daily in summer).

Places to Stay
Jönköping The *Park Hotel* (☎ 11 19 96) facing Rådhusparken at Kyrkogatan 6 is central with singles from 400 kr in summer. The *Good Morning Hotel* (☎ 16 41 00) on Strömsnäsgatan has doubles for 590 kr, which fall to 420 kr in summer.

Huskvarna The STF hostel *Rosendala* (☎ 10 59 98) is at Odengatan 10 (take bus No 4 from Djurläkartorget to Linnégatan).

Places to Eat
Lilla Krogen, at Barnapsgatan 2, can satisfy most appetites and budgets with solid fare but is closed on Sundays. *Istanbul* at Djurläkartorget with budget kebabs is open late. Some elegance in lunches and evening music is offered at *Maxim Café* in the match-museum precinct. *Café Louice* in the surrounds of Hamnparken is open late in summer and you can eat in the open.

Getting There & Away
Bus No 119 runs to Nässjö and No 120 runs to Gränna. Bus No 306 runs to Falköping and express bus No 839 to Karlstad.

Trains run from Jönköping to Nässjö to connect with the main Stockholm to Malmö trains, but there are also the Länståg rail connections to Nässjö via Vaggeryd, to Eksjö and Oskarshamn and to Halmstad. SJ trains to Falköping connect with services from Gothenburg to Stockholm.

Getting Around
Buses come to the end of the railway station on the shore of the lake. Bus No 4 runs regularly to and from the Huskvarna bus station at Viktoriaplan.

GRÄNNA & VISINGSÖ
The wooden town Gränna has avoided fire and looks today much as it did in the 18th century; walk the main street Brahegatan (take bus Nos 120 or 121 from Jönköping). To the north by the E4 is the impressive ruin

of the 16th century castle **Brahehus**. The tourist office at Torget off Brahegatan is open all year. The hostel *Elevhemmet Berghem* (☎ 0390-110 10) down the street is open only from mid-June to early August (reception is at the tourist office).

Ferries cross to the island **Visingsö** at least every hour in summer. The trip takes 30 minutes. On the island are the ruins of 16th century **Visingsborg** on the east shore near the ferry, attached to a **museum farm** and **herb garden** (15 and 10 kr). Nearby is the contemporary **Brahekyrkan** with beautiful interiors. The 12th century **Näs borg**, about seven km to the south near the islands and partly submerged, is probably the oldest castle in the country. A tourist office at the ferry berth is open daily from May to August.

EKSJÖ
The town of Eksjö suffered its share of fires but many of the precious wooden buildings and part of the medieval street plan have been preserved. The best of the wooden houses are directly north of Stora Torget. There is a tourist office open all year at the **Eksjö Museum**, in a period house with the STF hostel. Take bus No 320 or 321 from Nässjö, bus No 325 from Jönköping, or go by regional train (Länståget). *Hotell Eken* (☎ 0381-109 98), opposite the station, has very good singles for 350 kr.

SMÅLAND GLASSWORKS
Glassworks are associated with Småland and visitors stream in all year, many on day tours by air from Stockholm (730 kr, book at Stockholm Information Service). There are 16 glassworks in Småland, mostly between Växjö and Nybro. The best known manufacturer is Orrefors, based at the village of the same name 17 km north-west of Nybro.

Orrefors Glasbruk is in the village off road 31. There is a small museum of glass manufactures and demonstrations of techniques (open daily). Buses run daily from the railway station at Nybro.

The factory shop (open weekdays to 6 pm, Saturdays and Sundays to 3 or 4 pm) has seconds items, slightly imperfect, on sale. If you want to post crystal home, check that postal services in Sweden and your country recognise fragile packages.

KALMAR
The port of Kalmar was vital to Swedish interests until the 17th century and remains lively with traffic, although its main sights are relics of the earlier period.

Information
The tourist office is at Larmgatan 6 (open daily in summer, on weekdays from September to May).

Post & Telecommunications The post office is at Storgatan 21, although the post centre is across the canal off Esplanaden. The Telebutik is at Storgatan 11. The town's telephone code is 0480. All main banks have branches in Kalmar.

Emergency The duty pharmacy is at the medical centre on Stenbergsvägen, about three km west of the town centre, although there is another on Östra Sjögatan near the cathedral. Police are at Malmbrogatan 10, off Norra vägen.

Things to See
The once powerful Renaissance castle **Kalmar slott** on the water past the railway was the key to Sweden before lands to the south were claimed from Denmark. The documents creating the only unified, shortlived Scandinavia in 1397 and the imprisonment of women in crueller times were witnessed here. A **punishment museum** has been set up inside. The panelled **King Erik chamber** is the interior highlight. Entry costs 25 kr and the castle is open on Saturday and Sunday afternoons to 3 pm from November to March and daily from April to October.

Kalmar läns museum is in the old steam mill by the harbour on Skeppsbrogatan and the highlight is the exhibition of the flagship *Kronan*, which went to the bottom controversially off Öland in 1676 in a disaster to match the *Wasa*'s sinking. The museum is closed on Mondays from mid-August to mid-May (25 kr). Aft and slightly to port is the **Maritime Museum** at the end of Södra Långgatan 81 (open daily in summer, on Sundays only from mid-August to the end of September).

The Baroque **cathedral** on Stortorget is one of the best examples in the country and reflects Italian influences.

Places to Stay & Eat
The STF hostel (☎ 129 28) is attached to *Kalmar Lågprishotell* on Rappegatan, across the bridge from town off Ångöleden. The hotel rooms cost from 265/345 kr for singles/doubles (closed at Christmas and New Year). Singles at *Ritz Hotell* (☎ 155 40) at Larmgatan 6 cost 365 kr. At *Hotell Villa Ängö* (☎ 854 15), Baggensgatan 20, singles start at 300 kr. Private rooms can be booked at the tourist office (☎ 153 50) from 150/200 kr a single/double.

Getting There & Away
Trains run from Alvesta via Växjö to link with Malmö, Helsingborg and Stockholm. The regional bus station is near the railway station, although local buses come to the terminal at the north end of Östra Sjögatan. There are bus timetables at the railway station and services run to all main towns and to Oskarshamn connecting with the ferry to Gotland. Kristina Cruises has services to Helsinki in summer.

To/From Öland Buses run daily to north and south Öland as far as Borgholm and Mörbylånga (Nos 101 to 106, mostly via Färjestaden).

Gothenburg & Bohuslän

The sunny west coast is almost as island-studded as the east. Gothenburg (Swedish: Göteborg, which sounds rather different) has half a million residents. The city is wedded to its port and has a more Continental outlook than Stockholm. Many travellers prefer Gothenburg and hold that the waters that sustain it are every bit as refreshing as the capital's. The province of Bohuslän has fishing villages like Marstrand which offers the nearest possible thing to a summer idyll in the north.

GOTHENBURG
Sweden's second city Gothenburg is its most vital in character, an example (the inhabitants agree) of being half the size, and twice as personal when compared with the capital. On seeing the showpiece boulevard Kungsportsavenyn and the art museum on top of it on a summer's day, the whistle-stop traveller might leap to agree. But there is a lot to Gothenburg, not least its heavy industries and heritage as a port. There is plenty of interest apart from the finer things. The fun park Liseberg and its prominent 'space tower' is statistically Sweden's top attraction.

Orientation
The 17th century expansion and militarism of Gustaf II Adolf and his successors have left the kernel of the city within the remains of canal defences now well suited to sightseeing (its Dutch planners laid out many more canals that are now gone). Of the city towers that menaced the Göta älv only Skansen Kronan to the south remains intact, appropriately as a military museum.

An arm of the canals snakes its way to Liseberg (you can take the boat from near the railway station). A subway from there leads directly to the shopping hub, the boxed and packaged Nordstan. From the centre of the city, Kungsportsavenyn crosses the canal and leads up to Götaplatsen. Culturally speaking, this is the heart of the city with boutiques, restaurants, galleries, theatres and street cafés. The shipyards, showing the symptoms of decline, are on the island of **Hisingen**, which is reached by road from the monumental bridge Älvsborgs bron southwest of the city, by Götaälvbron near the central station, and the tunnel Tingstadstunneln.

Information

Tourist Offices City tourist offices are at Kungsportsplatsen 2 and in the Nordstan shopping complex (open daily, to 8 pm in the middle of summer). The main office of STF is at Östra Larmgatan 15, open weekdays from 9 am to 5.30 pm. There is a telephone guide to daily events, call 11 74 50.

The accommodation and sightseeing package Göteborgspaketet covers two summer nights (or a weekend at other times) in a double room and a Gothenburg card. Depending on your hotel, you will pay from 310 to 585 kr per adult (which will provide a free bed for two children).

Gothenburg Card The Gothenburg card, available separately for one, two or three days for 95, 170 and 225 kr, admits the holder to all museums, Liseberg and sightseeing by bus and canal boat and free travel (within the municipality, which may not include fares to an outlying youth hostel). There is also a free Denmark cruise. Children's cards are a little over half-price. If you cannot resist, you can see, absolutely free, a football local derby at the Ullevi arena! The package can be booked at the tourist office (☎ 10 07 40), the card is available there, at hotels, camping grounds and the Pressbyrå.

Money All main banks have branches open to 5.30 pm daily. The Forex bank (open from 8 am to 9 pm daily) is at the central station, Kungsportsavenyn 22 (to 7 pm weekdays, 3 pm Saturdays) and in the Nordstan complex. You can also exchange money at the ferry terminals or on the ferries.

Post & Telecommunications The central post office is at Drottningtorget 6, and others are in the Nordstan complex and at Kungsportsavenyn 12. The main Telebutik is at Hvitfeldsplatsen. The telephone code is 031.

Emergency The duty pharmacist is in Nordstan (press the button after hours). The hospital is Östra sjukhuset at the No 1 tram terminus. The police are at Skånegatan 5.

Liseberg

Spaceport Liseberg, which is 150 metres high, dominates the park. The ride to the top, attended by sound and vision, climaxes in a spinning dance at the top and a breathless view of the city. The other amusements and rides seem tame by comparison but there is no lack of variety. You can ride all day for 185 kr or select rides for between eight and 24 kr each. The park is open daily from mid-April to September but unfortunately closes by 4 pm. Admission costs from 35 kr early in the season to 40 kr in July (for all visitors aged seven years and over). Take tram No 5 from Brunnsparken.

Museums

After Liseberg the collected museums are the strongest attractions and, if several take your fancy, use Göteborg card or the special museum card for 100 kr available at any entry counter (valid for one year, if you need it).

The central museum **Östindiska huset** has archaeological, ethnographic and historical collections (25 kr, closed Mondays from September to April). **Kronhuset** (25 kr, closed Mondays) has changing art exhibitions.

The handicraft boutiques **Kronhusbodarna** are nearby in the square between Postgatan and Kronhusgatan. The workshops deal in pottery, glass, textiles and works of art and sell their wares in the shop; your visit is free.

Art museums The main collections are at **Konstmuseet** at the top of Götaplatsen. This museum has impressive collections of European masters and is notable for paintings by Rubens, Van Gogh and Rembrandt and characteristic (and uncharacteristic) works by Picasso in the modern and contemporary rooms. The sculpture is behind the main hall. Entry is 25 kr (closed Mondays from September to April). Take bus No 40 from Brunnsparken. **Röhsska konstslöjdmuseet**, Vasagatan 37, is devoted to all types of handcrafted work, especially classical and

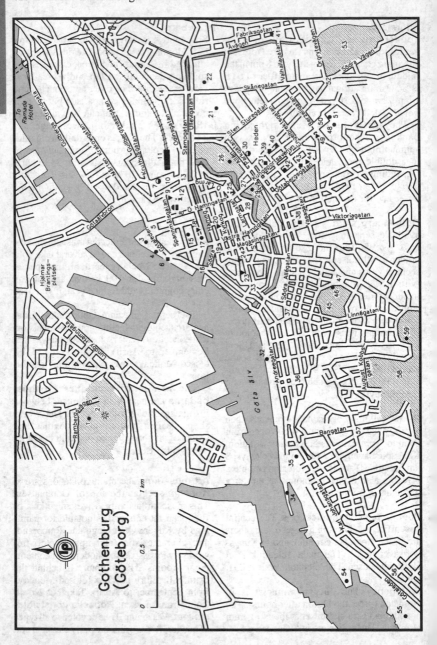

Gothenburg (Göteborg)

■ PLACES TO STAY

6   MS *Seaside*
38 Hotel Vasa
39 City Hotell
43 Maria Erikssons Pensionat

▼ PLACES TO EAT

9   Murveln
18 Museicafé
20 Simon's
23 Drottning Kristinas Jaktslott
24 Kungsgatan 20
40 Café Matkällaren
44 Pizzeria Royal
49 Brasserie Julien

OTHER

1   Keilerspark
2   Ramberget
3   New Opera
4   Göteborgs Maritima Centrum
5   Lilla Bommen
7   Main Bus Station
8   Post Office
10 Nils Ericsonsplatsen
11 Central Station
12 Nordstan Tourist Office
13 Drottningtorget
14 Odinsplatsen
15 Kronhuset & Kronhusbodarna
16 Skeppsbroplan
17 Östindiska huset & Museums
19 Lilla Torget
21 Police
22 Ullevi
25 Main Tourist Office
26 Trädgårdsföreningen
27 Kungsportsplatsen
28 Kungstorget
29 Stora Teater
30 Heden Bus Station
31 Post Office
32 Frederikshavn Terminal
33 Esperantoplatsen
34 Fiskhamnen & Auction House
35 Maritime Museum
36 Masthuggstorget
37 Järntorget
41 Industry Museum
42 Röhsskakonstslöjdmuseet
45 Skansparken
46 Skansen Kronan
47 Skanstorget
48 Concert Hall
50 Götaplatsen
51 Konstmuseet
52 Korsvägen
53 Liseberg
54 Kiel Terminal
55 Klippan Precinct
56 Jaegerdorfsplatsen
57 Djurgårdsplatsen
58 Slottsskogen
59 Natural History Museum

Oriental. Entry is 25 kr (closed Mondays from September to April).

Maritime museums The **Göteborgs Maritima Centrum** (35 kr) displays historical ships and is based around the submarine *Nordkaparen* and a frigate. The main museum of maritime history is **Sjöfartshistoriska museet** at Karl Johansgatan 1 near Stigbergstorget (25 kr, take tram No 3 or 4). The **aquarium** is attached. A museum depicting past waterfront life is the **Klippan precinct**, comprising 18th century sailor's cottages (take bus No 64 from Brunnsparken). Klippan is on Götaleden about 400 metres east of Älvsborgsbron.

Special museums The **Industry Museum**, at Åvägen 24, includes the first Volvo produced among exhibits of technical development, supplemented by working models. Entry is 25 kr (take tram No 5 to Liseberg). **Skansen Kronan** is the last of the city towers in any state of repair, sitting on Skansberget to the south-east of the business district with, naturally, a fine command. Uniforms and firearms dating back to the 17th century are the strongest collections (10 kr, open weekends only, take tram No 1).

Teaterhistoriska museet, on Berzeligatan off Kungsportsavenyn, is devoted to the development of presentation in the dramatic arts (10 kr, open weekdays from May to August, Tuesday to Friday only at other times).

Parks The prime botanic location is **Trädgårdsföreningen** on Nya Allén and you can visit the gardens. (Admission to the butterfly house costs 25 kr.) The 'lung' of the city is **Slottsparken**, where you can stroll or visit the **Natural History Museum** (25 kr, closed Mondays from September to May). From the heights of **Ramberget** on Hisingen is the best city view, but unless you take the city bus tour you are in for a climb. Bus No 31 from Hjalmar Brantingsplatsen takes you to the foot of Ramberget.

Activities

On the canal *paddan* you can cruise from Liseberg or Ullevigatan into the Göta älv to the fortress jail of **Nya Elfsborg** near the river mouth. From Kungsportsplatsen you can cruise in the harbour. The grand tour costs 55 kr and runs from May to mid-September. Göteborgs Sightseeing offers several harbour cruises and there are also vintage trams and a street train in summer (35 kr).

Less novel is the daily city bus tour ($1\frac{1}{2}$ hours from Kungsportsplatsen, 70 kr). There is a crayfish tour from Packhuskajen in summer for 235 kr (or get two tickets for the same price with Gothenberg card, book at a tourist office).

Places to Stay

The tourist office will book private rooms for a fee of 50 kr and hotels for 20 kr.

Camping *Göteborgs Camping Kärralund* (☎ 25 27 61) on Olbergsgatan is open all year and has sites for 110 and 145 kr. There are also hostel beds (150 kr) and four-bed cabins.

Hostels The STF hostel *Ostkupan* (☎ 40 10 50) at Mejerigatan 2 is the only choice in the city, offering two, three and six-bed rooms. Take bus No 64 from Brunnsparken. Out of town are two hostels. *Partille* (☎ 44 61 63) is on Landvettervägen just past Furulund about 15 km east of the city. Take the Partille

bus Nos 503, 513 or 514 from Heden; you'll pay 18 kr because they run outside the municipal district.

The STF tourist station *Torrekulla* (☎ 795 14 95), at Kållered about 13 km to the south, has hostel beds as well as singles/doubles for 310/500 kr (take bus Nos 710, 711 and 712 from Heden or No 730 from the central station).

The private *Nordengården* (☎ 19 66 31), at Stockholmsgatan 16, charges 75 kr a bed and 40 kr for floor space.

Hotels The better city hotels are included in Göteborgspaketet (see the previous Information section). For one-night stays there is budget hotel accommodation handy to the city. Private room services include Aveny Turist (☎ 20 52 86) and Cityrum (☎ 15 25 43).

Budget Hotels & Pensions Hotel Vasa (☎ 17 36 30), at Viktoriagatan 6, has singles/ doubles starting at 270/520 kr at weekends or in summer; the cheaper rooms lack only a shower. Singles are normally 420 kr during the week.

The *City Hotell* (☎ 18 00 25), at Lorensbergsgatan 6 in a fine location behind Kungsportsavenyn, has singles/doubles on weekdays from 275/350 kr and offers family rates.

For a little novelty consider the moored and renovated MS *Seaside* (☎ 10 10 35) at Packhuskajen, charging 175 kr a person in two to four-bed cabins, 250 kr for a private cabin (breakfast 45 kr).

Maria Erikssons Pensionat (☎ 20 70 30) at Chalmersgatan 27A offers rooms in apartment buildings. Singles/doubles range from 300/400 kr to 400/500 kr.

Marina The city visitors' harbour (☎ 11 83 08), right next to the business district at Lilla Bommen, is up to eight metres deep. The nightly charge is 60 kr.

Places to Eat

Simon's, a café at Korsgatan 11 near Kyrkogatan, makes very reasonably priced gourmet sandwiches and baguettes. *Brasserie Julien* at Götaplatsen is a lively bar with some mid-priced lunches and a pleasant open section on the street. *Kungsgatan 20* of that address is open for dinner every night and charges mid-range prices. *Drottning Kristinas Jaktslott*, up the ramp on Otterhallegatan is a novelty café in a restored 18th century building. *Murveln* is a steakhouse and bar in the busy Nordstan complex. It's reasonably priced if you scan the lunch board.

The *Café Matkällaren*, on the corner of Lorensbergsgatan and Kristinelundsgatan, is a budget spot for night owls that's open late on Fridays and Saturdays. The cheapest filling meal to find is at the small *Pizzeria Royal*, at Chalmersgatan 27, where you can eat for less than 50 kr. *Museicafé* at Östindiska huset would have one of the best sandwich lunches, although there are vegetarian dishes and soups among the lunches of the day.

Getting There & Away

Air Landvetter airport is 25 km east of the city and the airport bus from the central station costs 50 kr. The SAS office (☎ 94 20 20) is at Norra Hamngatan 20, Finnair (☎ 17 09 90) is at Fredsgatan 6 and the airport. There are regular services to Stockholm every day, daily direct flights to Helsinki, several daily flights to Oslo, daily flights (except on Saturdays) to Stavanger and flights most days to Amsterdam, Hamburg and Frankfurt. You can also fly to or from London daily with British Airways or SAS (see also the Sweden Getting There & Away section).

Bus Express bus Nos 800 and 802 run to Karlstad (take No 803 at weekends), Borlänge and Gävle, No 801 to Örebro, No 825 to Oslo (at weekends except Christmas) and No 830 to Jönköping and Norrköping. These buses leave from Nils Ericsonsplatsen. Swebus (☎ 771 82 00) is based in the city at Gullbergs Strandgata 34.

Train Direct trains go to Malmö via Åstorp and Hässleholm with connections to Helsingborg; the intercity trains from Oslo to Copenhagen use the ferry connection at Helsingborg. Direct trains to Stockholm depart almost every hour, some of them are the high-speed X2000s. The normal Stockholm intercity expresses take 4½ hours, but there are overnight sleepers as well. Luggage lockers at the central station cost 20 kr.

Car The E20 towards Stockholm begins on the south bank of the river, joining the E6 running to Helsingborg and Malmö in the south and Oslo in the north. It uses the tunnel after the interchange at Gullbergsmotet (road 45 to Trollhättan and Karlstad also begins here).

Boat There are several Continental ferry links and a UK service, all of which carry cars. Stena Line cruises between Gothenburg and Frederikshavn departing from Masthuggskajen (a free trip goes with the Gothenburg card) and Scandinavian Seaways sails to Oslo, Amsterdam and Harwich from Skandiahamnen on Hisingen (take bus No 28). The service to Kiel departs from Majnabbehamnen. (See also the Sweden Getting There & Away section.)

Göta Canal Göta Kanalbolaget cruises to Stockholm two or three times a week from June to August (and a few times in May); the trip takes four days (there are four stops) and costs from 5000 kr for a bed in a double cabin.

Getting Around

Free bus and tram travel goes with the Gothenburg card. To travel from one end of the municipality to the other will cost 13 kr. Cheaper and easy-to-use cards cost 50 and 100 kr. A day card for the city area costs 30 kr.

Bus Bus stations are at Nils Ericsonsplatsen near Drottningtorget and the central station, Heden, Hvitfeldsplatsen and Linnéplatsen. Blue GL express services run from Jonsered via Partille to Nils Ericsonsplatsen and

Linnéplatsen. Night buses Nos 592 and 593 run to Partille from Nils Ericsonsplatsen until 2.15 am Saturdays and Sundays.

Train Direct trains to Malmö stop at Mölndals Nedre and Kungsbacka to the south of the city. The GL train runs to Alingsås via Partille daily.

Taxi Two big fleets are Taxi Göteborg (☎ 65 00 00, with a 60 kr ceiling within the city) and Taxi Kedja (☎ 86 39 00). Luxuriously appointed motorcycle taxis are available also.

Boat The Älv-Snabben harbour craft are part of the transit system (use your coupons).

Tram The eight lines provide fast transit with trams running at least every 20 minutes. The lines converge at the central station and Brunnsparken.

MARSTRAND
The seaside village Marstrand, with its wooden buildings, conveys the essence of Bohuslän with its fishing villages. Marstrand is a popular weekend recreation and boating spot (it is crowded during the regatta season in early July). The fortress **Carlsten Fästning** reflects a martial and penal history (16 kr, open from June to August). You can arrive by bus and a ferry from Gothenburg.

Båtellet (☎ 0303-600 10) is a tourist hotel with multi-bed rooms, charging from 100 to 150 kr plus linen. Tourist information is dispensed here in summer.

ROCK ART OF TANUM
By no means a modern movement, the hällristningar pictures from Sweden's Bronze Age are well represented in Bohuslän. The most famous pictures are around the village of **Tanumshede**, where you can orient yourself at a marker opposite the church on the E6. The drawings, which are well signposted, are most striking at **Vitlycke**, two km south of Tanumshede. The **Litsleby** and **Fossum** pictures are within a few hundred metres of each other. Near the

Vitlycke site, two km east of the Tanum church, is a museum showing the pictures' origins and types. The tourist office is at Tanums Resecenter, Affärsvägen 13.

Skåne

The ancient province of Skåne, sometimes called Scania by English-speakers, was decidedly Danish until the middle of the 17th century: this is easily detected in the strong dialect. The flatlands have been the home of Swedish agriculture and the ports, the most intimate link with the rest of Europe.

MALMÖ
Malmö is a lively and personal city, perhaps influenced by Copenhagen across the Öresund. The dense boat traffic means you can shuttle to and fro by hydrofoil or ferry in less than an hour one way. Malmö is also a handy gateway to the country from the Continent.

Orientation
The square Stortorget is the focus of the city and the central station is outside the encircling canals. The ferry terminals are on Skeppsbron, beyond the station. Malmöhus guards the west end in its park setting and Limhamn lies beyond. The industrial areas are on the other side of the city centre.

Information
The tourist office is at Skeppsbron 2 in Börshuset (open weekdays from 9 am to 5 pm). The free booklet *Malmö this Month* is a useful general guide. The discount-card package Malmökort gives free bus travel in the city, two-for-the-price-of-one deals including journeys on City Jet Line to Copenhagen, some free trips on regional buses and free travel on Pågatågen trains between Malmö and Lund. There is also free entry to several museums, tours and the museum tram. The card costs 90 kr for a day, 160 kr for two days and 210 kr for three days.

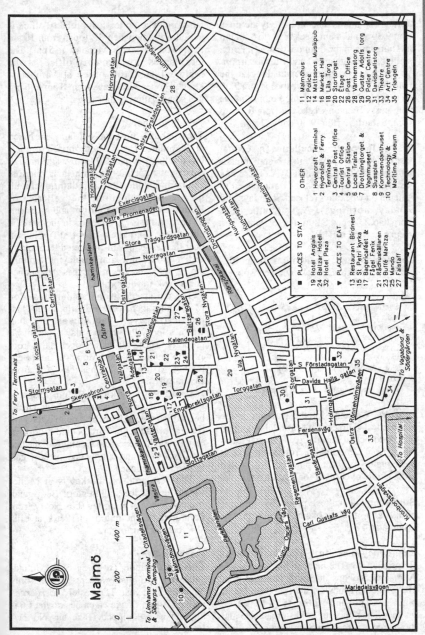

Malmö

0   200   400 m

PLACES TO STAY

19 Hotel Anglais
24 Baltzar Hotell
32 Hotel Plaza

▼ PLACES TO EAT

13 Restaurant Birdnest
15 St Petri kyrka
17 Fågel Fenix &
    Étage Café &
21 Rådhuskällaren
23 Buffé Maritza
25 Mando
27 Falstaff

OTHER

1   Hovercraft Terminal
2   Hydrofoil & Ferry
    Terminals
3   Central Post Office
4   Tourist Office
5   Central Station
6   Local Trains
7   Drottningtorget &
    Vagnmuseet
8   Slussplan
9   Kommendanthuset
10 Technology &
    Maritime Museum
11 Malmöhus
12 Police
14 Mattssons Musikpub
16 Market Hall
18 Lilla Torg
20 Stortorget
22 Étage
26 Post Office
28 Värnhemstorg
29 Gustav Adolfs torg
30 Police Centre
31 Davidshallstorg
33 Theatre
34 Art Centre
35 Triangeln

To Ferry Terminals

To Limhamn Terminal
& Sibbarps Camping

To Vagabond &
Södergården

To Hospital

Money The main banks in the city are open from 9.30 am to 4 pm weekdays (to 5.30 pm on Thursdays in the business district). Forex is at Norra Vallgatan 60 and Sturup airport. An exchange counter is open daily at the hydrofoil terminal on Skeppsbron from 7.30 am to 8 pm. You can exchange money at the main post office on weekdays from 8 am to 6 pm, Saturdays from 9.30 am to 1 pm.

Post & Telecommunications The central post office is at Skeppsbron 1 and another branch is at Stora Nygatan 31A. There is a postal counter at the central station open to 8.30 pm on weekdays (closed Saturdays and Sunday mornings). A Telebutik is at Storgatan 23 (open Saturdays to 1 pm). The telephone code is 040.

Consulates Any immigration difficulties can be cleared up at the following consulates:

Denmark
    Södra Promenaden 69 (☎ 12 33 44)
Finland
    Stortorget 17 (☎ 11 77 80)
Germany
    Lundavägen 142 (☎ 18 01 80)
Norway
    Norra Vallgatan 54 (☎ 12 35 00)
Poland
    Adolf Fredriksgatan 13 (☎ 26 87 86)

Laundry Welcome for the traveller is the laundrette Tvättoteket at Mariedalsvägen 60 on the corner of Kronborgsvägen (take bus No 11 from Centralplan). You buy tokens at the counter to wash, spin and dry, which costs a little over 50 kr for a full load.

Bookshops The best place for general books and guidebooks is Lundgrens at Östergatan 12.

Emergency The duty pharmacy is at Bergsgatan 48. The medical centre is at the Allmänna Sjukhus at Södra Förstadsgatan 101. An emergency doctor (☎ 33 35 00, at night 33 10 00) and dentist (☎ 33 10 00) are on duty. The police are at Västergatan 45 and the police centre is on Storgatan at Davids-

hallstorg. The police lost-property office is at Södra Promenaden 5B (open from 10 am to 2 pm on weekdays, Mondays to 5 pm). The local buses' lost-property office, at the Malmö Lokaltrafik office at Värnhemstorget, is open weekdays from 8 am to 6 pm and some Saturday mornings.

Things to See
The combined museums of Malmö are based at the moated castle **Malmöhus**. For combined entry you pay 30 kr to walk through the **royal apartments** with their interiors and portrait collections, **Stadsmuseet** with its Malmö collection, the galleries of **Konsthall** and the **aquarium** and **museum of natural history**. Included in the ticket is entry to the **Tekniska museet**, at Turbinbron near the castle, a well-presented technology and maritime museum displaying aircraft, motor vehicles, steam engines, telephones and a walk-in submarine.

The old arsenal **Kommendanthuset** on Malmöhusvägen keeps militaria, and the historic carriages of **Vagnmuseet** are also worth a look. Put aside a day to see it all properly. These places are open daily from June to August, closed Mondays from September to May (take bus No 20C from Centralplan).

Sankt Petri kyrka on Göran Olsgatan goes back to the 14th century, although it has been much rebuilt. The focal point is the 18th century **organ**. **Lilla Torg** behind Stortorget on the right is the restored remains of the late medieval town and is now occupied by galleries and boutiques.

The best produce **market** is at Möllevångstorget at the south end of Bergsgatan from Monday to Saturday (bus No 17 from Centralplan). The indoor market is at Lilla Torg behind Stortorget.

Places to Stay
Sibbarps Camping (☎ 15 51 65) at Strandgatan 101 in Limhamn accepts caravans only but is open all year. The hostel *Södergården* (☎ 822 20) on Bäckavägen beside the E6 is big and well equipped. Take bus No 21A from Centralplan.

A list of private rooms is available from City Room (☎ 97 99 27), prices start at 170 kr per head a night in a double. The tourist office (☎ 34 12 70) will also book hotel rooms from 500 kr a single during the week.

Hotel Plaza (☎ 771 00) at Södra Förstadsgatan 30 has singles from 440 kr and doubles for 740 kr at weekends and in July.

Baltzar Hotell (☎ 720 05) at Södergatan 20 has singles/doubles for 475/595 kr in July. The prime location belongs to *Hotel Anglais* (☎ 714 50) at Stortorget 15. It's a good city splurge for 395/595 kr a single/double in summer.

Places to Eat
The *Falstaff* at Baltzarsgatan 25 has steaks and fillets which aren't overpriced plus an Indian menu. *Rådhuskällaren* below the town hall at Stortorget is ideal for a splurge. *Buffé Maritza* at Södergatan 16 is mid-priced and has some vegetarian fare. *Vagabond* is a budget diner near the hostel which makes it also a natural watering hole. *Restaurant Birdnest* at Hamngatan 4 specialises in Oriental and vegetarian cooking. *Mando* at Skomakaregatan 4 is purely a steakhouse with specialities.

Cafés *Bagericaféet* and *Fågel Fenix* in the Saluhallen at Lilla Torg are good lunch or snack cafés with a range of inexpensive gourmet rolls, vegetarian fare and sandwiches.

Entertainment
The disco and club *Étage* at Stortorget 6 boasts a mobile glass roof and is a mildly expensive splurge (the upper age limit is 23 for women and 25 for men). *Mattssons Musikpub* on Göran Olsgatan is an earthier rock scene with live bands.

Things to Buy
The plethora of Swedish parish costumes is represented by Charlotte Weibull's dolls at Lilla Torg 1 (closed Saturdays after 2 pm and Sundays). These locally made dolls are mostly expensive but each comes with infor-

mation about its origin and from a reputable maker.

Getting There & Away
For a round tour of the Öresund or a visit to Copenhagen you can buy the Öresund Runt card for 125 kr, which gives free travel on ferries, the hydrofoil and the local trains for two days. The cards can be bought at the Pågatågen station in Malmö, the tourist office or some branches of Pressbyrån.

A three-day card that covers Länstrafiken Malmöhus buses and Pågatågen costs 145 kr, and a weekly card costs 245 kr.

Air Sturup airport is 31 km south-east of the city. (The airport bus trip costs 45 kr.) SAS has many nonstop flights to Stockholm daily and the hovercraft service to Kastrup near Copenhagen allows connections with anywhere in the world. There is also a daily flight to London's Heathrow airport. Braathens SAFE flies to Oslo on weekdays.

Finnair flies direct to Helsinki every day except Saturday. SalAir's partner Malmö Aviation flies to and from Hamburg every day except Saturday. KLM flies daily to Amsterdam. SAS/Linjeflyg (☎ 35 70 00) is at Baltzarsgatan 18 and Finnair (☎ 10 09 75) is at Baltzarsgatan 31.

Bus The länstrafik operates in zones with fares from 7 kr (60 kr from Malmö to Helsingborg). The airport bus No 110 runs from Malmö to Sturup. The intercity bus No 999 from Lund connects with Dragør ferries at Limhamn, stopping at Mälarbron on Norra Vallgatan. Regional buses stop there and at Slussplan.

Train The Pågatågen local trains run to Helsingborg, Landskrona and Höör (via Lund) and to Ystad (connecting for Simrishamn). The platform is at the end of the central station and you buy tickets from the machine. International rail passes are accepted.

SJ runs regularly to Helsingborg and Gothenburg via Lund and Eslöv. Direct trains run to Stockholm, but you can also change at Hässleholm for Karlskrona or to pick up the Helsingborg-Stockholm service.

Motorcycle MC-huset (☎ 21 04 35) at Jägershillsgatan 6 rents motorcycles from 1395 kr (one week maximum with a 3500 kr deposit). You must show an international licence.

Boat See the Sweden Getting There & Away section for details of ferries and hydrofoils to Denmark and Germany.

Getting Around
Most local transport queries can be answered at the transport information office in the main hall of the central station.

Bus Malmö Lokaltrafik offices are at Gustav Adolfs torg and Värnhemstorget. The letters after bus numbers denote route variations, sometimes only the direction of a ring route. Nattrafik, the night service, operates after about 10 pm on different routes. The excellent free bus map at the tourist office should sort out any confusion. The card Malmökortet includes bus travel and ferry and discounts on Pågatågen trains. Tickets are 11 kr for one hour's travel (16 kr at night) or you can buy a bus card for 100 kr that covers 12 journeys. There are also day family tickets for weekends and holidays for 17 and 25 kr. The bus stations are Centralplan (in front of the main station), Gustav Adolfs torg, Värnhemstorget and Triangeln.

Train Pågatågen stop at stations in southwest Skåne.

Taxi To order a taxi in the city dial 700 00 or 710 00.

LUND
In the 12th century Lund, then Danish, was the archiepiscopal centre of the northern countries and much of the medieval town can still be seen. The university was founded in the 1660s after Sweden took over Skåne and began to make it Swedish.

Information
At last report the tourist office had made camp at Klostergatan 11 (facing Bredgatan opposite the cathedral). The regional tourist authority Skånes Turistråd is at Skiffervägen 38. The student union is on the ground floor of Akademiska Föreningen on Sandgatan (open from 10 am to 3 pm weekdays, closed for lunch).

Money Some banks in the town are open until 5.30 pm on weekdays, but opening hours are shortened at some branches in summer. Then you can exchange money at the central post office.

Post & Telecommunications The main post office is at Knut den Stores gata 2. A Telebutik is at Klostergatan 6. The telephone code is 046.

Emergency The duty pharmacy at Mårtenstorget 12 is open only to 10 pm (to 8 pm at weekends). There is another pharmacy (☎ 10 10 00) at the hospital facing Getingevägen. The police are at Byggmästaregatan 1.

Things to See
The magnificence of Lund's Romanesque **cathedral** is well known but for a real surprise, visit at noon or 3 pm (1 pm on Sundays and holidays) when the astronomical clock strikes up *In Dulci Jubilo* and the figures of the three kings begin their journey to the Child. The main **university** building, which faces Sandgatan, is worth a glance inside and Scanian **rune stones** are arranged in the park nearby.

Museums The medieval museum of **Drottens kyrkoruin** (10 kr, open daily) is at Kattesund under the tourist office. The ruins of the church are visible from the street, but the underground museum has models and exhibits that fill in the details of Lund's past. The **history museum** in the university quarter at Kraftstorg 1 has interesting exhibits but is open only from 11 am to 1 pm Tuesday to Friday.

The biggest collections are in **Kulturen**

(25 kr, open daily) at Tegnérsplatsen and more rune stones are outside. There are guided tours in English on Sundays in summer. The **Arkivmuseum** at Finngatan 2 is part of the art museum (10 kr, closed Mondays) and has collected sketches and designs of public decorative art in Sweden and abroad. There's a good **planetarium** at Svanegatan 9 which has two shows every Tuesday evening for 30 kr.

Markets The open-air markets are at Mårtenstorget, where there is something to see daily during summer. The market hall (open daily) is also at the square.

Places to Stay

Källbybadets Camping, off Badarevägen at Klostergården three km south-west of the centre, is open only from mid-June to mid-August.

The novelty place to stay is the parked rail carriages of the *Tåget* hostel (☎ 14 28 20), a close but fun experience with old SJ blankets instead of the STF standard. The carriages are old sleeping stock with three bunks to a room. The hostel is open all year except at Christmas and New Year.

Private rooms can be booked at the tourist office (☎ 15 50 40) at rates between 100 and 150 kr a person plus a 40 kr fee. The *Hotell Ahlström* (☎ 11 01 74) at Skomakaregatan 3 has singles/doubles for 395/495 kr, but there is no breakfast. The *Good Morning Hotel* (☎ 30 31 20), on Förhandlingsvägen northwest of the city centre, has summer and weekend singles/doubles for 345/420 kr and singles for 495 kr the rest of the year.

Places to Eat

The most intimate surroundings (and full litres of fine ale) are at *Krog Filipinå* on Kyrkogatan, which is also open late. *Valvet* on Allhelgona kyrkogata near the arch has a fine mid-priced lunch although the bill will increase for dinner.

Petri pumpa opposite the library quarter has lunch specials. *Chrougen* is the university café and restaurant just inside the student union building. *Kattesunds Smørrebrød* on

Kattesund next to the tourist office is the best of the sandwich cafés.

Entertainment

For music and disco there is *Carlssons Trädgård* (enter at Mårtenstorget 6), although both upstairs and downstairs at *Glorias* on Sankt Petri Kyrkogatan is popular and there is no door charge. *Stadsparkens café* is an open lunch area in the city park where you can hire a chessboard and play as you relax.

Getting There & Away

Bus The main bus station is for SJ buses on Bankgatan behind Mårtenstorget. The intercity bus No 999 runs to Copenhagen by means of the ferry from Malmö, stopping on Botulfsgatan near Stortorget.

Train The SJ regular services run from Malmö in the direction of Stockholm, but the most frequent service is by Pågatågen to Helsingborg and Malmö.

Getting Around

The hubs for city buses are Botulfsgatan and Bangatan at the railway station. Taxis (☎ 11 70 20) gather there or at Mårtenstorget. City buses cost 9 kr.

TRELLEBORG

Trelleborg's few medieval remnants around Gamla Torg attract visitors but most of the traffic is through the port. The tourist office is at Hamngatan 4 (open daily from early June to mid-August). The post office is at Kontinentsgatan 2 and a Telebutik is on Nygatan at Stortorget. There are banks in town and Forex is at Sassnitzterminalen and Norra Kajgatan 20. The police are at Västergatan 4. The hostel (☎ 0410-533 20) on Hedvägen is open in summer.

Getting There & Away

Bus No 146 runs from Malmö to Övre Station. TS ferries running to Sassnitz in Germany leave from Sassnitzterminalen, TT-Line sails to Travemünde and TR-Line to Rostock.

SWEDEN

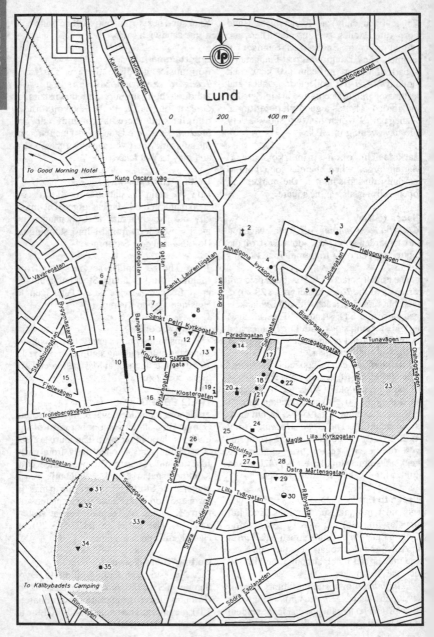

Lund

0   200   400 m

■ PLACES TO STAY

6 Tåget Hostel
24 Hotell Ahlström

▼ PLACES TO EAT

9 Petri pumpa
12 Glorias
13 Krog Filipinå
26 Kattesunds Smørrebrød
29 Carlssons Trädgård
34 Stadsparkens Café

OTHER

1 Hospital
2 Allhelgona Kyrkan
3 Zoology Museum
4 Valvet
5 Archive Museum
7 Clemenstorget
8 City Library
10 Railway Station
11 Post Office
14 University
15 Police
16 Bantorget
17 Chrougen
18 Tegnérsplatsen
19 Tourist Office & Medieval Museum
20 Cathedral
21 History Museum
22 Kulturen
23 Botanic Gardens
25 Stortorget
27 Market Hall
28 Mårtenstorget
30 Bus Station
31 Sports Centre
32 Swimming Pool
33 Planetarium
35 Stadsparken

YSTAD

In Ystad, there are many remnants of the medieval town, rambling cobbled streets and half-timbered buildings. Landmarks are **Gråbrödraklostret** on Klostergatan and the 16th century **Sankt Maria kyrka** at Stortorget. The hostel (☎ 0411-772 97) is two km east of town at Fritidsvägen (take bus Nos 304, 315, 572 and 573).

The tourist office, at Sankt Knuts torg, is open daily in summer. The post office is at Hamngatan 4 and there is a Telebutik at Maria Munthesgatan 1. Forex bank is at the ferry terminal. The SJ trains and Pågatågen run regularly from Malmö and regional buses come to Sankt Knuts torg. Ystad is a port for ferries to/from Bornholm (Denmark) and to Poland, see the Sweden Getting There & Away section.

LANDSKRONA

An outsized pencil at the corner of Östergatan and Järnvägsgatan helps make the claim that Landskrona is the centre of Europe (if only for map-makers). For travellers it is pleasant enough.

The 16th century castle and 18th century ramparts of **Citadellet** dominate the town and harbour. Now it is a lively handicrafts centre, open daily in summer. The **museum** at Kasernplan has displays on medicine, aviation and the interesting children's perspective of history.

The tourist office is behind the prominent Rådhus (open all year, daily in summer). The STF hostel *Barnavärn* (☎ 0418-120 63) at Kvarngatan 1 is open all year but you must book in writing (write to 261 40 Landskrona) from mid-September to mid-May.

Getting There & Away

Länstrafikenand SJ buses come to the railway station, which is served by Pågatågen trains from Helsingborg and Malmö. Ventrafiken ferries and the restaurant boats of Scarlett Line (☎ 0148-280 65) to Tuborg and Copenhagen depart from the main harbour off Kungsgatan (25 kr, and for 210 kr cars are carried).

VEN

The sleepy island of Ven is 25 minutes by ferry from Landskrona (48 kr return). Ferries arrive at the jetty at Bäckviken and a bus service links the villages (in summer there are weekend services from Råå near Helsingborg). The tourist office, open in summer, is at Landsvägen 2 above the ferry dock.

The astronomer Tycho Brahe worked here

in the 16th century and the attractions are connected with him. These include the ruined castle **Uranienborg**, the rebuilt observatory **Stjärneborg**, and the **Tycho Brahe museum**, all grouped on Landsvägen in the centre of the island (open from mid-May to mid-September).

HELSINGBORG

The busy port of Helsingborg is perched on the coastline of the Öresund and often experiences big winds. There is a summer boulevard atmosphere in Stortorget and the older buildings in the winding streets blend well with the newer shops. The seaside character is enhanced by the pastiche styles of the high beachfront houses. Denmark is only 25 minutes away by ferry. It's the obvious destination for a day's excursion, and you can see 'Hamlet's castle', Kronborg, on the other side of the Öresund at the sister city Helsingør.

Information

The tourist office is in the Knutpunkten complex (open weekdays to 5.30 pm).

Money Main banks have branches in the city, some open to 5.30 pm weekdays. You can exchange money at the ferry terminals. The Forex bank is at Knutpunkten.

Post & Telecommunications The central post office is at Norra Storgatan 17 by the square Stortorget. A Telebutik is at Bruksgatan 24. The telephone code is 042.

Consulates The following countries are represented in the city to sort out immigration queries:

Denmark
    Stortorget 16 (☎ 18 33 57)
Finland
    Bunkagårdsgatan 7 (☎ 29 62 25)
Germany
    ScandLines terminal (☎ 18 60 73)

Emergency The duty pharmacy is at the hospital (enter from Södra Vallgatan), but you can go to Drottninggatan 14 during the day (except Sundays). There, Cityklinik is open weekdays to 6 pm for visits (Saturdays from 9 am to 3 pm), after 6 pm there is emergency service (☎ 11 91 11) until 10 pm. At other times call 90 000 for assistance. The police are at Carl Krooks gata 24.

Things to See

The square medieval keep **Kärnan** dominates Stortorget from Terrassen above. The tower dates back to the defences of the 1300s and looked out from the heights over the Öresund to the Danish heartland and over past struggles that delivered the fortress finally to Swedish hands. Entry to the castle museum is 10 kr (open on weekdays to 4 pm, Saturdays until 4 pm and on Sundays from June to August until 5 pm).

The manor of **Pålsjö castle** in the forest north of the city originated in a different, more graceful time and retains its charm as a destination for walks, although there is no admittance. **Pålsjö mill** is actually a cottage by the pond at the north end of Strandvägen. The interiors are on display for a few hours on afternoons from May to August. More imposing is the 18th century manor at **Fredriksdals museum**, a park and museum village on Oscar Trapps väg immediately west of the city. In summer, highlights are performances in the open-air theatre. **Wildflowers** of the area are grown in the gardens.

The city museum **Stadsmuseet** at Södra Storgatan 31 is devoted to Helsingborg and Scanian history, but the city's **zoological house** is tucked behind in a separate building. It is a minor classic in old-fashioned taxidermic study. The nimble will clamber into the typical wooden south Swedish **millhouse** of bygone days, still seen in their hundreds but not so often accessible. Period houses and a **bakery** complete the layout. Entry to all this is 10 kr (closed Mondays).

Markets The weekday market is at Gustav Adolfs torg and some interesting flea markets are held at Mariatorget by the church on Saturdays.

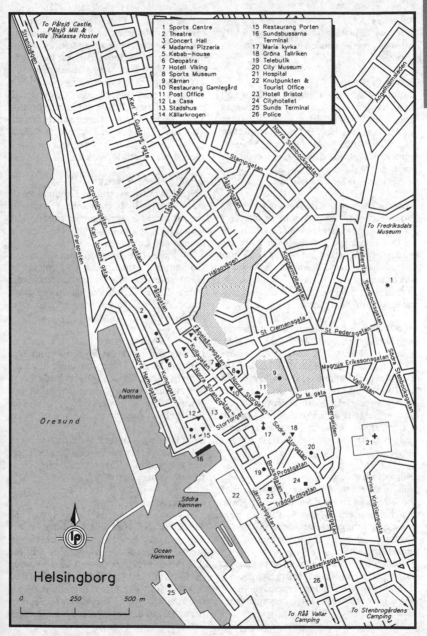

To Pålsjö Castle, Pålsjö Mill & Villa Thalassa Hostel

1   Sports Centre
2   Theatre
3   Concert Hall
4   Madarna Pizzeria
5   Kebab–house
6   Cleopatra
7   Hotell Viking
8   Sports Museum
9   Kärnan
10 Restaurang Gamlegård
11 Post Office
12 La Casa
13 Stadshus
14 Källarkrogen
15 Restaurang Porten
16 Sundsbussarna Terminal
17 Maria kyrka
18 Gröna Tallriken
19 Telebutik
20 City Museum
21 Hospital
22 Knutpunkten & Tourist Office
23 Hotell Bristol
24 Cityhotellet
25 Sunds Terminal
26 Police

To Fredriksdals Museum

Öresund

Norra hamnen

Södra hamnen

Ocean Hamnen

Helsingborg

0   250   500 m

To Råå Vallar Camping

To Stenbrogårdens Camping

Activities
Forest walks in **Pålsjö skog** north of the city are highly recommended by the nature-conscious.

Places to Stay
Camping *Råå Vallar Camping* on Kustgatan about five km south of the city centre is open from mid-May to August and charges 100 kr a site. Take bus No 1B from Rådhuset or (lågtrafik) No 41 from Söderport. *Stenbrogårdens Camping* on Rausvägen eight km south-east of the city (via Landskronavägen) is open all year for the same rate.

Hostels The hostel *Villa Thalassa* (☎ 11 03 84) is reached by the path from the bus No 7 (No 43 lågtrafik) terminus at Pålsjöbaden or on Dag Hammarskjölds väg. The villa and gardens are beautiful but you stay in huts around the grounds. The hostel is closed in December and mid-January. About three km farther north is the summer hostel *Nyckelbo* (☎ 920 05) on Skolvägen.

Hotels Two good budget hotels in the city are *Hotell Bristol* (☎ 11 46 60) at Prästgatan 4 with singles/doubles for 250/325 kr and *Cityhotellet* (☎ 13 64 35) at Trädgårdsgatan 19 where singles/doubles cost from 395/495 kr. The Bristol discounts its rates by up to 20% at weekends. More expensive hotels discount heavily at weekends or in summer and the *Hotell Viking* at Fågelsångsgatan 1 reduces its rates to 550/650 kr for singles/doubles.

Places to Eat
The friendliest surroundings for dinner are at the waterfront tavern *Källarkrogen* opposite the station at Kungsgatan 4. You can have more of a splurge at *Restaurang Porten* at Drottninggatan 1. There are reasonably priced specials.

Restaurang Gamlegård in the historic half-timbered building at Norra Storgatan 9 is basically a charming expensive lunch place, but consider the less extravagant specials.

Madarna Pizzeria, at Sankt Jörgens plats on the corner of Fågelsångsgatan, keeps its pizzas, sandwiches and salads modestly priced. For variety there is Mexican cuisine at *La Casa* on Badhusgatan near the station (predictably it is closed in the afternoon).

Cleopatra is a late-opening pizzeria on Roskildegatan that charges 35 kr for all pizzas. *Gröna Tallriken* at Södra Storgatan 12 is a good specialist vegetarian restaurant. The best of the budget food bars is *Kebabhouse* at Kullagatan 55, which offers a lunch special with drink for 36 kr.

Getting There & Away
The main transport centre is Knutpunkten on Järnvägsgatan by Inre Hamnen. The railway ferries and SFL ferries arrive there to link with SJ trains and buses and Pågatågen to Malmö and Lund.

SJ trains run direct to Stockholm and Gothenburg (sometimes you change at Hässleholm for the Malmö to Stockholm train). Länstrafiken Malmöhus has an office inside. Swebus No 833 runs to Jönköping and Norrköping.

Air Ängelholm airfield is 35 km north of Helsingborg (take the Flygbuss from Nya Knutpunkten). There are more than 20 Linjeflyg (☎ 0431-209 00) services a day to Stockholm to link with other internal flights. Northern Cross Airways (☎ 20 07 90) flies to Oslo from Ängelholm.

Boat For details of services to/from Norway and Denmark, see the Sweden Getting There & Away section. Return trips from Ven to Råå in summer cost 45 kr.

Getting Around
City buses converge on Järnvägsgatan and Knutpunkten. Those with low numbers run during the day, buses with numbers in the 40s are off-peak evening and weekend services (lågtrafik). For taxis there is Taxi Öresund (☎ 18 62 00) and Taxi Helsingborg (☎ 18 02 00). The lift to Terrassen from Stortorget is open daily to 8 pm in summer (from September to May to 6.30 pm weekdays and to 2 pm Saturdays, closed Sundays).

Baltic Islands

Gotland and Öland are basically summer resorts for most Swedes, and their tiny populations swell as millions of tourists pass through. These places are recognised bicycle paradises because of the landscape and concentration of sights. Campers and hostellers can virtually walk from place to place during July or August. The maps show camp sites and hostels for ease of planning, but some places are open only for six weeks a year. Beachgoers take advantage of steadily sunny weather at this time and hundreds of holiday cabins open up for visitors who've booked months ahead, so travellers' options may be limited. But for nature-lovers and those curious about the distant past spending a few days on either island is a must.

GOTLAND

Gotland is known for its many medieval church ruins, the odd limestone formations (*raukar*), which seem twisted rather than sculpted, and the walled medieval trading post of Visby. Bicycles rule on this island: Gotlands Turistservice in Visby arranges cycling packages for up to 10 days priced from 900 to 2500 kr including maps and hotel and hostel accommodation. Youth hostels are shown on the map.

Getting There & Away

Air Linjeflyg flies daily from Stockholm to the airfield three km north of the town.

Boat The main ferry operator to Gotland is Gotlandslinjen. The trips are relatively expensive (from 160 to 250 kr for a single journey) from Nynäshamn (south of Stockholm) and Oskarshamn. Gotlandslinjen services run between Visby and Nynäshamn and Visby and Oskarshamn (connecting by bus with Kalmar länstrafik to Kalmar). Birka Lines also sails to Bornholm from the ferry terminal. Kristina Cruises and Sally Lines sail to Helsinki and Baltic cities in summer.

Getting Around

Bicycles and motorcycles are favoured. You can hire bicycles for 50 kr a day or 225 kr a week at Team Sportia at Österväg 17 in Visby. MC-uthyrningen at Inre Hamnen rents mopeds from 150 kr a day and 500-cc motorcycles for 450 kr a day.

Visby

The walled and cobbled medieval port of Visby on Gotland is a living relic if there can be such a thing: more than 40 proud towers and the ruins of great churches attest Visby's former Hanseatic glories. Today it has much of the seaside resort about it in July and August, except when the costumes and re-enactments of medieval week take place during the second week of August.

Information You'll find Gotlands Turist-service (☎ 0498-2109 82) in the old restored half-timbered house at Strandgatan 9, open daily. The Telebutik is at Bredgatan 4.

Things to See The town itself is a noble sight, with its wall of 40 towers breached in only two places. The contemporary **ruins** of Drotten, St Nicolai, St Lars and St Carin are all within the town walls and contrast with the old but sound **cathedral** of St Maria. **Gotlands Fornsal** is the historical museum with a fine collection of the Gotland **picture stones** of the pre-Viking period (20 kr, open daily in summer).

The area of Fårö at the northern tip of the island is militarily restricted, although you can drive on the roads and visit the **Bunge open-air museum** inside the zone. But to stay a night there, you must apply to the Visby police (☎ 0498-29 35 00) at least 10 days in advance.

AROUND GOTLAND

The late medieval churches and church ruins number almost 100 and the church of the 12th century Cistercian monastery of **Roma kloster** in the centre of the island is one of the most popular sites for visitors. But most of the monuments of Gotland are older still,

SWEDEN

Legend:
- Restricted Area
- Protected Reserve
- ■ Place to Stay
- ♁ Historic Church
- ∴ Historic Site

FÅRÖ

Kappelshamnsviken

Fårösund

Bunge

Kappelshamn

Lärbro

To Nynäshamn

Martebo

Tingstädeträsk

Slite

Boge

Airport

Bro

Tjelvarsgrav

To Västervik

Visby

Vitviken

Källunge

Vibble

To Oskarshamn

Dalhem

Gothem

Roma

BALTIC SEA

Gnisvärd

Väte

Anga

Björkhaga

Klintehamn

Torsburgen

Fröjel

Lojsta

Garde

Ljugarn

Stånga

Lye

Sproge

Hemse

Rone

Havdhem

Grötlingbo

Gansviken

Näs

Burgsviken

Öja

Burgsvik

Gotland

0   10   20 km

such as the Bronze Age ship-setting known as **Tjelvars grav**, a few km west of road 146, and its surrounding landscape of standing stones, almost all linked with Gutnish legend. Mightier still is **Torsburgen** on the east of the island, a partly walled eminence that forms a fortification (the largest in Scandinavia) extending five km around its irregular perimeter.

ÖLAND

More windmills than Holland? There are 400 on Öland today, some lived in. Most are the characteristic wooden huts, on a rotating base. The more familiar 'Dutch' type is at **Sandvik** on the west coast, more than 30 km north of Borgholm, and in summer you can climb the eight storeys for a view back to the mainland. Also prominent are the **lighthouses** at the north and south tips of the island. Youth hostels and camp sites are indicated on the map.

Information

The Träffpunkt Öland centre is off the Färjestaden end of the bridge. The Historium, open weekdays (daily in summer) will explain Öland's past for 35 kr.

Getting Around

Bus Nos 101, 102 and 106 from Kalmar station run daily to Borgholm via Färjestaden. Bus Nos 103 and 105 run to Mörbylånga, but not as far as Eketorp, except late on weekdays, so do not rely on these buses for seeing the fort museum.

Gråborg & Ismantorp

The two Iron Age ring forts Gråborg and Ismantorp in the centre of the island are equally impressive, although Gråborg, with a diameter of 200 metres, is by far the larger. It is on the Norra Mockleby road about 10 km east of Färjestaden. Ismantorp, with its house remains and nine mysterious gates, is five km west of the Himmelsberga museum.

Himmelsberga

On the middle of the east coast at Långlöt, Himmelsberga is a farm village of the single-road type from a bygone age. This is not the only one on Öland, but here the quaint cottages have been fully re-equipped as a **museum**. They've been furnished and their painted interiors have been restored. The museum is open daily in summer.

Borgholm

The tourist office is in the park facing the water at Hamn. The attraction is **Borgholm slottsruin**, dominating the town from the hill just to the south. The castle was finally burned and abandoned early in the 18th century after being used as a dyeing works. In summer it is open for inspection.

Källa

The remains of the medieval fortified church **Källa odekyrka** at the little harbour off road 136 are fascinating, as it and other churches actually supplanted the mighty stone fortresses as defensive works. The broken **runic stone** inside shows the Cross growing from the pagan tree of life.

Karlevistenen

The Karlevi stone (Karlevistenen) looks over the water from a field six km south of Färjestaden on the coast road to Mörbylånga. It was raised in the 10th century for a Viking chieftain.

Mysinge & Gettlinge

The gravefield stretching out on the ridge along the main Mörbylånga road has graves and standing stones from the Stone Age to the late Iron Age, but the biggest single monument is the mound **Mysinge hög**, 15 km south of Färjestaden.

Eketorp Museum

Most southerly of the big ring forts, Eketorp,

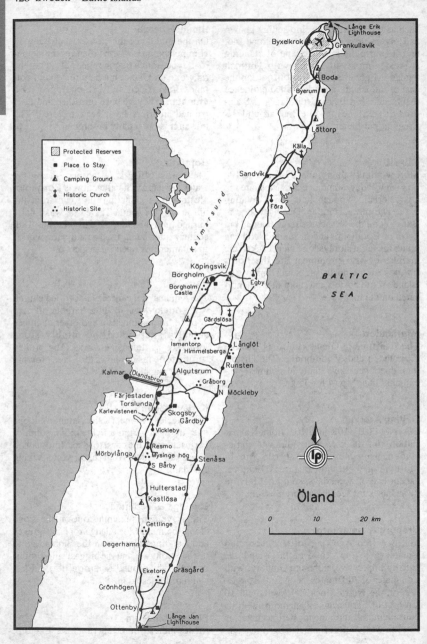

Länge Erik Lighthouse
Byxelkrok
Grankullavik
Boda
Byerum
Löttorp
Källa
Sandvik
Föra

Kalmarsund

Köpingsvik
Borgholm
Borgholm Castle
Egby
Gärdslösa
Ismantorp
Långlöt
Himmelsberga
Runsten
Algutsrum
Gråborg
N Möckleby
Kalmar
Ölandsbron
Färjestaden
Torslunda
Karlevistenen
Skogsby
Gårdby
Vickleby
Resmo
Mörbylånga
Mysinge hög
Stenåsa
S Bårby
Hulterstad
Kastlösa
Gettlinge
Degerhamn
Eketorp
Gräsgård
Grönhögen
Ottenby
Länge Jan Lighthouse

BALTIC SEA

Protected Reserves
Place to Stay
Camping Ground
Historic Church
Historic Site

Öland

0   10   20 km

three km south of Gräsgård, has been partly reconstructed as a museum to show what the fortified villages must have been like. The fort can be viewed at any time and the museum building is open daily in summer, but only at weekends during other times of year. The admission fee to the museum costs 30 kr.

Estonia

Estonia (Eesti) is just 80 km over the Gulf of Finland from Helsinki but a world away in many respects. Only fully independent of the Soviet Union since 1991, it is still piecing together a Western-style economy, and much of what the West takes for granted (food, phone calls, finding somewhere to stay) can be more complicated than expected. But the confusion also leads to some great bargains, and things are far less problematic than they were just a very few years ago.

Half the excitement of being in Estonia or the other Baltic states, Latvia and Lithuania, is witnessing the transformation taking place before your eyes. For a start you may be travelling there using a method that was impossible before 1990, when Estonia's only direct link with the world outside the USSR was a single ferry plying between its capital, Tallinn, and Helsinki.

Now there are seven or more craft crossing regularly between the two cities, plus direct flights and other new links with several Western capitals and even pleasure cruises calling at Baltic ports. And when you reach Estonia, there'll be none of the old Soviet restrictions which limited Westerners to just a few cities and excursions.

Estonia is the most northerly of the three Baltic states and the most Scandinavian in atmosphere. Ethnically the Estonians and Finns are cousins.

Estonia seems to have prepared a little more systematically for capitalism and independence than its Baltic siblings, which makes visiting it perhaps less of a shock to a Westerner and a good starting point for a trip through the Baltic states.

Estonia's German past lingers and Tallinn's medieval centre is a highpoint of any visit to the Baltic region. Tallinn is the hub of Estonian life in all ways but Tartu, the second city, Lahemaa national park, and Saaremaa island are among the other appealing destinations. There are also many islands and coastal areas newly opened to visitors.

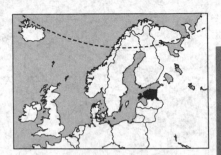

Facts about the Country

HISTORY
German Crusades

Estonia's pagan clans encountered Scandinavians pushing east and Slavs pushing west in the 8th to 12th centuries AD but were little influenced from outside until the 12th century, when German traders and missionaries were followed by knights unleashed by Pope Celestinus III's 1193 call for a crusade against the northern heathens. In 1202 the Bishop of Riga established the Knights of the Sword (also known as the Livonian order), whose white cloaks were emblazoned with blood-red swords and crosses, to convert the region by conquest. Within about a quarter of a century this 'unwholesome' brood had subjugated what is now Latvia and the southern half of Estonia. Northern Estonia fell to Denmark.

The Knights of the Sword were later subordinated to a second band of German crusaders, the Teutonic order, which by 1290 ruled the eastern Baltic area as far north as southern Estonia, and most Estonian islands. In 1346 Denmark sold northern Estonia to the knights, sealing Estonia's subordination to a German nobility until the early 20th century. This ruling class tightened its hold

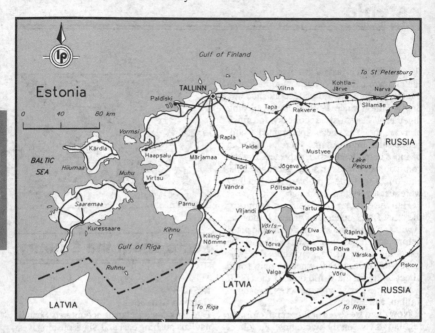

through military, religious and commercial might. Hanseatic towns like Tallinn, Tartu, Pärnu and Narva – on the routes between Russia and the West – often prospered, but the indigenous peoples in the countryside became serfs.

Swedish & Russian Rule
Sweden, a rising power, took northern Estonia between 1559 and 1564 and southern Estonia in the 1620s, consolidating Estonian Protestantism, which had taken root with the Reformation in the early 16th century. Some Estonians now look back on the Swedish era as a pre-Russian golden age but, although the Swedes tried to establish universal education, the frequent wars were devastating. Under Peter the Great, Russia smashed Swedish power in the Great Northern War (1700-21), and Estonia became part of the Russian empire.

Repressive government from Moscow and economic control by German landown-ers and burghers encouraged national self-awareness among the native Estonians. Serfs were freed in the 19th century, and improved education and wider land ownership pro-moted native culture and welfare.

Independence
Russia's new Soviet government, eager to get out of WW I, abandoned the Baltic region to Germany with the Treaty of Brest-Litovsk in March 1918. Estonian nationalists had declared independence on 24 February and the declaration was repeated after the German surrender in November. The Bol-sheviks then tried to win the Baltic states back but were beaten by local opposition and outside military intervention, in Estonia's case, a British fleet and volunteer forces from Scandinavia.

Damaged by the war and hampered by the disruption of trade with Russia and the world slump, independent Estonia suffered dire economic problems and the anti-communist, anti-parliamentary 'vaps' movement won a constitutional referendum in 1933. But Prime Minister Konstantin Päts outflanked it in a bloodless coup and took over as a moderate, fairly benevolent dictator.

Soviet Rule & WW II

The Molotov-Ribbentrop Pact of 23 August 1939, by which Nazi Germany and the USSR agreed on mutual non-aggression, secretly divided Eastern Europe into German and Soviet spheres of influence. The Baltic states ended up in the Soviet sphere and by August 1940 they were under occupation, Communists had won 'elections', and the states had been 'accepted' into the USSR.

Within a year or so, over 10,000 people in Estonia had been killed or deported. When Hitler invaded the USSR in 1941, many in the Baltics saw the Germans as liberators, but during the German occupation an estimated 5500 people died in Estonia's concentration camps. Some 40,000 Estonians joined the German army to try to stop the Red Army conquering Estonia at the end of the war and 70,000 fled, mainly to Germany or Sweden.

Between 1945 and 1949, with Stalinism back on course, agriculture was collectivised and industry nationalised, and around a further 60,000 Estonians were killed or deported. The *metsavennad* (forest brethren) partisans fought against Soviet rule until 1953.

New industries, technologically advanced in Soviet terms, helped give Estonia relatively high living standards but brought environmental problems and an influx of migrants, mostly from Russia, to work the new plants.

New Independence

There were demonstrations against 'Sovietisation' as early as 1980 by Estonian students. With *glasnost* (openness) in the late '80s, pent-up bitterness in the Baltic states was released and national feelings surged. By 1988 a reformist popular front had been formed in each republic to press for democratic change, virtually in alliance with the local communist parties. Estonia's, claiming 300,000 members, called at its first congress in October 1988 for autonomy, democracy and cuts in immigration. Like Latvia and Lithuania, Estonia paid lip service to *perestroyka* (restructuring) while dismantling Soviet institutions. On 23 August 1989, the 50th anniversary of the Molotov-Ribbentrop Pact, an estimated two million people formed a human chain across all three republics, many of them calling for secession from the USSR. In November Moscow granted the republics economic autonomy.

In 1990 attention focused on Lithuania as it declared itself independent, then suffered intimidation and economic blockade. Estonia followed a similar path more cautiously. In the spring nationalists won a big majority in the Estonian Supreme Soviet – now called the Supreme Council or parliament – and reinstated the pre-WW II constitution, but allowed a 'transition period' for independence to be negotiated. That independence came sooner and more suddenly than many expected in the aftermath of the attempted coup against Mikhail Gorbachov in Moscow. Estonia announced full independence on 20 August 1991 and first the Western world and then, on 6 September, the USSR recognised it.

Economic difficulties helped bring down the first government of independent Estonia when Prime Minister Edgar Savisaar, accused by some people of not moving fast enough towards a market economy, was replaced in January 1992 by Tiit Vähi.

Ethnic relations between Estonians and Russians were also a source of much tension early in the independence era: a February 1992 law decreed that those who were not citizens of the pre-WW II republic, or their descendants – in other words most of the large Russian population – could not apply for Estonian citizenship until they had completed two years' residence from 30 March 1990. They then had to wait one year for acceptance. Whether applicant citizens could vote in elections was still being debated as we went to press. If they could not, most of Estonia's Russian population would probably be excluded from the first elections to Estonia's new parliament, the Riigikogu.

GEOGRAPHY

With an area of 45,200 sq km, Estonia is the smallest of the Baltic states but is still bigger than Denmark. It's mainly low-lying, with extensive bogs and fens, but rises slightly in the eastern half. Suur Munamägi (318 metres) in the south-east is the highest point in any of the Baltic states. Nearly 40% of the land is forested, mainly with pine along the coasts and mixed forests inland.

Estonia's 3794-km coast is heavily indented. Offshore are over 800 islands, the biggest being Saaremaa and Hiiumaa in the west. Inland, there are over 1400 lakes, and Lake Peipus (3548 sq km) on Estonia's border with Russia, is the fourth biggest in Europe (though its maximum depth is only 15 metres).

GOVERNMENT

Legislative powers at the time of writing are exercised by a parliament called the Supreme Council (formerly Supreme Soviet), popularly elected under Soviet election rules in 1990 for a five-year term. Its chairman is the state president, an office held by Arnold Rüütel, a popular former high-ranking Communist. The Supreme Council is responsible for appointing an executive government, headed by the prime minister. But the authority of the Supreme Council is challenged by a nationalist assembly, the Congress of Estonia, elected in 1990 by citizens of the pre-WW II Republic of Estonia and their descendants.

A new draft constitution developed jointly by the Council and the Congress proposes elections to a new parliament, the Riigikogu, expected to be held in late 1992.

ECONOMY

Although from 1988 Estonia took a lead in encouraging private enterprise which created real opportunities for people with initiative, skills or contacts, most people were hit when independence came. This was because of a dire combination of rapid inflation, falling output, the end of cheap fuel and other supplies from Russia, shortages and unemployment. The winter of 1991-92 was probably the hardest economically since WW II, with the cost of living increasing tenfold in the year to March 1992 as state subsidies were removed. While there was more in the shops, most local people couldn't afford to buy it.

The hope is that the benefits of a market economy will be felt soon enough to make the problems of transition a bad dream. (The average wage was about US$20 in mid-1992.)

Trade between the three Baltic states and with the West is far less than with Russia. Nevertheless the Baltic states have the potential to be, like the Hanseatic cities centuries ago, a key gateway between Russia and the West. One obstacle they must overcome is industries which are outdated and products which are often low-quality in world terms. Another is the environmental problems of some of the industries developed in the Soviet era – Estonia rejected Moscow's plans for further development of the important electricity-producing oil shale fields in its north-east for these reasons.

In 1989, 50% of the workforce was in industry, forestry, construction or transport and 12% in agriculture.

POPULATION, PEOPLE & RELIGION

According to the 1989 Soviet census, 61.5% of Estonia's 1.56 million people were Estonian, 30% Russian, 3% Ukrainian and just under 2% Belorussian. A feeling among Estonians of being swamped by immigrant Russian workers since WW II gave rise to strong nationalist feelings which certainly helped Estonia gain independence but have also contributed to tensions in post-independence society. Russians are concentrated in the industrial north-east and in Tallinn.

Estonians are a Finno-Ugrian people, one of an ethno-linguistic group scattered across Siberia and along the Volga river. Their ancestors reached Estonia from the east between 2500 and 2000 BC. They're related closely to the Finns, and more distantly to the Sami or Lapps and even the Hungarians, but not to the Latvians and Lithuanians, who are Indo-European.

In a 1991-92 opinion poll, 23% of Estonians and 30% of Russians in Estonia claimed to have religious convictions. Lutheranism is the predominant faith of Estonians; Russian Orthodoxy, of Russians.

LANGUAGE

Estonians speak Estonian. Like Finnish, it's a Finno-Ugrian language, part of the Ural-Altaic language family, which sets it apart from Russian, Latvian and Lithuanian, which are in the Indo-European family. Using the odd word of Estonian goes down well with the locals.

Most waiters, taxi drivers and other people who come into contact with tourists, as well as many people who have had higher education, have a smattering of English, German or perhaps Swedish, but in general only the best educated people or those at higher levels in tourism can hold a conversation. Finnish and Estonian are related closely enough for their speakers to make some sense of each other.

The single most useful language if you're travelling through more than one of the three Baltic states is Russian. While few of the many Russians in Estonia speak much Estonian, nearly all Estonians speak Russian – a situation repeated in Latvia and Lithuania. But Estonians, Latvians and Lithuanians can be touchy about being addressed in Russian, so make an attempt to communicate in some other language first.

English	Estonian	Russian	Russian Pronunciation
Estonia	*Eesti*	Эстония.	ess-ton-ya
Hello.	*Tere.*	Здравствуйте.	zdrast-vooy-tye
Goodbye.	*Head aega.* ('hey-ahd ei-gah')	До свидания.	das-fi-da-nya
Excuse me.	*Vabandage.*	Извините.	iz-vi-nee-ti-ye
Thank you.	*Tänan.*	Спасибо.	spuh-see-ba
Please.	*Palun.*	Пожалуйста.	pa-zhahl-stuh
Yes.	*Jah.*	Да.	da
No.	*Ei.*	Нет.	nyet
Where?	*Kus?*	Где?	gdyeh
Do you speak English?	*Kas teie räägite inglise keelt?*	Вы говорите по-английски?	vih ga-var-ee-tye pa-an-glee-ski
Do you speak Russian?		Вы говорите по-русски?	vih ga-var-ee-tye pa-rooss-ki
How much?	*Kui palju?*	Сколько стоит?	skol-ka sto-eet
one, two	*üks* ('yooks'), *kaks*	один, два	ah-dyin, dva
three, four	*kolm, neli*	три, четыре	tree, chi-tir-yeh
cheap, expensive	*odav, kallis*	лешёвый, дорогой	desh-yov-y, da-ra-goy
hotel	*hotell*	гостиница	guh-stee-nit-suh
airport	*lennujaam*	аэропорт	ah-eh-ra-port
railway station	*raudteejaam*	вокзал	vahk-zahl
bus, bus station	*buss, autobussijaam*	автобус, автовокзя	uf-toh-boos, af-tah- vahk-zahl
seaport	*sadam*	порт	port
street, square	*tee, plats/väljak*	улица, площадь	ool-it-suh, plosh-id
avenue, road	*puiestee, maantee*	бульвар, шоссе	bool-vahr, shoss-eh

ESTONIA

The following sounds are specific to Estonian:

č	is pronounced 'ch'
š	as 'sh'
ž	as the 's' in 'pleasure'
ä	like the 'ai' in 'air'
õ	similar to the 'e' in 'bed'
ö	like the 'u' in 'fur' but with rounded lips
ü	like a short 'yoo'
b	is pronounced like 'p'
g	like 'k'
j	like the 'y' in 'yes'
oo	like the 'a' in 'water'
r	trilled

Lonely Planet's *Russian Phrasebook* by James Jenkin gives you many more Russian phrases.

Facts for the Visitor

VISAS & EMBASSIES
Visa regulations for any of the Baltic states are likely to be tinkered with at any time. Check the latest situation well ahead of your trip. At the time of writing all visitors to Estonia, except citizens of the states into which the USSR broke up, need a visa. Estonian visas are issued at Estonian missions in some countries, or on arrival at Tallinn seaport or airport. They're sometimes obtainable at other border points but don't count on it.

Normally you need to fill in a brief form and supply one photo. The usual charge for a single-entry visa is US$10 or a rough local equivalent. Multiple-entry visas, valid for a year, cost US$30 or a rough local equivalent. There are also transit visas available at embassies or borders and valid for three days, for US$5. If you could have obtained a visa before travelling to Tallinn but didn't, you are charged double. Embassy prices differ slightly from country to country.

Though Estonian embassies insist that confirmation of accommodation in Estonia is not needed when you apply for a visa, some travellers have been asked for this on arrival at Tallinn airport. It's therefore advisable to carry some papers showing that you have a hotel, hostel, college, home or whatever to go to. In May 1992 there were press reports that entrants from Russia would be issued visas only on the basis of invitations certified by the Estonian authorities. Whether this applied only to Russians or only to visas issued on the border itself and how the certification was supposed to happen was not clear.

In March 1992 the three Baltic states established a 'common visa space', which initially meant that a visa for any of the three states was also good for two days in each of the other two. This time limit may not always be rigidly enforced in any case. It may be possible to obtain an Estonian visa when you're already in Estonia through the Interior Ministry (☎ 66 36 76) at Pikk 61, Tallinn.

There are border posts on the land crossings between Estonia and Latvia, but in our experience scrutiny is light. Tighter control is being introduced on the Estonia-Russia border, at least at Narva, the main crossing point.

Estonian Embassies
Estonia is still setting up missions in other countries. New ones will be added and some existing ones may move. They are often open for limited hours so ring ahead and allow plenty of time to make contact. They include:

Canada
    Consulate, 958 Broadview Avenue, Toronto, Ontario, M4K 2R6 (☎ 416-461 0764)
Denmark
    Embassy, HC Andersens Boulevard 38, 1553 Copenhagen V (☎ 33 93 34 62)
Finland
    Embassy, Fabianinkatu 13 A-2, Helsinki 13 (☎ 63 35 48, 17 97 19)
France
    Embassy, 14 Boulevard Montmartre, 75009 Paris (☎ 1.48.010.022)
Germany
    Embassy, Bertha-von-Suttner-Platz 1-7, 5300 Bonn 1 (☎ 65 8276)

Lithuania
>Embassy, Turniškių gatvė 14, 232016 Vilnius
(☎ 76 48 96, 76 98 48)

Norway
>Embassy, Sankt Olavsgate 27, 0166 Oslo
(☎ 22 11 21 48)

Russia
>Embassy, Sobinovsky pereulok 5, 103009
Moscow (☎ 290 50 13, 290 31 78)

Sweden
>Embassy, Rädmansgatan 18, 11425 Stockholm
(☎ 10 9981)

UK
>Embassy, 18 Chepstow Villas, London W11 2RB
(☎ 071-229 6700)

USA
>Embassy, Rockefeller Plaza 9, New York, NY
(☎ 212-247 1450)

Foreign Embassies in Estonia

Foreign diplomatic representation in Estonia is also in its infancy. Some countries' ambassadors are still residing in nearby capitals like Stockholm or Helsinki. Check for likely future changes in the following addresses.

Canada
>Embassy Office Manager, Tolli 3 (☎ 44 90 56)

Denmark
>Ambassador, Rävala puiestee 9, Rooms 601-612
(☎ 69 13 61, 69 14 94)

Finland
>Embassy, Liivalaia 12 (☎ 44 95 22)

France
>Embassy, Toomkuninga 20
(☎ 45 37 84, consular department 45 16 49)

Germany
>Ambassador, Rävala puiestee 9
(☎ 69 14 72, 69 15 63)

Latvia
>Embassy, Tõnismägi 10 (☎ 68 16 68)

Lithuania
>Representative, Vabaduse väljak 10
(☎ 66 66 34, 44 89 17)

Norway
>Embassy, Pärnu maantee 8 (☎ 44 80 14)

Russia
>Representative, Pikk 19 (☎ 44 30 14)

Sweden
>Ambassador, Endla 4A (☎ 45 03 50)

UK
>Embassy, 2nd floor, Kentmanni 20
(☎ 45 53 28/9)

USA
>Embassy, Kentmanni 20 (☎ 45 50 05,
consular department 45 53 13)

DOCUMENTS & CUSTOMS

When you enter any of the three Baltic states you may be given a customs declaration to fill in. List your money and valuables (including jewellery) so that you can avoid paying duty when you take them out again. When you leave, you may have to fill in a new declaration showing what valuables you have then, or just produce the original one, or you may not be checked at all. If asked for a declaration you haven't got, since no one gave you one when you entered the country, all you can do is plead ignorance.

You'll be charged tax from 30% to 100% of the retail price for taking out of Estonia more than one litre of strong alcoholic drinks (up to 58% volume) and one litre of mild alcoholic drinks (up to 21% volume); or more than two litres of mild alcoholic drinks; or more than 10 litres of beer, 200 cigarettes, 20 cigars or 250 grams of tobacco. Currently there's a US$1000 limit on money taken in or out of Estonia duty-free, and a fluctuating limit on the value of purchases that can be exported duty-free.

MONEY
Currency & Prices

Estonia was the first of the Baltic states to introduce its own currency, the kroon, in 1992. This is Estonia's only legal tender, a 'hard' (freely convertible) currency, and is intended to be held close to a rate of eight kroons to one Deutschmark, making one kroon initially worth US$0.08.

Many prices went up because of a new sales tax introduced with the kroon. But hotel prices which were formerly quoted in dollars mostly went down. This move may make some things more expensive and others cheaper, but should certainly make everything simpler.

Previously Estonia had muddled along on a combination of Soviet roubles (at an exchange rate of R334 = US$1 in late 1992) and foreign 'hard' (freely convertible) currencies. Some purchases had a rouble price for Estonians and a hard-currency price for Westerners. There are amazing differentials between the two, designed to shield locals from the effects of economic reform: the same hotel room for instance might be offered for R85 (US$0.70) to a local but US$20 to a foreigner. But such 'foreigners' prices' were used somewhat haphazardly: cheaper hotels often dealt only in roubles, while rail tickets might cost hard currency if bought through a hotel service bureau or travel agent, but roubles if bought at the station.

Hopefully the two-tier prices will disappear with the arrival of the kroon. All prices in this chapter have been converted into US dollars.

Cash, Travellers' Cheques or Credit Cards?

At the time of writing travellers' cheques can only be exchanged at a very few places in Estonia. Cash US dollars are the best money to take, with Deutschmarks, pounds sterling or Finnish markka next best. Money can be changed at branches of the Bank of Estonia (Eesti Pank) and some other banks like Tartu Commercial Bank (Tartu Kommertspank) and Hansapank.

Only a few establishments like top-end restaurants and hotels accept credit cards, but the list of places accepting them can be expected to grow. Visa, MasterCard, Diners Club and American Express all crop up.

CLIMATE & WHEN TO GO

From May to September daytime maximum temperatures are usually between 14°C and 22°C. July and August, the warmest months, are also the wettest, with days of persistent showers. May, June and September are more comfortable.

April and October have cold, sharp, wintry days as well as mild spring-like or autumnal ones. There's usually snow on the ground from January to late March.

Temperatures in the east average 2°C colder than on the coast; the uplands have around 700 mm of precipitation annually, against 500 mm on the coast. Coastal waters average temperatures of 18°C in summer.

SUGGESTED ITINERARY

A suggested itinerary for one week could include:

Tallinn and either Tartu the south-east or Saaremaa and west coast, possibly also Lahemaa national park

TOURIST OFFICES

The first public tourist information office in the Baltic states was due to open in Tallinn in 1992. Travel agents and hotels in Estonia are also possible information sources.

The travel agencies Viron Matkapalvelu (☎ 66 35 63) of Mikonkatu 8, 00100 Helsinki, and Baltisches Reisebüro (☎ 59 6783, fax 52 5913) of Bayerstrasse 37/1, 8000 Munich 2, acted in 1992 as voluntary Estonian tourism information offices. They may well continue in following years.

Viron Matkapalvelu has an Estonia information line (☎ 9700 7017) for callers from Finland only (English spoken); Baltisches Reisebüro puts out an informative brochure in German.

BUSINESS HOURS & HOLIDAYS

Most shops are open from 9 or 10 am to 6 or 7 pm Monday to Friday, to 4 or 5 pm Saturdays, closed Sundays. Restaurants usually open from noon to around midnight, with two hours' break in the late afternoon or early evening.

Museums are open during varying hours but nearly always between 11 am and 4 pm. Normal office hours are from 9 am to 6 pm.

National holidays are:

New Year's Day, 1 January
Independence Day (anniversary of the 1918 declaration), 24 February
Good Friday (Easter Monday is also taken as a holiday by many people)
May Day, 1 May
Victory Day (anniversary of Battle of Võnnu, 1919), 23 June
Midsummer, 24 June
Christmas Day, 25 December
Boxing Day, 26 December

CULTURAL EVENTS

Estonia has a big calendar of festivals encompassing music, art, folk culture and more, especially in summer. Tickets are often easy enough to get, and some events are open to everyone free. A major event in 1993 will be the seventh Estonian Youth Song & Dance Festival, scheduled for 14 to 20 June.

Two regular events stand out. One is the Baltika international folk festival (see Lithuania, Facts for the Visitor), next due in Estonia in 1995. But most famous is the Estonian Song Festival which climaxes with a choir of up to 30,000 singing traditional Estonian songs on a vast open-air stage to an audience of 100,000 or more. Latvia and Lithuania hold similar events, all usually every five years, and their emotional charge has done much to foster Baltic national identities. The Estonia Song Festival is an experience not to be missed if you have the chance to attend it. Estonia's next one is in 1994 – tens of thousands of singers and dancers will perform in Tartu on 18 and 19 July, and in Tallinn from 30 June to 3 July.

At these festivals you'll see many people in Estonian traditional dress. Women sport long and colourful skirts, embroidered jackets, and an amazing variety of headgear from neat pillboxes to vast, winged fairy-tale creations.

POST & TELECOMMUNICATIONS
Post

Mail service out of Estonia isn't too bad, expect letters or cards to take about 10 days to Western Europe or North America. If you mark your mail 'via Finland' it may speed it up. Air-mail rates for letters or cards weighing up to 20 grams in mid-1992 were US$0.20 to European countries, the USA or Canada and US$0.35 elsewhere. For incoming mail, delivery times are very erratic. Have your mail sent to another country if you can.

Telephone

International International phone calls from Estonia can be frustrating to make, but at the time of writing are incredibly cheap. You need a private or hotel-room phone to make them from. It's starting to be possible to dial Scandinavia direct from some phones. Otherwise, hotel desk staff are usually willing to book calls for you, which can save a lot of aggravation.

On your own, dial 007 for the international operator, who may not speak English, to book the call. This may take some time, and you then have to wait an unspecified time for the operator to ring you back with the call – typically 30 minutes to two hours. Asking for a double-price *kiirkone* (quick call) may help. Each hotel room normally has its own individual number: ask the desk staff if you can't work out what it is. Mid-1992 tariffs per minute were: to Finland US$0.04, Sweden US$0.07, the rest of Europe US$0.15, USA or Canada US$0.27, and Australia or New Zealand US$0.35.

Local Calls within the city you're in can be made either from private or hotel-room phones (simply by dialling the number, without any area code) or from most public phone boxes. At the time of writing you need two one-kopeck coins, or one two-kopeck coin, or one 10-kopeck coin.

Within Estonia & the Ex-USSR Long-distance calls within Estonia, Latvia, Lithuania or anywhere else in the former USSR, are easiest from private or hotel-room phones: dial 8, wait for the dial tone, then dial the area code and number. You may have to wait up to a minute before the number rings. Most calls cost less than US$0.03 a minute. Area codes from Estonian phones include Tallinn 22, Haapsalu 247, Kuressaare 245, Narva 235, Põlva 230, Pärnu 244, Rakvere 232, Tartu 234, Viljandi 243, Riga 0132, Vilnius 0122, St Petersburg 812, Moscow 095.

There are also special long-distance phone booths (*Kaugekõneautomaadid*) in selected places. A third way of making a long-distance call is to book it at the town's telephone (*telefon*) office, and wait.

Calls to Estonia At the time of writing Estonia still uses the USSR country code, 7. From outside the ex-USSR, you precede this with your international access code (eg 010 in the UK), and follow it with 014, then the area code minus its initial 2, then the number. So, to reach Tallinn 76 54 32 from the UK, you dial 010 7 014 2 76 54 32. Getting through from Scandinavia or Finland can be even harder than from more distant countries since there's more demand on the lines. Pick times of day when both your country's and Estonia's lines are likely to be less busy.

If you're dialling Estonia from within the ex-USSR, including Latvia or Lithuania, you replace the initial 2 of the area code with 014. The code for Tallinn is thus 0142, usually preceded by a long-distance access code, 8.

Fax, Telex & Telegraph
Fax and especially telex can be good ways of reaching Estonia from other countries. But the only public outgoing fax service we found was at Tallinn Harbour Passenger Terminal, next to the Inreko ticket office, where you can fax Western Europe for US$3 a minute, or the USA for US$4 a minute.

Telegrams can be sent from any telegraph (*telegraaf*) office, often the same as post offices, and at the time of writing cost US$0.03 a word to Western Europe, US$0.07 to North America. Outgoing and incoming telegrams rarely take more than 24 hours.

TIME
Estonian, Latvian and Lithuanian time is GMT plus two hours, except from the last Sunday in March to the last Saturday in September when daylight saving is in force and it's GMT plus three hours. The 24-hour clock is used for rail, bus and air timetables.

BOOKS & MAPS
Books
The Singing Revolution: A Journey Through the Baltic States by Clare Thomson, a Michael Joseph hardback written not long before independence in 1991, takes a partisan anti-Soviet view of events and provides background on the Soviet era and earlier periods of outside rule.

The Baltic States: A Reference Book pub-lished jointly in 1991 by Estonian, Latvian and Lithuanian Encyclopaedia Publishers, is 260-plus useful pages of facts including history, culture, politics, arts and places to visit, useful organisations and who's who of important people in each country. You can get it at some Baltic embassies and one or two outlets in the Baltic states themselves for around US$20. It contains phrase lists for all three Baltic languages.

A Guide to the Baltic States edited by Ingrīda Kalniņš (Inroads Inc, Merrifield, Virginia, USA, 1990) contains background on the three countries as well as excellent information on places to visit, including lesser towns and the countryside. It's weaker on Estonia than on the other two states and is available in some travel bookshops and Baltic embassies or (for US$17.95 plus postage and handling or for US$2.75 in the USA) from Publishers Distribution Service, 121 East Front St, Suite 203, Traverse City, MI 49684, USA.

Maps
Lithuania, Estonia, Latvia (Cartographia, Budapest); *Estonia, Latvia, Lithuania* (Bartholomew, Edinburgh); and *Baltische Staaten* (Ravenstein Verlag, Bad Soden am Taunas, Germany) are similar 1:850,000 (1 cm = 8.5 km) maps of the three countries plus part of the Kaliningrad region. These should be adequate for most travellers. You can also pick up maps of individual states and towns in the Baltic states themselves, but beware of anything published before about 1989 since it's likely to contain deliberate Soviet distortions. *Eesti Maanteed – Estonian Roads* is a good 1990 road atlas covering the whole of Estonia at a scale of 1:200,000.

MEDIA
The admirable weekly *Baltic Independent* is an authoritative English-language digest of Baltic news and information, with an emphasis on Estonia, published in Tallinn. You can buy it for next to nothing at bookstalls or hotels in Tallinn, Riga or Vilnius. *Tallinn This Week*, published every two months in glossy booklet form, is packed with useful

and candid information for visitors not just to Tallinn but to Estonia as a whole. It costs around US$1, mainly from hotels. *Tallinn City Paper*, a quarterly, has similarly useful listings plus feature articles. The free monthly *What? Where? When? In Tallinn* gives comprehensive listings of theatre, concerts, exhibitions and sports events.

Western newspapers three or four days' old are sold at Tallinn's Hotel Palace.

FILM & PHOTOGRAPHY

Western print film is sold in some hotels and shops, along with some slide film (but rarely Kodachrome). There are a few quick print-processing outlets. Even in summer, sunlight can be at a premium, so make use of whatever you get.

HEALTH

Bring with you any medicines you think you'll need on the trip – even aspirin – as supplies can be very scarce. In an emergency seek your hotel's help first (if you're staying in one), the bigger hotels may have doctors on call. Your embassy should be able to recommend a doctor or hospital, but if things are serious be prepared to fly out.

Tap water in any of the three Baltic states can be dodgy – see Basic Rules, Water in the Health section of the introductory Facts for the Visitor chapter.

Because of coastal pollution, swimming was not recommended for several years at the Estonian resorts of Pärnu and Haapsalu. In 1992 we heard that Pärnu had been given the all-clear, but suggest you still take local advice about swimming anywhere on Baltic coasts.

DANGERS & ANNOYANCES

Theft from hotel rooms is a danger in all the Baltic states, but more significant in cheap hotels lacking much supervision. Carrying your own padlock can be a help. Keep valuables with you or in a hotel safe.

Most of the surly, rude, obstructive goblins employed in service industries in the Soviet era have miraculously changed character now that pleasing the customer has become worthwhile, but there are still one or two hangovers from the bad old days. When you encounter them, all you can do is grit your teeth and quietly persist.

Drunks on the streets and in hotels can be a nuisance in the evenings, especially at weekends. In Tallinn they're as likely to be foreign tourists as locals. Steer clear and don't get involved. Most restaurants, hotels, railway waiting rooms etc are wreathed in tobacco smoke.

ACCOMMODATION

The booklet *Eesti Hotellid ja Majutuskohad*, published by the Estonian Tourist Board, lists over 150 accommodation places of all types and grades throughout Estonia, with addresses and phone numbers. Try the tourist information office at Kinga 6 in Tallinn for a copy.

It's worth trying to book ahead, wherever you plan to stay. You can normally book by phone but language can be a problem. Consider booking into somewhere more expensive for your first night or two in Estonia, and make it a base for seeking out somewhere cheaper after you arrive. Agents in other countries as well as Tallinn itself can make bookings for you but they work mainly with the more expensive hotels and may charge commission. Still, they can be helpful when everywhere seems 'full'. In Finland they include Estum of Helsinki and Oy Saimaa Matkapalvelu of Lappeenranta; in Sweden Nordisk Reseservice and Estlands Resor of Stockholm should be able to help. See the Getting There & Away section for contact details. In Tallinn there's E-Sail (☎ 23 81 45 or 52 73 66, fax 23 79 45).

Keep any paperwork you receive in advance that shows you have somewhere to stay in Estonia, it may be helpful at immigration posts.

Camping

A dozen or so camp sites (*kämpingud*) around Estonia are listed in the Tourist Board accommodation guide. They typically have running water, toilets and some cooking facilities. Some have tiny wooden cabins as well as tent sites. Try to ring ahead for vacancies, especially if you need a cabin. Camp sites are usually open from June to August, and sometimes part of May and September. At local prices you'll rarely pay much more than US$1 a person to camp, perhaps a bit more for a place in a cabin. Estonian Holidays (see Tallinn, Information) may be able to provide some information on camp sites.

Hostels & Colleges

The Estonian Youth Hostels Project (Eesti Puhkemajade Sihtasutus), launched in 1991, has 10 hostels and more to come. They're mostly in rural areas such as Lahemaa national park or the west coast. Most have from 15 to 40 places; some are open only a few months a year. Accommodation is mainly in small two to four-bed rooms (sheets are usually provided) with prices between US$2.25 and US$5.75 a person except in Tallinn.

All hostels have cooking facilities; some can supply meals too. Hostel cards are not needed. Bookings are recommended four to six weeks in advance through the project's head office (☎ 44 10 96, fax 44 69 71) at Room 608, Kentmanni 20, EE0001 Tallin. At the time of writing, this office was open Mondays, Wednesdays and Fridays from 10 am to noon and 2 to 4 pm, Tuesdays 10 am to noon, and Thursdays 2 to 4 pm. The Youth Hostels Association of Finland (☎ 694 0377) in Helsinki can also provide some information.

Student rooms are another accommodation possibility, for around US$5 to US$12 a person. Booking ahead is particularly advisable. See Tallinn and Tartu, Places to Stay.

Private Homes & Flats

Family Hotel Service Network (☎ and fax Tallinn 44 11 87) offers accommodation ranging from US$6 to US$32 a person per night in more than 300 private flats throughout Estonia, mostly in town centres. It can confirm reservations by fax and its office address is Vana-Viru 13, EE0001 Tallinn.

Normally you stay with a family, which may also offer breakfast, but for longer stays entire flats are available. All flats have their own kitchen and bathroom with hot water.

You can also organise homestays in any of the Baltic states through some organisations in the West including Goodwill Holidays of Welwyn, England, for about US$27 a day with full board (see Getting There & Away for contact information), and Home & Host International (☎ 612-871 0596) of 2445 Park Avenue, Minneapolis, MN 55404, USA ('fully guided homestays' in any Baltic city for US$125 a day; bed and breakfast for US$80 (both of these with English-speaking hosts. Dorm stays cost US$40, apartment rental US$525 a week, student discounts available).

Hotels

Price differentials in the Baltic states at the time of writing were at perhaps their most absurd when it came to hotels, with US$6 the most you'd pay for a double room at rouble hotels, but US$25 the least you could hope for in hotels demanding dollars. You can try bargaining but don't *expect* success. With new local currencies, cheap hotels will probably become more expensive while expensive ones probably won't get much cheaper. Old Soviet hotels, in particular, can become pretty sleazy with drinking and prostitution.

Cheaper Hotels These are usually lower-grade old Soviet hotels with bare, dowdy, usually tolerably clean rooms. Some have private toilet, shower and basin; in others you share smelly facilities with other rooms. Often the staff will speak no English. In some places they may refuse to let Westerners stay, or only let you in after some persuasion. The stereotypical customer is a man in a vest, lying on his bed quaffing vodka, chain-smoking and watching TV. Hotels with a desk attendant on each floor are likely to have better security.

By 1992 some cheap hotels, usually the somewhat better ones, were demanding hard currency from foreigners and had thus become middle-price hotels. Their prices sometimes seemed to be plucked randomly out of the air when they realised they had a foreigner on their hands.

Expensive Hotels These are the better ex-Soviet hotels (usually former Intourist establishments) plus some new places (including some motels) built and at least partly run by Western companies. Prices for single/double rooms range from US$40/60 up to three or four times that. In all, the rooms are comfortable, with private bathrooms.

FOOD

There are numerous decent restaurants in all three Baltic capitals, and a few in most other sizeable towns. Make sure the door attendant realises you're a Westerner: it decreases your chances of a surly rejection. The restaurants of the old Soviet-era hotels remain as fallbacks, with their ear-splitting pop bands and groups of drunken revellers.

There are many good cafés, too, in the Baltics, especially in Tallinn and Riga. You can also usually supply yourself with basic foods without much trouble: bread is easy to get from bakeries for around US$0.05 a loaf, and fruit and vegetables are available at town markets, which function every day. Other food shops may not have a great variety, but they'll have something.

New local currencies are likely to make the present rouble restaurants (the majority) which may seem remarkably cheap in this book, more expensive.

Reservations may become more advisable as more locals begin to be able to afford to eat out: you can telephone or call in person at lunch time to reserve a table for the evening. Some hotels will do this for you.

Only a few of the best restaurants have all, or even most, of what's on the menu. At other places it's easier to find out what the waiter recommends. You'll usually be offered a choice from a few starters, a couple of soups, and two or three meat courses (which come with a few vegetables). The Russian custom of consuming large helpings of zakuski (hors d'oeuvres) such as tomato or cucumber salads, smoked fish or cold meats is alive and well in the Baltic states. Later courses tend to be smaller and more sloppily prepared than in the West.

Vegetarians may find life difficult. In Estonia keep saying *'taimetoite'* ('vegetarian dishes'); anywhere you can say 'vi-gi-ta-ri-AHN-yets' or 'bis MYA-suh' (Russian for 'vegetarian' and 'without meat'). Estonian specialities tend to be in the fishy realm, with smoked trout *(forrell)*, tra-

ESTONIA

English	Estonian	Russian	Russian Pronunciation
bread	leib	хлеб	khlyep
starters	eelroad	закуски	za-KOOSS-ki
salad	salat	салат	suh-LAHT
soup	supp	суп	soop
fish	kala	рыба	RIH-buh
meat or			
main dishes	liharoad	горячие блюла	gah-ri-ACH-i-yeh BLYOOD-ah
national dishes	rahvusroad	национальные блюла	nahts-ya-NAHL-ni-yeh BLYOOD-ah
chicken	kana	курица	KOO-rit-suh
vegetables	köögivili	овощи	OH-va-shchi
fruit	puuvili	фрукты	FROOK-ti
cheese	juust	сыр	seer

ditionally served with fried bread, one of the best.

DRINKS

Beer (*õlu* in Estonian, PEE-vah in Russian) is the favourite alcoholic drink in the Baltic states, but in restaurants and bars you usually have to pay US$1 or so for a can of imported beer. Easier to get are vodka and brandy ('kahn-YAHK') which in restaurants are sold by weight: a normal shot (bigger than the average Western measure) is 50 grams. Some Estonian cafés and bars serve *hoogvein* (mulled wine), a warming local speciality.

Tea (Estonian: *tee*, Russian: *chay*) and often coffee (Estonian: *kohv*, Russian: 'KOF-yeh') are easy to get throughout the Baltic states. A favourite soft drink is bottled mineral water (Estonian: *mineralveesi*, Russian: 'mi-ni-RAL-nuh-yuh va-DAH'). Tap water can be dodgy, see Health.

Getting There & Away

There are daily flights and numerous daily ferries between Helsinki and Tallinn. The land route, with a stop in St Petersburg (linked with Tallinn by rail, bus and air), is also appealing. But Helsinki can be a relatively expensive place to reach. If it's not on your itinerary in any case, consider the other options: direct flights to Estonia from several countries; a ferry from Sweden, or the Baltic corridor through Lithuania and Latvia, from which there are buses, trains and planes. Estonia also has direct connections with Warsaw, Moscow and Minsk. For any travel to or through parts of the CIS such as Russia, Belorussia or Kaliningrad, look into the visa situation well in advance.

TRAVEL AGENTS

Setting up a Baltic trip can be complicated, and travel-industry professionals can help smooth your path with bookings (including cheap flights), accommodation assistance, visa information, and so on. The following is a wide-ranging selection of agents specialising to some degree with travel in the Baltic states. Some deal with limited aspects of the subject, others are all-encompassing. Some offer expensive services, some are cheap. Some are tour operators as well. Some of those in North America didn't reply to our enquiries so may be defunct.

Australia
    Gateway Travel (☎ 02-745 3333),
    48 The Boulevard, Strathfield, NSW 2135
Canada
    Audra Travel (☎ 416-763 6279),
    2100 Bloor St West, Toronto, Ontario M6S 1M7
Denmark
    Fremad Rejser (☎ 31 22 04 04),
    Vesterbrogade 43, 1620 Copenhagen V
Finland
    Estum (☎ 62 92 99), Vuorimiehenkatu 23A, Helsinki
    Oy Saimaa Matkapalvelu (☎ 53300, 10066), Raatimiehenkatu 12, 53101 Lappeenranta
    Viron Matkapalvelu (☎ 66 35 63), Mikonkatu 8, 00100 Helsinki
Germany
    Baltisches Reisebüro (☎ 59 6783), Bayerstrasse 37/1, 8000 Munich 2
    Deutsches Reisebüro (☎ 95 8800), Emil-von-Bahring-Strasse 6, 6000 Frankfurt am Main 50
    Greif Reisen (☎ 24044), Universitätsstrasse 2, 5810 Witten-Heven
    Reisebüro Alainis (☎ 3582), Revalweg 4, 8940 Memmingen
    Schnieder Reisen (☎ 380 2060), Schomburgstrasse 120, 2000 Hamburg 50
Sweden
    Estlands Resor (☎ 11 0569), Wallingatan 32, Stockholm 11124
    Nordisk Reseservice (☎ 791 5055), Box 26030, S-100 41 Stockholm
UK
    Finlandia Travel Agency (☎ 071-409 7334), 2nd floor, 223 Regent St, London W1R 7DB
    Goodwill Holidays (☎ 043871-6421), Manor Chambers, The Green, School Lane, Welwyn, Herts AL6 9EB
    Progressive Tours (☎ 071-262 1676), 12 Dorchester Place, London W2 2BS
    Regent Holidays (☎ 211711), 15 John St, Bristol, BS1 2HR
    Rochdale Travel Centre (☎ 0706-31144), 66 Drake St, Rochdale, OL16 1PA
USA
    American Service Travel Bureau (☎ 312-238 9787), 9727 South Western Avenue, Chicago, IL 60643

Baltic-American Holidays, 501, 5th Avenue, New York, NY 10017

Baltic Tours (☎ 617-965 8080), 77 Oak St, Suite 4, Newton, MA 02164

Biruta's Tours (☎ 415-349 1622), PO Box 5410, San Mateo, CA 94402

Union Tours (☎ 212-683 9500), 79 Madison Avenue, New York, NY 10016

AIR
Routes
Western airlines and the national airline Estonian Air, which took to the air with former Aeroflot planes in 1992, operate scheduled flights in and out of Tallinn. At the time of writing Estonian Air flies to/from Moscow twice, and Helsinki once daily; Copenhagen, Kiev, Riga, Minsk, St Petersburg and Stockholm two or three times weekly; Budapest and Frankfurt once a week. Helsinki, Copenhagen, Stockholm, Budapest and Frankfurt are also served with equal or greater frequency by Finnair, SAS, Malev and Lufthansa respectively. LAL (Lithuanian Airlines) flies between Tallinn and Vilnius. The Western airlines offer worldwide connections via their hubs (Helsinki for Finnair etc).

Further new routes and airlines are likely to enter the picture but, equally, some services might be scaled down since some early Estonian Air flights carried far too few passengers because of the unpopularity of their Soviet-made aircraft.

Open jaws tickets – flying you into one city and out of another – are an option, see Fares.

Fares
Finding the best fare is very much a matter of ringing round to see who offers what. Sometimes the cheapest fares are sold by 'general sales agents' – travel agents (often Baltic specialists) appointed by an airline to sell reduced-price tickets on certain routes – so it's worth asking an airline's reservations department whether there are any such agents. For instance Regent Holidays has returns or open jaws on SAS or Finnair from London to Tallinn, St Petersburg, Riga or Vilnius for around US$510 to US$580 (some with Helsinki stopovers).

Tickets starting in Estonia can be more expensive than those starting elsewhere. Finnair has a US$83 Helsinki-Tallinn-Helsinki youth fare for under-25s, bookable not more than seven days before travel, or a US$92 'Superpex' return. But its cheapest Tallinn-Helsinki-Tallinn ticket is US$150. Estonian Air's regular Tallinn-Helsinki fare is US$118 one way.

SAS has cheap one-way youth fares, if you can comply with the booking restrictions, on its Scandinavia-Baltic state routes: Stockholm-Tallinn for instance is US$85 either way. Stockholm-Tallinn-Stockholm on an SAS Apex ticket is US$265; it's US$170 on an SAS 'Jackpot' fare (bookable seven to 14 days ahead).

Lufthansa offers an under-25s open jaw (Frankfurt-Vilnius and Tallinn-Frankfurt) for US$425. Frankfurt-Tallinn-Frankfurt on a Lufthansa or Estonian Air Apex is US$510, on a Lufthansa youth (under-25) fare it's US$460. Flights to/from Riga are US$54 one way, St Petersburg US$58, Moscow (Sheremetevo) US$87. Estonians buying Estonian Air tickets in Estonia are at present charged rouble fares equivalent to about one-tenth of the foreigners' fare. Estonian Air's first ticket outlet to open in another country was in Copenhagen (☎ 33 32 00 23). You should be able to buy its tickets from regular travel agents and perhaps from other airlines with which it shares routes. In Riga you can buy them from Latvian Airlines.

Charter Flights Individuals can often buy seats on charter flights, or in block bookings on scheduled flights, from tour companies or groups of emigrés returning to visit Estonia. Specialist travel agents and Estonian embassies are places to start asking. In 1992 Greif Reisen was offering Frankfurt-Tallinn round-trip flights from US$420. See Latvia, Getting There & Away for charter ideas from the UK.

LAND
Train tickets bought at stations in the former

USSR provide the cheapest form of long-distance transport in the Baltic states, so try to book them as early as possible. Buses are less heavily booked but this may change and it will pay to get tickets a few days ahead.

Bus

To/From Latvia, Lithuania & Kaliningrad
Between Riga and Tallinn (six hours, US$1.35) there are about four buses daily, via Pärnu. There are also daily buses to Viljandi and Tartu from Riga. There's a daily overnight bus each way between Tallinn and Vilnius (12 hours, US$2.50), plus daily services to/from Kaunas, Klaipėda and Kaliningrad.

To/From Russia
There are three daily buses each way between St Petersburg and Tallinn, taking eight hours for about US$1.

To/From Poland
In 1992 the Tallinn bus company Mootor (☎ 44 44 84) started a weekly bus to/from Warsaw, leaving Tallinn on Monday mornings and Warsaw on Wednesday mornings, taking 21 hours with a one-way fare of US$33. Tickets in Warsaw are sold at the Central bus station (near Zachodnia railway station).

Train

To/From Latvia, Lithuania, Belorussia & Poland
The 'Chayka' (train No 187/188) trundles each way between Tallinn and Minsk (Belorussia) daily in a scheduled 17 hours. Pulling carriages with four-berth couchette compartments, it sets out in the early morning and is supposed to arrive shortly before midnight. It stops at Tartu (3½ hours from Tallinn), Riga (7½ hours) and Vilnius (13½ hours). Between Tallinn and Riga, there's also an overnight couchette service (train No 651/652) taking 9½ hours via Tartu. The Tallinn-Riga couchette fare at the time of writing costs just US$1 southbound, US$0.60 northbound.

A daily through sleeping carriage runs both ways between Warsaw and Tallinn, taking 30 hours. The fare from Warsaw Central station ticket office is US$31. You may need a Belorussian visa on this train – see Lithuania, Facts for the Visitor.

To/From Russia
Between St Petersburg and Tallinn there are two overnight trains each way, taking nine or 10 hours for a soft-class sleeper fare of US$1.35. Overnight trains Nos 33/34 and 67/68 are the best between Moscow and Tallinn, taking from 15 to 16 hours.

Car & Motorbike
See the introductory Getting Around chapter for general comments on driving and riding in the Baltic states. From Finland it's easier to put your vehicle on a Helsinki-Tallinn ferry than to drive round via St Petersburg with possible delays at the Russia-Finland border. There's also a vehicle ferry from Stockholm, see the Sea section following. From Germany you can either approach through Lithuania and Latvia; or put your vehicle on the *Finnjet* to Helsinki or a ferry to Sweden, then on another ferry to Tallinn; or on the weekly Rostock-Helsinki-Tallinn freighter. For information contact DGSH in Rostock (☎ 36 62 28 02).

Taxi
Taxis in the Baltic states are so cheap by Western standards at the time of writing that they have become a mode of international transport. At the standard rate a taxi from Tallinn should cost about US$30 to Riga or St Petersburg. You may have to search for a driver willing to go so far and bargain over the price, but the trip will be quick if you succeed.

SEA

To/From Finland
By summer 1992 there were six to nine crossings each way daily to/from Helsinki, but it's still advisable to book a few days ahead. There are fewer services from September to April but, except maybe for a few days in December and January, some vessel is likely to be making the short voyage every day. Ships generally make the crossing in four hours, hydrofoils in two. In Helsinki

Viron Matkapalvelu can provide up-to-date information on schedules and make bookings. Main services (add US$7 travel tax to most prices for tickets bought in Finland) follow.

Georg Ots & Tallink These ferries are run by the Finnish-Estonian joint venture Tallink. There are three to six weekly sailings each in both directions almost all year round (one-way deck fares cost US$22 and US$27 on weekends); cabins are from US$11 to US$15 a person *(Georg Ots)*, from US$16 to US$37 *(Tallink)*. The *Tallink* takes cars for US$33 and motorbikes for US$11. Round-trip fares are double the one-way fare. Helsinki departures are from Olympia Terminal, South Harbour.

Georg Ots cabins can be occupied overnight in Helsinki before or after a crossing for US$11 to $US15. *Tallink* does 24-hour cruises from Helsinki, with accommodation on board at Tallinn, for US$33 to US$143. Make bookings at the following places:

Helsinki
> *Georg Ot*s at Saimaa Lines (☎ 65 87 33), Fabianinkatu 14, PL 8, 00130 Helsinki, or at the harbour (☎ 63 43 27), *Tallink* (☎ 602822)

Tallinn
> *Georg Ots* at the sea passenger terminal, *Tallink* at the Tallink office, Pärnu maantee, just down from Hotel Palace

Helta Line Finnish-run hydrofoils *Sinilind* and *Luik* each have a capacity for 94 people. There are two or more crossings daily each way from April to September (one way US$27, round trip US$40). Helsinki departures are from Magazine Terminal, South Harbour. Book at the terminals in both ports (☎ Helsinki 66 44 86 or 66 41 41, Tallinn 44 07 70 or 42 87 01).

Estonian New Line The hydrofoils *Liisa & Jaanika* make four crossings each way daily from June to September and up to two daily

during other months (one way US$22, round trip US$40). Helsinki departures are from Olympia Terminal, South Harbour.

The *Linda I* passenger and vehicle ferry makes one crossing each way daily all year round. Deck fare is US$11 one way, a cabin for two is US$11. Taking a motorbike costs US$11, a car US$27.

For bookings in Helsinki go to Yrjönkatu 23 A 2 (☎ 680 2499), or Travel Shop (☎ 62 44 34), Fabianinkatu 12, or Olympia Terminal. In Tallinn contact the Inreko ticket office (☎ 42 83 82) in the sea passenger terminal, or the Hotel Viru (☎ 65 08 71).

Kristina Cruises This company (☎ 62 99 68), at Korkeavuorenkatu 45, 00130 Helsinki sails each way several times weekly. It advertises 24-hour cruises to Tallinn costing from US$2, with round-trip deck passages from US$38.

To/From Other Countries
The Swedish passenger and vehicle ferry *Nord Estonia* sails overnight (15 hours) three or four times a week each way between Stockholm and Tallinn, year round. It's sometimes booked up two or three months ahead and the operator, Estline, may introduce a second vessel. One-way deck fare is US$65, with US$15 discount for students and senior citizens, but costs from US$11 to US$17 extra at weekends. A cabin costs from US$25 a person up to the sky, a car US$67. There are cruise deals too.

Make bookings in Stockholm at the Estline terminal (☎ 667 0001) in the Frihamnen (Free Harbour), or through travel agencies such as Bennett Resebureau or Nyman & Schultz. The Tallinn booking office is at Aia 5A (☎ 66 65 79, fax 44 12 19), open Monday to Friday from 9 am to 5 pm but for same-day departure you must book at the sea passenger terminal.

The *Baltic Star* (☎ Stockholm 23 8975), with an office at Vasagatan 4, S-111 20 Stockholm, runs four-day cruises from Stockholm to Tallinn.

ESTONIA

. A ferry service between Kiel (Germany) and Tallinn may start in 1992 or 1993.

TOURS

Some tours visit just one Baltic state, some visit all three and maybe Kaliningrad too, others add on St Petersburg and maybe Moscow. Some of the most imaginative trips are from Germany: in 1992 Greif Reisen offered a two-week bus trip taking in all three Baltic states plus Kaliningrad and Poland for about US$1000, while Deutsches Reisebüro had a 16-day Moscow-Klaipėda-Kaliningrad-Kaunas-Vilnius Riga-Tallinn-St Petersburg trip for US$1500 to US$1800, or a nine-day variation sticking to Lithuania, Latvia and Estonia for US$1170. Baltisches Reisebüro ran 17-day cruises from Travemunde to St Petersburg, Novgorod (Russia), Tallinn and Riga for US$1850.

From the UK, Regent Holidays plans tours typically costing around US$1400 for 12 nights in the three Baltic capitals, also one-off special-interest tours. Martin Randall Travel (☎ 081-994 6477), at 10 Barley Mow Passage, London W4 4PH, is to do tours focusing on art and related aspects of the Baltics.

Intourist, the Russian state travel company, still does Baltics tours. Contact its many branches in capital and major cities worldwide. In 1992 Intourist Reisen (☎ 030-88 0070) of Kurfürstendamm 63, 1000 Berlin 15, offered 10-day train trips to Kaliningrad, Liepāja, Riga and Vilnius for around US$850, while Intourist Travel (☎ 071-538 8600) of Intourist House, 219 Marsh Wall, London E14 9FJ, offered two-week tours to Moscow, St Petersburg and all three Baltic capitals for US$1075 to $US1400.

For Estonia only, Greif Reisen offered flights from Frankfurt and seven nights in Tallinn with half-board for around US$750. Possibilities with Baltisches Reisebüro included week-long trips combining Tallinn with Saaremaa or with Tartu and Pärnu for US$950 to $US1050. Leading travel firms in Tallinn (see Tallinn, Information) may be able to provide further information on tour firms going to Estonia from your country.

Getting Around

AIR

There are flights between Tallinn and Kuressaare on Saaremaa island. Flights to Kärdla on Hiiumaa may resume.

BUS

Long-distance buses serve all towns. They're a bit more expensive than trains, and on most routes are more frequent which cuts down queues and crowds. Still, it's advisable to book a day or two ahead. Most services are either *expres* or *kiir* (fast). An expres might be 20 minutes quicker on a three-hour trip.

TRAIN

The most frequent train services are on suburban routes to places of limited interest around Tallinn. Elsewhere, trains are slower and rarer than buses. Try to book a day or two ahead on long-distance trains, which may get fully booked.

TAXI

At the time of writing taxis are supposed to cost US$0.10 a km (which would get you anywhere around Tallinn for less than a dollar, and from Tallinn to Tartu for US$18.60) except at weekends and holidays when it's US$0.15. The meter ticks over at the outdated rate of 20 kopecks per km, and you multiply what it shows by 60 (or 90) to work out the fare.

To actually get the official rate, anywhere in the Baltic states, you must find a taxi with (a) a meter and (b) a driver who'll operate it honestly. The best bets are state taxis – those with a small chequered strip on the side, usually large Volga cars, often yellow. You can establish a multiplication rate by showing the driver a slip of paper with 'X 60', or whatever, written on it. Check that the meter is at zero when you start your trip.

CAR & MOTORBIKE
See the introductory Getting Around chapter for information on driving and riding in the Baltics and see Tallinn, Getting There & Away for information about car rentals.

BICYCLE
All the Baltic states are flat, with good roads and light traffic. But only Estonia has enough camp sites and youth hostels to provide fairly reliable cheap accommodation.

LOCAL TRANSPORT
Baltic cities and towns have good networks of buses, trolley buses and trams usually running from 5 or 6 am to midnight. You pay for your ride by punching a ticket in one of the ticket-punches fixed inside the vehicle. Tickets (Estonian: *pileteid*, Russian: *talony*) are sold from street kiosks displaying them in the window, which can be hard to locate, and by some drivers. Buy five or 10 at once: at the time of writing they cost less than US$0.01 each anywhere. Ticket inspection is rare but on-the-spot fines *can* be levied.

TOURS
Tour-group guides sometimes let outsiders tag along on day trips, which can be a good way to visit spread-out places like Lahemaa national park or Saaremaa. Look at the tour programmes posted up in hotel lobbies to see who's going where.

The service bureaux of Tallinn's Viru and Palace hotels, and the Tallinn Tourist Bureau (Tallinna Turismi Büroo), (☎ 66 60 07) at Toompuiestee 17A can hire you English-speaking guides for tours in or out of the capital. Also see the Tallinn Information section.

Tallinn

Tallinn (population 484,000) fronts a bay on the Gulf of Finland dominated by Toompea, the hill over which it has tumbled since the Middle Ages. The aura of the 14th and 15th centuries survives intact in central Tallinn's jumble of medieval walls and turrets, spires and winding cobbled hills; it's judiciously restored and fascinating to explore. Tallinn is also a national capital, with government buildings, a university, entertainment, and modern styles on its streets. Finns flock over from Helsinki at weekends.

Tallinn is on a similar latitude to St Petersburg and shares that city's summer 'white nights' and short, dark winter days.

History
The Danes set a castle and bishop on Toompea in 1219. German traders arrived and Tallinn joined the Hanseatic League in 1285, becoming a link between Novgorod, Pskov and the West. Exports included furs, leather and seal fat.

By the mid-14th century, after the Danes had sold northern Estonia to the German knights, Tallinn was a major Hanseatic town with about 4000 residents. The merchants and artisans in the Lower Town built a fortified wall to separate themselves from the bishop and knights on Toompea. Many of Tallinn's characteristic German-style buildings were constructed at this time. The city's German name, Revel or Reval, coexisted for centuries with the local name, Tallinn.

The prosperity faded in the 16th century as Swedes, Russians, Poles and Lithuanians fought over the Baltic region. Sweden held Tallinn from 1561 to 1710, then Russia took over. The city grew in the 19th century and by WW I had big shipyards and a population of 150,000. In 1944 during WW II, thousands of buildings were destroyed by Soviet bombing. After WW II industry was developed and Tallinn expanded fast, much of the population growth being due to immigration from outside Estonia. Only around half Tallinn's population today is Estonian.

Orientation
Tallinn spreads south from Tallinn Bay, which lies between two promontories jutting north into the Gulf of Finland. The city centre, just south of the bay, is essentially three parts: Toompea (or the Upper Town), the Lower Town and the New Town.

ESTONIA

ESTONIA

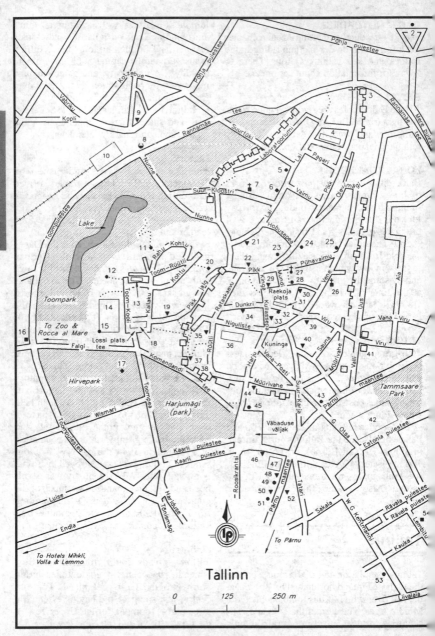

Tallinn

0   125   250 m

ESTONIA

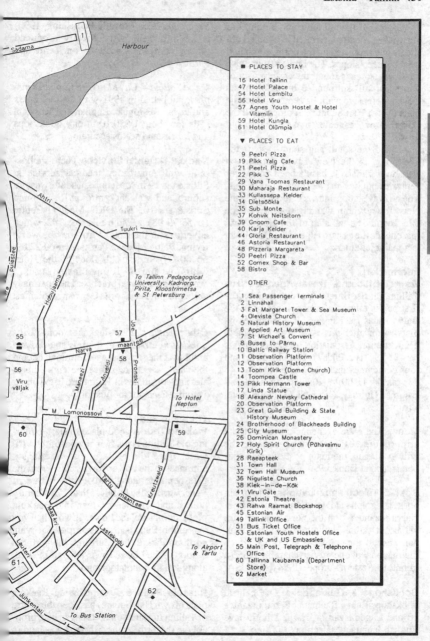

■ PLACES TO STAY

16 Hotel Tallinn
47 Hotel Palace
54 Hotel Lembitu
56 Hotel Viru
57 Agnes Youth Hostel & Hotel
   Vitamiin
59 Hotel Kungla
61 Hotel Olümpia

▼ PLACES TO EAT

9 Peetri Pizza
19 Pikk Yalg Cafe
21 Peetri Pizza
22 Pikk 3
29 Vana Toomas Restaurant
30 Maharaja Restaurant
33 Kullassepa Kelder
34 Dietsöökla
35 Sub Monte
37 Kohvik Neitsitorn
39 Gnoom Cafe
40 Karja Kelder
44 Gloria Restaurant
46 Astoria Restaurant
48 Pizzeria Margareta
50 Peetri Pizza
52 Cornex Shop & Bar
58 Bistro

OTHER

1 Sea Passenger Terminals
2 Linnahall
3 Fat Margaret Tower & Sea Museum
4 Oleviste Church
5 Natural History Museum
6 Applied Art Museum
7 St Michael's Convent
8 Buses to Pärnu
10 Baltic Railway Station
11 Observation Platform
12 Observation Platform
13 Toom Kirik (Dome Church)
14 Toompea Castle
15 Pikk Hermann Tower
17 Linda Statue
18 Alexandr Nevsky Cathedral
20 Observation Platform
23 Great Guild Building & State
   History Museum
24 Brotherhood of Blackheads Building
25 City Museum
26 Dominican Monastery
27 Holy Spirit Church (Pühavaimu
   Kirik)
28 Raeapteek
31 Town Hall
32 Town Hall Museum
36 Niguliste Church
38 Kiek-in-de-Kök
41 Viru Gate
42 Estonia Theatre
43 Rahva Raamat Bookshop
45 Estonian Air
49 Tallink Office
51 Bus Ticket Office
53 Estonian Youth Hostels Office
   & UK and US Embassies
55 Main Post, Telegraph & Telephone
   Office
60 Tallinna Kaubamaja (Department
   Store)
62 Market

Toompea is the hill on which Tallinn has always been centred, covered in cobbled old streets and protected on the north, south and west by steep slopes. The Lower Town, also medieval, spreads round the eastern foot of Toompea, still surrounded by much of its 2.5-km defensive wall. Its centre is Raekoja plats (Town Hall Square). Toompea and the Lower Town together make up the Old Town.

Around the south and south-east of the Old Town is the New Town, centred on Vabaduse väljak. It hasn't been 'new' for centuries but has lost most traces of its age. The railway station and the harbour are in the New Town within walking distance of the Old Town. The tall slab of the Hotel Viru, just outside the eastern edge of the Old Town, is a major landmark.

Information
Tourist Offices & Travel Agencies The Tallinn Tourist Bureau was due to open the first public tourist information centre in the Baltic states (at Kinga 6, just off Raekoja plats) soon after this book was published. The Estonian Association of Travel Agents (☎ 42 55 94) is at Pikk 71. Leading travel and tour companies include Raeturist (☎ 44 43 33, fax 44 11 00) at Raekoja plats 18 and Estonian Holidays (☎ 65 08 73) in the Hotel Viru.

Money There are exchange counters in the airport, the sea passenger terminal, the railway station, the main post office, major hotels, and at Dunkri 9.

Post & Telecommunications The main post, telegraph and telephone office is at Narva maantee 1 on the north side of Viru väljak. At Tallinn Harbour Passenger Terminal, next to the Inreko ticket office, is an international phone service charging US$3 a minute to Western Europe, US$4 to the USA.

Bookshops & Guidebooks The central bookshops Rahva Raamat at Pärnu maantee 10 and Lugemisvara at Harju 1 both have English-language selections. *Tallinn – A Practical Guide* (Revalia Publishing, 1990) is an informed, witty, locally produced guide, with short sections on Tartu and Pärnu.

Maps *Tallinn – City Plan with Public Transport*, published in 1991 with a street index and keys in Estonian, English and Russian, sells for about US$0.10 in city bookshops and kiosks and seems accurate.

Medical & Dental Services There's a hospital with emergency medical service at Sütiste tee 19 in Mustamäe, a south-western suburb, and accident centres at Ravi 18 and Sütiste tee 10. The DKN Medical Centre (☎ 55 79 08) at Pärnu maantee 102, which advertises in the Hotel Viru, may be worth trying. Baltic Medical Partners (☎ 60 22 00, 66 60 09), on the 4th floor of the Hotel Olümpia and at Toompuiestee 4, is a Western-style dental practice. The pharmacy at Rävala puiestee 7 sells German medicines.

Other There's a left-luggage room (*käsipakkide hoiurruum*) at the bus station, and another at the sea passenger terminal, behind the *Georg Ots* ticket office. Foreign embassies and consulates in Tallinn are listed under Estonia, Facts for the Visitor.

Things to See
Walking Tour A good place to start exploring old Tallinn is the twin towers of the **Viru Gate**, once the easternmost of the six entrances in the Lower Town walls. From the gate continue along Viru to the corner of Vene, surrounded by tall 15th to 17th century houses and warehouses, then into **Raekoja plats**, the heart of the Lower Town. Then you can climb Pikk jalg to **Toompea**, or walk north up Pikk to Fat Margaret, the northern bastion of the Lower Town, and return south along Lai or Laboratooriumi.

Raekoja Plats & Around Wide Raekoja plats (Town Hall Square) has been the centre of Tallinn life since markets began here probably in the 11th century (the last was held in

1896). It's dominated by the only surviving Gothic **town hall** (1371-1404) in northern Europe, the seat of medieval power in the Lower Town. Its spire is 17th century but Vana Toomas (Old Thomas), the warrior-and-sword weather vane at its top, has guarded Tallinn since 1530.

The **Raeapteek** (Town Council Pharmacy) on the north side of Raekoja plats is another ancient Tallinn institution: there's been a pharmacy or apothecary's shop here since at least 1422, though the present façade is 17th century. An arch beside it leads into short, narrow Saia kang (White Bread Passage), at the far end of which is the 14th century Gothic Holy Spirit Church (Pühavaimu Kirik), used by Lutherans. Its clock is the oldest in Tallinn, with 1684 carvings, and the tower bell was cast in 1433. Inside is a 1483 wooden altarpiece. A medieval merchant's home at Vene 17 on the corner of Pühavaimu houses the **City Museum** (Linnamuuscum), devoted mainly to Tallinn in the 18th and 19th centuries – open daily except Tuesdays.

Also on Vene, look for an 1844 Catholic church set back from the street with the inscription *'Hic Vere Est Domus Dei'*. A door in the courtyard leads into the **Dominican monastery** (Dominiiklaste Klooster), founded in 1246, which was home base for the Scandinavian monks who played a big role in converting Estonia to Christianity and starting education in Tallinn. Once wealthy, it was plundered during the Reformation in 1524 and burnt in 1531, but the cloister and surrounding rooms are rich in 15th to 17th century stonecarving. The monastery is open in summer only, daily except Mondays.

A minute's walk south of Raekoja plats, **Niguliste Church** has an early Gothic north doorway but is mostly 15th century. It is now used for organ recitals and as a museum of medieval church art – open Wednesdays from 2 to 9 pm, Thursday to Sunday 11 am to 6 pm, unless there's a concert on.

At the foot of the a slope below Niguliste is the carefully exposed wreckage of the buildings that stood here before the Soviet bombing of Tallinn on 9 March 1944. A sign facing Harju details the damage done to the city that night.

Toompea The best approach to Toompea ('TOM-pe-ah') is through the red-roofed 1380 **gatetower** at the west end of Pikk in the Lower Town, and up Pikk jalg (Long Leg). The 19th century Russian Orthodox **Alexandr Nevsky Cathedral** dominates Lossi plats at the top of Pikk jalg. Estonia's parliament meets in **Toompea Castle** at the west end of Lossi plats. Nothing remains of the original 1219 Danish castle, but three of the four corner towers of its successor, the Knights of the Sword's Castle, still stand, the finest being the 14th century **Pikk Hermann** (Tall Hermann) at the south-west. Sixteenth century shell scars are visible on its walls.

The Lutheran **Toom Kirik** (Dome Church) at the north end of Toom-Kooli dates mostly from the 15th and 17th centuries but the tower dates from 1779. Inside are many fine carved tombs. One of those on the right as you approach the altar bears lifesize figures of the 16th century Swedish commander Pontus de la Gardie and his wife. The Swedish siege of Narva, where de la Gardie died, is depicted on the side of their sarcophagus.

The marble Greek-temple-style sarcophagus belongs to Admiral Samuel Greigh, an 18th century Scot who joined the Russian navy and became a hero of Russo-Turkish sea battles.

A path leads down from Lossi plats through a hole in the walls to an open space where in summer artists paint portraits. One of the towers here, the **Virgin's Tower** (Neitsitorn), has been turned into a popular café, with good views. Nearby **Kiek-in-de-Kök**, a tall tower built in about 1475, is a museum with several floors of maps, weapons, models of old Tallinn – and more great views. Its name is Low German for 'Peep into the Kitchen' – from the upper floors a watch could be kept over the entire Lower Town, even the kitchens. It's open daily except Mondays.

Lower Town North Pikk, running north

ESTONIA

from Raekoja plats to the **Great Coast Gate** – the medieval exit to Tallinn port – is lined with the houses of medieval merchants and gentry, many of them built in the 15th century. Also here are the buildings of several old Tallinn guilds. Pikk 17 is the 1440 building of the Great Guild, to which the most important merchants belonged. Today it houses the **State History Museum** (Ajaloomuuseum) featuring Estonian history up to the mid-19th century, with labelling in English and is open daily except Wednesdays. One of the fine vaulted halls retains its original appearance.

Pikk 20, with statues of Martin Luther and St Canutus, dates only from the 1860s, but the site had already housed **St Canutus' Guild** for several centuries. Its members were mainly German master-artisans. Pikk 24 and 26 are the adjoining buildings of the **Brotherhood of Blackheads** and **St Olaus' Guild**. The Blackheads were unmarried, mainly foreign merchants who took their name from their patron saint, Mauritius. His head is between two lions on the building's façade (1597).

The tower of **Oleviste Church**, further north on Pikk, is a chief Tallinn landmark. The church is dedicated to the 11th century King Olav II of Norway but linked in local lore with another Olav (Olaf), the church's legendary architect, who fell to his death from the 120-metre tower. It's said a toad and snake then crawled out of his mouth. The incident is recalled in one of the carvings on the eastern wall of the 16th century Chapel of Our Lady, adjoining the church. Most of the church was rebuilt to resemble something close to its original Gothic appearance after a fire in the 1820s.

The Great Coast Gate is joined to **Fat Margaret** (Paks Margareeta), the rotund 16th century bastion which protected this entrance to the Old Town. Its walls are more than four metres thick at the base. Inside is the **Sea Museum** (Meremuuseum), open daily except Mondays and Tuesdays.

On **Lai**, roughly parallel to Pikk, the **Applied Art Museum** (Tarbekunstimuuseum), in a 17th century barn at No 17,

has excellent ceramics, glass, rugs, metal and leatherwork. It's open daily except Mondays and Tuesdays.

Suur-Kloostri leads past the former **St Michael's Convent** to the longest standing stretch of the **Lower Town Wall**, with nine towers marching back along Laboratooriumi to the north end of Lai.

Kadriorg To reach pleasant **Kadriorg Park**, two km east of the Old Town along Narva maantee in an area of pretty wooden houses, take tram No 1 or 3 or bus No 1 from Pärnu maantee in front of Tammsaare Park, to the Kohvik Kadriorg café on Narva maantee. The park itself and the 1718-36 **Kadriorg Palace** (Kadrioru Loss) in the park at Weizenbergi tee 37 were designed for the Russian tsar Peter the Great by the Italian Niccolo Michetti, soon after Peter's conquest of Estonia in the Great Northern War. The palace contains the **Estonian Art Museum** (Kunstimuuseum), with Estonian art from the 19th century to 1940, open daily except Tuesdays.

Maarjamäe & Pirita Two km north of Kadriorg Park on the inland side of Pirita tee is the 1870s **Maarjamäe Palace** (Maarjamäe Loss), containing the mid-19th century onwards section of the Estonia History Museum, open from Wednesday to Sunday.

Some 1½ km beyond Maarjamäe just before Pirita tee crosses the Pirita river, a side road leads down to Pirita Yacht Club and the **Olympic Sailing Centre** at the mouth of the river, the base for the 1980 Olympic sailing events. International regattas are still held here. In summer you can rent rowing boats beside the bridge where Pirita tee crosses the river. North of the bridge are a beach backed by pine woods, and the 15th century Swedish **Convent of St Birgitta**, ruined by war in 1577 – open daily except Mondays. Bus Nos 1, 8 and 34 run between the city centre and Pirita, stopping at Kohvik Kadriorg en route.

Along Paldiski Maantee Paldiski maantee leads west out of town from the Hotel Tallinn. A large, informal **bazaar** with many imported goods is held on Saturday and Sunday mornings at Mustjõe, three km out on the north side of the road. About one km further, Vabaõhumuuseumi tee branches right to **Rocca al Mare**, 1.5 km away, where wooden buildings from 18th and 19th century rural Estonia have been assembled in the **Estonian Village Museum**. You can walk in the woods or down to the sea. It's open daily, from May to October. On Saturday and Sunday mornings there are folk song and dance shows. Bus No 21 from the railway station and bus No 45 from Vabaduse väljak go to the bazaar and Rocca al Mare.

Places to Stay

Camping – Tallinn & Around The following sites are included in the Estonian Tourist Board's 1992 accommodation directory:

Kernu (☎ 77 16 30, fax 21 49 41), 40 km south on Pärnu road, built in 1991

Kloostrimetsa (☎ 23 86 86), Kloostrimetsa tee 56A, nine km north-east (three km east of Pirita), 136 places including cabins and a small restaurant, in shadow of 300-metre TV tower, bus No 34 from Viru väljak

Rannamõisa (☎ 71 63 32), at Rannamõisa, 15 km west near the coast, off Paldiski road, 132 places, bus No 108 or 126 from beside Tallinn railway station

Väänа-Jõesuu (no telephone), about 25 km west, two km south of Paldiski road and coast, 80 places, bus No 108 or 126 from beside Tallinn railway station

Hostels & Colleges – Tallinn & Around The *Agnes Youth Hostel* (☎ 43 88 70), at Narva maantee 7, has 34 beds in rooms with their own toilets for US$11.25 a person. Opening dates in 1992 were from 1 April to 25 August, making reservations two weeks ahead is essential.

The BATS (Baltic Accommodation & Travel Service) backpackers' hostel office (☎ 68 18 93) is at Sakala 11C, near the Hotel Palace. Take bus No 65 from the port.

The next nearest hostel to Tallinn is *Klooga II*, open from 1 April to 1 December at Klooga Beach, Laulasmaa, 35 km west. It

has up to 25 beds for US$4.50, plus 18 three-bed 'camping' cabins for US$3.40.

The International Relations Department (☎ 42 20 88, fax 42 53 39) of Tallinn Pedagogical University (Tallinna Pedagoogika-Ülikool), at Narva maantee 25 one km east of the Hotel Viru, can provide clean singles/doubles for around US$6/12 in a central student hostel. Try to contact the department two or three weeks in advance. Its office in the university building is room 215 on the 1st floor, with the sign *'Välis-suhted'* on the door. The Student Council office (Üliõpilasedustus) on the 2nd floor may be able to help with accommodation.

Private Homes See Accommodation in Estonia, Facts for the Visitor.

Cheap Hotels The drab 330-bed *Hotel Neptun* (☎ 21 54 31) at Asunduse 15, 2.5 km south-east of the centre, has clean, sizeable 'suites' – bedroom, sitting room with TV and phone, bathroom with shower, basin and toilet – for just US$6 a double. You may have to ward off other inmates excessively keen to share a few vodkas with you. Bus No 39 goes there from the corner of Tartu maantee and Pronksi.

The little *Hotel Lembitu* (☎ 44 12 91) at Lembitu 3 has basic singles/doubles with attached shower and toilet for US$1.70/2.50. The *Hotel Volta* (☎ 45 13 40) at Endla 31, 600 metres west of Toompuiestee, offered us a small, clean three-bed room, sharing a clean toilet with one other room, for just US$0.35 a person – but only when the management had overcome their astonishment at the sight of a Westerner. Endla 31 is a large pink block: enter at the back and look for the small *'gostinitsa'* ('hotel') sign in Russian.

Middle-Range Hotels The handy *Hotel Vitamiin* (☎ 43 85 85) at Narva maantee 7 has clean doubles/triples with attached toilet and shower, TV and phone for US$27/33. Go through the door next to the Vitamiin shop, up the stairs and through the door on the 1st floor.

The large Soviet-style *Hotel Kungla*

(☎ 42 14 60) at Kreutzwaldi 23 has small, fading rooms with attached bathroom and phone for US$35 a double including breakfast (no singles). The hot water is unreliable and the Kungla is poor value.

Better, though not certain to stay put for very long, is the *Hotel More* (☎ 60 15 02, fax 60 21 82; in Finland 949-24 76 58), which is in fact the old Soviet cruise ship *Vissarion Belinsky*, moored behind the Linnahall concert hall 10 minutes' walk from Tallinn passenger port. Tiny cabins each with a bathroom cost US$22/34/46 for a single/double/triple. Some English is spoken. Five km south-west of the city centre at Sõpruse puicstee 182 in the suburb of Mustamäe, the *Hotel Lemmo* (☎ 42 00 34) has double/triple 'suites' – bedroom, sitting room, bathroom – for US$24/29.

Expensive Hotels The *Hotel Sport* (☎ 23 85 98), on the seafront at Regati puiestee 1, Pirita, six km north-east of the centre, was designed as accommodation for the 1980 Olympics. Its clean, modern already-renovated rooms with balconies looking across Tallinn Bay are good value as far as the top end goes, at US$40/60 for singles/doubles. There are some cheaper unrenovated rooms, not meant for foreigners. The Galerie Bar at the top of the building serves good breakfasts for around US$1. Take bus Nos 1, 8 and 34 from the Pronksi stop on Narva maantee, 400 metres east of the Hotel Viru; all buses stop on Pirita tee a minute's walk from the hotel. A taxi from the city centre should cost under US$1.

Two comfortable places on the outskirts of the city might interest motorists in particular. The *Peoleo Motel* (☎ 55 64 69, fax 77 14 63), built in 1990 at Pärnu maantee 555, Laagri, about 14 km south-west of the centre. It has singles/doubles for US$50/66 including breakfast. The *Hotel Kelluka* (☎ 23 88 11, fax 23 73 98), eight km east of the centre at Kelluka tee 11, just north of Narva maantee, charges US$67 a single or double including breakfast and sauna. Bus No 5 from Tammsaare Park reaches the Kelluka. The best hotel is the 91-room *Hotel*

Palace (☎ 44 47 61, fax 44 30 98) at Vabaduse väljak 3, renovated to 'international four-star standard' by Scandinavian companies in 1989. The elegant, if not huge, rooms cost US$150/190 including breakfast, but at weekends there's usually a special rate of US$95/135. In Helsinki you can book through Arctia Hotel Partners (☎ 694 8022, fax 694 8471); in other countries, through Finnair Hotels or SAS Associated Hotels.

Other expensive hotels include the *Hotel Mihkli* (☎ 45 37 04) at Endla 23, 400 metres down the hill from Toompuiestee, with clean, bright rooms for US$35/55 but no atmosphere. There's also the former Intourist flagship *Hotel Viru* (☎ 65 20 93, fax 44 43 71) towering 22 storeys at Viru väljak 4, with comfortable pine-panelled rooms for US$80/105 and a long list of restaurants and bars.

The *Hotel Olümpia* (☎ 60 24 36/8, fax 60 19 07) 700 metres south of the Old Town at Liivalaia 33, is even taller than the Viru, but has smaller rooms (US$75/100 bed and breakfast) and the *Hotel Tallinn* (☎ 60 43 32) at Toompuiestee 27 on the western edge of the Old Town charges US$55 or US$75 a double.

Places to Eat

Tallinn's eating-out scene has improved beyond recognition since the last years of Soviet rule. There are now several quality restaurants which really have what's printed on their menus, plus a number of other places able to provide a reasonable meal. The Old Town's café (*kohvik*) scene is a big plus too. Most cafés close around 7 pm. The Central Market (Keskturg) at Keldrimäe 2 between Lastekodu and Juhkentali, beyond the Hotel Olümpia, is a good source of fresh fruit and vegetables.

Fast Food, Cafés & Bars *Peetri Pizza* has three outlets doling out tasty one-person pizzas for less than US$0.50 at almost any hour you might need one. Order two if you're really hungry, the pizza base is crisp but light. The locations are Pärnu maantee 22 (open from 10 am until 3 am); Lai 4 (10 am to 9 pm); and Kopli 2, behind the railway station, (from 11 am until 2 am).

Bistro at Narva maantee 6, half a km east of the Hotel Viru, serves up even cheaper pasta, burgers and salads, but tends to close in the early evening and doesn't always live up to its name (which is Russian for fast).

There's a reasonable stand-up snack bar in the east end of the railway-station building (enter through the suburban ticket hall), serving chicken legs for around US$0.15, beetroot salad, bread and so on.

On Toompea, *Kohvik Neitsitorn*, in one of the old towers of the city wall, serves good hoogvein (for less than US$0.50 a glass), coffee and snacks from 11 am to 10 pm. The views are great. In the Lower Town, *Kohvik Pärl* at Pikk 3 has good fare and lots of tables. *Maiasmokk Kohvik* at Pikk 16 does good pastries. There's a good café-cum-bar in the rear of the ground floor of the *Hotel Viru*, go down the stairs beside the main 1st-floor restaurant to reach it.

Karja Kelder at Väike-Karja 1 is a popular beer cellar in the Old Town, but only open till 7.30 pm. *Karikabaar*, nearby at the corner of Kuninga and Suur-Karja, is another popular cellar, with alcohol and dancing. It's sometimes hard to get into. The *Comex Pub*, downstairs next to the Comex shop across Pärnu maantee from the Hotel Palace, is open 24 hours. Hotel bars in general offer easy-to-get alcohol.

Restaurants The *Maharaja Restaurant* at Raekoja plats 13, open from noon to 5 pm and 7 pm to 2 am, is one of the best restaurants in the Baltic states, serving excellent Indian food. At the time of writing you can pay in roubles at lunch time (most main dishes cost the equivalent of US$0.50 to US$0.70) but you must use hard currency at night and pay around 10 times as much.

At Raekoja plats 8 is *Vana Toomas*, a large cellar restaurant serving a number of Estonian dishes. It has a cool jazz band at weekends. A large plate of hors d'oeuvres (*külmad road*) will be around US$0.75, main courses (*teised road*) about US$0.50 each: try roast pork with onion and mushroom garnish (*praetud sealiha seentega*) and vegetables or a fried fish and vegetable dish (*praetud kala*).

The *Gnoom* grill, a few steps from Raekoja plats at Viru 2, has a fine spacious 15th century stone interior and serves acceptable chicken, pork or beef dishes with vegetables for about US$0.75. The *Reeder Restoran* along the street at Vene 33 has similar fare and prices, and an equally intriguing interior done up in imitation of a sailing ship's dining room.

Just off Raekoja plats in another direction, *Kullassepa Kelder*, at Kullassepa 9, concentrates on grilled chicken and does it well – around US$0.90 a shot with vegetables.

The cheapest meals in central Tallinn must be at *Dietsöökla* on Dunkri, a cafeteria with much of its fare based on dairy products. It's open from 9 am to 7 pm (Sundays from 10 am to 5 pm). The food's no gourmet's delight, but you can get a meal for US$0.25. Offerings include rice and beef soups, egg mayonnaise, meatballs, buckwheat, tomato and cucumber salads, and various types of curd and curd cakes.

There's a gaggle of classier, dearer places down towards, and around, Vabaduse väljak. *Sub Monte* (☎ 66 68 71) in a medieval cellar at Rüütli 4, has international and traditional Estonian fare (open from noon to 6 pm and from 8 pm to 1 am). For the *Astoria* at Vabaduse väljak 5, seating over 100 with music and dancing at night, you can book tickets between 1.30 and 3.30 pm.

Pizzeria Margareta in the side of the Hotel Palace, entered from Pärnu maantee, does the best pizzas in town for around US$5, plus other dishes like pepper fillet and vegetables (US$8). The *Hotel Viru* has a 22nd-floor restaurant with good food and views; a meal costs around US$1.50. The hotel's all-you-can-eat buffet breakfast is good value at US$0.60.

Entertainment

In summer Tallinn is alive with festivals. On one visit we discovered four in a two-week period. They featured organ music, Irish and Estonian folk music, bands from Tallinn's

ESTONIA

German twin city Kiel, and international folk dancers and musicians gathered for the Baltika festival. Rock and folk concerts are fairly frequent, watch the posters around town.

The Estonia Theatre at Estonia puiestee 4 stages a range of classical operas and ballets in repertory, and the Estonia Concert Hall (Kontserdisaal) next door usually puts on several concerts a week. Both box offices are open till 7 pm daily except Sundays and tickets are cheap. There are regular organ concerts in Niguliste Church; tickets are sold at the church and at the Estonia Concert Hall. *What? Where? When? In Tallinn* and *Tallinn This Week* both list the upcoming cultural events. The Estonia State Symphony Orchestra and the Hortus Musicus Early Music Choir are among the best Tallinn musical ensembles.

Several restaurants have music and dancing – see the listings in *Tallinn This Week*, which will also tell you about current discos. The Palace Hotel has a casino.

Tallinn's basketball team Kalev plays to capacity crowds at Juhkentali 12.

Things to Buy

Prices for handicrafts are low by Western standards and more of Estonia's best work finds its way into shops than it used to. Firma Kauplus, a shop at Pikk 9, sells Estonian national costumes. For jewellery, ceramics or paintings check out Uku at Pikk 9; the Ars shops at Pikk 18, Vabaduse väljak 8, Liivalaia 12, Hobusepea 2, and on Viru; the shop at Kullassepa 13; or the galleries listed in *Tallinn This Week*. For records of Estonian choral singing and other music, visit the shops at Raekoja plats 15 and Kuininga 4.

Getting There & Away

Note that Tallinn is called Talinas in Lithuania.

Air For information on flights in and out of Tallinn see the Estonia, Getting There & Away and Getting Around sections. Airline offices in Tallinn include:

Estonian Air
    Vabaduse väljak 10 (☎ 44 63 82)
Finnair
    Liivalaia 12 (☎ 68 37 71)
    Airport (☎ 42 35 38)
SAS
    Airport (☎ 21 25 53)

Bus For bus information and advance tickets, go to the ticket office at Pärnu maantee 24, just down the street from the Hotel Palace. There's a big, easily understood timetable here, an information desk (charging a minuscule fee for each enquiry), and advance-booking ticket windows. Buses to places within 40 km or so of Tallinn, and Pärnu, go from the local bus station beside the railway station, but other services use the long-distance bus station (Maaliinide Autobussijaam) at Lastekodu 46, a km down Juhkentali from the Hotel Olümpia (take tram No 2 east from Tammsaare Park or tram No 4 south from Mere puiestee). The bus station has a big route map showing which buses go where, and more ticket windows.

Information on buses to places outside Estonia is given in the Estonia Getting There & Away section. Domestic services include:

Haapsalu – 100 km, 2½ hours, 10 buses daily, US$0.35
Kärdla – 160 km, five hours, one bus daily at 4.10 pm, US$0.85
Kuressaare – 220 km, 4½ hours, four buses daily, US$0.85
Narva – 210 km, four hours, two buses daily, US$0.75
Pärnu – 130 km, 2½ hours, about 12 buses daily, US$0.50
Tartu – 190 km, three hours, about 12 buses daily, US$0.65
Viljandi – 160 km, 2½ hours, three buses daily, US$0.55 or US$0.80

Train Tallinn's Baltic Station (Balti jaam) is at Toompuiestee 39, on the north-west edge of the Old Town. There are two ticket halls: one for longer-distance trains including to Tartu, Narva and places outside Estonia, and another (round the back) for 'suburban' trains, which includes some going as far as Viljandi.

Information about trains to places outside Estonia is given in Estonia, Getting There &

Away. Services within Estonia include four daily to Tartu (three to four hours, US$0.50 in unreserved general seating), two daily to Narva (from 3¼ to 4¼ hours), and an afternoon train to Viljandi.

Car & Motorbike There are Western-run petrol stations, with 99 octane and usually unleaded petrol, at Regati puiestee 1; Pirita (down past the Hotel Sport – look for the blue and green flags); at Pärnu maantee 141 and 552; and on Tartu maantee just north of the airport. Tallinna Autoinspektsioon (☎ 44 54 50) at Lastekodu 31 has English-speaking staff and can give information about motor-repair workshops and other car matters.

Rental Ideal Ltd (☎ 21 27 35, 21 92 22) at Tallinn airport rents self-drive Ladas for US$45 a day with unlimited km. A Toyota Corolla is US$35 a day plus US$0.35 per km, or US$280 for three days with unlimited km. You can book Ideal cars in Finland (☎ 949-24 79 50) or Sweden (☎ 063-12 78 60). Refit Ltd in the Hotel Olümpia (☎ 60 24 37) and at Magasini 20 (☎ 66 10 46) rents Corollas and Volvos. In the more expensive bracket are Finest Auto in the Palace Hotel (☎ 44 34 61) and at Pärnu maantee 22 (☎ 66 67 19) and Hertz (☎ 42 10 03) at Tartu maantee 13.

Boat See Estonia, Getting There & Away for information on the many ferries and cruises between Tallinn and Helsinki (Finland), Stockholm (Sweden) and Germany. Tallinn's sea passenger terminal is at the end of Sadama, about a km north-east of the Old Town. Tram Nos 1 and 2 and buses No 3, 4 and 8 go to the Linnahalli stop, five minutes' walk from the terminal.

Getting Around

To/From the Airport Tallinn Airport is on the Tartu road three km from the centre. Bus No 22 runs every 20 to 30 minutes to and from the bus station, the Tallinna Kaubamaja department store near the Hotel Viru, Vabaduse väljak, and the railway station.

City Transport The railway station and many hotels are an easy walk from the city centre. Buses and trams will take you everywhere else. One kiosk selling tickets (under US$0.01 each at the time of writing) is on Vabaduse väljak opposite the Astoria Restaurant.

LAHEMAA NATIONAL PARK

A rocky stretch of the north coast with numerous peninsulas and bays, plus 644 sq km of hinterland with 14 lakes, eight rivers and numerous waterfalls, forms Estonia's only national park (*rahvuspark*), Lahemaa, 60 km east of Tallinn. The landscape is 30% human-influenced, 66% forest or heath, and 5% bog. The Tallinn-Narva road crosses the park. There's a **tourist centre** (☎ 20 21 28) at Viitna near the eastern exit from the park, with a trail across the bogs. Roads crisscross the park to the coast and some old fishing villages. There's an 18th century **manor house** and park at Palmse, eight km from Viitna, **prehistoric stone barrows** at Kahala, Palmse and Vihula, and a **boulder field** on the Käsmu Peninsula.

Places to Stay

Two youth hostels are within the park: the 33-bed *Lahe* hostel (☎ 51 00 38), open from 1 May to 1 October in Lahe village in the east of the park, and the *Võsu Puhkekodu* (☎ 232-9 91 89) open all year round at Võsu, a coastal holiday spot. Võsu Puhkekodu has 16 beds from 1 June to 15 September and 40 for the rest of the year, with meals available. There are two small motels, the *Kadakas* (☎ 232-4 94 19) and the *Sõstra* (☎ 232-3 41 37) at Viitna. There are more places to stay in Võsu and at Valgejõe, Pedaspea, Viinistu, Kolgaküla, Leesi and Loksa in the central and western parts of the park.

Getting There & Away

If you don't have a vehicle, there are buses from Tallinn to Viitna, Käsmu, Võsu, Loksa, Leesi, Pärispea and elsewhere in the park. There's a bus at 6.40 am to Käsmu (1¾ hours, US$0.30), for instance, and one returning to Tallinn at 7.20 pm. Some of the excursion or service bureaux in Tallinn can organise guided trips (see Tours in Estonia, Getting Around), or you might be able to join a Western tour group.

NARVA

Estonia's easternmost town (population 82,000) is separated only by the Narva river from Ivangorod in Russia and almost entirely peopled by Russians. Narva was a Hanseatic League trading point by 1171. Later it became embroiled in Russia's border disputes with the German knights and Sweden. Ivan III of Muscovy founded Ivangorod, whose own big castle still stands, in 1492. Narva was almost completely destroyed in WW II.

Today the Narva region is blighted by phosphorite and oil-shale industries stretching from beyond Kohtla-Järve in Estonia to Kingisepp in Russia.

Things to See
Narva Castle guarding the road bridge over the river dates from Danish rule in the 13th century. Restored after being damaged in WW II, it houses the **Town Museum**, open Saturday to Tuesday. The Baroque **town hall** (1668-71) on Raekoja väljak, north of the bridge, is also restored.

Places to Stay
The better hotel is the *Vanalinn* (☎ 2 24 86) at Koidula 6 just north of the castle. The *Narva* (☎ 3 15 52) is at Puškini 6 just south of the castle.

Getting There & Away
Narva is 210 km east of Tallinn on the road and railway to St Petersburg, just 140 km away. From Tallinn there are at least two buses and two trains daily. The bus and railway stations are together at Vaksali 2. Walk north up Puškini to the castle (half a km) and the centre.

TARTU

Estonia's second city Tartu (population 115,000), formerly known as Dorpat, is 190 km south-east of Tallinn on the Emajõgi River, which flows into Lake Peipus. Tartu was the cradle of the 19th century Estonian national revival and still claims to be its spiritual capital. It's notable for its university, with over 5000 full-time students, and its classical architecture stemming from a comprehensive rebuilding after most of the town burnt down in 1775.

History
There was an Estonian stronghold on Toomemägi Hill around the 6th century AD. In 1030, Yaroslav the Wise of Kiev is said to have founded a settlement here called Yuriev. By the early 13th century the Knights of the Sword were in control, placing a bishop, castle and cathedral on Toomemägi Hill. The town that grew up between the hill and the river became a member of the Hanseatic League. In the 16th and 17th centuries Tartu suffered repeated attacks and changes of ownership as Russia, Sweden and Poland-Lithuania all vied for control.

The university, founded in 1632 during Swedish rule to train Protestant clergy and government officials, closed in about 1700 but reopened in 1802, and developed into a foremost 19th century seat of learning. It was the focus of the 19th century national revival. The first Estonian Song Festival was held in Tartu in 1869.

Orientation
The foci of Tartu are Toomemägi Hill and the area of older buildings between it and the Emajõgi River. At the heart of this older area are Raekoja plats (Town Hall Square) and Ülikooli, which runs across the west end of the square.

Things to See
Raekoja Plats The centrepiece is the beautifully proportioned town hall (1782-89), topped by a tower and weather vane, and based on the design of Dutch town halls. The buildings at Nos 6, 8, 12 and 16 are also early classical but No 2, one of the first to be built after the fire, is in an earlier style – late Baroque.

Ülikooli The main university building at Ülikooli 18, with its six Corinthian columns, dates from 1803-09. It contains Tartu's classical art museum. Further north, the Gothic brick **Jaani Church** (St John's) founded in 1330 but ruined in 1944, is being restored as a museum. It has rare **terracotta sculptures** around the main portal. The nearby **botanical gardens** at Lai 40 are worth a look.

Toomemägi Hill A 19th century English-style park covers much of the hill. The 13th century **cathedral** at the top was rebuilt in the 15th century, despoiled during the Reformation in 1525, and partly rebuilt in 1804-07 when the university library was installed in its choir (today occupied by the **University History Museum**, open Wednesday to Sunday).

Also on the hill and dating from the early 19th century are the **Angel's Bridge** (Inglisild), with a good view of the city; the Observatory (now a museum open daily except Tuesdays) on the old castle site; and the **Anatomical Theatre**.

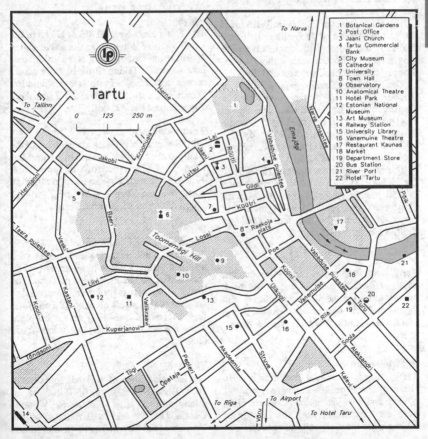

Tartu

0   125   250 m

To Narva
To Tallinn
To Riga
To Airport
To Hotel Taru

1 Botanical Gardens
2 Post Office
3 Jaani Church
4 Tartu Commercial Bank
5 City Museum
6 Cathedral
7 University
8 Town Hall
9 Observatory
10 Anatomical Theatre
11 Hotel Park
12 Estonian National Museum
13 Art Museum
14 Railway Station
15 University Library
16 Vanemuine Theatre
17 Restaurant Kaunas
18 Market
19 Department Store
20 Bus Station
21 River Port
22 Hotel Tartu

Other Museums The **Estonian National Museum**, with a collection ranging from ancient farm tools to modern national costume, is at Veski 32 just west of Toomemägi Hill, open Wednesday to Sunday. There's a City Museum, open daily except Tuesdays, at Oru 2.

Places to Stay

See the Estonia Facts for the Visitor Accommodation section for homestay possibilities. For accommodation in student hostels try Tartu University (☎ 3 48 66, fax 3 54 40), public relations office (☎ 3 54 21) at Ülikooli 18, Tartu 202400, preferably a few weeks before you visit.

The *Hotel Park* (☎ 3 36 63) at Vallikraavi 23, just south-west of Toomemägi Hill, is a pleasant old hotel with some cheapish singles for US$24/20 with/without toilet. Rooms with toilet and shower are US$60.

The *Hotel Pro Studiorum* (☎ 6 18 53), at Tuglase 13 and run by the university, has singles/doubles for US$33/52. The faded, Soviet-style *Tartu Hotel* (☎ 3 20 91) at Soola 2 is the biggest in town, with 250 beds, and will be cheaper as will the smaller *Hotel Salimo* (☎ 7 08 88) at Kopli 1.

The top place is the modern *Hotel Taru* (☎ 7 37 00, fax 7 40 95) at Rebase 9, which is 750 metres south of the centre, with singles/doubles for US$60/79 including breakfast. It's run by the same people as Tallinn's Hotel Palace.

Places to Eat

The *Kaseke* restaurant at Tähe 19, about a km south of Raekoja plats, is one of the best. More central are the *Volga* at Küütri 1, the *Tempo* at Küütri 6, the *Säde* at Küüni 2, the *Püssirohukelder* at Lossi 28, and the *Tarvas* at Riia 2.

Entertainment

Tartu stages an annual rock festival in October. The Vanemuine Theatre (Estonia's oldest) and the Vanemuine Concert Hall, both on Vanemuise near the corner of Ülikooli, are the main cultural venues.

Getting There & Away

About a dozen buses a day run to/from Tallinn, taking about three hours for US$0.65. There are also four trains daily, taking from three to four hours for US$0.50 in unreserved seating. See Estonia, Getting There & Away for information on train (and bus) services between Tartu and countries to the south. There should also be buses to/from Pskov in Russia and – if it hasn't sunk along with the old Soviet economy – a river-and-lake hydrofoil service there daily except Sundays, leaving Pskov in the early morning and Tartu in the afternoon.

SOUTH-EAST ESTONIA

Põlva

The *Hotel Pesa* (☎ 9 00 86) at Uus 5 in the small town of Põlva, in an attractive valley 40 km south-east of Tartu, is one of the best hotels outside Tallinn. Built in 1991, its 32 rooms cost US$56/74 for singles/doubles. Seven km north of Põlva the *Taevaskoja Youth Hostel* has 20 beds.

Suur Munamägi

The 29-metre observation tower on top of the Baltic states' highest peak, 318-metre Suur Munamägi, 17 km south of Võru (population 17,000), commands views of up to 50 km in good weather. There's a *Kämping* (☎ 4 12 16) at Männiku 43, Kubija, Võru.

Otepää

There's a 30-bed *youth hostel* (☎ 242-5 59 34) in the small, pretty town of Otepää, with a ruined bishop's castle in an area of many small lakes 40 km south-west of Tartu. The hostel is open year-round and reservations are essential. There's also the 72-bed *Hotel Otepää* (☎ 242-5 54 31) and a 50-place *Kämping* at Annimatsi, four km from Otepää.

VILJANDI

The lakeside town of Viljandi (population 24,000) is 160 km south of Tallinn on an inland route to Riga. Picturesque **Viljandi Castle**, near the lake, was founded by the Knights of the Sword. The town later joined the Hanseatic League, then was subject to the usual comings and goings of Swedes, Poles and Russians. There are good views of Lake Viljandi from the town's three hills.

Places to Stay
The *Hotel Viljandi* (☎ 5 38 52) at Tartu 11 has 26 rooms with private toilet and shower for US$15/29. Cheaper are the *Rendiettevõte Hotel* (☎ 5 28 15) at Riia maantee 38, and the *Kalevi Spordibaas* (☎ 5 47 70) at Ranna puiestee 6. *Viljandi Kämping* (☎ 5 23 71) is at Tallinna 6, Holstre-Nõmme, about eight km south-east.

Getting There & Away
There are three buses daily taking 2½ hours to/from Tallinn, plus one or two trains.

PÄRNU
The port and resort of Pärnu ('PAIR-noo', population 54,000) is 130 km south of Tallinn, straddling the mouth of the Pärnu River in the north-east corner of the Gulf of Riga. For some years swimming was considered unsafe because of pollution but it was hoped that a clean-up would render it safe again by summer 1992.

History
In the 13th century the Knights of the Sword built a fort at Pärnu, on what was then their border with Estonia to the north. It became a Hanseatic port in the 14th century and a resort in the 19th century.

Things to See
Resort Area The resort area is south of the river and has a wide, two-km-long beach. The biggest of Pärnu's parks – many of which are planted with foreign trees – is **Rannapark**, near the beach. The **Estonia Sanatorium** at Ranna puiestee 5 was built in the 1930s as the luxury Ranna Hotel. You can walk along the two-km breakwater at the mouth of the river, but beware tides.

Town Centre The **Red Tower** (Punane Torn) on Hommiku, open Wednesday to Sunday, was probably originally built by the Knights

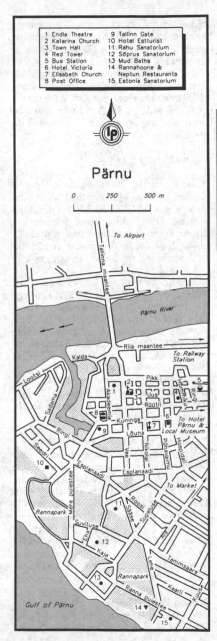

1 Endla Theatre	9 Tallinn Gate
2 Katarina Church	10 Hotel Estturist
3 Town Hall	11 Rahu Sanatorium
4 Red Tower	12 Sõprus Sanatorium
5 Bus Station	13 Mud Baths
6 Hotel Victoria	14 Rannahoone &
7 Elisabeth Church	Neptun Restaurants
8 Post Office	15 Estonia Sanatorium

Pärnu

0   250   500 m

ESTONIA

of the Sword. Parts of the 17th century Swedish moat and town walls, including the tunnel-like **Tallinn Gate** (Tallinna Värav) at the west end of Kuninga, survive.

The centre contains a few 17th and 18th century buildings. Rüütli is the busiest shopping street. The local **museum** at the corner of Rüütli and Aia displays handicrafts and local history, open from Wednesday to Sunday.

Places to Stay & Eat

The *Emmi Hotel* (☎ 2 20 43) at Laine 2 is a pleasant little 20-room hotel where singles/doubles with attached toilet and shower cost just US$3.50/5.50 at the time of writing. Other possibilities include the bigger, Soviet-style *Hotel Pärnu* (☎ 4 21 42) at Rüütli 44, the *Hotel Estturist* (☎ 4 23 38) at Seedri 4 and the *Hotel Vesiroos* (☎ 4 35 34) at Esplanaadi 42A.

The top hotel is the Art-Nouveau *Hotel Victoria* (☎ 4 34 12, fax 4 34 15) at Kuninga 25. It was renovated by a Swedish-Estonian joint venture and in 1992 joined the Best Western international hotel chain. Rooms cost US$67/90. English and Swedish are spoken. You can book through any Best Western office worldwide.

Pärnu's best known restaurant, with music and dancing at night, is the large *Rannahoone* at Ranna puiestee 3 near the beach. There are cafés on Rüütli.

Places to Stay & Eat – Around Pärnu

There are three youth hostels in south-west Estonia. West of Pärnu are the 21-bed *Tõstamaa Hostel* in Tõstamaa, 45 km from Pärnu (open from 1 May to 31 December in 1992) and the 25-bed *Varbla Hostel* (☎ 242-9 66 55) on Varbla Beach, 70 km from Pärnu, open from 1 May to 1 October. Forty km south are the *Lepanina Summer Houses* (☎ 244-9 84 77), four six-bed cabins in a forest 150 metres from the beach at Häädemeeste.

Getting There & Away

Pärnu is 2½ hours by bus from Tallinn. There are about a dozen buses daily, departing from beside Tallinn's railway station for US$0.50.

SAAREMAA

Estonia's biggest offshore island, Saaremaa (formerly Ösel), is a popular local holiday spot, but has only been open to foreigners since 1989. Visitors wanting to stay on Saaremaa may still need a permit, currently obtainable from the Hotel Viru service bureau in Tallinn for about US$10 but, with luck, this bit of bureaucracy will be eliminated altogether.

Things to See

Though low-lying and rocky, Saaremaa is a scenic island with pine woods, grasslands dotted with windmills, trees and juniper bushes, and virtually no industry. It fell to the German knights in the 13th century, when the castle in the biggest town, Kuressaare (now restored), and the Gothic churches at Poide, Valjala, and Karja (all in the east of the island) and Kaarma (north of Kuressaare) were built. At Valjala there are also the remains of a 12th to 13th century fortress of the native Saaremaa people.

Places to Stay

Kämping Saare (☎ 5 62 63) is on the coast 10 km west of Kuressaare. Other camp sites on the island include *Kadakas* (☎ 245-9 55 66, with 32 places) at Kuivastu maantee 44, Orissaare, and *Karujärve* (☎ 245-7 26 81, with 80 places) near Kärla.

The 15-bed *Virtsu Youth Hostel* (☎ 247-7 55 27) is in the village of Virtsu, on the mainland opposite Muhu island. It's open from 1 May to 1 October.

Kuressaare's *Hotel Lossi* (☎ 5 44 43) at Lossi 27 is more of a guesthouse than a hotel. Other small hotels include the *Hotel Mardi* (☎ 5 74 36) at Vallimaa 5A and the *Hotel Pangamaja* (☎ 5 77 02) at Tallinna 27. There's reportedly a new 17-room hotel called the *Männikäbi* with rooms for around US$25. Family Hotel Service Network (see

Accommodation in Estonia, Facts for the Visitor) has places on Saaremaa.

Agents in Kuressaare such as Thule (☎ 5 74 70) at Pargi 1, or the Saaremaa Travel Bureau (☎ 5 79 70) at Pärna 2, or agents in Tallinn, may be able to help with accommodation.

Getting There & Away

A vehicle ferry runs several times daily from Virtsu on the mainland to Muhu island, which is joined by a bridge to Saaremaa. Four buses daily travel each way between Tallinn and Kuressaare (4½ hours, US$0.85). There are also flights.

ESTONIA

Latvia

Latvia (Latvija), lacking Estonia's closeness to a Western country (Finland) or the fame that Lithuania achieved on its path to independence, is perhaps the least known of the Baltic states. Even those who visited it under Soviet rule usually saw less than in Estonia or Lithuania, since travel was restricted to just a few places around Riga, the capital.

Riga is the biggest, most vibrant city in the Baltic states. Several attractive already-known destinations lie with day-trip distance of it – among them the coastal resort Jūrmala, the Sigulda castles overlooking the scenic Gauja river valley, and the Rastrelli palace at Rundāle. Off the previously beaten track there's plenty more scenery and history to explore, but you'll be a pioneer – few places in provincial Latvia are used to Western visitors passing through, still less to them staying overnight.

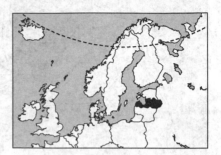

Facts about the Country

HISTORY

The idea of Latvia, a single political entity for the area inhabited by speakers of Latvian, did not become current until the late 19th century. For centuries, under various rulers, most of what's now Latvia had fallen into either Courland, the area west of Riga, or Livonia, the eastern half of Latvia and the southern half of Estonia.

German Rule

Peoples arriving in the south-east Baltic region from the south around 2000 BC introduced settled agriculture to Latvia and eventually grouped into what are called the 'Baltic' tribes, which were dragged into recorded history in the 12th century by the German *drang nach osten* (push to the east) of traders, missionaries and crusading knights. The Knights of the Sword (see Estonia, History – German Crusades), also known as the Livonian order, were founded in Riga in 1202 and subjugated Latvia within a quarter of a century.

In 1237 these knights, having been ticked off by the pope for brutality and defeated by Latvian and Lithuanian tribes at Saule (modern Šiauliai, Lithuania) in 1236, were reorganised as a branch of a second band of German crusaders, the Teutonic order, which by 1290 controlled the seaboard from modern Poland to Estonia, plus inland Latvia. The existing inhabitants became serfs to a German nobility which dominated until the early 20th century.

Polish, Swedish & Russian Rule

In 1561 Latvia came under Polish control after the Livonian order appealed to Poland-Lithuania for protection against Russia's Ivan the Terrible. In the 1620s Sweden took all Latvia except Courland, where the dukes of Jelgava, descended from the last Livonian grandmaster, maintained allegiance to Poland. Russia's Peter the Great destroyed Swedish power in the Great Northern War (1700-21), and most of Latvia became part of the Russian empire, the remainder following in the Partitions of Poland (see Lithuania History) towards the end of the 18th century.

Latvia, like Estonia, experienced an awakening of national awareness in the 19th century. Serfs were freed and native (non-

German, non-Russian) interests were promoted.

WW I & Independence
After WW I fighting between Latvian nationalists (who had declared independence in November 1918), Bolsheviks trying to incorporate Latvia into Soviet Russia, and lingering German occupation forces went on till 1920, when Moscow signed a peace treaty with the independent Latvian parliamentary republic. Latvia had lost about 40% of its population through death or emigration. Factories had been 'evacuated' to Russia, and trade through Riga in 1926 was only a tenth of what it had been in 1913. From 1934 Kārlis Ulmanis headed a non-parliamentary government of unity which tried to steer between right and left-wing extremes.

WW II & Soviet Rule
Between 1939 and 1941 events in Latvia followed a similar path to those in Estonia – the Molotov-Ribbentrop Pact, a 'mutual assistance pact' with the USSR, occupation by Soviet troops, a communist 'election' victory, incorporation into the USSR,

nationalisation, purges, about 35,000 deportations, and killings. Latvia was occupied partly or wholly by Nazi Germany from 1941 to 1945. Some Latvians collaborated in the murders of up to 90,000 Jews at the Salaspils death camp near Riga. Latvia's Jewish population was virtually wiped out.

Reconquest by the Red Army was followed by farm collectivisation and further nationalisation. An estimated 175,000 Latvians were killed or deported. There was some armed resistance until 1952. With postwar industrialisation, Latvia received an influx of migrant workers, mainly from nearby parts of Russia, Belorussia (Belarus) and Ukraine, which increased local resentment towards Soviet rule.

New Independence
The first significant public protest in the glasnost era was on 14 June 1987 when about 5000 people rallied at the Freedom Monument in Riga. Several big rallies on environmental, national and other issues were held in 1988, with 45,000 people joining hands along the Baltic coast in one anti-pollution protest. A reformist, pro-independence Latvian popular front was formed

which included the new Latvian Communist Party leadership. By 1989 the Latvian Popular Front had over 200,000 members. After its supporters won a big majority in the March 1990 elections to Latvia's Supreme Soviet (or parliament), the pre-WW II constitution was reinstated and the words 'Soviet Socialist' dropped from the republic's name. A transition period was envisaged for independence to be negotiated, but prospects for this faded as hardliners regained the ascendancy in Moscow in winter 1990-91. On 20 January 1991 Soviet Black Beret troops, trying to destabilise the Baltics, stormed the Interior Ministry building in Riga, killing four people.

The August 1991 coup attempt in Moscow turned the tables and Latvia declared full independence on 21 August. It was recognised first by the West then, on 6 September, by the USSR. But many Latvians feel that they will not be truly free until all members of the ex-Soviet armed forces have left Latvia. In mid-1992, about half the over 100,000 such troops in the Baltic states were in Latvia.

GEOGRAPHY

Green and rolling, Latvia covers an area of 63,700 sq km, a little smaller than Lithuania. Over half of this area is under 100 metres high, nearly all is under 200 metres. The four regions of Latvia are: Kurzeme, western Latvia; fertile and very low-lying Zemgale which is south and south-west of Riga; Vidzeme, east of Riga, with an upland of mixed farmland and forest that includes Gaizina kalns (311 metres), the highest point; and Latgale in the south-east, with more upland and over 40% of Latvia's several thousand lakes.

The Daugava, flowing across from Belorussia to the sea at Riga, is the biggest of Latvia's rivers. The Gauja, flowing down from the north-east, is the longest at 440 km. Pollution of rivers and the Gulf of Riga has reached serious proportions owing mainly to agricultural run-off and the city of Riga, which lacks a modern sewerage system.

Woodland still covers 40% of Latvia, half of it pine. Northern Kurzeme and northern Vidzeme are the most forested areas.

GOVERNMENT

Latvia intends to reintroduce a version of its pre-WW II parliament, the Saeima, by 1993. Until then, legislative power is exercised by a parliament called the Supreme Council (formerly Supreme Soviet) elected in March 1990. The chairman of the Supreme Council is the state president, a post currently held by Anatolis Gorbunovs. The executive government consists of a Council of Ministers led by a Prime Minister (Ivars Godmanis at the time of writing) and accountable to the Supreme Council.

A referendum on citizenship, and therefore on who could vote in elections for the Saeima, was due to be held among citizens of the pre-WW II Latvian republic and their descendants in 1992. The proposal likely to be put to them was that to be a Latvian citizen a person must have lived in Latvia for 10 years (which would include most of the Russians, Belorussians and Ukrainians living in Latvia) and have a reasonable knowledge of the Latvian language.

ECONOMY

Though Riga is the major industrial and commercial centre of the Baltic states, Latvia has suffered the same problems as Estonia and Lithuania which stems from the collapse of the Soviet economy, the introduction of a market economy, and independence. Price rises, the disruption of fuel and other supplies from Russia, falling output, old-fashioned technology, poor products and the reduction of subsidies were expected to lead to high unemployment during 1992. But it was hoped that the introduction of Latvia's own currency, the lat, and entry into the IMF would provide some stability for the economy. (In 1989 industry accounted for 60% of the gross national product, agriculture for 20%, construction, transport and communications for 13%.)

POPULATION, PEOPLE & RELIGION

Latvia's population according to the 1989 census was 2.7 million, over 70% of it in towns or cities. Only 52% is ethnic Latvian, which does much to explain Latvia's political landscape. Russians account for 34%, Belorussians 4.5% and Ukrainians 3.5%. Latvians and Lithuanians are the only surviving members of the Baltic ethnic family, an Indo-European but non-Slavic group whose third branch – the old Prussians – was exterminated by the Teutonic Knights.

Lutheranism is the main religious denomination of Latvians, though there are also significant numbers of Roman Catholics, mainly in the south once ruled by Poland. Russian believers are mainly Orthodox.

LANGUAGE

Latvians speak Latvian, one of the two languages of the Baltic branch of the Indo-European language family (the other is Lithuanian). Even more than Estonians, Latvians regard their language as an endangered species: only just over half the people in the country, and just over a third of the people in Riga speak it as their first language. Hence recent laws requiring varying levels of knowledge of Latvian for state employees.

The remarks in the Language section of our Estonia chapter about the use of English, Russian and other languages also hold true in Latvia. Here are some sounds specific to Latvian, followed by some useful words and phrases:

c	is pronounced as 'ts'
j	as the y in 'yes'
ā, ē, ī, ū	like the vowel sounds in 'bar', 'bare', 'he' and 'too'
ai, ei	as the vowel sounds in 'pine' and 'pain'
ie, o	like the vowel sounds in 'ear' and 'four'
č, š, ž	as 'ch', 'sh' and the 's' in 'pleasure'
ğ	as 'j'
ķ	as 'ch'
ļ	like the 'lli' in 'billiards'
ņ	as the 'ni' in 'onion'
r	trilled

Latvia	*Latvija*
Hello.	*Sveiki.*
Goodbye.	*Atā.*
Excuse me.	*Atvainojiet.*
Thank you.	*Paldies.*
Please.	*Lūdzu.*
Yes.	*Jā.*
No.	*Nē.*
Where?	*Kur?*
Do you speak English?	*Vai jūs runājat angliski?*
How much?	*Cik?*
one, two	*viens, divi*
three, four	*trīs, četri*
cheap, expensive	*lēts, dārgs*
hotel	*viesnīca*
airport	*lidosta*
railway station	*dzelzceļa stacija*
bus, bus station	*autobus, autoosta*
seaport	*jūras stacija*
street, square	*iela, laukums*
boulevard, avenue	*bulvāris, gatve*

Facts for the Visitor

VISAS & EMBASSIES

Always check the latest visa situation when planning your trip. At the time of writing visitors to Latvia, except citizens of the states into which the USSR broke up, need a visa. Latvian visas are issued at Latvian missions in some countries, or on arrival at Riga seaport or airport. You normally need to fill in a brief form and supply two photos. Single-entry visas from embassies or at borders cost US$20, transit visas cost US$5, or multiple-entry visas valid for six months usually cost around US$100 (embassy prices vary from country to country).

Latvia has a 'common visa space' with Estonia and Lithuania, established in 1992. This initially meant that a visa for any of the three states was also good for two days in each of the other two states. The two-day limit may be extended in the future and may not always be rigidly enforced in any case. It may be possible to obtain a Latvian visa once you're in Latvia through the Interior Ministry (☎ 37 38 28) at Raiņa bulvāris 6 in Riga.

Latvian Embassies

At the time of writing Latvia is still setting up missions in other countries. New ones will be created and some listed here will move. Latvian missions are often open for limited hours so ring ahead and allow plenty of time to make contact. They include:

Australia
Consulate, 38 Longstaff St, East Ivanhoe, Victoria 3073
Canada
Consulate, 19th floor, 700 Bay St, Toronto, Ontario M5G 126 (☎ 416-289 2617)
Denmark
Latvian Information Office, HC Andersens Boulevard 38, 1553 Copenhagen V (☎ 33 93 18 67)
Estonia
Embassy, Tõnismägi 10, Tallinn (☎ 68 16 68)
Finland
Embassy, Bulevarde 5A-18, Helsinki (☎ 60 56 40)
France
Embassy, 14 Boulevard Monmartre, 75009 Paris (☎ 48.01.00.44, fax 48 01 03 71)
Germany
Embassy, Bertha-von-Suttner-Platz 1-7, 5300 Bonn 1 (☎ 65 8276)
Lithuania
Embassy, Turniškių gatvė 19, Vilnius (☎ 77 85 32)
Russia
Embassy, ulitsa Chaplygina 3, Moscow 103062 (☎ 925 27 03)
Sweden
Embassy, Storgatan 38, Box 14095, S-114 55 Stockholm (☎ 667 3414, 667 3400, 105 024)
UK
Embassy, 72 Queensborough Terrace, London W2 3SP (☎ 071-727 1698)
USA
Embassy, 4325 17th Street NW, Washington DC 20011 (☎ 202-726 6757, 202-726 8213)

Foreign Embassies in Latvia

Foreign missions in Latvia are also in their infancy. Some ambassadors haven't found themselves embassies, while others are still residing in other countries. Some of the following details of missions in Riga can be expected to change:

Canada
Embassy, Elizabetes iela 45/47 (☎ 33 33 55)
Denmark
Embassy, Pils iela 13 (☎ 22 62 10)
Finland
Embassy, Teātra iela 9 (☎ 21 60 52)
France
Embassy, Hotel Ridzene, Endrupa iela 1 (☎ 32 59 79); expected to move to Raiņa bulvāris 9 during 1992
Germany
Embassy, Basteja bulvāris 14 (☎ 22 90 96)
Lithuania
Embassy, Elizabetes iela 2 (☎ 32 15 19, 32 09 48)
Norway
Embassy, Elizabetes iela 2 (☎ 32 31 88); plans to move to Zirgu iela 14 during 1992
Poland
Embassy, Elizabetes iela 2 (☎ 32 22 33)
Sweden
Embassy, Lāčplēša iela 13 (☎ 28 62 76)
UK
Embassy, Elizabetes iela 2 (☎ 32 07 37); expected to return to pre-WW II embassy at Raiņa bulvāris 2
USA
Embassy, Raiņa bulvāris 7 (☎ 22 70 45)

DOCUMENTS & CUSTOMS

See Estonia, Documents & Customs in the Facts for the Visitor section for information on customs declarations throughout the Baltic states. At the time of writing there are import limits of 250 grams of cigarettes or other tobacco products, one litre of spirits and two litres of wine, per person over 16 years of age. Up to 100% duty can be levied on antiques of artistic value.

MONEY
Currency & Prices

Latvia was due to introduce its own currency, the lat, in autumn 1992. This may make some things more expensive for visitors, and other things cheaper – but it will definitely simplify matters. Like the other two Baltic states, Latvia had previously muddled along on a combination of Soviet roubles (at R334 = US$1 in late 1992) and foreign 'hard' currencies with, additionally, visitors being

LATVIA

charged special high 'foreigners' prices' for some purchases.

All prices in this chapter have been converted into US$: those that were originally in roubles, which means most of those that look like bargains, may rise spectacularly.

Cash, Travellers' Cheques or Credit Cards?

At the time of writing it's difficult if not impossible to change travellers' cheques anywhere in Latvia. Cash US dollars are the best money to take, with European currencies like Deutschmarks, Swedish kronor or pounds sterling as a second choice. You can change money at special exchange offices. There's one at Riga airport and dozens around the city centre, look for signs saying 'Valūtas Apmaiņa'. Only a few of the more expensive establishments take credit cards, but the list will grow. Visa, MasterCard, Diners Club and American Express all crop up.

CLIMATE & WHEN TO GO

Latvia has a damp climate, with over 600 mm of precipitation a year. July, the warmest month, is also the wettest; temperatures reach up to 22°C but there are also persistent showers. Late June is noted for thunderstorms. May, the first half of June, August and September are usually the most comfortable times. Winter starts in November and lasts till late March, with temperatures rarely above 4°C, and snow usually on the ground from January to March in coastal regions. The east averages 1°C warmer than the coast in summer and 4°C colder in winter.

SUGGESTED ITINERARY

An itinerary for one week could include:

Riga; Jūrmala; maybe Kurzeme or Latgale; Sigulda, Līgatne and Cēsis

TOURIST OFFICES

In 1992 two German travel companies were acting as Latvian Tourist Offices in Germany (Lettische Fremdenverkehrsbüros in Deutschland) supplying information on transport, accommodation and so on, and a useful brochure in German. Hopefully they will continue this service in future years. Some of their staff speak English and it's worth contacting them even from outside Germany if you have specific queries. They are Schnieder Reisen (☎ 380 2060) of Schomburgstrasse 120, 2000 Hamburg 50, and Baltisches Reisebüro (☎ 59 6783) of Bayerstrasse 37/1, 8000 Munich 2. In other countries you may get information from Latvian diplomatic missions or Baltic specialist travel agents.

The Association of Latvian Travel Agents (☎ 32 72 54, fax 21 36 66, telex 161195 VENT SU) is at Torņa iela 9, Riga. The Latvian Tourist Board, a government department, may have some printed material available soon. It's unable to deal with casual visitors but you could contact it by phoning Riga 22 99 45, fax 28 45 72 or telex 161123 LRXC SU.

BUSINESS HOURS & HOLIDAYS

Shop, office, café and restaurant hours are as in Estonia (see Estonia, Facts for the Visitor). Latvia's national holidays are:

New Year's Day, 1 January
Good Friday (Easter Monday is also a holiday for many)
Labour Day, 1 May
Mother's Day, second Sunday in May
Ligo (Midsummer festival), 23 June
Jāni (St John's Day), 24 June
National Day (anniversary of proclamation of Latvian Republic, 1918), 18 November
Christmas Day, 25 December
Boxing Day, 26 December
New Year's Eve, 31 December

CULTURAL EVENTS

The 21st Latvian Song Festival is to be held from 2 to 4 July 1993 and the 11th Latvian Dance Festival will run concurrently with it; the Baltika folk festival is next due in Riga in July 1994. For background on these events, see Cultural Events in the Facts for the Visitor sections of the Estonia and Lithuania chapters.

Latvian traditional dress is on view at such

festivals. For women it consists of a long skirt, embroidered tunic-shaped blouse and colourful shawl. They often wear headgear, which represents a family's status, and amber and metal jewellery. Men traditionally wear flaxen shirts and trousers, embroidered tunics and brimmed hats.

POST & TELECOMMUNICATIONS
Post
The Latvian for post office is *pasts*.Mail for Scandinavia goes direct via Denmark so only takes a few days. Other mail goes via Moscow. Expect air-mail letters or cards to take about 10 days to Western Europe or North America; weighing up to 20 grams, they cost US$0.05 to Britain or the USA in mid-1992.

Delivery times for mail to Latvia are very erratic: it's best not to bother unless you'll be there for a long time. Addresses have a six-figure postcode with the town or city name.

Telephone
International Apart from a few direct-dial lines, international calls have to go via an operator and through Moscow. This gives you a choice of quick and expensive or cheap and frustrating.

At the time of writing the easiest way is to use one of the expensive-rate communications offices in Riga (see Riga, Information). The second easiest way is to get your hotel's desk staff to arrange the call for you. You'll probably have to spend an hour or two waiting in your room for the call to come through. There's no reason you shouldn't pay the same as anyone else (US$0.15 a minute to Britain, US$0.30 to the USA, US$0.35 to Australia at the time of writing) but you never know when you might be asked a 'foreigners' price'. Each hotel room has its own individual phone number: desk staff will tell you yours if you're in doubt.

The third method is to make the call from a public telephone (*telefons*) office. You normally need to book the call and pay on the previous day. When you return at the appointed time, you may have to wait for hours without explanation.

Local Calls within the city you're in can be made either from private or hotel-room phones (simply by dialling the number, without any area code), or from most public phone boxes. At the time of writing you need 15-kopeck coins.

Within Latvia & the Ex-USSR Long-distance calls within Latvia, Estonia, Lithuania or anywhere else that used to be in the USSR are easiest made with the help of hotel desk staff. If dialling yourself from a private or hotel-room phone, you usually need to dial 8 before the area code and number. Most calls cost under US$0.02 a minute. Area codes from Latvian phones include Riga 22, Bauska 239, Cēsis 241, Daugavpils 254, Jelgava 230, Liepāja 234, Valmiera 242, Ventspils 236, Vilnius 0122, Kaunas 0127, Tallinn 0142, St Petersburg 812, Moscow 095.

There are also long-distance phone booths (*starpilšetu telefonu automāti*) in selected places. You can make long-distance calls from telephone offices if you're prepared for a long wait.

Calls to Latvia At the time of writing Latvia still uses the old USSR country telephone code, 7. From outside the ex-USSR you precede this with your international access code (eg 010 in the UK, and follow it with 013, then the area code minus its initial 2, then the number. So, to reach Riga 72 63 54 from the UK, you dial 010 7 013 2 72 63 54). Getting through from Scandinavia can be harder than from more distant countries since there's even more demand on the lines.

When dialling Latvia from within the ex-USSR, including Estonia or Lithuania, replace the initial 2 of the area code with 013. The code for Riga is thus 0132. There's usually a long-distance access code, 8.

Fax, Telex & Telegraph
Except for one or two relatively expensive outgoing services from Riga (for details see Riga, Information) and a few organisations with satellite fax lines, telex (rather than fax)

LATVIA

is a more common way of communicating to or from Latvia.

International telegrams, inbound or outbound, usually arrive the same or next day. They can be sent from any telegraph (*telegrafs*) office (often the same as post offices) and at the time of writing cost US$0.03 a word to Western Europe, US$0.05 to North America. There's also a double-price urgent (*steidzama*) service.

TIME
See Estonia, Facts for the Visitor.

BOOKS & MAPS
See Estonia, Facts for the Visitor for some titles which cover all three Baltic states. The 1991 *Latvijas Ceļu Karte* atlas of Latvia, on sale in Latvia for US$0.50, is based on pre-WW II maps and therefore its 40 town maps and some of the highways marked are of limited use, but it's still a good buy, showing the whole country in 59 pages at 1 cm: 2 km. Some good new town maps have been produced.

MEDIA
The *Baltic Observer* published in Riga is a slightly more ponderous version of Tallinn's *Baltic Independent*, well worth picking up. It's sold for next to nothing at bookstalls, hotels and so on in Riga and the other Baltic capitals. *Riga This Week* is a thinner equivalent of *Tallinn This Week*, with information on things to see or buy, places to eat, entertainment etc, published every three months and worth US$1. There's a similar amount of information in the rival *Riga Success Guide*, in English and German.

A few Western newspapers three or four days old, and if you're lucky *Newsweek*, may be found at the De Rome or Metropole hotels in Riga.

FILM & PHOTOGRAPHY
See the comments in Estonia, Facts for the Visitor.

HEALTH
See the Estonia Health section for general comments on the three Baltic states. Drinking unboiled tap water is not advisable in Riga, residents boil theirs.

Swimming anywhere on Latvia's coast may be risky owing to pollution. No one chances it at the main seaside resort, Jūrmala.

DANGERS & ANNOYANCES
See the comments in Estonia, Facts for the Visitor.

ACTIVITIES
Canoe and bicycle trips for up to two weeks around Latvia run by the Latvian University Tourist Club are open to foreigners. The cost in 1992 for cycling trips was about US$7 per person per day, including bicycle, interpreter/guide and food; for canoe trips it's about US$10 a day. This would be a great way of seeing a side of the country that few tourists glimpse. For more information and bookings contact Latvijas Universitātes Tūristu Klubs (LUTK) (☎ 22 31 14, fax 22 50 39 or 22 74 11, telex 161172 TEMA SU) at Raiņa bulvāris 19, Riga 226098.

ACCOMMODATION
Latvia lacks Estonia's wide youth hostel network, and camp sites and homestays are harder to track down, but in Riga at least there are still adequate bottom-end accommodation possibilities. It's worth trying to book ahead, wherever you plan to stay, but particularly at Riga's top-end hotels, which are often full in summer. You can book in person by phone, fax or telex, or get an agency in your own country or Latvia to do it for you. Think about booking into somewhere more expensive than you'd normally consider for your first night or two in Latvia, and make it a base from which to seek out somewhere cheaper when you arrive.

Travel agencies such as TAS (☎ 22 46 98, fax 22 29 01) of Room 201, Hotel Riga, Aspazijas bulvāris 22, 226047 Riga, or Latvia Tours (☎ 33 28 46, fax 21 36 66, telex 161149 INLA SU) of Kalpaka bulvāris 1, 226010 Riga, can often book you into expensive or middle-range hotels at short notice when the hotels themselves say 'full'. The agent's price could be higher or lower than the hotel's own prices.

Camping

Latvia has some camp sites – mostly fairly basic – but no one, it seems, keeps lists of them. Town maps may help you locate them. Some new private-enterprise sites with superior facilities are said to be under development. Motorists can try asking at farms etc, for permission to camp.

Hostels & Colleges

The first backpackers' hostels sprang up in Latvia in 1992 but it is uncertain whether they will be summer-only or year-round. Places in college rooms in Riga can be found for US$6 to US$12 a person.

Private Homes & Flats

There are one or two enterprises offering flat or cottage rentals in Riga or Jūrmala, and more such places are likely to become available. The Latvian Tourist Board has been collecting information on farms willing to host visitors.

You can organise homestays in any of the Baltic states through organisations in the West – see Accommodation in the Estonia Facts for the Visitor section for some addresses.

Hotels

The information on hotels in Estonia, Facts for the Visitor also applies to Latvia. One type of accommodation likely to be developed in Latvia is forest or lakeside lodges for nature lovers or hunters.

FOOD

See the Food section of Estonia, Facts for the Visitor for general information on the food and restaurant scene in the Baltic states.

The Latvian diet leans heavily on dairy products, grains and fish, though you'll find meat in restaurants. *Šprotes* (sardines) crop up as a starter in many places. If they're *ar sipoliem*, they'll be with onions. *Siļķe* is herring, *līdaka* pike and *lasis* salmon. Soups and sausage *(desa)* are popular. In summer

and autumn good use is made of many types of berry. A few food words in Latvian follow:

English	Latvian
bread	*maize*
starters	*uzkoda*
salad	*salāti*
soup	*zupa*
fish	*zivis*
meat or main dishes	*gaļas ēdieni*
national dishes	*nacionālie ēdieni*
vegetables	*saknes*
fruit	*augļi*
cheese	*siers*

DRINKS

See Estonia, Facts for the Visitor for a few general comments on drinks in the Baltic states as a whole. Beer is *alus* in Latvian and one of Latvia's best is the thick Mērnieku Laiku, about US$0.80 a bottle in restaurants. Latvians also drink *kvas*, fermented rye-bread water. Dispensed on the streets from big wheeled tanks in summer, it's refreshing and mildly alcoholic. Also refreshing are tasty ice-cream and fruit-juice concoctions called *kokteili*.

Take care with tap water, see the Health section of this chapter. Tea in Latvian is *tēja*, coffee *kafija*, mineral water *minerālūdens*.

Getting There & Away

TRAVEL AGENTS

See Estonia, Getting There & Away for Baltic-states specialist travel agencies in Western countries.

AIR
Routes

At the time of writing Riga has scheduled flights to/from Copenhagen four times weekly and to/from Stockholm twice weekly with SAS; Helsinki three times with Finnair; Frankfurt five times with Lufthansa; Hamburg three times and Berlin Tempelhof twice with Hamburg Airlines. SAS, Finnair and Lufthansa offer worldwide connections.

LATVIA

476 Latvia – Getting There & Away

Latvian Airlines (Latvijas Avialinijas) began flying the same routes in 1992 with ex-Aeroflot planes and was due to add new services including to/from Düsseldorf.

Links between Riga and former Soviet republics by Latvian or other national airlines include Tallinn three times weekly; Moscow twice or more daily, St Petersburg six times weekly, Arkhangelsk twice weekly, and Minsk seven times weekly. There are also flights twice weekly between St Petersburg and Liepāja.

In summer 1992 a new airline, Baltia, was due to start direct flights between Riga and New York (JFK airport, five times weekly), Minsk, Kiev and Tbilisi (Georgia). Baltia (☎ 718-244 6916, fax 718-656 9084) is at Mail Room 342, Terminal 1, JFK International Airport, Jamaica, NY 11430.

Fares

The cheapest tickets may be offered not by the airlines themselves but by their 'general sales agents' such as Regent Holidays of Bristol, England, which has London-Riga returns (or open jaws through Tallinn, St Petersburg or Vilnius) for around US$510 to US$580 (see Estonia, Getting There & Away). SAS fares into Riga at the time of writing include:

Copenhagen
    'Jackpot' return (bookable 14 to seven days before travel) US$320,
    Apex return, US$400, youth (under 25 years) one-way fare (either way) US$160;
Stockholm
    'Jackpot' return US$250, Apex return US$310, youth one-way US$125.

Finnair's cheapest Helsinki-Riga-Helsinki fare is a US$215 'superpex', but the Riga-Helsinki-Riga lowest fare is a US$363 'excursion fare'. Lufthansa's Frankfurt-Riga-Frankfurt youth fare costs US$425 while its Apex fare is US$480.

Latvian Airlines' one-way economy fares from Riga include Copenhagen US$412, Stockholm US$370 and Helsinki US$282, with the cheapest return tickets around 50% to 60% dearer. One-way fares within the former USSR include to Tallinn US$53, Moscow US$86 and St Petersburg US$70. Return fares cost double that. As in Estonia and Lithuania, local citizens pay much lower fares at the time of writing.

Charter Flights Individuals can often buy seats on charter flights, or in block bookings on scheduled flights, from tour companies or emigré groups. For instance in 1992, Progressive Tours offered some charter seats London-Riga-London for US$585. Rochdale Travel Centre offered two and four-week return flights to any Baltic capital from Britain for around US$520. Schnieder Reisen of Hamburg had Hamburg-Riga-Hamburg tickets from US$245.

LAND

For any travel through Russia, Belorussia or Kaliningrad, look into the visa situation well ahead. Some information on Belorussian visas is given in Lithuania, Facts for the Visitor.

Bus

International buses into or between the Baltic states are generally quicker than trains, but as they tend to be more expensive they're generally less heavily booked. But still get tickets in advance if you can.

To/From Estonia & Russia About four buses run daily each way between Riga and Tallinn (six hours, US$1.35) mostly via Pärnu. There are also direct buses between Riga and Tartu and Viljandi. There's a daily Riga-Novgorod service, and St Petersburg bus services may begin operating.

To/From Lithuania & Kaliningrad There are four or five daily buses between Vilnius and Riga taking six hours for US$1.50, plus a few services daily to/from Kaunas, Šiauliai, Klaipėda and Kaliningrad. Direct daily buses also run between Klaipėda, Liepāja and Ventspils.

To/From Poland & Belorussia The weekly Warsaw-Tallinn bus (see Estonia, Getting

There & Away) can be used for journeys from Warsaw to Riga (17 hours, US$21.50), and probably vice-versa. Riga also has direct daily buses to/from Brest, on the Belorussia-Poland border, and Minsk.

Train

Train tickets bought at stations usually provide the cheapest form of long-distance transport in the Baltic states so book as early as possible. They may be only cost a fraction of tickets for the same route bought outside the former USSR or from local agents charging 'foreigners' prices'.

To/From Estonia & Russia In addition to the daytime 'Chayka', taking 7½ hours each way between Riga and Tallinn, there's also one overnight train each way. Both services go via Tartu. The fare in a four-berth couchette (with beds that convert to seats in the daytime) at the time of writing is US$0.60 northbound, US$1 southbound. There are three daily overnight trains each way between Riga and Moscow, taking about 14 hours, and two to/from St Petersburg taking 11 hours.

To/From Lithuania, Belorussia, Poland, Germany, Kaliningrad & Ukraine A daily through sleeping car operates between Berlin Hauptbahnhof and Riga via Warsaw Central and Vilnius, taking 32 hours from Berlin, 22 hours from Warsaw and eight hours from Vilnius. One-way fares in a four-berth couchette are US$115 from Berlin and US$27 from Warsaw (Central Station ticket office). At present this train is routed through Belorussia but there are plans for a direct Poland-Lithuania crossing.

Several trains daily run between Vilnius and Riga, including at least one overnight each way, and the daytime 'Chayka' which trundles back and forth between Minsk (9½ hours from Riga) and Tallinn. Travelling from Vilnius to Riga in a four-berth couchette is US$0.50 at the time of writing. There are also daily trains between Riga and Klaipėda (5½ hours), Kaliningrad (overnight, 10 hours), Kiev and Lvov.

Taxi

See Estonia, Getting There & Away.

Car & Motorbike

See the introductory Getting Around chapter for general comments on driving and riding in the Baltic states. The vehicle ferries to Riga from Sweden and Germany (see the next section) avoid any long delays at land borders (see Lithuania, Getting There & Away).

SEA

To/From Sweden

The Russian-owned Baltic Line operates the *Ilich* passenger and vehicle ferry between Stockholm and Riga. In 1992 sailings were once a week each way, taking 17 hours. One-way fares including breakfast range from US$127 to US$294 (but there are only a few places for US$127 and the next cheapest are US$181); a car is US$99, a motorbike US$36. You can book through Scansov Tours (☎ 782 9700) of Karlavägen 53, Box 5397 SA, S 10246 Stockholm, or CTC Lines (☎ 071-930 5833) of 1 Regent St, London SW1Y 4NN.

A more frequent, potentially cheaper option is to take Estline's *Nord Estonia* ferry between Stockholm and Tallinn (see Estonia, Getting There & Away), then local transport or one of Estline's own buses between Tallinn and Riga.

A third possibility between May and September is the hydrofoils of Lettline (☎ 11-12 33 39) between Norrköping and Riga.

To/From Germany

The *Mercuri-I* vehicle ferry began weekly sailings between Kiel (Germany) and Riga in 1992, taking 40 hours each way. One-way fares cost from US$135 to US$550 (full meals are US$50 extra); a car is US$125, a motorbike US$60. This ferry also does weekly sailings between Kiel and Klaipėda (Lithuania), enabling you to sail into Riga and out of Klaipėda or vice-versa. Round-trip fares are available whichever port you return from. Tickets are sold by the Karl Steder travel agency in Kiel (☎ 29 2604), or contact Schnieder Reisen of Hamburg or Baltisches Reisebüro of Munich (see Tourist Offices).

Cruises

Kristina Cruises from Finland and the *Baltic Star* from Sweden (see Estonia, Getting There & Away) are among the operators of cruises to Riga. There are also cruise packages on the *Ilich* (see To/From Sweden).

TOURS

Latvia Tours and TAS (see Accommodation in the Facts for the Visitor section) are among the main tour handlers at the Latvian end. They or the Association of Latvian Travel agents (see Tourist Offices in the Facts for the Visitor section) should be able to tell you of agents and tour companies in your country dealing with Latvia.

A typical week's tour of Latvia from Germany, staying in Riga with maybe a night or two in Liepāja or elsewhere, is likely to cost US$800 to US$900 including flights. Information on wider Baltic states tours is given in Estonia, Getting There & Away.

Getting Around

BUS

Buses link all the main towns in Latvia. On longer runs, they're generally a better option than trains, being more frequent, quicker, and still very cheap by Western standards.

TRAIN

A good network of suburban (*piepilsetas*) trains provides the best transport option for many places within about 50 km of Riga, but on longer routes rail services are generally poorer than bus services.

TAXI

At the time of writing taxis should cost around US$0.05 a km, which even makes them possible intercity transport for Westerners. Meters tick over at 20 kopecks a km and you multiply the result by 30, but no doubt a new system will set in when the lat is established. Of equal importance is finding a taxi driver who'll give you the proper rate – see Estonia, Getting Around for further information.

CAR & MOTORBIKE

See the introductory Getting Around chapter for information on driving and riding in the Baltics and see Riga, Getting There & Away for information on car rentals.

The Finnish company Neste runs two petrol stations which are open for 24 hours a day in Riga selling 99 octane and unleaded petrol, and oil.

BICYCLE, LOCAL TRANSPORT & TOURS

See the information under these headings in the Estonia chapter. Travel agents and hotel service bureaux are the places to ask if you're thinking of hiring an English-speaking guide.

Riga

With 916,000 people, Riga has more big-city excitement than anywhere else in the Baltic states. Its German connections are clear not just from its fine old German buildings (many now looking better-than-new after restoration) but also from the German-influenced fashions on its streets, the numbers of German visitors, and the clear German economic interest here.

Riga lacks that medieval feeling peculiar to Tallinn and Vilnius, but is still historically and architecturally fascinating – and even more of a cultural centre than either of the other Baltic capitals.

History

Riga was founded in 1158 as a river-mouth storehouse for Bremen merchants. Around 1200, Bishop Albert of Buxhoevden chose Riga as his seat. At his instigation, German knights soon conquered Livonia. Riga became an important fortified port, joining the Hanseatic League in 1282.

After the knights' decline in the 16th century, Riga fell under Polish, Swedish and then (in 1710) Russian control, though still dominated by the old German nobility. It grew into an important industrial and trading city, the population jumping from 28,000 in 1794 to about half a million before WW I, when it was Russia's third most important industrial city and the world's greatest timber port.

Seriously damaged in both world wars, Riga was turned into a Soviet technical and industrial centre after WW II, sprawling outwards as large numbers of migrants came to work the new industries.

Orientation

Riga straddles the Daugava river on the flatlands about 15 km inland from its mouth. The east bank holds all the interest. Here is Old Riga (Vecrīga), the city's 1.5-km-by-one-km historic heart, its skyline dominated by three steeples: from south to north, St Peter's (the tallest), the square bulk of the Dom cathedral tower, and the simpler St Jēkab's. East of the old city is a ring of parks and boulevards. Riga's axial street, running north-east from the October Bridge (Oktobra tilts), is called Kaļķu iela as it crosses the old city, then Brīvības bulvāris as it traverses the park ring, then Brīvības iela past the towering Hotel Latvija, about two km from the river.

The railway and bus stations are five minutes' walk apart on the south-east edge of Old Riga.

Maps Bookshops and kiosks sell (for US$0.15) a good 1 cm:250 metres *Riga City Map* published in 1991, with a closeup of the city centre. There's also a 1 cm:1.5 km map of Riga's surroundings, *Rīgas un Jūrmalas Apkārtne* (1991), useful for day trips out of the city.

Information
Tourist Offices & Travel Agencies See

Latvia, Facts for the Visitor for some information sources.

Money There are exchange offices at Riga airport, throughout central Riga, and in main hotels and banks. The only place we were told *might* change travellers' cheques in an emergency was the Rigas Komercbanka on Smilšu iela in Old Riga.

Post & Telecommunications You can make international phone, fax or telex calls straight away from 9 am to 6 pm daily at the 'Telex, Fax, Telephone' office on Dzirnavu iela immediately behind the Hotel Latvija. One minute by phone (minimum three minutes) or fax (minimum four minutes) costs US$1 to Europe, US$1.50 elsewhere.

Riga's main post, telephone and telegraph office at Brīvības bulvāris 21 is open 24 hours daily. There's another large office just to the right as you come out of the railway station, on Stacijas laukums. International phone calls can be made in a few minutes at the Brīvības office at, for example, US$2 a minute to Western Europe. The same office also has international fax lines.

Bookshops Centrālā Grāmatnīca at Aspazijas bulvāris 24, near the Hotel Riga, is one of the best bookshops; it has some guides in English. Globuss next door is the best place for maps. Makslas Gramata at Krišjāna Barona iela 31 is an art-book shop.

Medical & Dental Services There are hospitals at Maskavas iela 122/128 (☎ 24 17 70), and Veidenbauma iela 13 (☎ 22 48 64), and an emergency dental service (☎ 27 45 46) at Stabu iela 9. The pharmacy at Elizabetes iela 21 has some Western medicines.

Left Luggage There are left-luggage lockers (*automātiskas rokas bagāž as glabātuves*), open from 5 am to 1 am, in the long-distance section of the railway station. At the time of writing you have to pay US$0.01 to enter the locker hall. Then you find an open locker, put

LATVIA

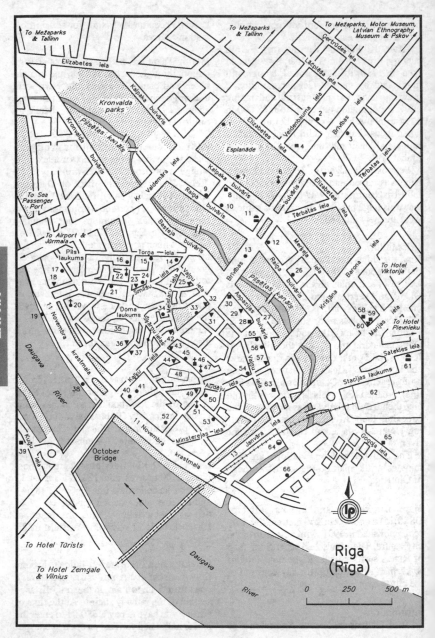

Riga
(Rīga)

0   250   500 m

■ PLACES TO STAY

4 Hotel Latvija
8 Hotel Ridzene
28 Hotel Riga
30 Hotel De Rome
39 Hotel Daugava
58 Accommodation Booking Office & Hotel Saulīte
59 Hotel Aurora
63 Hotel Metropole
65 Hotel Sport

▼ PLACES TO EAT

5 Sulas Coku Café
18 Kafe Pils
23 Kafejnica Magdalena
25 Ēdnīca Pulvertornis
29 Sena Rīga Restaurant
31 Cafe Forums
32 Elena Cafe
36 Pūt Vējini Restaurant
37 Pie Kristapa Restaurant
42 Kafe Balta Roze
43 Jever Bistro
44 Ridzene Café
49 Peter Gailis Café
57 Anre Café
60 Randevu Café-Bar

OTHER

1 Fine Arts Museum
2 Hard-Currency Telecommunications Office
3 MF Salons
6 Russian Orthodox Cathedral
7 Rainis Monument
9 Interior Ministry
10 US Embassy
11 Main Post, Telephone & Telegraph Office
12 Latvian Airlines
13 Freedom Monument
14 Powder Tower
15 Swedish Gate
16 Parliament
17 Museums of Latvian History, Foreign Art & Latvian Literature
19 Pier 2
20 Anglican Church
21 Three Brothers Houses
22 St Jēkab's Church
24 Rīgas Komercbanka
26 University
27 Opera House
33 Philharmonia Chamber Music Hall
34 Great Guild Building & Philharmonia Concert Hall
35 Dom Cathedral
38 Pier 1
40 Latvian Riflemen Monument
41 Latvian Riflemen Museum
45 Museum of Applied Arts
46 Eka Convent
47 St John's Church
48 St Peter's Church
50 House of Reitern
51 Protestant Church
52 House of Dannenstern
53 17th Century Warehouses
54 Centrālais Universālveikals (Department Store)
55 Centrālā Grāmatnica (Bookshop)
56 Globuss
61 Post, Telephone & Telegraph Office
62 Railway Station
64 Bus Station
66 Central Market

LATVIA

your bags in, turn the keys on the inside of the door to your chosen combination of one Cyrillic letter and three numbers, making a note of the combination and the number of the locker. Next you turn the knobs on the outside of the door to something other than your combination, put the right coin(s) (15 kopecks at the time of writing) in the slot, and finally shut the door.

To open the locker, turn the outside knobs to your combination and put the right coin(s) in the slot. The clown at the left-luggage office downstairs says you must pay 2% of the value of your luggage to store it.

There are also two left-luggage offices, open slightly different hours, at the bus station.

Other Foreign embassies and consulates in Riga are listed in the Latvia, Facts for the Visitor section.

Things to See
Old Riga The old city (Vecrīga) retains

whole squares or rows of German buildings that have stood since the 17th century or earlier. It's a protected, mainly pedestrian zone, made prettier by restoration. Walking its crooked streets is one of the chief pleasures of Riga.

Kaļķu iela neatly divides it into two halves, each focusing on a towering church: the Dom cathedral in the northern half, St Peter's in the south.

The brick **Dom cathedral** (Rīgas Doms), founded in 1211 for the Riga bishop, is now an all-in-one church, museum and organ concert hall. Its opening hours as a museum are from 1 to 5 pm Tuesday to Friday and 10 am to 2 pm Saturdays. There are services at noon on Sundays.

The cathedral is a 13th to 18th century architectural amalgam: the east end (the oldest) has Romanesque features, the 18th century tower is Baroque, and much of the rest is 15th century Gothic. The floor and walls are dotted with old stone tombs: a 1709 cholera and typhoid outbreak which killed a third of Riga's population was blamed on a flood that inundated these. The huge 1880s organ has 6768 pipes. The cloister contains the **Museum of the History of Riga & Seafaring**, open daily except Mondays and Tuesdays.

Riga Castle on Pils laukums dates in parts from the 13th century, when it was built for the German knights, but today most of it looks more recent. It houses the **museums of Latvian History, Foreign Art, & Latvian Literature**, all reached through the same door at Pils laukums 3. The history museum, up four flights of steps, spans the millennia with exhibits ranging from bronze body-ornaments more than 2000 years old to present-day items. It's open Wednesdays and Fridays from 1 to 7 pm, Thursdays, Saturdays and Sundays from 11 am to 5 pm.

Nearby at Mazā Pils iela 17, 19 and 21 is a quaint row of houses known as the **Three Brothers**. No 17 is a 15th century house, which makes it the oldest in Latvia. Jēkaba iela in front of **St Jēkab's Church** (originally 13th century) was still at the time of writing blocked by the barricades placed there in January 1991 against a feared attack by Soviet troops on Latvia's **parliament** next door.

The picturesque **Swedish Gate** at the junction of Torņa iela and Aldaru iela was built on to the city walls in 1698. The round, peaked 14th century **Powder Tower** (Pulvertornis) at the end of Torņa iela has changed little through incarnations as a gunpowder store, prison, torture chamber, Bolshevik Revolution Museum and now, the Latvian War Museum.

South of Kaļķu iela, the red-brick Gothic bulk of **St Peter's Church** (Pētera Baznīca) dates mainly from the 15th century, though the pink stone western façade is 17th century. Its famed spire has been built three times in the same Baroque form: originally in the 1660s, again in the 18th century after being hit by lightning, and most recently after destruction by the Germans in 1941.

The rest of the church was also badly damaged by the Germans, and much restoration has taken place. St Peter's has recently been in use as an exhibition hall, open daily except Mondays, though it may return at least partly to church use. There's a lift to the second gallery of the spire for a panorama of Old Riga.

A row of prettily restored buildings faces St Peter's on Skārņu iela. No 10/20, originally a 13th century church for the Knights of the Sword, is the **Museum of Applied Arts** (Dekoratīvi Lietišķās Mākslas Muzejs), full of outstanding Latvian work, open daily except Mondays. No 22 was the **Eka Convent**, built in the 16th century by the mayor, N Ekk. No 24, **St John's Church** (Jāņa Baznīca), is a 13th to 19th century Gothic, classical and Baroque amalgam.

New Riga East of Old Riga's jumbled streets, the city's old defensive moat, the **Pilsētas kanāls** (City Canal), snakes through parks laid between wide boulevards in the 19th century. On Brīvības bulvāris near the corner of Raiņa bulvāris stands the **Freedom Monument** (Brīvības Piemineklis), topped by a bronze Liberty holding aloft three stars. Erected in 1935, this monument was out of bounds in the Soviet years, when a statue of Lenin, facing the other way down Brīvības iela, was put up two blocks east (Lenin has now been removed). In the late 1980s the Freedom Monument became a hub of the Latvian independence movement, starting on 14 June 1987 when 5000 people rallied illegally there to commemorate the victims of Stalin's deportations.

In the section of park north of the monument, red stone slabs stand as **Memorials to the Dead of 20 January 1991**, when Soviet troops stormed the **Interior Ministry** nearby at Raiņa bulvāris 6.

The **Fine Arts Museum** at Krišjāna Valdemāra iela 10A, on the northern corner of the Esplanāde park, has permanent collections of Russian and Latvian work plus some interesting temporary exhibitions. It's open daily except Tuesdays.

The domed 19th century **Russian Orthodox cathedral** on the other end of the Esplanāde, fronting Brīvības bulvāris, returned to church use recently only after years as a Soviet planetarium. In the same park is the **Jānis Rainis Monument**, to Latvia's national poet, who Latvians say would have been world famous if he'd written in a less obscure language than Latvian.

Suburbs Riga's **Motor Museum** (Motormuzejs) at S Eizenšteina iela 6, eight km east of the Old Town along Brīvības iela then two km south, is a big hit for its cars that once belonged to Stalin, Khrushchev and Brezhnev, complete with wax images of the former Soviet leaders – an idea unthinkable a few years ago. The museum is open daily except Mondays from 10 am to 8 pm. A special bus service runs to it from beside the Orthodox cathedral on Brīvības bulvāris, signs at the stop give the schedule. Bus No 21 from the Orthodox cathedral goes to the Mežciems stop on Šmerļa iela, within half a km of the museum.

Over 90 buildings from rural Latvia, mostly wooden and from the 18th or 19th century, have been assembled together with thousands of artefacts at the open-air

Latvian Ethnography Museum beside lake Jugla on the eastern edge of the city. In summer, folk-dance shows and craft fairs are held. The museum is normally open daily from mid-May to mid-October, except the last day of the month. Take bus No 1 from opposite the Orthodox cathedral which is on Brīvības bulvāris.

Riga's biggest park is **Mežaparks** (Woodland Park), about seven km north of the centre, beside the lake Kišezers. Here you'll find playgrounds, a zoo, and pleasant pine woods. You can reach it by tram No 11 going north-east on Krišjāna Barona iela, or by river (see the next section).

River Trips

The public boats and hydrofoils plying the rivers and lakes around Riga are a minor attraction in their own right. In summer sailings from Pier 1 (Piestatne 1), by the east end of the October Bridge, include three or four a day to Mežaparks (1¼ hours); about eight a day to Majori in Jūrmala (one hour); and trips on to the Gulf of Riga and back (50 minutes). In spring and autumn services are reduced and in winter the river is frozen. Timetables are posted at the pier. On all routes you get a 'fish's-eye' view of the docks lining the river most of the way to the sea.

Places to Stay

Hostels & Colleges The *BATS backpackers' hostel*, charging $US9 in clean rooms with shared bathrooms, is at Grecinieku iela 28 facing the Riflemen Monument on the east side of the October Bridge. This hostel may close outside the summer travel season.

Youth Hostel Interpoint (☎ 01 38 48), one of about 30 summer travellers' hostels run by the YMCA Interpoint organisation around Europe, is at 10-12 Kalnciema iela, west of the October Bridge. Its clean, light and quite big rooms cost US$6 per person, plus US$4 for an Interpoint card if you don't have one. Some rooms have private baths and there's a café on the spot. Take tram No 4 or 5 from the Grecinieku Iela stop by the October

Bridge, and go five stops to the Kalneciema Iela stop. Expected opening dates in 1993 are 1 July to 1 September.

The Latvian University Tourist Club or LUTK (Latvijas Universitātes Tūristu Klubs) in the university building at Raiņa bulvāris 19, Riga 226098, has single, double and triple rooms in student hostels and university hotels around the city (some central) available for visitors from US$6 to US$12 a person. Some have private bath and toilet. Try to contact the club a couple of weeks in advance (☎ 22 31 14, fax 22 50 39 or 22 74 11, telex 161172 TEMA SU).

Private Homes & Flats Firmai Kiip (☎ 37 64 25) of Cēsu iela 8, Riga 226012, advertises flats for rent. Likely to be cheaper, since they're only advertised in Latvian and Russian, are the lodgings in private flats (Russian: *chastny kvartira*) offered by Ko-op Viesis (☎ 22 28 02) at Merķeļa iela 12, next to the Hotel Saulīte, two minutes' walk from the railway station. Travel agents like TAS (see Accommodation in the Facts for the Visitor section) may be able to organise flat rentals or homestays at a couple of weeks' notice.

Cheap Hotels The *Hotel Aurora* (☎ 22 44 79) at Marijas iela 5, facing the railway station, has double rooms with washbasin for US$0.55 – if you can convince the desk staff that a Westerner really wants to stoop to their hostelry. Rooms are clean enough but the shared toilets smell.

Round the corner from the Aurora, Ko-op Viesis (see Private Homes & Flats) runs a same-day booking service for other hotels. It's open from noon to 2 pm and 3 to 9 pm, Monday to Friday. Its sign says *'Viesnīcu Tresta izzinu birojs'*. Only Latvian and Russian are spoken. The cheapest rooms we were offered cost US$0.55/1.10 for singles/doubles in the *Hotel Viktorija* (☎ 27 23 05) at A Čaka iela 55 or the *Hotel Plavnieki* (☎ 13 70 40) on Salnas iela.

The Viktorija, 1.5 km north-east of the station by trolley bus No 11, 18 or 23, has rooms with TV and washbasin but toilets are shared and none too fragrant. The Plavnieki has some rooms with shower and toilet and is eight km east of the centre: take bus No 17 from the bus station or No 52 from the railway station, to the Liepiņas stop on Deglava iela.

Behind the railway station at Gogoļa iela 5 is the dingy *Hotel Sport* (☎ 22 67 80) with 'suites' – bedroom, sitting room, TV, bathroom – at US$10 for two, or ordinary rooms (sharing shower and toilet with other rooms) for US$5 a double.

Middle-Range Hotels The *Hotel Tūrists* (☎ 61 54 55) a large, former Soviet trade-union tourism hotel, bigger and less seedy than the Sport, has clean but faded rooms with private shower and toilet for US$18 a double, or suites (with sitting room and TV) for US$30. It's at Slokas iela 1, about a km west of the October Bridge. Take tram No 4 or 5 to the Rainberga Bulvāris stop. *Hotel Saulīte* (☎ 22 45 46) at Merķeļa iela 12 near the railway station has clean rooms at US$20 for Westerners and US$0.10 for Latvians.

Expensive Hotels Riga's biggest hotel is the *Hotel Latvija* (☎ 21 26 45) at Elizabetes iela 55 on the corner of Brīvības iela. Its 27 storeys poke uglily into the sky. The service is moderate but the eating options are adequate, and the views are great. Singles/doubles are US$88/105 from April to October, US$66/84 during other months – expensive for the size of room. TAS (see Facts for the Visitor, Accommodation) was quoting from US$10 to US$15 lower when we last checked.

The *Hotel Riga* (☎ 21 60 00) on the edge of Old Riga at Aspazijas bulvāris 22, is more human in scale, but there's little to choose between its rooms and the Latvija's. Singles/doubles cost US$70/110.

Better is the smaller, modern (1991) *Hotel De Rome* (☎ 33 28 46), at Kaļķu iela 28, created with foreign businessfolk in mind. There's good service, direct-dial phones, fax machines, and mini bars in tasteful rooms. The price of this hotel's comforts is US$136/174. The *Hotel Metropole* at

Aspazijas bulvāris 36, a centre of diplomatic intrigue and espionage in the 1930s, was due to reopen in 1992 after renovation by a Swedish company as probably the best hotel in Baltic states.

Places to Eat

The large central market on Nēgu iela behind the bus station has plenty of fresh food.

Restaurants The *Sena Rīga* (Old Riga) at Aspazijas bulvāris 22 beside the Hotel De Rome will give you a decent meal for under US$1, not counting drinks, if you can get in without agents, bribes or 'foreigners' prices', which might multiply your costs several times. It's easier to get in at lunch time than in the evening. We enjoyed *Vistas Galas Kotletes Kurzeme*, a good chicken schnitzel with vegetables (US$0.55).

The German-run *Jever Bistro* at Kaļķu iela 6 in Old Riga serves German beer from 11 am to 3 am, and is crowded most of the time. It also does meals: fish main courses US$7.50 to US$11, steaks from US$13 to US$15. *Cafe Forums*, nearby in the court-yard at Kaļķu iela 24, is a shiny café-restaurant with waiter service and a young clientele and usually live music in the evenings. It's open from noon to 6 pm and 7 pm to midnight. Get there early in the evenings. Food includes salads (up to US$0.30), and meat and fish dishes around US$0.50. Portions aren't huge but it's decent fare.

Pūt Vējini (☎ 22 88 41) is a small, quiet upstairs restaurant, at Jauniela 1 near the Dom cathedral. It has quick service and good, well-priced food. The menu is incomprehensible, so ask the waiters' advice – we ended up with hors d'oeuvres followed by trout with a mushroom side dish. Most meals cost under US$1 a head not counting drinks. This place is popular, so reservations are advisable, try in person or by phone at lunch time to book for the same evening.

Across the road at Jauniela 25/29, the *Pie Kristapa* is equally busy, rowdier and more expensive. The food and the live pop music are both reasonable. *Kafejnica Magdalena* nearby on Smilšu iela does reasonable meals

including fish or chicken dishes from US$0.50 to US$0.70. The upstairs section is quieter than the ground floor.

Ēdnīca Pulvertornis on Vaļņu iela in the old city, open 7 am to 6 pm, can manage a better meal than most such basic cafeterias, for about US$0.25. Queue up and point to what you want. Offerings include meat and two veg, borsch with sausage, semolina and salads. The food is hotter and the queues shorter if you have an early lunch.

The *Restorāns* upstairs in the suburban half of the railway station, open from 11 am to 11 pm, serves perfectly respectable fare including beef stroganoff, mashed potato and beetroot for US$0.40. *Restorāns Selga* at Čaka iela 55, in the same building as the Hotel Viktorija, is a good fish restaurant. Booking is advisable.

Hotels The easy-to-walk-into *Hotel Latvija* offers the easiest pickings to non-residents. It has lots of snack bars plus the waitress-service Express Bar (through the lobby of the Zala Zale restaurant, then down a floor) where you can put together a snack meal for US$0.50 or so, and the Kafejnica Dzintars (through the Zala Zale itself), with slightly better and dearer snacks. For a full meal you can either book into the Zala Zale (Green Hall), with its loud 'entertainment', or the Nacionala Zale, a Latvian-food restaurant, or the cloud-level Fireplace Restaurant.

You can put together lunch in the *Hotel Riga* 1st-floor snack bar for US$0.50, or breakfast in the *Hotel Tūrists* ground-floor cafeteria for even less.

The best hotel food of all is reportedly found on the 3rd floor of the Hotel Riga, converted by Swedes into a hotel-within-a-hotel called the *Eurolink*.

Cafés It's worth queueing to get into the *Kafe Balta Roze* on Meistaru iela near the corner of Kaļķu iela in Old Riga. This small upstairs café has good coffee and really tasty snacks which you can build into a lunch. If you arrive outside the door 15 minutes before it opens or reopens, you'll shorten your waiting time. Other atmospheric and popular places in Old Riga include the *Ridzene* at Skārņu iela 9 and the tiny *Peter Gailis* at Skārņu iela 21.

The *Anre* café at the corner of Aspazijas bulvāris and Audēju iela does excellent cakes and pastries. The stand-up *Sulas Coku*, on Elizabetes iela half a block south-east of the Hotel Latvija, doles out good cheap kokteili – varieties include plum *(plumju)*, apple *(abolu)* and grape *(vinogu)*.

Entertainment

Riga has a lively cultural life: two good what's-on poster sites are the square where Kaļķu iela meets Meistaru iela in Old Riga, and Basteja bulvāris opposite Torņa iela.

The Dom cathedral's acoustics, as well as its huge organ, are spectacular, and the frequent organ and other concerts there are well worth attending. The ticket office is opposite the west door. The Opera & Ballet Theatre at Aspazijas bulvāris 3 has a good reputation. The Latvia Philharmonia's concert hall at Amatu iela 6 is in a fine 1330 merchants' meeting hall; its Chamber Music Hall is at Kaļķu iela 11A.

Some discos are listed in *Riga Success Guide*; others, and rock concerts, are advertised on posters around town. Several restaurants have live music and dancing: the jazz trio we heard in the Cafe Forums on our last visit was well worth the price of the meal.

Riga stages quite a variety of festivals, especially in summer, from classical music or theatre to jazz or rock, and there are numerous art galleries, listed in *Riga This Week* and *Riga Success Guide*.

Casino Riga at Kaļķu iela 24 is open daily from 4 pm to 4 am, with admission costing US$3 including one free drink, drinks half-price from 7 to 8 pm. Admission for women is free on Mondays and Wednesdays. There's also a casino in the Hotel Riga.

Things to Buy

Undoubtedly the best of Riga's many craft and souvenir shops in our experience is MF Salons on Brīvības iela, half a block past the Hotel Latvija. Somehow much of the best Latvian craft work has found its way into this one shop. It includes unique ceramics, paintings, prints, leatherwork, and long chunky amber necklaces for around US$35 to US$50. Hours are Monday to Friday from 10 am to 2 pm and 3 to 7 pm. There are also reportedly some good buys at the crafts fairs at the Ethnography Museum.

Centrālais Universālveikals, near the Hotel Riga on the corner of Vaļņu iela and Audēju iela, is the main department store.

Getting There & Away

Riga is spelt Riia in Estonia and Ryga in Lithuania.

Air Flights in and out of Riga are covered in the Latvia Getting There & Away section. Airline offices in Riga include:

Finnair
    Airport (☎ 20 70 10)
Hamburg Airlines
    Mārstaļu iela 12, a/k 541 (☎ 22 76 38)
Latvian Airlines & other ex-Soviet states' airlines
    Raiņa bulvāris 11 (☎ 22 33 05, 22 98 08, 20 76 61)
Lufthansa
    Airport (☎ 20 71 83)
SAS
    Airport (☎ 20 70 55)

Bus Buses to/from other towns and cities use Riga's main bus station *(autoosta)* at Prāgas iela 1, behind the railway embankment just beyond the south edge of the old city. The staff at the information office *(izziņu birojs)* here don't speak English but are much more communicative than the ticket clerks.

Information on buses to/from other countries is given in Latvia, Getting There & Away. Domestic services include to:

Bauska – 65 km, 1½ hours, 14 buses daily, US$0.25
Cēsis – 90 km, two hours, 10 buses daily, US$0.35
Daugavpils – 230 km, four hours, three buses daily, US$1
Jelgava – 40 km, one hour, 14 buses daily, US$0.15 (microbus US$0.25)
Liepāja – 220 km, four hours, five buses daily, US$0.90
Rēzekne – 245 km, 4½ hours, two buses daily, US$1.20
Sigulda – 55 km, one hour, four buses daily, US$0.20

Ventspils – 200 km, four hours, several buses daily, US$0.70

Train Riga station on Stacijas laukums is divided into two parts: one for long-distance trains and one for 'suburban' trains which may go as far as Jelgava or Cēsis. Timetables are clearly displayed and your only problem may be finding the right window to buy your ticket at. Those marked *Bilešu noformiēšana vilciena atiešanas dienā* are for same-day trips only. If you're having problems, try asking at window 36 in the suburban section; the staff there seem used to handling foreigners.

Suburban A huge wall chart shows the stations on each line and the fare zones they fall into. Līgatne for instance is on the Sigulda-Cēsis-Valmiera line, in zone seven, which at the time of writing costs US$0.05 one way. The suburban lines are :

Ķemeri-Tukums Line – about one train an hour to each of Ķemeri, Sloka and Tukums II, 4 am to midnight, all calling at Majori

Jelgava Line – one or two trains an hour, from 5.30 am to 12.30 am

Ogre-Krustpils Line – eight trains to Ogre from 4.40 to 9.05 am, six trains from 2.20 to 6.25 pm; a few to Aizkraukle, Lielvārde or Krustpils

Sigulda-Cēsis-Valmiera Line – 11 trains daily to Sigulda or beyond

Saulkrasti-Aloja Line – one to three trains an hour to different destinations from 4.50 am to 9.20 pm

Long-Distance Trains go from Riga to Liepāja three times daily, taking from 4½ to 5½ hours; Ventspils twice daily, 4½ hours; Daugavpils twice daily, 3½ hours; Rēzekne once daily, 4½ hours. Information on international trains is given in Latvia, Getting There & Away.

Car & Motorbike The Finnish company Neste runs two 24-hour petrol stations, with 99-octane and unleaded petrol, in Riga: Latvian Traffic Service at Pērnavas iela 78 near the corner of Vagonu iela (two km east of the railway station) and Traffic Service Jugla at Brīvības gatve 386 (the Sigulda and Pskov road) eight km east of the centre. The

workshop at the Motor Museum (☎ 55 27 77) can do Volkswagen and Audi repairs; the garage at Vogonu iela 35 in the eastern suburb Berġi can handle Volvos.

Rental One car hire outfit is Lat Inter Auto (☎ 38 30 42, fax 38 39 39) at Uriekstes iela 3. Another, in the Hotel Latvija (☎ 21 25 05), rents VW Passats and Ford Transits.

Boat See Latvia, Getting There & Away for sailings from Sweden, Germany and Finland. Riga's sea passenger port is at Eksporta iela 1 which is 1.5 km north of the October Bridge.

Getting Around

To/From the Airport Riga Airport (Lidosta Rīga) is at Skulte, 14 km west of the city centre. Bus No 22 runs there about every 20 minutes from Arhitektu iela off Raiņa bulvāris next to the university building. A metered taxi between the airport and the city centre costs around US$0.60.

City Transport The *Riga City Map* shows the routes of buses, trolley buses and trams. All use the usual ticket-punching system. One kiosk selling tickets (for less than US$0.01 at the time of writing) is in the middle of Brīvības bulvāris at the Raiņa bulvāris junction.

JŪRMALA

Jūrmala (Seashore) is the combined name for a string of small towns and resorts stretching 20 km along the coast west of Riga. It's an easy, enjoyable day trip from the city, or possibly a fresh-air base for day trips *to* the city. Jūrmala's long sandy beaches are backed by dunes and pine woods, its shady streets lined with low-rise wooden houses. Holiday-makers have been coming here since the 19th century, but at the time of writing the Baltic waters are so polluted that swimming has been stopped. One study reported a four-metre layer of pollutants on parts of the bed of the Gulf of Riga. Nevertheless, a relaxed holiday atmosphere

LATVIA

remains and the land environment is pleasant.

Orientation & Information

Jūrmala lies between the coast, which faces north, and the Lielupe river which runs parallel to it, a km or so inland, for over 20 km. The Jūrmala townships are, from the east (Riga) end: Lielupe, Bulduri, Dzintari, Majori, Dubulti, Jaundubulti, Pumpuri, Melluži (on the coast) and Valteri (two km inland), Asari, Vaivari, Kauguri (on the coast) and Sloka (two km inland), and Jaunķemeri (on the coast) and Ķemeri (six km inland). All except Valteri, Kauguri and Jaunķemeri have railway stations. The hub is the four or five km between Bulduri and Dubulti, centred on Majori and Dzintari.

Majori's main street is pedestrians-only Jomas iela, across the road from Majori station, then to the right. Streets and paths lead through the woods to the beach.

Jūrmala has the Riga telephone area code. You drop the initial bracketed digit if dialling from within Jūrmala.

Things to See

To walk the beach, the dunes, and the woods is reason enough to come to Jūrmala. The highest dunes are at Lielupe. In Majori, at Pliekšāna iela 7 between Jomas iela and the beach, the poet **Jānis Rainis' country cottage**, where he died in 1929, is now a museum. There's an **art exhibition hall** (izstāžu zāle) at Turaidas iela 11, opposite the east end of Jomas iela. The **Latvia Philharmonia's Dzintari Concert Hall** (Koncertzāle), functioning from June to August, is at the beach end of Turaidas iela. Many sanatoria are in the quiet streets behind the beach from Majori to Bulduri.

Places to Stay

In Soviet times, many of Jūrmala's visitors came to sanatoria and holiday homes (*pansionaty*) run by their trade unions, factories and so on. The 1988 Russian-language tourist map *Yurmala Turistskaya Skhema*

shows hosts of such places, some of which are likely to be opened up to a wider range of visitors.

There's a camp site at Vaivari and up to 1988 at least there were two others: the *Melluž i* near the Lielupe river at Slokas iela 113/115, Valteri, and the *Pumpuri* near the beach at Upes iela 2, Pumpuri.

The *Hotel Jūrmala* (☎ 22-(7)6 42 76) at Jomas iela 47-49 has decent single/double rooms with private shower and toilet for just US$4.20/5.80, though management said prices would rise in the peak summer season. The hotel has a casino and also a branch (☎ 22-(6)5 11 57) at Viļņu iela 3, Lielupe. Other hotels (some open in summer only) include the *Majori* (☎ 22-(7)6 13 80) at Jomas iela 29, Majori; the *Pumpuri* (☎ 22-(7)6 75 54) at Upes iela 2, Pumpuri; and the *Vaivari* (☎ 22-(6)3 63 92) at Atbalss iela 1, Vaivari.

In 1992 the travel agency TAS (see Facts for the Visitor, Accommodation) was offering five-bed Jūrmala cottages for US$200 a night, but it may well be possible to find cheaper such places locally.

Places to Eat

The *Orients Restorāns* at Jomas iela 86 in Majori is good and popular, so try to make a reservation for an evening meal in summer. A table full of zakuski – tasty salads, cold meats, smoked fish – followed by a hot shashlyk (kebabs) or fish dish with vegetables, plus a couple of brandies, will set you back about US$4.50. The *Jūrmala* restaurant in the Hotel Jūrmala is another of the better places in Majori. Several cafés are dotted along Jomas iela and Turaidas iela and in the woods behind the beach.

The *Juras Perle (Sea Pearl)*, by the beach at Bulduri, is another top restaurant. In the evenings you may have to pay extra for a floor show with scantily clad performers. Again, a booking is helpful. From Bulduri station, walk back beside the railway in the Riga direction to the level crossing, then go left towards the sea along Vienības prospekts.

Getting There & Away

About three trains an hour run from Riga to Jūrmala along the Ķemeri-Tukums line, but they don't all stop at every station. From Riga to Majori costs US$0.03 for a journey of about 40 minutes.

In summer there are also hydrofoils from Riga to Majori (one hour, about US$0.20 – see Riga, River Trips). Some stop at Lielupe en route. In Majori the jetty is just downstream from the railway station.

Getting Around

Bus No 4 from Dubulti station to Sloka runs closer to the coast than the railway does.

KURZEME

Kurzeme is known in English as Courland and in German as Kurland. **Kuldīga**, 165 km west of Riga on the Venta river, has an Old Town with numerous 16th to 18th century buildings, often used as a movie location, and some picturesque waterfalls. It was briefly, from 1561 to 1573, the first capital of the Duchy of Courland. The *Hotel Kursa* (☎ 233-2 24 30) is at Pilsetas laukums 6.

Talsi, 50 km north-east of Kuldīga in an area of lakes and small hills, has several **medieval buildings** and a regional **museum** at Rožu iela 7. There's a hotel (☎ 232-2 26 89) at Kareivju iela 16. Between Talsi and the northern tip of Kurzeme, **Cape Kolka**, where there are remains of an old **lighthouse**, is a 13th century castle at **Dundaga**. At **Vidale**, the road north-east from Dundaga descends the Slītere precipice, a 35-metre cliff which is 15 km long.

On the Gulf of Riga coast there are a number of small fishing villages between **Mērsrags** and Jūrmala. On the Baltic coast, **Liepāja** (population 115,000) is Latvia's second port and has an annual pop and rock festival in August. **Ventspils** further south suffers bad industrial pollution.

JELGAVA

Jelgava (population 75,000), 42 km southwest of Riga, is the biggest town in Zemgale. It was once the capital of the dukes of Courland – one of whom, Duke Jacob (1642-82), had his own navy, counted Tobago and The Gambia among his possessions and laid plans to colonise Australia. The dukes' 18th century riverside palace beside the Riga road in the north-east of town has the unmistakable Baroque touch of Bartolomeo Rastrelli, architect of many of St Petersburg's most magnificent buildings including the Winter Palace. It has been rebuilt twice after destruction in 1919 and in WW II and is now a college.

RUNDĀLE & BAUSKA

The lovely palace at Rundāle, 65 km south of Riga, was another Rastrelli creation for the dukes of Courland. Rundāle is 11 km west of Bauska, which is on the Vilnius road near the Lithuanian border and served by buses from Riga. The palace and its park are open from 11 am to 6 pm Wednesday to Sunday. The palace has been restored to house a museum of 17th and 18th century art and furniture. Bauska has an old town and a big 15th century knightly castle, both under restoration.

Places to Stay

On the highway just north of Iecava, a little more than half-way from Riga to Bauska, is the reportedly comfortable and expensive *Brentis* motel. There's a hotel (☎ 2 47 05), with an excursion bureau (☎ 2 29 07), at Slimnīcas iela 7 in Bauska.

SALASPILS

Somewhere between 55,000 and 87,000 Jews, including nearly all Riga's 45,000 Jewish population, and thousands of other people were murdered in this Nazi death camp 18 km south-east of Riga. Gaunt, giant sculptures stand as a memorial, and there's also a museum here. From Riga, take a train on the Ogre-Krustpils line to Dārziņi. A path leads from the station to the memorial (Latvian: *piemineklis*, Russian: *pamyatnik*).

SIGULDA & GAUJA NATIONAL PARK

One of the best trips from Riga is to Sigulda (formerly Segewold), 50 km east on the southern lip of the picturesque wooded Gauja valley. In 1207 this area was divided between the Knights of the Sword, who got the land south of the Gauja river, and the Archbishop of Riga, who got the land north of the river. The valley sides are dotted with caves and castles. At Sigulda you can cross the valley by cable car or road bridge.

Descending the escarpment between Sigulda and the river you enter the 920-sq-km Gauja National Park (Gaujas Nacionālais Parks), which stretches either side of the Gauja valley up to beyond Cēsis. There are several camp sites in the park.

Sigulda & Around

Bits of the knights' 1207 **Sigulda Castle**, among woods on the north-east edge of Sigulda, have survived the numerous wars to which the area has been subject. The evocative ruins are approached by a bridge across the now overgrown moat. Nearby stands a

former residence of the Russian prince Kropotkin, known as the **New Castle**, now a cardiovascular sanatorium.

A good circular walk on this south side of the valley is to the **Satezele Castle Mound**, a refuge of the Finno-Ugrian Liv tribes who lived here before the knights came, the **Pētera Cave**, and panoramic **Gleznotāju Kalns** (Artists' Hill). On the north side of the valley, a track leads up from near the bridge to the ruined **Krimulda Castle** (1255-73), once a guesthouse for visiting dignitaries. In the bottom of the valley, the **Gūtmaņa Cave** is covered with graffiti going back to the 16th century – including the coats of arms of long-gone hunters. The water of the stream flowing out of the cave is supposed to remove facial wrinkles.

The bishops' **Turaida Castle** on the northern lip of the valley was founded in 1214 but blown up by a lightning strike in the 18th century. What we see today is mostly the

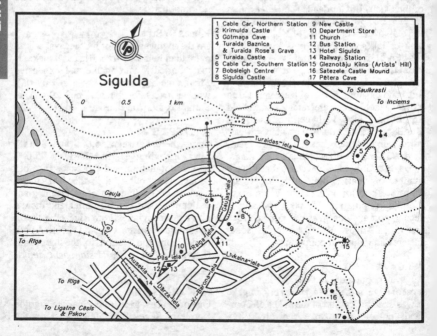

1 Cable Car, Northern Station
2 Krimulda Castle
3 Gūtmaņa Cave
4 Turaida Baznīca
  & Turaida Rose's Grave
5 Turaida Castle
6 Cable Car, Southern Station
7 Bobsleigh Centre
8 Sigulda Castle
9 New Castle
10 Department Store
11 Church
12 Bus Station
13 Hotel Sigulda
14 Railway Station
15 Gleznotāju Kalns (Artists' Hill)
16 Satezele Castle Mound
17 Pētera Cave

Sigulda

0   0.5   1 km

To Saulkrasti
To Inciems

Turaidas-iela

Gauja

Gaujas-iela

To Riga

Pils-iela

Raiņa-iela

Livkalna-iela

Kr-Barona-iela

Darza-iela

Ausekļa-iela

To Riga

To Ligatne Cēsis & Pskov

result of recent rebuilding. It's open daily from 10 am to 5 pm. There's a museum, and good views from the 42-metre tower. Near the small **Turaidas Baznica** church on the path from the car park, two lime trees shade the grave of 'Turaida Rose' – a legendary local beauty who met an untimely death in the Gūtmaņa Cave, after events which tour guides relate at great length.

Līgatne & Cēsis
At the **Līgatne Recreation & Research Park** (just south of the river 15 km north-east of Sigulda but eight km north of the town of Līgatne on the railway to Cēsis) are elk, deer, boar and bison in open-air enclosures, and nature trails.

Cēsis (formerly Wenden), 38 km north-east of Sigulda, was once the headquarters of the Knights of the Sword and a member of the Hanseatic League. It has been destroyed and rebuilt several times over the centuries. Part of the old town, with narrow streets, is preserved. Some of the castle stands in its own park, open from 10 am to 5 pm daily except Mondays. The regional history and arts museum is at Pils iela 9. The *Hotel*

Tērvete (☎ 2 23 92) is at Vienības laukums 1.

On an island in **Āraišu Ezers** (Āraiši lake), seven km south of Līgatne, you can visit a 9th century dwelling under excavation. Further south-east is the **Vidzeme upland**, the highest part of Latvia.

Getting There & Away
Trains and buses run from Riga to Sigulda, Līgatne town, Āraiši (two km from the lake) and Cēsis. Trains are probably more convenient for getting to Sigulda and Līgatne, buses for Cēsis.

LATGALE
Daugavpils, with only 10% to 15% of Latvians in its 128,000 population, is Latvia's second biggest city owing to industrial development since WW II. Some of the best scenery in the Latgale lake region is around **Rēznas Ezers** (Rēzna Lake) and **Ezernieki**. The church at **Aglona** is a Roman Catholic centre and big crowds descend on it for the festival of the Assumption on 15 August. There are hotels in Krāslava, Rēzekne and Ludza.

Lithuania

The southernmost Baltic state is in many ways the most vibrant, as it showed the world by its daring, emotional drive for independence. Lithuania (Lietuva) owes much to the rich cultural currents of Central Europe: with neighbouring Poland it once shared an empire stretching nearly to the Black Sea, and still shares the Roman Catholicism which sets it apart from its Baltic neighbours.

Vilnius, the historic, lively capital, is the obvious base for visitors. But Lithuania has other sizeable cities such as Kaunas, briefly its capital this century, and the seaport Klaipėda, formerly the German town Memel. Other intriguing places include the Neringa sandspit on the coast, the strange Hill of Crosses near Šiauliai, and the forests and castles of the south.

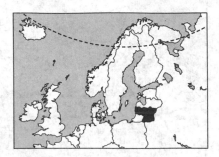

Facts about the Country

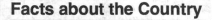

HISTORY
Beginnings
By the 10th century AD the south-east Baltic was occupied by three related groups of tribes: the Lettish in present-day Latvia, the Prussians in the present Kaliningrad region of Russia and modern north-east Poland, the Lithuanians in between.

German Invasion & Lithuanian Expansion
In the 1220s the German crusading Teutonic order was invited into Mazovia in northern Poland to protect it against the marauding Prussians. By 1290 the order had exterminated most of the Prussians, settling Germans in their place, and ruled the eastern Baltic from around modern Gdańsk to southern Estonia. But the Lithuanians, protected by forests, restricted them to a coastal strip.

Gediminas, leader of a united Lithuania from 1316 to 1341, profited from the decline of the early Russian state based in Kiev to push Lithuania's borders south and east, but found his own willingness to accept Christianity opposed by pagan kin. After his death his son Algirdas, based in Vilnius, pushed the borders past Kiev, while another son Kestutis, at Trakai, fought off the Teutonic Knights.

Union With Poland
In 1386 Algirdas' son and successor Jogaila married Jadwiga, Queen of Poland, becoming Wladyslaw II of Poland and a Christian, forging an alliance against the knights and initiating a 400-year bond between the two states. Together they won control of a huge swath of land from the Baltic Sea to the Black Sea by the turn of the 16th century. But Lithuania ended up the junior partner, its gentry adopting Polish culture and language, its peasants becoming serfs.

In 1410 Jogaila and Kestutis' son Vytautas, who governed Lithuania, decisively defeated the Teutonic order at the battle of Grünwald (also called Tannenberg or Žalgiris) in modern Poland. Kazimieras IV of Poland (1447-92), also Grand Duke of Lithuania, reduced the knights' realm to a small area, itself under ultimate Polish control. The Reformation sent a wave of Protestantism across Lithuania and Poland but it petered out by the 1570s and the

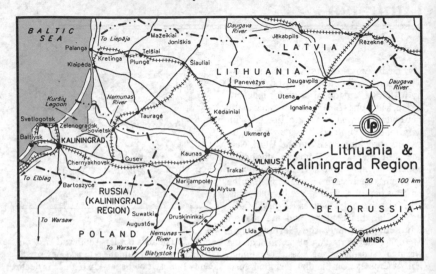

Lithuania & Kalfrom Region

country remains predominantly Catholic to this day.

Russian Control

Polish and Lithuanian forces briefly took Moscow in 1610 but in 1654 Russia invaded in return and took significant territory. In the 18th century divisions in the Polish-Lithuanian state, with factions calling in Russian help from time to time, so weakened it that it finally vanished from the map when Russia, Austria and Prussia (successor to the Teutonic order) carved it up in the Partitions of Poland (1772, 1793 and 1795-96). Most of Lithuania went to Russia.

In the 19th century, while Vilnius became a bastion of Polish culture and a focus of uprisings against Russian rule, there was a growth of Lithuanian national consciousness in the countryside, encouraged by the abolition of serfdom in 1861.

Independence

With the collapse of the old order in eastern Europe in 1917-18, Lithuanian nationalists declared independence on 16 February 1918 and managed to fend off an attempted Soviet

takeover in the next two years. Independent Lithuania's capital was Kaunas, since it had been Polish troops who took Vilnius from the Red Army in 1919. Vilnius was a constant source of inter-war Lithuanian-Polish tension.

The new democracies in the war-damaged Baltic states couldn't withstand the world slump and the rise of fascism. Lithuania suffered a military coup in 1926 and from 1929 was ruled along similar lines to Mussolini's Italy.

Soviet Rule & WW II

In 1940, following the Molotov-Ribbentrop Pact and subsequent events (see Estonia, History) Lithuania found itself part of the USSR. Within a year around 40,000 Lithuanians were killed or deported. A further 150,000 to 300,000-plus, mostly Jews, died in concentration camps and ghettos during the 1941-44 Nazi occupation. Lithuania had had a Jewish population of around 300,000.

Between 1945 and 1952, with Soviet control re-established, an estimated 200,000-plus people were killed or deported. The Lithuanian forests were the centre of armed resistance to Soviet rule, which may have involved tens of thousands but was crushed by 1952.

New Independence

In the late 1980s Lithuania came to lead the Baltic push for independence after candidates supporting its popular front, Sajūdis, won 30 seats in the March 1989 elections for the USSR Congress of People's Deputies. In December 1989 Lithuania was the first Soviet republic to legalise non-communist parties. Mikhail Gorbachov visited Vilnius in January 1990 but could do nothing to dissuade Lithuania from its clear independence course. In February Sajūdis was elected to form a majority in Lithuania's new supreme soviet, now 'parliament', which on 11 March declared Lithuania independent and stated that its 1918 constitution had never lost its validity.

Moscow shunted troop convoys around Vilnius and cut off Lithuania's fuel supplies. The heat was finally taken off after 2½ months, when Lithuania's music-professor-turned-president, the Sajūdis leader Vytautas Landsbergis, agreed to a 100-day moratorium on the 11 March declaration in exchange for independence talks with the USSR's government.

The independence momentum flagged as the Baltic republics' economic reliance on the USSR became clear and Lithuania's talks with Moscow bogged down. Then in January 1991 Soviet troops and paramilitary police stormed key buildings in Vilnius, apparently to pave the way for a communist coup and Soviet crackdown. Thirteen people were killed in the storming of the Vilnius TV tower and many more hurt. Lithuanians barricaded their parliament, the violence drew heavy condemnation from the West, and the threat subsided.

Lithuania and the other Baltic states were finally brought real independence by the failed coup in Moscow in August 1991, which resulted in Western and then, on 6 September, Soviet recognition of Lithuanian independence.

GEOGRAPHY

Lithuania, covering an area of 65,200 sq km, is the biggest of the three Baltic states. Retreating glaciers formed a rolling landscape with higher areas in the north-west (the Žemaičių upland), across the south-east (the Baltic highlands), and in the east (stretches of the Lithuanian-Belorussian uplands including the country's highest hill, 294-metre Juozapinės). The central lowland, a north-south band up to 100 km wide, is the most fertile region. Forest (38% pine, 21% spruce, 21% birch) covers a little over a quarter of the country as a whole, but about half of the south.

Half Lithuania's short coastline is on Neringa, a spit stretching 90 km north from near Kaliningrad with high dunes and pine forests. The Nemunas river, which drains most of Lithuania, flows into the semi-salt Kuršių Lagoon behind the spit. Inland Lithuania is dotted with over 4000 mostly shallow lakes.

GOVERNMENT

Lithuania's legislature is the Supreme Council (formerly Supreme Soviet) or parliament. Its chairman (Vytautas Landsbergis since 1990) is also the country's president. Parliament is responsible for the constitution and elections, and appoints the prime minister (Kazimiera Prunskienė 1990-91, then Gediminas Vagnorius) and other members of the executive government, who are accountable to it.

Parliament became paralysed in mid-1992 when the right-of-centre Sajūdis block supporting Landsbergis and Vagnorius lost its majority and decided to boycott proceedings, rendering parliament inquorate, as it pressed for new elections.

ECONOMY

By mid-1992 Lithuania was experiencing the same economic scenario as the other Baltic states: unprecedented opportunities for some and more in the shops for those who could afford it; but an overall picture of inflation, shortages, unemployment, poor technology and products, and frightening

LITHUANIA

dependence on trade with Russia. The average monthly wage in spring 1992 was US$22. Lithuania planned to introduce its own currency, the litas, to replace the rouble during 1992.

Like Latvia and Estonia, Lithuania was industrialised after WW II. Nearly a quarter of the Lithuanian workforce was engaged in agriculture which was collectivised between 1949 and 1952 and is now being returned to private ownership. There's an emphasis on dairy products, meat and cereals. The major industries are machine building, metalworking and food processing. Lithuania reputedly had one of only two toilet paper factories in the Soviet Union, which should give it a major export market now!

POPULATION & PEOPLE

Lithuania's population in 1989 was 3.68 million, easily the biggest of the three Baltic states. Lithuanians form 80% of the population (a far higher proportion than Latvians in Latvia or Estonians in Estonia) which seems to give rise to greater ethnic harmony. There are reckoned to be over a million Lithuanians in other countries, mainly the USA.

The main minority groups in Lithuania are Russians (345,000) and Poles (260,000). Nearly all the Poles live in the two south-eastern districts of Vilnius and Šalčininkai. A further 220,000 Poles left Lithuania for Poland between 1945 and 1958.

LANGUAGE

Lithuanians speak Lithuanian, one of only two surviving languages of the Baltic branch of the Indo-European language family (the other is Latvian). See the Estonia Language section for information on the use of English, Russian and other languages in the Baltic states. Here are some sounds specific to Lithuanian:

ą	is pronounced like the 'a' in 'father'
ę	like the 'ai' in 'air'
į & y	like the 'ea' in 'heat'
ų &ū	like the 'oo' in 'boot'
ė & ei	like the 'a' in 'late'
o	like the 'o' in 'home'

ai	like 'i' in 'high'
ie	like the 'ea' in 'hear'
ui	like 'wi' in 'win'
č	as 'ch'
š	as 'sh'
ž	as the 's' in 'pleasure'
j	as the 'y' in 'yes'
r	trilled

Lithuania	*Lietuva*
Hello.	*Labas.*
Goodbye.	*Viso gero.*
Excuse me.	*Atsiprašau.*
Thank you.	*Ačiū.*
Please.	*Prašau.*
Yes.	*Taip.*
No.	*Ne.*
Where?	*Kur?*
Do you speak English?	*Ar kalbate angliškai?*
How much?	*Kiek?*

one, two	*vienas, du*
three, four	*trys, keturi*
cheap, expensive	*pigus, brangus*
hotel	*viešbutis*
airport	*aerouostas*
railway station	*gelež inkelio stotis*
bus, bus station	*autobus, autobusų stotis*
street, lane	*gatvė, skersgatvis*
square, avenue	*aikštė, prospektas*

Facts for the Visitor

VISAS & EMBASSIES
Visas

The only certainty about Lithuania's visa rules is that you should double-check the situation well before your trip. At the time of writing, visitors to Lithuania (except UK passport holders and citizens of former parts of the USSR) need a visa. Lithuanian visas (normally single-entry, valid for 10 or 14 days) are usually issued at Lithuanian missions in some countries, or on arrival at Vilnius airport. Transit visas obtained at embassies or borders are free, single-entry visas cost US$15 at an embassy and US$25 at a border, and multiple-entry visas from embassies cost US$15. The UK has a reciprocal arrangement with Lithuania, allowing each other's passport holders entry without visa.

For nationalities that do need visas, Lithuania is, at the time of writing, in one of its diplomats' words, 'trying to introduce an invitation system'. This seems to mean that visa applicants should preferably have an invitation from someone in Lithuania, but that if they don't it may not matter. A letter from an organisation in your country explaining the nature of the visit would 'help', the diplomat told us, adding unhelpfully, 'We are trying to find out where people are travelling'. It all sounds like the Soviet system Lithuania has just taken such pains to escape from. The other requirements are a photo, a completed application form, and a fee usually around US$15.

Lithuania has a 'common visa space' with Estonia and Latvia. When established in 1992 this meant that a visa for any of the three states was also good for two days in each of the other two. This time limit may be extended in the future and may not be rigidly enforced in any case.

Poland & Belorussian Visas Many travellers reach Lithuania through Poland and/or Belorussia (formerly the Soviet republic of Belorussia) though Belorussia might be avoided if a promised direct Poland-Lithuania rail link materialises.

Some nationalities need visas for Poland. There's a cheap transit-visa option for travellers staying less than 48 hours in Poland who have an onward visa. The Belorussian visa situation is, if that's possible, even less clear than Lithuania's. Ask everybody you can think of. The *Baltic Independent* reported a section of the Lithuanian foreign ministry as saying that a Lithuanian visa will get you across Belorussia, but some train travellers through Belorussia report being asked to show Belorussian or CIS visas. Some say these will be issued at borders for about US$25: to get one in advance it's best to have a travel agent's help but if you don't, start at your local ex-Soviet embassy, applying as early as you can.

Lithuanian Embassies
Lithuania is still establishing missions in other countries. Some listed here may move. Missions are often open for limited hours so give yourself plenty of time to make contact. At the time of writing they include:

Australia
    Honorary Consul, 26 Jalanga Crescent, Aranda, ACT 2614 (☎ 06 253 2062)
Canada
    Honorary Consul, 235 Yorkland Boulevard, Willowdale, Ontario M2J 4Y6 (☎ 416-494 4099)
Denmark
    Embassy, Det Baltiske Informationskontor, HC Andersens Boulevard 38, 1553 Copenhagen V (☎ 33 93 48 17)
Estonia
    Representative, Vabaduse väljak 10, 200001 Tallinn (☎ 66 66 34, 44 89 17)
France
    Ambassador, 14 Boulevard Montmartre, Paris 75 009 (☎ 48.01.00.33)
Germany
    Embassy, Bertha-von-Suttner-Platz 1-7, 5300 Bonn 1 (☎ 0228-65 82 76)
Latvia
    Embassy, Elizabetes iela 2 (☎ 32 15 19, 32 09 48)
Norway
    Honorary Consul, Stranden 3, Aker Brygge, 0250 Oslo 2 (☎ 22 83 35 10)
Poland
    Embassy, aleje Ujazdowskie 13-12, Warsaw (☎ 62 3194, 694 2487)
Russia
    Embassy, ulitsa Pisemskogo 10, Moscow 121069 (☎ 291 26 43)
Sweden
    Embassy, Sturegatan 29, 11436 Stockholm (☎ 613 0040)
UK
    Embassy, 17 Essex Villas, London W8 7BP (☎ 071-938 2481)
USA
    Embassy, 2622 16th St NW, Washington DC 20009 (☎ 202-234 5860)

Foreign Embassies in Lithuania
These too are in their infancy at the time of writing. Some of the following embassies in Vilnius will undoubtedly change:

Canada
   Hotel Draugyste, Čiurlionio gatvė 24
   (☎ 66 17 31)
Denmark
   Kosciuškos gatvė 36 (☎ 62 80 28)
Estonia
   Turniškių gatvė 14 (☎ 76 48 96, 76 98 48)
Finland
   Hotel Draugyste, Čiurlionio gatvė 24
   (☎ 66 16 35)
France
   Daukanto aikštė 3/8 (☎ 22 29 79)
Germany
   Hotel Draugyste, Čiurlionio gatvė 24
   (☎ 66 16 27)
   Consular Section, Sierakausko gatvė 24/8
   (☎ 66 01 88)
Latvia
   Turniškių gatvė 19 (☎ 77 85 32)
Norway
   Hotel Draugyste, Čiurlionio gatvė 24
   (☎ 66 17 95)
Poland
   Aušros Vartų gatvė 7 (☎ 22 44 44)
Sweden
   Jogailos gatvė 10 (☎ 22 64 67)
UK
   Antakalnio gatvė 2 (☎ 22 20 70)
USA
   Akmenų gatvė 6 (☎ 22 30 31,
   consular section 65 08 28)

DOCUMENTS & CUSTOMS

See the Estonia Documents & Customs
section for information on customs declarations throughout the Baltic states.

Lithuania limits amber exports but a few
necklaces as souvenirs or gifts should be OK.
You're supposed to get a Culture Ministry
permit, and pay duty, to export artworks of
special worth – the procedure takes a few
days.

MONEY

Currency & Prices

Lithuania planned to introduce its own currency, the litas, in 1992. This will be simpler
than the previous combination of Soviet
roubles (at R334 = US$1 in late 1992, with
a small, risky black market giving R370) and
foreign 'hard' currencies with, additionally,
special high 'foreigners' prices' for some
purchases.

Prices in this chapter have been converted

into US dollars. Those that were originally
in roubles, which means most of those that
look like bargains, may rise spectacularly.

Cash, Travellers' Cheques or Credit Cards?

At the time of writing you can change foreign
cash or traveller's cheques at main branches
of the Bank of Lithuania (Lietuvos Bankos)
including in Vilnius, Kaunas and Klaipėda,
and in some other banks and major tourist
hotels. Cash US dollars are the easiest currency to change, but you can take some of
your money in travellers' cheques as a safeguard. Banks tend to charge 4% or 5%
commission for immediate encashment of
travellers' cheques. Other European currencies like Deutschmarks or pounds sterling
would be a second choice. Only a few expensive hotels, restaurants, shops etc take credit
cards, but the list will grow. Visa,
MasterCard, Diners Club and American
Express all crop up.

CLIMATE & WHEN TO GO

Lithuania's climate is similar to Latvia's with
the warmest period, late June to early
August, being also the wettest. Temperatures
at this time reach up to about 22°C but there
are days of persistent showers and some
thunderstorms. The months either side of this
period tend to be more comfortable. In
winter, temperatures may not rise above
freezing from mid-December to late February. Winter lasts about six weeks longer in
the inland east of the country than the coastal
west. Annual precipitation ranges from 540
mm in the central lowland to 930 mm in parts
of the Žemaičių upland. Winter is foggy.

SUGGESTED ITINERARY

An itinerary for one week could include:

Vilnius, Trakai, Kaunas or the coast, Hill of Crosses

TOURIST OFFICES

Possible tourist information sources include
Lithuanian embassies and specialist travel
agents in other countries, and hotels and
travel agents in Lithuania.

BUSINESS HOURS & HOLIDAYS

Shop, office, café and restaurant hours are similar to Latvia and Estonia (see Estonia, Facts for the Visitor). Lithuania's national holidays are:

New Year's Day, 1 January
Day of Restoration of Lithuanian state (anniversary of 1918 independence declaration), 16 February
Easter
Mother's Day, 1st Sunday in May
State Holiday (commemoration of coronation of Grand Duke Mindaugas, 13th century), 6 July
National Day of Hope & Mourning, 1 November
Christmas Day, 25 December
Boxing Day, 26 December

CULTURAL EVENTS

The next Lithuanian Song Festival is due in summer 1995 (for background see Estonia, Facts for the Visitor). The Baltika international folklore festival, which has taken place annually in each Baltic state in turn since 1987, is due in Vilnius in mid-July 1993. This week of music, dance, exhibitions and parades focuses on folk traditions and is well worth catching if you're in the region. Many people wear picturesque traditional dress.

The southern town of Birštonas holds an international spring jazz festival around the end of March in even-numbered years. Other festivals of music, art, crafts and so on pop up, especially in Vilnius and Kaunas during summer.

POST & TELECOMMUNICATIONS
Post

Mail to the West takes from 10 days upwards. In 1992 it was estimated the Baltic states would need five years to develop a postal service of Western quality. Air-mail cards or letters weighing under 20 grams to other countries cost US$0.06. The Lithuanian for post office is *astas*.

Delivery times for mail to Lithuania are so unpredictable that it's hardly worth bothering to have mail sent to Lithuania unless you'll be staying a long time. Addresses have a postcode, usually six figures, with the town or city name.

Telephone

International The easiest way to make an international call is to get your hotel's desk staff to arrange the call for you. You'll probably have to spend an hour or two waiting in your room for the call to come through. Costs are US$0.20 a minute to Poland, US$0.25 to the rest of Europe, US$0.50 to the USA and US$0.60 to Australia, but check in advance that you won't be charged a 'foreigners' price'.

Alternatively you can make the call from a public telephone *(telefonas)* office in any town. At the main telephone office in Vilnius, estimated waiting time after you've given the number to the counter clerk is one hour. In Vilnius there's also an office where you can get international calls (for special prices) with only a few minutes' wait.

A third option is to book the call yourself from a private or hotel-room phone. The number for the international operator (who may take half an hour or more to reach and who might not speak English) is 07. By this method it's very hard to chase up calls that don't come through.

Local Calls within the city you're in can be made either from private or hotel-room phones (simply by dialling the number without any area code) or from public phone boxes where, at the time of writing, you need 15-kopeck coins despite the fact that they say it costs 2 kopecks.

Within Lithuania & the Former USSR Long-distance calls within Lithuania, Latvia, Estonia or anywhere else that used to be in the USSR are easiest with the help of hotel desk staff. From a private phone, you usually need to dial 8 and wait for a dial tone, before you dial the area code. Most calls cost about US$0.01 a minute. You can also make long-distance calls from telephone offices, identifiable by long motionless queues of glum people.

Area codes from Lithuanian phones include Vilnius 22, Druskininkai 233, Kaunas 27, Klaipėda 261, Palanga 236,

Šiauliai 214, Trakai 238, Riga 0132, Tallinn 0142, Moscow 095, St Petersburg 812.

Calls to Lithuania At the time of writing Lithuania still uses the old USSR country telephone code, 7. From outside the ex-USSR you precede this with your international access code (eg 010 in the UK), and follow it with 01, then the area code, then the number. So to reach Vilnius 45 36 27 from the UK, you dial 010 7 01 22 45 36 27. You're likely to have to dial several times before you get through.

When dialling Lithuania from the ex-USSR, including Latvia or Estonia, add 01 at the start of the area code, making the Vilnius code 0122, usually preceded by a long-distance access code, 8.

Fax, Telex & Telegraph
Fax is still in its infancy in Lithuania and only a few businesses and hotels have it. Telex is a more usual way of communicating. International telegrams (incoming or outbound) usually arrive the same or next day and can be sent from any telegraph (*telegrafas*) office which are often the same as post offices and cost, at the time of writing, US$0.04 a word to Western Europe, US$0.09 to North America.

TIME
See Estonia, Facts for the Visitor.

BOOKS & MAPS
See Estonia, Facts for the Visitor for some titles covering all three Baltic states. New, seemingly accurate, town and regional maps can be picked up for a few US cents in bookshops, hotels and kiosks.

MEDIA
The Vilnius-published *Lithuanian Weekly* is a weekly English-language newspaper on the lines of Tallinn's *Baltic Independent* and Riga's *Baltic Observer*, but slimmer and focused much more on its home country. All three papers are sold at news kiosks in Vilnius for the equivalent of a handful of US cents. In hotels you may pay more. *Vilnius*

In Your Pocket is a 64-page compendium of valuable information on similar lines to *Tallinn This Week*, and is updated five times a year.

The occasional Western newspaper (several days' old) turns up at the Neringa or Astorija hotels in Vilnius.

FILM & PHOTOGRAPHY
See Estonia, Facts for the Visitor.

HEALTH
See Estonia, Health for general comments on the three Baltic states. Drinking unboiled tap water is certainly not advisable in Vilnius judging by the smell it sometimes exudes. Swimming anywhere may be risky owing to pollution.

DANGERS & ANNOYANCES
See Estonia, Facts for the Visitor.

ACCOMMODATION
Accommodation can be heavily booked, especially in summer, and it's worth trying to book ahead particularly for the first night or two. If you don't, you'll probably find something but it may not be what you want. In smaller provincial places the few available options might occasionally be booked right out.

Camping
There are camp sites at holiday towns like Palanga and Druskininkai but collected information on them seems non-existent. Some sites apparently have small cabins as well as tent places. Those that do exist may be heavily booked in July and August. Town maps may help you locate sites. Motorists can try asking at farms etc, for permission to camp.

Hostels & Colleges
There are possibilities of staying in fairly cheap hostels or student accommodation in Vilnius and possibly Kaunas and on the coast. Check with youth hostel organisations in Estonia, Latvia, Scandinavian countries and Poland (PTSM, suite 423, 4th floor, ulica

Chocimska 28, Warsaw – near Lazienkowski Park) about hostel developments. The first backpackers' hostels sprang up in 1992, some initially uncertain whether they'd be summer-only or year-round.

Private Homes & Flats

At least one agent offers accommodation in private flats, see the Vilnius Places to Stay section. He may be able to fix you up in other places too, given a few days' notice. You can also organise homestays through organisations in the West. See Estonia, Facts for the Visitor and Tours in Lithuania, Getting There & Away for more details.

Hotels

The information on hotels in Estonia, Facts for the Visitor also applies to Lithuania. One travel agency that can get you into some of the better hotels at short notice is Lithuanian Tours (☎ 61 51 38, telex 261261 GERMA SU) of Šv Ignoto gatvė 10/32-8, Vilnius.

Other

Some tour groups, especially those coming from Germany, stay in sanatoria or holiday homes at coastal places like Klaipėda, Juodkrante or Nida. Most of these places were built for the rest and recreation of members of Soviet institutions like trade unions or factories. The best ones, which tend to be the ones booked for foreigners, are just as comfortable as hotels.

FOOD

See Estonia, Facts for the Visitor for general information on food and restaurants in the Baltic states.

Common Lithuanian starters include herring (silkė) and mushrooms (grybai), which may come together, also salads and sprats (šprotai). cold beet soup (šaltibarščiai) is also popular and traditionally comes with boiled potatoes. Dairy products like cottage cheese (varške) and sour milk (rūgusis pienas), and potatoes (possibly in pancake form or as kugelis, a potato pudding) are among the mainstays of the ordinary diet, though meat and other vegeta-

bles are standard in restaurants. Another standby is virtinukai, small ravioli-style dumplings stuffed with cheese, mushrooms or meat.

English	Lithuanian
bread	duona
salad	salatos, mišrainė
soup	sriuba
fish	uvis
meat or main dishes	mėsos patiekalai
national dishes	nacionaliniai patiekalai
vegetables	daržovės
fruit	vaisiai

DRINKS

See Estonia, Facts for the Visitor for some general comments on drinks in the Baltic states. Beer is alus in Lithuanian. Lithuanians also drink mead (midus), and gira, made from fermented grains or fruit.

Take care with tap water, see the Health section. Tea in Lithuanian is arbata, coffee kava, mineral water mineralinis vanduo.

THINGS TO BUY

You can buy amber jewellery in Latvia, Russia, and elsewhere but the main sources of this light, translucent, fossilised tree resin are the coast of Lithuania – where it may wash up after storms or be brought up in fishing boats' nets – and the neighbouring Kaliningrad region of Russia, where deposits of it are mined. Some amber is produced by a heat treatment that compresses small pieces into bigger ones – pieces with imperfections such as grains of dirt or vegetation inside are more likely to be original.

Getting There & Away

Lithuania has cheap air, bus and rail links with Warsaw, which in turn has flights, trains and cheap buses to/from many Western European cities. In Polish, Vilnius is Wilno; in Lithuanian Warsaw is Varšuva. You can also easily reach Lithuania overland through

Latvia, by air or sea from Germany, or by air from Scandinavia.

Book as far ahead as you can on any transport: buses and trains either way between Warsaw and Vilnius, and trains between Berlin and Vilnius, seem particularly heavily booked.

TRAVEL AGENTS

See Estonia, Getting There & Away.

AIR
Routes

Lithuanian Airlines (LAL, Lietuvos Avialinijos) was the first independent Baltic-state airline to take wing (in December 1991). Flights in and out of Vilnius at the time of writing include: Berlin Schönefeld three times a week with LAL; Berlin Tempelhof and Hamburg twice a week with the German Hamburg Airlines; Budapest once weekly each with Malev and LAL; Copenhagen three times a week each with SAS and LAL; Frankfurt three times a week each with Lufthansa and LAL; Vienna twice a week with Austrian Airlines; Warsaw three times a week each with LOT and LAL; and Zurich weekly with Swissair and LAL. LAL was also due to start flights to/from London in 1992, and Finnair was expected to add Helsinki-Vilnius flights. Some LAL services might be scaled down since LAL sometimes attracted far fewer passengers than airlines flying the same routes with non-Soviet-made aircraft.

LAL also links Vilnius with Moscow (twice daily), Tallinn, Kiev and St Petersburg; Kaunas with Moscow; and Palanga with Moscow and St Petersburg.

Fares

Youth tickets (for under-25s) are one way of flying into Vilnius and out of somewhere else in the region. SAS has one-way youth tickets between Stockholm or Copenhagen and all three Baltic capitals, at half the cost of its cheapest return fare, the 'Jackpot', but booking conditions are limited. A Copenhagen-Vilnius-Copenhagen Jackpot (which must be booked seven to 14 days ahead) is US$320, the one-way youth fare US$160. (SAS's regular Copenhagen-Vilnius Apex return, originating in either city, is about US$450.)

Lufthansa has a useful youth open-jaw ticket for under-25s: Frankfurt-Vilnius and Tallinn-Frankfurt for about US$420. Regent Holidays of Bristol, England, has London-Vilnius returns and Tallinn, St Petersburg or Riga open-jaw options, for around US$510 to US$580. Other airline 'general sales agents' like Regent – travel agents appointed to sell reduced-price tickets – may offer the best deals from other countries too, so it's worth pressing airline reservations departments about them.

A Warsaw-Vilnius-Warsaw 'Superpex' return (fixed dates, advance payment, valid for one month) with Lot or LAL (both bookable through Lot) is US$95. A similar ticket Vilnius-Warsaw-Vilnius is US$130. Lot has worldwide flights into Warsaw – worth considering, wherever you're coming from.

Apex returns on the LAL Vilnius-Berlin Schönefeld route are about US$300 starting from either end. Returns to/from Frankfurt or Hamburg are generally US$500 or so, but Lufthansa's Frankfurt youth fare for under-25s is US$420.

The cheapest fare we found from London is a US$420 fixed-date non-refundable return via Warsaw with Lot, bought from Progressive Tours. If LAL begins London flights, check the fares offered by Rochdale Travel Centre and Regent Holidays.

One-way fares to Moscow, St Petersburg and Kiev are all around US$80. Return fares cost double.

At the time of writing, as in Estonia and Latvia, local citizens paid much lower fares for air tickets bought in Lithuania.

Charter Flights Individuals can often buy seats on charter flights, or in block bookings on scheduled flights, from tour companies or emigré groups. For instance Rochdale Travel Centre does two and four-week return flights to any Baltic capital from the UK for around US$520. Check with Baltisches Reisebüro for charter flights from Germany.

LAND
Bus

To/From Poland & the West There are at least two bus services between Warsaw and Vilnius and more may spring up if the new Kalvarija crossing point between Suwałki (Poland) and Marijampolė (Lithuania) is finally opened. In the meantime buses either use the crossing at Lazdijai, north-east of Augustów (Poland), which is small and subject to long delays, or go via Grodno in Belorussia (see Visas & Embassies).

One Warsaw-Vilnius service is run by Bus-Tour (☎ 22 4710, 22 4811) of Aleje Jerozolimskie 144, Warsaw, every morning from Warsaw Central bus station (near Zachodnia railway station). The one-way fare is US$16 plus US$4 for luggage, and tickets are sold at the bus station. Tickets for a daily Polish bus from Vilnius to Warsaw are sold at Vilnius bus station for US$15. This bus is regularly booked-up for 10 to 14 days ahead.

There's also an overnight bus by the Polish state travel company Orbis three times a week, taking about 11 hours. Tickets are US$18.50 one way, US$27 return from the Orbis offices at Puławska 31 and Marszałkowska 142 in Warsaw. In Vilnius they cost US$27 one way, US$37 return from Turistinė Firma Erelis (☎ 22 53 92) in the lobby of the Pergalė Cinema at Pamenkalnio gatvė 7/8.

Daily buses, also booked up some days in advance, run between Vilnius and Białystok (US$13 from Vilnius) and Gdańsk (overnight, US$18). There's also a German-run bus linking Vilnius once a week with Copenhagen (US$88 from Vilnius), Berlin (US$50) and Warsaw(US$25). Tickets for all these are sold at Vilnius bus station.

Buses between Warsaw and other European cities are a cheap way of approaching or getting away from Lithuania. Warsaw Central bus station and the Orbis offices at Marszałkowska 142 and ulica Bracka 16 in Warsaw sell a variety of these. Fares to/from London (36 hours) are typically US$130 one way, US$210 return. Conact Polish tourist offices in Western capitals for information.

To/From Latvia & Estonia There are four or five daily buses between Vilnius and Riga taking six hours for US$1.50, plus Riga buses to/from Kaunas, Šiauliai, and Klaipėda. Vilnius, Kaunas and Klaipėda all have overnight services to/from Tallinn, 12 hours for about US$2.50.

To/From Belorussia & Kaliningrad Seven buses leave Vilnius for Minsk daily, two for Brest and three for Kaliningrad. There are also likely to be services to these places from Kaunas, and from Klaipėda to Kaliningrad.

Train

To/From Germany & Poland A daily through sleeping car operates between Berlin Hauptbahnhof and Vilnius via Warsaw Central and Grodno (Belorussia), taking 22 hours from Berlin and 12 hours from Warsaw. There are three or four other daily trains, some overnight, just between Warsaw and Vilnius. The one-way fare in a four-berth couchette – which is what most of the accommodation consists of – from Warsaw (Central Station ticket office, not Orbis, which may charge more) is US$18. See Lithuania, Facts for the Visitor on the Belorussian visa situation but there are reportedly plans also to start direct Lithuania-Poland trains.

To/From Latvia, Estonia & Belorussia Several trains daily run between Vilnius and Riga, taking six to eight hours, including at least one overnight each way. The only train as far as Tallinn (13½ hours) is the daytime 'Chayka' which trundles back and forth from Minsk (3½ hours) via Vilnius and Riga. Vilnius-Riga in a four-berth couchette (converting to seats during the day) costs just US$0.50 at the time of writing. There are also daily trains between Klaipėda and Riga (5½ hours).

To/From Kaliningrad, Russia & Ukraine Vilnius is linked by *greit* ('fast') trains with Kaliningrad (six hours) twice daily (Kaunas is also on this line); St Petersburg (13 to 15 hours) three times, two of them overnight;

Moscow (12 hours) five times, four overnight; and Kiev once overnight.

Taxi

Taxis are so cheap by Western standards at the time of writing that they have become a mode of international transport. At the standard rate a taxi from Vilnius to Riga should cost about US$20 if you can find a driver willing to go so far.

Car & Motorbike

See the introductory Getting Around chapter for general comments on driving and riding in the Baltic states. The wait for private motorists on the Lithuania-Poland border at Lazdijai (see the Bus part of this section) can be as long as 24 hours, while the Grodno route isn't open to private motorists at the time of writing. One Lithuanian travel agent advises drivers from Poland to take the Brest-Minsk route through Belorussia, an extra 300 km but usually with quicker border crossings. Check the Belorussian visa situation before taking this route. The Kaliningrad region may open up to motorists as another route into Lithuania but meanwhile the vehicle ferry from Kiel to Klaipėda may well be the easiest way of getting a vehicle in from the south. The Klaipėda-Vilnius road is good. Another option is to take a ferry from Sweden or Finland to Riga or Tallinn and drive down.

SEA

The *Mercuri-I* vehicle ferry began weekly sailings between Kiel (Germany) and Klaipėda in 1992, taking 31 hours each way. Fares and ticket information are as for its Kiel-Riga route, see the Latvia Getting There & Away section. In Klaipėda contact LITMA (☎ 5 78 49, fax 5 34 66, telex 278141 LITMA). There's talk of new ferries to/from Lübeck (Germany) and Copenhagen from 1993.

TOURS

From Germany, Baltisches Reisebüro, Schnieder Reisen, Greif Reisen and Reisebüro Alainis offer stays in a variety of hotels, private homes, sanatoria and holiday homes at Klaipėda, Palanga, Nida or Juodkrante. Including flights to/from Hamburg or Hannover, a week costs from US$550 to over US$900 a person. A week in Vilnius through Baltisches Reisebüro or a week split between Vilnius, Kaunas and Klaipėda from Intourist Reisen is around US$800 to US$900 including flights. For information on wider Baltics tours see Estonia, Getting There & Away.

Getting Around

AIR

Check with LAL about possible Vilnius-Palanga flights.

BUS & TRAIN

Buses link all the main towns and cities, and are generally more frequent and quicker than trains. They're also a bit dearer, though still very cheap by Western standards, and therefore tend to be less crowded. From Vilnius to Kaunas for instance there are 20 buses a day (US$0.60), compared with just a handful of trains.

TAXI

At the time of writing a taxi should cost around US$0.05 a km. Meters tick over, as in Estonia and Latvia, at 20 kopecks a km and you then multiply the result by 30. Some drivers won't accept the official fare and you have to bargain with them – see Estonia, Getting Around for some tips. At these low fares you can consider taxis as possible intercity transport.

CAR & MOTORBIKE

See the introductory Getting Around chapter for information on driving and riding in the Baltics, and the Vilnius Getting There & Away section for car rentals. There's at least one Western-run petrol station in Vilnius.

BICYCLE, LOCAL TRANSPORT & TOURS

See Estonia, Getting Around.

Vilnius

The greenest and prettiest of the Baltic capitals, Vilnius (population 592,000) lies 250 km inland on the Neris river. The winding streets of old Vilnius are a pleasure to explore, and there are many reminders of the city's pivotal role in the campaign for Baltic independence. Vilnius' historical links with Catholic Poland perhaps contribute to a less austere atmosphere than in Riga or Tallinn. Direct evidence of the Polish connection can be seen in the many Catholic churches and the array of central European architectural styles from past centuries.

History

According to tradition Vilnius was founded in the 1320s by Gediminas but it may well have already been a political and trade centre, with river access to both the Baltic and Black seas, by then. Fourteenth century Vilnius was on the slopes of Castle Hill, with upper and lower castles and the townspeople's houses all protected by a moat and walls. The Teutonic Knights attacked at least six times between 1365 and 1402 but their defeat in 1410 at Grünwald launched Vilnius into an era of prosperity. Many Gothic buildings went up and merchant and artisan guilds were formed. Following Tatar attacks, a 2.4-km stone wall was built between 1503 and 1522 around the new part of the town south of Castle Hill. Sixteenth century Vilnius was one of the biggest cities in eastern Europe, with 25,000 to 30,000 people. It blossomed with buildings in late Gothic and Renaissance styles as the Lithuanians Žygimantas I and II occupied the Polish-Lithuanian throne. The university was founded in 1579.

In the 17th and early 18th centuries Vilnius suffered fires, war, famine and plague, and shrank in population and importance, but in the 19th century it grew again as industry developed, and became a refuge of dispossessed Polish-Lithuanian gentry, and thus a Polish cultural centre. It was devastated, however, in WW I when the Germans occupied it for 3½ years and by the subsequent Soviet/Polish/Lithuanian fighting.

When the shooting died down, Vilnius found itself in Poland, where it remained till 1939. By now its population was one-third Jewish (between 60,000 and 80,000 people) and it developed into one of the world's three major centres of Yiddish culture (the others being Warsaw and New York), earning the nickname 'Jerusalem of Lithuania'. WW II saw another three-year German occupation and nearly all the Vilnius Jews were killed in its ghetto or the Paneriai death camp. Much of the city was wrecked in the six-day battle by which the Red Army recaptured it towards the end of the war.

New residential and industrial suburbs sprang up all round the city after WW II. According to some estimates the population today includes up to 100,000 Poles and 110,000 Russians.

Orientation

Central Vilnius is on the south side of the Neris River and its heart is Katedros aikštė, the cathedral square with Castle Hill rising behind it. South of Katedros aikštė are the streets of the old city; to the west Gedimino prospektas is the axis of the newer part of the centre. The railway and bus stations are just beyond the south edge of the old city, 1½ km from Katedros aikštė. Hotels are dotted around the central area and its fringes.

Information

Money You can change money at the Bank of Lithuania at Gedimino prospektas 6 or Vilniaus Bankas at Gedimino prospektas 12, both open Monday to Friday from 9 am to 12.30 pm, the main post office (Monday to Friday from 9 am to 6 pm) and the airport (daily from 10 am to 5 pm). Some hotels including the Lietuva also exchange money.

Post & Telecommunications The main

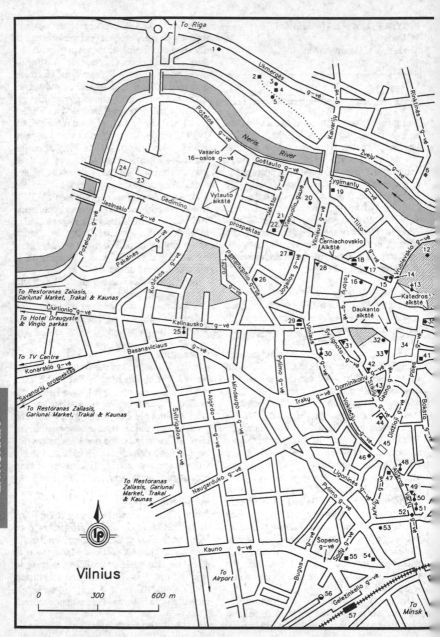

Vilnius

0   300   600 m

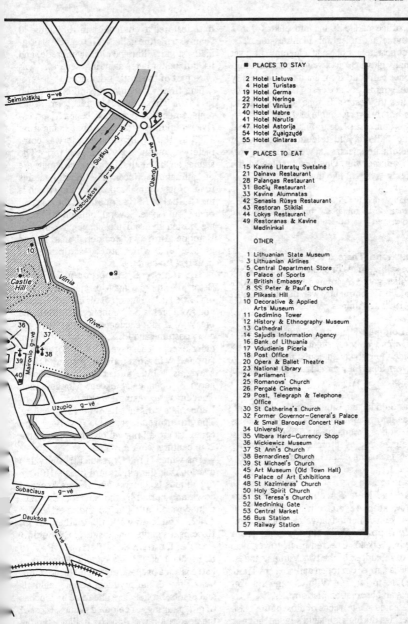

■ PLACES TO STAY

2 Hotel Lietuva
4 Hotel Turistas
19 Hotel Germa
22 Hotel Neringa
27 Hotel Vilnius
40 Hotel Mabre
41 Hotel Narutis
47 Hotel Astorija
54 Hotel Zvaigzdė
55 Hotel Gintaras

▼ PLACES TO EAT

15 Kavinė Literatų Svetainė
21 Dainava Restaurant
28 Palangas Restaurant
31 Bočių Restaurant
33 Kavinė Alumnatas
42 Senasis Rūsys Restaurant
43 Restoran Stikliai
44 Lokys Restaurant
49 Restoranas & Kavinė
   Medininkai

OTHER

1 Lithuanian State Museum
3 Lithuanian Airlines
5 Central Department Store
6 Palace of Sports
7 British Embassy
8 SS Peter & Paul's Church
9 Plikasis Hill
10 Decorative & Applied
   Arts Museum
11 Gedimino Tower
12 History & Ethnography Museum
13 Cathedral
14 Sajudis Information Agency
16 Bank of Lithuania
17 Vidudienis Piceria
18 Post Office
20 Opera & Ballet Theatre
23 National Library
24 Parliament
25 Romanovs' Church
26 Pergalė Cinema
29 Post, Telegraph & Telephone
   Office
30 St Catherine's Church
32 Former Governor-General's Palace
   & Small Baroque Concert Hall
34 University
35 Vilbara Hard-Currency Shop
36 Mickiewicz Museum
37 St Ann's Church
38 Bernardines' Church
39 St Michael's Church
45 Art Museum (Old Town Hall)
46 Palace of Art Exhibitions
48 St Kazimieras' Church
50 Holy Spirit Church
51 St Teresa's Church
52 Medininkų Gate
53 Central Market
56 Bus Station
57 Railway Station

LITHUANIA

post office at Gedimino prospektas 7 has telephone and telegraph facilities too. The newer post, telephone and telegraph office at Vilniaus gatvė 33 is always open for long-distance calls and from 8 am to 11 pm daily for telegrams. Its fax desk (US$2 for three minutes to Western Europe) only seems to open briefly every couple of days.

The quickest place to make international phone calls is the telephone station at Savanorių prospektas 28, with an average 10 to 15-minute wait. One local explained the charging 'system' like this:

Officially it may be US$2 a minute to England, for a minimum three minutes – but you might find, however short your call is, that you're timed at five minutes ...

Bookshops There are a few bookshops, some selling maps or a few titles in English, on Pilies gatvė. A foreign languages bookshop, Five Continents, was due to open in mid-1992 at Vilniaus gatvė 39.

Left Luggage There are left-luggage offices (*saugojimo kamera*) either side of the stairs outside the railway station's main entrance. Between them they should provide a 24-hour service.

Other Sajūdis, the Lithuanian popular front, has an information agency facing the cathedral. Notice boards on its Tilto gatvė side sometimes display information on upcoming events including entertainment.

Things to See
Katedros Aikštė & Around The **Gedimino Tower**, atop 48-metre-high **Castle Hill** (Pilies kalnas) behind the cathedral, is a good starting point. Walk up the path from Katedros aikštė. The red-brick tower was part of the upper of the two Vilnius castles. Inside is a museum (open daily except Tuesdays) featuring old Vilnius, and on top there's an observation platform.

Katedros aikštė, scene of most of the mass gatherings during Lithuania's independence campaign, is dominated by **Vilnius Cathedral**, restored to church use in 1989 after 30 years as a picture gallery. The cathedral originally stood within the old lower castle, and its tall bell tower, standing separate, was once part of the castle's defences.

The first, wooden, cathedral burnt down in 1419. The original Gothic form of its replacement has vanished beneath successive rebuildings – the major one being from 1783 to 1801, when the outside was completely redone in today's classical form. The statues on the south side facing the square are of Lithuanian princes. The interior retains more of its original aspect: the showpiece is the **Chapel of St Kazimieras** at the east end of the south aisle. Several Lithuanian princes are buried beneath the chapel. Its present Baroque form, with coloured marble and granite and white stucco sculptures, is mainly 17th century.

The **History & Ethnography Museum** (Istorijos-Etnografijos Muziejus) at the foot of Castle Hill just north of the cathedral takes you from prehistoric amber ornaments to the pre-WW II independence period. There are good costume and folk art sections. It's open daily except Tuesdays. The **Decorative & Applied Arts Museum** (Taikomosios Dailės Muziejus) a little further along at Arsenalo gatvė 3, open daily except Mondays and Tuesdays, is testament to the skills of Lithuania's artisans since the 15th century. The furniture, tapestries, jewellery and ceramics are all marvellous. Don't miss the 20th century work upstairs.

The white **Three Crosses** (Trys Kryžiai) overlooking the city from Plikasis Hill are old Vilnius landmarks which were knocked down and buried by the Soviet authorities, then symbolically dug up and re-erected in 1989. You can walk up to them from Kosciuškos gatvė. The inside of **SS Peter & Paul's Church** (Šv Petro ir Povilo Bažnyčias) at the far end of Kosciuškos gatvė is a sea of sparkling white stucco sculptures of real and mythical people, animals and plants, broken here and there by touches of gilt, paintings or coloured statues. Most of the decoration was done by Italian sculptors between 1675 and 1704.

The tomb of the Lithuanian noble who founded the church, Mykolas Kazimieras Pacas, is on the right of the porch as you enter. If you don't want to walk, trolley bus No 2, 3 or 4 will take you there from the Gedimino stop on Vrublevskio gatvė near the cathedral.

Old City The area stretching a km or so south from Katedros aikštė was built up in the 15th and 16th centuries. Some buildings have been polished to a pristine state they never knew in the past, while others remain evocatively dilapidated. The focal streets are Pilies gatvė and its southward continuation, Didžioji gatvė.

The streets west of Pilies gatvė were once the heart of Vilnius' **Jewish Quarter**, and in WW II its ghetto. In the 1950s and '60s the Soviet authorities tried to obliterate all traces of Vilnius' Jewish past, even recycling Jewish gravestones as paving, but there are now reportedly plans for a Jewish museum and new memorials.

The central buildings of **Vilnius University** occupy most of the block between Pilies gatvė and Universiteto gatvė. The university produced many notable scholars in the 17th and early 19th centuries, but was closed from 1832 to 1919. Today it has about 16,000 students. The 12 linked courtyards can be entered by several passages and gates: the southern gate on Šv Jono gatvė brings you into the Didysis or Skarga Courtyard, with three sides of galleries in the early 17th century Mannerist style and **St John's Church** (Šv Jono Bažnyčia) which has an outstanding 18th century Baroque main façade.

The arch through the 16th century building opposite St John's leads to a two-domed observatory whose late 18th century façade is adorned with reliefs of the zodiac. The other main courtyard, reached from the north side of the Didysis Courtyard, is the Sarbievijus Courtyard, whose exit to Universiteto gatvė brings you out opposite the 18th and 19th century **Governor General's Palace** on Daukanto aikštė. Both Napoleon and his Russian adversary General Mikhail Kutuzov used this palace. At its far end is a pleasant, secluded public garden.

East of Pilies gatvė, the old rooms of the Polish Romantic poet Adam Mickiewicz (1798-1855) at Pilies skersgatvis 11 are now a **Mickiewicz museum**, open Fridays from 2 to 6 pm and Saturdays from 10 am to 2 pm. Mickiewicz grew up near Vilnius and studied at its university from 1815 to 1819 before being exiled for anti-Russian activities. Much of his work, which inspired 19th century Polish nationalists, is set in the Vilnius region.

Across Maironio gatvė from the east end of Pilies skersgatvis, stands the fine 1581 brick façade of **St Ann's Church** (Šv Onos Bažnyčia), a highpoint of Lithuanian Gothic architecture with its sweeping curves and delicate pinnacles. The austere church behind it was part of the city's defensive wall.

Southern Didžioji gatvė widens into a plaza which was long one of the centres of Vilnius life, with markets from the 15th century. The **Old Town Hall** here is now the **Lithuanian Art Museum** (Lietuvos Dailės Muziejus) showing 20th century Lithuanian work. Its classical exterior dates from 1785 to 1799. The modern **Palace of Art Exhibitions** (Dailės Parodų Rūmai) behind the town hall at Vokiečių gatvė 2, shows interesting contemporary art and also has a café, art and craft shop, and video centre showing foreign films.

The large **St Kazimieras' Church** (Šv Kazimiero Bažnyčios) opposite the Hotel Astorija is Vilnius' oldest Baroque church, built by the Jesuits between 1604 and 1615. Under Soviet rule it spent two decades as a museum of atheism.

Pretty **Aušros Vartų gatvė** leads up to the **Medininkų Gate** (or Aušros Vartai, Gates of Dawn), once the start of the Moscow road, the only one of the nine gates in the town wall still intact. On the east side of the street, just above a 16th century house which has been turned into the Restoranas & Kavine Medininkai, is the big, pink, domed 17th century **Holy Spirit Church**, Lithuania's chief Russian Orthodox church. The streetside Catholic **St Teresa's Church** (Šv Teresės Bažnyčios), above the Church of the Holy Spirit, is early Baroque (1635-50) outside and more elaborate late Baroque inside.

Shortly before the Medininkų Gate, a door on the left gives on to a staircase up to a little 18th century chapel directly over the gate arch, which houses a supposedly miracle-working icon of the Virgin thought to have been souvenired from the Crimea by Algirdas in 1363. It draws a constant bustle of people coming, going and saying prayers.

New Town The main street of modern Vilnius, laid out in 1852, is **Gedimino prospektas**, running about 1.5 km west from Katedros aikštė to the river. At the time of writing many of the barricades erected at its west end on 13 January 1991 to protect the **parliament** from Soviet troops are still in place. Thousands of people gathered here to defend parliament after troops had stormed the Vilnius TV tower and centre earlier that day, but in the end the feared attack never materialised. The rooftop satellite dish was set up to bring foreign TV reports on Lithuania to the people of Vilnius after Soviet troops had taken over Lithuania's own TV installations.

Just over a km south-west of parliament, at the west end of Čiurlionio gatvė, is Vilnius' biggest city park, the pleasant **Vingio parkas**, whose huge stage is the usual setting for the Lithuanian Song Festival. The 326-metre **TV tower**, where Soviet tanks and troops killed 13 people and hurt many more as they fought through the crowd encircling it on 13 January 1991, is in the suburb of Karoliniškes, across the river from Vingio parkas. Carved wooden crosses stand as memorials to the victims. Trolley bus No 7 from the railway station to Justiniškės goes within a couple of minutes' walk of the tower. More crosses stand outside the **TV & Radio Centre**, also stormed by Soviet troops that night, at the corner of Konarskio gatvė and Pietario gatvė, 2.5 km west of the city centre.

Beyond the Hotel Lietuva on Ukmergės gatvė, the **Lithuanian State Museum** (Lietuvos Valstybės Muziejus), open daily except Mondays and Tuesdays, has folk costumes and artefacts, including many fine carved crosses, saints and suns from the 19th and early 20th centuries. On our last visit, one floor was devoted to the events of January 1991.

Gariūnai This is the name given to the big free-for-all market held daily up to about 11 am just off the Kaunas road on the western fringe of Vilnius. Poles are among the main traders and this is where Lithuanians come to get things the shops don't sell – a fascinating insight into the country's real economy. 'Gariunų Turgavietė' or 'Turgavietė' buses ferry shoppers from Vilnius station from early morning. The 'Lazdynai' turning 11 km along the Kaunas road from Vilnius centre leads to the market, which soon appears on your left.

Paneriai About 100,000 people, mostly Jews, are reckoned to have died in the Nazi death camp at Paneriai on the south-west edge of Vilnius. The site of the camp is a wooded valley about 10 km from the city centre, off the Trakai road. It's now reportedly crisscrossed by neat paths – the pits where thousands of bodies were burned are grassed over. There's a small museum. Bus No 8 to Aukštieji Paneriai from Vilnius railway station should get you close. Ask for *muziejus* (museum) or *paminklas* (monument).

Places to Stay
Hostels & Colleges *The BATS backpackers' hostel* (☎ 63 08 91 daytime and ☎ 76 55 18 evening) is at Geležinio Vilko gatvė 27 (formerly Konarskio gatvė 36) out in the west of the city. Prices are from US$9 to US$11 per person. Take trolley bus No 15 or 16 from the railway station to the 'Kaunas' stop near the Kaunas shop, but ring first to check that the hotel hasn't moved or temporarily closed.

Vilnius University Student Representation (VUSA) (☎ 61 44 14, (☎ /fax 61 79 20, telex 261212 VU SU) can offer single or double rooms in university accommodation. When we visited, it was still finalising plans but similar accommodation in Estonia and Latvia costs around US$6 to US$12 a head. You may be sharing a shower and toilet with people in other rooms. VUSA would like to be contacted a month ahead but probably won't turn you away if you arrive at shorter notice. It has access to accommodation on the coast as well as in Vilnius. Its office is in the main university block at Universiteto gatvė 3, ask for *Studentų Atstovybė* (Student Representation).

Private Homes & Flats A kiosk beside the railway station proclaiming *Hotel Ekspres* offers double rooms in flats for around US$3 a day. The people inside have a card written in English telling you what to do if you're interested.

Mr Vaclovas Sakalauskas (☎ 35 20 32 or 61 35 80), a friendly ex-diplomat, will fix you a comfortable flat in Vilnius with or without a family for US$20/30/40 a single/double/triple in the city centre, or US$15/20 a single/double about 10 minutes' bus ride out. On our last visit to Vilnius Mr Sakalauskas found us a comfortable, clean, spacious flat a minute's walk from the cathedral which was far better value than most upper-range hotels.

Cheap Hotels The small *Hotel Narutis* (☎ 62 28 82) at Pilies gatvė 24, a good location in the old city, has rooms that are clean enough for US$1.80/2.35. Toilets are shared and not very savoury. Also central is the large *Hotel Vilnius* (☎ 62 41 57) at Gedimino prospektas 20 where clean, sizeable rooms with washbasin and TV are US$2.75/4, which is good value – if you can avoid any inflation to a foreigner's price. Rooms with private bathroom, we were told, are US$40/60.

Convenient for rail and bus travellers and big enough (200 rooms) to have vacancies, but without many other plus points, is the *Hotel Gintaras* (☎ 63 52 51) on Naujoji gatvė in front of the railway station. Small, faded singles/doubles with private bathroom

go for US$4.50/6; *'lyux'* rooms are US$7.50/11.25. Security seems notably slack.

Five km north of the centre, near the river at Verkių gatvė 66, is the *Hotel Trinapolis* (☎ 77 89 13), reportedly decent value at about US$3 a double. Going by taxi is the easiest way to find it.

Expensive Hotels Fairly central and reasonable value at the lower end of the top bracket are the *Hotel Germa* (☎ 61 72 32) at Vilniaus gatvė 2 and the larger 230-bed *Hotel Turistas* (☎ 73 32 00) just north of the river at Ukmergės gatvė 14. The Germa, once reserved for top Communists, has singles/doubles for US$36/54. The Turistas, in the shopping precinct next to the Hotel Lietuva, is US$40/46 but there are also suites (with an extra room) for US$56. Rooms in both have TV, phone and private bath.

The *Hotel Astorija* (☎ 62 99 14) at Didžioji gatvė 35 in the old city, now Norwegian-run, has rooms from US$25/35 (with washbasin only) to US$60/70 (with attached bathroom), plus suites for US$100. The *Hotel Neringa* (☎ 61 05 16) at Gedimino prospektas 23 charges US$50/60 for clean but ordinary rooms.

The *Hotel Mabre* (☎ 61 41 62) at Maironio gatvė 13 consists of three multi-level apartments holding up to five people each in an interesting, modernised old city building. German is spoken here and you'll pay US$60/99 for single/double occupancy, including breakfast.

Vilnius' biggest hotel is the towering, 330-room *Hotel Lietuva* (☎ 35 60 92) at Ukmergės gatvė 20, a 15-minute walk northwest of the centre. This is where most Western tourists stayed in the Soviet era. Prostitution is rampant and there's a reputation for theft, but the views are good, the staff overall helpful, and there's a selection of restaurants, bars and cafés where you can get food at most times of day. Rooms are comfortable enough at US$56/70 including breakfast.

The 150-bed *Villon Country Club*, a Lithuanian-British joint venture which was due to open on the Riga road 20 km north of Vilnius, looks set to outstrip anywhere in the city with its swimming pool, tennis, riding, two saunas, gym, three bars, café, restaurant, resident doctor, hairdresser and casino. Single/double rooms are US$49/88 and there are suites for US$132. Book through Villon Tours (☎ 65 13 85, fax 26 17 18) at Ševčenkos gatvė 31, Vilnius.

Places to Eat

Old City The *Restoranas Stikliai* (☎ 62 79 71) at Stiklių gatvė 7 is still one of the better restaurants in the Baltic states, though portions have shrunk since we visited in 1989. The Stikliai aspires to old-fashioned elegance, waiters wearing bow ties; *you* don't have to dress up but dirty clothes get dirty looks. It's open daily from noon to 10 pm: for the evening, book by phone from 10 am (English is spoken). There's an English-language menu and a typical three-course meal comes to US$8 or US$10 plus 15% service charge. Main courses include trout, veal and steak and there are choices for vegetarians. Italian pancakes are a tasty dessert. Near the Stikliai are the *Lokys* on Stiklių gatvė, which specialises in game, and the *Senasis Rūsys*, a cellar restaurant at Šv Ignoto gatvė 16, which is cheaper than the Stikliai – main courses typically cost US$0.60 – but with less variety.

You can fill up without much fuss at the *Amatininkų Užeiga* at Didžioji gatvė 19 on the corner of Stiklių gatvė. Despite language difficulties, two of us cobbled together a cheap meal of six fried eggs, fish, chips, vegetables, sliced tomato and two extra plates of greasy chips.

A café popular with students is the *Kavinė Alumnatas* at Universiteto gatvė 4, where the coffee comes under a thick layer of cream. The *Restoranas Medininkai* on Aušros Vartų gatvė is in a converted 16th century house with a sculpture garden. The *Kavinė Medininkai* next door does good snacks.

Elsewhere One uncomplicated, central place to feed is *Vidudienis Piceria* on Gedimino prospektas where reasonable one-person pizzas (including a solid egg, ham, tomato and cheese variety) cost from just US$0.25 to US$0.50. Hours are from noon to 9 pm.

At Gedimino prospektas 1 (the cathedral end) the *Kavinė Literatų Svetainė* has a long trilingual menu but not much that's 'on'. Still, you can get a fair meal of salads followed by meat with vegetables and a dessert for around US$1. At Gedimino prospektas 23 next to the Hotel Neringa, the *Kavinė Neringa* will do a fair meal for around US$1 including a drink.

Two convenient eating options in the *Hotel Lietuva* are the bars on the main lobby floor. For the other eateries you may need to book. In the floor-22 restaurant you pay US$1 for a floor show or disco in addition to the meal price of around US$2 for a good spread.

The *Restoranas Žaliasis* (☎ 65 32 33), similar in style to the Stikliai but cheaper and if anything better, is in just about the last place you'd expect to come upon a classy restaurant – an industrial estate on the southwest edge of the city. Little English is spoken but try to muddle through with a telephone booking. We gave the thumbs-up to the chicken Kiev *(kijevo kotletas)* and *bifštekas angliškai* ('English beefsteak', not beef but respectable) main courses. If you're very hungry order two or three starters as portions could be bigger, but even so a three-course meal with a drink is unlikely to cost over US$4. The restaurant is on Titnago gatvė north-west off the main Kaunas road, Savanorių prospektas. The turning is seven km from the city centre. You may have to bargain with a taxi driver to bring you here, US$1 should be enough, and book the same driver to go back as there's little passing traffic!

Entertainment

The local evening paper *Vakarinis Kaujienos* may help you work out what's on. The Lituanika Festival (usually held in July) has a sizeable rock, blues and jazz component. Keep your eyes open for performances by the internationally known Lithuanian jazz saxophonist Petras Vyšniauskas.

The Lithuania Chamber Orchestra and the Kaunas Philharmonic Choir have high reputations. The Lithuania Philharmonia runs an orchestra and three string quartets: the Lithuanian, the Vilnius and the Mikalojus Čiurlionis. Concert halls include the Philharmonic at Didžioji gatvė 45, and the Small Baroque at Daukanto aikštė 1. The Lithuania Opera & Ballet Theatre, a modern building with poor acoustics at Vienuolio gatvė 1, stages several mainly classical productions in repertory.

You can sometimes catch foreign as well as good Soviet films at the video centre in the Palace of Art Exhibitions.

Things to Buy

Dailė, next door to the Kavinė Literatų Svetainė on Gedimino prospektas, sells amber jewellery (necklaces cost from US$50 to US$100) and interesting pottery. You'll find a few souvenir shops on Pilies gatvė. The main department store is in the precinct by the Hotel Lietuva.

Getting There & Away

International connections to/from Vilnius are covered in Lithuania, Getting There & Away. If regular ticket outlets fail you, the Kelionių Biuras (travel bureau) in the sunken square beside the Hotel Lietuva may be able to help, at inflated prices. People also use its doorway as an informal ticket exchange board.

Air Airline offices in Vilnius include:

Austrian Airlines, SAS & Swissair
    Airport (☎ 66 20 00)
LAL
    Ukmergės gatvė 14 (☎ 75 25 88)
Lot
    Room 108, Hotel Skrydis at the airport
    (☎ 63 01 95)
Lufthansa
    Airport (☎ 63 60 49)
Malev
    Room 103, Hotel Skrydis at the airport (tickets
    also sold by LAL)

Bus The long-distance bus station is just south of the old town at Sodų gatvė 22 near the railway station. The ticket hall on the right as you enter is for same-day departures; the one on the left is for advance bookings. With buses to nearby destinations (on the left side of the platform) you can pay on board. For the longer-distance red buses you need a ticket.

Timetable information is clearly displayed in the ticket halls (green letters indicate a microbus), and on the platform. International services are discussed in Lithuania, Getting There & Away. Domestic departures from Vilnius include:

Druskininkai – 125 km, 2½ hours, six buses daily,
    US$0.80
Kaunas – 100 km, two hours, 20 buses daily, US$0.60
Klaipėda – 310 km, 6½ hours, 11 buses daily, US$2
Palanga – 340 km, seven hours, three buses daily,
    US$2.15
Šiauliai – 225 km, 4½ hours, eight buses daily,
    US$1.40

Train The railway station is just south of the old city on Geležinkelio gatvė. Timetable displays are poor: 'Ryga-Kijevas 21.21' means that the train from Riga to Kiev will leave Vilnius at 9.21 pm. Intermediate stops aren't shown. Most of the better trains are listed *greit* (fast). Ticket queues at weekends can be long. Information on international trains is given in Lithuania, Getting There & Away. Within Lithuania, buses are usually more frequent and quicker. There is a handful of daily trains to Kaunas (1½ to two hours), Klaipėda, Šiauliai and Trakai.

Car & Motorbike There's a Western-run petrol station with higher grade fuel on Savanorių prospektas, the main Kaunas road out of Vilnius.

Rental The Eva car rental firm (☎ 64 34 28) has Volvos and Audis from US$50 a day plus US$0.30 a km, or US$120 a day with unlimited km. Its Ladas cost only US$36 a day plus US$0.20 a km, but tend to be booked-up well ahead.

LITHUANIA

Getting Around

To/From the Airport

Vilnius airport is six km south of the centre in the suburb Kirtimai. Bus No 1 runs between the airport and railway station, bus No 2 between the airport and the north-western suburb of Šeškinė via the city centre and the Hotel Lietuva. A taxi from airport to city centre should be about US$0.35.

City Transport

From the railway and bus stations, trolley bus No 2 goes to Katedros aikštė, Gedimino prospektas, then up Kosciuškos gatvė to the north-east suburb Antakalnis; No 5 to Gedimino prospektas at Černiachovskio aikštė then over the river and north up part of Kalvarijų gatvė (you can use it for the Lietuva and Turistas hotels). Bus and trolley bus tickets cost less than US$0.01: one kiosk selling them is at the east end of the railway station forecourt, with the sign *'Bilietai važiuoti miesto transportu'*. Two useful taxi ranks are on Katedros aikštė and in front of the old town hall on Didžioji gatvė.

TRAKAI

Gediminas reputedly made Trakai, 26 km west of Vilnius, his capital in 1321. Its two lakeside castles were built within the next 100 years to fend off the German knights. Today it's a small, quiet town on a north-pointing peninsula between two lakes. From the railway station, follow Vytauto gatvė north to the central square, then continue north along Melnikaitės gatvė to the main points of interest.

Things to See

Among the wooden cottages along Melnikaitės gatvė is a 19th century **Kenessa** (prayer house) of the Karaites or Karaimai, a Judaist sect originating in Baghdad and adhering only to the Law of Moses, some of whom were brought to Trakai from the Crimea by Vytautas around 1400. Some 150 Karaites still live in Trakai, and there's a small **Karaites museum** at Melnikaitės gatvė 22.

The remains of Trakai's **Peninsula Castle** are towards the north end of town, in a park close to the shore of lake Luka. It's thought to have been built between 1362 and 1382 by Vytautas' father, Kestutis. The painstakingly restored Gothic red-brick **Island Castle** probably dates from around 1400 when Vytautas found he needed stronger defences. It stands east of the north end of the peninsula, linked to the shore by footbridges. The moated main tower has a cavernous central court and a range of galleries, halls and rooms, some housing the **Trakai History Museum**.

Getting There & Away

About 18 buses daily run from Vilnius bus station to Trakai, but there are spells of two or three hours with no buses. There are trains too.

DRUSKININKAI

Druskininkai, 125 km south-west of Vilnius, is a spa and resort town on the Nemunas river in a pleasant area of lakes and pine forests. The outstanding Lithuanian painter and composer Mikalojus Konstantinus Čiurlionis grew up at Čiurlionio gatvė 41 and the family house is now a museum (closed Mondays).

There's a *Camping* (☎ 5 25 77) at Nemuno gatvė 26 and the *Hotel Druskininkai* (☎ 5 25 66) is at Kudirkos gatvė 41.

RUMŠIŠKĖS

The **Lithuanian Country Life Museum** at Rumšiškes, 80 km west of Vilnius just off the Kaunas road, has a large collection of 18th and 19th century country buildings and artefacts. On summer Sundays there are folklore performances.

KAUNAS

Lithuania's second city is 100 km west of Vilnius at the confluence of the Nemunas and Neris rivers. Kaunas' 430,000 population is about 90% Lithuanian. The city is a cultural centre with a big student population and some fine architecture, museums and galleries. Founded in the 11th century, it's said to have been reduced to ashes 13 times before WW II, in which it received one more battering. It was an important river-trade town in the 15th and 16th centuries, and Lithuania's capital between WW I and WW II, when Vilnius had been taken over by Poland.

Orientation & Information

Kaunas' historic heart, Rotušės aikštė (City Hall Square), is on the point of land between the two rivers, at the west end of the city centre. The heart of modern Kaunas is the mostly pedestrianised Laisvės alėja, further

east. Around here you'll find most of the main shops, hotels, restaurants, galleries and museums. Most of the latter are open from noon to 6 pm daily except Mondays, though a few also close on Tuesdays. The central post office is at Laisvės alėja 102. You can change money at the Bank of Lithuania at Maironio gatvė 25. Dailė, at Rotušės aikštė 27, is a good handicrafts shop.

Things to See

Rotušės Aikštė Many 15th and 16th century German **merchants' houses** round

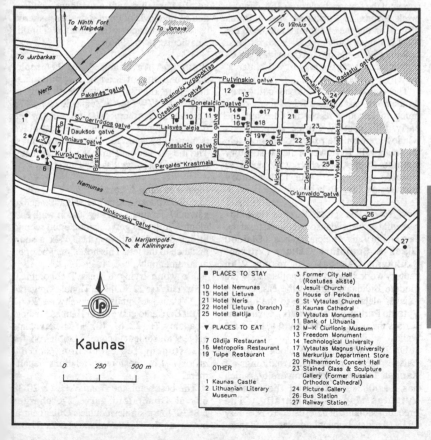

LITHUANIA

Kaunas

0   250   500 m

■ PLACES TO STAY	3 Former City Hall
10 Hotel Nemunas	(Rostušes aikštė)
15 Hotel Lietuva	4 Jesuit Church
21 Hotel Neris	5 House of Perkūnas
22 Hotel Lietuva (branch)	6 St Vytautas Church
25 Hotel Baltija	8 Kaunas Cathedral
	9 Vytautas Monument
▼ PLACES TO EAT	11 Bank of Lithuania
	12 M–K Ciurlionis Museum
7 Gildija Restaurant	13 Freedom Monument
16 Metropolis Restaurant	14 Technological University
19 Tulpe Restaurant	17 Vytautas Magnus University
	18 Merkurijus Department Store
OTHER	20 Philharmonic Concert Hall
	23 Stained Glass & Sculpture
1 Kaunas Castle	Gallery (Former Russian
2 Lithuanian Literary	Orthodox Cathedral)
Museum	24 Picture Gallery
	26 Bus Station
	27 Railway Station

Map labels: To Ninth Fort & Klaipėda; To Jonava; To Vilnius; To Jurbarkas; Neris; Pakalnės gatvė; Savanorių prospektas; Putvinskio gatvė; Žemaičių gatvė; Radastu gatvė; Ožeškienės gatvė; Donelaičio gatvė; Sv Gertrūdos gatvė; Dauksos gatvė; Laisvės alėja; Maironio gatvė; Vilniaus gatvė; Birštono; Kurpių gatvė; Kestučio gatvė; Daukanto gatvė; Mickevičiaus gatvė; Gedimino gatvė; Vytauto prospektas; Pergalės Krastmala; Nemunas; Griunvaldo gatvė; Minkovskių gatvė; To Marijampolė & Kaliningrad the pretty square have been restored, some with cafés or souvenir shops. The fine, white Baroque former **city hall** in the square is late 18th century.

In the south-west corner stands a **statue of Maironis**, or Jonas Maculevičiaus, the Kaunas priest and writer whose works were banned by Stalin but is now Lithuania's national poet. The **Lithuanian Literary Museum** is in the house behind, where Maironis lived from 1910 to 1932. The south side of the square is dominated by an 18th century twin-towered **Jesuit church**, now back in religious use after years as a school.

On Aleksotas gatvė, off the south-east corner of the square, the curious 16th century brick **House of Perkūnas** was built as offices, on the site of a former temple to the old Lithuanian thunder god Perkūnas. Just beyond, backing on to the river, is **St Vytautas Church**, the biggest in Lithuania, built by Vytautas about 1400.

The single-towered **Kaunas cathedral**, on the north-east corner of the square, owes much to Baroque reconstruction, but the early 15th century Gothic shape of its windows remain. **Maironis' tomb** is outside the south wall. The tower of the 11th century **Kaunas Castle** is a short walk north of Rotušės aikštė, with the 15th century **Bernardinu Church** behind it.

New Town The former Russian Orthodox cathedral on Nepriklausomybės aikštė, at the east end of Laisvės alėja, houses a **Stained Glass & Sculpture Gallery** (Vitrazo-Skulpturos Galerija) with mainly 20th century work. Next to it is a gallery showing modern Lithuanian art. At the east end of Laisvės alėja is an entrance to the hillside **Vytauto Parkas** (Vytautus Park). Next to the park is the oak forest **Ąžuolynas**, good for walks.

On Daukanto aikštė, a block north of Laisvės alėja, are the main buildings of **Kaunas Technological University**, which has 14,000 students, and the smaller **Vytautas Magnus University**. The Freedom Monument here, dated 16 February 1918 (the day Lithuania declared independence), was erected in 1928, hidden during the Stalin era, and put back in place on 16 February 1989. Nearby are the **Lithuanian History Museum** at Donelaičio gatvė 64 and the **M-K Čiurlionis Museum** at Putvinskio gatvė 45. The latter has a good collection of 17th to 20th century Lithuanian art, including the Romantic, symbolic paintings of Mikalojus-Konstantinus Čiurlionis (1875-1911), Lithuania's greatest artist, who was a composer too. The **picture gallery** at Donelaičio gatvė 16 has mainly Western art including work by Rubens, Goya and Cézanne.

At Putvinskio gatvė 64 is the popular **Velnių Muziejus** with a worldwide collection of hundreds of devil statuettes gathered by the landscape artist Antanas Žmuidzinavičius (1876-1966).

Ninth Fort An estimated 80,000 people, including most of Kaunas' Jewish population, were killed in the Nazi death camp in this former WW I fort at Žemaičių plentas 73 on Kaunas' northern outskirts. One of the prison buildings remains and the mass grave is marked by stark, monumental sculptures. The museum at the entrance now has material on Soviet as well as Nazi atrocities.

Places to Stay & Eat

The *BATS backpackers' hostel* is at Prancūzų gatvė 59. From the railway station walk east along Čiurlionio gatvė and take the second bridge over the railway, then walk a short distance to the left. This hostel may be open in summer only.

It's worth trying Kaunas Technological University (☎ 22 70 44) at Donelaičio gatvė 73, Vytautas Magnus University (☎ 20 67 53) at Daukanto gatvė 28, or Kaunas Medical Academy (☎ 22 61 10) at Mickevičiaus gatvė 9 for student accommodation. Ask for the student representation (*studentų atstovybė*) or the foreign relations department.

The best hotel, the *Hotel Neris* (☎ 20 38 63) at Donelaicio gatvė 27, charges US$30/40 for singles/doubles. Other central hotels are the *Hotel Nemunas* (☎ 22 31 02) at Laisvės alėja 88, the *Hotel Lietuva* (☎ 20 59 92) at Daukanto gatvė 21, with a branch (☎ 22 17 91) at Laisvės alėja 35, and the newer *Hotel Baltija* (☎ 22 36 39) at Vytauto prospektas 71, said to have a good restaurant.

The *Gildija* at Rotušės aikštė 2 is one of the better restaurants. There's a café serving cheery little liqueur-based cocktails on the first corner past the side of the cathedral, going from Rotušės aikštė.

Getting There & Away

Some international bus and rail connections are mentioned in the Lithuania Getting There & Away section, and the frequent buses and rarer trains to/from Vilnius in Vilnius, Getting There & Away. There are also buses at least daily to/from Klaipėda. and Šiauliai. Passenger flights were in disarray at the time of research but there are possibilities of flights to/from Moscow, St Petersburg, Minsk, Riga or Tallinn. Contact LAL on 5 33 31.

KLAIPĖDA

The port of Klaipėda, the third biggest city in Lithuania with 207,000 people, and a centre of amber-ornament production, is 315 km west of Vilnius, at the mouth of the Kuršių Lagoon. Before the Soviet era Klaipėda was a German-populated town called Memel – part of it, since its founding in 1252 by the Teutonic Knights of East Prussia. In 1923 Lithuania seized it from the Western allies who had been administering it pending a decision on its post-WW I fate. Hitler annexed it in 1939 and it was wrecked towards the end of WW II when the Red Army took it.

Orientation & Information

The north end of the town fronts the open Baltic Sea, but most runs back from the Kuršių Lagoon, into which the Danės river flows. Some old areas south of the river have been restored and contain a number of shops, cafés and restaurants. You can change money at the Bank of Lithuania at Turgaus gatvė 1. The central post and telegraph office is at Liepų gatvė 16.

Things to See

An important landmark, on a square opening off Turgaus gatvė, south of the river, is the 1819 **Klaipėda Theatre**. A tall **fish warehouse** at Aukštoji gatvė 3, typical of the old Memel buildings known as 'Fachwerk', has been restored as an exhibition hall.

If it's museums that interesrt you, there's an **ethnography museum** at Liepų gatvė 7, a **folk-art museum** at Pakalnės gatvė 6, and a **maritime museum & aquarium** at Smiltynė on the northern tip of Neringa, the narrow spit dividing the Kuršių Lagoon from the open sea. Ferries run half-hourly to Smiltynė.

Places to Stay & Eat

The central *Hotel Klaipėda* (☎ 1 69 71, fax 5 39 11), at Naujo Sodo gatvė 1 and used by most tour groups, has rooms with attached bath for US$25/36, two restaurants and a couple of coffee shops and bars.

Other hotels include the *Hotel Baltija* (☎ 1 49 67) at Janonio gatvė 4, the *Hotel Pamarys* (☎ 1 99 43) at Šaulių gatvė 28, the *Hotel Vėtrunge* (☎ 5 48 01) at Taikos prospektas 28, and the *Hotel Viktorija* (☎ 1 36 70) at Šimkaus gatvė 12.

Some German groups stay in the modern *Sanatorium Pajūris*.

Restaurants include the *Meridianas* in a former sailing ship moored on the Danės River next to the main bridge. The *Regata* is nearby at Danės krantinė 15. There are markets at Turgaus aikštė 5 and Taikos prospektas 80.

Getting There & Away

International connections including a ferry from Germany are mentioned in Lithuania, Getting There & Away. There may be flights too, contact LAL (☎ 6 22 95).

See the Vilnius section for buses and trains from there. There's also a bus service from Kaunas.

The Vilnius-Kaunas-Klaipėda road is among the best in the Baltic states.

PALANGA

The seaside resort of Palanga is 30 km north

LITHUANIA

of Klaipėda on a 10-km **sandy beach** backed by dunes and pine woods, with a long wooden pier. The resort area, with sanatoria and rest homes, is south of the Ronze river; the town is north. The landscaped **botanical park** on Vytauto gatvė contains an **amber museum** in the former palace of the Polish noble Tyszkiewicz family.

Places to Stay
There are camp sites at Vytauto gatvė 8 (☎ 5 35 33) and Užkanavės (☎ 5 16 76). Some German groups use the *Hotel Alka*. The *Hotel Pajūris* (☎ 5 33 45) is at Basanavičiaus gatvė 9.

Getting There & Away
LAL (☎ 22 81 76) may start flights to/from Vilnius. Buses from Vilnius take seven hours. The bus station is at Jasinskio gatvė 1.

NERINGA
There's a passenger and vehicle ferry about half-hourly between Klaipėda and the northern tip of Neringa, the sandy spit between the Baltic Sea and the Kuršių Lagoon. The northern half of the spit is Lithuanian, the south is Russian, and a road runs the whole 90-km length to Kaliningrad. The spit is an attractive combination of sand dunes and pine woods. Much of it is a national reserve, with a US$0.30 entry fee. The main settlement is **Nida** (formerly German Nidden), a popular resort near the Russian border. The German writer Thomas Mann had a house (now a museum) at Nida in the 1930s. Further north is **Juodkrantė** (formerly German Schwarzort) with a fine stretch of elk-inhabited forest. German tour companies use holiday homes at both places, also private homes at Nida.

ŠIAULIAI
Šiauliai (population 150,000), 80 km west of Panevėžys and 150 km east of Palanga, is Lithuania's fourth biggest city. Most of the town dates from after 1872 when it was burned down in a great fire. Pedestrianised Vilniaus gatvė is its heart. The white 16th and 17th century **SS Peter & Paul Church** has one of the the tallest spires in Lithuania.

There are **museums** of history and ethnography (Aušros aleja 47), bicycles (Vilniaus gatvė 139), cats (Žuvininkų gatvė 18) and photography (Vilniaus gatvė 140).

The *Hotel Šiauliai* (☎ 3 73 33) is at Draugystės prospektas 25, with a branch (☎ 3 29 33) at Vytauto gatvė 74. Buses and/or trains run from Vilnius, Kaunas, Jelgava, Riga and elsewhere: the bus station is at Tilžės gatvė 109, the railway station at Dubijos gatvė 44. With your own vehicle you could stop off at the Hill of Crosses in an easy day's drive between Riga and any Lithuanian city.

Hill of Crosses
About 10 km north of Šiauliai, a km east off the road to Meškuičiai and Riga, the strange Hill of Crosses (Kryžių Kalnas) is a place of national pilgrimage, a hillock covered in a forest of thousands of crosses – large and small, expensive and cheap, some devotional, some memorial (many for people deported to Siberia). Some crosses are finely carved folk-art masterpieces.

Crosses have been planted on the hillock, said to have been originally a fortification, for centuries. It was the focus of revolts in the 19th century.

At least three times in the Soviet era the crosses were bulldozed, only to spring up again. Easter brings the biggest flocks of pilgrims. Buses from Šiauliai to Meškuičiai, Joniškis, Jelgava and Riga pass the entrance road.

Kaliningrad Region

A disconnected wedge of Russia too strategic to have been left in anyone else's hands, the 21,000 sq km of the Kaliningrad region (population 900,000 plus an estimated 200,000 to 400,000 military) lies between Lithuania, Poland and the Baltic Sea. From the 13th century until 1945, Kaliningrad was German, part of the core territory of the

Teutonic Knights and their successors the dukes and kings of Prussia. Its capital, now named Kaliningrad, was the famous German city Königsberg.

After WW I, East Prussia (the northern half of which the Kaliningrad region approximates) was separated from the rest of Germany. Hitler's desire to reunite it was one of the sparks that lit WW II. The three-month campaign by which the Red Army took it in 1945 was one of the fiercest of the war, with hundreds of thousands of casualties on both sides.

Until 1990 the Kaliningrad region was closed to Western tourists. Now it's open, and trying to become a free-trade zone. The practicalities of travel seem to change from week to week. Both group and individual travel are possible. Rooms in the better hotels are in short supply, so advance bookings are advisable.

The currency is the Soviet rouble, worth slightly under US$0.01 at the time of writing. Kaliningrad time is GMT plus one hour from the last Sunday in September to the last Saturday in March, GMT plus two hours for the rest of the year. If you can read German, try to get hold of the excellent guide *Königsberg Kaliningrad* by Henning Sietz (Edition Temmen, Bremen, 1992).

VISAS

Some travellers have obtained visas for Kaliningrad from Russian missions without meeting the standard Russian requirement for prior confirmed accommodation. But others are told that this rule still holds. If a travel agency is involved in organising your trip, get it to get you a visa too – its fee will be well worth the red tape and queues it saves you. At least ask whoever sells you your ticket about the current visa rules and how to get a visa.

Supervision at border crossings from Lithuania is reportedly slack, so it might be possible to get in from that side without a visa at all but visa scrutiny by hotel staff may be more thorough than elsewhere in Russia because of the region's military importance.

GETTING THERE & AWAY

Tours & Travel Agents

Most Western tourists come in groups to Kaliningrad, from Germany.

In 1992 Greif Reisen, Baltisches Reisebüro, Reisebüro Alainis and Schnieder Reisen (see Estonia, Getting There & Away for contact details) all offered trips with accommodation in Kaliningrad, Zelenogradsk or Svetlogorsk. A week's visit typically costs from US$800 to US$900 including flights, US$500 to US$700 by bus. Some firms may be able to book accommodation only.

Rail Tours Mochel Reisen (☎ 07821-43037) of Georg-Vogel-Strasse 2, W-7630 Lahr/Schwarzwald offers a return train trip from Berlin plus a week in Kaliningrad or Svetlogorsk for US$600 to US$1050 or a lightning in-and-out trip with just 12 hours in Kaliningrad for US$185 to US$570.

Intourist, the Russian state-tourism giant with offices in capitals and major cities worldwide, can book individuals into the Hotel Kaliningrad for around US$80/90 singles/doubles. If you can arrange to end up staying at the Motel Baltika or Pension Stroitel (Svetlogorsk), it will be cheaper. Other German firms dealing in Kaliningrad travel and accommodation are Skan-Tours (☎ 05371-8930) of Eyffelkamp 4, 3170 Gifhorn, and Ost-Reise-Service (☎ 0521-14 2167) of Artur Ladebeck Strasse 139, 4800 Bielefeld 14.

Air

The only scheduled flights at the time of writing are to/from the CIS with Aeroflot (Moscow twice daily).

In 1992 Schnieder Reisen and Greif Reisen offered return charter flights from Hamburg and Hannover respectively for US$245 to US$425.

Kaliningrad airport is at Chrabrovo, 25 km north of the city. A bus runs about half hourly to/from Kaliningrad bus station.

Bus

There are cheap daily buses from the main Lithuanian cities and Riga and Tallinn. In summer 1992 a daily bus service was due to begin between Gdańsk (Poland) and Kaliningrad for US$40 return, three hours each way. Contact the Hewelius tourist office (☎ 41 32 51) in Gdańsk. If and when the road borders with Poland at Mamonovo and Bagrationovsk are opened, more bus services can be expected to start.

Train

Apart from the Berlin train, the only trains to Kaliningrad at the time of writing are from the Baltic states and the CIS (Moscow and St Petersburg daily).

Car & Motorbike

The planned vehicle ferry from Germany offers motorists the only potential way in from the south until the road borders open. The Lithuanian border is more promising and the road down the Neringa sandspit was suggested by one Lithuanian travel specialist. Check carefully on the advisability of taking a vehicle into Kaliningrad, and the availability of petrol.

Sea

Weekly ferries from Kiel (Germany), Karlskrona (Sweden) and Gdynia (Poland) were planned to start in 1992. The Kiel route was to be serviced by the *Mercuri-I* vehicle ferry (see Latvia, Getting There & Away), the others by the Swedish Corona Line (☎ 46600 Karlskrona, 21 70 72 Gdynia). In 1991 there were hydrofoil day trips from Gdynia to Kaliningrad, which may resume. A hydrofoil from Elblag (Poland) may also start.

KALININGRAD (KÖNIGSBERG)

Founded as a Teutonic order fort in 1255, Königsberg joined the Hanseatic League in 1340 and from 1457 to 1618 was the residence of the grand masters of the Teutonic order and their successors the dukes of Prussia. The first king of Prussia was crowned here in 1701. The city was nearly flattened by British air raids in 1944 and the Red Army assault from 6 to 9 April 1945. Many of the surviving Germans were sent to

Siberia – the last 25,000 were deported to Germany in 1947-48. The city was renamed, rebuilt and repeopled mostly by Russians. Today it has 400,000 residents and a lot of drab Soviet architecture and desolate empty space where cleared areas haven't been rebuilt, but also has evocative remnants of the German era.

Orientation & Information

The two arms of the Pregolya river, both west-flowing, meet around the island where Kaliningrad's old cathedral stands. From here Leninsky prospekt heads about 1.25 km south to Kaliningrad South railway station (Yuzhny Vokzal) and the bus station, and north to the city's two main squares – Tsentralnaya ploshchad (about 250 metres) and ploshchad Pobedy (1.25 km) with Kaliningrad North station.

You can change money Monday to Friday from 9 am to 6 pm at Investbank, Leninsky prospekt 28, and Gosbank, ulitsa Shillera 2. Rubin at Leninsky prospekt is a good shop if you're looking for amber. The Kaliningrad telephone area code is 0112.

Things to See

The outstanding German remnant is the red brick Gothic shell of the **Dom**, or cathedral, founded in 1333. The **tomb of Immanuel Kant**, the 18th century philosopher who was born, studied and taught in Königsberg, is on the outer north side. The fine old **stock exchange**, now a blue-painted 'Sailors' Culture Palace', is just across the river south of the cathedral.

At the east end of wide Tsentralnaya ploshchad, on the site of the 1255 castle (whose ruins were dynamited in 1965), stands the unfinished upright-H-shaped **House of Soviets** (Dom Sovietov), acclaimed as one of the ugliest creations of Soviet architecture (no mean achievement). Just north of Tsentralnaya ploshchad, on ulitsa Universitetskaya near the university, is the much visited **Bunker Museum** (Muzey Blindazh) in the 1945 German command post (open daily).

North of the House of Soviets stretches the

Lower Pond (Nizhny Prud), in German times a favourite city beauty and leisure spot, the Schlossteich. Kaliningrad's **History & Art Museum** is housed in a reconstructed 1912 concert hall on the east bank. Waterfalls connect the pond's north end with the larger **Upper Pond** (Verkhny Prud), at whose south-east corner, on ploshchad Marshala Vasilevskogo, are the **Dohnaturm**, a bastion of the city's old defensive ring now housing the fine **Amber Museum**, open daily except Mondays, and the **Rossgärter Tor**, one of the gates through the old defences. Another bastion, the **Wrangel-Turm**, stands near the south-west corner of the pond. From here ulitsa Profesora Baranova heads west to ploshchad Pobedy, passing the **Central Market** on ulitsa Chernyakhovskogo just to the south.

On **Ploshchad Pobedy** (formerly Hansaplatz) remain the 1930 **Kaliningrad North Station** (Severny Vokzal) and the 1923 **city hall**. About 300 metres west along prospekt Mira is the 1927 **Kaliningrad Drama Theatre**, restored in 1980, and about a km further is **Kalinin Park**, once the Luisenwahl, a favourite Königsberg park.

Places to Stay

Hotel standards are poor. Many groups stay in the *Hotel Kaliningrad* (☎ 46 94 40), handily placed on Tsentralnaya ploshchad at Leninsky prospekt, an ordinary 1970s Soviet hotel awarded two stars out of a possible four by Intourist. Rooms have private bathrooms. Some renovations began in 1991. Better is the already renovated *Hotel Turist* (☎ 46 08 01), run by a Russian-German joint venture, at ulitsa Alexandra Nevskogo 53 on the east side of the Upper Pond, just over a km north of the Amber Museum. Walk beside the ponds to the centre or take tram No 1 or 8.

The *Hotel Moskva* (☎ 27 20 89) at prospekt Mira 19 just past the Stadion Baltika is probably the next best central hotel, though it's dilapidated. There are others on ploshchad Pobedy and ulitsa Razina.

The *Motel Baltika* (☎ 43 79 77), on the east edge of the city shortly past the ring road on Moskovsky prospekt, the road to Gvardeysk, is run by the same joint venture as the Hotel Turist. Rooms have private shower and toilet. Bus Nos 25 and 27 go to/from the Hotel Kaliningrad, No 28 to/from ploshchad Pobedy.

Places to Eat

Most restaurants have loud music in the evenings. The best is reckoned to be the *Olshtyn* at ulitsa Olshtynskaya 1 near Kaliningrad South station, with a popular café as well as a restaurant.

The *Kafe Vstrecha* at prospekt Mira 10 is a quiet, slow but good restaurant whose two rooms have separate entrances. You can get a reasonable, quiet lunch (but beware of drunken revellers in the evening) at the *Brigantina* at Leninsky prospekt 83 just south of the cathedral-island, the *Kafe Kamenny Tsvetok* at ulitsa Klinicheskaya 25 near the Lower Pond, and the *Kafe Solnechny Kamen* in the Rossgärter Tor. The hotels mentioned have restaurants and some have cafés too.

OTHER PLACES IN KALININGRAD REGION

Parts of the region are still restricted for visitors but the rules have been easing, especially for groups. **Baltiysk** (formerly German Pillau), at the mouth of the Kaliningradsky Lagoon and the base of Russia's Baltic fleet, was opened to former German residents in 1992.

Foreigners have been able to visit and stay in one coastal resort, **Svetlogorsk** (formerly German Rauschen) since 1991 and were admitted to another, **Zelenogradsk** (Cranz) in 1992. **Yantarny** (Palmnicken) with its **amber mines**, on the coast north of Baltiysk, and the Neringa peninsula, could both be visited by groups at least in 1992.

Electric trains run from Kaliningrad North to Zelenogradsk (30 minutes) and Svetlogorsk (from 60 to 80 minutes). Of Svetlogorsk's two stations, Svetlogorsk-II is nearer the beach. Two partly renovated hotels used for foreigners in Svetlogorsk are the *Hotel Volna* (☎ 011533-3005), on

LITHUANIA

Kaliningradsky prospekt five minutes' walk from Svetlogorsk-II, and the *Hotel Baltika*.

There are trains to Gurievsk (Neuhausen), Polessk (Labiau), Sovietsk (Tilsit), Gvardeysk (Tapiau) and elsewhere from both North and South stations in Kaliningrad. If you want to join a group trip to places out of Kaliningrad, you could try Rossgärter Tours at ulitsa Sergeeva 2, a local partner of Greif Reisen.

Appendix I – Alternative Place Names

The following abbreviations are used:

(D) Danish
(E) English
(Est) Estonian
(F) Finnish
(Far) Faroese
(G) German
(Lat) Latvian
(Lit) Lithuanian
(N) Norwegian
(P) Polish
(R) Russian

DENMARK
Danmark

Copenhagen (E) – København (D), Kööpenhamia (F),
    Köpenhamn (S)
Helsingør (D) – Elsinore (E)
Jutland (E) – Jylland (D)
Funen (E) – Fyn (D)
Zealand (E) – Sjælland (D), occasionally Sealand (E)

FAROE ISLANDS
Færoe Islands (E), Færøerne (D), Føroyar (Far)

FINLAND
Suomi

Åland (S) – Ahvenanmaa (F), formerly Åbo (S)
Hämeenlinna (F) – Tavastehus (S)
Haparanta (F) – Haparanda (S)
Helsinki (F) – Helsingfors (S)
Kokkola (F) – Karleby (S)
Lappeenranta (F) – Villmanstrand (S)
Naantali (F) – Nådendal (S)
Oulu (F) – Uleåborg (S)
Pietarsaari (F) – Jakobstad (S)
Tampere (F) – Tammerfors (S)
Tornio (F) – Torneå (S)
Tornionjoki (F) – Tornealv (S)
Turku (F) – Åbo (S)
Vaasa (F) – Vasa (S)

ICELAND
Ísland

NORWAY
Norge

North Cape (E) – Nordkapp (N)

SWEDEN
Sverige

Gothenburg (E) – Göteberg (S)
Haparanda (S) – Haaparanta (F)
Stockholm (S) – Tukholma (F)

ESTONIA
Eesti

Tallinn (Est) – Talinas (Lit), formerly Reval or Revel
Tartu (Est) – formerly Dorpat
Saaremaa (Est) – formerly Ösel

LATVIA
Latvija

Cēsis (Lat) – formerly Wenden (G)
Kurzeme (Lat) – formerly Courland (E), Kurland (G)
Riga (E) – Rīga (Lat), Riika (F)
Sigulda (Lat) – formerly Segewold (G)

LITHUANIA
Lietuva

Klaipėda (Lit) – formerly Memel (G)
Juodkrantė (Lit) – formerly Schwarzort (G)
Nidda (Lit) – formerly Nidden (G)
Vilnius – Wilno (P)

MISCELLANEOUS
Belorussia (E) – Belarus (R)
Lübeck (G) – Lyypekk (F)
Kaliningrad (R) – formerly Königsberg (G)
Kiev – Kijevas (Lit)
St Petersburg – Pietari (F),
    formerly Leningrad (R)
Vyborg (R) – Viipuri (F)
Warsaw (E) – Varšuva (Lit)
Zelenogradsk (R) – Cranz (G)

Appendix II – European Organisations

	Council of Europe	EC	EFTA	NATO	Nordic Council	OECD	WEU
Austria	✓	–	✓	–	–	✓	–
Belgium	✓	✓	–	✓	–	✓	✓
Cyprus	✓	–	–	–	–	–	–
Denmark	✓	✓	–	✓	✓	✓	–
Finland	–	–	✓	–	✓	✓	–
France	✓	✓	–	✓	–	✓	✓
Germany	✓	✓	–	✓	–	✓	✓
Greece	✓	✓	–	✓	–	✓	–
Iceland	✓	–	✓	✓	✓	✓	–
Ireland	✓	✓	–	–	–	✓	–
Italy	✓	✓	–	✓	–	✓	✓
Luxembourg	✓	✓	–	✓	–	✓	✓
Malta	✓	–	–	–	–	–	–
Netherlands	✓	✓	–	✓	–	✓	✓
Norway	✓	–	✓	✓	✓	✓	–
Portugal	✓	✓	–	✓	–	✓	–
Spain	✓	✓	–	✓	–	✓	–
Sweden	✓	–	✓	–	✓	✓	–
Switzerland	✓	–	✓	–	–	✓	–
Turkey	–	✗	–	✓	–	✓	–
UK	✓	✓	–	✓	–	✓	✓
Yugoslavia	–	–	✗	–	–	✗	–

✓ – *full membership*
✗ – *associate membership*

Council of Europe

Established in 1949 the Council of Europe, based in Strasbourg, aims to promote European unity, protect human rights, and assist in the cultural, social and economic development of its member states. Founding states were Belgium, Denmark, France, Ireland, Italy, Luxembourg, the Netherlands, Norway, Sweden and the UK. Estonia, Latvia and Lithuania were expected to join in autumn 1992.

European Community (EC)

Founded by the Treaty of Rome in 1957, the European Economic Community, or Common Market, has broadened its scope far beyond mere economic measures and is now generally referred to as the European Community. Its original aims were to develop and expand the economies of its member states by abolishing customs tariffs, coordinating transport systems and general economic policies, establishing a common economic policy towards nonmember states, and promoting the free movement of labour and capital within its borders.

Further measures included streamlining of telecommunications, abolishment of border controls and linking of currency exchange rates. Since the Maastricht treaty of December 1991, the EC is committed to establishing a European Union with an even larger degree of political integration, a single currency and one central bank. The EEC's founding states were Belgium, France, (West) Germany, Italy, Luxembourg and the Netherlands (the Treaty of Rome was an extension of the European Coal and Steel Community founded by these six states in 1952). Full economic union was achieved in 1969.

Denmark, Ireland and the UK joined in 1973, Greece in 1981, and Spain and Portugal in 1986; Greenland, a self-governing member of the Kingdom of Denmark, voted by referendum to leave the Community in 1982. The main EC organisations are the European Parliament (elected by direct universal suffrage, with growing powers), the European Commission (the daily 'government'), the Council of Ministers (ministers of member states who make the important decisions), and the Court of Justice. The European Parliament meets in Strasbourg, Luxembourg is home to the Court of Justice, and the other EC organisations are based in Brussels.

European Free Trade Association (EFTA)

Established in 1960, EFTA aims to eliminate trade tariffs on industrial products between member states, though each member retains the right to its own commercial policy towards nonmembers.

EFTA is in effect a watered-down version of the EC, without supranational powers. The two are working towards a European Economic Area, which them in economic matters and will create a single market. Denmark and the UK left EFTA to join the EC in 1973. Its headquarters are in Geneva.

North Atlantic Treaty Organisation (NATO)

This is a defence alliance established in 1949 between the USA, Canada and several European countries to safeguard their common political, social and economic systems against external threats (read: against the powerful Soviet military presence in Europe after 1945). An attack against any member state would be considered an attack against them all. NATO is based in Brussels.

Nordic Council

Established in 1952, the Nordic (or 'Norden') Council aims to promote economic, social and cultural cooperation among its member states. Since 1971, the Council has acted as an advisory body to the Nordic Council of Ministers, a meeting of ministers from the member states responsible for the subject under discussion. Decisions taken by the Council of Ministers are usually binding, though member states retain full sovereignty. Environmental, tariff, labour and immigration policies are often coordinated.

Organisation for Economic Cooperation and Development (OECD)

The OECD was set up in 1961 to supersede the Organisation for European Economic Cooperation, which allocated US aid under the Marshall Plan and coordinated the reconstruction of postwar Europe. Sometimes seen as the club of the world's rich countries, the OECD encourages economic growth and world trade. Its 24 members include most of Europe, as well as Australia, Canada, Japan and the USA. Its headquarters are in Paris.

Western European Union (WEU)

Set up in 1955, the WEU was designed to coordinate the military defences between member states, to promote economic, social and cultural cooperation, and to encourage European integration. Social and cultural tasks were transferred to the Council of Europe in 1960, and now the WEU is touted as a future, more 'European', alternative to NATO. Its headquarters are in London.

Appendix III – Telephones

Dial Direct
You can dial directly from public phone boxes from almost anywhere in Europe to almost anywhere in the world. This is usually cheaper than going via the operator, and you don't even need a pocketful of coins if you use one of the phone cards which have recently become more common.

To call overseas you simply dial the overseas access code (OS) for the country you are calling from, the country code (CC) for the country you are calling to, the local area code (dropping the leading zero if there is one) and then the number. If, for example, you are in Norway (overseas access code 095) and want to make a call to the USA (country code 1), San Francisco (area code 415), number 123 4567, then you dial 00-1-415-123 4567. To call from Denmark (009) to Australia (61), Sydney (02), number 123 4567, you dial 010-61-2-123 4567.

Home Direct
You can, from many countries, dial directly to your home country operator and then reverse charges, charge the call to a phone company credit card or perform other credit feats. Simply dial the relevant Home Direct number to be connected to your own operator. For the US there's a choice of AT&T, MCI or Sprint home direct services. Home Direct numbers vary from country to country – check with your telephone company before you leave, or with the international operator in the country you're ringing from.

In some places, you may find dedicated Home Country Direct phones where you simply press the button labelled USA, Australia or whatever for direct connection to the relevant operator. Note that the Home Direct service does not operate to and from all countries.

Dialling Tones
In some countries, after you've dialled the overseas access code, you have to wait for a dialling tone before dialling the code for your target country. Often the same applies when you ring from one city to another within these countries: wait for a dialling tone after you've dialled the area code for your target city. If you're not sure what to do, simply wait three or four seconds after dialling a code – then keep on dialling.

Phone Cards
In major locations you may find phones which accept credit cards: simply swipe your card through the slot and the call is charged to the card. Phone company credit cards can be used to charge calls via your home country operator.

Stored-value phone cards are becoming increasingly common all over Europe. You buy a card from a post office, phone office, newsagent or other outlet and simply insert the card into the phone each time you make a call. The card saves the problem of finding the correct coins for calls (or lots of correct coins for international calls) and sometimes gives you a small discount.

Call Costs
Avoid ringing from a hotel room, unless you really don't care what it's going to cost. The cost of making an international call varies widely from one country to another. A US$10 call from Germany or Switzerland would cost you US$15 from France or US$20 from Italy. Choosing where you call from can make a big difference to the budget. The countries listed below are rated from * to *** in ascending order of cost – * is cheap, **** is expensive. Note that to make a call from Estonia, Latvia or Lithuania without an interminable wait, you may have to use special, much dearer phone services. Reduced rates are available at certain times, though these vary from country to country and should make little difference to relative costs – check the local phone book or ask the operator.

TELEPHONE CODES

	CC	cost (see text)	OS	IO
Andorra (via Spain)	34738	***	0	19
Andorra (via France)	33628	**	0	19
Austria	43	*	00	09
Belgium	32	**	00	1324
Cyprus	357		00	
Cyprus (Turkish)	905			
Czechoslovakia	42		00	0131
Denmark	45	*	009	0015
Estonia	7 (370)	*	(see text)	
Faroe Islands	298		009	0017
Finland	358	*	990	92022
France	33	**	19(w)	19(w)33
Germany †	49	*	00	0010
Gibraltar	350		00	100
Greece	30	**	00	161
Hungary	36		00(w)	09
Iceland	354		90	09
Ireland	353	*	00	114
Italy	39	***	00	15
Latvia	7 (371)	*	(see text)	
Liechtenstein	41		00	114
Lithuania	7 (372)	*	(see text)	
Luxembourg	352		00	0010
Malta	356		00	94
Morocco	212		00(w)	12
Netherlands	31	**	09(w)	060410
Norway	47	**	095	091
Poland	48		0-0	900
Portugal	351	**	00	099
Romania	40			071
Spain	34	***	07(w)	9138 9
Sweden	46	****	009(w)	0018
Switzerland	41	*	00	114
Tunisia	216		00	
Turkey	90		9(w)9	248888
UK	44	*	010	155
Yugoslavia	38	**	99	901

CC – Country Code (to call that country)
OS – Overseas Access Code (to call abroad from that country)
(w) – wait for dialling tone
IO – International Operator (to make enquiries)

Other country codes: Australia 61, Canada 1, Hong Kong 853, India 91, Indonesia, 62, Japan 81, Macau 853, Malaysia 60, New Zealand 64, Singapore 65, South Africa 27, Thailand 66, USA 1

† The eastern part of Germany is still being amalgamated with the western German phone system. The old East Germany country code was 37, the old overseas access code 06 or 000.

Appendix IV – International Car Codes

The following is a list of official country abbreviations that you may encounter on vehicles in Europe. Other abbreviations are likely to be unofficial, often referring to a particular region, province or city. A motorised vehicle entering a foreign country must carry a sticker identifying its country of registration, though this rule is not always enforced.

A –	Austria
AL –	Albania
AND –	Andorra
AUS –	Australia
B –	Belgium
BG –	Bulgaria
CC –	Consular Corps
CD –	Diplomatic Corps
CDN –	Canada
CH –	Switzerland
CS –	Czechoslovakia
CY –	Cyprus
D –	Germany
DDR –	German Democratic Republic (the former East Germany)
DK –	Denmark
DZ –	Algeria
E –	Spain
ET –	Egypt
F –	France
FL –	Liechtenstein
GB –	Great Britain
GBA –	Alderney
GBG –	Guernsey
GBJ –	Jersey
GBM –	Isle of Man
GBZ –	Gibraltar
GR –	Greece
H –	Hungary
HKJ –	Jordan
HR –	Croatia
I –	Italy

IL –	Israel
IND –	India
IR –	Iran
IRL –	Ireland
IRQ –	Iraq
IS –	Iceland
J –	Japan
KWT –	Kuwait
L –	Luxembourg
LAR –	Libya
M –	Malta
MA –	Morocco
MC –	Monaco
MEX –	Mexico
N –	Norway
NA –	Netherlands Antilles
NL –	Netherlands
NZ –	New Zealand
P –	Portugal
PAK –	Pakistan
PL –	Poland
RIM –	Mauritania
RL –	Lebanon
RO –	Romania
RSM –	San Marino
S –	Sweden
SCV –	Vatican City
SF –	Finland
SLO –	Slovenia
SME –	Surinam
SN –	Senegal
SU –	The former Soviet Union (including the Baltic states)
SYR –	Syria
TN –	Tunisia
TR –	Turkey
USA –	United States
VN –	Vietnam
WAN –	Nigeria
YU –	Yugoslavia
ZA –	South Africa

Appendix V – Climate Charts

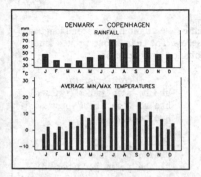

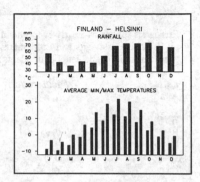

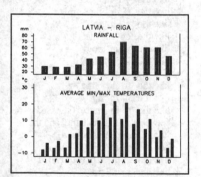

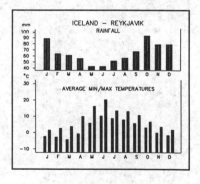

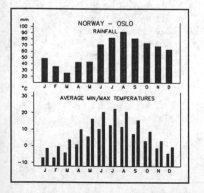

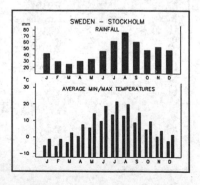

Appendix VI – Russian Alphabet

Russian is spoken by nearly everyone in the Baltic states, though as a second language by Estonians, Latvians and Lithuanians themselves. The chart shows printed letters, transliterations (Latin-letter equivalents) and common pronunciations.

Letter	Transliteration	Pronunciation
А, а	A, a	like the 'a' in 'father' (stressed)
		like the 'a' in 'about' (unstressed)
Б, б	B, b	like the 'b' in 'but'
В, в	V, v	like the 'v' in 'van'
Г, г	G, g	like the 'g' in 'god'
Д, д	D, d	like the 'd' in 'dog'
Е, е	Ye, e	like the 'ye' in 'yet' (stressed)
		like the 'ye' in 'yeast' (unstressed)
Ё, ё	Yo, yo	like the 'yo' in 'yore'
Ж, ж	Zh, zh	like the 's' in 'measure'
З, з	Z, z	like the 'z' in 'zoo'
И, и	I, i	like the 'ee' in 'meet'
Й, й	Y, y	like the 'y' in 'boy'
К, к	K, k	like the 'k' in 'kind'
Л, л	L, l	like the 'l' in 'lamp'
М, м	M, m	like the 'm' in 'mad'
Н, н	N, n	like the 'n' in 'not'
О, о	O, o	like the 'o' in 'more' (stressed)
		between the 'a' in 'hang' and the 'u' in 'hung' (unstressed)
П, п	P, p	like the 'p' in 'pig'
Р, р	R, r	like the 'r' in 'rub' (but rolled)
С, с	S, s	like the 's' in 'sing'
Т, т	T, t	like the 't' in 'ten'
У, у	U, u	like the 'oo' in 'fool'
Ф, ф	F, f	like the 'f' in 'fan'
Х, х	Kh, kh	like the 'ch' in 'Bach'
Ц, ц	Ts, ts	like the 'ts' in 'bits'
Ч, ч	Ch, ch	like the 'ch' in 'chin'
Ш, ш	Sh, sh	like the 'sh' in 'shop'
Щ, щ	Shch, shch	like the 'shch' in 'fresh chips'
ъ		('hard sign')
Ы, ы	Y, y	like the 'i' in 'ill'
ь		('soft sign')
Э, э	E, e	like the 'e' in 'end'
Ю, ю	Yu, yu	like the 'u' in 'use'
Я, я	Ya, ya	like the 'ya' in 'yard' (stressed)
		like the 'ye' in 'yearn' (unstressed)

Index

536 Index

Keep in touch!

We love hearing from you and think you'd like to hear from us.

The Lonely Planet Newsletter covers the when, where, how and what of travel. (AND it's free!)

When...is the right time to see reindeer in Finland?
Where...can you hear the best palm-wine music in Ghana?
How...do you get from Asunción to Areguá by steam train?
What...should you leave behind to avoid hassles with customs in Iran?

To join our mailing list just contact us at any of our offices. (details below)

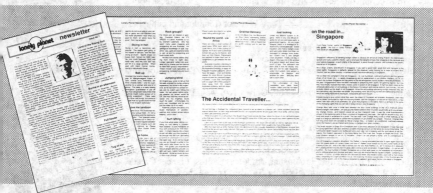

Every issue includes:

* *a letter from Lonely Planet founders Tony and Maureen Wheeler*
* *travel diary from a Lonely Planet author - find out what it's really like out on the road*
* *feature article on an important and topical travel issue*
* *a selection of recent letters from our readers*
* *the latest travel news from all over the world*
* *details on Lonely Planet's new and forthcoming releases*

Also available Lonely Planet t-shirts. 100% heavy weight cotton (S, M, L, XL)

LONELY PLANET PUBLICATIONS

Australia: PO Box 617, Hawthorn, 3122, Victoria (tel: 03-819 1877)
USA: Embarcadero West, 155 Filbert Street, Suite 251, Oakland, CA 94607 (tel: 510-893 8555)
UK: Devonshire House, 12 Barley Mow Passage, Chiswick, London W4 4PH (tel: 081-742 3161)

Lonely Planet guides to Europe

Twenty years ago Maureen & I set out on the trip across Asia which led to the very first Lonely Planet guidebook. Since then our reputation has been built on boldly going where no guidebook publisher had gone before. Now after all these years it has been a delight to return to Europe; culminating with the launch of our Europe series.

We deliberately didn't try to produce one monster Europe volume. Instead we've divided Europe into regions, sometimes overlapping, which has enabled us to include more maps and information – all the detail you've come to expect from a Lonely Planet book.

We're certain our readers are going to enjoy travelling with these books just as much as we enjoyed researching, writing and publishing them.

– Tony Wheeler (founder and publisher)

Eastern Europe on a shoestring
This guide has opened up a whole new world for travellers – Albania, Bulgaria, Czechoslovakia, eastern Germany, Hungary, Poland, Romania and Yugoslavia.
'...a thorough, well-researched book. Only a fool would go East without it.' – *Great Expeditions*

Mediterranean Europe on a shoestring
Details on hundreds of galleries, museums and architectural masterpieces and information on outdoor activities including hiking, sailing and skiing. Information on travelling in Albania, Andorra, Cyprus, France, Greece, Italy, Malta, Morocco, Portugal, Spain, Tunisia, Turkey and former republics of Yugoslavia.

Western Europe on a shoestring
This long-awaited guide covers all of Western Europe's well-loved sights and provides routes for cycling and driving tours, plus details on hiking, climbing and skiing. All the travel facts on Andorra, Austria, Belgium, Britain, France, Germany, Ireland, Italy, Liechtenstein, Luxembourg, Netherlands, Portugal, Spain and Switzerland.

Finland – travel survival kit
Finland is an intriguing blend of Swedish and Russian influences. With its medieval stone castles, picturesque wooden houses, vast forest and lake district, and interesting wildlife, it is a wonderland to delight any traveller.

Iceland, Greenland & the Faroe Islands – travel survival kit
Iceland, Greenland & the Faroe Islands contain some of the most beautiful wilderness areas in the world. This practical guidebook will help travellers discover the dramatic beauty of this region, no matter what their budget.

USSR – travel survival kit
Invaluable advice on getting around and beating red tape for individual and group travellers alike. This comprehensive guide includes an unsanitised historical background and complete information on art and culture. Over 130 reliable maps, and all place names are given in Cyrillic script. (includes the independent states)

Trekking in Spain

Aimed at both overnight trekkers and day hikers, this guidebook includes useful maps and full details on hikes in some of Spain's most beautiful wilderness areas.

Trekking in Turkey

Few people are aware that Turkey boasts mountains with walks to rival those found in Nepal. This book gives details on treks that are destined to become as popular as those further east.

Also available:
Eastern Europe phrasebook

Discover the most enjoyable way to get around and make friends in Bulgarian, Czech, Hungarian, Polish, Romanian and Slovak.

Mediterranean Europe phrasebook

Ask for directions to the galleries and museums in Albanian, Greek, Italian, Macedonian, Maltese, Serbian & Croatian and Slovene.

Scandinavian Europe phrasebook

Find your way around the ski trails and enjoy the local festivals in Danish, Finnish, Icelandic, Norwegian and Swedish.

Western Europe phrasebook

Show your appreciation for the great masters in Basque, Catalan, Dutch, French, German, Irish, Portuguese and Spanish (Castilian).

Moroccan Arabic phrasebook

Essential words and phrases for everything from finding a hotel room in Casablanca to asking for a meal of *tajine* in Marrakesh. Includes Arabic script and pronunciation guide.

Turkish phrasebook

Practical words and phrases that will help you to communicate effectively with local people in almost every situation. Includes pronunciation guide.

Russian phrasebook

This indispensable phrasebook will help you get information, read signs and menus, and make friends along the way. Includes phonetic transcriptions and Cyrillic script.

Also:

Look out for *Lonely Planet travel survival kits* to the Baltic states, France, Greece, Hungary, Ireland, Italy, Poland and Switzerland.

Lonely Planet Guidebooks

Lonely Planet guidebooks cover every accessible part of Asia as well as Australia, the Pacific, South America, Africa, the Middle East, Europe and parts of North America. There are five series: *travel survival kits*, covering a country for a range of budgets; *shoestring guides* with compact information for low-budget travel in a major region; *walking guides*; *city guides* and *phrasebooks*.

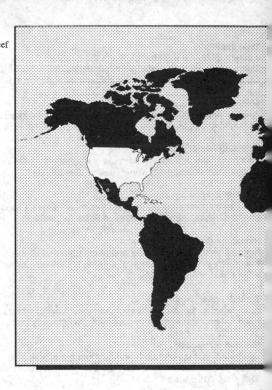

Mail Order

Lonely Planet guidebooks are distributed worldwide. They are also available by mail order from Lonely Planet, so if you have difficulty finding a title please write to us. US and Canadian residents should write to Embarcadero West, 155 Filbert St, Suite 251, Oakland CA 94607, USA; European residents should write to Devonshire House, 12 Barley Mow Passage, Chiswick, London W4 4PH; and residents of other countries to PO Box 617, Hawthorn, Victoria 3122, Australia.

Indian Subcontinent
Bangladesh
India
Hindi/Urdu phrasebook
Trekking in the Indian Himalaya
Karakoram Highway
Kashmir, Ladakh & Zanskar
Nepal
Trekking in the Nepal Himalaya
Nepal phrasebook
Pakistan
Sri Lanka
Sri Lanka phrasebook

Africa
Africa on a shoestring
Central Africa
East Africa
Kenya
Swahili phrasebook
Morocco, Algeria & Tunisia
Moroccan Arabic phrasebook
Zimbabwe, Botswana & Namibia
West Africa

Mexico
Baja California
Mexico

Central America
Central America on a shoestring
Costa Rica
La Ruta Maya

North America
Alaska
Canada
Hawaii

Europe
Eastern Europe on a shoestring
Eastern Europe phrasebook
Finland
Iceland, Greenland & the Faroe Islands
Mediterranean Europe on a shoestring
Mediterranean Europe phrasebook
Scandinavian & Baltic Europe on a shoestring
Scandinavian Europe phrasebook
Trekking in Spain
USSR
Russian phrasebook
Western Europe on a shoestring
Western Europe phrasebook

South America
Argentina, Uruguay & Paraguay
Bolivia
Brazil
Brazilian phrasebook
Chile & Easter Island
Colombia
Ecuador & the Galápagos Islands
Latin American Spanish phrasebook
Peru
Quechua phrasebook
South America on a shoestring
Trekking in the Patagonian Andes

The Lonely Planet Story

Lonely Planet published its first book in 1973 in response to the numerous 'How did you do it?' questions Maureen and Tony Wheeler were asked after driving, bussing, hitching, sailing and railing their way from England to Australia.

Written at a kitchen table and hand collated, trimmed and stapled, *Across Asia on the Cheap* became an instant local bestseller, inspiring thoughts of another book.

Eighteen months in South-East Asia resulted in their second guide, *South-East Asia on a shoestring*, which they put together in a backstreet Chinese hotel in Singapore in 1975. The 'yellow bible' as it quickly became known to backpackers around the world, soon became *the* guide to the region. It has sold well over half a million copies and is now in its 7th edition, still retaining its familiar yellow cover.

Today there are over 100 Lonely Planet titles – books that have that same adventurous approach to travel as those early guides; books that 'assume you know how to get your luggage off the carousel' as one reviewer put it.

Although Lonely Planet initially specialised in guides to Asia, they now cover most regions of the world, including the Pacific, South America, Africa, the Middle East and Europe. The list of *walking guides* and *phrasebooks* (for 'unusual' languages such as Quechua, Swahili, Nepalese and Egyptian Arabic) is also growing rapidly.

The emphasis continues to be on travel for independent travellers. Tony and Maureen still travel for several months of each year and play an active part in the writing, updating and quality control of Lonely Planet's guides.

They have been joined by over 50 authors, 48 staff – mainly editors, cartographers, & designers – at our office in Melbourne, Australia and another 10 at our US office in Oakland, California. In 1991 Lonely Planet opened a London office to handle sales for Britain, Europe and Africa. Travellers themselves also make a valuable contribution to the guides through the feedback we receive in thousands of letters each year.

The people at Lonely Planet strongly believe that travellers can make a positive contribution to the countries they visit, both through their appreciation of the countries' culture, wildlife and natural features, and through the money they spend. In addition, the company makes a direct contribution to the countries and regions it covers. Since 1986 a percentage of the income from each book has been donated to ventures such as famine relief in Africa; aid projects in India; agricultural projects in Central America; Greenpeace's efforts to halt French nuclear testing in the Pacific and Amnesty International. In 1991 $68,000 was donated to these causes.

Lonely Planet's basic travel philosophy is summed up in Tony Wheeler's comment, 'Don't worry about whether your trip will work out. Just go!'